IRISH SAINTS
IN ITALY

IRISH SAINTS IN ITALY

BY

Fra ANSELMO M. TOMMASINI, o.f.m.

with introduction by
The Rev. Father GREGORY CLEARY, d.d., o.f.m.

Translated with some additional notes by J. F. Scanlan

LONDON
SANDS AND COMPANY
(PUBLISHERS) LTD.
15 KING STREET, COVENT GARDEN
76 CAMBRIDGE STREET, GLASGOW

Ex parte Ordinis nihil obstat quominus imprimatur.

Romæ, e Collegio S. Antonii de Urbe, die XV novembris MCMXXXIV.

Fr. Leonardus M. Bello,
Min. Glis O.F.M.

NIHIL OBSTAT :

Josephus Long,
Cen. Lib.

IMPRIMATUR :

✠ Andreas Joseph, o.s.b.
Archiep : S : Andr : et Edim
die 10 Jan. 1935

First Published 1937.

PRINTED IN GREAT BRITAIN BY
THE STANHOPE PRESS LTD.
ROCHESTER : : KENT

PREFACE

Fra Anselmo Tommasini's work on the Irish Saints in Italy was published at Milan in the summer of 1932, shortly before the International Eucharistic Congress of Dublin. It was the approach of the welcome of Ireland to the representatives of the Catholic world, and of the celebration of the fifteenth centenary of St. Patrick's mission, that led him to choose this time for giving to his fellow-countrymen this account of Italy's debt to the Irish missionaries of the Middle Ages.

The author described his work as "a humble, but loving tribute to the Island that had done such good service to Christian civilization" and expressed the hope that it might lead other students of history to undertake more complete researches on the subject with which he dealt. But the author's researches seem to be absolutely exhaustive; and very little, we think, is now to be garnered.

I have been honoured by the invitation to write a brief introduction to the English translation of Fra Tommasini's masterly treatise. I trust this translation will have the success it so thoroughly deserves; and will be widely welcomed by a large number of readers, not only in Catholic Ireland, but also among the millions of the English-speaking lands.

Its author underestimates the importance of his book; for it is no mere popular compilation from the already available works on the history with which he deals. It gives us the results of many years of original research, to which he was attracted during visits to all parts of Italy, when he was engaged in the successful professional career which he abandoned to take the habit of St. Francis; for he is now a simple lay-brother in Rome—another Michael O'Clery!

He was first interested in these studies through gradually realizing how widespread in Italy is the devotion to Irish saints. He found more than two hundred and twenty parochial churches dedicated to them, besides hundreds of minor churches, chapels and shrines. In our school-books we were informed that there were "twenty-nine" places in Italy dedicated to Irish saints!

Often among the people, even of obscure villages, the author heard of traditions and legends of St. Patrick and St. Brigid, and of the Irish monks who had spread their fame in the land to which they devoted their lives.

Turning to modern times, the author finds historians very disappointing. Christian Europe was being re-created in the Middle Ages; but it was mainly Irish saints who did the work. He feels that very inadequate references have been made to the labours of Irish saints. His work is the vindication.

He informs us that many of these historians have something to tell us of St. Columbanus, whose church and tower still make Bobbio a place of pilgrimage. But they have nothing more to say about the other heroic Irish saints who worked in Italy. Not even about St. Cathaldus (Cathal of Kerry), the most popular saint in southern Italy, whose fame was from the Alps to Sicily.

In his detailed introduction to his subject, our author traces in outline the religious history of Ireland from the earliest period; treating specially of the influence of the Irish missionaries on the Europe of the Middle Ages. To quote St. Bernard, treating of Bangor alone and its branches, he observes: "Into foreign lands swarms of [Irish] saints poured as though a flood had arisen" (*Life of St. Malachy*).

His last chapter is devoted to an interesting comparison of the outburst of missionary zeal in the early days of Catholic Ireland and the first age of the Franciscan missions. In the closing pages there is a reference to the good work done for the spread of the Faith by priests who followed the tide of Irish emigration to so many countries beyond the seas.

This book is the result of ten years of patient observation and research. Not only the general reader, but Irish historians and hagiographers must feel themselves deeply indebted to Fra Tommasini. His work marks an epoch in Irish hagiography.

GREGORY CLEARY, O.F.M.

CONTENTS

PREFACE 7

INTRODUCTION 13

§ 1. General bibliographical indications—§ 2. Meaning
of the word *Scots*—§ 3. The Scotch historians and the *Scots*
saints—§ 4. Plan of this book—§ 5. Reason for its publication

PART I

THE IRISH RELIGIOUS MOVEMENT

I THE CONVERSION 31

§ 1. The Celts of the British Isles—§ 2. The origins of
Christianity in Great Britain. St. Germanus of Auxerre.
Ninian. The Anglo-Saxon Invasion—§ 3. The beginnings
of Christianity in Ireland. Palladius. St. Patrick—§ 4.
Monasticism: its origin and development in Ireland—§ 5.
St. Brigit of Cell-dara—§ 6. *Insula Sanctorum*

II THE APOSTOLIC AND ASCETIC EXPANSION . 63

§ 1. The beginning of the apostolic emigration. St.
Brendan—§ 2. St. Colum-cille of Iona—§ 3. St. Aidan of
Lindisfarne—§ 4. St. Columban and St. Gall—§ 5. The
disciples of St. Columban in Gaul. St. Fursa—§ 6. The
Irish in Belgium and the Germanies—§ 7. Pilgrimages *ad
limina*—§ 8. Scotic foundations in Europe—§ 9. Scotic
foundations in Italy—§ 10. Celtic particularism

III THE CULTURAL EXPANSION . . . 101

§ 1. Irish monasteries the earliest centres of culture. Latin
and Greek—§ 2. The Irish schools. Biblical and canonical
studies—§ 3. The Irish Manuscripts. The Library at
Bobbio—§ 4. The Scots in the Carolingian renascence

IV FROM THE DANISH TO THE ANGLO-NORMAN
CONQUEST 128

§ 1. The Danish conquest—§ 2. The decline in religion
and morals—§ 3. The Danish Churches in Ireland. The
supremacy of Canterbury—§ 4. Máel Maedóc Úa Morgair
(St. Malachy)—§ 5. The Cistercians in Ireland. The
achievement of ecclesiastical reform—§ 6. The Anglo-
Norman Conquest. The discredit cast on Ireland

V THE INFLUENCE OF CELTIC LEGEND ON THE
MEDIÆVAL POETRY OF EUROPE . . 157

§ 1. Characteristics of early Celtic literature: adventure,
vision, and quest—§ 2. The Voyage of St. Brendan—§ 3.
The Visions of Fursa, Tundale, and Owen (St. Patrick's
Purgatory)—§ 4. The Welsh epic and the legend of King
Arthur—§ 5. Contrast between Celtic legends, the chansons
de geste, and the Scandinavian cycle of romances—§ 6.
The Normans as propagators of Celtic legends.

CHAPTER   PAGE

VI THE MARTYRDOM OF IRELAND . . . 190

§ 1. Ireland from the Anglo-Norman Conquest to the
English breach with Rome—§ 2. The Reformation and
Henry VIII—§ 3. Under Edward VI and Elizabeth—
§ 4. The "Flight of the Earls," the Plantation of Ulster,
and the Great Rebellion to 1649—§ 5. Oliver Cromwell—
§ 6. From the Restoration until the accession of James II—
§ 7. Under William III—§ 8. The Penal Laws—§ 9. From
1760 until the Union—§ 10. The agitation for Catholic
Emancipation—§ 11. Catholic Emancipation and after

PART II

THE IRISH SAINTS IN ITALY

VII ST. PATRICK 234

§ 1. St. Patrick in Italy—§ 2. Cult of St. Patrick in
Genoa—§ 3. In Pavia—§ 4. In Vertova (Bergamo)—§ 5.
In San Patrizio di Conselice—§ 6. In Tirli (Firenzuola)—
§ 7. In Bologna—§ 8. In Torre San Patrizio (Fermo)—
§ 9. St. Patrick's Well at Orvieto—§ 10. In Rome

VIII ST. BRIGIT OF CELL-DARA 244

§ 1. St. Brigit Virgin of Ireland and St. Bridget Widow
of Sweden—§ 2. Cult of St. Brigit Virgin in Piedmont. The
Scots' Hospice in Vercelli—§ 3. In Liguria—§ 4. In
Lombardy. The Hospital of St. Brigit in Pavia—§ 5. In
Emilia. The Church of St. Brigit and the Hospital for
Irish pilgrims in Piacenza—§ 6. In the Trentino—§ 7.
Geographical limits of the cult of St. Brigit Virgin

IX ST. GALL 252

§ 1. Relations between the Swiss abbey and Italy—
§ 2. Cult of St. Gall in Piedmont—§ 3. In Liguria—§ 4. In
Lombardy—§ 5. The Monastery of Val di Tolla—§ 6. In
the Padovano, the Veronese, the Trentino and Soligo—
§ 7. The Abbey of Moggio—§ 8. In Strassoldo and Istria—
§ 9. In Florence

X ST. URSUS OF AOSTA 265

§ 1. Various saints of the name honoured in Italy—
§ 2. Biographical particulars concerning St. Ursus of Aosta.
The Apostle of the Valdostani—§ 3. The chronology of St.
Ursus—§ 4. Memories and cult of St. Ursus in the city
of Aosta—§ 5. In the diocese of Aosta—§ 6. In the diocese
of Ivrea. The Hospital of the XXI—§ 7. In the other
dioceses of Piedmont—§ 8. In France and Switzerland

CHAPTER   PAGE

XI St. Gunifort of Pavia 280

§ 1. The Legend of St. Gunifort Martyr—§ 2. The texts
—§ 3. The historical value of the Legend—§ 4. The translations of the sacred body—§ 5. Cult of St. Gunifort in
Pavia—§ 6. Elsewhere in Lombardy

XII St. Columban of Bobbio 289

§ 1. Italian bibliography of St. Columban—§ 2. Other
saints of the same name—§ 3. Cult of St. Columban in
Piedmont—§ 4. In Liguria—§ 5. In Lombardy—§ 6. In
Emilia—§ 7. In the Veneto—§ 8. In Tuscany—§ 9. Memories
of St. Columban in Corsica—§ 10. Observations with
regard to the propagation of the cult of St. Columban in
Italy

XIII St. Cummian of Bobbio 315

§ 1. The relics of St. Cummian at Bobbio—§ 2. Biographical particulars and cult

XIV St. Fulco di Piacenza "ex gente Scota" 320

§ 1. Life of St. Fulco Scotti—§ 2. Erroneous connections
between St. Fulco and St. Donatus of Fiesole, both Scots—
§ 3. The traditional genealogy of the Scotti family of
Piacenza—§ 4. Observations relative thereto—§ 5. Probable
Irish origin of the family—§ 6. Families of Scotti appear
in many parts of Italy in eminent positions about the end of
the twelfth century—§ 7. Probable common Irish origin
of them all. Irish lay diaspora over Europe in the early
Middle Ages

XV St. Emilian of Faenza 341

§ 1. The Legend of St. Emilian—§ 2. Vicissitudes of his
cult in Faenza—§ 3. Historical sources

XVI St. Pellegrino delle Alpi di Garfagnana 346

§ 1. The Legend of St. Pellegrino delle Alpi—§ 2. Its
historical value—§ 3. The vicissitudes of the Shrine—
§ 4. Great variety of saints of the same name—§ 5. Cult
of St. Pellegrino in the neighbourhood of the Shrine—
§ 6. In Parma and Reggio—§ 7. In Modena—§ 8. In
Bologna—§ 9. In Valle del Santerno—§ 10. In Liguria—
§ 11. In Viterbo—§ 12. In the Trentino

XVII St. Fridian of Lucca 360

§ 1. St. Gregory the Great and St. Fridian—§ 2. Life of
St. Fridian—§ 3. The texts—§ 4. The chronology of St.
Fridian—§ 5. St. Fridian and St. Finnian of Mag-Bile—
§ 6. The translations—§ 7. The Monastery of St. Fridian
and the Lateran Canons of St. Fridian—§ 8. Cult of St.
Fridian in Lucca—§ 9 In other cities of Italy—§ 10 Parishes
dedicated to him—§ 11. Various particulars relative to the
cult of the saint

CHAPTER   PAGE

XVIII   St. Silaus of Lucca 378
§ 1. The Legend of St. Silaus—§ 2. Observations relative thereto—§ 3. The Monastery of St. Giustina in Lucca. Translations of the saint—§ 4. His cult

XIX   St. Donatus of Fiesole 383
§ 1. The age of St. Donatus—§ 2. Biographical particulars—§ 3. Miracles attributed to him—§ 4. The literary activities of St. Donatus—§ 5. Translations and cult

XX   St. Andrew of Fiesole 395
§ 1. Biographical particulars—§ 2. The Monastery of St. Martin at Mensola—§ 3. Particulars relative to the cult of the saint

XXI   St. Brigit at Opaco 399
§ 1. Particulars with regard to this saint

XXII   St. Cathal of Taranto 401
§ 1. Introductory—§ 2. The Legend of St. Cathal—§ 3. Invention and Translation—§ 4. The chronology of St. Cathal—§ 5. His episcopate at Rachau—§ 6. His episcopate at Taranto—§ 7 Donatus of Lecce—§ 8. Prophecies attributed to Cathal—§ 9. Cult of St. Cathal in Liguria—§ 10. In Lombardy—§ 11. In Emilia—§ 12. In the Veneto—§ 13. In Tuscany—§ 14. In Latium—§ 15. In the Marches—§ 16. In the Abruzzi—§ 17. In Campania—§ 18. In the Puglie—§ 19. In Basilicata—§ 20. In Calabria—§ 21. In Sicily—§ 22. In Malta and France—§ 23. Observations on the propagation of the cult of St. Cathal

XXIII   The Blessed Tadhg Machar of Ivrea . 433
§ 1. Introductory—§ 2. Biographical particulars—§ 3. Translations and cult

Part III

The Irish Religious Movement and the Franciscan Movement

XXIV 442
§ 1. Improper comparisons between St. Francis and St. Columban—§ 2. St. Francis and Bobbio—§ 3. The Rule of St. Columban contrasted with the Rules of St. Benedict and St. Francis—§ 4. Genuine similarities between the Irish movement and the Franciscan movement—§ 5. Probable reasons for such similarities and differences—Conclusion

Appendix 493

Index 501

INTRODUCTION

§ 1

THE exceptionally interesting phenomenon of the Irish apostolic expansion over the continent of Europe from the sixth to the twelfth century has not generally received the attention it deserves.

H.H. Pope Pius XI, in his letter addressed in 1923 to the Most Eminent Cardinal F. Ehrle, Papal Legate to the celebrations held in Bobbio in honour of St. Columban, wrote as follows: "The more light is thrown on the dark places of the early Middle Ages by the patient investigations of scholars, the more manifest it becomes that the re-birth to Christian wisdom and civilization in various parts of France, the Germanies, and Italy is due to the labours and the zeal of Columban—a striking testimony to the merits of the priesthood and more particularly of Catholic Ireland." And a little further on His Holiness recalled that with Columban began "those successive waves of emigration from Ireland which were destined in the course of the ages to bring such profit and advantage to such a multitude of peoples."[1]

It were impossible to begin with more august and authoritative testimony.

The masterly and exhaustive work of Dom Louis Gougaud, Benedictine monk of St. Michael's Abbey, Farnborough, *Christianity in Celtic Lands*,[2] provided with an abundant bibliography, maps, and an excellent index, presents the student with a picture clear, organic, and complete, though still perfectible in details, of the Irish expansion and serves to introduce the reader to all the various fields in which it brought forth such precious fruit. Dom Gougaud, however, has not had occasion to follow the tracks of the Irish movement in Italy very far, and yet

[1] Cf. *Civiltà Cattolica*, August 1923.
[2] Sheed & Ward (London), 1932.

there are certain saints, extremely popular in certain
provinces of the peninsula, who are intimately associated
with it. There is only one work dealing in particular with
the Irish saints in Italy, that of Miss Margaret Stokes, *Six
Months in the Apennines, or a Pilgrimage in Search of Vestiges of
the Irish Saints in Italy*.[3] Miss Stokes, however, deals at length
with only a few of them (St. Fridian, St. Silaus, St. Columban, St. Donatus, St. Andrew and St. Brigid of Fiesole); she
scarcely mentions the others even to name them. The
critical spirit of her inquiry also leaves much to be desired,
as she is inclined to treat fantastic legends on the same
footing with the ascertained facts of history and to confuse
persons historically distinct. It has therefore occurred to me
that a work a little more up-to-date and, if possible, more
comprehensive, on the subject of the Irish saints in Italy,
might still present a certain interest.

Unfortunately, such Italian writers as have concerned
themselves with these saints, in the majority of cases with the
sole object of composing panegyrics in praise of local patrons,
have brought to their task an inadequate stock of learning
as regards not only the history of the Irish religious movement, but also the civil or secular history of Ireland, and not
infrequently as regards the plain meaning of the word *Irish*,
which is too often considered as synonymous with *Scotch*
or *English*.[4] Local investigations into the history both of the
Irish saints and Irish foundations conducted in a genuinely
historical manner are rare indeed; and as regards the Irish
foundations, even in Rome itself, historians—ordinarily so
competent and trustworthy as, e.g., Huelsen—have fallen into
grievous error. Irish writers, on the other hand, have in
many cases neglected to take into account Italian historical

[3] Bell & Sons (London), 1892.
[4] Local Italian hagiographers have some excuse, but what can be said for
the published catalogue of the MSS. in the Royal Library at Brussels, in which
Irish annals and other historical documents are indexed under the rubric
Angleterre? "In Switzerland [the Irish Traveller] will be told at St. Beatenberg
by the guide-books that St. Beatus was British, and by local tradition that he
was Scotch. At the shrine of S. Pellegrino in the Apennines [cf. ch. XVI] he
will hear praises of a Scotch king's son. At Rome he will learn that England
was 'the isle of the Saints.' Against these ignorances his training in Ireland
gives him no protection." (Mrs. A. S. Green, *The Old Irish World* (Dublin
and London), 1912, p. 47.)

sources, and so created fresh confusion by erroneously identifying their own saints gone to Italy as *peregrini* with saints of similar or analogous names who played important parts in the religious life of the country of their birth.

Irish hagiography emerged as a science in the seventeenth century largely owing to the labours of the Irish Franciscans and, more particularly, of those who had taken refuge during the Protestant persecution in the famous College of St. Antony of Padua, founded in 1606 by Philip III at Louvain at the instance of the Franciscan Flaithri O MáilChonaire, otherwise known as Florence Conry (1560-1629), provincial of his order and archbishop of Tuam, who spent the greater part of his life in exile and died in Spain. "The Irish Franciscans," writes Dom Gougaud,[5] "were the first to get into direct contact with the early sources of the ecclesiastical history of their country. Between 1632 and 1636 in the convent of Donegal the lay-brother [Tadhg, or in religion Micháel Ó Cléirigh] Michael O'Clery, assisted by three principal collaborators, compiled the *Annals of Donegal* (generally known as the *Annals of the Four Masters*, a title given to them by Colgan) from old Irish chronicles, some of which are now lost. These Annals extend from the year of the world 2242 to A.D. 1616. . . ."

"Michael O'Clery also compiled various genealogies [*Réim Rioghaide*, 'Succession of Kings'] and a martyrology of Irish saints drawn from earlier martyrological writings." This compilation, the *Félire na naomh nÉrennach* or *Calendar of the Saints of Ireland*, was completed on 19th April, 1630, in the convent of the friars in Donegal and is therefore known as the Martyrology of Donegal. Finally O'Clery published after his return to Louvain in 1643, *Foclóir nó Sanasán nua* or *New Glossary* of the more obscure and difficult Old and Middle Irish words he had met in the course of his reading. "The Franciscan John Colgan (1592-1658) made use of the Latin and Irish materials supplied to him by Bollandus, by his fellow workers O'Clery and Hugh Ward and by Brendan O'Connor and Stephen White in the publication of his two famous hagiographical collections: (i) *Acta Sanctorum veteris*

---

[5] *Christianity in Celtic Lands*, p. xviii et seq.

et majoris Scotiae seu Hiberniae Sanctorum insulae (1 vol. ff.,
Lovanii, 1645); and (ii) *Triadis Thaumaturgae seu divorum
Patricii, Columbae et Brigidae . . . acta*, 1 vol. ff., Lovanii,
1647." Another Franciscan, Christopher, or in religion
Patrick, Fleming (1599-1631), deputed to make transcripts
or to collect originals of manuscripts wherever they could
be found in Europe, had gathered before his tragic death—
he was murdered, together with a deacon named Matthew
Hoar, by some Lutheran peasants outside Prague on 7th
November, 1631, when the Protestant army under the
Elector of Saxony advanced against that city—an important
collection of documents concerning St. Columban published
later (1667) in Louvain by Thomas Sirinus, i.e., O'Sherin,
one of Colgan's disciples: *Collectanea sacra seu S. Columbani
Hiberni abbatis . . . necnon aliorum . . . Sanctorum acta et opuscula.*
The work of these Irish Franciscans was a forlorn attempt to
save some fragments of their country's recorded history
from the disaster which they saw impending upon a civilization doomed to extinction. A thorough study of their heroic
labours still remains among the innumerable *desiderata* of
Irish history, but the curious reader may refer to (i) *The
Rise and Fall of the Irish Franciscan Monasteries and Memoirs of
the Irish Hierarchy*, by C. P. Meehan, Dublin, 1877; (ii)
*L'archéologie irlandaise au couvent de St. Antoine de Padoue à
Louvain*, by Victor de Buck, in *Études religieuses, historiques et
littéraires de la Compagnie de Jésus*, XXII, 1869, pp. 409-37,
586-603; (iii) *The College of the Irish Franciscans at Louvain*,
by Denis Murphy, in the Journal of the Royal Society of
Antiquaries of Ireland, 5th series, II, 1898, pp. 237-50; and
(iv) *The Return of the Irish Franciscans to Louvain*, in *Studies*,
XIV, 1925, pp. 451-8.[6]

Interest in ecclesiastical history and religious antiquities
on the Continent had been given a fillip by the publication
at Magdeburg of the notorious *Centuries* and was strong at the
time. Cesare Baronius had just completed his twelve great
volumes of *Annales ecclesiastici a Christo nato ad annum* 1198
(Rome 1588-1607), written at the request of St. Philip Neri

---

[6] Cf. also a note by Fr. F. O'Brian, O.F.M., in *Antonianum*, 1927, pp. 500-504,
on the "Restitutio Collegii S. Antonii, Lovanii."

in reply to the Lutheran Centuriators. The Bollandists, who had been anticipated in a field which they were to make peculiarly their own by the publication in 1611 of a *Catalogus praecipuorum sanctorum Hiberniae*, made by Henry Fitzsimon (1569-1643), a Dublin man, "the son of an alderman of good account, and by his profession a priest and a Jesuit,"[7] were about to begin the vast undertaking which Gibbon described in words most characteristic of the Age of Enlightenment and therefore rather less than true, as "communicating through the medium of superstition and fable much historical and philosophical instruction," and in 1643 the first volume of the *Acta Sanctorum quotquot toto orbe coluntur* was published in Antwerp and Brussels. Their labours were suspended for a time (1794-1837), but have long since been resumed,[8] and to the *Acta* are now added a *Bibliotheca hagiographica latina* and a periodical *Analecta Bollandiana*. The Society has recently (1925) made available to students a *Miscellanea Hagiographica Hibernica*, three Lives of early Irish saints edited by the late Dr. Charles Plummer, formerly Fellow and Chaplain of Corpus Christi College, Oxford, and dedicated in moving terms to the pious memory of John Colgan[9] and Michael O'Clery. Gratitude is no less due to

[7] The description is taken from the account of his arrest furnished by the Lord Chancellor Loftus and Thomas Jones, bishop of Meath, to Whitgift, Archbishop of Canterbury, 7th April, 1600, in Calendar of State Papers, Ireland, pp. 76-7. Fitzsimon's mother was a Lancashire woman, and he, a convert from Protestantism and educated at Oxford and Paris, was sent on the Irish mission at his own request. Cf. His *Life* by Fr. E. Hogan, Dublin, 1881.

[8] The Bollandists were long without a specialist in the Irish language and literature, and such an edition of the *Codex Salmanticensis* of the *AA. SS. Hiberniæ* as was published (Edinburgh and London, 1888) through the munificence of the late Marquis of Bute, by Frs. De Smedt and De Backer, S.J., suffers exceedingly from this ignorance. The advent of Fr. Paul Grosjean, S.J., a pupil of Dr. Plummer's, has made a world of difference.

[9] Dr. Plummer had written earlier (*VV. SS. Hib.* I, p. 10, n. 3): "There is, indeed, hardly to be found in the history of literature a more pathetic tale than that of the way in which Colgan and his fellow workers [. . .] strove, amid poverty, and persecution, and exile, to save the remains of their country's antiquities from destruction." About a hundred years later, when *etiam periere ruinae*, a Scotch priest, Thomas Innes (1662-1744), the first Scotch writer of history to apply a little critical intelligence to the fables of which the popular history of Scotland consists (cf. *A Critical Essay on the Ancient Inhabitants of the Northern Parts of Britain or Scotland*, reprinted from the original edition published in 1729, *The Historians of Scotland*, Vol. VIII, Edinburgh, 1885), working not uncomfortably in Edinburgh, and, in the words of a contemporary observer,

the memory of Dr. Plummer, who in 1910 published *Vitae Sanctorum Hiberniae partim hactenus ineditae* (2 vols., Oxford) and in 1922 *Bethada Náem nÉrenn* (2 vols., Oxford), scholarly editions of the more important lives of Irish Saints, both in Latin and in Irish.

Two very recent works of capital importance are Dr. J. F. Kenney's indispensable collection: *The Sources for the Early History of Ireland*, Vol. I, *Ecclesiastical* (Columbia University Press, New York, 1929) and Fr. John Ryan's *Irish Monasticism* (Dublin, The Talbot Press, 1931).

Most of the Italian publications are, as might be expected, local in character and never attain to these supreme sources. They confine themselves to repeating legends and particulars gathered from works predominantly of the sixteenth and seventeenth centuries in which, amongst other things objectionable, the Irish are frequently presented, partly through ignorance and partly in bad faith, as Scotch.

§ 2

It is essential that the reader should acquire from the outset definite ideas on this fundamental point.

The ancient Latin name for Ireland, first encountered in Julius Caesar's commentaries on the war in Gaul, was *Hibernia*. The word *Scotti*[10] makes its first appearance in Latin texts of the second half of the fourth century[11] in connection with the frequent incursions of Irish freebooters into the Roman provinces of Britain. From the fourth to

"mostly in the Advocates' Library in the hours when open, looking over books and manuscripts," querulously reproached the wretched Irish (pp. 276-9) for not publishing, "as other polite nations have done and daily continue to do," their chronicles and annals, to "serve for a solid bottom to a true history of Ireland since the fifth age that would do honour to the nation."

[10] Professor MacNeill (*Phases of Irish History*, Dublin, 1919, p. 145) thinks that *Scottus* "was originally a common noun meaning a raider or reaver, a depredator who worked by rapid incursions and retirements. It was probably a Gaulish word. . . ."

[11] "The first time, then, that we find the Scots mentioned in any ancient author yet known is in Ammian Marcellin, towards the latter end of the fourth age [*History*, XX, cap. 1, *c.* A.D. 380]. All former writers . . . never call them but Hiberni . . . such are Caesar, Diodor the Sicilian, Strabo, Mela, Ptolemy, Tacitus, Pliny, Solinus." (Innes, *A Critical Essay, etc.*, p. 283.)

the tenth century *Scottia* or *Scotia* means Ireland, and *Scotti* or *Scoti* the Irish.[12]

Contemporary Scotland at that time had no existence as a nation. Its ancient name was Caledonia, but it was generally described as North Britain. It was inhabited by various fierce and savage tribes, including the Picts, against whose attacks the Romans built their two great walls.

In the fifth century, perhaps even earlier, a colony of Scots from the north-east of Ireland crossed the sea, and settling in Britain, south of the kingdom of the Picts, called the land they occupied by the name of the land they had left, *Dál Riada*, roughly corresponding to the present shire of Argyll (*Airer nGaidhel*, the land of the Gael). This Scots colony became so powerful that the name *provincia Scottorum, septentrionalis provincia Scottorum*, i.e., the province of the Irish, or the *Scotti* settled in Britain, was applied by foreign writers to its territory, and as such it is described by the Venerable Bede in the eighth century. At that time *Scotia* properly so-called meant solely Ireland.[13] Scotland was but a part of Britain.

In the ninth century Cinaedh, son of Aïlpin, called in English writings Kenneth Mac Alpin (844-858), king of the Scots of Dál-Riada, either, according to some accounts, as a result of successful wars, or, according to others, because of his dynastic connections, brought the kingdom of the Picts also under his sway and extended further north both his own dominion and the name of his people. The amalgamation of the Scots and the Picts with two other groups of peoples, the Britons, who, driven north probably as a result of the Anglo-Saxon invasions, had settled between the Solway Firth and the Firth of Clyde, and the Angles, who, in the second half of the sixth century, had overrun the Lothians and occupied the present shires of Selkirk, Peebles and

[12] The Irish name for Britain up to the tenth century and later, before it became restricted to Scotland, was 'Alba,' in Greek 'Albion.'

[13] "St. Laurence, Archbishop of Canterbury in the beginning of the seventh age, is the first that I find who gives to Ireland the name of Scotia, in his letter mentioned by Bede (*H.E.*, II, ch. IV] to the bishop and clergy of that kingdom. After him Isidore, in the same age, and Adamnan in St. Columba's life." (Innes, op. cit., p. 286.) It was not until the immigrant *Scotti* had absorbed the Picts in the ninth century that their name began to prevail in the country.

Roxburgh, later gave rise under King Duncan (1034)—the Duncan of Shakespeare's *Macbeth*, who, in the imagination of the poet, bore 'his faculties so meek' and was 'so clear in his great office'—to the kingdom and nationality of Scotland as it is known to-day.

A distinction was then drawn between *Scottia major* or Ireland and *Scottia minor* or Scotland.

The appellation *Scotti* became the exclusive appanage of the Scotch only towards the end of the twelfth or thirteenth century in the time of Giraldus Cambrensis (1147-1223), when the power and influence of the real Scots were declining in Ireland under the increasing pressure of the Anglo-Norman invasion, and the mother island resumed to distinguish herself her old Latin name *Hibernia*.[14]

The word *Ériu*, the Gaelic name for the country (of which *Erin* is merely the dative case, and the primitive meaning of which was probably 'hill' or 'height') gradually assumed different forms, *Eri*, *Eire*, *Ire* (Greek *Ierne*) and ultimately yielded to derivatives on the Anglo-Saxon model *Eireland*, *Irland*, which began to appear in the eleventh and twelfth centuries.[15] The oldest chronicle in which the name 'Ireland' is found is believed to be that composed by Adhémar, a monk of St. Eparchius [St. Cybar] in Angoulême.[16]

[14] "And as to the application of the name Hyberni, or Irish, to the Scots in Britain, besides other examples, we find, as far down as the fourteenth age, the name of Irishery given to the Highlanders of Scotland, because of their origin from Ireland and of the Irish language that they still continue to speak." (Innes, op. cit., p. 356, quoting Archdeacon Barber, in the *Life of King Robert of Bruce*. Cf. the Spalding Club edition, Preface, p. xviii.) The unity between Erin and Alba was first broken by the Scandinavian invasions which drove, as it were, a wedge between them. The divorce, spiritual and literary, was made absolute by the Reformation. While the Irish language was proscribed in Ireland, the Scotch Reformers were ironically compelled to have recourse thereto for a written language wherewith to corrupt the Irishery in Scotland, and the translation of Knox's Liturgy, if the word be not misapplied, prepared in 1567 by Bishop Carsewell, the translations in the following century of the metrical version of the Psalms, of Calvin's Catechism and of the Bible printed in Gaelic by the Synod of Argyll and by the Rev. R. Kirke, of Balquhidder, "were thoroughly Irish in form, and the latter was simply taken from the Irish version of the Bible." (Cf. *Celtic Scotland*, by W. F. Skene, Edinburgh, 1887, II, p. 463.)

[15] Cf. Dom Gougaud, "Les noms anciens des îles Britanniques," in *Revue des Questions Historiques*, 1907, pp. 537-47; *Christianity in Celtic Lands*, pp. 2-3; Montalembert, *The Monks of the West*, Edinburgh, 1875, III, pp. 162 et seq.; and the *Encyclopædia Britannica*, 14th ed., 1929, Vol. XX, p. 154.

[16] 'His temporibus [sc. *c.* 1031] Normanni [i.e. the Northmen] Hiberniam

In texts or documents of the eleventh or twelfth century
the name *Scottia* may therefore mean at one time Ireland
and at another Scotland; each case must be considered on
its merits with particular regard to the native country of the
writer. From the pen of an Irish writer it probably means
Ireland, from that of an English or Scotch writer more
probably Scotland.[17]

In the thirteenth century it generally meant Scotland.
The famous Michael Scott (1175-1232), the magician, 'well-
practised in the game of magical deceptions,' placed by
Dante in Hell[18] and mentioned by Boccaccio,[19] Fra Salimbene and Fazio degli Uberti, although Dempster, who
gravely informs us that he had heard in his youth that his
magical books were still preserved, but could not be opened
without danger on account of the malignant fiends thereby
invoked, maintained that in his case Scotus was the name
of his nation and not of his family, was almost certainly
Scotch. John Duns Scotus (1266-1308), 'the Subtle
Doctor,' was also Scotch and contested by Ireland only so
long as it was impossible to prove by documentary evidence

insulam quae Irlanda dicitur ingressi sunt.' (Labbe, *Nova. Bibl. MSS.*, II,
p. 177.)

[17] A typical difficulty occurs in the 'Vita S. Forannani († 982) auctore
Roberto,' in *AA. SS. Boll.* III (April), pp. 808-14, Robert being the abbot of
Waulsort, and the date of his composition, *c.* 1140. Forannan came 'from
Scotland,' but was undoubtedly an Irishman, and succeeded another Irish-
man Cadroe as abbot of Waulsort. Cadroe, whose life was written, *c.* 995
(*AA. SS. Boll.* I (March), pp. 469-80), by one Reimann or Ousmann, is said
to have been of the Irish colony in Scotland, but to have been educated at
Ardmacha before setting out "on his pilgrimage." It is presumed, therefore,
that in some contexts *Scotia* may also mean the Irish colony in Scotland.
Cf. Bédier, *Les légendes épiques*, Paris, 1917, II, p. 426; and Kenney, *Sources*,
etc., pp. 609-10. Scotia clearly meaning Scotland in the Life of an Irish saint
would be excellent evidence of a late redaction.

[18] *Inferno*, XX, 115-117.

[19] "A great master of necromancy hight Michael Scott for that he was of
Scotland . . ." (*Decameron*, 8th day, Nov. 9. Mr. J. M. Rigg's translation,
Routledge, London, n.d. Cf. also *The Lay of the Last Minstrel* (II, XIII):

> ". . . the wondrous Michael Scott;
> A wizard of such dreaded fame,
> That when in Salamanca's cave,
> Him listed his magic wand to wave,
> The bells would ring in Notre Dame!"

And Sir Walter Scott's own notes, pp. 178-81 of the *Poetical Works*, Edinburgh,
1820, I.

that in his case also the epithet 'Scotus' was indicative of nationality.[20]

But the important point for the reader to bear in mind, let it be repeated, is that well into the eleventh century *Scotus* means an Irishman, and *Scotia* means Ireland. *"Scotti or Scoti,* Celtic inhabitants of Ireland, frequently referred to in the late Roman epoch on account of their incursions into the Roman province of Britain, settled as early as the fourth century in the northern part of Great Britain, which owes to them its present name of Scotland. Such appellation, which began to appear in the eleventh century, became a term of common use only in the twelfth and thirteenth centuries. The name of the inhabitants, *'Scotti,'* became the name of the country they inhabited, *Scottia, Scotia*— Ireland."[21]

§ 3

About the end of the twelfth century, when the word *Scoti* began to mean the Scotch, the latter took advantage of the equivoque and seized the opportunity to pass themselves off as the real founders of the *monasteria Scottorum* on the Continent of Europe, and so, gradually usurping the place of the Irish in these convents, proceeded to oust the lawful owners.[22] But the injury which the Scotch attempted to inflict and with partial success on the unfortunate Irish in the sixteenth and seventeenth centuries was ever so much greater. A group of Scotch writers, including John Lesley, Bishop of Ross,[23] David Chambers,[24] "Principal of the

[20] Cf. Fr. Gregory Cleary, O.F.M., 'St. Francis and Ireland,' in *Studies*, Dublin, March 1927, p. 65; P. Stefano Simonis, 'De vita et operibus b. Joannis Duns Scoti,' in *Antonianum*, 1928, p. 451, et seq.; and P. A. Callebaut, 'À propos du Bx. Jean Duns Scot de Littledean,' in *Arch. Franc. Hist.*, July 1931, pp. 305 et seq. Chambers (*De Scotorum fortitudine*, III, p. 186) had no doubt about it, but discusses the question at length with a great parade of authorities: "patria Scotus unde et a theologis communiter Scotus a patria nominatur. Natus est hic Dei famulus in ea Scotiae provincia cui Merchia [i.e. Berwickshire] nomen in oppidulo Duns nomine, etc."

[21] *Paulys Realencyklopadie*, Stuttgart, II, Vol. III, p. 838.

[22] Cf. Gougaud, *Christianity in Celtic Lands*, p. 184.

[23] Leslaeus (1527-1596), author of *De Origine moribus et rebus gestis Scottorum libri X, Romae*, in *aedibus populi Romani*, MDLXXVIII, and described by his compatriot Chambers as a "Historiographus praeclarus: scripsit enim nostrae gentis historiam aliaque opera praeclarissima." Some of the fables retailed

Scots College, Paris, in 1637, and probably earlier, who died still holding that post in 1647," and above all Thomas Dempster,[25] set themselves with an utter disregard for truth and a degree of ignorance remarkable even at that time, and not otherwise to be explained than by the fact of their nationality, to extol their own country in the most extravagant terms at the expense of Ireland. The Irish, in spite of the disastrous political and religious conditions by which they were oppressed, did not take this attack lying down, and Luke Wadding (1588-1657), one of the foremost scholars of his day,[26] Aedh Mac an Bhárd, otherwise known as Hugh Ward (1590-1635), Stephen White (1574-1646), David Rothe (1573-1650) and Christopher (or Patrick) Fleming (1599-1631) strove hard to re-establish the truth and to expose the dishonest machinations of their opponents.[27] But the mischief sown by these unscrupulous

by this illustrious historiographer are discreditable as *e.g.* the tale of the goose which grew upon a tree, a tale which two centuries earlier had greatly provoked the curiosity of Aeneas Sylvias Piccolomini when he visited Scotland. The beast was called a 'claik,' qui *ex arboribus gigni creditur*, p. 31. He probably conveyed it like much else in the earlier part of his illustrious history, straight out of Boece. On this particular fable, cf. Max Muller's *Lectures on the Science of Language*, 1871, Vol. II, pp. 583-604.

[24] Camerarius, author of *De Scotorum fortitudine, doctrina et pietate, etc.*, another work of fiction, published in Paris in 1631 and dedicated "Invictissimo serenissimoque Carolo Primo Magnae Britanniae etc Regi," "the successor of 108 Scottish Kings." The Scotch, according to this romancer, among other notable achievements, founded the universities of Paris, Pavia, Oxford and St. Gall, and, as time went on, were generous enough to admit the local inhabitants. That he was Rector of the Scots College, Paris, has been shown by Mr. M. V. Hay, from whose excellent study *The Blairs Papers* (Sands & Co., London and Edinburgh, 1929) the words quoted are taken (cf. pp. 110-11). This Chambers should not be confused with his namesake David Chambers, Lord Ormond (1530-1592), another Scotch historical *farceur*, whose '*Abbrégé*' des Histoires de tous les roys de France Escosse et Angleterre avec l'Epitome des Papes et Empereurs joincts ensemble en forme d'harmonie was published in Paris in 1579. On his performance, cf. Innes, *A Critical Essay, etc.*, pp. 171-6.

[25] "Thomas Dempsterus (1579-1625) juris utriusque doctor ac saepius professor in humanioribus litteris nulli secundus; Primarius in Bononia Italiae Professor: Obiit in eadem Bononia et sepultus est ad D. Dominici ubi cippus ejus hoc insigne praefert Elogium"—which is too long to transcribe. Such is the opinion of Mr. David Chambers (op. cit., p. 45).

[26] He founded the Irish Franciscan College of St. Isidore at Rome, wrote the *Annales Ordinis Minorum* (8 vols., 1626-1650) besides much else, and projected a History of Ireland, which he was compelled to abandon. See Cleary, *Father Luke Wadding and St. Isidore's College, Rome* (Rome, 1925, pp. 53-72).

[27] Cf. O'Hanlon, *Lives of the Irish Saints*, 9 vols., Dublin, 1879 et seq., Vol. I, p. 35 et seq.; and Mrs. Concannon, *The Life of St. Columban*, Dublin, 1915, p. 21.

Scotch propagandists succeeded in taking root, and the influence of the notorious Dempster, a clever rascal of considerable erudition, was particularly harmful. Dempster lived for a long time in Italy, teaching at Pisa and Bologna (where, as already mentioned by Chambers, he died and is buried). In Italy he wrote and published numbers of books, the catalogue of which, drawn up by himself, is most imposing. Many bore faked dedications to kings and other exalted personages, and thus gained for their author a great reputation. The best known of his works and those which have had such a baleful influence upon local Italian hagiographers are: (i) *Apparatus ad historiam Scoticam. Accesserunt Martyrologium Scoticum Sanctorum et Scriptorum nomenclatura* (Bologna, 1622); (ii) *Historia ecclesiastica gentis Scotorum, sive de Scriptoribus Scotis,* including his own none too veracious autobiography (Bologna, 1627; and Edinburgh, ed. D. Irving, for the Bannatyne Club, 2 vols., 1829); and (iii) *De Etruria regali* (published posthumously in Florence in 1724).

There is not a single Irish saint, beginning with those in Italy, but Dempster, trading upon the general ignorance as to the historical significance of the word *Scotia,* attempted to pass him off as Scotch. This 'peerless professor of humane letters', as his compatriot described him, perverted facts, invented quotations from non-existing books and documents, and attributed to existing authors passages they had never written. Many instances of his methods will occur in the course of this book. No reliance can be placed on any statement of Dempster's, and it may be sufficient in this connection to quote only two judgments, those of Dom Gougaud and Mgr. Lanzoni. It is Dom Gougaud's opinion that:[28] "Perhaps no writer has ever handled historical questions so recklessly and with such utter absence of impartiality and restraint as Dempster," while Mgr. Lanzoni,[29] confronted with three hexameters of Dempster's fabrication and interpolated by him in a ninth century text of Alcuin, writes as follows: "Dempster did not shrink from betraying the truth

[28] Cf. *Christianity in Celtic Lands,* p. 21.
[29] Cf. *Le Diocesi d'Italia,* Faenza, 1927, I, p. 597.

in order to magnify and extol the saints and famous men of
his own country and was a forger of conviction."

Considering how rife vanity, local interest and sycophancy
were among seventeenth century writers even upon sacred
things[30]—to say nothing of the traffic in forgeries—the
gravity of the evil influence exercised by Dempster on Italian
hagiography can easily be realized.

This consideration has contributed to persuade me that a
book on the Irish saints in Italy in accordance with the
most recent Italian work done with an exacting sense of
historical criticism by, e.g., the present Pontiff, Pius XI,
during his illustrious tenure of office at the Ambrosiana,
and such scholars as Lanzoni, Savio, Majocchi, Gianani,
Guidi, Lugano, and Blandamura might still offer some
interest.

§ 4

The present work is divided into three parts. In Part I
(six chapters) it has seemed best to set out succinctly the
history of the whole Irish spiritual movement down to the
present day in order to show how deeply Italy is indebted to
it, to place the figure of each single Scots saint to be encountered in Italy in appropriate relation to the background
of history, and to avoid the necessity of having to give an
account of the circumstances surrounding each which would
perforce in the event be merely fragmentary. The first four
chapters are based largely on Dom Gougaud's *Christianity
in Celtic Lands*, passages from which I have summarized and
occasionally reproduced, always excepting Italy, which
does not come within the learned Benedictine's purview.

Part II, consisting of seventeen chapters, is devoted to
such of the Irish saints as receive a cult in Italy, a chapter
being allotted to each. The first three, St. Patrick, St.
Brigid and St. Gall, did not die in the Italian peninsula,
but enjoyed and still enjoy, great popularity there, both on
their own account and by reason of a number of institutions
which have arisen under their names. The remaining
fourteen all either died or are buried in Italy. I believe that

[30] Cf. Lanzoni, ibid., I, p. 21.

I have omitted none. But as the Scots *peregrini* were numerous and not all, e.g., St. Emilian, have received from Irish writers the attention they deserve, there is always the possibility that one or two less important figures may have escaped my attention, although I have carefully examined various hagiographical dictionaries. I have not mentioned such Irish *peregrini* as only *passed* through Italy without leaving any trace. One of the saints I have taken into consideration, St. Fulco Scotti, cannot, strictly speaking, be regarded as Irish at all because he was undoubtedly born in Piacenza; but the fact that some writers have related him to St. Donatus of Fiesole, a pure Scot, has given me the opportunity of broaching the interesting subject of the origin of the various Scotti families found flourishing in many Italian cities in the twelfth century, and suggesting, in my opinion, an important Irish secular *diaspora* all over Europe, provoked mainly by the Danish invasions.

Dom Mauro Inguanez, O.S.B., archivist of Montecassino, has kindly communicated to me the name of an Irish priest, Father Braughall, who died in the odour of sanctity at Montecassino about a century ago. He was born in Ireland at Kildare in 1780, the son of a Protestant father and a Catholic mother. Educated at Carlow College, which had been founded in 1793, Braughall completed his ecclesiastical studies in Salamanca, where he was ordained priest. After serving as curate for four years at Grange in County Kilkenny (*c.* 1807), he spent seven years administering the parish of Raheen and was then appointed parish priest, first at Newbridge for a short time and then again at Grange. In 1822 he fell ill and vowed that if he recovered he would make a pilgrimage to the Holy Land. Seven years later he was at Lisbon, having given up his parish. From Lisbon he made his way to Montecassino, where he died, as already stated, in 1847. The most recent manifestations of Irish sanctity admirably illustrate the most ancient, which are in many cases misunderstood and being misunderstood are laughed at. The like of Father Braughall throws some light upon the like of the blessed Tadhg Machar, and he in turn reflects the like of the legendary St. Silaus.

I would here draw attention to another group of saints from the British Isles, whom I have left aside as not being Irish. They are not so much British as pure Anglo-Saxon, and they seem to be distributed over a rather restricted area between Latium and Campania. They are St. Harduin of Ceprano, St. Bernard of Rocca d'Arce, St. Fulk (Folco) of Santopadre, St. Gerard of Gallinaro, St. Eleutherius of Arce, and St. Grimoald of Pontecorvo; and to their number may be added, although he was very much later and flourished elsewhere, St. Berthold of Parma, a pure Anglo-Saxon.

As regards each of the seventeen saints taken into consideration, besides giving hagiographical particulars brought up to date as far as possible in accordance with the most recent studies, I have endeavoured to collect every memorial preserved in Italy in the form of churches, convents, chapels, hospices, geographical and topographical nomenclature and folk-lore, with references wherever available to their cult, past and present. The list of the parishes of Italy and their respective titular saints contained in the last edition published of the *Annuario delle Diocesi e del Clero d'Italia*, [31] and the general index to the map of Italy issued by the Italian Touring Club have been of the greatest assistance to me.

In the third and last part, in one somewhat protracted chapter, I have dealt—and by way of summarizing the whole book—with an admirable subject, already broached, but cursorily, and, as I think, erroneously, by some foreign writers, viz., the similarities between the Irish religious movement and the Franciscan movement.

§ 5

Nobody is more conscious than I am of the defects of the work here presented, due both to my own insufficiency and to the unfavourable conditions in which I have been compelled to carry it through.

These deficiencies have been made good to some extent by the comity of scholars who have helped me in my investigations by providing me with books and information

[31] Rome, Tip. Vaticana, 1924.

and giving me valuable indications as to persons and places: of their number it is my duty publicly to thank Mgr. Faustino Gianani, Mgr. Pantaleone Micheletto, Count Emilio Nasalli-Rocca, Professor Giulio Scotti, Dom Placido Lugano, Mgr. Enrico Carusi, Mgr. Giuseppe Blandamura, Don Stefano Rebolini, Don Annibale Maestri, Don Gio. Battista Baggi, Padre Raffaele M. Vitale, S.J., Fr. Ferdinando Antonelli, O.F.M., Fr. Aniceto Chiappini, O.F.M., Fr. Benvenuto Bughetti, O.F.M., Fr. Teodorico Asson, O.F.M., Commendatore Fortunato Pintor, and the Marchese Francesco Carandini.

Even so, the book makes no pretence of being devoid either of omissions or errors. The careful reader will notice also that with regard to certain institutions I have been able to provide detailed information, with regard to others only the barest indications. The fault is not altogether mine. In work necessarily involving recourse to the assistance of others by correspondence, my experience has been that some persons send the most exhaustive and detailed replies, others, replies which are incomplete and vague, others again, 'not so much as a line.' Lanzoni records that Ughelli and he had the same experience.

For all that, I believe that this book may usefully be offered to the public as it is. It may serve in the first place to bring the merits of the Irish saints before the faithful of the one hundred and twenty parishes in Italy where prayers are offered and honour is paid to them every day, but in the majority of cases as to beings wrapt in mystery. In the second place it may be an incentive to local antiquarians to collect such particulars of record as now lie hidden beneath the dust of archives and are still to seek with regard to both the Scots saints and the Scotic foundations, and encourage them to conduct their investigations on historically exact lines—a habit which not all of them have yet acquired. There is not a chapter, nay, not a paragraph in this book (more particularly Ch. II, § 9, Ch. XIV and Ch. XXIV) which could not easily give rise in the hands of anyone who cared sufficiently about it to a whole book which would certainly not be absolutely lacking in interest.

PART I

THE IRISH RELIGIOUS MOVEMENT

CHAPTER I

THE CONVERSION

§ 1

THE Celtic inhabitants of the British Isles may be divided into two groups: Gaels or Goidels and Britons or Brythons.[1]

The Gaels were the first to arrive in the islands, probably about 800 B.C., and imported the use of bronze: the unknown race which preceded them and may have been Turanian was ignorant of the use of metals. The second Celtic invasion, the British invasion, took place only some five or six centuries later (about 200 B.C.). These new invaders, Gauls of the Belgian branch, introduced the use of iron into the British Isles, and gradually substituted their own British language for the Gaelic, which remained a native language only in Ireland, where there were no British settlements of any importance, and in the colonies of the Irish.

Ireland, we know, was called Ériu in old Irish, but its Latin name down to the twelfth and thirteenth centuries was *Scotia*, the land of the Scots, another name for the Gaels.

The Roman legions in the two expeditions of Julius Caesar (55 and 54 B.C.), the expedition of Claudius (A.D. 43) and the expedition of Agricola (A.D. 83 and 84), ultimately penetrated Great Britain to the furthest north; but

---

[1] Cf. H. d'Arbois de Jubainville, *Les Celtes depuis les temps les plus anciens jusqu'en l'an 100 avant notre ère*, Paris, 1904; G. Dottin, *Manuel pour servir à l'étude de l'antiquité celtique*, Paris, Champion, 1906; and J. Loth, 'La première apparition des Celtes dans l'Ile de Bretagne et en Gaule,' in the *Revue Celtique*, XXXVIII, 1920-21, pp. 259-88. An excellent summary of the present state of our knowledge with regard to the origin and migrations of the Celts down to Roman times, according to the investigations of Déchelette, Rice Holmes, Fleure, Obermayer and Peake, may be found in an article by Canon Patrick Power, 'The Problem of the Celts,' in *Studies*, a quarterly review, Dublin, March 1927, pp. 99-114. Reference should also be made to Professor Eóin MacNeill's *Phases of Irish History*, Dublin, 1919; and to Cecile O'Rahilly's *Ireland and Wales: Their Historical and Literary Relations*, London, 1924.

Rome never succeeded in bringing the barbarians of Caledonia within her civilizing influence, and, although Tacitus[2] records that he had often heard his father-in-law Agricola say that the other island could have been conquered and held with one legion and a handful of auxiliary troops, the Roman eagles in the providence of God never flew over Ireland. That country retained its modest independence until the ninth century and then for the first time felt the yoke of the foreigner imposed by the Northmen.

To protect themselves against ceaseless incursions from the turbulent and savage north, the Romans raised huge fortifications in Britain as elsewhere on the marches of the Empire. Hadrian's Wall was built in 122, the Antonine Wall in 142; the former was reinforced apparently by Septimius Severus in 208, the latter, a mere breakwater to stem the heavy tide of invasion flowing from the north, was abandoned before the century was out.[3] The most formidable of these northern peoples were the Picts or Pitts who dwelt in present-day Scotland, the northern Picts north of the Grampians, the southern between the Grampians and the Firth of Forth. Their origin is obscure. Sir John Rhys has suggested that they may have been the representatives of some pre-Aryan race speaking a language akin to Basque. Other scholars think they may have been Celts and would connect them with the Breton branch of that wide-spread family.

The Roman conquest of Great Britain within the Wall was, it was once thought, tedious and difficult, long protracted and never fully carried out. No such assimilation, it was imagined, ever took place in the island as created the Gallo-Roman type of civilization in Gaul, and, it was

---

[2] Cf. *Vita Agricolae*, cap. xxiv. The first Irishman known to history makes his appearance in the pages of Tacitus. He was a petty king *unus ex regulis gentis*, who, having been driven out by some domestic insurrection, sought refuge with Agricola and was detained *specie amicitiae in occasionem*. Agricola, who knew his business, was not expressing an idle opinion to his son-in-law. The Irishman's adventure was repeated eleven hundred years later with disastrous consequences for the peace of Ireland.

[3] When this wall was first built the Romans had a harbour a little lower down the Clyde, probably at Dumbarton. This, too, appears to have been abandoned some time before the wall itself was given up, *c.* A.D. 185, a clear proof of the increasing menace of the Scots from Ireland.

even suggested, the British language continued to be commonly spoken throughout the country. The investigations of contemporary archæologists have dissipated this flattering belief, and the evidence that Agricola, who was recalled in 85, after only seven years' residence, romanized Britain, has by a most distinguished archæologist[4] been declared to be "nothing short of overwhelming."

§ 2

As in nearly all the provinces, so also in Britain the Roman occupation served as a vehicle for the propagation of the Christian religion. An ancient legend preserved in the apocryphal Gospel of Nicodemus related that the first apostle to England was Joseph of Arimathea, the 'noble counsellor' of St. Mark's Gospel, who, fleeing the persecution of the Jews, brought with him, it was believed, all that he had of value—a few drops of the Blood of Christ. This Joseph landed with twelve companions in western England and settled in a place afterwards famous in the religious history of the country—Glastonbury. The relic of the Blood of Christ, believed to have been brought by this disciple, gave rise later to the legend of the Holy Grail (san greal), and the monastery where, it was believed, King Arthur had been buried, endured until 1539, when Henry VIIIth's agent, Thomas Cromwell, a rascal money-broker, had Richard Whiting, its last abbot, quartered on Glastonbury Torr and his venerable head exposed above the gateway of his own abbey in horrible warning to any who should defy the royal inquisitors.[5]

[4] Sir George Macdonald in his presidential address to the English Classical Association at Reading in 1931. Cf. also *The Romanization of Britain*, by F. J. Haverfield, 4th ed., revised by Sir George Macdonald, Oxford, 1923. An excellent summary of recent work with full bibliography is given by M. Cary, 'La Grande Bretagne Romaine,' in the Sept.-Dec. number, 1928, of the *Revue Historique*, pp. 1-22.

[5] Cf. Cardinal Gasquet, *The Last Abbot of Glastonbury, and Other Essays*, Bell, London, 1908. The interesting story of the discovery of what was alleged to be Arthur's tomb is told by Giraldus Cambrensis in his *Speculum Ecclesiae* and elsewhere. Cf. Gibbon's *Decline and Fall*, cap. LXX, n. 86. It is not therefore surprising to find Lesley (op. cit., *Paraenesis ad nobil. populumque Scoticum*, p. 31) writing almost lyrically about it: "Loquitur Glassimburia antiquissima civitas in qua sedem fixit [Josephus]: loquitur templum longe magnificentissi-

The earliest positive fact, however, to which sober history can refer is the presence of five British ecclesiastics including three bishops, Eburius of York, Restitutus of London, and Adelfius of Colchester,[6] at the council of Arles in 341, a year after the Edict of Milan had proclaimed the freedom of the Christian Church. Three prelates from Britain also attended the Council of Rimini in 359, and on this occasion distinguished themselves by accepting, on the score of poverty, the Emperor's offer to put them up at the public expense.[7] The Church in Britain at the time would appear to have consisted mainly of Roman citizens and others who had followed the armies; the native population, according to Gildas,[8] showed little enthusiasm for the precepts of Christ.

In 367 the Picts and Scots swept over the country, destroyed the towns and ravaged the villas. Hadrian's Wall was abandoned in 395 and in 409 Honorius bade the 'cities' of Britain to look after themselves. A year later, 24th August 410, the capital of the world fell to Alaric the Goth. The occupation of Rome was comparatively benign,

mum, sedei ibi fixae monumentum relictum, loquitur ipse tumulus in quo puritatem suae religionis, imitationem sui facti, gloriam sui Christi in omnem aeternitatem conservari voluit." Cf. also with reference to the Abbey of Glastonbury, the cluster of legends which gathered round it, and the results of the most recent archæological excavations, an important article by M. Edmond Faral in the *Revue historique* for Jan.-April., 1929, pp. 1-49, and the bibliography given by Vismara, 'Storia benedettina,' in *Aevum*, 1931, pp. 573-4.

[6] Mansi, II, 476-7 reads "de civitate colonia Londinensium," for which Lingard had conjectured Lincoln and Haddon & Stubbs, Caerleon-on-Usk. Mr. S. N. Miller (*English Historical Review*, 1927, 79-80) has neatly emended the passage to read 'Camulodunensium' Colchester.

[7] The others thought it unbecoming, but "tres tantum ex Britannia, inopia proprii, publico usi sunt, sanctius putantes fiscum gravari quam singulos." Sulpicius Severus, *Hist. Sac.*, II, 41; Migne, *P.L.*, XX, 159-76.

[8] "De Excidio, etc.," in Migne, *P.L.*, LXIX, 337. Other patristic texts on the origin of Christianity in England are Tertullian, *Adv. Judaeos*, cap. VIII: "In quem enim alium universae gentes crediderunt nisi in Christum qui jam venit? Cui enim et aliae gentes crediderunt? . . . et Galliarum diversae nationes et Britannorum inaccessa Romanis loca, Christo vero subdita, et Sarmatarum et Dacorum et Germanorum . . . et quae enumerare minus possumus?" Migne, *P.L.*, II, 649-50 (the date is *c.* 200-206); St. Irenaeus, Adv. Haer., L.I, C.X, ibid., vii 554. Origen, *Homilia IV in Ezech*, *Hieron*, *interpr.* (*c.* A.D. 239); Migne, *P.G.*, XIII, 698; *Commentar. Series*, in Matt. xxiv, *sec Vet. Interpr.* (*c.* A.D. 246); ibid., 1655; *Homilia VI in Luc*, I, 24; *eodem interpr.*, ibid., 1816 (*c.* A.D. 230-46). Lesley (*De origine, etc.*, p. 18) refers both to Tertullian 'antiquissimus auctor,' and to Origen, but from the tone of the references it would not seem as though he were familiar with either of them.

but in desolate Britain the barbarian raids increased in intensity, the country districts were laid waste, the towns fell one by one, until finally in 442 the Roman occupation of Britain came to an end, and the Britons were left free but unprotected.[9] Meanwhile St. Germanus of Auxerre had landed in Britain a year after the first appearance (428) of the Saxons whom the wretched Britons had invited into their country to protect them against their other oppressors. Christianity at that time would seem to have been fairly wide-spread among the natives, for there is record of the great missioner preaching, not only in churches to the faithful, but also at cross-roads and in fields, such was the afflux of the curious to hear him. Certain passages in the letters of St. Jerome[10] bear the construction that pilgrims from Britain were not infrequent visitors to the Holy Places in Rome and even wandered as far afield as Palestine.

In the first half of the fifth century the Pelagian heresy endangered the integrity of the faith among the Britons, but not among the Scots of Ireland upon whom it apparently took no hold. Pelagius, who is presumed to have been born in Britain of Scots parents,[11] left his native country to settle in Rome under the pontificate of Damasus († 384), or at the latest, under that of Anastasius (399-401), but it was not until he had established himself in the Eternal City that he began to expound the erroneous doctrines concerning the nature of divine grace which he later propagated in Sicily, Africa and the East. His heresy was imported into Britain by one Agricola, the son of Severian, a Pelagian

[9] Cf. J. Loth, *La fin du monde antique*, 1927, pp. 236-7; and H. Stefan Schulz, 'The Roman Evacuation of Britain,' in the *Journal of Roman Studies*, XXIII, 1933, I, pp. 36-45.

[10] Cf. (a) Ep. XLVI, *Paulae et Eustochii ad Marcellam*, § 10 (c. A.D. 386): "Quicunque in Gallia fuerit primus huc properat: divisus ab orbe nostro Britannus si in religione processerit occiduo sole dimisso quaerit locum [sc. Jerusalem] fama sibi tantum et scripturarum relatione cognitum" (Migne, *P.L.*, XXII, 489; and (b) Ep. LXXVIII, *ad Oceanum de morte Fabiolae:* "Xenodochium in Portu Romano situm totus pariter mundus audivit. Sub una aestate didicit Britannus quod Aegyptus et Parthus noverant vere," ibid., 697. Fabiola, whose death is deplored, had together with Pammachius charitably founded a hostel at Ostia.

[11] As to the native country of Pelagius, cf. also Karl Müller in the Appendix to his *Der heilige Patrick*, Berlin, 1931; and M. Esposito, "Notes on Latin Learning," etc., in *Hermathena*, 1929.

bishop, and made such rapid progress that the orthodox Britons, feeling incapable of controverting it successfully unaided, begged assistance from the Church in Gaul. A synod was held and appointed Germanus, bishop of Auxerre, as most fitted to bring the British Pelagians back to the orthodox fold, and Pope Celestine himself, at the request of the deacon Palladius, confirmed the bishop selected for so important a task and gave him for associate St. Lupus, Bishop of Troyes. The two bishops discharged their duty admirably between 429 and 431 and reconverted many of the heretics. But they had no sooner taken their departure than the heresy raised its head again, and St. Germanus was compelled to cross the Channel once more in 447, accompanied on this occasion by Severus, Bishop of Treves. This second campaign extinguished Pelagianism in Britain.

At some date unknown, but before the first mission of St. Germanus, a Briton, who had been instructed in the Faith and Holy Scripture at Rome, journeyed across Gaul and England to bring the light of the Gospel to the peoples of the north, the Britons of Strathclyde and the Picts of Galloway; his name was Nynias (Ninian) and he was a bishop. He settled in the peninsula of Galloway and there built himself a church called *Candida Casa* (A.S., *Hwit-aern*, now Whithorn), from the light colour of the stone used, "a thing unusual among the Britons." Ninian's foundation developed into a flourishing school of missionaries (*Monasterium Rosnatense*), who spread the Faith in Strathclyde, and was much resorted to by the Irish and the Welsh, but the task of extending the kingdom of the Gospel further north was reserved for Colum-cille and his disciples and successors, the monks of Iona and Lindisfarne.[12]

[12] Cf. Bede, *H.E.*, III, 4, repeated in the *Anglo-Saxon Chronicle*, a.a. 560. Ninian's life was written in the twelfth century by Aelred, Abbot of Rievaulx, who adds that Ninian visited St. Martin at Tours and, receiving the news of Martin's death (A.D. 397) while his church was building, dedicated it to his memory. Cf. Karl Strecker, 'Zu den quellen für das leben des hl. Ninian', in *Neues Archiv.*, XLIII, 1920, pp. 1-26, and criticism in *Ana. Boll.*, XL, 1922, III-IV. All that we really know of Ninian is what we are told by Bede, but Strecker thinks that Aelred's 'source' was a Latin poem similar to the 'Miracula Nyssiae episcopi,' in *M.G.H., Poetae lat. aev. car. iv*, Berlin, 1923, 943-62. Dempster (*H.E. Scot.* II, 502) took it into his head to ascribe to him *Meditationes Psalterii* and *De Sententiis Sanctorum*.

The havoc wrought among the British Christian communities by the Anglo-Saxon invaders was devastating: "public as well as private structures were overturned; the priests were everywhere slain before the altars; the prelates and the people, without any respect of persons, were destroyed with fire and sword; nor were there any to bury those who had been thus cruelly slaughtered . . . some, with sorrowful hearts, fled beyond the seas. Others, continuing in their own country, led a miserable life among the woods, rocks, and mountains. . . ." The earliest invaders from the lower Weser and the lower Elbe[13] established in 455 the Saxon kingdom of Kent and were succeeded by other hordes which established in 477 the kingdom of Sussex and in 495 those of Wessex and Essex. The Britons fought desperately and the figure of King Arthur later became the personification of the resistance to the invaders and the centre of the famous cycle of chivalrous legends named after him. Other Germanic peoples, the Angles, followed close on the heels of the Saxons, and settling north of them expelled the Britons and established the three kingdoms of Northumbria (roughly present-day Yorkshire), divided into Bernicia and Deiria, East Anglia and Mercia. These seven Anglo-Saxon kingdoms constituted the so-called 'heptarchy.' The name of the Angles was applied to the whole country without regard to any of the other races, and so it came to be known as Engel-seaxna-land, Engla-land, England—Angleterre—Inghilterra. German paganism thus dominated the country until the coming of Augustine in 597.

The Anglo-Saxon encroachments drove the Britons into the West. Those in Strathclyde (in the neighbourhood of the present city of Carlisle), hemmed in between the Picts and the Anglians of Bernicia, defended their independence against their two formidable neighbours down to the ninth century. Others held out in ancient Cumbria (Lancaster), south of the former, but it was in Wales, Cornwall and Armorica ('little Britain,' modern Brittany) that the language and traditions of the fugitives found a most secure refuge and lingered longest.

[13] Ibid., I, 15.

Celtic and Saxon elements mingled in varying degrees in the territories adjoining these main refuges of the Celts, and recent progress in linguistic study has revealed the existence in the counties now known as Somerset, Gloucester and Cumberland of a mixed population which might be described as Anglo-Celtic.[14]

The consequence of these events was that the Britons dwelled in almost complete isolation from the rest of Christendom. No echo of the great Arian, Nestorian and monophysite controversies which divided East and West in the fifth and sixth centuries ever disturbed their intellectual tranquillity. They were left unmoved by the dogmatic, disciplinary and liturgical development. Everything around them was a-stir, they remained stock-still, so that, when towards the end of the sixth century and the beginning of the seventh, Augustine and his monks from Rome came into contact with them, they looked upon the Britons as foreigners, almost as heretics.[15]

§ 3

Their commercial relations with the insular Britons and the peoples of the European continent, their raiding expeditions across the sea, and the establishment of their settlements in Britain, more particularly in South Wales, the slave trade in which they were forever engaged and the capture in war of slaves for the most part Christian, had almost certainly brought the Scots of Ireland into contact with the Gospel as early as the end of the fourth century. In 431 Pope Celestine sent the Irish believing in Christ, *ad Scottos in Christum credentes*,[16] their first bishop in the person of one Palladius whom he had consecrated, a mission which would seem to suggest that the Christian communities in that country had already attained to some degree of

[14] Cf. the articles by J. Loth in the *Revue Celtique*, XXIX, 1907, 281-2, XXX, 1908, 287; and R. E. Zachrisson, *Romans, Kelts and Saxons in Ancient Britain*, Uppsala, 1927, p. 64 and *passim*.

[15] Cf. Gougaud, op. cit. 20-27: Cabrol, op. cit. 21-43.

[16] 'Epitoma Chronicon,' ed. Mommsen, in *M.G.H.*, *Auctores antiquissimi*, IX (*Chronica Minora*, I), p. 473.

importance. But Prosper of Aquitaine, our informant, adds in another work in praise of Celestine that the same Pope, while striving to keep the Roman island Catholic (an allusion to the anti-Pelagian mission of St. Germanus to Great Britain), exerted himself also to christianize the barbarous, i.e., non-Roman island, Ireland: "dum romanam insulam studet servare catholicam, fecit etiam barbaram christianam,"[17] an activity which would seem to indicate that the island of the Scots, lying outside the pale of civility, had not at that time made any notable progress in the Faith. Such is also the impression left by the writings of St. Patrick. The apostolic labours of Palladius in Ireland found no chronicler. Only a well preserved tradition[18] relates that he was inhospitably received, that after founding three churches he put to sea, was driven out of his course by a storm and compelled to take refuge somewhere in Scotland. There, it was believed, he founded a church at Fordun in the Mearns, and there, perhaps, he also died. His mission at all events was of short duration. The title of 'the apostle of Ireland' was reserved for another.

St. Patrick was born in Britain in the last quarter of the fourth century. He tells us himself, in the *Confessio* which he wrote towards the end of his life in passionate justification of his apostolate, that he was the son of one Calpornius, a deacon, who was also a *decurio*, and the grandson of Potitus, a priest, who was stationed at a *vicus*, which, variously written Banaven Taberniae and Banaventa Berniae, has not been satisfactorily identified. He had an estate hard by called Enon where Patrick, a lad of about sixteen at the time, was taken captive with "some thousands of others" in 401 by raiders from Ireland under the command of the high-king of Ireland, Níall *nói-gíallach*, Niall of the Nine Hostages. He was sold into slavery to one Miliucc moccu Buain, a small Pictish chieftain, lord of the territory of Dál Buain, towards the Lagan, in the country east of Lough Neagh, and employed in tending his master's flocks and herds. Looking back upon his captivity in old age,

---

[17] *Contra Collatorem*, c. 437, Migne, *P.L.*, LI, 271.
[18] Colgan, *Triad. Thaum.*, p. 5.

he reproached himself bitterly for having lived until then forgetful of the Lord and regardless of his duties as a Christian, but the miseries of bondage and exile, he considered, turned his heart to God. The love of God and the fear of Him (*timor* not *metus*) grew more and more, faith increased, and the spirit stirred, so that in one day, according to his own account, he offered up to the number of a hundred prayers and by night likewise, even while he stayed in the woods or on the mountain. During his servitude he learned Irish, which was later to prove of such service to him. His native tongue, it may be presumed, was Brythonic.

This first period of captivity lasted fully six years. Then one night he heard a voice telling him that he did well to fast as he would return presently to his own country. A little later he heard an answer—he describes these ghostly admonitions as answers—saying: "Your ship is ready," whereupon he left his master and made his way to the coast about two hundred miles distant. God directed his steps and he had no fear. A ship was on the point of sailing and the captain at first refused to take the fugitive on board. Patrick however prayed as he made his way back to the hut where he had taken shelter, and, before he had finished his prayer, he heard one of the men shouting after him: "Come back. These fellows are calling you," and he returned immediately. They set sail and after three days at sea made land and tramped across a desert for eight and twenty days until their provisions gave out and hunger overcame them. The captain turned to Patrick and, taunting him, asked if he could not pray to his great and omnipotent God to help them in their distress, and Patrick bade them be converted to his God to Whom nothing was impossible, if he wanted Him to send them food. And with God's help so it fell out. A herd of swine came before them on the road and the stranded sailors killed a number of them and ate their fill of pork and were greatly refreshed, because many of them had fainted and been left half-dead by the way. They also found wild honey in the woods and one of his mates offered some to Patrick, but, as he did so, remarked: "This shall be for a sacrifice," and Patrick therefore would have none of it. A little later he was taken captive a second time in circumstances which have not yet been satisfactorily explained, but he heard a divine answer telling him that in two months he would be free, and on the sixtieth night God delivered him out of the hands of his captors, so that eventually he was able to return home and see his relatives once more. They adopted him as a son and implored him after all the hardships he had undergone not to leave them again.[19] But one night at home he had a dream in which he saw a man coming as it were from Ireland with innumerable letters, one of which he handed to Patrick. Patrick read the beginning of the letter containing the Voice of the Irish and, as he read it aloud, he thought that at that very moment he heard the voice of those who dwelt by the wood of the Ulaid,[20] near the western sea, crying out as one: "We beseech you, holy youth, to come and walk amongst us once again," and he was so moved that he could read no more and sleep left him. He had no doubt then of his vocation. The affection of his family was powerless to detain him and he resolved, God governing him, to go and preach the gospel to the heathen of Ireland, to sacrifice his free-born condition for the sake of others, but first to acquire some direction in the spiritual life, some instruction in the scriptures and divine law before engaging in the new adventure.

[19] Lanigan (*Ecclesiastical History of Ireland*, I, p. 128, n. 179) and Bury conceived the text "eram cum parentibus meis qui me ut filium susceperunt et ex fide rogauerunt me ut . . . nusquam ab illis discederem" to mean that his parents were dead. Professor MacNeill, *St. Patrick*, C.T.S. of Ireland, Dublin, 1932, p. 28, controverts this view, but has overlooked the peculiar meaning of 'suscipere' in the fourth and fifth century. It means to adopt as a client, e.g. in the *Code of Theodosius*, XI, 24, 1, 3, 4. So Servius commenting *Aeneid*, VI, 609, observes, "Clientes quos nunc susceptos vocamus." Patrick, if this interpretation is right, was therefore adopted as a son. Dr. White translates (S.P.C.K., London, 1918) 'ex fide' both above and in § 18 as 'in good faith.' This is certainly wrong; the words in both cases simply mean 'on my honour.'

[20] Professor MacNeill has emended the 'Focluti,' of the text to 'Uluti,' the Wood of the Ulaid, now Killultagh, east of Lough Neagh. Even so, is it quite certain that this is what Patrick wrote? The words "quae est prope mare occidentale" have all the appearance of a gloss inserted by somebody (Tirechán?) to explain an emendation made by him of something which he did not understand. The shadow cast upon the whole passage by Acts xvi, 9 is oppressive.

The most important centre of spiritual life and learning at the time was the monastery founded in 410 by St. Honoratus in Lérins, a little island off the coast of Provence. Thither Patrick made his way and there in all probability he became a monk. It was his intention to complete his studies in Rome, but something happened, and he went instead to Auxerre. Lérins and Auxerre were closely connected in the bond of a common antagonism to Pelagianism, and Lupus, Bishop of Troyes in 426, Faustus, Bishop of Riez in 456 and himself a Briton, had both been schooled at Lérins. Of Patrick's life at Auxerre there is no record beyond the pious platitudes of his seventh century biographer, Muir-chú moccu Machthéni. He prepared himself at leisure, "like Paul at the feet of Gamaliel," for his self-imposed mission in devotional exercises and study under Amator the bishop, who died in 418, and Germanus, his successor, the same who, at the instance before the Pope of the deacon Palladius, had been sent to evangelize Britain. The story told by Muir-chú is far from clear,[21] but it would seem not unreasonable to suppose that Patrick, knowing Irish and having spent six years in Ireland, was deputed by Germanus to go and assist Palladius as a priest and was given for companion another priest, Segetius, who was to be his 'witness.' The two set out together but had reached no further than a place described as 'Eboria,' which some have taken to be 'Ebroicum' (*Ebroicorum civitas*), the modern Evreux in the Eure, although why they should have taken that route is not so clear, when the news reached them that Palladius had died. They retraced their steps to Auxerre. Patrick was thereupon consecrated bishop by Germanus and in 432 set sail for Ireland. *Et non ego sed Christus Dominus qui me imperavit ut venirem.*

The country to which Patrick thus returned after an absence of twenty-five years was a land of lake and mountain

---

[21] Unlike many hagiographers ancient and modern, Muir-chú candidly admits that his competence is unequal to his task, that his sources are uncertain (anonymous?), his memory unreliable, and his intelligence feeble. He complains of the diversity of opinions among his predecessors and begs to be excused the incoherence of his narrative on the ground that his intentions are pious and that he is obeying the order of a superior. *Vit. Trip.*, p. 269.

and fen, of broad pastures and primitive agriculture, divided into rather more than a hundred little states, *tuátha*, small communities of people inhabiting a limited extent of territory and arranged in seven groups with an over-king above the petty king of each *tuáth*, and a high-king above all.[22] Each was autonomous and the kingship was elective, not hereditary. Each was a religious unit in which the recognized ministers of religion were the Druids. They were a priesthood whose members presided at the sacrifices, lit the fire at religious festivals and burned the offerings, interpreted dreams and acted as exorcists, defied the elements, acted as the councillors of the king and were his ambassadors. They were the official intermediaries between the spiritual world and men and they wielded of course a formidable power of excommunication. Secular learning was represented by the *filid* whom the classical writers called οὐάτεις, the Greek transcription of the Gaulish word *uatis*, Latin *vatis*, which has survived in Irish as *fáith*, prophet. The *filid* were learned men and seers, adepts at divination, skilled in magic. A powerful confraternity, they embraced all the arts and crafts, the profession of medicine and the humbler trades of the smith, which always seems to have had something magical about it, the wright, the founder and the architect. They were the custodians of the national traditions, they knew the local legends, the *senchas*, of each *tuáth* by heart. They travelled all over the country reciting tales of gods and heroes at festivals and feastings wherever

[22] "A Tuath was a community of people not necessarily united by ties of blood, and therefore *not* to be called a tribe, which is *always* a misnomer wherever used in reference to Celtic Ireland." R. A. S. Macalister, *The Archæology of Ireland*, London, 1927, p. 25. Cf. also Eóin MacNeill, *Phases, etc.*, pp. 289 et seq. Mr. Christopher Dawson (*The Making of Europe*, London, 1932, p. 69) remarks that "the reluctance to accept this definition is, of course, due to the suggestion of cultural inferiority which the word 'tribe' carries with it." It must, however, be observed that the degree of culture is not in question, and that the idea of 'tribes' is simply a piece of modern fiction. The Ancients who, after all, were the best judges, never speak of 'tribes,' much less of the absurd 'clans.' Cæsar always refers to 'civitates Germanorum'; Tacitus to 'gentes,' 'civitates,' 'populi,' 'nationes,' while Strabo writes of ἔθνη. Even Giraldus Cambrensis, who noticed most things remarkable in Ireland and imagined others, never took it into his head to anticipate some seven or eight centuries and to describe 'clans.' The Latin for 'tuáth,' which Zeuss translates 'populus,' is more probably 'civitas,' a word which means merely a 'community.'

they could find an audience. They enjoyed and abused rights and privileges of entertainment and hospitality and maintained schools in which they taught large numbers of pupils drawn from all over Ireland to listen to teachers who enjoyed a national renown. A subsidiary body of the *filid* was composed of *brithemin* who, though Patrick conceived them to be judges and describes them as such, were not so much judges as jurisconsults, the repositories of precedents in law, the arbiters of vexed questions, whose decision or opinion was usually accepted as binding. The lowest class of all the lettered folk was made up of the bards, humble minstrels, dependent only on their wits to earn a livelihood, outcasts before the law, but feared by the commons because of their bitter tongues and the talent for sorcery with which they were believed to be endowed. The *filid* broke the bounds of the *tuáth* and spread over the nation. As a corporation they owed their allegiance to an *árd-ollamh*, the high *fili* of Ireland, who presided over the whole body, and the ideals of the nation found their earliest forms of expression, the sense of national unity its most effective support, in the *scéla* of the *filid*. They and the Druids were naturally rival institutions, and Patrick, apparently, with the intuition of genius, made it his first business to enlist the sympathy and gain the support of the *filid*.

He began his labours in Down among the Ulaid, but travelled far through the dominions of Dál Cuinn, from the western coasts of Ulster to Connacht, into the remotest parts beyond which no man dwelt and to which none had ever gone before to baptize or ordain clergy or confirm the people. He went very willingly for their salvation and inaugurated everything. He was conciliatory and gave presents to the *brithemin* in all the countries he visited to the value of no less than the price (an *eiric* or *wergild*) of fifteen men; he gave presents also to the kings over and above the rewards he distributed to their sons who walked along with him, eager to hear him expound the strange new gospel. He was exposed to many perils, however, and was arrested on one occasion with his companions and placed in irons. His captors robbed him of all his possessions and would have killed him, "but the time had not yet come," "and on the fourteenth day the Lord delivered him out of their power." Travelling everywhere like an itinerant *filé*, he preached his gospel, his *su-scéla*, as though it had been the marvellous improvisation of some preternaturally gifted member of the corporation, so that when he came in due course to the court of the *árd-rí*, Laoghaire, son of Níall, at Tara, Dubhthach, the *filé*, *poeta optimus*, was the first to rise up in his presence, although forbidden by his master to do so, and greeted the stranger, thus doing obeisance to one whom he acknowledged as his master in the art, the homage of Natural Law to the Law of the Letter. Dubhthach's pupil Fíacc became the first Bishop of Leinster, *mirabilis episcopus*, and his remains were venerated at Slébte (Sletty). The fruits of Patrick's labours were remarkable and the first tangible evidence of the success which attended his mission is to be found in an entry in the Annals of Ulster: "In the year 439, Secundus, Auxilius, and Serninus, all three bishops, were sent to Ireland to help Patrick." Secundus or Secundinus established his see at Domnach Sechnaill, now Dunshaughlin about five miles from Tara, and died in 447; Auxilius his at Cell-Usailli, now Killossy, near Naas. He died in 459. Iserninus his at Áth Fadat, now Aghado in Carlow. He died in 468. Patrick, working in the territory of Dál Cuinn, chose Árd-macha, close to the ruins of the ancient stronghold of Emain-Macha which the Dál Cuinn had overthrown, to be the base of his operations, and "the holy city on the hill" became in course of time the ecclesiastical metropolis of Ireland. It is now known as Armagh.

At some time before 459 the three surviving bishops issued a pastoral letter which throws a certain light on the circumstances of the *plebs Dei* living under their care in a country still predominantly pagan. Assuming clerics to be inmates of religious houses and recognizing some, not unnaturally, to be married, it forbade Christians to consult witches and soothsayers or to accept alms from the heathen. It imposed light penances on sins confessed.

Patrick himself had been trained in a monastery. It was

only natural therefore that he should commend life in community under a rule to the more ardent and devoted of his new converts, the sons and daughters of the petty kings of the Scots, who, in numbers too great for him to reckon, had become monks and virgins of Christ. But he was also and primarily a missionary bishop who had come from Gaul to lay the foundations of a new ecclesiastical system, and the oft repeated statement[23] that the basis of the Irish Church was monastic is, like so much else written about the achievement of the Saint, mere figment. He had decreed before he died that there should be a bishop in every *tuáth*, but on his death, while there may have been some fifty bishops consecrated, only about four or five sees had been duly constituted. *Tantae molis erat. . . .* There were, it is important to observe, no towns in Ireland.[24]

His laborious episcopate came to an end in A.D. 461, but its very success had aroused jealousy, and before he died accusations were being circulated against him of want of education, arrogance, and self-seeking. He was even charged with avarice and greed, and thought it necessary to defend himself. He had baptized thousands, he declared with indignation, and never required from anyone so much as the smallest silver coin. God through his poor instrumentality had ordained priests everywhere, but he never took anything for having conferred the sacrament, not even the price of his shoe-leather. The Christian brethren to whom he ministered, the virgins of Christ to whom he had given the veil, the women who, under his direction, had taken a vow of continence, spontaneously made him little presents and threw their ornaments upon the altar at which he had

---

[23] C.f., e.g., G. T. Stokes, *Ireland and the Celtic Church*, London, 1907, a book stuffed with glaring errors, of which the title is not the least, and yet purporting to be revised in its sixth edition by H. C. Lawlor, D.D., and A. R. MacEwen, *History of the Church of Scotland*, London, 1913, Vol. I, which among other *ineptiae*, observes (p. 85) of the community at Iona: "Of violence, contentiousness and dogmatism, the besetting sin of monks, they showed no sign . . . their intense zeal, their genuine humility, their scriptural and evangelical fidelity are attested by every witness . . ." so unlike other monks; and contrives in a chapter (IX) on 'Church Life and Worship' not to mention the word 'Mass' except once in a footnote, and then with inverted commas.

[24] Giraldus Cambrensis, also, had been impressed by this singularity: "Non urbe, non vicis, non castris cohabitant, sed quasi solitarii silvis inhaerent." Cf. DK., *Opera* (Rolls Series) ed. Brewer and Dimock, V, 17, p. 200.

offered his Mass, but he returned them all and, although
they were offended at his doing so, he did so from prudence
and not to give the heathen any ground for spreading
stories to his disparagement. It was not the heathen he
needed have feared.

After his death the memory of the great missionary seems
to have faded. There is no mention of him in the literary
remains of Columban, none in Bede. The reference to
him in the second preface of Adamnán is perfunctory.
Cogitosus, who wrote the life of Brigid, is silent. Only in the
diptychs of his own church at Armagh does his name seem
to have been held in honour. It was one of the first communities to be established on a monastic basis, one of the
earliest to collect such traditions as were current about its
patron. In the seventh century a cloud of legend began to
gather about the head of the Saint and in succeeding
centuries grew until the features of the man were lost to
sight dazzled by the portentous halo. He was likened to
the Messiah, to Moses and the Prophets, to Joseph and the
other Worthies of the Old Testament. A fantastic genealogy
was devised for him and he was declared to have been
thirteenth in the line of descent from Brittus, the first King
of the Britons,[25] or again to have been the nephew on his
mother's side of St. Martin of Tours.[26] An ideal itinerary
was invented for him, and there was no place in Ireland
boasting a church of any antiquity but he had visited it,
placed a priest in charge and given him an *abgitorium* or
abecedary, of which he was said to have written out with
his own hand the suspicious number of 365, before passing
on to the next. Marvellous tales were told of his encounters
with the Druids, the champions of the ancient paganism,
in contests of magic, of his battles with demons and the
fauna of Irish mythology. He became the national hero,
the most powerful patron of the people, and at the Last
Assize, it was believed, Patrick, sitting by the right hand
of Christ, would judge his own in the valley of Josaphat.[27]

[25] Cf. the 'Leabhar Breac' in the *Vit. Trip.*, II, 432.
[26] Cf. Colgan, *Vita IV* *auctore Probo*, and Marianus Scottus, *PL*, CXLVII,
623 anno 410. [27] Cf. Fr. Paul Grosjean, S.J., 'A Tale of Doomsday Colum-
cille should have left untold,' in *Scottish Gaelic Studies*, III, 1929, pp. 80-81.

Seven years before that *dies irae*, Ireland would be engulfed in the ocean and its people spared the persecution of the Antichrist—another boon St. Patrick had obtained from the Lord.[28] However, the confession which he made before he died so that his brethren and relations should know his quality and be able to discern the desire of his soul is testimony enough. Born a freeman according to the flesh, he sold his nobility, without shame or regret, for the benefit of others. He did not want to go to Ireland and be reviled by the heathen. He had no *natural* compassion for the people who had enslaved him and slaughtered the men and women on his father's estate; but the Spirit moved him, unworthy though he felt himself to be, and he went. The heathen were not so unkind as the fellow Christians who scoffed at him, and he remained. He, whose dearest friend had deserted him in the crisis of his life, ran the gauntlet of the jeers of his enemies and, old man though he was and worn out with his labours, he would not be silent about the signs and wonders shewn to him by the Lord many years before they came to pass. He, "an alien and a stranger," laid the country in which he laboured uninvited under an incalculable debt of obligation. He had his reward—after death. His work endures and he abides in the memory of the people he converted, unchallenged and unchallengeable, the first and greatest of the apostles of Ireland, a lonely, suffering man.[29]

§ 4

St. Patrick, it was observed, had come from Gaul to lay the foundations of a new ecclesiastical system in a country which had never known the administrative system of the

[28] 'Additamenta ad Tirechanum' in *Vit. Trip. II*, p. 331, et seq.

[29] The most valuable of recent contributions to the history of St. Patrick has come from Germany: *Der heilige Patrick*, by Karl Müller, *Nachrichten von der gesellschaft der wissenschaften zu Göttingen*, Weidmannsche Buchhandlung, Berlin, 1931. The learned author, affirming that the birthplace of the saint is to be sought in the estuary of the Severn, doubts, very reasonably, if anything can be definitely asserted touching his residence in Gaul and Italy. Mr. G. H. Wheeler, however, has recently (*Eng. Hist. Rev.* Jan., 1935, pp. 109-113) suggested Bewcastle as the birthplace of the Saint. The claims of Dumbarton, still sometimes obtruded, have always been negligible.

Roman Empire. He came to preach in an island which had no towns a religion which had grown and developed in towns—a religion which, as some of its modern opponents unceasingly reiterate, made a peculiar appeal to the proletariat, in a country which had the happiness of having no proletariat. The Catholic Church under the Empire had been slow to penetrate the countryside, and 'pagan,' it is common knowledge, was merely another word for 'peasant.' By the end of the fourth century, however, it had outgrown its obscure and modest beginnings, defined its dogma and established its hierarchical organization, which though the names of its officers still continued to be Greek, was modelled on the administrative system, the towns and provinces, of Rome. The town (*urbs*) had become the ecclesiastical unit and, together with its surrounding and dependent territory, was placed under the jurisdiction of an *episcopus*, bishop. They formed his *parouchia*, parish.[30] The provincial high-priest of paganism was gradually ousted and the Catholic bishop, who took his place, assumed also his title of *pontifex* or *sacerdos*.[31] As his flock became more numerous and his duties more onerous, it became impossible for the bishop to oversee everything in his *parouchia* or *diocesis*, as his district was also called,[32] and another bishop was appointed by him as his deputy (*visitator, circuitor*) to go round and superintend the countryside. This chorepiscopus, χώρας ἐπισχοπος or country bishop, lingered on until the tenth century on the Continent, but in Ireland survived until the twelfth, when he was abolished.

The task of converting the pagans in the countryside devolved therefore upon a new institution, the monastery.

[30] The word does not mean a place, but is merely the collective noun to designate the community of Christians living as strangers and sojourners in this world under their bishop, and only afterwards was applied to the area in which they dwelt. So 'pieve' in modern Italian derives from 'plebs Dei.' The word 'parouchia' in Irish was rendered 'fairche.'

[31] Until the end of the sixth century at least *sacerdos* always means a bishop. Gregory of Tours uses the words *episcopus* and *sacerdos* indifferently. *Archiepiscopus*, however, an uncommon form, makes its first appearance, it is believed, in the *acta* of the Council of Macon, A.D. 581.

[32] Cf. St. Jerome, *Ep. CIX ad Riparium presbyterum: Miror sanctum episcopum, in cujus parochia esse presbyter dicitur, acquiescere furori ejus. P.L.*, XXII, 908, ubi parochia sumitur pro diocesi. The later differentiation apparently was that *diocesis* was reserved for the province of an archbishop.

D—i

The solitary life, much practised in the East, would seem
to have been discouraged by authority in the West, and
solitaries exhorted to associate at least for devotions in a
monasterion, a word which came to mean the exact opposite
of its etymology. Bishops were not responsible for their
establishment. They grew spontaneously to meet an eternal
human need. Two things only were required: a patch of
land and some relics, the bones of the canonized founder
in many cases constituting the principal relic.[33] The
monastery also had this singularity that it knew no distinction
of persons: all were eligible for admission alike, bond and
free.[34] The monasteries in his territory were subject to the
jurisdiction of the bishop,[35] but the community elected its
own abbot and vowed him only absolute obedience. The
first monastery in the West was founded by St. Martin at
Ligugé,[36] near Poitiers, and the movement received a
powerful impulse from the writings of St. Athanasius. It
spread to Britain and Germanus of Auxerre is said to have
ordained Illtud, the founder of the famous monastic school
of Llan-Illtud and "the first great abbot of the British
Church."[37] Llan-Illtud was the school which produced St.
Samson of Dol, one of the most famous saints of Brittany,
St. Pol Aurélien, Bishop of Léon, the gloomy Gildas himself,
perhaps, but, most important of all, Dewi Sant, the national
saint of Wales, and the founder of the see of Mynywd,
called in Latin *Menevia*, whose popularity in his own country
under the Hebraized form of his name, David, down to the
Reformation, rivalled that of St. Patrick in Ireland or St.
Martin in Gaul. St. Cadoc founded the monastery of
Llan-carvan, but the greatest of the Welsh monasteries was
beyond question that of Bangor-is-Coed on the Dee, in which,

[33] Cf. Gregory of Tours, *Miracula Martyrum*, 33, 39, *De gloria confessorum*, 50,
and almost *passim*.

[34] But the slaves had first to be redeemed or have received their owners'
permission. Cf. *Vita Bercharii*, 14, in Mabillon, *AA. SS.*, II, 480: "Pretio
suscepit captivas puellas octo quas Deo dicatas ibi manere constituit."

[35] By the Council of Arles, A.D. 554, art 2: "Ut monasteria, vel monachorum
disciplina ad eum pertineant episcopum in cujus sunt territorio constituta."

[36] "Monasterium Locociagense quo congregatam monachorum catervam
locaverat vir beatus," writes Gregory, *Miracula Martini*, IV, 30, suggesting a
concentration at Ligugé of isolated groups of hermits.

[37] Ryan, *Irish Monasticism*, p. 110.

it was reported, "there was so great a number of monks that, the monastery being divided into seven parts, with a ruler over each, none of those parts contained less than three hundred men, who all lived by the labour of their hands."[38]

Relations between Wales and Ireland had always been close and continuous. St. Patrick himself was born in South Wales, and from Wales came the impulse to the extraordinary development of monasticism in Ireland in the sixth century. The hierarchical organization which Patrick would have imposed found no natural basis in the political system of the country, and the great saints of the sixth century, having grown up at a time when only its ruins reminded them of the old Roman system, and being left to their own devices owing to the chaos on the Continent, seem to have wrought a revolution in the polity of the Irish church and substituted the monastery for the continental 'city' as the centre of ecclesiastical life and culture. The name, as often happens, survived though the substance was different, and the monastery and its dependence together formed the 'civitas.'[39] Bishops were not abolished. They were indispensable to perform their own peculiar functions in cases where the abbot was not himself a bishop. They continued on also in the *tuátha* to found (*longo intervallo*) the medieval Irish sees, but their multiplication was a source of weakness at home and an embarassment when their peregrinating proclivities drove them abroad.

An extraordinary number of monasteries sprang up all over Ireland in the sixth century, and in the seventh increasing numbers of solitaries withdrew from the society of men to lead the religious life in seclusion. Nowhere, except, perhaps, in Egypt in the time of the Fathers of the Desert, did the monastic institution develop so rapidly or produce types so singular and in such abundance of sanctity so authentic and assured.

Killeany (Cell Enda), the earliest of these monastic

[38] Bede, *H.E.*, II, 2, Everyman trs., p. 68.
[39] The word requires some care. It does not mean a place but, primarily, a community associated by a common purpose, united by a common bond.

foundations, and the oldest of those centres of learning, which, from the first half of the sixth century onwards, are reputed to have been the glory of Ireland, was thought to have been founded by St. Enda[40] on Aran mor, the largest of the Aran Islands at the entrance to the Bay of Galway. Unrecorded in the annals, Enda seems to have lived in the first half of the sixth century, and, according to the legend, received a grant of Aran from a King of Munster. He acquired fame as a teacher and numbered among his pupils Finnian, Brendan of Clúain-ferta, Ciarán of Clúain-moccu-Nóis, and Colum-cille of Iona, all destined in their turn to be founders of monasteries and all enrolled as early as the eighth century in the *Catalogue of the Saints of Ireland*. Another Finnian, moccu Telduib, who died in 549, founded Clúain-Iráird, 'Erard's meadow' in the 'midlands,' Meath, which also became a school of great renown and is said to have attracted 3,000 disciples. In 540 St. Enda's pupil, Finnian moccu Fiatach, founded the abbey of Mag-Bile (Moville) on the Strangford Lough in Ulster. About 544 or 548 St. Ciarán *mac in tsair*, the humble son of a carpenter, collected a little company of eight and built a monastery on the left bank of the Shannon, "in a quiet watered land, a land of roses," afterwards known as the "Meadow of the race of Nois," and now called Clonmacnoise. It became the Westminster Abbey of the Gael, "And the warriors of Erin in their famous generations slumber there." In 546 Columcille set up Dair-mag, 'Oak-plain,' now Durrow in Offaley, and Daire-Calgach, 'Calgach's Oak-wood,' now Derry. Glendalough in the valley of two lakes amid the mountains of Wicklow was founded *c.* 550 by Coemgen (*anglice* Kevin), of the royal house of Leinster, Clúain-ferta, 'the meadow of graves,' in Connacht, by St. Brendan the Navigator *c.* 564, and Bend-chor, the modern Bangor, on the southern shore of the Belfast Lough, *c.* 559, by St. Comgall of the Dál Araide, the master of St. Columban and the intimate friend of Colum-cille. He died in 602.

[40] St. Enda, it should be observed, was associated with St. Ninian's foundation at Whithorn in Wigtownshire, the Rosnat of Irish tradition, and representative, therefore, of an influence distinct from, and secondary to, the stronger current flowing from South Wales.

The Irish monasteries bore no resemblance to the imposing Benedictine abbeys of the Middle Ages. Like primitive pioneer settlements or the rude dwellings of the Egyptian laura, they consisted of groups of huts, each harbouring one or more of the community, and oratories. The buildings were of wattle and thatch, poles and rods being first woven together in a wicker-work, then coated with clay. Undressed stone[41] was used wherever it was plentiful, uncemented, and the building, oval or rectangular in shape, was roofed, like the *trulli* (*Gk. troullas*, dome-shaped) in Puglia, with a dome or cupola by the progressive imposition of one layer upon another. The abbot in most cases, like the captain of a battleship, and for the same reason, lived apart in a hut placed upon a little eminence. The church (*tech mór*) and the oratories were equally unpretentious in structure and dimensions, and a kitchen (*cuicenn*), a refectory (*praind-téch*), and a guest-house (*téch-n-oiged*), presided over by its own special officer (*airchindech-tige-oiged*), the chief of the guest house, made the monastic state complete and self-sufficient.[42]

A monastery of the sort was quickly established. The founders in Ireland usually selected the site of some old pagan stronghold, as in other countries that of a fortified enclosure dating back to the days of the legions. The rampart of the fort or *castrum*, *rath* in Irish, became the enclosure of the new monastery. The earliest monastic settlements in the East and in Gaul were formed in the same way and surrounded by a *vallum*.

The Irish monks rivalled the solitaries of the desert in the asceticism of their lives and the rigour of their discipline. Manual labour at the plough or in the smithy was the least of the mortifications they practised. Liturgical prayer, based substantially upon the Psalter, absorbed a great part of the day and night and in many cases was accompanied by gestures of adoration, demonstrations of penitence such as plunging into the ice-cold waters of rivers and loughs, prostrations and genuflexions (on occasion three hundred

---

[41] The first stone church in Ireland is traditionally said to have been built at Duleek (Daimliac = 'house of stone'), by St. Cianan.

[42] Ryan, *Irish Monasticism*, pp. 285-94.

by day and three hundred by night), and long stations with
the arms outstretched in the form of a cross (*cross-figell=
crucis vigilia*). Of St. Coemgen of Glendalough it is related
that he remained for seven years standing upon a board in
the *crossfigil* posture, without closing an eyelid day or night,
and so rigid that the birds, *ut ferunt*, nested in his hands.
Their diet was as frugal as their religious devotions were
austere. They ate no meat and fish but seldom; their staple
was vegetables seasoned with salt, and the little monastic
loaf, the *paxamation*, the classic fare of the East. Many of
them took themselves off at intervals or for good to live a
life of solitude in the woods or among the rocks in the
Irish *disert*, an appetite difficult for us at the end of our old
and decaying civilization to understand. But at the end
of the fourth and fifth centuries Western Europe renewed
its youth, and "after the breakdown of strict society, the
love of hermitage also grew passionately . . . that it must
return soon or late is certain; it is of permanent recurrence
in the history of mankind."[43] The solitary would sometimes
become an incluse enclosed in his *carcair* (Lat. *carcer*) close
to some church or monastery, but there is no trace in the
Irish records of any solemn ceremony of immuration such
as attended the walling-up of an incluse in the Middle Ages.
The hermit or anchorite was invested with particular regard
and consideration, and down to the twelfth century and
even later the practice of withdrawing from commerce with
the world to commune only with the spirit and contemplate
divine things in solitude was much in vogue in Wales.[44]

The extraordinary development of monasticism in Ireland
has been attributed to a diversity of causes. In Dom
Gougaud's opinion[45] there are chiefly two: "The burning
zeal of the apostles of the country, themselves very often
monks, who from the outset set their hearts on promoting
monastic institutions. . . . A large number of the baptized
had scarcely felt the regenerating touch of the sacramental
waters, when they were drawn to follow the evangelic

[43] H. Belloc, *The Cruise of the Nona*, London, 1925, pp. 20-21.
[44] Giraldus Cambrensis, *D.K.*, Opp. VI, 204; Gougaud, op cit., 99-100;
Cabrol, op. cit., 182-95; and Albers, *Aforismi di storia monastica*, 125-44.
[45] *Christianity in Celtic Lands*, p. 65.

counsels: once become Christians, they were impelled by holy zeal to vow themselves forthwith to the Christian religion in its entire extent." And the learned Benedictine quotes the observation of Frédéric Ozanam:[46] "The first ardours of faith which everywhere else led Christians to martyrdom impelled the Irish converts to the monastery." The second cause was the political and social condition of the country. "When it came to pass that a chieftain was converted, he would grant the missionary a site not only for a church, but also for a monastic settlement. . . ." Founder's kin in the little state enjoyed a unique privilege; the abbacy became hereditary in the family of the *regulus* who had granted the land or in that of the abbey's holy founder. A third cause, and, it is suggested, not the least, was the practical necessity of training clergy, teaching Latin, expounding doctrine, producing copies of the Old and New Testament, providing the essential vestments and vessels for offering the Holy Sacrifice in every little station where a priest had been ordained to baptize and instruct the heathen. Patrick, according to the hymn composed in his honour in the late fifth century and attributed to Secundinus, showed the sound practical sense which distinguishes all great missionaries in his solicitude for the provision of such things in Ireland, and the sacred Scriptures especially are said to have "multiplied like manna in his hands."

§ 5

Ethne the Fair and Fedelm the Red, daughters of Leogaire, the obdurate pagan, believed and were baptized. A veil was laid upon their heads and they received the Eucharist of God and fell asleep in death; and they were laid on a couch under the one covering. Their friends bewailed them with loud cries . . . and when the days of mourning were ended, the King's daughters were buried, near the spring where they had come to bathe, in a round pit such as the pagans used to make. So Tírechán tells

[46] *La civilization chez les Francs*, Paris 1849, p. 97.

the story of the conversion of the daughters of the High-King of Ireland.

They were legion, these sons and daughters of the kings of the Scots who became monks and virgins of Christ. But it was against their fathers' will that they so dedicated themselves, and they were forced to endure persecution and reviling from their parents. Yet their number increased and included widows and matrons who lived continent lives in wedlock. The lot of the bondwomen, according to St. Patrick, was specially hard, but they endured in constancy in spite of intimidation and threats, for God gave grace to many of his handmaids and, though forbidden to do so, they steadfastly followed the example set before them. So Patrick felt justified in calling those who but lately had worshipped "only idols and filthy things," a *plebs Domini* and "children of God."

Women converts living in the heart of a society still predominantly pagan naturally inclined to draw together for protection and mutual support under the direction of the churchmen who had initiated them into the spiritual life.

The origins of women's convents in Ireland are obscure, but certain aspects of the character and career of the great St. Brigid would suggest that there had been a primeval cult of fire tended perpetually by Vestal Virgins, as in Rome, so that the transition from one form of conventual life to another under the Law of the Letter would present no difficulties once the initial obstacles had been overcome.

Nunneries (*monasteria puellarum*) were flourishing in the time of Colum-cille, A.D. 597, and in the century following it was Aidan, a Scot from Iona and first abbot of Lindisfarne, who gave the veil to Heiu, the abbess of a little convent at Hereteu, now Hartlepool, and the first woman in Northumbria to take the veil. She was succeeded by Hilda, a lady of exalted lineage, who built a double monastery at Whitby and ruled a sisterhood of nuns and a confraternity of monks under her maternal authority.[47]

Of Irish virgins much the most remarkable was Brigid

[47] Bede, *H.E.*, III, 24; IV, 23.

of Cell-dara, 'the Church of the Oak,' now known as Kildare, in the territory of the Lagan, the men of Leinster. Her life[48] was written by one Cogitosus, whom some conceive, but doubtfully, to have been the father of Muir-chú, the author of the earliest life of St. Patrick. Drawing copiously upon a rich store of myth and popular legend, Cogitosus conceived his heroine to have been the daughter of a slave in the household of one Dubhthach, who, rejecting the suitors attracted by her beauty, succeeded in taking the veil at the hands of a bishop Macaille and founded a convent, which presently became an ardent centre of religious life. A bishop Conlaed was associated with her in the performance of sacerdotal functions for her community, and his remains were preserved with hers under the high altar in the church, "spacious and lofty, adorned with mural paintings, containing three ample *oratoria* and partitioned by painted walls," of the double monastery she governed. Cell-dara and its dependence together formed a *civitas*, ruled jointly by the bishop and the abbess, so that, in the words of her biographer, it was "a see at once episcopal and virginal." Cogitosus is the only biographer of the sainted abbess who relates the story of the double monastery and, no other example of such an institution having been found among Irish Christians, doubts have been expressed as to its existence in his time. The church, however, survived down to the Norman invasion and was visited by Giraldus Cambrensis, who has left an interesting description of it.[49] Brigid died in 524 or 521. The martyrologists, beginning with Bede, enter her name on the 1st February. Her popularity among the Scots, who looked upon her as a Patron and Protector of Ireland second only to the great apostle, was extraordinary. She early became a particular patron of the *filid*, a 'goddess of poets,' and her feast was certainly celebrated in Ireland in the eighth century. Devotion to her was carried over to, and propagated throughout, Europe by the Scots *peregrini* wherever they

[48] Cf. Migne, *P.L.*, LXXII, 775-90; and M. Esposito, 'Notes on Latin Learning,' etc., in *Hermathena*, 1929.

[49] Top. Hib. XXXIV-XXXVI.

settled,[50] and their propaganda in her favour attained dizzy heights. In the Book of Leinster[51] Brigid was compared to Our Lady and acclaimed as "the Prophetess of Christ, the Queen of the South, the Mary of the Gael." In the hymn *Ni car Brigit*, attributed to Broccán,[52] she is described as "the mother of my High-King," while in Ultan's hymn *Brigit be Bithmaith*,[53] she is exhorted to "extirpate in us the vices of our flesh, she, the branch with blossoms, the mother of Jesus," a flight of imagination testifying by its very extravagance to the fabulous sanctity of the abbess of Cell-dara and to the potency of her influence upon the religious and monastic life of Ireland.[54]

§ 6

The Church in Ireland, it has often been observed,[55] had no martyrs, and for the obvious reason that in no country in Europe was the division between Church and State so absolute. No violent conflict was waged with heathenism which was quickly absorbed only to re-appear transfigured. The comparatively rapid and bloodless conversion of the country, the subsequent burgeoning of a collective life, animated by such intense and profound Christian feeling, into an efflorescence continuous and unparalleled through three or four centuries of sanctity in heroic types of men and women, exhibiting a loyalty to Rome, unbroken and unique, through fifteen centuries of indescribable martyrdom, are facts of history which provoke

---

[50] Cf. Gougaud, *Gaelic Pioneers*, p. 104 et seq.

[51] Cf. Whitley Stokes, *Lives of Saints from the Book of Lismore*, pp. 51, 198.

[52] Cf. the Irish *Liber Hymnorum*, ed. Bernard and Atkinson, London, 1898; I, 112; II, 40.

[53] Ibid, I, 110; II, 39.

[54] Colgan reprints (*Tria. Thaum, app. VI, ad vitas beat. Brig.*, p. 600, col. 2) the office of St. Brigit printed in Paris in 1622:

"*Lectio sexta:* Tunc vir quidam sanctus in Synodo dormiens vidit visionem et surgens ait: Haec altera Maria quae habitat inter nos.

"*Respons:* Virgo deportatur, honor ei amplius cumulatur: synodus instabat, nona Brigida stella micabat. Sacra cohors plaudit, quia signum celitus audit.

"*Vers:* Praesbyter hanc aliam denuntiat esse Mariam."

[55] Notably and *in primis* by Giraldus Cambrensis, 'Top. Hib.' in *Opp.* V, 174: "unde et omnes sancti terrae istius confessores sunt et nullus martyr quod in alio regno Christiano difficile erit invenire."

the wonder of anyone who, considering them, should also seek to explain them.

It would almost appear as though Tertullian's trite description of the *anima naturaliter christiana* could find no more fitting application than to the Celtic race. Ernest Renan, himself a Breton, once wrote an essay much applauded in its day (1855), *La poésie des races celtiques*, in[56] which he declared that "that gentle little race was naturally Christian." Sober history comes to no such comfortable conclusion. The Christian virtues encountered and encounter obstacles no less formidable in the heart of the Celt than in any other of the children of Adam, and such fugitive glimpses as can be caught of the pagan Celt display him in no serene light. The ancient Irish worshipped stocks and stones, offered children in sacrifice to ensure their milk and corn, and celebrated the funeral of a great warrior by burying captives alive. Patrick, we are told, waged unceasing war against the machinations of the Druids, but paganism and its crudities are congenial to the natural man, man unsanctified by grace, difficult to eradicate, and never, perhaps, wholly extirpated. Man continues to be man, *ni ange, ni bête*, and God, it has been finely said, need be in no hurry, for He, having eternity to work in, can afford to wait. Renan, however, for all his sentimentality, may have stumbled upon something more important when he remarked that "never had a human family lived more apart from the world and been freer from all alien admixture," that the Celtic family "had drawn everything out of itself, lived solely on its own capital." There is, perhaps, an element of truth in this, and, if it be taken into consideration with that other fundamental truth of Christian teaching, man's first disobedience and his fall, it may be possible to discern the secret of the Irish phenomenon. "It should always be borne in mind that the first age of felicity, when man had a true and proper conception of God, Who revealed Himself to man, as Holy Writ securely testifies, was followed by a state of barbarism in which, however, the conception pre-

[56] Republished in *Essais de morale et de critique*, 10th ed., Paris, Calman-Lévy, 1929.

served in the primitive tradition could not, in spite of subsequent errors with regard to religion and God, be wholly
effaced even among the most thoroughly barbarized peoples.
The proper conception to hold, therefore, is not that of a
religion in process of *formation*, but rather that of a religious
tradition in process of *deformation*, the faculty of rising from
created things to their Creator always retaining its primitive
spontaneity, at least as a generic idea, in nations and individuals alike."[57] The ethnographical investigations of Fr.
Wilhelm Schmidt, the eminent anthropologist, have bril-
liantly confirmed these truths as against the too facile
simplifications of merely materialist evolutionary theory.
The Gaels had dwelt in isolation, since about 800 B.C., in
the Ultima Thule of Ireland and had not therefore undergone any of the progressive and profound *deformations* of
continental paganism or experienced any of the refinements
of Oriental and Græco-Roman corruption, so that when
they found themselves in the fifth century confronted with
primary truth in the person of St. Patrick, they recognized
it for what it was and did it reverence with an extraordinary
ardour of zeal. Some analogy may be found in the sphere
of individual experience. As great converts, once they
acquire by the touch of Grace the *sensus Christi* and realize
its capacity to turn all values topsy-turvy, attain at a bound
to the conception of Christianity as a *heroic* conception of
life, and simply *cannot help* abandoning all things to follow
and serve Christ—"Lord, what will you have me do?" (Acts
ix, 6)—so the Irish nation, the solitary instance in history,
collectively manifested such an unexpected, radical, and
ineffaceable regeneration and transformation. "Lord, what
will you have me do?" it exclaimed with one voice at the
end of the fifth century. And an army of saints of heroic
stature and original character rose in that privileged island
and thence marched over the world, bringing to the
remotest lands their unwearying apostolic fervour and
humble aspiration after martyrdom. Dom Gougaud[58] has

[57] Cf. *Civiltà Catholica*, 1st Nov., 1930, pp. 246-7.
[58] 'Les conceptions du martyre chez les Irlandais,' in *Revue bénédictine*, 1907,
p. 360.

shewn how ardent the longing for, and how fervent the cult of, martyrdom were among the earliest Irish saints, beginning with St. Patrick, and has recalled the names of St. Fingar and his companions, the Virgin Dymphna and Gerebern her guide, St. Kilian, and St. Blathmac, all of whom incarnadined the ancient pages of the island martyrology. Circumstances summoned but few of them to the glory of the martyrdom of blood, *derg mártra*, the red martyrdom as they called it, but hosts of others took their excellent revenge by crucifying their flesh in exemplary fashion in the long drawn out white martyrdom (*ban mártra*) of abnegation and chastity,[59] and in the grey-green martyrdom (*glas mártra*) of the most austere penance and the most rigid mortification.[60]

The eminent virtues and imposing numbers of these heroic servants of God earned for Ireland the distinguishing title of *Insula Sanctorum*, a description first found in the *Chronicon* of Marianus Scottus, the incluse of Fulda († 1083), and adopted ever since by innumerable writers upon the history of that country.[61] In the nineteenth century the English attempted to arrogate the title to themselves,[62] but

[59] "Habet et servata pudicitia martyrium suum," wrote St. Jerome in Ep 130 *ad Demetriadem, P.L.*, XXII, 1110; cf. Lugano, *S. Colombano*, p. 14, note, who recalls the significance of the colour white in the habit of many monks, the Irish included, and the *martyrum candidatus exercitus* in the *Te Deum*, which some would deny to Nicetas a Remesiana, included also in the Antiphonary of Bend-chor, *P.L.*, LXXII, 587. The *Te Deum*, it may be observed, almost certainly came to Ireland from Lérins, having reached there from Milan. White was originally the sole colour of the martyrs—the angels in Albrecht Dürer's plates illustrative of the Apocalypse (*c.* 1498) are depicted giving white robes to the martyrs, while a fiery rain of stars falls from Heaven—and red but a later development. The distinction is properly drawn in the Vesper hymn for the Festival of All Saints: "vos, purpurati martyres, vos, candidati praemio confessionis."

[60] Green, according to the *Leabhar Breac*, the 'Speckled Book,' compiled (*c.* 1411) by one of the MacEgans in north Tipperary, was the liturgical colour of mourning, because it recalled the greensward over the grave at the end of life. Cf. also with regard to the three kinds of martyrdom, Ryan, *Irish Monasticism*, p. 107 et seq.

[61] Cf. Cardinal Moran, 'Ireland: the Island of the Saints,' *Australasian Catholic Record*, October, 1909, p. 444; and Mons. J. Hogan, *Insula Sanctorum la storia d'un titolo usurpato*, Roma, Ferrari, 1910. It may be as well to give the text: "Hibernia insula sanctorum sanctis mirabilibus perplurimis sublimiter plura habetur." Anno 696 (DCLXXIV), *P.L.*, CXLVII, 751.

[62] The question has been exhaustively discussed by Dom Gougaud in an article in *Studies*, XIII, 1924, pp. 363-80. The modern mischief would seem to have begun with Lingard, whose *History and Antiquities of the Anglo-Saxon*

Mgr. Hogan, while endeavouring to explain why some confusion in the matter should have arisen on the Continent at the time, has triumphantly vindicated Ireland's right to this glorious and most ancient appellation.

Church was first published in 1808. Cf. the 3rd ed., London, 1845, II, 90. The error is reproduced by Abbot Cabrol, op. cit., 288, and Dom Ursmer Berlière, *L'ordre monastique des origines au XIIe siècle*, 3rd ed., Lille-Paris, 1924, 26. Cardinal La Fontaine, Patriarch of Venice, repeated it in a New Year letter to his clergy, as reported in *The Catholic Times* of 6th January, 1933.

CHAPTER II

§ 1

THE sanctity which flowered in Ireland immediately after the conversion was, it has been said, animated by an ardent spirit of proselytism and stirred by a great force of expansion. The converts of yesterday became the apostles of the morrow, and the enthusiasm of the monks inspired them with the desire to transport their ascetic practices overseas.

The Irish emigration to Armorica was insignificant in comparison with that from Wales, which assumed responsibility for the ecclesiastical organization and religious development of the peninsula in which the Britons expelled by the Anglo-Saxon conquest had taken refuge, and need not here be further dwelt upon.[1] The main stream of Irish expansion, which began to flow as early as the sixth century, was directed into other channels, to the north of Great Britain and the centre of Gaul, whence it spread into neighbouring continental countries until it ultimately reached Italy.

The emigration of the Irish was always accompanied by the love of art and letters. The Irish saints have always vividly realized the divine origin of all forms of beauty and both in moral oppression and physical suffering have always sought consolation, not only—as was but natural—in divine teaching and the doctrines of the holy Fathers, but also in the great prose writers and poets, and they were all with few exceptions in their varying degrees poets themselves.

"Sint tibi divitiae divinae dogmata legis
    Sanctorumque Patrum castae moderamina vitae,

[1] Cf. Gougaud, op. cit., pp. 109-28.

Omnia, quae dociles scripserunt ante magistri,
Vel quae doctiloqui cecinerunt carmina vates;
Has cape, divitias semper contemne caducas,"

was the counsel given by Columban to his disciple Set.[2]

Two phases, however, may be distinguished in this
expansion: a first phase, extending from the sixth to the
end of the seventh century, when the emigrants were
dominated almost exclusively by the thought of asceticism
and the desire to preach the Gospel among the pagans and
the Arians; and a second phase, beginning in the Carolingian epoch and developing after the first Danish invasion,
when Irish churchmen and scholars crossed over to the
mainland of Europe to devote themselves principally to
the culture of their own minds and imparting their learning
to others.

Illustrious examples of the earlier migratory movement
are to be found in Italy in the persons of St. Ursus of Aosta,
St. Columban of Bobbio, St. Fridian of Lucca, and St.
Cathal of Taranto; of the later in Dungal of Pavia and St.
Donatus of Fiesole.

During the first phase, the subject of this chapter, the
emigrants, the great majority of whom were monks, looked
upon voluntary expatriation as a supreme act of *self-sacrifice*,
supremely apt to perfect the work of renunciation to which
they had set their hands. The love of the Irish for their
island and their families, it should be observed, is as strong
as their tendency to leave both; and the dominant note of
their popular songs, even at the present day, is the heartfelt
homesickness of her sons in distant lands at the recollection
of their home and the mother that begat them.[3] To leave
their country 'for the love of God' (*peregrinatio pro Dei
amore*), 'for the name of the Lord' (*peregrinatio propter nomen
Domini*), 'for the love or the name of Christ' (*ob amorem, pro
amore, pro nomine Christi*), 'for the good of their soul' (*pro
remedio animae*), 'to attain the heavenly home' (*pro adipiscenda
in coelis patria, pro aeterna patria*), are the expressions com-

[2] Cf. also Ryan, *Irish Monasticism*, pp. 365-83.
[3] Ibid., p. 262.

monly used by the biographers of these holy travellers to describe the motives determining their subjects' peregrinations. They describe themselves as *peregrini*, i.e. aliens, voluntary exiles. They denied themselves, in most cases for life, any return home; and they are therefore likened by hagiographers to Abraham. They all seemed to have heard the voice which spoke to the patriarch: "Egredere de terra tua et de cognatione tua."[4]

The Irish monks were early visitors to the northern seas. Some, eager for absolute solitude, sought a place of retreat in wastes inaccessible to man. Of such was Cormac úa Liatháin, for whom Colum-cille of Iona obtained from Brude, King of the Picts, the protection of the Prince of the Orkneys, his suzerain. Cormac landed on those islands and, finding them inhabited, was certainly the first missionary to preach the Gospel to the natives.

The Irish geographer Dicuil, a fugitive from Iona, who completed his treatise, *De mensura orbis terrae*, in 825, declares that Irish monks had visited the Faroe Isles, situate almost half-way between the Orkneys and Iceland, and that, about a hundred years earlier, i.e. *c.* A.D. 795, some sixty-five or seventy years before the date generally accepted for its discovery by the Scandinavians, they had discovered the latter island, which he calls Thile. Dicuil's testimony is confirmed by the Icelandic tradition preserved in the *Islendígabók* and the *Landnámabók*.[5]

It is not improbable that St. Brendan the Navigator, the founder of the monastery at Clúain-ferta (552), and his companions to whom legend attributes a series of marvellous adventures (*immrama*), to be noticed in Chapter V, really

---

[4] On the spirit animating these wandering ascetics, cf. also Hans von Campenhausen, *Die asketische Heimatslosigkeit im altkirchlichen und frühmittelalterlichenmoenchtum*, Tubingen, Mohr, 1930. On the word *peregrinus*, cf. Ducange. *Peregrinatio*, it should be observed, does not mean 'wandering about,' but rather 'being abroad,' an exile for Christ's sake, and is best exemplified in the well-known entry in the Anglo-Saxon Chronicle for the year 891: "Three Scots came to King Alfred in a boat without any oars from Ireland whence they stole away, because they would live in a state of pilgrimage, for the love of God, they recked not where. . . . They were thus named: Dublslane, and Macbeth, and Maclinmun."

[5] On Dicuil and his work, cf. Mr. Esposito's severely critical essay in *Studies*, III, 1914, pp. 651-76.

did carry out voyages in far distant seas for some object now beyond our knowledge. Their odysseys exercised a spell of extreme fascination on the people of the Middle Ages and translations or adaptations of their epics are to be found in nearly every medieval European tongue.

It has even been averred that the adventurous coracles of the Irish monks, driven by currents or sped by favouring winds, reached the continent of America eight or nine centuries before Christopher Columbus; but the theory has failed to commend itself to modern criticism.[6]

§ 2

The settlement of Colum-cille in the little island of Iona was the first stage of the Irish expansion into the north of Great Britain.

Colum-cille,[7] the most illustrious in lineage of the saints of Ireland, was born in 521 (?), a prince of the royal line of the Uí Néill. He was educated in letters and trained in religion first at Mag-bile and later at Clúain Iráird, and became in his turn a founder of monasteries. Daire Calgaich (now Derry) and Dair-mag (now Durrow) were the most important of his Irish foundations, which tradition estimated at thirty-seven.[8]

Colum-cille left Ireland in 563 (?) "wishing to be an exile

[6] Cf. the bibliographical note in Cabrol, op. cit., p. 187; Gougaud, op., cit. 138; and Fridjof Nansen, *In Northern Mists*, London, 1911, I, 162-7.

[7] Cf. Vismara, 'Storia benedettina,' in *Aevum*, 1931, p. 510; a bibliography of the more recent work on St. Colum-cille (cf. 809-15 *bis*); and some observations on the controversy aroused by Dr. W. Douglas Simpson's *The Historical St. Columba*, Aberdeen, 1927, reference to which will be found also in *Analecta Bollandiana*, 1928, p. 410. Dr. Simpson argues that the Northern Picts received Christianity from Candida Casa, Bend-chor and Glasgow, not from Colum-cille, a thesis disposed of by Dr. Duke in the appendix to his *The Columban Church*.

[8] He was called Colum-cille (his baptismal name was Criomthann), because when he was a child under instruction at Dubhglaise in Tir Luighdheach in Cineall Conaill (now Temple Douglas) . . . "the children of the district . . . when they beheld him coming towards them from the monastery, used to lift their hands for joy and say with one voice, 'Here comes the Colum, or dove of the Church' . . . and the teacher . . . deemed it to be God's will that he should be always called by that name which was in the mouths of the innocent children." Cf. Keating, *Foras Feasa*, III, 101, Dineen's trans., London, 1908, and Dr. Reeves's note, p. 225, to his edition of Adamnán, Dublin and Edinburgh, 1857.

for Christ." The Irish Scots had settled early in the fifth century—as already mentioned in the Introduction—in Albion, in a country south of the Picts, called by them Dál Riada. The Picts who dwelt in the most northern, least accessible part, of the island beyond the Grampians, were still pagans. They and the Scots settlers in Dál Riada, his kinsmen, were in the mind of Colum-cille when he left Ireland.

He settled within reach of both these peoples on a small island three miles in length, belonging to one of them, but under the suzerainty of the other. Both renounced their rights in his favour, and the exile established himself in full security. The little island, some seventy miles north of Ireland, is separated from the mainland of Scotland by the island of Mull, and from Mull by a strait about a mile in width. It was called I or Hii, whence the adjectival form Iora which, by a scribal error, was corrupted into Iona, a name which has clung to it ever since. The 'island soldier,' *insulanus miles*, as Adamnán described him, lived in that solitude for thirty-four years.

On leaving Ireland he was accompanied by only twelve monks, but disciples soon flocked to Iona in large numbers. Other monasteries or hermitages soon sprang up in the adjoining isles of *Ethica*, *Elena*, *Hinba* and *Scia* (Skye).[9] These houses, together with those on the mainland of Scotland, whose number is said to have amounted in all to fifty-three, and those in Ireland, which their holy founder still continued to direct, formed one vast monastic confederation described as the *muintir Colum-cille*, the *familia Columbae*.

There is little positive record of the actual labours of Colum-cille and his monks among the Picts, but it may be taken for granted that the greater part of the thirty-four

[9] The Latin names, all adjectival forms, are Adamnán's. "Ethica terra [or insula] . . . has been conclusively identified with the low-lying and fertile island of Tiree, the Tireth, or 'land of corn.' . . . The name Hinba or Hinbina seems to designate the group of islands called the Garveloch Isles . . . which were the Imbath or 'sea surrounded' [or perhaps Canna or Uist]. The most westerly of the four islands which constitute this group is termed Elachnave and Eilean na Naomh, or the Island of Saints, i.e. Elena." Cf. Skene, op. cit., II, p. 128.

years during which the saint's *peregrinatio* lasted was absorbed in the difficult and dangerous task of evangelizing Dál Riada, whose King Aedhán mac Gabhráin was consecrated at Iona in 574 by Colum-cille himself. Colum-cille's eloquence (he was himself a poet, the friend and patron of the *filid*), the prestige of his family connections, his own austere example, must all have made a profound impression upon the barbarians and strewn his path with conversions. When he died in 597 Scotland was partly converted, and he well deserved his title of the Apostle of Caledonia: his disciples carried on and completed his work.

The name of Colum-cille, according to Adamnán, was venerated in distant Spain, the Gauls and beyond the Apennines in Rome itself, 'the capital of all cities.' England especially owes him a deep debt of gratitude for the work which his sons performed for her advantage, as we shall now see.[10]

[10] Cf. Gougaud, op. cit., pp. 133-36; and Cabrol, op. cit., pp. 46-48. Dr. G. G. Coulton has prefaced his latest volume *Scottish Abbeys and Social Life* (Cambridge University Press, 1933) with a disquisition on Celtic Monachism which this is not the place to appraise. After a disingenuous reference to Columba as a Scot of Ireland, "at a time when the Irish were perhaps more often called by that name than the inhabitants of North Britain" (p. 12), he tells his audience that the community at Iona "celebrated the Lord's Supper comparatively seldom . . . they lived at a time when the popular word 'Mass,' which in itself is descriptive of nothing, had not yet entirely superseded the earlier and accurately descriptive Christian terms of 'Eucharist,' or 'Holy Mysteries,' or 'Breaking of Bread.' The Lord's Supper is indeed spoken of as 'Missarum solemnia' by Adamnán; but the ordinary evening service is also called 'Missa,' as in other writings of about that time." Well, well! It does not seem to have occurred to the learned writer that Colum-cille and his disciples spoke Irish, that in Irish "the popular word 'Mass' " is unknown, that 'Mass' in Irish is *oifrenn* (Latin *offerendum*), in Welsh *offeren* (cf. the prayer: *Has oblationes . . .* IMMOLAMUS *tibi Domine Jesu Christe . . . pro animamus* (= *animabus*) *carorum nostrorum;* and the canon in the late seventh century Stowe Missal and Dom Gougaud's article in the *Dict. d'archéol. chrét. et de liturgie*, II, ii (1910), 2969-3032), and that, therefore, if the community at Iona had lived at a time when, etc., etc., the supersession would have left them entirely indifferent. The Holy *Sacrifice* is commonly described in Latin texts for short as 'Missa,' a comprehensive word (cf. Ducange, s.v.), and a cursory perusal of Adamnán's text *ad hoc* in *P.L.*, LXXXVIII, 725-76 shows: "audiens presbyterum sacrae Eucharistiae mysteria conficientem, quem ideo fratres . . . ad Missarum elegerant peragenda solemnia quia valde religiosum aestimabant . . ." (col. 737); "Christi corpus ex more conficere" (col. 740); "sacra celeriter Eucharistiae misteria praeparentur, hodie enim natalis Brendini est dies. Quare, ait minister, talia Missarum solemnia hodierna praeparari praecipis die?" (cols. 764-65). As to "the ordinary evening service" at Iona, little is known, but it may be suspected that, as the chief occupation of monks in all places is the celebration of the divine office, it was not substantially different

§ 3

The prime mover in the conversion of England was, as everybody knows, Pope Gregory the Great. The British monks had been unwilling, even if they had not lacked the power, to take any steps for the redemption of those who had massacred or enslaved their countrymen. St. Gregory, a former Benedictine monk, entrusted Augustine and forty other Roman Benedictines from the monastery of St. Andrew on the Coelian Hill with the honourable task of evangelizing the German invaders.[11] It has been suggested by Dom Lugano[12] that the example of St. Columban's foundations in Burgundy may have prompted Gregory to send not isolated monks or a small band, "but a complete monastery, which from the outset should offer pagan society the spectacle of Christian life in practice as it was preached."

Augustine landed in England in 597 (the year in which Colum-cille died) and found a powerful ally in Bertha, the wife of Ethelbert, King of Kent, and the daughter of the Frank Charibert, King of Paris, herself a devout Catholic. On Ethelbert's death in 604 or 605, two kingdoms of the heptarchy, Kent and Essex, had been won to the Faith: Essex was very soon lost again. The Roman monks continued the struggle unaided until 633; in 627 they had converted Edwin,

from the compline sung in any monastic house to-day, although complines as such did not exist in the primitive *cursus*. On one occasion, not a Sunday, when the brethren had shod themselves and were about to begin their several tasks about the monastery, Colum-cille, with a foreboding of the death of Columban, a bishop in Ireland, bade them make it a day of rest, "sacraeque oblationis obsequia praeparari . . . meque ait hodie sacra oportet Eucharistiae celebrare mysteria" (col. 763). The time was afternoon. What Dr. Coulton has not observed is that there was a curious rite of confraction practised at Iona, unless the celebrant happened to be a bishop. On this singularity cf. Dom Gougaud, loc. cit., and *Christianity in Celtic Lands*, p. 328 and notes 1 and 2.

[11] Cf. Cabrol, op. cit., p. 93 et seq.: Grisar, *S. Gregorio Magno*, Rome, Desclée, 1898, p. 233 et seq., Berlière, 'L'ordre monastique,' etc., and Fr. Paul Grosjean, 'Quelques textes irlandais sur Saint Grégoire le Grand,' in *Revue celtique*, 1929, pp. 223-251.

[12] 'S. Gregorio Magno e S. Colombano nella storia della cultura latina,' in *Riv. Stor. Benedettina*, 31st August 1915.

the powerful King of Northumbria, and the course seemed to be set fair for the entrance of the new religion into the other two kingdoms of the Angles, when all hopes were dashed by the defeat and death of Edwin at Ashfield in Yorkshire, fighting bravely against Penda, the heathen King of Mercia, and Caedwalla, King of the Britons (12th October, 633). The monks were forced to flee from Northumbria, and the converts, deprived of instruction, relapsed into their old idolatry.

Edwin was succeeded on the throne by Prince Oswald (633-642), a son of Adelfrid, the predecessor of Edwin, who had concealed himself in his youth from the jealousy of that prince and spent the time of his exile in learning from the Irish monks of Dál Riada or Iona the principles of the Gospel. They had baptized him and, ardent Christian that he was, he determined from the day of his accession to restore the Faith in his kingdom. He turned to Iona and solicited a supply of missionaries. The Irish, who had suffered none of the terrible losses of the invasion and, unlike the Britons, harboured no resentment against the Anglo-Saxons, sent him one Corman, a monk of severe and unbending temper, who speedily returned to his monastery in disgust and despair. A private monk of the name of Aidan was next selected, and the issue of his labours justified the wisdom of the choice.

Aidan settled in 635 on a little island in the North Sea, still accessible from the mainland at low water, and facing the royal palace at Bamborough. It was called Lindisfarne and is now known as Holy Island. It was *more Hibernico* both the seat of a monastery and a bishopric and for thirty years, down to the Synod of Whitby in 664—when the Irish religious predominance in the country came to an end—the most powerful centre of religious influence in England.

With the backing of the pious King Oswald, who, when occasion arose, acted as his interpreter, Aidan displayed such apostolic activity that Lightfoot[13] has unhesitatingly

---

[13] *Leaders of the Northern Church*, London, 1890, p. 9. The exaltation by certain writers of the 'Celtic' achievement may, however, not improperly be regarded as inspired mainly by the desire to belittle the Roman missionary effort.

declared that "it was not Augustine, but Aidan who was the apostle of England." Bede,[14] our sole authority for his life, speaks in the highest terms of praise of the virtues and labours of the holy bishop.

Aidan died in 651 and was succeeded by another Scot, Finan, "who built a church in the Isle of Lindisfarne, the episcopal see; nevertheless, after the manner of the Scots, he made it not of stone, but of hewn oak and covered it with reeds, and the same was afterwards dedicated in honour of St. Peter the Apostle by the reverend Archbishop Theodore."[15] Finan helped to spread Christianity beyond the frontiers of Northumbria: he baptized two heathen kings, Peada, the son of Penda, King of the Middle Angles in Mercia, and Sigbert, King of the East Saxons in Essex. He sent four priests into Mercia: "Cedd and Adda, and Betti and Diuma, the last of whom was by nation a Scot, the others English." The aforesaid priests, arriving in the province with the prince, "preached the word, and were willingly listened to; and many . . . were baptized daily." Cedd and Diuma were both later raised to the episcopate, the former in Sigbert's dominions, the latter among the Middle Angles, where his episcopate was of short duration. He died and was succeeded by yet another Scot, Cellach.

Finan's successor in the see of Lindisfarne was again another Scot, Colman.

Many of the Anglo-Saxons, beginning with Wilfred (634-709), who about that time entered into direct relations with Rome and gave their infant church a definitely Roman and anti-Scotic orientation, had been educated and moulded at Lindisfarne. "The Celts," in the words of Abbot Cabrol, "handed on to the Saxons, along with the Faith, the torch of learning."[16]

The South of England boasted two monastic foundations made by Irishmen: the little monastery of Bosham in modern Sussex, "encompassed with the sea and woods,"

[14] *H.E.*, III, 3, s. Cf. also for the history of the conversion of the Anglo-Saxons, Mons. Duchesne, *L'Église au VIème siècle*, Paris, E. De Boccard, 1925, pp. 591-624.
[15] Bede, *H.E.*, III, 23.
[16] Op. cit. p. 90.

which had been founded by a certain Dicuil, "for five or
six brothers, who served Our Lord in poverty and humility;
but none of the natives cared either to follow their course of
life, or hear their preaching"; and Malmesbury in Wiltshire, founded by Máel-dubh, the teacher of St. Aldhelm.[17]

§ 4

Although it is more than probable that some Irish churchmen crossed over to the continent of Europe in single spies
early in the first half of the sixth century,[18] St. Columban
may be regarded as the great pioneer of the Irish monastic
and apostolic emigrations.   He was born in Leinster—
Lagenorum terra—about 540.   A religious woman having
counselled him to abandon the world and serve the Lord,
he had recourse first to the school of the pious Abbot Sinchell at Cell-Achid, now Killeigh in Ofalley, and moved
thence to the great monastery of Bend-chor in Ulidia,
founded by Comgall of the Dál Araide in 558.   There he was
ordained priest in 572 and spent a number of years devoted
to asceticism, literary studies and sacred learning.   Duly
fashioned and finely tempered, Columban left Ireland about
589 with twelve companions,[19] like Colum-cille, to preach
the Gospel to other nations.   He made first for Britain,
insular or continental—we have no means of telling—and
disembarked on the coast of Gaul.   He arrived in Burgundy
about 590, and there founded in succession the monasteries
of Annegray, Luxeuil and Fontaines.

Luxeuil, through the novelty of its rule, the ardent zeal
and personal ascendancy of its founder, soon began to
exercise a powerful influence upon the neighbourhood, and

[17] Cf. Bede, *H.E.*, IV, 13; Gougaud, op. cit., pp. 137-39; and C. H. Slover,
'William of Malmesbury and the Irish,' in *Speculum*, 1927, II, pp. 268-83.
Bede (*HE.*, V, 18) refers to the monastery "quod Maildulfi *urbem* nuncupant."
By a false analogy with Eadelmesburg (Aldhelm's *civitas*) the *Maldubia civitas*
was rendered 'Meadelmesburg,' and so Malmesbury.   Máel-dubh and his
pupil are together commemorated, but by accident, in the name.
[18] Cf. Kenney, op. cit., p. 183.
[19] Their names have been preserved.   They were, according to Fleming,
Gall, Deicola (Dicuil?), Sigisbert, Columban junior, Cummin, Eunoc, Ecconan,
Equonam or Aegnon, Domitialis, Culian, Naemias, Lua or Potentinus, and
Flaithri or Florentinus.

the Rule of St. Columban became the object of such veneration that towards the middle of the seventh century many
monasteries in Gaul adopted it together with that of St.
Benedict. "In the annals of monasticism," writes Dom
Gougaud, "we do not think that any other example can be
found of an amalgamation of rules differing so widely in
spirit."[20] In Part III we will deal with the supersession
which presently took place of this double rule or single rule
of St. Columban by the single Rule of St. Benedict.

Expelled from Burgundy in 610 by Brunhilda, Columban
resumed his wanderings. They were not barren of consequence. His example, his exhortations, his mere blessing on
occasion, bestowed on the child of some notable who had
given him shelter, produced a crop of precious vocations
destined to bear fruit later in a harvest of monastic foundations. The progress of monasticism in seventh century Gaul
may well be traced by simply following the itinerary of the
saint. The monasteries of Faremoutiers (627), Jouarre
(630), and Rebais (c. 636), all in the Brie, owed their origin
to his friends and disciples. In later days the Irish remembered the fact, and we learn from the *Vita Agili* (St. Ayeul),
the first Abbot of Rebais, that his house became a favourite
stopping place for Irish pilgrims on the road to or from
Rome. They rested there and left behind them such of
their number as were exhausted by the hardships of the
journey.[21]

Faro (who died in 672), the alleged brother of St. Fara
or Burgundofara, the foundress of Faremoutiers, whom
St. Columban had blessed as a child when he stopped with
her parents on his expulsion from Burgundy,[22] was also very
hospitable to Irish travellers when he became Bishop of
Meaux. At his suggestion, two of them settled for good in
Gaul, St. Kilian at Aubigny near Arras, and St. Fiacra
in the hermitage of Broilum, which later grew into the
monastery at Breuil near the city of Meaux.[23]

[20] *Christianity in Celtic Lands*, p. 141.
[21] Cf. *AA. SS. Boll.*, Aug., VI, cap. xxiv, p. 586.
[22] Cf. Jonas, *Vita Columbani*, I, xxvi.
[23] Cf. 'Vita Faronis,' 98-99, ed. Bruno Krusch in *M.G.H., Script. R.M.*, V.,
1910, p. 194; 'Vita Killiani Albiniacensis,' ed. A. B. Poncelet, S.J. (*Anal. Boll.*,

The foundations attributable to the wanderings of St. Columban and his white monks in German lands and Italy are particularly well known. After stopping for a time at Bregenz on the Lake of Constance, he set out for Italy. But St. Gall, one of his companions, who had learned the dialect of the country and redeemed many of the natives from idolatry, was seized by a sharp attack of fever and, unable to continue the journey, begged leave to remain where he was (612). He built himself a cell some distance from the lake, and with a companion or two led the life of a hermit. After his death a church was erected on the spot in his honour and before the middle of the eighth century had grown into a monastery, with St. Othmar for its first

XX, 1901, pp. 432-44) and 'Vita Fiacrii' in *AA. SS. Boll.*, Aug., VI, p. 605. The word Burgundofaro, Faro for short, is used three times in the Chronicle of the pseudo-Fredegarius in contexts which leave no doubt that the word merely means 'a grandee of Burgundy.' Of St. Faro we know that he was referendary to Dagobert I, became Bishop of Meaux, 'pontifex Meldensis urbis' (*Vita Columbani*, II, 21) in 626 and that he was still living in 668 when Hadrian, the tutor to Theodore of Tarsus, spent the winter with him (Bede, *H.E.*, IV. 1). His life, written in 869 by Hildegaire, one of his successors in the see of Meaux (855-76), is a sorry piece of work appraised by M. Bédier as follows: "Tout ce qu'on peut contrôler est erroné, douteux ou mensonger." It derives largely, as Mabillon had already observed, from the 'Liber historiae Francorum,' written by a monk of Neustria (726-27), *M.G.H., Script. R.M.*, ed. Krusch, II, p. 313, and borrows extensively anecdotes from the lives of other hagiographers' heroes. Hildegaire also refers to a 'Vita B. Chilleni viri Scothicae gentis' (i.e. St. Killian of Aubigny), an early seventh century (?) form of the name, now lost. The Bollandist 'Vita Killiani,' which also contains much that is absurd, is a late composition (eleventh century (?) but cf. *Anal. Boll.*, XX (1901), pp. 433-4) and makes its hero a contemporary of St. Vaast who died in 540, fifty years before 'Faro' was born. St. Fiacra might have lived forever, 'per ora virum,' if the taxi-cab had not superseded the 'fiacre' in France and, although he enjoyed a prodigious reputation in the Middle Ages, it cannot be said that his historical remains are satisfactory. On St. Faro cf. M. Bédier's admirable essay in *Les Légendes épiques*, Paris, 2nd. ed. 1921, pp. 290-335—To the west of the Bay of Nigg, a parish in the extreme north-seat of Kincardine-shire, stand the ruined and roofless walls of the old church of St. Fittack, and some distance south of the church is a spring dedicated to the saint, 'St. Fiackres well,' to which the citizens of Aberdeen, in defiance of the fulminations of the kirk-session, resorted "in ane superstitious maner for seiking health to thameselffis or bairnes" down to the beginning of the nineteenth century. A similar practice prevailed in the village of Saint-Fiacre, Crécy, Seine et Marne, and in Alsace (cf. Dom Gougaud, *Gaelic Pioneers*, pp. 136-7), and in 1641 Anne of Austria made the pilgrimage in thanksgiving for the birth of a dauphin. A seventeenth-century Italian monograph, printed at Florence, fathered the saint on 'Eugenius IV, King of Scotland,' and placed his *floruit* in the first half of the seventh century. Is it possible that the Kincardineshire dedication is a fifteenth century importation from France adapted to some local patron? The ramifications of the cult of St. Fiacre are endless.

abbot. This was the humble origin of the famous abbey and later city of St. Gall.[24]

The other companions of St. Columban who retired to lead a hermit life, one on the banks of the Doubs, and the other in the Grisons, were the remote founders of the Swiss monasteries of St. Ursitz (St. Ursanne), near Délémont, and Dissentis. St. Beatenberg on the Lake of Thun also takes its name from a holy Irish hermit, while St. Fridolin of Säckingen, another Irishman who founded the monastery in Baden, became the patron saint of Glarus with a widespread cult in Switzerland, Southern Germany and Austria.

Columban, meanwhile, with the rest of his band, had crossed the Alps and was hospitably received in Milan by the Lombard King Agilulf and Queen Theodolinda. He was an Arian, she a devout 'Roman' Catholic. At the suggestion of a certain Jucundus, who drew Agilulf's attention to a wild tract of land in the valley of the Trebbia, at the confluence of the torrent Bobbio, and the site of a ruined church once dedicated to St. Peter, the king granted the place to Columban, who betook himself there in 614 and began forthwith to build his celebrated monastery, later justly renowned as the Monte Cassino of northern Italy. The main lines of the topography of the early monastery are still discernible in the configuration of the present little town of Bobbio.

A year later, on Sunday, 23rd November, 615, the dauntless monk, '*velut olim Dryadum princeps,*' entered into his eternal rest.[25]

St. Gall and Bobbio in succeeding centuries became the

---

[24] Cf. J. M. Clark, *The Abbey of St. Gall as a Centre of Literature and Art*, Cambridge University Press, 1926; Maud Joynt, *The Life of St. Gall*, London, S.P.C.K., 1927, and A. Faeh, *Die Stiftsbibliotek in St. Gallen*, St. Gall, Fehr, 1929.

[25] The words are John of Trittenheim's, quoted by Ussher from the other's 'De Script. Eccles.' in his *Sylloge*, Whole Works, IV, p. 407: The Abbé Martin (*Saint Colomban*, Paris, 1905, p. 197) has an interesting note on the iconographical characteristics of the great saint which still need to be fixed by some Irish artist. He should have his Irish tonsure, bow-shaped on the forehead, carry a *cambuta*, and wear a satchel suspended from the neck. The habit should be white. In *Franche Comté* he is depicted in a white habit, but in *Bregenz, St. Gall and Bobbio* as a Benedictine, in the one case with a bear which he is supposed to be taming, in the other with a sun upon his breast in allusion to his mother's dream. In France he is 'un moine q uelconque,' in Italy 'un moine absolument fantaisiste,' in Ireland —?—.

goal of pious pilgrimages on the part of the Irish. In the ninth century an Irish bishop, Marcus, returning from Rome, came to visit St. Gall—*tamquam compatriotam suum.* "He was accompanied by his sister's son Moengal, whom we afterwards called Marcellus. This man was exceedingly learned both in sacred and secular knowledge, and taught his pupils the seven liberal arts, music especially. The nephew was elected to our community and the bishop was asked to remain in our place for some time. They deliberated long and finally, but with reluctance, consented. . . . The bishop gave his horses and mules to such persons as he selected by name ; his books, his gold and his clothes he kept for himself and for St. Gall. When at last the time came for them to say good-bye, he put on his stole and came down to bless his departing companions [his fellow pilgrims returning to Ireland]. So with many tears on both sides they parted. The bishop and his nephew and a few servants of his own tongue remained with us. Moengal—we called him Marcellus—was given charge of the cloister schools, with Notker —afterwards nicknamed Balbulus [the Stammerer]—and other boys who had entered the monastic life."[26] Eusebius, another Irishman, also came to St. Gall about the middle of the ninth century, but soon retired to the solitude of the Viktorsberg beyond the Rhine and lived there for thirty years the life of a recluse, dying in 884.[27] The Necrology of St. Gall[28] has preserved the names of some twenty Irish monks who died there, while at Bobbio there is record of a Cummian in the eighth and a Dungal in the ninth century, not to mention other monks bearing Irish names.[29]

§ 5

The personal influence brought to bear on Gaul by St. Columban was considerable.[30] After his death his essentially

[26] Cf. Ekkehard IV: First Continuation of the *Casus S. Galli (c.* A.D. 1030), *M.G.H., SS.,* II, 74-147; Kenney, op. cit., p. 596. 'The Necrology of St. Gall' (*M.G.H., Necrologia, I* (1888), 481) records the death of Moengal: 'II. Kal. Oct. obitus Moengal cognomento Marcelli viri doctissimi et optimi': (qu. in 887?).
[27] Ratpert, *Casus S. Galli,* Migne, PL. CXXVI, 1057-80.
[28] Cf. J. M. Clark, op. cit., p. 31 (and *passim*).
[29] Cf. Gougaud, op. cit., p. 144.   [30] Cf. Kenney, op. cit., pp. 186-209.

Irish ideas on the necessity for frequent confession and recourse to a spiritual director (*anmchara*), and the exemption of monasteries from episcopal jurisdiction, continued to spread through the zeal of his own numerous immediate followers and their disciples. "Up to the seventh century the monks in Africa and Gaul had made only timid efforts to free themselves from the jurisdiction of the diocesan bishops. The movement towards emancipation had begun to make itself felt before the arrival of the Scots on the Continent; but to St. Columban and his disciples, who propagated the Irish tenets, was certainly due the remarkable progress made thenceforth by the principle of the exemption of regulars."[31] "The case of Bobbio calls for special notice. Abbot Bertulf in 628 besought its exemption from the Holy See. It was granted him by a privilege of Honorius I declaring the abbey freed from all episcopal jurisdiction and placing it immediately under that of the Pope. This is the earliest privilege of the kind."[32]

Many exalted personages of the time, who, under Scotic influence, abandoned the Frankish court for the cloister or were raised to the episcopate, high officials such as Faro, Eligius (better known as St. Éloi), Bishop of Noyon, Wandregisilus (St. Vandrille), and Philibert, Abbot of Jumièges, seem to have valued highly the ascetic discipline of Luxeuil and to have striven to propagate it.[33]

St. Vandrille (c. 668) resigned his position at Court and devoted himself in solitude to prayer and the practice of austerities (the recitation of the entire Psalter with genuflexions and immersions in ice-cold water), singularly reminiscent of the mortification of the Irish monks. He spent some time by the tomb of St. Ursicinus, the disciple already mentioned of St. Columban, was carried in spirit by an angel to Bobbio, and even harboured the intention of going to Ireland.

St. Philibert of Jumièges seems to have been affected by the same influence. He first followed the Rule of St. Colum-

[31] Cf. Gougaud, op. cit., p. 224.
[32] Ibid., p. 226.
[33] St. Dado, Audoenus or Ouen, Bishop of Rouen, was an exception. He set himself to maintain the old discipline in his diocese. Cf. Gougaud, op. cit., ibid.

ban at Rebais, made visits to Luxeuil and Bobbio, and
dedicated one of the altars in Jumièges to St. Columban
before proceeding to found his own monastery at Noirmoutier on an island in the mouth of the Loire.[34]

St. Éloi, a master of the royal mint under Dagobert I,
built the monastery of Solignac in the diocese of Limoges
and had it exempted from the jurisdiction of the bishop and
placed under that of the Abbot of Luxeuil. The foundation
charter prescribed according to the custom of the time that
the joint rule of SS. Benedict and Columban should govern
the religious life of the house.

Two former officials of the court of Clothair II and
Dagobert I were in direct contact with the Scotti: St. Cyran
(† *c.* 655), who became Abbot of Longrey in the Berry and
owed his conversion to his meeting an Irish Bishop Failbe
(*latine* Folvius), who took him on a pilgrimage to Rome,
and Desiderius (Didier) of Cahors, who had friendly relations
with an Irish recluse named Arnanus.

Mommelin, the successor of St. Éloi in the see of Noyon,
was a monk of Luxeuil: as were also St. Walaricus (Valéry) of
Leuconoe ('white thoughts') in Picardy, who had known St.
Columban, St. Audomar (Omer) of Thérouanne and St.
Bertin, the second abbot of Sithiu. These missionary
monks planted the traditions of Irish monasticism all over
northern Gaul. To Luxeuil also came Bathilda, the wife of
Clovis II (639-57), who had been a slave in the household of
Erchinoald, when she wanted a first abbot for the monastery
which she had founded at Corbie at her own expense; and
from the double monastery at Jouarre she sought a first
abbess for the double monastery at Chelles, near Paris,
which she had restored.

These foundations had not been long established when an
Irishman, who had been living for some time 'a stranger for
our Lord' in Britain in a little monastery, 'pleasantly situated

---

[34] The 'Vita Filiberti' (ed. Levison), *M.G.H., SS., R.M.,* V (1910), pp. 568-
604, contains an interesting reference (p. 603) to a ship from Ireland coming up
the Loire with merchandise. The brethren were supplied with an abundance
of shoes and clothing. It is curious to think that the name of the French composer Camille Saint Saëns should be merely that of one of Philibert's disciples,
an Irishman Sidonius or Saëns, who founded the monastery of Saint
Saëns in the diocese of Rouen.

in the woods and with the sea not far off,' within the area of
a castle, 'which in the English language is called Cnobheresburg,' now Burgh Castle in Suffolk, came to settle on the
banks of the Marne at Lagny. This was St. Fursa, of whose
life in France only this is known that he won the high esteem
of Erchinoald, mayor of the palace of Neustria. He was
attracted, perhaps, by the fame and example of St. Columban,
and the prosperity of the monastic establishments in the Brie,
but his career was of short duration, for he died at Mézerolles
in the Somme, leaving a profound impression on the minds
of his contemporaries by reason of the curious visions with
which he was favoured, [35] and which will be mentioned later.
"The same Erchinoald took his body and deposited it in
the porch of a church he was building in his town of
Péronne, till the church itself should be dedicated," which
happened twenty-seven days after. The activity of Fursa
is not to be compared with that of Columban, yet his name
deserves to be recalled on account of the visits paid to his
tomb by hosts of his countrymen. They erected the first
monastery on the continent reserved for the exclusive use
of the Scotti, Perrona Scottorum, the abbots of which down
to 774 at any rate were all Irish. Foillan, the elder brother
of Fursa, who arrived in Gaul some time before 652, was
succeeded, when he left Péronne at the request of St. Gertrude of Nivelles to assume the government of the abbey at
Fosses in the diocese of Liège, by yet another brother
Ultán, and Ultán in turn by Cellan, the correspondent of
Aldhelm, who died in 706. Foillan is said to have been
murdered by robbers in 655, but his monastery remained
in Irish hands until its destruction by the Norsemen in 880.
The Four Masters (a.a. 779) record the death in 774 of
Moinan mac Cormaic, abbot of 'Fursa's Community in
France.' [36]

---

[35] Cf. Bede., *HE.*, III, 19.

[36] Cf. Dom Berlière 'La plus ancienne vie de St. Foillan' in *Revue Bénédictine*
IX (1892), 137-39; Gougaud, op. cit., pp. 146-48, and Albers, op. cit., pp.
115-24.

§ 6

The Irish *peregrini* had already penetrated before 800 into many other regions in the continent of Europe near to and far from their early spheres of influence. The seventh century found them scattered over modern Belgium. Romold or Rombaut preached the Gospel in Malines, Livin or Liévin, if that dim figure was not in fact an Englishman, in the neighbourhood of Ghent, where he is reputed to have been martyred. Celestinus became abbot of the monastery of St. Peter of Mount Blandin in Ghent (*c.* 683); St. Roding or Rouen, *Scotorum prosapia ortus*, founded the abbey of Beaulieu in the Argonne, while St. Disibod, another phantom figure, is credited with having founded the monastery of Disibodenberg between Tréves and Mainz at the confluence of the Nabe and the Glan, not far from Bingen.[37] St. Kilian preached the Gospel in Franconia and fell a victim to his apostolic zeal at Würzburg, where he and his two fellow-workers, Colman and Totman, were murdered.[38]

The monasteries of Honau, a little island then situate in the Rhine, near Strasburg, but now completely submerged, and Altenmunster in the diocese of Freising, also owed their foundation to Irish monks. Ferghil, Abbot of the monastery of Achadh-bó—Cainnigh (Aghaboe) in Ossorey,

[37] His life, a fabulous composition, was written by Hildegard, the famous Abbess of Rupertsberg, also known as 'the Sibyl of the Rhine (cf. Migne, P.L., CXCVIII, 1095-1116), who declared that she wrote under divine inspiration, but in this particular exaggerated. Her prediction that the world would come to an end in 1180 greatly alarmed Vincent of Beauvais. Cf. *Spec. hist., Epilog* cc. CVII and CVIII. Dempster, *H.E.*, I, 205, professes to have seen a book written by Disibod upon the 'Proficiency of Monks in their Solitary Estate,' but even admitting that there ever was such a work, the authorship is at the least doubtful.

[38] Kilian became a common baptismal name in Franconia. In 1155 Kilian of Limberg, one of the four free lords of Germany, made a descent into Italy with a numerous armed band to assist the Norman King William in his campaign against Adrian IV, and received from the king as a reward for his services the grant of territories at Castromediano, Pietrapertosa and Castrobellotta in Basilicata, with the right to assume the title of Castromediano, the most considerable of the estates conferred upon him. Cf. Brizio De Sanctis in a 'Cenno biografico' appended to *Memorie del Duca Sigismondo Castromediano* (who died in 1895), Lecce, 1895, Vol. II. At the back of the courtyard in the feudal palace of the Castromediano family at Cavallino, near Lecce, stands a statue, commonly known as the Giant, of this Kilian, the founder of the family.

went into voluntary exile (*c.* 742) 'for the love of Christ,' and after residing for some time in Gaul settled in Salzburg, where he became Abbot of the monastery of St. Peter and changed his name to Virgil. There he fell foul of St. Boniface, who accused him to Pope Zachary of sowing hatred between himself and Virgil's patron, Duke Odilo of Bavaria, and further suspected the orthodoxy of Virgil's doctrines about the antipodes, which in fact contained nothing very novel. The Irishman, however, was too securely established to be easily dislodged, and in the end became the ecclesiastical administrator of Salzburg (767-84). He was not, however, consecrated bishop but, until after the death of St. Boniface, had a countryman Dub-dá-chrich, also called Dobdagrecus, sometimes even 'Tuti Graecus,' who was a bishop, to perform a bishop's sacramental functions on his behalf. Dub-dá-chrich later became abbot of a monastery at Chiemsee in Upper Bavaria.

The Franks also chose more than one bishop from among these strangers. In 747 Pippin the Short, on the advice of St. Boniface, summoned an Irishman named Abel from the monastery at Lobbes in Hainault, to the archiepiscopal see of Rheims, an appointment which later received the approval of Pope Zachary. Abel, however, was turned out of his see by his deposed predecessor Melo, and, returning to Lobbes, became its abbot.[39] These island Celts penetrated even into regions beyond the Loire. Reference has already been made to Arnanus, the protégé of St. Didier of Cahors. Ansoald, Bishop of Poitiers, in the surviving fragment of his will, records how he found the monastic house of Mazerolles on the river Vienne deserted: "I completely restored

---

[39] Flodoard, *Hist. Eccl. Remensis*, II, xvi, Migne *P.L.*, CXXXV, 27-406, and Folcuin, *Geste abbatum lobiensium*, ibid, CXXXVII, 548-82. Flodoard tells a curious story of an Irishman, 'Scotigena,' who, having set out to go to Rome, 'orationis causa,' was murdered by some robbers on the banks of the Aisne and buried by his companions in the graveyard of one of the two churches of St. Hilary in Rheims. Dissatisfied with this accommodation, he appeared to a rustic and bade him tell the Bishop Artold that he wanted his body brought inside the church. "Quod idem rusticus intimare timens neglexit mandatum." The holy man lost his temper and, picking up a stone, broke the rustic's jaw, and he "capitis dolore per dimidium fere vexatus est annum." The Irishman was very insistent that his name should be preserved to posterity. So be it. It was Morolilanus.

F—i

it, and placed over it a holy *peregrinus* of God of Irish race, Bishop Ronanus (Ronan), with his fellow *peregrini*, directing that the *peregrini* should abide there permanently."[40] The see of Angoulême was twice held by Irishmen at an interval of about one hundred years, a certain Tomianus (*c.* 668) and 'Helias Scotigena' (? Ailill), who died in 860.

§ 7

Charlemagne was a patron of the Irish monks.   When those of Honau had been despoiled of part of their property, he issued a decree dated 772-74 ordering it to be returned without delay: "Si quis eorum hoc non fecerit, recognoscat se regis preceptorum non obaudire, quia reges Francorum libertatem dederunt omnibus peregrinis Scotorum, ut nullus rapiat aliquid de rebus eorum, nec ulla generatio praeter eorum generationem possideat ecclesias eorum."[41] He was so fond of the *peregrini* and so liberal in entertaining them, says his biographer Einhard, in a passage[42] which an eminent French critic[43] has suspected of revealing a personal malice, that presently the multitude of them became *non inmerito* a nuisance in the palace and a burden to the nation. "Ipse tamen prae magnitudine animi hujuscemodi pondere minime gravabatur cum etiam ingentia incommoda laude liberalitatis ac bonae famae compensaret."

One consequence of the intimate relations between the Carolingians and the Holy See was that the pilgrimage to Rome became more popular as the difficulties in the way

---

[40] Cf. Pardessus *Diplomata*, II, 239, and Kenney, op. cit., p. 499. Dr. Kenney suggests that it is just possible that this Ronan was he, who, 'a Scot by nation, but instructed in ecclesiastical truth, either in France or Italy,' zealously defended the true Easter against the Irish at the Council of Whitby in 664 and 'convinced many." Cf. Bede, *H.E.*, III, xxv.

[41] Cf. the text in *M.G.H, Dipl.Kar.*, I (1906), pp. 110-11; Migne, *P.L.*, XCVII, 927.

[42] Cf. 'Vita B. Caroli Imperatoris,' in Migne, *P.L.*, XCVII, cols. 25-62, cap. 21.

[43] M. Louis Halphen in *Études critiques sur l'histoire de Charlemagne*, Paris, 1921. This solicitude found practical expression in the establishment of hospices at the termini of the great pilgrim routes, the 'Schola Francorum' in Rome and St. Mary of the Latins, "nobilissimam habens bibliothecam studio praedicti imperatoris" in Jerusalem.   Rome, Jerusalem and Aix-la-Chapelle were his predilection. And the *peregrini* repaid him, this semi-barbarous German, 'à la barbe florie,' as no one else could. They made him immortal. Cf. *La Légende de Charlemagne* in Bédier, op. cit., IV, pp. 437-69.

diminished. Although the *peregrini* from the island were not, as already observed, 'pilgrims' in the modern sense of the term, many among them directed their footsteps, either from the outset or as opportunity presented itself, to some predetermined shrine. St. Gall, Bobbio and Péronne, after the death of their founders, drew many of their compatriots. Even as late as the tenth century Cadroe began his *peregrinatio* with a visit to the tomb of St. Fursa, while Móel-Brigte (Marianus Scottus) had himself ordained priest in the basilica of St. Kilian at Würzburg in 1059. The *limina Apostolorum* naturally held the greatest fascination for the devout imagination of the islanders. St. Mo-lua *vir vite venerabilis de provincia Mumenie*, who died *c.* 609, earnestly desired to make a pilgrimage to the tomb of the Apostles, according to his biographer, and went to his master St. Maedóc to ask permission. The elder offered some objections, which the saint brushed aside, expressing the warmth of his desire by the stark simplicity of his retort: "Nisi videro Romam, cito moriar."[44]

Rome was therefore frequently visited by Irish pilgrims: but the Anglo-Saxons showed still greater eagerness to make their way to the Eternal City and ingratiate themselves with the Pontiffs. They were the originators of Peter-pence, the *Romescot*, the origin of which is involved in obscurity,[45] and the alacrity with which kings, prelates, monks and nuns

[44] Corrado Ricci, *Santa Cristina e il lago di Bolsena*, Milan, Treves, 1928, p. 24, referring to the Church of St. Stephen in the island of Martana and to the grant of it by Paschal I to the church of S. Stefano dei Mori 'presso il Vaticano,' continues: "Leo IX [1049-54] had but recently confirmed the grant when the Irish King Donnchad III landed there in the humble garb of a penitent and shut himself up as a monk. He left it only to go to Rome, to throw himself at the feet of the Pope and offer him the suzerainty of Ireland and to die in the monastery of Santo Stefano Rotondo . . ." where his bones still rest. The episode is referred to by Keating, III, p. 353. Sigr. Ricci's statement (cf. p. 347) must, however, be regarded as based upon a fable, the fable being Keating's own fiction, for three reasons: (*a*) the Donough in question was only king in Munster, (*b*) he could not therefore have had any authority to offer the Pope the suzerainty of Ireland, (*c*) he fled from Ireland (*c.* 1064) and was dead long before the Pope Urban II (1088-99) to whom Keating assigns the offer in 1092, of the suzerainty of Ireland, was elected Bishop of Rome. A restored monument on the Monte Casteltomond (this Donough O'Brien was King of Cashel and Thomond) to the north-west of the lake, near Latera, still commemorates the incident, but a recent visitor to the spot has reported that the stone is missing, that the origin of the monument is unknown, and that the name Casteltomond has disappeared from the locality.

[45] Cf. Cabrol, op. cit., Appendix II.

set out from England upon the long and laborious journey is surprising.[46]

The letters of St. Boniface and those of Charlemagne provide many instructive details of the habits of the pilgrims and pseudo-pilgrims of the time and acquaint us also with the many abuses and irregularities to which the pilgrimages gave rise.[47]

A monk in sound health, who did not travel on foot, rendered himself liable to excommunication in terms of his Rule. St. Kentigern, St. Ceadda and St. Aidan are known for a fact to have gone their long missionary circuits on foot.[48] Abstention from horseback or vehicle was considered to be in the apostolic tradition and sometimes placed on a level with continence and self-mortification. It is not improbable that the Irish missionaries and ascetics had to conform to this custom on the Continent. The texts do not say so explicitly, but the extreme weariness of which numbers of the travellers complain, the poverty of the majority, the destitution to which they protest they are reduced through lack of baggage, all force the conviction that they had no other means of transport than their own legs. Men of the distinction of Clement, Dungal and Sedulius are every minute compelled to implore the benevolence of a king, a prelate, or some magnate of the realm on behalf of themselves or a needy compatriot.[49]

[46] The road to Rome was from Mount Cenis via Susa and Turin or from the Great St Bernard via Ivrea, through Pavia and Piacenza, down the Via Emilia through Modena and Imola, across the Apennines at Bagno; the Via Cassia was picked up at Arezzo and led through Viterbo and Sutri to Rome. You had the option of leaving the Via Emilia before Parma, crossing the Apennines at Cisa and then continuing your journey through Pontremoli, Lucca, Siena and Viterbo. Cf., e.g., the itinerary of Sigeric, Archbishop of Canterbury († 994) in Memorials of Dunstan, ed. Stubbs, 1874, pp. 391 et. seq., and Jung's commentary in Mittheilungen . . . für österreichisehe Geschichtsforschung, Vol. XXV, 1904, p. 1.

[47] Cf., e.g., Ep. 78 in M.G.H., Epist., III, pp. 354-5, and Labbe, Concilia, VI, 1565.

[48] Theodore of Tarsus ordered Ceadda to make his diocesan round on horseback. The holy man protested his 'morem majorum,' but Theodore was not the man to stand any such nonsense. He lifted the bishop bodily and planted him in the saddle (Bede, H.E., IV, 3). Mgr. Duchesne, L'Église au VIème siècle, p. 622, regards the incident as "pleasingly typical of the religious situation" and reflects that the votaries of the Celtic discipline, owing to their prolonged fasts, must have been light-weights.

[49] Cf. Gougaud, op. cit., pp. 173-7.

§ 8

A number of bishops, some of whom have been already mentioned, distinguished themselves by their zeal in helping the Irish emigrants: Faro of Meaux, Didier of Cahors, Ansoald of Poitiers, Hartgar of Liège, his successor Franco and the Bishops of Cambrai. Other prelates used their influence to have restored to them the hospices or shelters which they had established in the places most frequented by their compatriots and of which they had been unjustly deprived. These were hostels specially intended for the refreshment of wayfarers and pilgrims (*hospitalia Scottorum*) or monasteries exclusively reserved for such *Scotti* as wished to end their days in retreat in a foreign land (*monasteria Scottorum*). A number of institutions simultaneously fulfilled both functions.

Many sprang up under the Merovingians and the Carolingians. Péronne and Honau are perhaps the earliest examples of *monasteria Scottorum*. In 845 the Council of Meaux ordered certain Scots' hospices, which had been usurped towards the end of the reign of Charlemagne, to be reorganized and given back to their legitimate administrators and owners. Charles the Bald (the most outstanding protector of the Scots after Charlemagne) confirmed at the Diet of Epernay in 846 the measures taken at Meaux for the restoration of the *hospitalia Scottorum*.[50]

From the middle of the ninth century Irish monasteries and hospices multiplied more particularly outside the western kingdom of the Franks. In 883 Charles the Fat granted a villa called Rotis to the monastery of St. Gall at the instance, according to Ratpert,[51] of an Irish solitary named Eusebius, who had retired there twenty-nine years earlier, for the maintenance on Mount St. Viktor of a hospice for twelve pilgrims making the journey to Rome.

In the tenth century the Teutonic sovereigns scattered similar foundations throughout their dominions, and the Scots are found established (*c.* 945), at St. Michael's abbey in

---

[50] Mansi, *Concilia*, XIV, 227-8; *M.G.H.*, *Leges:* Sec. II, cap. II, p. 408.
[51] 'Casus S. Galli,' in Migne, *P.L.*, 1077 and note.

Thierache and at Waulsort, near Dinant, in the Ardennes. Cadroe, Abbot of Waulsort, having been summoned to Metz by the Bishop Adalbero I (929-62) to reform the abbey of St. Clement in that city (953), was succeeded by another Irishman, Forannan, who negotiated with Thierry, Adalbero's successor, the annexation to his own monastery of the neighbouring abbey of Hastières.[52]

Adalbero II (984-1005) showed himself no less willing than his predecessors to entrust the monastic establishments in his diocese to the islanders. "Scotti et reliqui sancti peregrini semper sibi dulcissimi habebantur," observes his biographer Constantine, the Abbot of St. Symphorien at Metz, and in his time an Irishman Fingen was Abbot of the monastery of St. Clement in that same city. Adalbero begged him to take over the government of St. Symphorien which had been destroyed long before, probably by the Northmen. Fingen restored it, and Irish influence under his administration became predominant. Two charters, one from Pope John XVII, the other from the Emperor Otto III, prescribed that only Irish monks should be received there as long as possible, but that, should the number from Ireland fail, recruits of other nationalities might be admitted. Fingen ended his reforming career at the monastery of St. Vannes in Verdun, a very poor church, where he had "only seven Irish monks under his abbacy." He died in 1005 and was buried "in the church of St. Felix outside the walls of the city of Metz."[53]

Cologne also contained a considerable Irish colony about

---

[52] The 'Vita Cadroae' (AA. SS. Boll., Mart, I, pp. 468-81) was composed (c. 1000) by one Reimann or Ousmann, who is lost to fame and dedicated 'Venerabili in Christo Patri Immoni,' who may have been Abbot of Waulsort. Cadroe was born of a noble family in Scotland but went to Ireland according to Mabillon (Annal. Bened. ad ann. 944) to be educated at Ardmacha, there being no schools in Scotland at the time. He left Ireland as a result of a vision, landed near Boulogne after a storm, and made his way with thirteen companions to the tomb of St. Fursa at Péronne. A pious matron, 'Hersendis nomine,' fell in with the little band and offered them the oratory of Saint Michel en Thiérache. There they settled and chose 'Malcallan, natione Hibernicus' to be their abbot, whose death as such is recorded by Flodoard in his Annals under the year 978. For the part played by Waulsort in the composition of the 'chanson de geste' Raoul de Cambrai, cf. M. Bédier's criticism in op. cit., II., pp. 337-438.

[53] Cf. Kenney, op. cit., p. 612.

this time. In 975 the Archbishop Eberger assigned the monastery of St. Martin to the Scots in perpetuity. Móel-Brigte (Marianus Scottus), who lived there from 1056-58, records in his *Chronicle* the names of the abbots from 975 to 1061: they are all Irish. In the time of the Abbot Elias, another monastery in Cologne, that of St. Pantaleon, passed in its turn into the hands of the Scots (1042).

They were warmly welcomed in the eleventh century in other monasteries also than their own, for they were looked upon as holy men, and the skill of their penmanship in the work they did to repay their hosts made their presence the more valuable. Fulda, under Abbot Richard († 1039), was particularly eager to receive them as guests, and kept some as incluses.

A marked inclination for the solitary life was, it has been observed, a distinguishing feature of Irish monasticism from the beginning. The same yearning for solitude animated St. Findan even in the eleventh century. Taken prisoner by the Vikings and carried off to the Orkneys, he succeeded in making his escape, entrusted himself to the ocean, and landed among the Picts. He fulfilled a vow to make a pilgrimage *ad limina*, and on his return stopped with certain anchorites dwelling on the island of Rheinau in the Rhine, near Schaffhausen. Their manner of life pleased him and he abode with them as an incluse for twenty-seven years until his death (*c.* 878).[54]

The practice of asceticism became more common in the eleventh century, and Fulda received two Irish incluses in succession: Anmchad, a monk of Inis-Celtra, banished by his superior for some transgression, died there in 1043, while Móel-Brigte (Marianus Scottus), also banished, had himself walled up there from 1059 to 1069. Transferred by order of the Abbot of Fulda and the Bishop of Mainz to the latter city, he had himself walled up again in the monastery of St. Martin, until in 1082 *de hac luce ad lucem migravit perennem*. Móel-Brigte records in his *Chronicle* the distressing fate of a

[54] The 'Vita Fintani,' published by Mabillon in *AA. SS. o.s. B.*, IV, i, 377-82, is largely fabulous but of interest as containing one of the earliest references to "those pathetic relics of a lost Celticity," the once much discussed Céli Dé (anglice Culdees).

brother Irishman, a certain Paternus, who was burned
alive in his cell at Paderborn in Westphalia after many
years of solitude (1058).[55] When Muiredach macc Robartaig, the Latin namesake of the incluse of Fulda and Mainz,
arrived in Bavaria (c. 1075), he encountered a compatriot
named Muirchertach, who was also an incluse. One of his
travelling companions, known to us only by the name of
John, was smitten presently with a similar desire. He walked
out of Bavaria and, wandering down the valley of the Danube,
lingered for a little at Melk (where the saintly Emperor
Henry II had erected a tomb only half a century before in
honour of another Irishman, St. Colmán, murdered at
Stockerau in 1012 while making a pilgrimage to Jerusalem),
until at the last he found at Göttweich in Lower Austria the
perfect solitude for which his soul craved.

Muiredach macc Robartaig's intention had been to make
the pilgrimage to Rome. But the welcome he received at
Ratisbon, the counsel of the incluse Muirchertach, the offer
made to him of the priory of Weih-Sanct-Peter, kept him and
his companions in the Bavarian city. Together they formed
the nucleus of a Congregation destined to endure in spite of
some interruption and many vicissitudes down to living
memory, the so-called Scottish Benedictine Congregation
(Schotten Congregation), whose superior-general was the
Abbot of St. James of Ratisbon.

The building of this Jakobs Kirche as a shelter for the
Irish monks, who had rapidly grown in number, was begun
(c. 1090) with the help of the Landgrave Otto, carried on
through the munificence of the neighbouring gentry and the
wealthy inhabitants of the city and the donations of Conor
O Brien, King of Munster, and brought to completion by
the proceeds of sale of a consignment of furs, which a monk
named Mauricius, who had visited Kieff in Russia and
established a mission there, brought back with him when he
returned.

The Schottenring, which is such a familiar feature in

[55] Migne, *P.L.*, CXLVII, 786. Paternus had prophesied that a great fire
would break out in the house and it did, but he "ambiens martyrium pro
nullo foris exivit sed in sua clausola combustus per ignem pertransivit in
refrigerium."

Vienna, takes its name from the neighbouring Schottenhof, a considerable group of buildings which once formed the Irish monastery in Vienna. The story of this foundation is not without interest. When the city of Vienna had fallen so low in the twelfth century that all hope of revival seemed to have disappeared, a group of merchants from Ratisbon were invited by the Court to settle there. They agreed but on condition of being accompanied by some Irish monks. This stipulation was accepted, and the Abbot Gilla-na-Naemh took up his quarters with a small band of his brethren within the orbit of Vienna in the north-west. This monastery was the seed out of which in centuries later grew the famous Schottenhof.[56]

It is a curious coincidence that, in the Germanies, those countries which have remained predominantly Catholic down to this day (the Rhineland, Bavaria and Austria) are precisely those in which the Irish missionary effort was most intense and Irish monastic foundations most numerous.

The foundation of St. James of Ratisbon inaugurated a new era in the history of Irish monastic institutions on the Continent, but one much less interesting and animated than the preceding. The Germanies were thenceforth the only

[56] Cf. Gougaud, op. cit., pp. 180-4, Card. Moran, 'Ireland, the Island of Saints,' *Australasian Catholic Record*, October 1909, p. 495, and the bibliography with regard to the Schottenkloster in Vienna, given by Vismara, 'Storia Benedettina,' in *Aevum*, 1931, pp. 576-7 (cf. 1184-87). Dr. Kenney notes, op. cit., p. 787, that a new foundation at Kieff contemplated by Irish monks from Vienna in the twelfth century was abandoned because of a Mongol invasion in 1241. The Irish monastery of St. James of Ratisbon (Regensburg), founded in 1135 the Irish monastery of St. James of Würzburg (cf. Gougaud, op. cit., p. 183), a member of which was one David Scotigena or David Scottus, whom the Emperor Henry V took with him "pro morum pietate omnique liberalium artium peritia," when he invaded Italy in 1110 as historiographer of the expedition. According to Ekkehard the Chronicler David acquitted himself admirably of the task, composing three books "stilo tam facili, qui ferme nichil a communi loquela discrepet," Migne, *P.L.*, CXLIV, 1019. William of Malmesbury, however, gives a different account. David, according to him, was Bishop of Bangor, and "magis in regis gratiam quam historicum deceret acclinis. . . . Ego interim, ne bonum virum verbo videar premere statuo diligendum quia non historiam sed panegyricum scripsit," *P.L.*, CLXXIX, 1375. Odericus Vitalis describes him as "Irensis quidam scholasticus" (cf. Pertz, *M.G.H.*, *SS.*, VI, 243, xx, 67), but he was more probably Welsh. In any event he is erroneously described as Scotch in the French translation of Hefele's *Conciliengeschichte*, V., Paris, 1912, p. 510, and it is difficult to believe Dempster's statement (*HE.*, IV., nn. 362, 383) that in his time some of this David's theological writings were preserved in the library of Corpus Christi College, Cambridge. Cf. also Kenney, op. cit., pp. 355 and 619-20.

country to which the religious migration continued, while the number of emigrants steadily declined. One nationality was substituted for another in the monasteries, and the Scotch, trading on the actual identity of their name in Latin with the old Latin name for the Irish, succeeded in passing themselves off as the real founders of the *monasteria Scottorum* and gradually usurped the place of the Irish in houses where they had not been forestalled by German monks.[57]

§ 9

The Irish foundations in Italy have been left to the last. They have been neglected, and for the reason, perhaps, that they were undoubtedly less numerous and important than those in French and German territory.

Colgan, the prince of Irish hagiographers, had composed a treatise in four books on the missionary labours of the Irish abroad which has unfortunately disappeared. Walter Harris, the translator and editor of *The Whole Works of Sir James Ware concerning Ireland* (three vols. Dublin, 1739-64), saw the manuscript at the College of St. Anthony in Louvain some

[57] Cf. Gougaud, op. cit., p. 174, and *Gaelic Pioneers*, p. 68. Historical study in Scotland has made very little progress in four hundred years, and in 1873, Hill Burton, the historiographer royal, could write with unrebuked effrontery of the Schottenkirche at Ratisbon: "The local authorities were clear that the Scots monastery belonged to Scotland and treated the partial possession of it by Irish ecclesiastics as an invasion. They were finally driven out in 1516. Leo the Tenth issued a bull restoring it to its proper owners, the inhabitants of Scotland." (*History of Scotland*, Edinburgh, 1905, I, p. 203). The first Scotchman appointed by Leo X was a certain John Thompson, a secular priest. He sent all the Irish monks back to Ireland and filled their places with his own compatriots. Ninian Winzet succeeded him as abbot and found the house in a ruinous condition and inhabited by only one monk and a novice. He died in 1592 and was succeeded by John White. The last abbot was an Arburthnot, and in 1855 the monks were reduced to two, the survivor of whom was Anselm Robertson. In 1864 the monastery and its property were transferred to the Bishop of Ratisbon by the Bavarian Government, the Scotch hierarchy receiving £10,000 in compensation. Dom Anselm Robertson returned to Scotland in 1860, served in the archdiocese of Glasgow until 1878, when he retired to the Benedictine house at Fort Augustus, died at Fochabers on 19th November, 1900, aged 76, and is buried in Bellic churchyard. On the work of the Irish missionaries in Europe, cf. also W. Finsterwalder, 'Wege und Ziele der irischen und angelsachsischen Mission im frankischen Reich,' *Zeitschrift fur Kirchengeschichte*, 1928, pp. 203-26; G. Goyau, 'Missionaires d'Irlande dans l'Europe mérovingienne 'in *Revue générale*, 1928, pp. 129-46; and A. De Moreau, 'L'Irlande et le monachisme de Saint Benoît,' in *Revue liturg. et monast.*, 1928, pp. 30-7.

time before 1745.[58] It was probably transferred thence to the Convent of St. Isidore in Rome (Wadding's foundation) and destroyed during the Napoleonic régime, when the French troops used that convent as a barracks. A few surviving fragments are still preserved in the Franciscan convent at Merchants' Quay, Dublin, including the index to Book IV, which dealt "De Monasteriis pro veteribus Scotis seu Hibernis per suae gentis viros sanctos, vel alios, extra patriam suam olim fundatis, vel eisdem post fundationem traditis." This index, a valuable record in itself, was first published by Charles MacDonnell,[59] and subsequently by Sir J. T. Gilbert,[60] and shows that Colgan had taken into consideration ten monasteries in Scotland, eight in England, sixteen in Armorica, six in Gaul, nine in Belgium, seven in Lorraine, four in Burgundy, sixteen in Rhaetia, Switzerland, and Suabia down to the Danube, seventeen in Alsace, five along the left bank of the Rhine from Alsace into Gueldres, six in Franconia, Thuringia, and the adjoining regions on the right bank of the Rhine down to the Danube, sixteen in Bavaria and adjoining regions on the right of the Danube, and, lastly, six in Italy.

"De coenobiis per Scotos sive Hibernos vel pro iisdem in Italia fundatis: (cap. 1) De coenobio Scotorum Romano S. Trinitatis dicto. (cap. 2). De Latino S. Endei coenobio. (cap. 3). De monasterio S. Cannechi. (cap. 4). De Lucensi S. Fridiani archicoenobio. (cap. 5). De Bobiensi nobilissimo coenobio. (cap. 6). De Messulano S. Martini coenobio."

The first, i.e. the monastery of the Holy Trinity of the Scots in Rome, will be considered presently; the fourth, i.e. the monastery of St. Fridian in Lucca, in Chapter XVII, § 7; the fifth, i.e. the monastery of St. Columban in Bobbio, already mentioned in our preceding § 4, in Chapter III,

[58] According to a communication kindly made to the author by Fr. O'Brian, O.F.M.
[59] In *P.R.I.A.*, Vol. VI (1853-7), Dublin, 1858, pp. 103 et seq.
[60] In the *Fourth Report of the Royal Commission on Historical Manuscripts*, Pt. I, Report and Appendix C, 857 (London, 1874), pp. 599-613.

§ 3, and in Chapter XII; the sixth, i.e. the monastery of St. Martin in Mensola, in Chapter XX.

Here something will be said of the second and third.

Endeus or Enda is the Irish saint already referred to in Chapter I, § 4.[61] The Bollandists observe in their *Commentarius praevius* (p. 267) that no trace or mention of any Latin monastery founded by St. Enda is to be discovered except in the Life of St. Enda (*BHL* 2543), and that Colgan, in situating it in Italy, must have been confused by the ambiguity of the Irish word *Leta*, which may mean either *Latium* or *Letavia*, i.e., Armorica. That the monastery founded by St. Enda must be sought in Armorica, if anywhere, appears from the life of the saint's sister and teacher, St. Fanchea (*AA. SS.* 1st January).

Cannechus or Cannicus (St. Cainnech) is another Irish saint considered by the Bollandists in *AA. SS.* Oct. V, 54-6 and 642-6. They make no mention of any monastery founded by him in Italy, but say only that, according to the lesson in the office of St. Cainnech, as it was recited in his church of Cell-Cainnich (Kilkenny) in 1509, the saint, while travelling in Italy, fell among thieves, who stripped and would have murdered him; but their arms were miraculously palsied into rigidity and restored to their native mobility only by the intercession of the saint, to whom the bandits hastened to do reverence. The Bollandists observe that Colgan must have had at his disposal, in addition to the texts which have come down to us, other *acta* of the saint, because he quotes, both in the *AA. SS. Hiberniae* and in the *Triad. Thaum.*, on more than one occasion, from a *vita* of the saint which he contemplated publishing for 11th October, if death had not intervened. That it differed from the texts which have come down to us is clear from the fact that he quotes extracts from it elsewhere which are missing in our texts, and I have been unable to find any

---

[61] Cf. *AA. SS. Boll.*, Mart, III, pp. 266-74, and Colgan, *AA. SS. Hiberniae*, pp. 705-10. The pedigrees of Enda, all very fanciful compositions, agree in making him the son of Conall Derc of Airgialla (d. 615). Another sister attributed to him, but on quite fictitious grounds, is Cáirech Dérgain, the reputed founder of a community of nuns at Clúain-Boirenn (Clonburra), in Roscommon.

mention of a monastery founded by St. Cainnech in Lubin, [62] Kehr [63] or Cappelletti. [64] It may be that the *vita* which Colgan had at his disposal referred to some monastery founded in connection with the story of the saint's encounter with the brigands. But any such monastery, even assuming that Colgan has not been misled with regard to it as he was with regard to St. Enda's alleged foundation, cannot have been of any consequence. [65]

Of the six mentioned by him, the certain foundations are therefore reduced to four: the monastery of the Holy Trinity in Rome, that of St. Fridian in Lucca, that of St. Columban in Bobbio, and that of St. Martin in Mensola.

To these foundations may be added the hospice for Irish pilgrims founded in Piacenza in 850 by St. Donatus of Fiesole and mentioned also by Dom Gougaud. [66] This hospice, which was attached to a church dedicated to St. Brigid, will be dealt with in Chapter VIII, § 5, and also in Chapter XIV, § 2. There was another Scots hospital in Vercelli, the oldest, apparently, among the various hospitals in the city and still functioning in 1140; it, too, was attached to a church dedicated to St. Brigid and will be considered in Chapter VIII, § 7. Pavia also had a hospital of St. Brigid mentioned in the *Libellus de descriptione Papie* of Opicino de Canistris, [67] but it is impossible to say with certainty whether it was a Scots foundation, however probable that may be (cf. Chapter VIII, § 4). Local investigations have been too few to ascertain whether any, and if so which, of the numerous hospices which sprang up round the tombs of the two Irish saints Ursus and Pellegrinus, bore a definitely Scots character (cf. Chapters X and XIV).

[62] *Abbatiarum Italiae brevis notitia.*
[63] *Italia Pontificia.*
[64] *Le chiese d'Italia.*
[65] The story of Cainnech's trip to Italy is, to say the least of it, very doubtful. This great neglected saint (*c.* 521-*c.* 599) was the contemporary and companion of Colum-cille, is mentioned several times by Adamnán, and spent part of his life in the western islands of Scotland, where his cult became very popular and his name survives as 'Kenneth.' His principal church was in Achad-bó, now Aghaboe, and was not displaced by Cell-Cainnech until after the coming of the Anglo-Normans.
[66] Cf. op. cit., p. 180.
[67] Cf. F. Gianani, *Opicino da Canistris, l'Anonimo Ticinese*, Pavia, Fusi, 1927, pp. 90 and 131.

Lanzoni[68] has shown that the Archbishop of Ravenna had a deanery in the territory of Senigallia entitled *S. Maria degli Scotti*, and that in Ravenna itself a monastery in the city was called *S. Pietro degli Scotti*: both, according to Lanzoni, were foundations intended for the reception of Irishmen. The relative documents are parchments belonging to the archiepiscopal archives of Ravenna, published by Fantuzzi[69] to illustrate the Bavarian Codex,[70] and from these it would appear that the *diaconia sce marie scotorum* was situate near the farm of Serbiniano in the territory of Senigallia and the parish of S. Giuseppe. As for the monastery in Ravenna, a document dated 1049 mentions "omnes res cum mansionibus et curtibus et ortis q. detinebant de jure Mon. S. Petri q.v. Scotorum ante Portas S. Andree Apostoli q.v. majoris in Civit. Rav. Regione S. Andree majoris," and a document dated 1190 mentions "mansiones Rav. in Regione Herculana prope Pontem Candavarie viam q. vadit ad S. Petrum Scotorum et ad stradam de Gazzi."

To sum up: to the four certain foundations in Italy under Irish auspices mentioned by Colgan, only four others can be added: Vercelli, Piacenza, and the two dependences from the diocese of Ravenna.

The Irish foundations in Rome have up to the present been wrapped in a cloud of obscurity and uncertainty: and the subject positively cries out for investigation and consideration.

Among the medieval churches in Rome, three are mentioned with the addition Scottorum: *S. Benedicti Scottorum, S. Salvatoris Scottorum, S. Trinitatis Scottorum*.

The church *S. Benedicti Scottorum* is recorded in the list drawn up by Cencio Camerario (1192), and, according to both Huelsen[71] and Armellini,[72] is the same as a puzzling

---

[68] 'Le Vite dei Quattro SS. Protettori di Faenza,' *RR. II. SS.*, new edition, Zanichelli, 1921, Vol. XXVIII, Part III, p. 333.

[69] Cf. *Monumenti ravennati de' secoli di mezzo*, Venice, 1801, Vol. I., pp. 52, 393 and 397.

[70] Cf. Bernhart's edition of the Bavarian Codex, *Codex traditionum ecclesiae ravennatensis*, Munich, 1810.

[71] *Le chiese di Roma nel Medio Evo*, Florence, Olschki, 1927, pp. 211 and 587.

[72] *Le chiese di Roma*, Tip. Ed. Rom., 1887, pp. 153 and 155.

church called *S. Benedicti Sconchi* or *Sconchii* or *Sconzi*; but whereas Armellini considers Sconchi to be a corruption of Scotti, Huelsen considers Scotti to be a corruption of Sconchi. Armellini, adopting as certain a conjecture by Grimaldi (in Martinelli), identifies it also with *S. Benedicti de Arenula*, which stood on the site of the present church of the SS. Trinità dei Pellegrini; Huelsen corrects this statement and declares that *S. Benedicti Sconchi* stood not very far from the Ponte S. Angelo. Grimaldi and Armellini are both of the opinion that the church derives its name not from the Scots nation directly, but rather from the Roman baronial family of Scotti which was domiciled in the rione della Regola. I will show in its proper place the probability that this family derived its name from the country of origin of its founder (cf. Chapter XIV). Amayden and Bertini[73] say that *Dominus Gottifridus de Scottis de regione Arenulae*, who died in 1452, was buried in the church of *S. Salvatore in Campo* or *de (Domno) Campo*. Neither the name nor the history of this church is very clear.[74] "The medieval church," writes Huelsen, "did not stand on the site of the modern one"; Ciampini relates that the ancient church was *e conspectu ecclesiae Smae. Trinitatis Convalescentium*, and that the remains of tombs belonging to it were excavated in 1690 *in via quae a platea Montis Pietatis ad ecclesiam S. Trinitatis ducit* (the present via dei Pettinari). It was demolished in 1639 to make room for the Palazzo del Monte di Pietà. I have the idea that it would be just as well to bear this church in mind in any investigation into the history of the churches *S. Benedicti Scottorum* and *S. Salvatoris Scottorum*.

As regards the exact site and the vicissitudes of the church *S. Salvatoris Scottorum*[75] nothing is certain. It is also recorded in the list drawn up by Cencio Camerario. Huelsen thought he had found the same title in the Paris catalogue, but in the form *Salvator de Scrote in cavill(is)* which, he suggested, should be amended to read *Salvatoris de Scotis in harenula*, *de Scotis* being a reference to the family before mentioned.

---

[73] *La storia delle famiglie romane*, Rome, Collegio Araldico, Vol. II, p. 191.
[74] Cf. Huelsen, p. 434; Armellini, p. 594.
[75] Ibid., p. 601.

Armellini also is inclined to refer the attribute *Scotorum* to the family of that name, but Dom Wilmart,[76] on the other hand, refers it to the Scots nation and is inclined to suspect that it may have been, as is indeed very probable, a dependence from the *Trinitatis Scottorum*.

The church *S. Trinitatis Scottorum*, with the abbey attached, which undoubtedly belonged to the Scots nation, is mentioned in the lists drawn up by Pietro Mallio, John the Deacon and Cencio Camerario.[77] Huelsen, following an error transmitted by Forcella to Armellini and Calvi, identifies it with the church of St. Thomas of Canterbury which belonged to the English College in the via Monserrato, thus confusing absolutely independent foundations belonging to different nations.

This almost inexplicable error was first cleared up by Dom Wilmart (loc. cit.), who pointed out[78] that the English had two establishments at Rome in succession. In the eighth century they had a *Scola Saxonum* with a hospice in the *Vicus Saxonum*, near the Vatican, and a church, S. Maria *in Sassia*, which still survives in the Borgo S. Spirito.

This institution declined for various reasons in the twelfth century, and in 1204 was abolished by Innocent III, who converted it into a hospital which he handed over to the Confraternity of the Holy Ghost. After the Jubilee in 1350 a new institution sprang up entirely independent of that which Innocent III had abolished, the *societas pauperum Anglorum*, which established itself in the via Monserrato under the title of the Trinity and later of St. Thomas, and which, towards the end of the fifteenth century, absorbed yet another English hospice started in 1396 in the via dei Genovesi in Trastevere under the title of St. Chrysogonus and St. Edmund Martyr, the headquarters still remaining in the via Monserrato. It became the residence, after the schism, of the English College founded in 1575 by Cardinal Allen, and canonically established by Gregory

[76] 'La Trinité des Scots à Rome et les notes du Vat. Lat. 378,' in *Revue Bénédictine*, July 1929, p. 218.

[77] Cf. Huelsen, p. 493; Armellini, p. 645.

[78] Cf. Cardinal Gasquet, *A History of the Venerable English College*, 1920.

XIII in 1580 under the title of the Holy Trinity and St Thomas.[79]

These English foundations, therefore, never had any connection with the Trinità degli Scoti. Dom Wilmart situates the *S. Trinitatis Scottorum* in the south-east corner of the Palatine and identifies it with the *S. Trinitatis* near the hill of Scaurus,[80] mentioned in the *Mirabilia* (the twelfth century redaction), the Turin catalogue (*c.* 1320), and the list drawn up by Signorili (*c.* 1425). In certain notes to *Cod. Vat. Lat.* 378, which contains a martyrology for the use of the neighbouring church of S. Maria in Palladio (now S. Sebastiano al Palatino), the learned Benedictine found two rolls of the members of the community of the Trinità degli Scoti at the end of the eleventh and the beginning of the twelfth century. As this monastery does not appear in the great catalogue of Pope Leo III (806), the notes to *Cod. Vat. Lat.* 378, although comparatively very late, may be presumed to be the earliest documents containing any reference to it. It was a small community consisting of an abbot, two provosts, six monks and seven *commensales* which, as such, had already ceased to exist in 1249, when Pope Innocent IV, by a privilege addressed from Lyons to the Abbot of the Monastery of San Gregorio *in clivo Scauri de urbe*,[81] canonically acknowledged the various possessions of that monastery including *Sancte Trinitatis de Scotis . . . (ecclesiam) cum omnibus pertinentiis (eiusdem)*. It must have been quickly absorbed by S. Gregorio in the beginning of the thirteenth century. The last explicit mention of the name Trinità degli Scoti occurs, according to Dom Wilmart, in a

---

[79] The Welsh, it should be observed, claimed the first foundation of this college to have been by a British king for the perpetual behoof of his country-men. It was "the Palace of Cadwalladr, Prince of Wales . . . who by his last will . . . gave his House or Palace . . . to be a hospital for Welsh pilgrims . . . and ordained that certain priests of his country should have the rule and govern-ment of this hospital for ever" (cf. Owen's *Running Register*, 1626, p. 17). The Warden of this hospital became the first rector of the new College. Dissensions, however, soon broke out, the English students resenting the old rector's prefer-ence for his Welsh compatriots. The Jesuits fanned the flames of strife, Dr. Morris, the Welsh rector, was removed, and a Jesuit Aggazzari voted in by a majority of the English over Dr. Bristowe of Rheims, the Welsh candidate.

[80] Cf. Huelsen, p. 493, n. 11.

[81] Cf. A. Gibelli, *L'antico monastero dei SS. Andrea e Gregorio al clivo di Scauro sul monte Celio*, 1892.

G—i

bull of Boniface VIII dated the 17th June, 1299, and confirming that of Innocent IV. In a *vita* of St. Fridian cited by
Mgr. Guidi,[82] who dates it "not earlier than the thirteenth
century" (MS No. 880 in the Public Library of Lucca), I
have discovered the following interesting passage: "Pauca
de pluribus quae de vita et moribus et genealogia beatissimi
Fridiani a viris litteratis et orthodoxis Scotiae limina Apostolorum et Romanam ecclesiam visitantibus accepimus,
videlicet Araldo, electo Virginensis Ecclesiae et Catholico
Priore Sanctae Mariae Vallis Salutis et Malachia Priore
Sanctae Trinitatis, quae sita est Romae, atque Dionisio
germano suo sacerdote quoque et canonico Sancti Brandani,
ad posteritatis memoriam, sicut in vita eius legitur, quae in
insulis Scotiae solemnis habetur, et nobis studiose inquiren-
tibus diligenter narrarunt, auribus fidelium intimare
curavimus." The "S. Mariae Vallis Salutis" referred to may
perhaps be the Cistercian house of the name founded at
Baltinglas in 1148 or 1151 by Diarmait Mac Murchadha,
King of Leinster (cf. Chapter IV, § 5). Dom Wilmart had
observed (p. 225) that about the end of the eleventh century
the name of St. Fridian had been inserted in the martyrology
(18th March), which had been adapted at that time to the
needs of the little community on the Palatine. The canons of
St. Fridian (cf. Chapter XVII) in the twelfth century administered the Lateran Basilica, S. Croce in Gerusalemme,
S. Maria Maggiore and other basilicas, and were therefore
in continual relations with Rome, and, it may be presumed,
—the church of St. Fridian of Lucca still being a lively
centre of attraction for the Irish—with the *Scoti* in Rome.
It is a calamity that the archives of St. Fridian of Lucca,
which may perhaps have contained records of inestimable
value for such investigations as these, were burned to the
ground in 1596:[83] but a search among the papers of the
churches of Rome and other Italian cities formerly administered by the said canons might still reveal something
of importance.

[82] Cf. Guerra and Guidi, *Compendio di storia ecclesiastica lucchese*, Lucca, 1924,
p. 45.

[83] Cf. Guerra and Guidi, op. cit., p. 95.

Dom Wilmart declares that the monastery *S. Trinitatis Scottorum* "can never have been in a very flourishing condition: the Island of the Saints was too far off, despite the wandering proclivities of the race, to provide this remote foundation with such a stream of recruits as would guarantee a future for it conformably with its origins."

The deductions and opinions of the learned Benedictine scholar carry great weight and deserve the highest respect, but it may still be permissible to point out that there is a wide difference between the slight importance attributed by him to the monastery on the Palatine at the end of the twelfth century and the fact that the Trinità degli Scoti is at the same time reckoned by Mallio and John the Deacon among the twenty greater abbeys in Rome, whose churches, like the greater basilicas, paid the ecclesiastical tax of two *soldi*. It is to be hoped that further investigation may confirm the suggested site and throw some light upon the origin of the Irish abbey, which must date back probably to the eighth or ninth century. It is also to be hoped that further information may be forthcoming some time about the other two churches, *S. Benedicti* and *S. Salvatoris Scottorum*, the probability being that in addition to an abbey in the vicinity of the Lateran patriarchate, the Irish had also a hospice close to St. Peter's for their numerous pilgrims. Mr. H. J. Marrou, in an essay, 'Autour de la bibliothèque du Pape Agapit,' in *Mélanges d'archéologie et d'histoire*, Paris, 1931, p. 169, situates the *Ecclesia Sanctae Trinitatis in Clivo Scauri* between S. Gregorio and SS. Giovanni e Paolo, on the site of the ancient library which Pope Agapetus built upon the ruins of the *xenodochium* of Pammachius, but his arguments have been controverted by Dom Wilmart (cf. 'Finian parmi les moines romains de la Trinité des Scots,' *Revue Bénédictine*, 1932, p. 359).

§ 10

It will be well to warn the reader before bringing this chapter to an end that intentionally no reference has been made to an important factor in the history of the Christian communities in Celtic lands, viz. the tenacious particularism they displayed in certain questions and the almost incredible confidence they reposed in the absolute validity of some of their own insular traditions. No such reference has been made because the detailed knowledge of the particularism and traditions referred to, which, be it said, never in the least impaired their solid dogmatic orthodoxy, is unnecessary to illustrate the features of the Irish saints in Italy, with the single exception of St. Columban. The character and achievement of that great saint cannot, however, be adequately appreciated in a work so limited in scope as this present. It must therefore suffice to say that such questions did exist, and the reader curious with regard to the story of the long and embittered quarrel about the computation of Easter, the Celtic form of the tonsure, the administration of baptism and episcopal consecration, which terminated in the early eighth century, when the relations of the Irish bishops with the Anglo-Saxon Church and the churches on the Continent had made them more familiar with Roman usages, in the complete submission of the Celtic Christian communities, is referred to the admirable exposition of the subject by Dom Gougaud in Chapter VI of *Christianity in Celtic Lands*.

CHAPTER III

THE CULTURAL EXPANSION

§ 1

BRITAIN had been a Roman province and it is therefore no matter of surprise that its monks even in the sixth century—such as, e.g. Gildas, the Jeremiah of the Britons—should have retained some classical culture. But, Dom Gougaud asks, "how did Ireland, a land which had never been incorporated in the empire, acquire the knowledge of letters?"

The earliest missionaries from Britain or the Continent to bring the faith to the Irish in the fifth century had no doubt not the leisure to engage in study or to concern themselves to any great extent with the diffusion of secular learning, but the cultivation of the liberal arts soon imposed itself as a necessity upon the native clergy. If Mass was to be celebrated at all, the Scriptures to be read with intelligence, the truths of the new religion to be explored and expounded, some knowledge of Latin was essential, and the works of the ancient authors were gradually imported into Ireland, together with Biblical texts and the writings of the Fathers, both from the neighbouring island and the Continent. The great number of monasteries contributed to the rapid progress of intellectual culture, and Mag-Bile, Clúain-moccu-Nóis, Clúain-ferta-Brénaind, Clúain-Iráird and Bend-chor, all sixth-century foundations, soon became flourishing centres of learning, which attracted persons eager for instruction from all quarters of the Irish world and overseas.

One interesting feature of the Irish monastic culture, which distinguished it throughout the ages from every other type of similar intellectual discipline, deserves special mention.

When Christianity first penetrated Ireland, it came into contact with a flourishing national, religious, historical and poetical tradition transmitted orally by the three orders of learning: the Druids, the *Vates* or seers, among whom the *brithemin* were the repositories of legal tradition and judicial precedents, and the *filid*, the custodians of the literary traditions of the nation, who survived as a powerful corporation down to the fourteenth century.[1] The Christian missionaries introduced into this national culture of Ireland through the Britons and, more particularly, St. Finnian of Clúain-Iráird and St. Cadoc of Llan-carvan, the Western culture of Lérins, where, along with Holy Scripture and theology, profane literature also was studied as of indispensable assistance to the complete acquisition of the Latin language and, generally, to the full understanding of the sacred texts.

Irish monasticism so far differed from the systems which flourished elsewhere, e.g. in Gaul, where churchmen were disposed to be contemptuous of the vulgar tongue, which, because it was still inchoate and unformed, they considered to be fit only for the unlettered laity, that it gradually effected a fusion of the two cultures, the indigenous and the exotic from Lérins, by means of the Gaelic language which the monks themselves spoke and used to address the people. The *filid* gradually became Christian, and Colum-cille, himself a *file* of the highest rank, made a memorable intervention at the momentous *mórdail* of Druim-Cetta in 575 to help them retain the privileges which they abused and, incidentally, to prevent their banishment from Ireland.[2] The national intellectual patrimony of the race had thitherto been transmitted only orally, the preceding attempts of the *filid* to transmit their lore in writing (ogham script) having failed to achieve their literary object; the monks, however, while retaining Latin as their model, succeeded in developing a system of orthography—it may be said to have become

---

[1] Cf. Ryan, op. cit., p. 369, and Kenney, op. cit., pp. 1-7.
[2] "O'Donnell . . . informs us that about the year 586 of Christ, it was decreed . that all the race of the bards or antiquaries should be banished . . . and their discipline abolished; but that St. Columba (a very likely tale) was pleased to intercede for them." So Innes, op. cit., p. 263, but with sarcasm misplaced.

stereotyped about the end of the seventh century—which made Gaelic as easy to write as Latin, and so rendered possible the emergence and preservation in record of a real Gaelic literature.[3] The successful fusion of the two cultures secured therefore for the Irish monks a privileged position of religious and intellectual predominance both at home and abroad. By accepting, assimilating, and promoting the national culture, they acquired an immense influence at home; by assimilating the classical culture which the Church had preserved for Europe, they were able to spread over the Continent and to play a great part in making good the intellectual losses entailed by the barbarian invasions.

The nature or the value of the teaching of such as Finnian of Clúain-Iráird or Comgall of Bend-chor will never be known, for the authentic works of these masters have not survived. But from the writings of their disciples, Columcille of Iona, for example, to whom an ancient tradition attributes a Latin hymn, *Altus prosator*, a kind of early 'Paradise Lost,' and Columban of Bobbio, it may be inferred that it was possible to acquire in sixth-century Ireland an extensive and practical knowledge of Latin to the point of being able to write the language, if not with simplicity and grace, at any rate correctly, and even to compose verses in a diversity of metres.[4] The literary remains of St. Columban include a *carmen navale* or boat song in eight stanzas of three hexameters each, another set of hexameter verses of exhortation to Sethus on the vanities of life, an acrostic in hexameters, *Columbanus Hunaldo*, on the contempt of worldly pleasures, and, most famous of all, a discourse in Horatian vein addressed *Fidolio fratri suo* in 159 Adonic lines, *bipedali*

---

[3] Cf. Ryan, op. cit., p. 377.

[4] The question of Latin culture in Ireland to which M. Roger, *L'enseignement des lettres classiques d' Ausone à Alcuin*, Paris, Picard, 1905, and Sigr. L. Schiaparelli in the introduction to *Note paleografiche intorno all' origine e ad alcuni caratteri della scrittura e del sistema abbreviativo irlandese* (Archiv. stor. Ital., 74, II, 1916, pp. 3-126) had already devoted a scholar's careful examination, has been established on a rational foundation by Mr. Mario Esposito in *Notes on Latin Learning and Literature in Medieval Ireland*, Hermathena, 1929, XX, pp. 225-60, and 1932, XXII, pp. 253-71. Reference should also be made to two papers by Dr. Eóin MacNeill, 'Beginnings of Latin Culture in Ireland' in *Studies*, XX, March and September, 1931.

condita versu, and six hexameters on the evils that flow from gold and the wisdom of discarding cares.   The works of the most eminent Latin Fathers and the Bible in particular were the object of serious study, while the profane writers of the Empire were no less sedulously read and commented. Quotations or reminiscences may be found in the works of Columban from or of Virgil, Ovid, Horace, Persius, Juvenal and Prudentius.   The few short pieces which have survived of Cellanus of Péronne, the correspondent of Aldhelm, and Adamnán show some knowledge of Virgil, and Adamnán may well have been the compiler of the Berne collection of Scholia upon the Bucolics and Georgics of the master poet. St. Cadoc, that curious Welsh character who founded Llan-carvan and who was reputed to be at once hermit, abbot, bard, and feudal chieftain, was educated at Liss-mor and had a passion for Virgil, whom he taught his pupils to learn by heart.   "One day, while walking with his friend and com-panion the famous historian Gildas, with his Virgil under his arm, the abbot began to weep at the thought that the poet whom he loved so much might be even then perhaps in Hell. At the moment when Gildas reprimanded him severely for that 'perhaps,' protesting that without any doubt Virgil must be damned, a sudden gust of wind tossed Cadoc's book into the sea.   He was much moved by this accident and, returning to his cell, said to himself 'I will not eat a mouthful of bread, nor drink a drop of water before I know truly what fate God has allotted to those who sang upon earth as the angels sing in Heaven.'   After this he fell asleep and soon after, dreaming, heard a soft voice addressing him, 'Pray for me, pray for me,' said the voice; 'never be weary of praying.   I shall yet sing eternally the mercy of the Lord.' The next morning a fisherman of Belz brought him a salmon, and the Saint found in the fish the book which the wind had snatched from his hands." [5]

The works of Pliny the Elder, Cicero, Frontinus, Vegetius, Valerius Maximus, Macrobius, Donatus, Priscian, Chari-

[5] Cf. Montalembert, op. cit., III, p. 69, and compare the verses "Ad Maronis mausoleum, Ductus [sc. Paulus] fudit super eum Piae rorem lacrimae 'Quem te,' inquit, 'reddidissem Si te vivum invenissem Poetarum maxime!' " quoted in Comparetti, *Virgilio nel medio evo*, I, pp. 128 et seq.

sius and Boethius had penetrated into Ireland before the ninth century. By that time the number of Irishmen, settled for the most part on the Continent, who took to writing Latin verses, was legion, and among the best known names are Sedulius Scottus, John the Scot (*Eriugena*), Dungal, and Joseph the Scot.

In the ninth century also, the progress of Greek studies took a notable step forward in the island world, and we shall find traces of it in Part II with reference to Donatus of Fiesole. Five or six Irishmen then resident in the Frankish empire had more than an elementary notion of Greek and Græco-Latin glossaries, and paradigms of Greek declensions, Biblical texts and psalters in Greek, to say nothing of Latin translations of Greek proverbs made by the Scots of the day, are still preserved. There was no better Greek scholar than John the Scot. He wrote Greek verses and is known to have translated into Latin—but after a residence of some years in France—the works of the pseudo-Dionysius the Areopagite which had not thitherto found a competent translator in the West. John's version was entrusted for examination and correction to Anastasius the papal librarian, who returned it to Charles the Bald, the Irish scholar's patron, with his comments and a most complimentary letter: "Mirandum est quomodo vir ille barbarus, in finibus mundi positus, talia intellectu capere in aliamque linguam transferre valuerit." [6]

[6] Cf. Gougaud, op. cit., p. 309. On the knowledge of Greek in Ireland in the early Middle Ages, cf. chapter VII, pp. 55-67, of the same author's *Gaelic Pioneers of Christianity*, Dublin, 1923, and Eóin MacNeill, *Phases, etc.*, pp. 243-4. John the Scot had the wit to anticipate criticism of his effort and referred any reader who might be doubtful of his rendering to the original Greek codex: "there, perchance, he will find whether it is so or not." 'Ep ad Karolum.' Anastasius did object that the translation was too literal and to remedy this John provided a commentary, part of which has survived. Cf. Migne, *P.L.*, CXXII, 125-266; Kenney, op. cit., pp. 580 and 582. The translation and commentary had one curious result. Frequently commented by the doctors of the early Middle Ages, notably Hugh of St. Victor, they inspired the artists who sculped the nine orders of angels on the southern portal of the Cathedral at Chartres. Not every work is thus forever commemorated in stone.

§ 2

Religious education and the teaching of letters went hand in hand therefore in Ireland. The liberal arts, the study of the ancient languages, all profane culture were regarded from the beginning as ancillary to the main business of religious discipline, and the primary object was to make men's minds fit for the *lectio divina*, i.e. the study of the Divine mind as revealed in its scriptural and traditional expression. Calligraphy and miniature painting, arts held in the highest esteem in Ireland, were employed almost exclusively to multiply and adorn religious books, liturgical texts and Bibles. Colum-cille of Iona in the seventy-third year of his age, and on a day when his mind was heavy with the presentiment that he was about to die, went on for the last time with his work of transcribing a psalter. "When he came to that verse where it is written 'Inquirentes autem Dominum non deficient[7] omni bono,' he stopped. 'Here,' he said, 'I think I can write no more: let Baithin write what follows.' Baithin was the steward at Iona, the cousin and intimate friend of Colum-cille, and succeeded his master as abbot."[8]

Early in the seventh century crowds of foreigners began to flock to the schools of Ireland and to those which the Scots opened outside their island. The names of many of these studious foreigners have come down to us. They include "a certain bishop called Agilbert, by nation a Frenchman, but who had then [A.D. 635] lived a long

---

[7] The Vulgate now reads instead of 'deficient,' 'minuentur,' which suggests that the Irish, even as late as Adamnán's time, continued to read the old Latin version of the Scriptures. Cf. Lanigan, *Ecclesiastical History of Ireland*, Vol. I, 247, n. 225.

[8] Cf. Adamnán, 'Vita S. Columbae,' *P.L.*, LXXXVIII, col. 772, and Skene, op. cit., pp. 141-5, who comments that Montalembert (*Monks of the West*), III, p. 269, accepted without question the whole of O'Donnell's biography of St. Columba, described by Lanigan as "that great repository of doubtful traditions," and entirely misunderstood Adamnán's expression (Pref. 2) 'insulanus miles.' It is to be regretted that Skene did not always exercise the same care in his judgment of Montalembert. Manus O'Donnell, however, wrote his *Life of St. Columba* (1532) with "but a fragment of the book which Holy Adamnán compiled [of it] in Latin," the *Life of Adamnán* having been lost until Stephen White discovered it at Reichenau in 1625 and copied it for Colgan. O'Donnell's *Life* has been edited and translated by A. O'Kelleher and G. Schoepperle: *Betha Colaimchille*, Illinois, 1918.

time in Ireland for the purpose of reading the Scriptures," and who later became "bishop of the city of Paris": Egbert, "who long lived a monastic life . . . in Ireland, praying, observing continence, and meditating on the Holy Scriptures"; Wigbert, "famous for his contempt of the world . . ." who "went abroad and arrived in Friesland, preaching the word of salvation for the space of two years successively . . . but reaped no fruit of all his great labour among his barbarous auditors"; Willibrord, "the holy bishop of the Frissians"; Hewald the Black and Hewald the White, "both piously religious, but Black Hewald was the more learned of the two in Scripture," and both martyred in Friesland; Haemgils the hermit, "supporting his declining age with coarse bread and water"; Chad, later bishop of Lichfield; Ethelhun, who died of the great plague in A.D. 664, and Ethelwin, his brother, later second Bishop of Lindsey; Eahfrid, the correspondent of Aldhelm, and the Northumbrian princes, Oswald, Oswy and Aldfrid. A Pictish bishop also went to study in Ireland but his name has not been preserved, and the number of English attracted to the holy city of Armagh by the renown of its schools was such that one of the three wards into which it was divided was called the Saxon third. Aldhelm, in a letter to his friend Eahfrid, whoever he may have been, but lately returned home from Ireland,[9] refers with some bitterness to the *Scotici scioli*: "Why, I ask you, *misellus homuncio* that I am, should Ireland *quo catervatim isthinc lectores classibus advecti confluunt* be exalted above herself by some ineffable privilege, as though *didascali Argivi Romanive quirites* are not to be found on the fruitful sod of Britain *qui coelestis tetrica enodantes bibliothecae problemata sciolis reserare sciscitantibus valeant*?" The country in Ireland, he continued, was rich in scholars *vernansque ut ita dixerim pascuosa numerositate lectorum*: it was the duty of Englishmen to patronise the schools at home. Another writer reckons in thousands the number of persons engaged

---

[9] Epist. III, 'Aldhelmi ad Eahfridum ex Hibernia in patriam reversum, Migne, *P.L.*, LXXXIX, col. 92. The first fifteen words of this "angry, macaronic' and ridiculous" letter would all begin with the letter 'p,' but for the inevitable intrusion of a small 'sub.' As to his identity, cf. A. S. Cook, 'Who was the Ehfrid of Aldhelm's letter?' in *Speculum*, October 1927, pp. 363-73.

in teaching in Ireland: *Scotti multa millia paedagogorum habebant.* The Scots treated their foreign pupils with rare generosity. "Many of the nobility and of the lower ranks of the English nation were there at that time [*sc.* A.D. 664, the year of the great plague, described in the Irish Annals as *buidhe chonnuil*[10]] . . . who forsaking their native island retired thither, either for the sake of divine studies or of a more continent life. . . . The Scots willingly received them all, and took care to supply them with food, as also to furnish them with books to read, and their teaching, gratis."[11]

All these pupils resorted to the schools of Ireland for instruction in the art of asceticism and the learning of Holy Writ. The 'Celtic' churchmen, Patrick, Gildas, Columban, Cummian, Aidan, Adamnán and Sedulius, were all nourished on the Scriptures.

The Latin Biblical texts in use among the Christian communities in Celtic countries were pre-Vulgate versions. St. Jerome's translation was introduced gradually into Ireland and England in the sixth century and made its way under Columban, Cummian and Adamnán. The *Collectio Hibernensis*, the Irish collection of canons, was compiled under Roman auspices early in the eighth century.

Texts of the Vulgate belonging to the Irish family were not confined to the island, and manuscripts carried off to their own countries by foreigners, who had gone to study in Ireland, or by Scots emigrants, are found scattered all over the Continent, so that the pure Irish text may be read in Biblical manuscripts from such different sources as Tours, Angers, Le Mans, Epternach, St. Gall, Reichenau, and Bobbio.

The most ancient memorials of the Old Irish language are some Biblical glosses, not a few of which date as far back

[10] Cf. *The Four Masters*, ed. O'Donovan, I, p. 275 note: "The one medical detail which has been preserved . . . is not incompatible with the hypothesis of bubo-plague, and is otherwise unintelligible." Charles Creighton, *A History of Epidemics in Britain*, Cambridge University Press, 1891, p. 8, who attributes the earliest mention of "yellow plague" to an ancient life of St. Gerald of Mayo in Colgan's *Acta Sanctorum* at the calendar date of 13th March. Cf. also Plummer's *VV. SS. Hib.* I, pp. lxxi, et seq., II, 107-15.

[11] Bede, *H.E.* Cf. also W. G. Hanson, *The Early Monastic Schools of Ireland*, Cambridge, Heffer, 1927, and Th. Allison, *English Religious Life in the Eighth Century as illustrated by Contemporary Letters*, London, S.P.C.K., 1929.

as the eighth century. They are relatively numerous. But more important than the glosses, particularly from the point of view of language, are the commentaries properly so-called on the books of the Bible written or transcribed by the Irish. These are of inestimable value in enabling us to understand their method of interpreting the Holy Scriptures. They include a treatise, *De mirabilibus sacrae scripturae*, which, although preserved and published among the works of the great Augustine of Hippo, is without doubt the composition of an 'Augustinus' who was an Irish priest of the seventh century and an inmate, perhaps, of the monastery of Clúain-moccu-Nóis. It is a work of very great interest as throwing light on the theories current in Ireland at the time in natural philosophy—the problem of the tides is treated at great length—theology—as God ceased from creation on the seventh day, the work He continues to do is merely governance (*gubernatio*), and any new miracle is merely the evocation of some principle normally concealed in the depths of nature—and exegesis—the author excludes from the canon of Scripture the story of Bel and the Dragon and the two books of Maccabees.[12] Other Irish codices contain a Latin commentary on Job and an abstract (*Egloga*) of Pope Gregory the Great's *Moralia in Job*, one of the most popular works in Ireland as elsewhere in medieval Europe, made by a certain Laid-cend (*c.* 640), a monk apparently of Clúain-ferta-Molua.

The Psalter, the basis both of liturgical and private prayer, was the object of specially sedulous study by the monks and learned by heart. Jonas of Susa, who wrote the *Life of St. Columban*, tells us that such was the riches of the treasure of Divine Scripture which his hero had laid up in his heart that he composed, while still a young man in Ireland, a learned commentary on the Psalms. Copies of the

[12] The lucky accident of the name 'Augustinus' ensured the preservation of the work. Cf. Migne, *P.L.*, XXXV, 2149-200. It is inscribed: "Venerandissimis urbium et monasteriorum episcopis et presbyteris maxime Carthaginensium, Augustinus per omnia subjectus, optabilem in Christo salutem" (there is a twelfth-century MS. in Balliol College, Oxford), and Lanigan first made the suggestion that 'Cluanensium' or 'Corcaginensium' was the proper reading for 'Carthaginensium,' the almost inevitable correction by a continental scribe who knew only one Augustine.

work existed at St. Gall and Bobbio in the ninth and tenth centuries, according to the old catalogues of those monastic libraries, but Fleming in the seventeenth century could find no traces of it. A century later Muratori found and published what he believed to be the authentic commentary, in a ninth-century manuscript, now known as *C.* 301 inf. and preserved in the Ambrosian Library at Milan. Another commentary upon the Psalter written by an Irish hand in the eighth century is contained in *Cod. Pal.* 68 of the Vatican.

Joseph the Scot, "Joseph abbas Scottus genere," the pupil of one Colcu and the disciple of Alcuin, wrote a commentary on Isaias compiled from St. Jerome at Alcuin's request, which has never been printed. There are various works on the Gospel and the Epistles of St. Paul. Sedulius has left a *Collectaneum in omnes beati Pauli epistolas* and another treatise *in Matthaeum*, both still unpublished, besides notes of the arguments and other matter prefixed to the Gospels, and John the Scot a homily on the prologue to the Gospel of St. John, four considerable fragments of a commentary on the same evangelist, and a commentary, now in the Vatican and still in manuscript, on the Old Testament.

These brief indications may suffice to show that the Christian mind of the old Irish was saturated with the Bible.

The growing development of the Church imposed the necessity for disciplinary canons, some of which were traditionally ascribed to the age of St. Patrick himself, but the best known collection is that described for short as the *Hibernensis*, and compiled by Rubin of Dair-Inis, in the Blackwater, not far from Youghal († 725), and Cu-Chuimne of Iona, surnamed 'the wise.' Irish and British canonical texts crossed the seas in the latter half of the eighth century and played a considerable part in moulding the legislation of the Frankish Church. The *Hibernensis*, unlike other contemporary collections such as the *Dionysiana* and the *Hispana*, which were made up of texts emanating from some official authority such as the councils or the Pope, was welcomed on its merits as a practical book of reference for the teaching of the Church on matters of administration, discipline, and the care of souls, classified under sixty-five main headings and many sub-headings.

Disciplinary canons brought in their train penitentials, manuals containing a schedule of the expiatory works to be imposed for the various sins for which penitents might desire to make atonement. These, taking their origin among the Christian communities of Celtic lands, later passed by way of Irish missionaries to the Anglo-Saxons and then by way of both Irish and Anglo-Saxon missionaries, notably Columban and his disciples, to the Continent.[13] The latter kindled the ardour of the people among whom they laboured *ad medicamenta penitentiae*, in the words of Jonas of Susa, and strove to make the practice of confession more frequent not only in monasteries but also among the devout laity living in the world. The *Regula coenobialis*, the *Poenitentiale*, the *Ordo de vita et actione monachorum* of St. Columban,[14] the *Regula cujusdam patris ad virgines*, a rule based on St. Columban's *Regula coenobialis* which St. Donatus of Besançon drew up in the seventh century for the *monasterium puellarum* which he had established in that city, the customs of Faremoutiers, all, impregnated with the spirit of Luxeuil, prescribe frequent confession for religious men and women. In Ireland the confessor was described by a name which deserves to be noted; he was called in old Irish *anmchara*, 'the soul friend,' and a gloss on the Martyrology of Oengus (*c.* 800) records a comment by St. Comgall of Ben-chor that 'a man without a soul-friend is like a body without a head.'

§ 3

Occasional reference has been made to the esteem in which the arts of writing and miniature illumination were held in Ireland. It would be impossible in a chapter dealing with the expansion of culture not to dwell for a moment on this

---

[13] The English called the *Poenitential* the '*Doom-book*' and the various compilations in use in England were all superseded by that composed by Archbishop Theodore. Cf. Lingard, op. cit., I, pp. 304-10. The *Poenitential*, it may be observed, was only one volume in the essential library of the early medieval priest who had care of souls.

[14] Cf. Lugano, op. cit., pp. 24-7.

subject or to omit any mention of the libraries formed in the great foundations abroad, more particularly in the Italian city of Bobbio.

Before the introduction of Christianity, books, it may be said, were lacking in Ireland. The sudden necessity of supplying them in large quantity to meet the needs of the extraordinary monastic development, which followed the establishment of the new religion in the sixth century, accounts for the rapid increase in the bibliographical patrimony of the Irish. In the work of copying and decorating religious manuscripts, the native scribes, however, exhibited such patience, ingenuity, resourcefulness and invention as have never been surpassed, and many of the Irish codices in respect of calligraphy and illumination rank among the most beautiful examples of their kind.

The Irish had a secular regard for learning, and scribes were held in the highest esteem, both in the monasteries and among the laity, and ranked in dignity with an abbot or a bishop. A team of subaltern copyists worked in silence under the strictest discipline in the *scriptorium* of the monastery under the orders of the chief scribe. Parchment of sheepskin, calfskin, or goatskin was the material most in use, but of a coarser texture than that commonly employed on the Continent between the seventh and tenth centuries, and the pen was the quill of a swan, goose or raven.

Irish script derives from the Latin, and is of two kinds: a half-uncial of a rather peculiar type (less rounded than the Roman half-uncial), and a very fine pointed minuscule, with sharp capitals and special ligatures. "To Ireland," writes Mr. E. A. Lowe,[15] "belongs the credit of having been the first to develop a minuscule in the true sense of the word.... But before creating a minuscule Irish calligraphers had created a majuscule, the Irish half-uncial as it is styled, of which the *Book of Kells*, a work of unsurpassed skill and artistry, is the most eminent example." This remarkable work, the *Codex Cennanensis*, may reasonably be assigned to

[15] Cf. the article 'Handwriting' in *The Legacy of the Middle Ages*, ed. C. J. Crump and E. F. Jacob, Oxford, p. 209. Mr. Lowe cites the *Antiphonary of Bend-chor*, written between 680 and 691, as having all the characteristics "that we associate with minuscule."

the eighth century. Wherever the Irish went they took their
script with them and taught it to their pupils; it varied but
little down to the threshold of the Middle Ages, so that the
dating of Irish MSS., wherever found, is a difficulty for
palæographers, and it was ousted only because of their
"cardinal virtue of clearness" by the continental minuscules.
Mr. Lowe thinks that "the particular type of half-uncial
which served as a model must have come by way of Gaul,"
and that "there is nothing inherently improbable in the
supposition that a half-uncial type with numerous uncial
adhesions was still largely in vogue in Gaul in the first half
of the fifth century. The evidence of palæography would
seem to confirm the testimony of hagiography, both as to the
period and the instrument of Ireland's conversion."

Irish manuscripts are not confined to the British Isles:
precious exemplars may also be found in Paris, St. Gall,
Turin, Milan, Dresden, Berne, Carlsruhe, Zürich, Vienna
and the Vatican Library. The *scriptura Scottica*, so propagated
as aforesaid, became very familiar to continental scribes
from the eighth down to the tenth century.

The English script derives from the Irish, but the English
were apt pupils and it is extremely difficult in certain cases
to distinguish the two types. Although the English is now
seen to be "less bizarre, clearer and less crowded," they were
confused in the seventeenth century under the common
appellation *scriptura Saxonica*, and it was not until the beginning of the nineteenth century that the distinction was
securely established, and the priority of the *scriptura Scottica*
finally settled by the patriotic investigations of Dr. Charles
O'Conor.

The decoration of the Irish manuscripts is characteristic,
and the *Book of Kells*, which contains the Eusebian canons,
breves causae, *argumenta*, and the four Gospels with some
lacunæ, is a marvel of richness and a triumph of art. The
pen and brush together achieved an almost incredible
degree of perfection, intricacy and harmony in the Irish
monasteries. The colours most frequently used are red,
yellow, and green: gold, surprisingly, never; they were
blended with exquisite taste to produce a dazzling result

H—I

and after the lapse of twelve centuries are still wonderfully fresh.[16]

The weakest feature in Irish illumination is the representation of the human figure and animals. Genuine Irish art apparently drew no element of inspiration from the vegetable kingdom, but when it ceased to be a mere matter of copying living things or natural objects, when the artist was free to dive down into his own imagination and to bring up complex and varied combinations of decorative motifs, his achievements in interlaced designs with loops and spirals upon the letter T or Z or a saltire as a ground are unsurpassed and unsurpassable. He revelled in Leonardesque labyrinths of ribbons and straps endlessly unrolled in a maze of infinite criss-cross which, though its lines are extremely complicated and varied, never wearies the eye or offends the mind with the least suggestion of disorder or confusion.

St. Columban on his arrival in Italy is traditionally said to have brought with him in a wallet hanging from his neck a codex of the Gospels, which on his death was preserved in his monastery at Bobbio. This *Codex Bobbiensis*, copied in uncial script by a careless scribe, an old Latin text with some Vulgate additions, familiar to scholars as G.VI 15, under the symbol K, is preserved to this day in the National Library of Turin. This single book was the fruitful seed out of which in course of time grew the famous library of that monastery.

A document dating back to a period in the ninth century, when one Wala was abbot (833-35), and enumerating among the more important duties in the monastery those of the librarian and the *custos cartarum*, proves the existence thus early of a library and archives.

The growing library received additions both from passing Irish *peregrini* and from monks who, having been driven out of their country by the Danish invasions, had settled

---

[16] The decoration has recently been analysed with patient thoroughness by Mlle Françoise Henry in her admirable book, *La sculpture irlandaise pendant les douze premiers siècles de l'ère chrétienne*, two vols., Paris, Leroux, 1933. Mlle Henry has come to the conclusion that a whole team of artists was engaged on the work at intervals over a considerable extent of time.

there, as well as from various private donors such as Amale-fred, Dungal *praecipuus Scottorum*, Petroald, Boniprand, the Abbot Agilulf, Theodore, two monks of Luxeuil named Peter and William respectively, and others who took care to transmit their names to posterity by inscribing com-memorative verses on the books they presented.[17] Some scholars, notably Rudolf Beer and Paul Lejay, have sug-gested that many books in the library at Bobbio came from the monastery at Vivario, to which Cassiodorus, the illustrious senator and chief minister to Theodoric, had transported his own celebrated collections from Ravenna and Rome.[18]

Besides such additions as were derived from external sources, the products of the Bobbio scriptorium itself, busily at work from the ninth century onwards, must also be taken into account. Codices certainly copied at Bobbio as early as the eighth century are now preserved in the Ambrosian Library at Milan, and the names of at least four of the amanuenses, George, Amandus, Nazerius, and Ermen-garius, all members of the ancient school, have come down to us. It had its own characteristic features and decorative motifs borrowed from the schools of Ireland, and its manu-scripts bear comparison with those from the sister institu-tions at Luxeuil and St. Gall.

The library, like other monastic libraries of the time and later, contained works reflecting the divers ecclesiastical disciplines (Biblical texts and commentaries, liturgical books, the writings of the Fathers, hagiographical com-positions, theological and polemical treatises), as well as profane works (treatises on grammar and the works of the more eminent Latin poets and prose-writers), with this singularity, that as the Bobbio monks had taken upon themselves the task of controverting Arian heretics, who at the time of their foundation were predominant in North

[17] As e.g. Dungal in the lines quoted by Muratori:
"Sancte Columba, tibi Scotto tuus incola Dungal
Tradidit hunc librum quo fratrum corda beentur
Qui legis ergo Deus pretium sit muneris ora"
which would suggest that Dungal ended his days at Bobbio.
[18] Cf. also A. Van der Vyver, 'Cassiodore et son œuvre,' in *Speculum*, VI, 1931, p. 283.

Italy, they naturally laid in a store of Arian literature of various kinds, homilectic, dogmatic, and polemical.[19] The rarity, or rather the absence, of Greek manuscripts is noteworthy: most of the leaves from the earliest Bobbio collection are palimpsest belonging to much older codices and in some cases the old Greek script is overlaid with a Latin script, itself of such antiquity as to induce the belief that such was the condition in which they were received at Bobbio.

A catalogue of the library, which Mr. Mario Esposito[20] considers to be a tenth-century copy of a document written in the second half of the ninth (probably between 862 and 896), contains no less than six hundred and sixty works and yet shows many lacunæ; even so, it is far from giving us any adequate idea of what the library was like in the golden age of the monastery. It must always be remembered that when parchment was scarce or too expensive, as it was during the seventh and eighth centuries, or there was a dearth of scholars capable of appreciating at their proper value texts such as Ulfilas's excessively literal Gothic version of the Scriptures and profane authors such as Cicero, Lucan, Plautus and Fronto, pages were erased for some more practically useful text to be substituted. "The obvious way of saving vellum," writes Mr. E. A. Lowe, "was to write more on a page. One way of getting more on a page was to make narrow instead of broad letters, to write a smaller script, in short to write minuscule. It is this forced economy which made the Irish, probably an impecunious race even in the seventh and eighth centuries, squeeze more into a page than a decent regard for the reader's convenience would warrant, or good taste dictate. . . . How thoroughly the lesson of thrift had been inculcated in the followers of St. Columban and St. Gall, and how badly in need they were of writing material . . . may be surmised from the frequency with which the monks of St. Gall and Bobbio made use of membranes that had already been written upon. It was not out of contempt for the classics that

[19] Cf. J. Zeiller, *Les Origines chrét. dans les Prov. Danubiennes*, etc., Paris, 1918, pp. 491-9, who gives a list of the chief texts.
[20] 'The ancient Bobbio Catalogue,' in *Journ. of Theol. Studies*, 1931, pp. 337-44.

Cicero's *De Republica,* Fronto's *Letters,* Lucan and Juvenal were erased—for biblical and patristic texts suffered a similar fate—but out of sheer need of writing material." Other works which had become unserviceable through too frequent usage were used again, but as fly leaves and covers for the binding of new books.

This is the reason why so many palimpsests were found among the MSS. from Bobbio and so many fragments of ancient scripts in such volumes as have survived.

The gradual decline of monastic life in the venerable abbey was followed by the dissolution and dispersal of its library.

The humanists of the fifteenth century, Pomponius Laetus in chief, turned the library at Bobbio into a quarry from which to cart away codices and classical antiquities to enrich the libraries of Florence, Wolfenbüttel, Naples, Vienna, Paris, Nancy and the Escurial.

Cardinal Federico Borromeo, the founder of the Ambrosian Library at Milan, endowed it about 1606 with fully seventy-three codices from Bobbio, including the famous *Antiphonary of Bend-chor,* a gift to which the Ambrosiana "is indebted for much of the prestige it enjoys among learned men and scholars, it would be no exaggeration to say, all over the world."[21]

Pope Paul V, fired perhaps by the example of Borromeo, succeeded in 1618 in securing twenty-eight volumes for the Vatican Library, which are now known as Nos. 5748-76 of the *Codices Vaticani Latini,* and include the famous palimpsest of Cicero's *De Republica* discovered by Cardinal Mai and published by him in 1822. Some seventy other volumes found their way to Turin during the reign of Charles Emmanuel I. In 1801 the French took possession of the library of St. Columban and in 1803 dealt it the *coup de grâce,* when such of the volumes as escaped the flames passed into the hands of secularized monks, private citizens, or agents of the Republic, not one being then confided to the care of any public library. Owing to the zeal and intelligence of an

[21] Cf. Achille Ratti, *Le ultime vicende della biblioteca e dell'archivio di S. Colombano di Bobbio,* Milano, Hoepli, 1901, p. 10.

eminent classical scholar, the Abbé Peyron, many fragments and some sixty manuscripts were, however, recovered between 1820 and 1824 and assembled in the National Library of the University of Turin, but, unfortunately, they were either destroyed or seriously damaged in the fire which broke out in the University on 26th January, 1904. [I am indebted for some of these particulars to Mgr. Grammatica's *La Biblioteca di Bobbio*[22] and to the before-cited article by Mgr. A. Ratti (now H.H. Pius XI). They may serve to illustrate the importance to the world of culture of this great Irish foundation. Mgr. Giovanni Mercati, the eminent prefect of the Vatican Library, has recently prefaced his photographically-reproduced edition of the famous Bobbiese palimpsest containing the *De Republica* of Cicero (*M. Tulli Ciceronis De Re Publica Libri e codice rescripto vaticano latino 5757 phototypice expressi*, Romae, ex Bibl. Ap. Vaticana, 1934) with a lengthy dissertation on the vicissitudes of the famous library, which is undoubtedly the most complete and exhaustive account now available.]

This parenthesis concluded, it will be well to resume the thread of the narrative and to consider the part played by the Irish in the Carolingian renaissance.

§ 4

The period from the beginning of the seventh century until the middle of the eighth is generally considered to have been one of unparalleled ignorance throughout the Western world, the long dark night preceding the dawn of the twelfth century. The picture commonly presented, it may be permitted to believe, lacks proportion and is overdrawn. Ecclesiastical and literary studies, it is alleged, had sunk to an incredibly low level; the classical tradition, however, embodied in the Latin language still survived and continued to be cultivated, although few of the laity, even among the upper classes, could read or write. The religious

[22] In *Scuola cattolica*, 1923. Cf. also C. G. Mor, 'Bobbio, Pavia e gli Excerpta bobiensia,' in *Contributi alla storia dell' Università di Pavia*, Pavia, 1925, pp. 45-55, and Kenney, op. cit., pp. 85-6.

outside the monasteries, we are told, knew very little Latin and no Greek, but they were still sufficiently under the influence of the old imperial culture to look down upon the vernacular languages then in painful process of being brought to birth. The 'secular' clergy, however, possessed but few books for purposes of study and, having no formal education, were content to thumb the well-worn missals, lectionaries, and psalters used at Mass and other religious offices. Charlemagne, a semi-barbarous German, who valued letters the more because he was himself illiterate, was seized with the desire to raise the general level of education in order to impress his influence upon the empire of his dreams,[23] and threw himself energetically into the task of restoring education by organizing schools with a generous breadth of view and sound practical sense. Scholars and theologians gathered at his court from all parts of the great Emperor's dominions: Theodulf,[24] judge, scholar, poet and theologian, who disliked the Irish exceedingly but as bishop founded the schools at Orleans, and Agobard, a doughty controversialist, who fell foul of the Jews for their insolence and the outrages they committed in Lyons where he was archbishop, these two from the Narbonnese; Peter of Pisa, of whom John of Salisbury[25] said that "nullus aut vix similis alter erat in curia," Paul the deacon, best known for his *History of the Lombards*, although he also wrote some charming verse and may have been the author of "Ave

[23] Einhard has a familiar little anecdote of the great man going to bed with his slate under his pillow so that, if he were restless during the night, he could sit up and make pot-hooks, "sed parum prospere successit labor praeposterus et sero inchoatus." *Vita B. Car. Mag.*, cap 25, Migne, *P.L.*, XCVII, 62.

[24] He could write of Charlemagne:
> "O facies, facies ter cocto purior auro,
> Felix qui potis est semper adesse tibi!"

and denounce the Scot no less fervently as:
> "Res dira, hostis atrox, hebes horror, pestis acerba . . ."

and much else, but he will be forgiven because he enriched the liturgy with the hymn, "Gloria, laus, et honor, tibi sit, Rex Christe, Redemptor," still sung on Palm Sunday. He wrote it in prison under suspicion of treason, and one would like to believe the story that the Emperor Louis, riding past one Palm Sunday morning, heard him sing it and was so impressed that he ordered Theodulf's immediate release. For the verses against the unknown 'Scottellus' who so provoked him, cf. Migne, *P.L.*, CV, 322.

[25] Cf. *Polycraticus*, VIII, § 3, Migne, *P.L.*, CXLII, 645.

Maris Stella," and Paulinus of Aquileia, styled "gram-
maticae artis magister," and the author likewise of some
noble hymns: these three from Italy; Claudius, a fiery
zealot, travelled from Spain, while from England came
Alcuin, Sigulf, Abbot of Ferrières, much too fond of reading
Virgil, Witto and Fredegisus, the pupil and friend of Alcuin,
his successor as Abbot of Tours. This band of scholars,
poets and theologians received the addition of two Irishmen
in 782. One was called Clement and is not to be confused
with his heretical namesake, the other is presumed to have
been Dungal of Pavia. The story told by the Monk of St.
Gall[26] is a familiar one: two Irishmen came to France in
the company of British merchants; they cried their wares
in the market place with the others, but their wares were not
the same. They had wisdom to sell: *si quis sapientiae cupidus
est, veniat ad nos et accipiat eam.* The news came to the ears of
Charlemagne and the Emperor made haste to summon
them to the palace and inquired at what price they might
be willing to place their knowledge at the disposal of the
youth of his empire. Needy men are never exigent, and
philosophy for sale is usually cheap. They wanted nothing
more, they said, than "loca tantum opportuna et animos
ingeniosos, et sine quibus peregrinatio transigi non potest,
alimenta et quibus tegamur." And so the bargain was
agreed. Clement remained to succeed Alcuin as master of
the palace school and after the death of Charlemagne was
conffrmed in his functions by Louis the Pious, numbering
among his pupils the future Emperor Lothair. He left his
post only to go to Wurzburg to visit the tomb of St. Kilian
and there, it would appear from the Necrology, he died.

Dungal rose to greater fame. Many references to one
bearing this appellation and many compositions, which he
either begot himself or had fathered on him, have been
preserved to us. It was long the accepted opinion that the
corpus was to be ascribed to a single individual: but as a
result of the labours of L. Traube,[27] Dungal was later split

[26] Cf. 'De gestis Karoli Magni' in Migne, *P.L.*, CXVIII, 1371-1410 (*c.* A.D.
883-87), usually attributed to Notker the Stammerer.
[27] 'O Roma nobilis' in *Abhandlungen der K. Bayer. Akad der Wissenschaften*, I
Cl., XIX, Bd., II, pp. 323-37, Munich, 1891.

into four, five, and finally six different persons.[28] The first
was a 'Bishop Dungal,' so described in a letter written
(*c.* 792) by Alcuin to congratulate the monks of Ireland on
the excellent reports the writer had received with regard to
them; the second a recluse in the famous monastery of St.
Denis, a few miles north of Paris, the friend of Charlemagne
and the writer of a letter to the Emperor with reference to
an eclipse of the sun in 810 and the putative author of various
poems current under the name of '*Hibernicus exul*'; a third
Dungal of Pavia, appointed by Lothair in 825 to be head of
the school established at Pavia, and the author of a reply in
827 to the iconoclastic Spaniard, Claudius, Bishop of
Turin; a fourth, a more shadowy figure, but a poet belonging
to the circle of Sedulius and the composer of some verses
addressed to one Baldo, hailed as '*Dei famule, clare magister*'; a
fifth, an abbot resident on the Continent and the addressee
of verses, ' . . . *praesulis Dungalo abbati*,' preserved in the
Carlsruhe *Codex Augiensis* CXCV f. I[v.] ; a sixth, the '*Dungalus praecipuus Scottorum*,' the monk of Bobbio already
mentioned among the donors of books to the monastic
library.

Mr. Mario Esposito,[29] however, after a patient and
penetrating examination of the various documents, has
recently re-assembled all these different characters into one
single person.

Dungal, then, would appear to have been an Irish bishop
already settled on the Continent some time before 804.
Ingratiating himself with Alcuin, he succeeded in obtaining
the latter's recommendation to the patronage of Charlemagne. He stopped for some time and was employed in
teaching at the monastery of St. Denis and there wrote
poems, describing himself as a *peregrinus*, in honour of Hildoard, Bishop of Cambrai (790-816), a locality where
Irish influence was very strong, and Hilduin, Abbot of St.
Denis, who died in 840. The Baldo, '*Dei famulus clarus
magister*,' the addressee of the poem by the shadowy Dungal,

---

[28] Cf. Kenney, op. cit., index, p. 796.
[29] Cf. 'The Ancient Bobbio Catalogue,' in *Journal of Theol. Studies*, 1931, pp.
337 et seq: "The poems of Colmanus 'nepos Cracavist' and 'Dungalus praecipuus Scottorum,' " ibid., 1932, pp. 113, et seq.

would, if Mr. Esposito's suggestions are well founded, then be Waldo, Abbot of St. Denis (806-13), and no longer, as hitherto conjectured, an obscure scribe in Salzburg: and there would be no inherent improbability in this same Dungal having been the author of his own epitaph, published by Dummler[30], in which he describes his occupation as teaching.

Dungal earned some reputation for himself also as a student of astronomy. A letter addressed to him (*c.* 809) by Charlemagne, requesting information as to the nature of darkness and nothingness apropos of a treatise, '*De substantia tenebrarum et nihili,*' sent to the Emperor by Fredegisus, has been preserved but not the answer returned by Dungal. There is extant instead a dissertation from his pen composed in 811 in explanation, scientifically based on the Ptolemaic system, of two solar eclipses in the preceding year, in answer to yet another request to the astronomer made by the Emperor through Waldo, the Abbot of St. Denis. Dungal by that time had removed to Pavia to teach in the monastery of St. Augustine, and there laid the foundations of his subsequent great reputation.

Lothair, as everybody knows, conceived the ambition to raise the level of culture in Italy also, and in 825 promulgated a famous Edict (the *Constitutiones Olonnenses*) establishing nine schools for youths in nine Italian cities (Pavia, Ivrea, Turin, Cremona, Florence, Fermo, Verona, Piacenza and Cividale del Friuli).[31] The Irishman was invited to

[30] *M.G.H., Poet. lat. aevi Carol. I* (1881), 404-7, no XVII of the *Hibernicus exul*, vv. 19-24. Mr. Esposito suggests (p. 125 of the second article quoted) that the *Hibernicus exul* ought on the whole to be identified rather with Dicuil than with Dungal. The text is printed by Migne, *P.L.*, CV, 460, as

"Epitaphium Dungali: Quisquis es hunc cernens titulum dic pectore puro,
 Sit requies illi, lector opime, precor. . . .

19.   Discipulos proprios illustrat lumine sacro
      Ceu posita in celso clara lucerna loco
      Scripturas promit casto de pectore sacras
      Edocet infirmos et validos pariter.
      Lacte rigans pueros et dat capientibus escam

24.   Hinc lac ut capiant, inde cibum pariter."

[31] The text of the Edict is in *M.G.H., Leges*, I, 1835, pp. 248-53, and trs. in Miss Stokes's *Six Months in the Apennines*. Cf. also A. Solmi, 'Sul capitolaro di Lotario dell' anno 825 relativo all' ordinamento scolastico in Italia,' in *Contributi alla storia dell' Università di Pavia*, Pavia, Tip. Co-operativa, 1925.

take charge of the school at Pavia and his fame was thence-forth assured. "In Papiam conveniunt ad Dungalum de Mediolano, de Brixia, de Laude, de Bergamo, de Novaria, de Vercellis, de Tortona, de Aquis, de Janua, de Aste, de Cuma." This list of the centres from which his pupils came may be sufficient to show the importance of the mission entrusted to him and serve as a measure of the esteem in which the teacher was held. In Part II it will appear that another Irishman, St. Donatus, Bishop of Fiesole, very probably bore a not inconsiderable share in the establish-ment of the academy instituted in Florence by the same Edict for the whole district of Tuscany, which would suggest the likelihood of relations between Donatus and Dungal.

In 827 Dungal published his famous treatise against the Spanish iconoclast Claudius, who in 816 had been appointed Bishop of Turin by Louis the Pious. This Claudius had no sooner taken possession of his diocese than he proceeded to have all crucifixes, 'holy' pictures, and statues of saints removed from the churches, and, when remonstrated with by his friend Abbot Theutmir, indignantly defended his proceedings in 824 in an "Apologeticum atque Rescriptum," condemning the invocation of saints, the veneration of relics, and pilgrimages to the Holy Places. "Ego distruere solus cepi;" he boasted, "et idcirca aperuerunt omnes ora sua ad blasphemandum me et nisi Dominus adjuvisset me forsitan vivum deglutissent me," so great according to his own confession was the resentment his tactless activities aroused. The *Dungali responsa contra perversas Claudii Taurinensis episcopi sententias* (A.D. 827) are important not only as an excellent defence of an immemorable practice in the Church against the vagaries of puritans, but also because of the extensive use the writer, "ob divinae crucis contemptum zelans . . . blasphemiamque sanctorum surda aure transire nequiens," makes of the Christian poets such as Prudentius, Paulinus of Nola, Fortunatus of Poitiers, that engaging character and earliest of Court poets whose noble hymn, "Pange, lingua, gloriosi praelium certaminis," he cites, and Sedulius, the author of the *Carmen Paschale*, quoting passages from their work at some length, which might not otherwise have been preserved. Dungal makes reference also to the epigram composed by St. Ambrose for the burial of his brother Satyrus and concludes: "Haec pauca de sanctis libris assumens collegi, si necesse fuerit ad resistendum diabolo, Christo opitulante, his alia prout ipse dederit, adjuncturus."

At some date unknown, but which cannot have been later than 830, Dungal quitted his post in Pavia and retired with his collection of manuscripts to Bobbio. There is no documentary evidence, but it is not improbable, in Mr. Esposito's opinion, that he became abbot of that house, for the name of the abbot immediately preceding Wala is missing (833).[32]

The last act known to us in the career of Dungal is a gift by him of twenty-nine volumes to the library of his monastery. He would appear to have been the most distinguished of the Irish emigrants to end his days in Bobbio.[33]

About the end of the eighth century and the beginning of the ninth, Cambrai and Laon seem to have been the favourite resorts of the *Scotti* in France, but there were colonies of them also in Rheims, Soissons and Liège.

The most famous emigrant of his day (ninth century) was John the Scot (*Eriugena*), already mentioned as a talented Latin and Greek scholar, who made a protracted stay at Laon teaching in the palace school of Charles the Bald and in friendly relations with Bishop Hincmar, the younger, the nephew of the Hincmar who was Archbishop of Rheims. It became the fashion then, through John and his companion *Scotti*, to affect Greek in conversation. John's was undoubtedly one of the strongest intellects of the early Middle Ages, but the boldness of his speculations in the famous predestination controversy which raged round the head of the unfortunate Gottschalk led him into errors—he seems to have held as a fundamental principle the neo-Platonic doctrine of the non-existence of evil, that sin and

[32] Cf. Cipolla and Buzzi, *Cod. Dipl.*, I, p. 28.

[33] Cf. also with reference to Dungal F. Savio, *Gli antichi vescovi d'Italia, il Piemonte*, pp. 301-19, and *La Lombardia*, I, p. 916, Miss Stokes's *Six Months in the Apennines*, pp. 201-26, and C. G. Mor, *Bobbio, Pavia, e gli Excerpta bobiensia*, pp. 54 et seq.

punishment being mere privation, God could not foresee them nor in consequence predestine to punishment, that the pains of the damned were only their sins or the tormenting recollection of them, and so forth—which evoked various anathemas.[34] "While his contemporaries were only lisping in philosophy . . . Eriugena in the ninth century worked out a complete philosophical synthesis. . . ." "He reads like a pantheistic contemporary of St. Thomas," observes De Wulf,[35] and the traces of his philosophical teaching are discernible throughout the eleventh and twelfth centuries in St. Anselm, Hugh of St. Victor, and Honorius of Autun, as those familiar with the writings of the early schoolmen are aware. It has been suggested that he sojourned for some time at Vercelli, and that the establishment of a *Studium Generale* in that city is due to his efforts. It seems improbable.[36]

Another considerable figure of the Irish emigration in the middle of the ninth century is Sedulius Scottus, who, arriving in Liège (c. 848,) was warmly welcomed by Hartgar, the bishop of that diocese, and settled as a teacher in the school of St. Lambert. A copious versifier, at once facile and agreeable, Sedulius succeeded in arousing the interest of kings and other exalted personages of the time in his distressing economic situation. His house, he complained in one set of verses addressed to his patron Hartgar, was dark, more fit for moles than philosophers; he had no key; the draughts were dreadful and the beer abominable.[37] His knowledge of Greek, though not to be compared with that of John the Scot, was still substantial; but his learning, like his, was encyclopædic. He wrote a commentary on the "Art of Discerning Conjugations" by Eutyches, at the request, as he says, of his brethren, which is believed by some to have been composed before he left Ireland, commentaries

---

[34] His theses were condemned by the Council of Valence in A.D. 855, and the Council of Langres in A.D. 859, which denounced John's arguments as 'diabolical inventions,' and 'old wives' tales.'

[35] *History of medieval philosophy* (trs. Coffey), 1909, p. 167.

[36] Cf. Pastè, 'Sulle traccie dei Monaci di San Gallo,' in *Scuola Cattolica*, 1913, Vol. III, pp. 223-30.

[37] 'Carm ii,' 4, p. 169, in *M.G.H., Poet. lat. aevi Carol III* (ed. Traube), 1886, pp. 151-237. The Irish exiles make many complaints of the quality of the Belgian beer, 'pessima cervisia,' and it is still bad.

on Priscian and Donatus, and composed for Louis II, emperor after 855, or possibly for Lothair II, his brother, a treatise *De rectoribus Christianis* on the duties of Christian rulers, the forerunner of that long series of 'Mirrors for Princes,' so popular in medieval and early modern times.[38]

The Irish writers of this generation, it should be borne in mind, derived much profit from their sojourn on the Continent. Dungal, John the Scot, Dicuil, and Sedulius, all perfected in Europe the knowledge of patristic literature, geography, philosophy, and profane letters which they had acquired in their native island. But from the testimonies of their contemporaries to the learned men who came from Ireland—and to the known names there falls to be added a host of obscure monks who taught the elements and grammar, expounded the Holy Scriptures, brought over from Ireland and copied on the Continent Biblical and liturgical manuscripts, canons, and penitentials—it would appear that contemporaries themselves considered the learning of the sons of Erin to be superior and realized that the progress made in spiritual and intellectual life was largely their achievement.

The venerable Bede had a high appreciation of the excellence of the traditions of piety and doctrine inculcated into the English by the monks of Lindisfarne, and of the unexampled generosity with which the Irish welcomed to their shores, during the seventh and eighth centuries, foreigners eager for instruction. Other writers were compelled to use superlative terms in order to express their admiration for the learned *Scotti*. The Welsh biographer of St. Cadoc,[39] writing about the end of the eleventh century, depicts his hero going to the schools of Ireland, especially Liss-mor, "until he had acquired the complete knowledge of the

---

[38] Thus anticipating by some centuries the *De regimine principum*, part of which at least may be the work of St. Thomas. The political speculations of Sedulius (Migne, *P.L.*, CIII, 291-332) have been overlooked and the only work in English to notice them at all is, it is believed, *A History of Medieval Political Theory in the West*, by R. W. and A. J. Carlyle, Edinburgh, 1903, I, pp. 215-62. His list of ideal rulers is interesting: Augustus, the Antonines, Constantine, the two Theodosii, Charlemagne of course, and Louis the Pious. There is no indication in the text that the author had lived in Ireland. Cf. Hellmann, *Sedulius Scottus*, Munich, 1906.

[39] 'Lifris, Vita Cadoci,' 7, in *AA. SS. Boll.*, Jan., III, 217-20.

West," and mentions also the skill of an Irish wood-worker, Liuguri (= Lóiguire), so cunning in his craft that his fellow-labourers killed him in jealousy. Alcuin recalls the services rendered to Christendom by "the very learned Irish masters, who enabled the Church of Christ in Britain, Gaul and Italy to make such great progress,"[40] and Notker the Stammerer, the monk of St. Gall, depicts Clement and his companion Dungal as men "incomparably well versed in literature both sacred and profane."[41] Another representative of German erudition in the ninth century, Ermenrich, a monk of Ellwangen, afterwards Bishop of Passau, writing to Grimald, Abbot of St. Gall (841-72), extols the island "whence such brilliant luminaries have come to us . . . for teaching philosophy to little and great alike, they have filled the Church with their learning and doctrine."[42]

Such quotations, even discounting the high pitch of their general commendatory tone, are nevertheless useful indications of the great value set on the learning of the Irish by those most competent to appraise it in its Golden Age.[43]

[40] *M.G.H., Epist.*, IV, ep. 280, p. 437. In his *Versis de sanctis Euboricensis ecclesiae* he makes a reference (based obviously on Bede) to a raid made on the "gentes Scottorum" always on friendly terms with the English, "Anglis et semper amicas," by Egfrid of Northumbria, Migne *P.L.*, CI, 829-30.
[41] *M.G.H., SS.*, II, p. 731.
[42] *M.G.H.*, Ep., V, 1899, p. 575.
[43] Cf. L. Maître, *Les écoles épiscopales et monastiques en occident avant les Universités* (768-1180), Paris, Picard, 1926.

CHAPTER IV

§ I

In the ninth century unhappy Erin fell a prey to the Vikings, who on their first appearance were known to the Irish chroniclers by the simple name of Gentiles or heathen, but were later distinguished, as they became more familiar visitors, into the *Lochlannaigh* or *Fingall*, who were fair and Norse (Lochlainn was Norway), and the *Dubhlochlonnaig* or *Dubhgail*, who were dark and Danes. The monasteries were sacked, the great schools at Armagh, Cashel, Dun-da Leathglais and Liss-Mor abandoned, and their teachers compelled to flee from a distracted country in which learning could no longer earn its professors a livelihood. Emigration at will was succeeded and intensified by an emigration perforce.

One of the first places on the English coast facing the North Sea to be attacked by the pirates from Scandinavia was the monastery at Lindisfarne. That venerable pile was pillaged and destroyed in 793; Jarrow was ravaged in the following year.

The Vikings made their first appearance on the coasts of Ireland in 795, when the little island of Raghlin was laid waste. Inis Pátraic was plundered and devastated in 798, and a few years later the Isle of Man was occupied. The Gentiles made a settlement there and it remained in their power for centuries. The first attacks were naturally directed against the sparsely populated little islands, and Iona, which had been sacked once in 795, was plundered again in 798 and 802, when Adamnán's reconstructed abbey was burned to the ground, and afterwards repeatedly. The fury of the heathen in 806 was such that the number of the community was reduced to sixty-four.[1] The remains of St. Colum-cille, like those of St. Martin in Gaul and St. Cuthbert in Northumbria, were in perpetual motion all through the ninth century. Diarmait, the superior, carried them over to the mainland of Scotland to escape the rapacity of the sea-rovers and in 831 brought them back to Ireland, only to take them back to Scotland again, when Ireland in turn fell a prey to the invaders. The relics (*minda*) of Colum were brought to Ireland in 878 and found a final resting-place in Down.

The first aggression of the Vikings in Brittany ended with the sack of Nantes in 843. They began to settle in northern France about the beginning of the tenth century and gradually became converted to Christianity. In 912 Rollo, one of the most arrogant of the invaders, was baptized by the name of Robert, and making a treaty with Charles the Simple, acknowledged him as his liege lord over all the territory later known as Normandy, thus paving the way for the eventual assimilation of the Normans into the kingdom of France.

Wales seems to have been spared until the latter half of the ninth century. Anglesey was first ravaged in 853 and thereafter the attacks became more frequent. The monasteries of Llan-Badarn, Mynyw (Menevia or St. David's), Llan-Iltud, Llan-Carvan, Llan-y-doch (St. Dogmael's), all went up in flames in 989. St. David's would seem to have held a special attraction for the heathen, and two of its bishops were slaughtered, Morgeneu in 999, whose death was considered a judgment upon him because he had eaten meat in Lent,[2] and Abraham in 1078.

The attacks upon England succeeded one another with increasing intensity of violence all through the ninth century and culminated in the great invasion of 870, when St.

---

[1] Opposite the passage of St. Mark's Gospel in the *Book of Armagh* (*c.* 807), containing Christ's prophecies of the miseries of the destruction of Jerusalem (Mark xiii, 20), somebody has written the name 'Cellach.' Cellach was Abbot of Iona 802-15 and fled to Ireland when his monastery was sacked and sixty-eight of the 'family' slain by the Northmen.

[2] Giraldus Cambrensis tells a story of his ghost wandering above the sea and bewailing this transgression in *Itinerarium Kambriae*, *Op.* II, 1 (Rolls Series, VI, p. 104).

Edmund, the last king of the East Angles, sacrificed himself to the enemies of his country. He was seized by the Danes and slain because he would not abjure his faith, and thirty-three years after his death his remains were translated from Hoxne, about twenty miles east of Thetford, to Beadorices-worth, about ten miles south, and there in course of time the magnificent abbey of Bury St. Edmunds was raised above his bones.[3] Northumbria and Strathclyde were ravaged in 875-76, and it seemed as though all England would become a conquered Danish province, but Alfred the Great (871-90) succeeded in maintaining the independence of Wessex and the south and secured a spell of tranquillity to the distracted country. Alfred, however, could not do more than hold a part of the land, and on his death the struggle began again and was carried on by his successors in East Anglia, Essex and Mercia. A fresh period of invasion, with further ferocious slaughter and rapine, opened in 988 until, finally, Canute, who had been baptized in 1013, in 1016 became sole master of England. Once secure upon the throne, Canute proved a devout and liberal monarch, governed his English kingdom according to the traditions inherited from his Anglo-Saxon predecessors, duly made his pilgrimage to Rome in 1026, and on his death in 1035 left two sons, Harold and Hardicanute, by his wife Emma, the widow of his predecessor Ethelred the Unready. Ethelred's son, St. Edward the Confessor, invited over from Normandy, where he had languished as a child, by his half-brother Hardicanute, a year later (1042) succeeded him. St. Edward was the last Anglo-Saxon king of the old royal line and with him the English monarchy perished (1066). His other half-brother Harold was defeated and slain by William, Duke of Normandy, surnamed the Conqueror, at the Battle of Hastings (14th October, 1066). William received the submission of the English nobles and, on the Christmas

[3] Cf. F. Hervey: *The History of King Eadmund the Matryr and of the Early Years of His Abbey*, Oxford, The University Press, 1929. He became one of the most popular of English saints as the survival of his name indicates, Canute being particularly devoted to him, and some sixty English churches from Durham to Devon were dedicated to him. Cf. Miss Arnold Foster's *Studies in Church Dedication*, II, p. 327.

Day following, was crowned King of England in the Abbey at Westminster, which St. Edward had rebuilt.

In Ireland also the invasions of the Vikings from the early ninth century onwards became the more extensive as their knowledge of the geography of the country, its harbours and navigable rivers, increased. In 807 they effected a landing and, penetrating as far as Roscommon, destroyed it and laid waste the surrounding country. They returned in 812 with a great fleet, engaged in battle with the Scots and, being defeated, according to Einhard, with great slaughter, shamefully returned home. The respite, however, was only momentary. They returned again in hordes and running their ships, which were propelled by oars as well as sail, up the rivers and dragging them overland, where need was, to the inland loughs, cast anchor there and sallied forth to plunder churches and monasteries. Not one of the great religious houses which had flourished so peacefully in the eighth century escaped their rapacity. Liss-mor was ravaged in 821, Bend-chor in 823, and Mag-Bile in 824. They slaughtered or dispersed the inmates everywhere, seized any precious object of gold or silver, threw relics—which meant nothing to them—into the water and burned the libraries.

In 832 the Viking leader Thorgest (Turgesius), who had first landed in 818, entered Armagh and plundered it three times in the course of one month; but, while the foreigners were thus laying their country waste, the Irish were at strife among themselves, and Fedelm Mac Crimthan, King of Munster, devastated the country from Birr to Tara and carried off some of the clergy of Armagh. In 845 Thorgest attacked the holy city once more, and Forannan, its abbot, fled with his antiquities and the survivors of his community to Limerick, while the Viking leader extended his sway over all the north of the island.

There was an interval of comparative peace until the Northmen, returning again in force about the middle of the ninth century, renewed the war. This time they established fortified settlements in the country. Dublin,[4] *Ath-Cliath* in

---

[4] The (tenth-eleventh century) 'Vita Coemgeni' in *AA. SS., Boll.*, June 1, 310-22, contains an interesting but obviously anachronistic reference to Dublin

Irish, 'the ford of the hurdles,' was established (c. 840) on the boundary between two of the greater kingdoms, Leinster and Bregia, and followed in 914 by Port Lairge (Waterford), and in 920 by Luimneach (Limerick), at the estuary of the Shannon. The conquest of the country was facilitated by the divisions between the local sovereigns, who continued to carry on their domestic feuds instead of making common cause against the invader: and throughout the dreary tenth century "the Norse settlements . . . if they went to war in Ireland, as often as not, it was in alliance with one Irish king against another."[5]

A heroic champion of the national cause finally emerged in the person of Brian *bóroimhe*, Brian 'of the tribute,' head of the Dal gCais, the ruling race in northern Munster, who compelled the *árd-ri* of all Ireland, Máel-Sechlainn of Meath, to abdicate in his favour in 1002, and decisively defeated the Danes at Clontarf (Clúain-tarbh, 'Bull Meadow'), on the outskirts of Ath-Cliath, on Good Friday, 23rd April, 1014. A heavy price was paid for the victory. Brian, who, during his royal progress throughout Ireland in 1004, had had himself described in the Book of Armagh as Emperor of the Irish (*imperator Scottorum*), *manibus et mente ad Deum intentus*, was slain at the age of eighty-eight, and with him perished his son Morough, his grandson Turlough and many of the petty kings of Munster and Connacht. The advance of the invaders was stayed, but no advantage accrued to the internal peace of Ireland. Máel-Sechlainn became High-King once more, but was unrecognized as such by Ua Brian and the people of Munster, while the Norse settlements under the rule of Ivar, 'king of all the Northmen of Ireland and Britain,' accepted the status of principalities within the Irish political system and remained. In 1015 Máel-Sechlainn attacked the Danes and burned Dublin, and in 1022, the year in which Sitric, the Norse king, was overthrown

---

(cap. xxix): "St. Garban dwelt near the city [*civitatem*] of Ath-Cliath which is in the northern territory of the Leinstermen, situated on a gulf of the sea. Its name in Irish [*scotice*] is Duibh Linn, which means in Latin *nigra terma:* and it is a powerful and warlike city, where ever dwell men fierce in battle, and skilled in the handling of fleets."

[5] Cf. MacNeill, *Phases*, etc., p. 265.

with great slaughter, he retired to a monastery to make his peace with God. The Norse kingdoms survived until the invasion of the Franks, the rank and file of whom were Welsh and Flemish, in a piratical adventure known to history as the Anglo-Norman conquest.

§ 2

These wars with their inevitable political upheavals wrought the greatest injury to the Church in Ireland. Learning decayed for lack of books and teachers, and we are told[6] that when Brian, after freeing his people from the domination of the Danes of Limerick and establishing himself as King of Munster, sought to restore civilized life in the country, "he sent for professors and masters to teach wisdom and knowledge: and to buy books beyond the seas and the great ocean; because their writings and their books in every church and in every sanctuary where they were, were burned and thrown into water by the plunderers from the beginning to the end; and Brian himself gave the price of learning and the price of books to everyone separately who went on this service." The fact remains that the fugitive monks carried their precious manuscripts off with them to the Continent, and that while well over fifty specimens, complete or fragmentary, are extant, only about ten of later date than the year 1000 are estimated to have survived on Irish soil.[7] It would be a mistake, however, to conclude that the fire of intellectual life was burnt out in the tenth and eleventh centuries, for the national reaction showed itself in the devotion of the clergy to the literature and history of their country, but in Irish at the expense of Latin (it was about this time that the term *fer léiginn*, 'man of

[6] 'Cogadh Gaedhel re Gallaibh,' *The War of the Gael with the Foreigner*, ed. and trs. J. H. Todd, London, Rolls Series, 1867, pp. 138-9.

[7] The *St. Gall Priscian*, which, it has been inferred by L. Traube, *O Roma nobilis* (Munich, 1891), 50 (346) et seq., was in the hands of the Circle of Sedulius, at Liège (*c.* 860), and had been transcribed in Irish minuscule in Ireland about the middle of the ninth century, contains among its *marginalia* written in a different hand a significant little poem in Irish:

> "Bitter is the wind to-night: it tosses the ocean's white hair;
> I fear not the coursing of the clear sea by the fierce heroes from
> Lochlann." *Thes. palaeohib.*

reading,' displaced *scriba* as the appellation of the head of
the intellectual activities of the monastery), and the plastic
arts still continued to be cultivated.

Monasticism, however, had fallen from its high estate. It
had suffered the common fate of that institution in feudal
Europe and become laicized. St. Bernard doubtless exaggerated when he wrote that, prior to the reforms of Mael-
Máedóc Ua Morgair and the introduction of the Cistercians
into Ireland, monks were known there (whatever 'there' may
mean) only as a memory from the past; but that there was
laxity in Ireland, although probably to a less extent than in
England and Europe at large, in that ebb of faith in the
tenth century, before the tide was turned by the reformers
of Cluny, can hardly be denied.

The Anglo-Saxon Church "presented a very melancholy
spectacle to the friends of religion. (i) The laity had resumed
the ferocious manners of their pagan forefathers; (ii) the
clergy had grown indolent, dissolute and illiterate; (iii) the
monastic order had been apparently annihilated."[8]   Bad
as it may have been in England, religion was in a still worse
plight on the Continent.

In Ireland the capture of Armagh by Thorgest had preluded the establishment of a regular Viking state and been
followed by the installation of the worship of Thor in the
holy city. The country, his informants told St. Bernard,
had relapsed into a barbarism hardly less degraded than
that which had predominated before the coming of St.
Patrick, and the word 'barbarous'[9] keeps recurring to the
pen of this last of the Fathers as an epithet appropriate to a
people whose institutions he did not understand, but whose
morals it had been his friend Mael-Máedóc's task to reform.
The letters written by the two archbishops of Canterbury,

    [8] Lingard, op. cit., II, p. 217.
    [9] Alcuin also writing (*c.* 800) a friendly letter "ad patres Mugensis ecclesiae,"
the English monks who had accompanied Colmán of Lindisfarne to Ireland
and established themselves in Mag-nEo na Sachsan, 'Mayo of the Saxons'
(cf. Bede, *H.E.*, IV, 4), urges them to devote themselves to their studies and
"to let their light shine forth in the midst of a most barbarous people." (Dümmler, *M.G.H.*, *Epistolarum*, IV, CCLXXXVII, 445-6.) 'Barbarous' thus early seems to
have become as much a conventional epithet as 'savage' with its variant 'wild'
in the sixteenth century. Cf. Mrs. Green, *The Making of Ireland and Its
Undoing*, Appendix, p. 556.

Lanfranc (1070-93) and St. Anselm (1093-1109), read with care and due attention to the motives inspiring them, throw some light upon the chief evils of the time, laxity in marriage relations which seems to have meant in practice marriage within certain degrees not then prohibited in the country, and the too numerous consecration of bishops.[10]

The ecclesiastical hierarchy, which had been so laboriously erected in the West, had always been a precariously frail structure in Ireland. Bishops, consecrated only by one bishop, continued to grow in number without cause and without sees to fill. The abbot in most churches had become a lay lord, *airchinnech* (*anglice*, erenach), whose family held the office and the property from generation to generation; no parochial organization existed, and there was a dearth of priests. "The lack of diocesan and metropolitan organization, which in earlier times had not entailed any very deplorable consequences owing to the zeal and faith which animated the clergy," Dom Gougaud observes, "had now in the midst of general disorder and demoralization resulted in complete anarchy. Even when the liturgy was not once and for all given up, a spirit of independence and arbitrary caprice laid down the law."[11]

The Annals of Ireland naturally give but scanty information with regard to the religious history of the Scandinavians. The conversion of several of their kings to Christianity, notably that of Olaf Cuaran, King of Dublin and Northumbria (934-81), who laid down his kingship in 943 and retired to lead a life of religious seclusion in Iona, set an example which doubtless led many of their subjects to embrace the Faith, while intermarriage with the Irish, which appears to have been common in Ireland—as witness the

[10] This seems to have particularly scandalized St. Bernard: "Nam quod inauditum est ab ipso Christianitatis initio sine ordine, sine ratione, mutabantur et multiplicabantur episcopi . . . ita ut . . . singulae paene ecclesiae singulos habeant episcopos." 'Vita S. Malachiae,' in Migne, *P.L.*, CLXXXII; X, col. 1086. It was not, however, such an unheard of thing as St. Bernard, whose knowledge of history did not excel that of his contemporaries, would have his reader believe. In the early centuries of the Church it was literally true that every church had its own bishop ('nulla ecclesia sine episcopo'). The practice of fixing bishops in small towns was first forbidden, it is believed, by the Council of Sardica, A.D. 343-344. Cf. Hefele, *Conciliengeschichte*, I, pp. 503-16.

[11] Gougaud, *Christianity in Celtic Lands*, p. 396.

still surviving Norse names—undoubtedly hastened the diffusion of the Christian religion among the worshippers of Thor, when such unions were not, as is frequently the case, followed by disastrous consequences to the beliefs of the Christian spouses. Out of the intercourse between the two peoples an Irish Nordic culture was born which exercised a strong influence upon the art and literature of Scandinavia.[12]

§ 3

About 1040 the Danish colony in Ath-Cliath felt itself sufficiently strong in the Faith to have a bishop of its own, and one Dunan was chosen to be the first occupant of the see. He founded the cathedral of the Holy Trinity, now Christ Church, and died *c.* 1074. The clergy and people then elected as his successor one Patrick, who was sent to Lanfranc for consecration, bearing a letter[13] in which Dublin was described as "the metropolis of the island of Ireland." Patrick was duly consecrated in St. Paul's in London, and took an oath to obey Lanfranc, 'primate of the Britains,' and his successors 'in all things appertaining to the Christian religion.' The people of Port Lairge (Waterford) in 1096 thought they might have a bishop too and selected Máel Isu Ua hAinmire, otherwise known as Malchus, an Irishman by birth, but by breeding a monk of Winchester, and he also was consecrated at Canterbury by Anselm with the assistance of Ralph, Bishop of Chichester, and Gundulph, Bishop of Rochester. On his return to Waterford Malchus built a cathedral and consecrated it to the Holy Trinity. It was to Canterbury and not to Armagh that these Danish Christian communities of the towns turned for their bishops, and although Keating maintains that "it was through a feeling

[12] Cf. MacNeill, *Phases*, pp. 212 and 249-73, and for the Irish influence on Icelandic culture, Vigfusson and York Powell's *Origines Islandicae*, two vols., Oxford, 1905. Professor Olrik's *Viking Civilization*, ed. H. Ellekilde, English trs., London, 1930, pp. 107-20, considers that the Irish Christian influence which made that culture, a phenomenon in itself, "an enrichment and expansion of the native north European stage of civilization," rather impeded the absorption of the north into Christian Europe. The development of the saga he attributes specifically to Irish poets.

[13] Ussher, *Sylloge*, no. xxv; *Whole Works*, IV., 488-9.

of friendship for the people of Normandy who sprang from their own race that the prelates of these places gave jurisdiction and authority to the Archbishop of Canterbury over them," and a fear "that their side would not have an equal chance, as in the election the Gael would have a larger popular vote than any of them,"[14] it may more probably be conjectured that they simply wished to regularize their position in the eyes of the universal Church and to be independent of the neighbouring Irish *comarbai*, the lay heirs of the saintly founders of monasteries, in a country which still lacked a proper (i.e. Western) diocesan organization. An 'imperialist' prelate such as Lanfranc, an Italian by birth, but a Norman by breeding, 'vir divinae simul et humanae legis peritissimus,' was not slow to seize for his own advantage the opportunity thus presented to him of extending his jurisdiction, and the first five bishops of Dublin, Malchus of Waterford, and Patrick of Limerick, were all consecrated by, and made their professions of canonical obedience to, the Primate of England. Through these Danish Christian communities the Roman influence gradually penetrated into Ireland, and it was a bishop of the Danish settlement in Luimneach, Gilla-easpuic or Gillebert, a former Abbot of Bend-chor and the firm friend and humble admirer of St. Anselm, whose acquaintance he had made in Rouen in 1087, who became the first Legate of the Holy See in the island.

Rome had never ceased to be considered as the Mother Church, the capital of the Christian world, and the Pope, however mysteriously distant and remote, as the supreme head of the ecclesiastical hierarchy. But Rome rarely made its influence felt and local hierarchies remained vague and ill-defined, and ineffective in the superior degrees. They rarely received unsolicited any opinion or explicit direction from the Holy See. The Church in Ireland, therefore, in comparison with the Anglo-Saxon Church, which was bound to the Holy See by ties so close and filial, and had been so thoroughly shaped and moulded by Rome, might well have struck an unintelligent observer, more particularly one

[14] Cf. Keating, *Foras Feasa*, III, 301.

brought up on the ideals of Cluny, as almost independent and autonomous. Reform brooked no delay, if doubtful practices, inconsistent with forms prevalent elsewhere in the Christian world, were to be abolished, abuses to be checked, and innumerable omissions to be rectified in religious discipline, liturgy, and custom.

The impulse came from Canterbury. Considering on the one hand, most improperly, that Gregory the Great, in giving St. Augustine primatial authority as legate over "all the bishops of Britain,"[15] had included the Bishops of Ireland also in such a designation, and having regard, on the other, to the ill-defined and therefore insecure nature of the supremacy of Armagh, the Archbishops of Canterbury, inspired by the astute and unscrupulous Lanfranc, ambitious also to serve his royal master, proceeded to assert their supremacy in things spiritual, not only over Ireland, but also over the rival English see of York, the whole of Scotland, and the adjacent isles. Lanfranc who, in 1070, had succeeded a deposed Englishman on the throne of Canterbury, acting like the good judge, succeeded in bringing the newly formed Scandinavian dioceses in Ireland within his jurisdiction, and Eadmer, a monk of Christ Church, Canterbury, and the friend and confidant of St. Anselm, explicitly attaches the diocese of Waterford to the province of Canterbury,[16] and informs us also that in 1115 Gillebert, the Bishop of Limerick, assisted the Archbishop of Canterbury and other English prelates, as a suffragan, at the consecration in the Church of the Blessed Peter at Westminster on 19th September 1115, of Bernard, one of the queen's chaplains, to the

[15] Bede, *HE.*, I, xxvii. Augustine had asked: "How are we to deal with the bishops of France and Britain?" And the Pope replied: "We give you no authority over the bishops of France, because the Bishop of Arles received the pall in ancient times from my predecessor, and we are not to deprive him of the authority he has received. . . . 'Britanniarum vero omnes episcopos tuae fraternitati committimus,' that the unlearned may be taught, the weak strengthened by persuasion, and the perverse corrected by authority." 'Everyman' trs. By no stretch of imagination could Ireland be reckoned among the 'Britanniae.'

[16] "Rex Hiberniae Murchertachus nomine [i.e. Murierdach or Morlough, the son of Tourlough] et Dofnaldus episcopus cum ceteris episcopis . . . ipsius insulae miserunt nuntios ac literas ad Anselmum innotescentes ei civitatem quamdan Waterfordian nomine in una suarum provinciarum esse." Eadmer, *Historia novorum in Anglia*, Migne, *P.L.*, CLIX, 395-6.

bishopric of St. David's.[17] Anselm's own letters[18] to the bishops of Ireland are the letters of a metropolitan to his suffragans. He invites their prayers, urges them to consult him in their difficulties, exhorts them to extirpate evils, specifying the consecration of bishops but making no complaint with regard to any other Irish practice, and vigorously to discharge the duties of their office. He rebukes Samuel Ua h Anglé (O'Hanley), Bishop of Dublin, the nephew of that Donough who had died of the plague in 1095, and himself a former Benedictine monk of St. Albans, for giving to strangers the books, vestments, and furniture which Lanfranc had presented for the use of the church, for dispersing and expelling the monks, when it was his duty rather to assemble the scattered than to scatter the assembled, and for his presumption in having a cross borne in front of him on his walks abroad, a privilege reserved to archbishops who had received the *pallium* from Rome. He thanks his friend Gillebert for his congratulations on the successful issue of the investiture struggle with William Rufus and a gift of pearls.[19]

It was Gillebert, not unnaturally, who took the initiative in the reform movement in Ireland. In 1109 he addressed a letter, *De usu ecclesiastico*, to the bishops and priests of the country, stating that not so much at the request, as by the positive injunction, of many among them, "vestrae cupiens parere piissimae jussioni," he had attempted to write down the canonical customs in the observation of the hours and the performance of the offices of the whole ecclesiastical order. The letter, which would seem to have been simply a copy of the Roman Use, covered a treatise of his com-

[17] Eadmer describes Bernard as "vir probus et multorum judicio sacerdotio dignus" (ibid., col. 495). Giraldus Cambrensis, however, to whom Roger Bacon's bitter comment on Vincent of Beauvais "numquam fuit dignus auctoritate" may in many cases be applied, objected to Bernard as "the first French Bishop of Menevia," and, strange to relate, found fault with his "pompositas et ambitio." Cf. *I.K.* (Opp. Rolls series, VI), pp. 105-6.

[18] They are most conveniently collected in Ussher's *Sylloge* (XXXI-XXXIX) *Whole Works*, IV, pp. 515-27.

[19] A charming little letter accompanied the pearls: "Munusculum paupertatis meae et devotionis transmitto viginti quinque margaretulas inter optimas et viliores et rogo ne sitis immemor mei in orationibus vestris in quibus post divinam largitatem confido." Ussher, *Sylloge*, no. XXI, *Whole Works*, IV, pp. 511-2.

position, *De statu Ecclesiae*, explaining an accompanying graphic representation of the Church and all its officials, doorkeepers, exorcists, sub-deacons, deacons, priests, bishops, archbishops, primates, patriarchs and Pope, with appropriate observations on their inter-relations. Obviously based on ideal European conditions, this curious missive must have presented an oddly incongruous appearance in the Irish climate.[20]

This untoward zeal attracted the attention of Rome, and Gillebert was presently appointed Legate of the Holy See in Ireland, the first to hold that office. As such he was invited to preside at the synod of Rath-Breasail, held in 1110 or 1111, at which it was decided that Ireland should be divided on the model of England into twenty-four dioceses, exclusive of Dublin, which was left subject to Canterbury, twelve, including Cashel, for the southern province (Leath Mogha), and twelve, including Armagh, for the northern (Leath Cuinn), Armagh retaining its supremacy "over the bishops of all Ireland." "The reason why Ath-Cliath is not counted here," says Keating,[21] who gives the list, "is that it was not customary with its bishop to receive consecration except from the Archbishop of Canterbury in England."

§ 4

Gillebert had referred to the *pallium* in his *De statu Ecclesiae*, although that sacred emblem, which St. Augustine had received from Pope Gregory the Great and Egbert, Bishop of York, from Pope Gregory III in 735, was unknown in his day and for some time afterwards in Ireland.[22] It was Máel Máedóc Ua Morgair or Malachy who, in 1139,

[20] The little treatise is well summarized by Dom Gougaud. Cf. also Ussher's *Sylloge*, XXX, *Whole Works*, IV, 500-10. Ussher's printers were unable apparently to reproduce these attractive charts. A reference to Purgatory, interesting for the time, should be noted: "Purgatorius videlicet ignis qui corpore statim egressos et minus per lamenta poenitentiae purgatos ad plenitudinem recipit purgandos."

[21] *Foras Feasa*, III, p. 299.

[22] Jocelyn of Furnes, writing *c.* 1180, among other fables, pretends that St. Patrick had received the *pallium* from Rome and is followed in this particular by Colgan, *Tria. Thaum.*, pp. 306 et seq.

according to St. Bernard, took the first step to have the pall, *quod est plentitudo honoris*, granted to the metropolitans of his country. Thanks to the friend who wrote his life, no other Irish personality of the time is so well known to us as Máel Máedóc.

He was born, we are told, among a 'barbarous' people but of gentle parents—they were "genere et potentia magni juxta nomen magnorum qui sunt in terra"—at Armagh in 1095, his father, Mugrom Ua Morgair, having been probably *árd fer légind*, chief professor in the school there. He placed himself at an early age under the spiritual direction of, and was trained in piety by, Imar Ua hAedhagáin, a recluse and promoter of reform, who turned his thoughts to an ecclesiastical career. Before the age of twenty-five he was ordained priest by Cellach, Archbishop of Armagh and grandson of Móel Isu, the brother and immediate predecessor of Domnall, *comarba* of St. Patrick, who, under the influence of the reform movement, had had himself ordained. In 1123 Máel Máedóc was consecrated to the see of Coindire (Connor) and became abbot also of Bend-chor, which had been abandoned as a result of the Viking wars. Driven out in 1127 by a political disturbance, he retreated to Munster and there founded the monastery of Iveragh in what is now Kerry. On Cellach's death in 1129 he found himself nominated to the primatial see, although the old succession of *comarbai* still continued, and was forced in spite of his reluctance, for he longed all his life for the quiet of the cloister, to accept the charge imposed upon him. The struggle continued for five years and ended with the triumph of Máel Máedóc. St. Bernard gives a vivid description of the moral degradation of his flock. "When the man of God began to perform the duties of his office, he discovered that he had been appointed not to men but to wild beasts. He had never experienced any such in any state of barbarity howsoever depraved. He had never found any so wanton in morals, so uncouth in their religious observances, so godless in belief, so barbarously disposed towards law and order, so stubbornly opposed to discipline, so filthy in their lives, nominal Christians but in reality pagans. They would not pay tithes or offer first-fruits; they would not contract marriage in due form of law;[23] they would not go to confession. There was nobody to be found seeking to do penance nor anybody to impose it. There were very few priests at the altar, and no voice was to be heard in church either preaching or singing."

Máel Máedóc set himself immediately to reform the morals of his flock, to revive the liturgy, to re-introduce psalmody into churches where it had been discontinued, and to restore ecclesiastical discipline. He ruled his see for three years, restored liberty to the Church, and then resigning his primacy in favour of Gilla-meic-Liag, otherwise known as Gelasius, the *comarbadi* of Colum-cille at Derry, returned to the peace of his beloved Bend-chor. He divided his diocese into two provinces, Down and Connor, reserving Down, the less important one, for himself, and from his retreat took in hand more resolutely than ever the reformation of the Church in Ireland. Two points claimed his particular attention: to have the elevation of Cashel to the status of a metropolitan see confirmed by the Pope, in Rome, and to obtain the *pallium* both for his successor, the Archbishop of Armagh, and the new archbishop of the south, should the Holy See consent to recognize the latter. In 1140 Máel Máedóc set out for Rome to make his two requests in person

[23] As Giraldus Cambrensis (*Top. Hib.*, III, *c.* 19) also remarked that the Irish did not contract matrimony, it should be explained that the Irish form of marriage, until after the Council of Trent, was not "sponsalia de praesenti in facie ecclesiae," which *ipso facto* made the marriage valid and indissoluble, but "sponsalia de futuro" (sc. formal betrothal), which was dissoluble if not followed by consummation within a reasonable time (normally two years), and this ceremony, however much St. Bernard may have disapproved of it, duly consummated, made a marriage as valid in Ireland as anywhere else in Europe, where it had not been prohibited by canon law. One J. Good, an English schoolmaster in Limerick, *c.* 1566, from whom William Camden derived much of his information concerning the Irish and who *more suorum* also traduced his hosts, noted that in his time the practice as to the form of marriage in Ireland was "sponsalia de futuro." As to St. Bernard's other charges, it may be sufficient to observe that tithes were not imposed until the Council of Cennanas prescribed them in 1152, and little, if at all, exacted until after the triumph of the English power; that the Irish clergy seem not to have extended the impediments of consanguinity or affinity beyond those mentioned in Leviticus, and that the precept prescribing the use of confession at certain times was not enjoined until the Lateran Council in 1215. The religious condition of Ireland at the time would be seen in better perspective if considered with that of Scandinavia, which Adrian IV did so much to reform.

to the Pope. Travelling by way of Scotland, he went to York, where there came to greet him an Augustinian monk of Kirkham, whom St. Bernard describes as 'Wallenus nomine,' not knowing that he was Waldeve, the step-son of King David, destined later to become Abbot of Melrose. Distressed at the sight of the archbishop's sorry retinue— five priests, a few clerks and servants, twelve, perhaps, in all *secundum morem*, with only three horses among them— Waldeve generously offered Máel Máedóc his own poor nag,"saying he was vexed that it should be such a screw, *runcinus dure portans*." Máel Máedóc gratefully accepted the brute and kept it for nine years. It throve under his care and presently became *pretiosissimus palfreus*, a miraculous transformation according to St. Bernard. On his way south Máel Máedóc made another halt at Clairvaux (*Clara Vallis*) in the Aube, and there his lively faith, unaffected goodness, absolute disinterestedness and exquisite simplicity completely won the heart of his host, who, moved by the memory when he later came to write the story of Máel Máedóc's life, set his recollection down with feeling: "I too had the privilege of seeing the man in this life and I was refreshed by the sight of him and by the words that he spoke, and I delighted in him as in everything delightful. And I too, sinner though I am, found favour in his eyes at the same time and thereafter until his death. . . . Our brethren, also, were greatly edified by his presence and his discourse; he accepted the place and us along with it, and taking us to his heart of hearts, he bade us farewell and went his way."[24]

Máel Máedóc was received with particular benevolence by Pope Innocent II, and besought the Pontiff with tears in his eyes to be allowed to spend the rest of his days at Clairvaux. The Pope refused his consent, and, during the month that they spent in Rome visiting the holy places and seeing the sights, plied his Irish visitors with questions about the state of the Church in the distant country from which they had come. Confirmation of the new metropolitan status of Cashel was readily granted, and Máel Máedóc,

[24] Ibid., cap. XXXVII, col. 1094.

emboldened, broached the question of the two palls. The Pope was not hasty. "The granting of palls is a matter which involves some circumspection," said the supreme Pontiff. "Summon your bishops and priests and the notables of your country to a general council, and if, with the common consent and by the express desire of all, you solicit the palls *per honestas personas*, they shall be granted you." Then, taking the mitre off his own head, he placed it on that of his visitor, and, giving him the stole and maniple which he wore himself when celebrating, he embraced him and bade him good-bye.[25] So Máel Máedóc returned, but not before the Pope, having learned that Gillebert was now old and infirm and unable to carry out his duties, had conferred upon him, as a manifest token of his good will, the legateship of Ireland.

He returned as he had come and on his way north was entertained by King David in his castle at Carlisle. He cured the king's son of a malady, and, while waiting at Port Yarrock in Wigtownshire for a boat to take him across to Bend-chor, built himself a little oratory constructed of twigs woven into a hedge, surrounded it with a wall, and blessed the enclosed space for a cemetery. It became a shrine of great resort, and miracles were said to have taken place there after his death.

For some unknown reason seven years elapsed before the Council required by the Pope could be summoned. It was held at last at Inis-Pátraic (off Skerries on the eastern coast) in 1148, and decided that the Legate should return to Rome and remind the new Pope Eugenius III of the promise made by Innocent II.

Máel Máedóc undertook the long journey again, hoping to meet the Pope in France. He sailed to Scotland and was warmly welcomed by King David at Carlisle, paid a visit to the canons at Gisbourne Priory in Cleveland, and, denied passage by King Stephen, who, having some dispute with the Pope, would not allow any bishop to cross the Channel, took sail from some port in Yorkshire. He went no further on this occasion than Clairvaux. Arriving there

[25] Cf. Ibid., cap. XXXVII, col. 1095.

on 13th or 14th October to spend a few days only with the
community he loved so well, on the 18th he fell sick. He
knew that his end was near. "I have greatly desired," he
said, "to eat this pasch among you, and, thanks to the
supreme Goodness, I have not been deprived of my desire,"
and on All Souls' Day, 2nd November 1148, "at the place
of his election and at the time he had foretold, Malachy,
bishop and legate of the holy and apostolic see," died in the
arms of St. Bernard, in the fifty-fourth year of his age.

§ 5

A friend of monks and himself a former abbot, the Irish
prelate had been so impressed by the life of the Cistercians
and the sanctity of St. Bernard, that, on his return from his
first visit to Rome, he had left four of his following at Clairvaux for the purpose of learning its rules and regulations
and qualifying in due course to introduce them into Ireland,
and they, "having been tried and found worthy, were made
monks." When he returned to Ireland he dispatched more
novices to be trained in the Cistercian discipline, and in
1142 St. Bernard was able to send back a first contingent
with some of his own *ad numerum abbatiae*. Not all the French-
men persevered—to St. Bernard's displeasure—but one
Robert did, and became the architect of the first Cistercian
house in Ireland, Mellifont, 'Honey Fountain,' about five
miles from Drogheda. It conceived, in St. Bernard's words,
and brought forth five daughters: Bealach *alias* Baltinglass
(*De valle Salutis*), built by Diarmiad Mac Murchadha in the
diocese of Leighlin (1151), Bective (*De Beatitudine*), built
by the descendants of Máel-Sechlainn in the diocese of Meath
(1151), Boyle (*De Buellio*) in the diocese of Elphin, Nenay
(*De Magio*) in the diocese of Limerick, Newry (*Viride Lignum*,
at Ibar-cind-trachta, 'the yew tree at the head of the strand')
in the diocese of Dromore (1156-60), on land granted by,
and under the protection of, Muirchertach Ua Lochlainn
King of Ireland. The *Vita S. Malachiae* was written at the
request of Congan, Abbot of the Cistercian (?) house of Inis-

lounaght on the Suir, which appears to have been in existence before 1148.

Until the arrival of the Cistercians, the Irish monks had in all probability adhered to the practice of their own native rule. The Rule of St. Benedict was certainly known in Ireland through literature in the seventh and eighth centuries, but no surviving document attests its observance in any Irish monastery before the arrival of the Cistercians.

It may be taken for granted that, immediately after the death of his friend Máel Máedóc, St. Bernard would see that the wishes of the Church in Ireland were conveyed to Pope Eugenius III in Rome, and the more expeditiously, as that Pope was an old pupil of his. At all events Cardinal John Paparo was commissioned as Legate *a latere* to bring the palls to Ireland. He reached England in 1150 but, denied a passport by King Stephen unless he would take an oath to do nothing prejudicial to the interests of the kingdom of England in Ireland, declined and returned to Rome. Setting out once more, he made this time for Scotland, was honourably received by King David about Michaelmas 1151, and thence crossed over to Ireland.

In 1152 "a famous council was held at Cenanans [Kells] in the season of spring about the time of 'Laetare Jerusalem' Sunday, in which Lord John, Cardinal Priest of St. Lawrence in Damascus, presiding over twenty-two bishops and five bishops-elect and over many abbots and priors, on behalf of the holy apostles Peter and Paul and of the Apostolic Lord Eugenius, entirely rooted out and condemned simony and usury, and commanded by apostolic authority the payment of tithes. He gave four *pallia* to the four archbishops of Ireland, to wit, to those of Dublin, Cashel, Tuaim and Ard Macha. Moreover, he appointed the Archbishop of Ard Macha as primate over the other bishops, as was meet. And this Cardinal John, immediately after the council was over, took his departure, and on the ninth of the calends of April [24th March] set sail." [26]

It still remained to improve certain points of discipline, of liturgical observance, and the administration of the sacra-

[26] Cf. Keating, *Foras Feasa*, III, pp. 315-7.

ments, in conformity with the practice of the Western Church and the expressed wishes of Lanfranc and St. Anselm, and these and kindred matters were settled at another synod convened for the purpose at Cashel in 1172 at the instance of Henry II, and under the presidency of Giolla Criost O'Conaire, Bishop of Liss-mor and Papal Legate at the time. The decrees of this synod were confirmed by Henry, represented thereat by a number of English ecclesiastics, and the reformation of the Church in Ireland in essentials was there completed.

§ 6

Shortly after the Council of Cenannas, from which the Church in Ireland emerged reinvigorated and refreshed, there took place the most important political event in the history of the island, the consequences of which have endured to this day, its conquest by the Anglo-Normans (1169-71) under Henry II Plantagenet (1154-89) whereby the destinies of England and Ireland were linked together for the next eight centuries.

It had been only natural for the Church in Ireland, undergoing reformation according to the ideals of Clairvaux, to turn to Rome for counsel and direction, and thus, however unconsciously, to thwart the imperialist pretensions of Canterbury; but Norman aggression was not to be so lightly held in check. The secular power intervened to support ecclesiastical pretensions, and solemn application was made to the Pope, the supreme arbiter at the time of Christian morals, for permission to conquer Ireland and restore religion and morality. An odd circumstance favoured the ambitions of the imperialists.

The reigning Pope was a certain Nicholas, a poor Englishman who, born perhaps at Abbots Langley in Hertfordshire, to one Robert, a humble clerical official, later a monk at St. Albans, had been rejected when he too sought admission to that house. Crossing over to the Continent, and describing himself *a Brakespeare*, a hamlet in the parish of St. Michael's, Hertfordshire, this Nicholas wandered from school to school. After sheltering for a time in Paris and listening to the lectures of one Marianus, an Irishman who later became a monk at Ratisbon, and whom he did not forget, Nicholas took to the road again and wandered on until he came at last to the abbey of St. Rufus, then near Avignon, where he was received as a lay brother and remained until his industry earned him election as abbot. The rigour of his rule provoked the idle canons to revolt, and Nicholas repaired to Rome to plead his cause in person. His wisdom and modesty there attracted the attention of Pope Eugenius III, who, on the occasion of a second appeal, bade the fractious canons elect an abbot of their own "with whom they might have peace, for the Englishman would be a burden to them no longer," retained Nicholas in his own service and appointed him Cardinal Bishop of Albano (1146). As *legatus a latere* he travelled through the Scandinavian kingdoms, winning golden opinions by the tact and celerity with which he laboured to establish a proper hierarchical organization and to introduce much needed reforms, and on his return to Rome loaded with gifts and with such a reputation as never foreigner had earned before, Nicholas was elected Pope, after the death of Eugenius' successor Anastasius IV, and assumed the title of Adrian IV. Rome accepted what St. Albans had rejected, and the Englishman's compatriots were overjoyed. He had risen *de pulvere ad sedem Petri*, from a humble village in Hertfordshire to the City of the Seven Hills. [27]

In the year 1155 he issued to his friend Henry a privilege, *Laudabiliter satis et fructuosae*, in which, after reciting the pious and praiseworthy desire of his magnificence to propagate the glorious Name throughout the world, and to lay up for himself the reward of eternal felicity in Heaven, he gave

[27] Unhappy Adrian! He would never have left his native England, he told John of Salisbury (*Polycraticus*, VIII, 23, ed. C. C. J. Webb, Oxford, 1909) or quitted the cloister of the blessed Rufus, had he known what was in store for him. He had found such misery in the chair of Peter that all former bitterness seemed pleasant in comparison. The chair of Peter was so thorny and girt about with so many pricks as to wear out the strongest shoulders. It was only because they burned like fire that the crown and tiara (*phrygium*) were worth having, but God had always hammered him on an anvil, and he dared not struggle against the divine ordinance.

his kind and grateful assent to the king's petition: "ut pro dilatandis ecclesiae terminis, pro vitiorum restringendo decursu, pro corrigendis moribus et virtutibus inserendis, pro Christianae religionis augmento" he might be allowed to invade "insulam illam," and there prosecute "quae ad honorem Dei et salutem illius terrae spectaverint. . . ." He was further exhorted to "gentem illam bonis moribus informare," and so to conduct himself, "ut decoretur ibi ecclesia, plantetur et crescat fidei Christianae religio. . . ." This concession was confirmed by a second privilege granted by Pope Alexander III (1159-81), who, following, as he said, in the footsteps of the venerable Adrian, ratified and confirmed "concessionem eiusdem super Hibernici regni dominio vobis [*sc.* to Henry] indulto . . . quatenus eliminatis terrae illius spurcitiis, barbara natio quae Christiana censetur nomine, vestra diligentia morum induat venustatem et redacta in formam . . . gens ea per vos Christianae professionis nomen cum effectu de cetero consequatur."

Floods of ink have been spilt in discussing the authenticity of these famous documents. Irish ecclesiastics (e.g. Cardinal Moran[28] and Mgr. Hagan[29]) have argued rather *a priori* that the very content of them is sufficient to impugn their genuineness, and the latter especially contends that a country which throughout the early Middle Ages had produced such a galaxy of saints and scholars from St. Columban to John the Scot could not have been the subject of slanders at once so gross and so gratuitous, and that it is inconceivable that a mission of religious propaganda could ever have been entrusted to the murderers of St. Thomas Becket. Dom Gougaud, on the other hand, considers that the arguments put forward by those who uphold the authenticity of the bull *Laudabiliter* are the stronger. "Although the Bull is not drawn up in strict conformity with the rules followed at the time by the Papal Chancery, it can neverless be proved that in substance it is in accord with other contemporary and uncontested witnesses."[30] The popular

---

[28] *Irish Ecclesiastical Record*, 1872.

[29] *Insula Sanctorum*, pp. 11 et seq.

[30] Cf. *Christianity in Celtic Lands*, p. 408.

text-books by R. Dunlop,[31] and M. Hayden and G. A. Moonan,[32] also admit the greater cogency of the arguments in favour of authenticity.[33]

The fact, however, remains that an abominable campaign of defamation was launched against Ireland and a sustained effort made to obliterate every trace of her glorious past as effectively as though it had never been, and that the promoters of this undertaking were Englishmen who, in spite of an initial period of opposition to the Normans, had doggedly maintained their position and gradually conconquered their conquerors. The Anglo-Saxons had obliterated nearly every trace of the Roman civilization in England, and their language triumphed with their arms, yielding but reluctantly to the more profound Latin influences. The imprint of its double origin is on the English speech to this day.

The latent hostility of the Anglo-Saxons towards the *Scotti*, to whom they were yet so heavily indebted, was no new thing, and the state of the case is well expressed by Dom Gougaud: "Thus, even after they had finally yielded the field in the domain of discipline, Scots and Britons found themselves invested, down to the ninth century and even later, with a vague suspicion, if not of actual heresy, at any rate of being rash and too free and easy in their opinions and

[31] Cf. *Ireland from the Earliest Times to the Present Day*, Oxford University Press, 1922, pp. 27 and 32.

[32] Cf. *A Short History of the Irish People*, Longmans, Green & Co., 1927, p. 116.

[33] Dom Gougaud's note refers *inter alia* to Miss Kate Norgate's article, 'The Bull *Laudabiliter*,' in the *English Historical Review*, VIII, 1893, pp. 18-52, in which the question is threshed out, and to Fr. Herbert Thurston's articles, 'The English Pope and His Irish Bull,' in *The Month*, April and May, 1906. The authenticity of the Bull was first impugned apparently, after the lapse of three hundred years, by Stephen White (1574-1646) in his *Apologia pro Hibernia adversus Cambri calumnias*, ed. Kelly, Dublin, 1849, pp. 184-206, and John Lynch (*Gratianus Lucius*) (1599-1673) in his *Cambrensis Eversus* (Celtic Society: Dublin, 1848-52), ii, pp. 184-206. The matter has only an academic interest, but nothing, it is suggested, can explain away the formal testimony of John of Salisbury, to make no mention of any other arguments. The fable that the Pope had jurisdiction over islands in virtue of the Donation of Constantine, which, first forged by Anastasius, the papal librarian, to serve his own sinister ends, lay dormant until about the middle of the eleventh century, does not seem to have been thought of until some time after the Normans had settled in Ireland, and the Irish may have come to believe it in the fond hope that if the Pope had any such jurisdiction, he had powers also to turn their oppressors out. Cf. the Abbé MacGeoghegan's *Histoire d'Irlande*, II, p. 106.

methods, a suspicion which the freedom of their manners and their frankness of speech appear to have helped to establish. Their neighbours, the Anglo-Saxons, were the chief to cast discredit on them, instigated by principle, by differences of temperament, and very likely also by jealousy. . . . Their impulsive nature and proneness to extremes were an offence to the sober Anglo-Saxons, imbued with the Roman spirit and ever on the look-out for the minutest direction emanating from the Roman Curia. If (as there is room for believing) the Holy See laid in its stock of information concerning the life of the Celtic Churches from that furnished by the English churchmen who were incessantly plying to and fro between their country and the Eternal City, it is easy to account for the prejudices to which more than one Roman document testifies."[34]

When the Anglo-Normans, after their conquest of Ireland, felt the necessity of justifying their aggression and accrediting in some way their malignant accusations against the Emerald Isle, they found an agent ready to hand in a certain Girald de Barri, commonly known by his Latin name of Giraldus Cambrensis (1147-1223). This light-hearted, pert-witted, most entertaining raconteur was the fourth son of a Norman noble, William de Barri, and kin on the maternal side to Rhys ap Theodor, Prince of South Wales, and most of the powerful families in the principality. Educated in Paris, where he acquired some distinction in literature despite the importunity of his creditors, and ordained priest on his return home in 1172, Gerald received a commission from Richard, Archbishop of Canterbury in 1175, to raise the level of instruction and reform the morals of the Welsh clergy. He proceeded to discharge his task with a vigour and boldness which involved him in many disputes and made him not a few enemies, from whom he sought refuge in an appointment as chaplain to the king, Henry II, and as tutor to Prince John he accompanied that prince in 1185 on the filibustering expedition to Ireland, of which his uncle

[34] "Angli, qui maxime familiariores apostolicae sedis semper existunt" (*Gesta abbatum Fontanellensium*, ed. S. Loewenfeld (Hannoverae, 1886, p. 42).

and patron in chief, David Fitzgerald, Bishop of St. David's, was one of the most zealous promoters. Between 1185 and 1190, Gerald, who was almost as credulous as he was vain and pompous, composed and dedicated to his royal master a *Topographia Hibernica* in three parts or 'distinctions,' written in a nimble, lively style and full of the most malicious calumnies. Malignity, vanity and conceit made up for his deficiencies of knowledge. "He picked up every idle story that he met with among the foreign adventurers, basely distorted the nature and circumstances of customs innocent in themselves, and has related heaps of fables, many of which he was forced to acknowledge that he did not believe himself."[35] The book enjoyed an immense success and had a no less sinister repercussion upon the fair fame of the country its author so recklessly defamed. Commenting on the fact that the Faith had been planted in Ireland from the time of St. Patrick, he expressed his astonishment "quod gens haec in fidei rudimentis hactenus manserit tam inculta," but found the explanation in the savage life lived by the people: "Est autem gens haec gens silvestris, gens inhospita: gens ex bestiis solum et bestialiter vivens, gens a primo pastoralis vitae vivendi modo non recedens . . . agriculturae labores aspernens et civiles gazas parum affectans. . . . Gens igitur haec gens barbara et vere barbara . . . et omnes eorum mores barbarissimi sunt." The Irish were "gens spurcissima, gens vitiis involutissima, gens omnium gentium in fidei rudimentis incultissima." He had an equally ready explanation for the numbers of blind, halt, and maimed he professed to have seen in Ireland: "nec mirandum si de gente adultera, gente incesta, gente illegitime nata et copulata, gente exlege . . . tales interdum contra naturae legem natura producat." The 'natives' always had an axe ready to hand, and again he had an explanation: "Est etenim gens haec gens inconstans, gens varia; gens versipellis et versuta: gens sola instabilitate stabilis, sola infidelitate fidelis: est igitur longe fortius timenda eorum ars quam Mars: eorum pax quam fax, eorum mel quam fel, malitia quam militia, proditio quam expeditio, amicitia defucata quam inimicitia

[35] Lanigan, *An Ecclesiastical History of Ireland*, Dublin, 1822, IV., 279.

despicata. Hic enim horum sententia: dolus an virtus quis in hoste requirat [Virgil, *Aeneid*, II, 310]; hi mores Nec in bello fortes, nec in pace fideles."[36]

Gerald became, in Keating's phrase, "the bull of the herd for them for writing the false history of Ireland." He provided the pattern, set the tone, became the model for later English writers on that country such as Edmund Campion, the Jesuit martyr,[37] (1540-81), who wrote in 1571 'A Historie of Ireland' for Holinshed's *Chronicles* (London, 1577),[38] his friend Richard Stanyhurst (1547-1611), a Dublin man and the uncle of Archbishop Ussher, who contributed 'A Plain and Perfect Description of Ireland' to the same collection, and later published two romances, *De rebus in Hibernia gestis* (1584), a history of Ireland to the time of Henry II, and *De vita sancti Patricii* (1587). A third was a certain Fynes Morison who, visiting Ireland in the autumn of 1600, became secretary to Sir Charles Blount, Lord Mount-joy, and published his *Itinerary* in 1617;[39] and a fourth,

[36] Cf. also *Expugnatio Hibernica*, II, 39, and *Descriptio Kambriae*, II, 9 (Rolls Series).

[37] He was hanged, drawn and quartered at Tyburn on 1st December, 1581. His friend Stanyhurst, an Englishman born in Dublin, the first of that wretched class, was more (or less) fortunate. He escaped to the Continent and spent the last forty years of his life in exile. Both had become Catholics. Stanyhurst had three defects, according to Keating (Introduction, I, p. 43), for writing the history of Ireland: (1) youth, (2) blind ignorance, (3) ambition and "expectation of obtaining advantage from those by whom he was invited to write evil concerning Ireland." In this last particular he was disappointed.

[38] "The people are thus inclined: religious, frank, amorous, ireful, sufferable, of pains infinite, very glorious, many sorcerers, excellent horsemen, delighted with wars, great almsgivers, passing in hospitality. . . . Clear men they are of skin and hue, but of themselves careless and bestial. Their women are well-favoured, clear-coloured, fair-handed, big and large. . . . So light they are in believing whatsoever is with any countenance of gravity affirmed by their superiors, whom they esteem and honour, that a lewd prelate within these few years, needy of money, was able to persuade his parish that St.Patrick in striving with St. Peter to let an Irish gallowglass into Heaven, had his head broken with the keys, for whose release he obtained a collection. . . . They honour devout friars and pilgrims. . . . To rob and prey their enemies they deem it none offence . . ." and so forth (1633 ed., cc. V and VI.).

[39] "The wild, and as I may say, mere Irish, inhabiting many and large provinces, are barbarous and most filthy in their diet. . . . They devour great morsels of meat unsalted, and they eat commonly swine's flesh, seldom mutton. . . . They willingly eat the herb Shamrock, being of a sharp taste, which as they run and are chased to and fro, they snatch like beasts out of the ditches. . . I trust no man expects among these gallants any beds, much less feather beds and sheets . . . they make a fire in the midst of the room, and round about it they sleep upon the ground, without straw or other thing under them . . . and, their bodies being naked, they cover their heads," etc. (III, iii, 162-4).

among many lesser fry, the poet Edmund Spenser (1552-99), who offered a *View of the Present State of Ireland*, written in or before 1598, but not published until Ware took it in hand in 1633. They all drew lavishly upon their unsympathetic imagination to describe conditions as unfamiliar to their experience as they were repugnant to their prejudices, and, as 'superior persons' bred in a certainly alien but doubtfully superior culture, they made no effort to understand a civilization which, because they had wronged it, they despised. To salve their consciences, they exaggerated the defects and vices of the lowest classes in an alien society, and systematically omitted anything that might in common justice have been said to the honour and credit of those who deserved it. St. Bernard had never been in Ireland, knew nothing of its history, and wrote at second hand to praise and magnify his hero's achievement: the Tudor chroniclers were in Ireland and wrote to defame the people whom they had outraged and dispossessed.[40]

Here I would take leave to interpose a brief parenthesis with regard to the origin of the Fitzgeralds, whom some historians have derived from Italy.

The new edition of Luke Wadding's *Annales Minorum*[41] reproduces an interesting fragment from a manuscript by Antonio de Terrinca, O.F.M., preserved in the convent of Ognissanti (All Saints) in Florence, according to which two Franciscan friars from Florence made their way to Ireland in 1230, "cum quibusdam nobilibus de Gerardis e patria [*sc.* Florence] rebellis" (*sic*). These nobles were Maurice and his brothers Gerard and Thomas, and, on their arrival in England, they were, according to this account, kindly

[40] Keating (*Foras Feasa ar Éirinn*, I, 3, 55) compares them to beetles: "For it is the fashion of the beetle . . . not to stoop towards any delicate flower that may be in the field . . . but it keeps bustling about until it meets with dung of horse or cow, and proceeds to roll itself therein. . . . Let us consider the rough folk of Scotland, the rabble-rout of Great Britain, the plebeians of Flanders, the insignificant fellows of France, the poor wretches of Spain, the ignoble caste of Italy and the unfree tribe of every country besides, and a multitude of ill-conditioned evil ways will be found in them: howbeit, the entire country is not to be disparaged on their account. . . . Since it is thus that Fynes Morison has acted, writing about the Irish, I think it is not allowable he should have the repute of an historian; and so I say also of Campion . . ."

[41] *Quaracchi*, 1931, II, p. 734.

received by Henry II and presently enrolled among his forces. Maurice was dispatched to the conquest of Ireland and, having accomplished his task to the king's satisfaction, received a grant from his Majesty of vast estates in perpetuity in the county of Kildare. This Maurice de Gerardis was the founder, according to De Terrinca, of the noble Irish house of the Geraldines, later known as Fitzgerald, and was the first to welcome the Friars Minor into Ireland and to build them convents. Finally he himself abandoned the world and its riches, entered the Order, and died a holy death in the convent at Youghal in 1257.[42]

That the Mendicant Orders were introduced into Ireland and largely patronized by the Anglo-Normans, who sought to monopolize their activities, is exact:[43] but De Terrinca in this passage has merely echoed rumours and confused events separated by a wide interval of time. The first Norman invasion of Ireland with the assistance of a Maurice Fitzgerald, accompanied by a Robert Fitz-Stephen, took place in 1170, but the earldom of Kildare was not conferred on the Fitzgeralds until 1318.[44] Reference to the probable Florentine origin of the Fitzgerald family is occasionally found in English text-books,[45] but the tale is devoid of historical foundation. Count Alessandro Pecori Giraldi of Florence has courteously informed me that his family records show no connection between the Irish Fitzgeralds or the French family of Géraldy (which also professes to be of Italian origin) and the Giraldi. A branch of the Giraldi family migrated to Portugal in the seventeenth century and one member rose to be Viceroy of Brazil. The branch which remained in Florence became extinct in the second half of the eighteenth century, when the patrimony and the name passed to the Pecori.

[42] Cf. 'Materials for the History of the Franciscan Province of Ireland, A.D. 1230-1450,' by Fr. E. B. Fitzmaurice, O.F.M., and A. G. Little (Vol. IX of the *British Society of Franciscan Studies*), Manchester, The University Press, 1920, p. 27. Mr. Little notes (p. 2) that the story told by Wadding, II, 250-1, about the foundation of the house at Youghal has not been traced to its original source. The earliest mention of it in contemporary record is 1290.

[43] Cf. also Hayden and Moonan, op. cit., p. 147.

[44] Ibid, pp. 111 and 161.

[45] Eg. *Leading Events in the History of the Church by the Sisters of Notre Dame*, Washburn, London, 1910, IV, 226.

The famous group of families, Fitz-Gerald, Fitz-Stephen, Fitz-Henry, De Barry and others, known in Irish history by the name of Geraldines, is of Cambro-Norman origin. The Maurice Fitz-Gerald, who led the expedition of 1170 and was the brother of the Bishop of St. David's before referred to, was of mixed Welsh and Norman blood, and he and Robert Fitz-Stephen were the sons, by different fathers, of the Welsh princess Nesta, the record of whose numerous adventures occupies a disproportionate place in the chronicles of the time.[46]

Emboldened by the example of the English, the Scotch seized the opportunity to profit by the name they had acquired to confuse and distort the reality of history, to appropriate to themselves the ancient glory of the *Scotti* of Ireland, by pretending that they were Scotch, and also to appropriate—as before mentioned—their foundations on the Continent.

Under the weight of the heavy Anglo-Norman yoke, the poor island, which had already suffered so sorely from the Danish invasions, entered on a period of degradation such as it had never before experienced. But before the fair blossoms of Celtic piety and culture were shrivelled by the rude blasts from overseas, the Celts caught and held the imagination of Europe under another kind of spell: the spell of the harps played by their bards. The imaginations of the nations rivalled one another in hastening to drink from the springs of poetry which had gushed forth from the little race which lay politically strangled, and the Celtic romances, so full of dreams and mystery and melancholy and passion, acted like a quickening ferment on the nascent literatures of the Continent. This was another great service which the Celts rendered the world.

In the following chapter the nature of these romances will be briefly touched upon, with special reference to their influence upon the literature of Italy.

[46] Cf. Hayden and Moonan, op. cit., p. 109; Dunlop, op. cit., pp. 28-9.

CHAPTER V

§ 1

THE Celtic legends which so vividly affected the imagination
of early medieval Europe belong to well-defined types of the
old Irish literature, the *immram* or voyage along the enchanted coasts of pagan mythology, and the *aisling* or vision
of, and adventures in, its underworld.

Little enough is known, in spite of much speculation and
conjecture, of the religion which the Celtic invaders brought
with them into Ireland. Belief in the survival of the soul,
common among many Indo-European races, was not
peculiar to the Celts, but these impressed early observers by
their doctrine of the transmigration of souls, and Pythagoras,
who expounded the same teaching, was popularly believed
to have been initiated into their magical practices by the
Druids, "the sole repositories," in Lucan's words, "of knowledge or ignorance concerning the gods and the divinities
above."

The minds of the seafaring peoples of antiquity were
haunted by the tradition of an island remote and inaccessible,
where the souls of the departed dwelled in peace, the
makaron nesos of Hesiod, the *fortunatae insulae* of Plautus.
Thither the souls of all who had lived their lives in a manner
pleasing to the gods were shepherded after death by
Hermes *psychopompos*, the escort of souls. Many attempts
were made by the living to discover this abode of the blessed,
and its situation was variously conceived, at one time off
the west coast of Africa, as by Strabo and Pomponius Mela,
at another in the heart of Libya, as by Plutarch and Polybius. Leuke, a lonely uninhabited island in the Black Sea,
whose chalk cliffs face the mouth of the Danube, became

identified in Greek tradition with the island Elysium to which the souls of Achilles and a few choice heroes had been rapt. It was thickly covered with woods in the heart of which stood a temple, cleansed every morning by birds which bathed their wings in the sea, and in the temple an oracle, operated, according to Arrian, by no human agency, foretold the future to anyone who consulted it. No man could live on that island, and the sailors who landed there by chance had to leave before nightfall, because at night the spirits of the dead roamed free. *Nox clausas liberat umbras.* Leuke for centuries was visited by pilgrims in thousands.

Most famous of all was the attempt made by Sertorius to discover the fortunate isles. Some Spanish seamen had told him in a port of the West that they were "two in number, divided from one another only by a narrow channel, and distant from the coast of Africa ten thousand furlongs." Rain fell there seldom. The soil was rich for ploughing and planting, and produced spontaneously an abundance of delicate fruits, so that the inhabitants enjoyed all things without trouble or labour. The firm belief prevailed even among the barbarians that there was the seat of the blessed, and that those were the Elysian Fields celebrated by Homer. When he heard this account, Sertorius "was seized with a wonderful passion for these islands, and had an extreme desire to go and live there in peace and quietness, and safe from opposition and unending wars; but his inclinations being perceived by the Cilician pirates, who desired not peace nor quiet, they immediately forsook him and sailed away into Africa. . . . This sudden departure noways discouraged Sertorius."[1]

The uninhabited islands off the coast of Britain provoked the curiosity of the Romans, and Plutarch relates[2] how one Demetrius was sent by the Emperor to get information about them. He returned with a story that in one of them Chronos was imprisoned with Briareus keeping guard over him while

---

[1] Plutarch: 'The Life of Sertorius.' The translation is by John Dryden, revised by A. H. Clough in the Everyman edition of *Plutarch's Lives.*

[2] *De defectu Oraculorum,* c. XVIII. On the subject generally, cf. Erwin Rohde, *Psyche, Seelencult u. Unsterblichkeitsglaube der Griechen,* fourth ed., Tubingen, 1907, pp. 350 et seq., and F. G. Welcker, *Kleine Schriften,* II, pp. 19 et seq.

he slept, sleep being the bond forged for Chronos. Chronos in Greek mythology was the lord of Elysium, and it has been suspected that Demetrius had heard a tale of Cernunnos, the divine ancestor of the ancient Celts, and conceived him to be his own more familiar Chronos, as some centuries later Cernunnos became identified with Bran, the son of Febal, and Bran in turn with Brons, the Fisher King and Keeper of the Grail.

The Greek and Celtic conceptions of the otherworld were very similar, and a specifically Breton belief recorded by Pomponius Mela[3] finds an echo in the *History* of Geoffrey of Monmouth.

The earliest Christian missionaries to Ireland, anticipating the politic advice tendered some centuries later to Serenus, Bishop of Marseilles, and the Abbot Mellitus upon his departure for Britain, by the great Pope Gregory, and pursuing the common practice of the Church in pagan lands, had tolerated what was tolerable in the country to which they had been sent, and, baptizing them, enlisted in the service of the new faith old associations ineradicable from the hearts of the people. The Gospel which Patrick preached was welcomed by the *filid*, and in Ireland it was the *filé* who, under the habit of the monk, continued to bestow his patronage upon his humble brother the bard, the monk who continued to transcribe the myth in which the animal creation and the bird-flock of Faery, no less than the children of Adam, yearned for and acclaimed the advent of the Apostle. The *immram* and the *aisling*, each containing in practice much that was common to both, were specially suitable for Christian treatment, and while the *immram* was thinly disguised with a veneer of Christian eschatology, the *aisling*, transformed into the *Fis*, and composed mainly for edification, borrowed many of its elements from the same source. The new religion brought them into contact with the general literature of early medieval Europe, and they in turn contributed their own distinctive characteristics to the common stock.

[3] *De Chorographia*, iii, 5. Mela was not unknown to the Irish in the Middle Ages.

The Irish imagination, ever tugging against the fetters of reality and revolting against the tyranny of fact, sought and found release in the tale of adventure and the vision of the underworld, in the legend of St. Brendan the Navigator and the visions of Tundale and Owen in the purgatory of St. Patrick. Obsessed by the dream of a happier and better world immune from the sorrows and miseries of this, and clinging stubbornly to the conviction, patent in the legend of Judas's weekly rest and the persistent tradition of the periodical respite of the damned, that souls could be got out of Hell and the irremediable remedied, if only the means thereto, existing somewhere, could be found, it indulged its fancy in yet another type of tale, the Quest, the hero of which journeyed underground to the land of shades to bring back talismans, and among them the inexhaustible vessel of plenty and rejuvenation.

Peredur thus went below in search of a magic lance and sword with which to avenge a kinsman, and in the underworld met Bran, the son of Febal. In the apocryphal epistle of Nicodemus it was related that Our Lord had given the cup which He had used at the Last Supper to Joseph of Arimathea, and how it had come to Glastonbury in charge of Joseph's brother-in-law, Brons, or his son Josephe. Two strands of legend became inextricably interwoven, and the object of the old heathen quest, christianized in the hands of Robert de Boron at a time when the cult of relics was most intense, and interest, aroused by the crusades, centred on those of the Passion, became confused with the lance with which Longinus had pierced Our Lord's side,[4] and the talisman was transformed first into the chalice which He had used at the Last Supper and ultimately into the vessel ("gradalis . . . scutella lata et aliquantulum profunda") in which Joseph of Arimathea had collected the drops of Precious Blood which fell from the Wound. A moral tendency, the inspiration of which was, it has been suggested, Cistercian, then invaded the *Queste del Saint Graal*, and a new hero, known in English as Sir Galahad, was introduced to

[4] Cf. *The Legend of Longinus*, by Miss R. J. Peebles, Baltimore, 1911.

typify the virtue of chastity.[5] Wolfram von Eschenbach (c. 1210), a man of deep religious feeling, wove new elements into the old story and transformed the Grail still further into "a precious stone fallen from Heaven, yielding all manner of food and drink, and sustained in its power by a dove which every week laid a Host upon it." Wolfram based the conception of his Parzival[6] not upon chastity exclusively but also upon loyal observance of the marriage bond, and the Grail in his poem became transformed into a spiritual symbol of human striving and love in their noblest manifestation.

The legend owes its preservation at the present day to Richard Wagner. The German composer contributed to his *Bühnenweihfestspiel* the figure of Kundry, the Herodias whom Christ doomed for her laughter to wander until He should come again. Her mission is to tempt and lure the warriors of the Grail to their destruction, and yet she would find release from her torment and salvation for her soul could but one man resist her spell. The German Parsifal, 'the perfect fool,' 'the guileless one,' succeeds in resisting physical desire for the temptress, and thus becomes the symbol of Our Saviour. Wagner, accepting the sacramental nature of the Grail, turned the feast of its warriors with much luscious music into a drama which affect some listeners as an odious parody of the Last Supper and the daily continuing Mass.

§ 2

The *immram* type of romance reached the highest point of conscious art in the *Navigatio Brendani*.[7]

[5] Cf. Alfred Nutt, *Studies on the Legends of the Holy Grail*, London, 1888; Albert Pauphilet, *Queste del Saint Graal*, Paris, 1921, and some recent articles by Mme Myrrha Lot-Borodine in *Romania*, 1930 and 1931, pp. 147-205. M. Pauphilet is concerned only with the Galahad Quest, and the suggestion that the introduction of the new element under Cistercian auspices is a consequence of the triumph of a pre-Thomist 'affective' mysticism was first made by M. Gilson. Cf. his article on 'Le mystique de la grâce' in *Romania*, 1925.

[6] He is Perceval in the French romances, but the Welsh substituted their own Peredur, a warrior of the sixth century.

[7] There is a good text in Jubinal *La légende latine de S. Brandaines*, Paris, 1836, but no attempt has been made above to give a coherent or consecutive account based on the *Vitae* and the later *Navigatio*. Only a few typical incidents have been selected. The Bollandists originally rejected a *Vita* as too fabulous

Brénaind moccu Altai, otherwise known as Brendan, the patron saint of the Ciarraige, an ancient people scattered over the western part of Ireland, Connacht and Munster, was a disciple of St. Jarlath, founded his own chief monastery, Clúain-ferta-Brénaind, 'Brendan's meadow of graves,' at Clonfert in the county of Galway in 558 or 564, and died, according to the Annals of Ulster, in 577 or 583.

He lived therefore at a time when the overseas movement of the Irish ascetics, who went forth seeking in foreign or desert places an abode where they might lead in peace an exalted religious life, was at its height, and himself, fired by their example, "peregre proficisci ardenti volebat desiderio." Colum-cille had sailed for Iona, Columban was contemplating his departure to Gaul, Cormac úa Liatháin, in the words of Adamnán, "no less than thrice had painfully sought a hermitage in the ocean," *nec tamen invenit*. Cormac, however, had visited Colum-cille in the island of Hinba, and with him were Comgall of Bend-chor, Cainnech of Achad-bó and Brendan of Clúain-ferta. Brendan also determined to put to sea.

He prayed for a land 'secret, hidden, secure, delightful and apart from men,'[8] whither he might retire 'on pilgrimage,' and in such a mood, falling asleep, dreamed that an angel directed him to repair to Sliabh Daidche, now Brandon Hill in Kerry, build himself a ship, and commit himself with his fourteen *comilitones* to the ocean. Brendan did as he was bade and out of a pine-tree hollowed a boat which he covered over with skins. Forty days elapsed in preparations before the little company were ready to put out to sea. They had only been fifteen days on the ocean, when the wind failed and they were compelled to take to their oars. They laboured manfully until they came at last to an island 'very high and rocky,' round which they cruised for three days before finding a landing place. There they

for comment—even Vincent of Beauvais, who could stomach much pious romancing, was moved to reject what he described as "deliramenta apocrypha" —but it may be permitted to think that a reconsideration of the story in the light of increased knowledge would concede to the tradition at least a nucleus of historical truth.

[8] Cf. the translation by Whitley Stokes in *Anecdota Oxoniensia*, Pt. V, and the texts in Dr. Plummer's *VV. SS. Hib.*, I, 44-95; II, 44-92, 328-37.

kept Easter with the birds which sang in chorus, flapping their little wings, "Te decet ympnus in Syon et tibi reddetur votum in Jerusalem." Going down to the sea again, they came upon another island which terrified his companions when it began to move, and Brendan, rebuking them, told them that it was not in truth an island, but that Almighty God, "unto Whose bidding every creature was obedient, had made a huge whale raise its back above the sea, so that there might be a place suitable for His servants to dwell on for the night of His resurrection." The whale was most suitable as the lordliest of all fishes.

> "Leviathan which God of all His works
> Created hugest that swim the ocean stream."

It was ever attempting to join its tail and head, but was unable to do so owing to its great length, and Casconius was its name. The monster bore them off across the ocean, and food, miraculously sent, sustained them the while, until at last Brendan encountered the Devil and held converse with the Fiend whom none of the others could perceive. He told the Saint that he was 'vilely housed in the dark places of the sea,' but was so far prevailed upon as to guide Brendan to the gate of Hell which no man could look upon and thereafter continue to live. Brendan looked and saw "the camps of poisonous demons and the handsmiting of the sinful folk; and a gloomy, mournful life in cores of pain, in prisons of fire, in streams of the rows of eternal fire in the cup of eternal sorrow and death" (trans. Stokes), in a land of black swamp and fiery mountains. One of the little company, bolder than the rest, asked that he too might be permitted to have a glimpse. His wish was granted and he immediately dropped dead. Brendan, however, succeeded in resuscitating him, "non tamen sine magno labore," and they proceeded on their way. The sound of wailing through the mist next caught Brendan's ear, and, peering, he espied the figure of a man, naked and unkempt, clinging desperately to a rock though sorely buffeted by the waves. He had a veil of some cloth or other across his face and kept groaning in a dull, raucous voice, "Dicens: 'Ha! Jesu pie, si fas esset,

ad te clamarem. Ha! Jesu, rex in majestate, venietne
unquam terminus mali? . . .' " Brendan, grief stricken and
appalled at the spectacle of such anguish, raised his hand,
fortified his little company with the sign of the cross, and
drew near. And as he drew near, the wind suddenly became
still, and the sea ceased heaving and moaning and lay quiet.
"I conjure you to tell me who you are," he began, but he
could say no more, for his voice choked. "I am Judas,"
said the figure on the rock, "I am he who betrayed the Master
Whom I served: I am he who sold my Lord and hanged
myself." And Judas proceeded to explain that he enjoyed
a weekly respite which, beginning on the Sabbath evening,
lasted all Sunday, but late on that day he was doomed to
return to his torment. He had other holidays, he continued,
fifteen days at Easter, Pentecost, and the feasts of Our Lady.
Brendan and his companions listened to his dolorous story
and when they left him they were amazed.[9]

They next descried a great strand and drawing near beheld
a maiden dead with a deep wound between her shoulders.
She was of vast stature, a hundred feet high. "The dutiful
father (*pius pater*) prayed to God for her in his heart, and his
prayer was heard, because he revived and baptized her. He
asked her what country she came from and who were her
people, and she answered: 'I am of the dwellers by the sea
and our hope is for a common resurrection.' Brendan thereupon said to her: 'Choose now one of two things: do you
want to return to your own folk or will you go to Heaven?'
The maiden answered in a tongue which only the elder
(*senior*) could understand: 'I want to live with my king
and to see him every day and to dwell together with the

---

[9] On Judas's Sunday rest, cf. D. Bergamaschi, 'Giuda Iscariota nella leggenda, nella tradizione e nella Bibbia' in *Scuola cattolica*, 1909, Vol. XV, pp. 299
et seq, and a comprehensive paper by Paull Franklin Baum in the *Modern
Language Review*, Vol. XVIII (1923), pp. 168-82. That there was holiday in
hell at Easter-tide was a pious belief in the early Church and found beautiful
expression in some verses of Prudentius, *Cath.*, V, 125 et seq., with which
cp. St. Augustine, *Encheiridion*, *c.* 112: "Poenas damnatorum certis temporum
intervallis existiment, si hoc eis placet, aliquatenus mitigari, dummodo intel-
ligatur in eis manere ira Dei, hoc est ipsa damnatio." The fancy failed to
commend itself to Bellarmine, and Fabricius described it as "a Spanish fabrication." Cf. also Dom Gougaud's 'La croyance au répit periodique des damnés'
in *Mélanges bretons . . . offerts à J. Loth*, Rennes, 1927, p. 67.

angelic spirits praising him without interruption.' And forthwith, after choosing Mary's part, she returned once more to rest in peace without difficulty or pain, and they buried her where they had found her."

Landing on another island, they were greeted by an old man of wondrous gravity whose face was radiant and whose hair was white as snow. He escorted them to a marvellous monastery, where in the refectory they refreshed themselves with loaves wonderfully white and roots incredibly sweet. The abbot told them that in that island there was no need of fire for cooking or warmth, for there was neither extreme heat nor cold to depress them. The lamps in the house lit spontaneously *divina insufflatione* as though an arrow of fire had been shot through the window and the oil never grew less. There was no sickness of body or sadness of soul. An absolute stillness reigned and everyone knew the appointed hour of his death. All this had endured ever since the time of St. Patrick, who had ordained it so. There was a noble church on the island where Brendan and his companions joined their hosts in praising the Lord. After many more extraordinary adventures and visits to other islands, they returned home after seven years' absence to tell the Irish of all the wonderful things they had seen.

The spirit of unrest, however, was not yet laid, and Brendan set out on the ocean once more, this time with a different object. His ship for this second adventure was timber-built by cunning smiths and artificers, and he went forth not to seek a retreat in which to lead the anchoritic life but, emboldened by his former experiences, to discover *Tir tairngiri*, the Land of Promise of the Saints. A certain Abbot Barinthus[10] had fired him by his description of that elysium. The brother of Barinthus, it appeared, one Ternoc, *pauper fugiens laboris sollicitudinem perrexit in solitarium locum*. This, too, was an island *contemplationi satis apta*. Other solitaries had been attracted to Ternoc's foundation, and Barinthus had gone to visit them. He was received with charity

[10] This Barinthus of the *Vita S. Brendani*, who was familiar also to Geoffrey of Monmouth, is merely Barrfind, 'White Crest,' another marine saint whose name has been preserved in Kilbarran (*Cell Bairrfind*), near Ballyshannon. His maritime exploits, alas! have found no chronicler.

unfeigned, and the description he gave Brendan may be regarded as the Irish monk's ideal of the contemplative life. "Although there were many separate dwellings (*mansiones*) therein, yet the intercourse among the brethren was animated by one single spirit in faith and hope and charity; there was only one church, one refectory.   They ate only the roots of herbs and the fruits of trees, and they drank water only to slake their thirst.   The brethren took such recreation as God sent them, and, when they had said compline, returned according to custom, each to his own cell, and there abode until cockcrow."

In one of the islands, which he visited on this second voyage, Brendan came upon an old man covered with white hair, 'like a dove or sea-mew,' and speaking almost in the tones of an angel.   The old man bade him enter into the plains of Paradise, "a land of odorous flowers, smooth, bland, of many melodies, musical, shouts for joy, unmournful," where there were "health without sickness, delight without quarrelling, union without wrangling, princedom without dissolution, rest without idleness, freedom without labour, luminous unity of angels, delights of Paradise, service of angels and feasting without extinction" (trs. Stokes), and all things else whatsoever that could appease the tortured heart of man.   The canonical hours were strictly observed, psalms were sung, prayers said, and penances punctiliously performed by all the inhabitants, human and superhuman.   The birds[11] in that paradise had been the angels who, when Lucifer rebelled, did not rebel and yet were not loyal to God, but *per se foro*.   Their lot, in the Irish tale, was happier than that bestowed upon them by Dante, for they were merely relegated to that island, where they suffered no pain and kept the canonical hours, until such time as the trumpet should sound for the general resurrection.

The Brendan legend was transmitted to the continent of Europe from Wales through Brittany, and by the early

---

[11] Birds play a prominent part also in Greek mythology, and the companions of Diomede were transformed into birds to be his servants on the island inhabited by his spirit. Cf. Pliny, *N.H.*, X, 78 and 127.

tenth century had contributed, among other features, the whale episode[12] to the *acta* of St. Machutus or Malo, in which Brendan became transformed into the Welsh abbot of Llancarvan and Machutus into his disciple. Irish *peregrini*, numerous at the time in the lower Rhine valley, may also have contributed to its diffusion throughout Europe.[13]

The Latin text of the *Navigatio Sancti Brendani*, a work of high accomplishment, written in Ireland by an Irishman in the first half of the tenth century,[14] was followed by innumerable translations and adaptations into all the vernacular languages of Europe. In Italy Villari published an Italian redaction, 'La leggenda di San Brandano' as an appendix to his 'Antiche leggende e tradizioni che illustrano la Divina Commedia,' reprinted by Battelli in his *Le più belle leggende cristiane* (Hoepli, Milan, 1928), pp. 436 et seq., with some interesting notes. Arturo Graf provides copious bibliographical particulars in Vol. I, pp. 184-5 and 266, and Vol. II, p. 395 of his *Miti, leggende e superstizioni del Medio Evo*. The same authority cites an Italian *Vita* of St. Brendan noted by Lami, and an Italian text of the legend contained in codex No. 1008 of the library at Tours, as to which cf. *Bibliothèque de l'École des chartes*, 1878, pp. 385-6. This text was edited recently by the late Mr. E. G. R. Waters: *An Old Italian Version of the Navigatio Sancti Brendani*. (Oxford University Press, 1931), who considered it a thirteenth-century vulgarisation in Lucchese dialect. Brendan, in this interesting version, was born in Venice. Graf (I, 184) warns his reader not to confuse the legend of the Irish St. Brendan with the legend, still current in Tuscany in popular sheets, of Brendan of Siena, who flourished in the

---

[12] The report of the appearance of a whale off the coast of Norway reached Radulphus Glaber in his monastery at Cluny (*c.* 1033) and launched him off on a summary and inaccurate account of Brendan's voyage. Brendan, according to him, was "an eminent confessor of the East Anglians," *Histories*, II, ii, *P.L.*, CXLVII, col. 644.

[13] To the great irritation of such as Nicholas de Bibera, who accused the Irish at Erfurt of proclaiming St. Brendan to be "dean of the college of saints," "the brother of God" and "the son of St. Brigit." Cf. the 'Carmen Satiricum' quoted by Dom Gougaud in *Gaelic Pioneers*, pp. 104-5.

[14] Mr. Mario Esposito would date it even earlier, to the seventh century, and attributes its diffusion on the Continent to the activities of the Irish *peregrini* in the ninth century. Cf. his 'Notes on Latin learning,' etc. (VII, 'An Invocation to St. Brendan') in *Hermathena*, 1929.

sixteenth century. Novati, who thinks that the Italian texts derive from a single thirteenth or fourteenth-century translation made in the Venetian dialect, has published *La Navigatio Sancti Brendani in antico veneziano* (Bergamo, 1892). The legend still flourishes among the seafaring folk along the coast of Liguria, and a redaction in Loanese dialect has been picked up and published by G. Vitaletti in the *Giornale Dantesco* for 1923, fasc. II. The most recent works on the subject are Carl Wahlund's *Die altfranzösiche Prosaübersetzung von Brandans Meerfahrt*,[15] (Upsala and Leipzig, 1900), which contains a good survey of the enormous literature, and Wilhelm Meyer's *Die Ueberlieferung der deutschen Brandanlegende* (Gottingen, 1918). Dom Gougaud, *Gaelic Pioneers*, pp. 119-20, records some popular traditions concerning St. Brendan in various European countries.

Relics of the saint, it may be of interest to note, were preserved in the fourteenth century in Pavia,[16] in the Church of S. Maria Capella, of which De Canistris became parish priest in 1323, and of which all that remains to-day is the frame of the façade looking west in the bay of the via Rezia.

The island which St. Brendan set out to discover became a fixed idea in medieval geography and continued to be marked on charts of the Atlantic until the eighteenth century. It was claimed by the Portuguese but afterwards ceded to Spain, and the last expedition to set out in quest of it was in 1721.

The *immram* type of romance thus came to an end, but the otherworld tradition persisted to inspire a work in the rival genre of the *Fis* which, although far inferior as a literary composition, almost rivalled the *Navigatio Brendani* in the popularity it achieved in medieval Europe and the influence it exercised upon later writers, artists and even sculptors.[17]

[15] Wahlund, op. cit., p. 225, quotes a remark attributed by the *Revue bleue*, 22nd August, 1896, to Paul Verlaine: "Je dis que Judas est damné . . . damné pour s'être pendu de désespoir, pour avoir mis en doute l'infinie misericorde de Dieu."

[16] Cf. Gianani, *Opicino de Canistris*, Pavia, Fusi, 1927, pp. 55, 82 and 126.

[17] E.g. in the portals of Saint Maclou (appropriately enough) at Rouen, built 1432-72, and the Cathedral at Nantes, built 1434-80. The sculptures would naturally come towards the end of the period, and M. Mâle would date them c. 1470. The Church took a long time to adopt these old legends.

This was the *Visio Tundali*, written *c.* 1149 in his convent at Ratisbon, by an Irish monk named Marcus.[18]

§ 3

The idea of purgatory, as the learned Dr. Thomas Wright long ago pointed out,[19] first assumed concrete and definite form in the West in the literature of the Irish. The earliest descriptions of that state are nearly all by Irishmen or by Anglo-Saxons who had lived in Ireland, St. Fursa or Drihthelm, the Northumbrian monk, who related his experiences to Haemgils, then a hermit in Ireland, who told them in turn to Bede.[20] The vision which Fursa beheld probably during the solitude of his ocean retreat, is the earliest example of its type in the Christian literature of the Irish. Rapt up on high by the angels he was ordered to look back upon the world. "Upon which, casting his eyes downwards, he saw as it were a dark and obscure valley underneath him. He also saw four fires in the air, not far distant from each other. Then asking the angels what fires those were, he was told they were the fires which would kindle and consume the earth."[21] They were the fires of falsehood, discord, covetousness and iniquity. Fursa in the course of his adventures received much instruction in theology and morals which he was bidden to impart to the princes and prelates of Ireland before he was conducted back to his body.

The vision of Fursa, however, was eclipsed by the vision of Tundale.

Tundale—Tnúthgal or Tnúdgal is conjectured to have been the proper form of his name—was a soldier of Cashel

---

[18] He paid a visit to Clairvaux shortly after the death in 1148 of St. Malachy, and was doubtless one of the sources from which St. Bernard drew his information as to the condition of Ireland (cf. Seymour, *P.R.I.A.*, XXXVII, 1926, C. 90-1).

[19] Cf. *St. Patrick's Purgatory: an Essay on the Legends of Purgatory, Hell and Paradise current during the Middle Ages*, London, 1844. A more recent book is Archdeacon J. D. Seymour's *Irish Visions of the Otherworld*, London, S.P.C.K., noticed in *Analecta Bollandiana*, 1932, pp. 418 et seq.

[20] *H.E.*, V, 12. He retired afterwards to Melrose and died according to the Anglo-Saxon Chronicle in A.D. 693. The laconic entry: "In this year also Drihthelm retired from the world" would be unintelligible without Bede.

[21] Bede, *HE.*, III, 19, Everyman tr., pp. 133-4. Cf. also Mabillon, *AA. SS. o.s. B.*, II, 291.

who had served under Cormac Mac Carthaigh, King of
Munster. He was "noble of blood but bloody of deeds;
fair as to the body but careless about his soul. Fierce and
terrible towards the Church, for he would endure none of
the poor folk of the Lord in his sight." While on a visit
once to a friend in Cork, he fell on a Wednesday into a
trance, while sitting at table, and during this trance beheld
the vision which he related to Marcus.[22]

When his soul left his body, Tundale was welcomed as
one of their own by great hordes of demons who tore at him
with their talons and taunted him with his sins. His guardian
angel at last came to him in light, like a star,[23] and, bidding
him welcome from God, bade him also follow and remember
firmly whatever he should see. They set out together in
darkness, lighted only by the radiant garments of the guide,
until they came to a glen 'darkened with the mist of death,'
and filled with sparks of fire. It was crowded with a huge
multitude of souls burning 'till they were melted like garlic
in a pan,' because in life they had been parricides and
slayers of their kin. Another glen was black as pitch and
fetid with a mist uprising, so that Tundale could only smell
the stench and hear the wailing of the souls tormented
there. The angel bore his guest across a plank between the
two mountains bounding the glen, and on they went through
dark and tortuous ways until they came to the monster
Acheron, which devoured the covetous. "Its eyes were like
hills of flame; its mouth, wide yawning, might contain a
legion of armed men." Flames issued from its mouth and
troops of souls were driven into it by demons with scourges,
and from the monster's belly came the sounds of wailing.

[22] The summary in the text follows the summary of the Irish version contained in *La Vision de Tondale*, V. H. Friedel and Kuno Meyer, Paris, 1907,
made by Mr. C. S. Boswell in *An Irish Precursor of Dante*, London, 1908, pp.
213-24, but the opportunity of reading two French prose versions has not
been neglected. The Irish version is a translation made in 151- by Muirges
mac Paidin úi Maoil-Chonaire from the original Latin (ed. Schade, Halle,
1869) into the language in which, it was conceived, the tale was first told to
Marcus.

[23] Cf. Dante, *Inf.*, IX. The Latin text reads "longe venientem velut stellam
lucidam," which Signor d'Ancona, *I Precursori di Dante*, Florence, 1874, p.
55, n., compares to the wonderful simile of the approach of the angel in *Purgatorio*, XII, 89 et seq., "nella faccia quale Par tremolando mattutina stella."

Tundale was driven in with the rest and found himself along with many other souls, bitten by vipers and scourged by demons, while suffering the extremes of heat and cold. He emerged presently to be rejoined by his angel guide, who escorted him to the shores of a stormy lake, where monsters innumerable sought to devour the wretched souls. There was a bridge studded with iron nails to be traversed by all who had ever stolen anything, bearing on their backs a burden commensurate with the magnitude of the theft, and Tundale, who had once stolen a cow, was forced to cross like the others carrying a wild cow on his back. His feet bled with the spikes, and his angel guide explained to him that this was because he had been one of 'those whose feet were swift to shed blood.' He was then handed over to the demons standing in the flames of a burning house and armed with axes, scythes, and 'all other instruments whatsoever useful for cutting.' They seized him and tortured him until he confessed that he had suffered no more than he deserved, and upon that confession he found himself alone and in a dark place, free from pain.

The angel re-appeared and after expounding to the bewildered Tundale, as well he might, the saying 'Misericordia Domini plena est terra,' delivered him over to another horrible monster with two feet and many necks, beaks and talons, who dipped the wretched souls into an icy lake and swallowed them again in his mouth of perpetual fire. This was the punishment reserved for monks, canons, nuns, all who had broken their vows, and such as had defiled themselves with their inordinate lust. This punishment also Tundale was compelled to endure. They journeyed on, and after divers horrible adventures, in the course of which the unhappy Tundale was seized with their tongs by a succession of smiths and cast into a series of fiery red furnaces where souls were forged into one solid mass, and although screaming for death, were denied that relief, arrived together at the gate of hell. Tundale would have turned away, but his feet clave to the floor and in frenzy he began to tear himself with his nails. The angel rescued him from the demons who surrounded him, threatening and reviling, and he was told to look. He looked and saw the Prince of Darkness himself, "black as a raven from head to foot with more than a thousand hands on him. . . . Every limb was covered with chains of iron and bronze. As he lay there roasting, tossing from side to side filled with rage and fury, he grasped the souls in his rough, thick hands, bruising and crushing them, as a man would crush grapes to squeeze out the wine." With his fiery stinking breath he scattered the souls about hell, and, as he drew it in again, he swallowed them down with it, and those whom his hands could not reach he lashed with his tail.[24] Tundale stared at the appalling sight and was horrified to perceive numbers of his own friends and kin.

On leaving Hell they entered into a great light and came to a wall with men and women perched thereon and beaten by wind and rain. These were the Laodiceans, who *senza infamia e senza lodo* had led a 'variegated' life compounded of equal good and evil, and they patiently endured their exposure to the elements and hunger and thirst in the hope, to be accorded to them in the end, of entering into eternal life.

The travellers next penetrated a forest, and, passing through an open door, found themselves in a plain covered with flowers and fragrant with sweet-smelling herbs, and saw the Well of Life in the midst of it. This was the dwelling place of the good while they waited to join the heavenly host. There Tundale recognized Donnchad and Conchobar Ua Briain, King of Munster (d. 1142), who, having formerly been at feud, were now reconciled and at peace. He saw also his King Cormac Mac Carthaigh (d. 1138),[25] whose subject he had been in Desmond, sitting on a yellow throne

[24] The description of Hell and Satan in the *Visio Tundali* was one of the principal texts which the fancy of artists in the fifteenth century took to embroidering. The passage above was illustrated with a great wealth of imagination in the introduction of further horrors in the *Très Riches Heures* formerly belonging to the Duc de Berry and now at Chantilly. Cf. E. Mâle, *L'Art religieux de la fin du Moyen Age en France*, Paris, 1908, pp. 502-18.

[25] Cormac had been deprived of his kingship in 1127 by Turlough O'Conor, King of Connacht, his brother Donogh being set up in his stead. He led a life of penance in pilgrimage, until he was reinstated by Conchobar and his brother banished to Connacht. He was murdered in 1138 by his son-in-law Diarmid at the instigation of Turlough (cf. St. Bernard, *Vita Mal.*, c vii).

and surrounded by priests and deacons clad in rich vestments as though about to sing a Mass. Tables were set out, covered with vessels of gold and silver and ivory, and preparations were being made as though for a royal banquet. The whole company presently fell on their knees and repeated the verse, "Labores manuum tuarum manducabis; beatus es et bene tibi erit." The angel told him, when he expressed surprise that none of those serving Cormac were the king's own people, that Cormac was being served by the poor and pilgrims of the Lord whom in life he had relieved.

Even as they watched, it suddenly grew dark in the house, and Cormac left it. Tundale, following him, saw the king don a hair-shirt and enter a fire where he spent three hours every day to expiate the breach of his marriage vow. He wore the hair-shirt because he had once murdered a nobleman under the protection of St. Patrick, and made a false vow. All his other sins he had expiated.

Tundale next encountered men and women in silken robes, with shining faces and hair like gold, who passed him singing 'Alleluia.' These were the saints "who had macerated their bodies for God's sake, washed their robes in the Blood of the Spotless Lamb, turned their backs upon the world, and crucified their wills in the service of God."

The travellers, proceeding on their way, were greeted by the sounds of every kind of music from castles and pavilions hung with the richest draperies. It was played by people of devotion, who, submitting their own will in lowliness and humility to God, had been obedient to their superiors, and finding savour only in spiritual things, had bridled their tongues. A little further on they met choirs of saints, full of gladness and rejoicing, perpetually praising the Trinity. These were they who had been faithful in wedlock and had distributed their goods among the poor. They were waiting for Christ to say to them: "Venite benedicti Patris mei, possidete regnum quod vobis paratum est ab origine mundi." The nine orders of angels and the saints consorted with them and the words the travellers heard were sweet beyond record. Tundale at last had a glimpse of the supreme vision, and "from that moment forth he asked nothing of the angel, for to himself was given from God knowledge of what he desired to know." In that glory he beheld St. Patrick and a number of bishops whom he had known in the world, Cellach, *alias* Celestine, Archbishop of Armagh (d. 1129), Máel Máedóc Ua Morgair (d. 1149), Nehamiah Ua Moriertach, Bishop of Clúain-uama (Cloyne), who according to this text died in 1148, and Gilla-Criost (Christian) Ua Morgair, the brother of Máel Máedóc and Bishop of Clogher and Louth (d. 1138).[26] He saw also a great tree laden with blossom and all manner of fruit. Vast flocks of birds thereon sang every kind of song, the air was fragrant with every sort of sweet-smelling herb, and round the tree were multitudes of men and women with golden crowns on their heads and golden wands in their hands, singing and praising the King. The tree was the prop and stay of the Church and those about it were they, who, in their lives, had united to support and defend the Church.

The vision over, Tundale begged to be allowed to stay where he was, but the angel told him he must return to his body, remember what he had seen and deliver it to people in the world. It was a Saturday when Tundale came to his senses again. He received Holy Communion, gave thanks to God, and after distributing all his goods among the poor, assumed the cross, and turned his back on his former life. He had the angel's promise to protect and counsel him.

This Vision of Tundale, with the exception of the Voyage of St. Brendan, became the most widely popular of all the stories of early medieval Ireland. It was translated into French, German, Italian, Anglo-Norman, Middle-English and Norse. It exercised an immense influence on art.[27]

[26] Cellach (Archbishop of Armagh in 1105) was the first clerical archbishop after a series of eight laymen. St. Bernard describes him as "vir bonus et timoratus." Nehemiah, whose death the Four Masters attribute to the year 1149, is described by them as "a bishop of the South of Ireland, wise, devout, and chaste."

[27] The anticipations of Dante in this brief and inadequate summary of Tundale's Vision will be apparent to anyone familiar with the *Divina Commedia*—and the difference between the two. The Italian poet took the poor dross of the Irish visionary's prose and turned it into the pure gold of poetry. Marcus had read the 'Vision of St. Paul' (cf. 'Io non Paolo sono' in *Inf.* II, 32) and was familiar with the legends of the voyage of St. Brendan, but, as M. Mâle (op. cit., p. 509) says: "On ne peut pourtant lui refuser une imagination originale. Quelle étonnante facilité d'invention dans l'horrible! Dante ne le dépasse

Villari published in the appendix to his book before mentioned a 'Libellus de raptu Tundali et ejus visione tractans de poenis inferni et gaudiis paradisi,' and an Italian redaction, 'La Visione di Tantolo,' identical with one inserted in many ancient editions of the *Vite dei Santi Padri*. Other Italian redactions have been published by Giuliani, *Il libro di Theodolo ovvero la visione di Tantolo*, Bologna, 1870 (Scelta di curiosità letterarie Disp. 112), and Corazzini, *Visione di Tundalo*, Bologna, 1872 (Sc. di cur. lett. Disp. 128). Arturo Graf (op. cit., I, 268) cites the *Visio Tungdali*, ed. D. Schade, Halle, 1869; in II, 122, the *Visio Tundgali Lateinisch und altdeutsch*, ed. Albrecht Wagner, Erlangen, 1882, and in II, 123, *Sulla visione di Tundalo* by A. Mussafia in Sitzungsb. d. k. Akad. d. Wissenschaft, philos. hist. Cl. LVII, Vienna, 1871.

The best known of the three is the legend of St. Patrick's Purgatory. When it first emerges into the light of history (*c.* 1153) it is found situate on one of two little islands in Lough Derg in Southern Donegal, the larger of which, Oilean na Naomh, was occupied by a community of Augustinian canons, who at some time between 1130 and 1134 had established themselves upon the remains of an ancient monastery under the patronage of, and perhaps founded by, St. Da-Bheóc. They were the guardians of the holy place.

In 1153 one Owen, *miles quidam*, and an Irishman who had served for many years under King Stephen in England, came on furlough to visit his parents in Ireland. This Owen had led an ungoverned life from his cradle, 'being ever intent on burning things and looting' (*incendiis semper vacaverat et rapinis*), violating churches, and making free with ecclesiastical property, but in Ireland he suffered a change of heart, made full confession of his iniquities to a bishop, and

---

pas. Mais l'oeuvre de Dante a la beauté architecturale. L'Italien enferme la pitié, la haine et l'amour dans la forme parfaite du cercle. Le pauvre poète celte rêve sans art, comme l'enfant qui regarde vaguement dans le foyer des paysages de feu"—an admirable simile. It may also be observed that these tales of hell and its torments, the origin of which is incontrovertibly Oriental and more immediately Greek, were essentially popular, and it is not without significance that St. Thomas, the most impersonal of philosophers, who yet must have been well aware of them, almost studiously ignores them. Cf. *Summa Theologica*, Pars. III, supplementum. *Qu*. XCVII, art. 11.

resolved to do penance for his sins by making a descent into the pit of the Purgatory. The bishop sought to dissuade him from so perilous an adventure, but Owen, in his agony of remorse, was in no mood to listen, and duly went off to present himself to the abbot in charge. He made a preliminary retreat of fifteen days in prayer and fasting, and, when the appointed day came, heard Mass, received Holy Communion, and was ceremoniously escorted to the edge of the pit. Making 'the sign of the life-giving Cross upon his forehead,' the hero, dauntless, went down.

On his return Owen told the story of his adventures in the underworld to Gilbert, a monk of Louth in Lincolnshire under a promise of secrecy, but the burden of the revelation was too great for Gilbert to bear, and he communicated the disclosures to a Cistercian monk of Saltry in Huntingdon whom Matthew Paris called Henry. This Henry of Saltry (c. 1190) composed his 'Tractatus de purgatorio Sancti Patricii Hibernorum apostoli,' and captured the imagination of Europe.[28]

After referring to another Patrick, an abbot, who, because he found the Irish fractious and troublesome, withdrew from their country c. 850 and went to settle in Glastonbury, where he died 'on St. Bartholomew's Day,' Henry begins with a story of how the great St. Patrick was preaching to the multitude one day about Heaven and Hell, when a sceptic in the audience remarked that what he said might well be true, but that his account would carry more conviction if someone were permitted to experience *tormenta illa malorum*, instead of having to take the saint's word for them. Patrick thereupon fasted and prayed and the Lord Christ appeared to him, brought him to a desert place, showed him a round cave dark within, and said: "Whosoever, truly penitent and constant in the faith, shall enter this cave and spend a day and night there, shall be purged of all the sins he ever committed in his life against God, and if he pass through it, he shall see, if he persevere in the faith, not only

[28] The summary in the text follows the reprint in Migne, *P.L.*, CLXXX, 975-1004, from Messingham's *Florilegium*. It is a crude production of little worth as literature, but Dante did not disdain to read it, and certain anticipations of the *Inferno* have been noticed which give it an interest.

the torments of the damned, but also the joys of the blessed."
Such, according to Henry, was the origin of St. Patrick's
purgatory.

To return to Owen in the bowels of the earth. It grew
darker and darker as he groped his way underground, but
he went forward cautiously, until presently he was assailed
by a party of horrible demons. He escaped from their
clutches by repeating the name of his master, Christ, and,
exposed to further onslaughts, extricated himself in similar
fashion until, emerging at last from the tunnel, he saw
before him a series of four consecutive plains. As he traversed
these, he saw they were appropriated to various forms of
torture: "et omnia genera tormentorum quae excogitari
possunt ibi visa sunt." The writer's poor imagination failed
him, and his torments are mostly of the conventional kind.
The damned were plunged in molten metal deep as their
sins were heinous.[29] Some were congealed in ice,[30]
others gnawed by serpents,[31] others again buried in flaming
trenches fanned by gales.[32] In the third plain Owen noticed
numbers of souls clamped to the ground with red-hot iron
nails,[33] and, to his horror, like Tundale and Dante, recognized among them friends and acquaintances whom he had
known in life. He went on and the demons tossed him on a
wheel of fire across a river, which was 'broad and fetid and
stank,' a very Phlegethon choked with a multitude of demons.
Underneath lay Hell. Crossing the bridge which spanned it,
he came at the end to a wall of crystal in which was a gate
decorated with various enamels, adorned with precious
stones, and radiant with a marvellous splendour. Two

[29] Cf. *Inferno*, XII and XXXII-XXXIV.

[30] Cf. *Inferno*, XXXII-IV. Alternations of intense heat and cold seem
to be a favourite form of torture for the damned, an interpretation, no doubt,
of Job, xxiv, 19: "Let him pass from the snow waters to excessive heat, and his
sin even to hell." Cf. Shakespeare's "fiery floods" and "thrilling regions of
thick-ribbed ice,"

> "To be imprisoned in the viewless winds,
> And blown with restless violence round about
> The pendent world;"

in *Measure for Measure*, III, i.

[31] Cf. *Inferno*, XXIV-V.

[32] Cf. *Inferno*, IX and V.

[33] Cf. *Inferno*, XXIII, iii et seq.

M—i

dignitaries there accosted him who looked like archbishops.
The gate, they said, led to the Earthly Paradise, the sojourn
of spirits purified from sin and awaiting their final perfection.
There Owen felt neither heat nor cold and saw nothing
which could hurt or offend. Everything was peaceful and
placid and pleasing, "et multo plura quam ipse aut aliquis
hominum peritissimus lingua aut calamo posset explicare
delectabilia jucundaque prospexit." As he gazed enraptured
at the inenarrable vision of what eye hath not seen nor ear
heard, a multitude of the elect passed him singing God's
praises, and "as star differs from star in brightness, so was
there a harmonious difference in the beauty of the brightness
of their garments and features."

The two archbishops discoursed to their guest upon the
nature of the Earthly Paradise and conducted him to a
hill-top, whence he might obtain a Pisgah view of the gate
of Paradise. He said it shone like gold burning in a furnace.
Owen, entranced, would fain have stopped there, but his
advisers bade him return to earth, and, with a flash of fire
from heaven, the vision ended.

This legend became immensely popular all over Europe
and was early recorded in the works of Jacques de Vitry, the
Dominican († 1240), who firmly believed that those who
came out never smiled again, in the *Dialogues* of Caesarius
von Heisterbach, his contemporary, in the *Polychronicon* of
the Cistercian Ralph Higden of Chester († *c.* 1363), and in
the *Quattuor Novissima* of Denis the Carthusian (1402-71),
who not only incorporated the story of Owen in his treatise,
a preacher's text-book, but also reproduced almost word
for word the vision of Tundale.

The little island in Lough Derg drew pilgrims from the
remotest parts of Europe, even from Hungary, and the
English archives still contain records of certificates given by
Edward III and Richard II to eminent foreigners testifying to
to their due accomplishment of the purgatorial ritual. Pope
Alexander VI, however, in 1497 ordered the Purgatory to
be closed, but the order would seem to have been but imperfectly executed, for twenty years later Francesco Chieregato, apostolic nuncio in England, wrote (10th July, 1517) to

Isabella d'Este, Marchioness of Mantua, announcing his intention of going to Ireland "to see St. Patrick's Purgatory and all the other wonderful things which are said and written about that island."[34] He came and, a month later (28th August), gave his correspondent an interesting account of his experiences.[35] In 1632 the chapel and all the buildings on the island were demolished to the order of the English government in Dublin by the Protestant bishop of Clogher, one James Spottiswood, who described the purgatorial cave as 'a poor beggarly hole,' and pilgrimages to the place in the reign of Queen Anne were proclaimed 'riotous and unlawful assemblies.' In 1790 the cave was finally filled up, but the nineteenth century saw a recrudescence of the popular devotion, which was consecrated in 1931 by the erection of a church ranking as a minor basilica.[36]

The legend of the Purgatory and the terrifying adventures of Owen was as widespread in Italy as elsewhere in Europe, and in the fourteenth century had become a common topic with preachers. It was first popularised by Jacopo da Voragine, the Dominican Bishop of Genoa (*c.* 1230-*c.* 1298)

[34] *Calendar of Venetian State Papers*, 1509-19, p. 401. The Nuncio, before going, had had a stormy interview with Wolsey, who pleasantly threatened him with the rack for having had the audacity to communicate with the King of France. In Ireland he was under English escort and was stuffed with some extraordinary stories, as, e.g. that the people were communists and lived by thieving, that in the north they went naked, lived in caverns, and ate raw flesh, all of which he duly transmitted to Rome. An Italian account of his career and the text of the letter are given by Morsolin, 'Francesco Chiericati, vescovo e diplomatico nel sec.' XVI, in *Atti dell' Accademia Olimpica di Vicenza*, 1873. That "the wild Irish, as unreasonable beasts, lived without any knowledge of God or good manners, in common of their goods, cattle, women, children and every other thing" would seem to have been a popular opinion in England at the time. Cf. e.g. *Il Pellegrino inglese nel quale si difende l'innocente e la sincera vita del pio e religioso re d'Inghilterra Henrico ottavo*, Bologna, 1552, the record of a discourse made by one William Thomas, a fugitive Welshman, to some Italian gentleman after the death of that monarch. The words quoted are taken from J. A. Froude's edition, *The Pilgrim: A Dialogue on the Life and Actions of King Henry VIII*, London, 1861, p. 67.

[35] The letter is translated and reproduced in *Isabella d'Este, Marchioness of Mantua*, 1474-1539, by Julia Cartwright (Mrs. Ady), London, two vols., 1906, and reprinted in Mr. Shane Leslie's *St. Patrick's Purgatory*, London, 1932. Mr. Leslie, for some reason not immediately apparent, conceives the Augustinian canons to have been an Anglo-Norman foundation. There is no evidence of this. Cf. also Fr. John Ryan's article, 'St. Patrick's Purgatory' in *Studies*, September 1932, pp. 443 et seq.

[36] *St. Patrick's Purgatory*, contains a comprehensive survey of historical and literary references to the pilgrimage.

and the compiler of the *Golden Legend*.   In 1411 Antonio
Mancini, a Florentine merchant, made the descent and
wrote a solemn account of his experiences published in the
Giornale storico della letteratura italiana, VIII, p. 154.   He was
followed by Fazio degli Uberti, another native of Florence.
Ariosto in *Orlando Furioso*, X, str. 92, mentions:

> ". . . Ibernia fabulosa, ove
> Il santo vecchiarel fece la cava
> In che tanta mercè par che si trove
> Che l'uom vi purga ogni sua colpa prava"[37]

and Tassoni, in his burlesque poem, 'La secchia rapita'
(Paris, 1622), also refers to the tradition.

Villari published an Italian text of the legend as an
appendix to his book, and this has recently been re-
published by Battelli in *Le piu belle leggende cristiane*, Hoepli,
Milan, 1928, p. 436, with some interesting notes.   Another
Italian text was published by Grion in the *Propugnatore*,
Vol. III, part I, pp. 116-49, while a 'Viaggio nel Pozzo di
S. Patrizio' has been repeatedly printed in Italy (Haym,
Biblioteca Italiana, II, 624).   Arturo Graf refers to the legend
in Vol. I, pp. 92 et seq. of his book before mentioned, and on
p. 181 gives an Italian bibliography, citing (*inter alia*)
*Il Purgatorio di S. Patrizio secondo Stefano di Bourbon e Uberto
da Romans* by L. Frati (*Giorn. str. della letteratura italiana*).
It may, in conclusion, be recalled that the legend furnished
Calderon with both the subject and the title of his tragedy,
El Purgatorio de San Patricio.

§ 4

The literature of the old Irish world flowered with the
florison of the old Irish Church and shared its summer; the

---

[37] "He next for Ireland shaped his course,
And saw the fabulous Hibernia where
The goodly sainted elder made the cave
In which men cleansed from all offences are
Such mercy there, it seems, is found to save."
                    Trs. W. S. Rose, Bohn's edition, London, 1858.
The 'he' in question is Roger.   The poem was first translated into English by
Sir John Harrington (1591), who, visiting Aedh O'Neill in 1599 with Sir
William Warren, presented his two sons with a copy.   The Earl had some of it
read to him and said he liked it well.

literature of the other branch of the Celtic family in Wales was not so fortunate. With the withdrawal of the legions from Britain darkness falls upon the island, but certain figures may still be faintly discerned moving stealthily in the gloom. The Britons beyond the Roman frontier, not having been conquered by Rome, had remained uncivilized, and Cunedda Wledig, one of their rulers, appears to have invaded Wales. A son of his, the King of Dumbarton, the Alcluith of Bede, established himself there in the principality still called after him, Ceridigion, Cardiganshire.[38] A formidable pirate, this Coritic, *guleticus* or *wledig*, it would seem, of a hegemony among the barbarians, led his mixed force of Picts and miscreant Scots on one memorable raid upon the coasts of Ireland, fell upon a number of Patrick's neophytes the day after their anointment with the chrism of baptism, butchered some, carried the rest off into slavery, and evoked from the Saint the angry remonstrance contained in the *Epistola*. Coritic, however, established the Welsh nation, and the native language, driven underground during the Roman occupation, emerged once more. The great Welsh saints of the sixth century have already been mentioned. The bards were no less prominent, and Taliesin, Myrrdin, Talhaiarn and Llywarch Hen animated with their strains the rising hopes of their people. The Cymry, however, as they now began to call themselves, were harried again by a succession of fresh invaders, Saxon and Angle, Jute and Dane, and, driven further and further into the remote corners and extremities of the island and overseas to 'little Britain,' clung the more desperately to the language and literature embodying their traditions as the menace to their national life became more insistent, and the prospect of a national resurrection grew ever fainter. Shunning their pagan oppressors, they refused even to assist in saving their souls by lending a hand to the new missionaries who had come from Rome to convert them. Before the reality of present oppression, they too sought refuge in dreams of a future deliverance by an

---

[38] Cf. the Life of St. Carantoc in *AA. SS. Boll.*, May, III, 585-7: "Keredic held Keredician, i.e. Keredigan, and it was named after him. And after he had held it, the Irish came and fought with him and seized all the country"; and Canon Doble's monograph, *St. Carantoc* (XIV), Shipston-on-Stour, 1928.

ancient hero whose return to them was to set all things right. This persistent Breton folly was familiar to, and laughed at by, their more practical neighbours, but the son of Geoffrey Plantagenet was tactfully christened Arthur in homage to it.

Few national heroes owe less to reality than Arthur. There is no mention of him in Gildas or in Bede, none in the Anglo-Saxon Chronicle; the reference to him in the Book of Taliesin is trivial. His very existence has been doubted.[39] Tradition would make of him a warrior of the late fifth or early sixth century, who, as *comes Brittanicus*, played a predominant part—*ipse erat dux bellorum*—in the wars waged between the Britons and the Saxons. He may have fought at the momentous battle of Mt. Badon, he was betrayed by his wife and some near relative, son or nephew, and fell in battle. He makes his first appearance as a Christian warrior in panoply in the pages of the obscure and enigmatic Nennius, the pupil of an early ninth-century bishop of Bangor, who worked over the materials of his composition, the *Historia Britonum*, in the first half of that century, but three centuries more were to elapse before he attained his full stature as an ideal hero of romance in the hands of Geoffrey of Monmouth. This Geoffrey, a canon of Oxford and later Bishop of St. Asaph, wrote his *Historia Regum Britanniae* in 1135, and was more a Breton than a Welshman.

Geoffrey's Arthur is the son of Uther Pendragon and Igerna, wife of Gorlois, Duke of Cornwall. His sister Anna, the wife of Lot, is the mother of his nephew Gawain and Mordred. A great warrior, after crushing the Saxons, he turns against the Picts and Scots, captures Alcluyd and, victorious in three pitched battles, reduces the northern country. He then takes to wife Guinevere (Gwenhwyvar), 'a lady of noble Roman family,' and proceeds the following year to the conquest of Ireland and Iceland. These triumphs are followed by twelve years of unbroken peace, during which Arthur lives in splendid state and holds his

[39] Cf. *Arthur of Britain*, by E. K. Chambers, London, Sidgwick and Jackson, 1927.

regal court at Caerleon-on-Usk, presiding over the feast at Christmas or Whitsuntide, and surrounded by hundreds of knights and beautiful ladies, patterns of valour and virtue, of breeding and grace. Arthur himself, in most of the romances, is a somewhat shadowy figure, and the stories are told not of him, but of his knights Gawain or Perceval, Lancelot or Pelleas or Pellinore. They all go forth sooner or later in search of adventure, to protect women and the weak, to chastise oppressors, to liberate the enchanted, and to do battle with giants.

This halcyon period came to an end when Arthur conceived the ambition to conquer all Europe. He began his campaign by subduing Norway and then crossed over into Gaul. During his absence he left Britain to the care of Guinevere and Mordred, and, crossing the Channel, did battle with a marvellous giant at St. Michael's Mount, routed with great slaughter the Romans who had come to oppose him in Gaul, and was about to pass into Italy when news was brought to him of Mordred's treachery. Returning at once, he engaged the traitor in a great battle at Richborough, in which Gawain was killed, and drove him back on Winchester. Guinevere, meanwhile, had entered a convent at Caerleon and, repentant, taken the veil. Arthur, pursuing the retreating Mordred, entered Cornwall, and at another great battle on the Camel fought and killed him: "but the illustrious Arthur, too, was wounded to the death and was borne from the battlefield for the healing of his wounds to the island of Avallon in the 542nd year after the incarnation of Our Lord." Avallon was the Welsh equivalent of the Irish Tír na n-Og, the land of youth, the *makaron nesos* of Greek mythology—the Paradise of the Blest.[40]

The story came to Italy very early from Brittany, and the late Signor Pio Rajna discovered in Italian documents of the early twelfth century the attestation of witnesses bearing

[40] Cf. Chambers, op. cit., and *The Vulgate Version of the Arthurian Romances, edited from Manuscripts in the British Museum,* by H. Oscar Sommer, seven vols. and index, Washington, Carnegie Institution, 1908-16. Dr. Sommer's choice of manuscripts has not, however, escaped criticism. Of the attempt being made in recent years, notably by American scholars, to establish a direct affiliation between Arthurian romance and early Irish tradition, it would, perhaps, be premature to speak, but the resemblances are striking.

the names Arthur and Gawain.[41] The Duomo at Modena was built in the eleventh century, and the sculptor in chief is known to have been one Wiligelmo (1099-1184); on the archivolt of the Porta della Pescheria a scene is sculped representing a tower besieged by armed knights, and among them are Arthur, Meriadoc, Caradoc, Gawain, Kay and Ider.[42] Similar work is to be found at Bari in the Cathedral of St. Nicholas, and in the mosaics in the Cathedral of Otranto, "a rough jumble of figures evoked by the popular imagination out of old bestiaries and the legends of *Re Artù*."[43]

The 'Arturi regis ambages pulcherrimae,' as Dante calls them in the *De vulgari eloquentia*, spread as far south as Sicily. Gervase of Tilbury, who had followed the Norman King William there about 1190, tells in the *Otia Imperialia* (*c.* 1211), which he wrote for the entertainment of his master, the Emperor Otho IV, 'on the authority of the natives,' the story of how a groom in the service of the Bishop of Catania, pursuing a horse which had bolted among the steep places of Mount Etna, 'a mountain which they also call Mongibel,' climbed up a very narrow path and suddenly came upon a plain full of all manner of delights. He there found Arthur lying in bed in a palace of marvellous construction. The king inquired of the astonished intruder (*advena et peregrinus*) what had brought him there and, on being told the reason, forthwith had the bishop's palfrey brought to the astonished groom. He told him, moreover, of his battle with Mordred and Childeric, the *dux Saxonum*, and how he had been wounded, and that his wounds broke

[41] Cf. 'Gli eroi Brittoni nell' onomastica italiana del secolo XII' in *Romania* XVII, 161, 355. The name survives in modern Italian as 'Galvani.'

[42] On the Duomo at Modena cf. 'Storia dell' arte italiana' by Pietro Toesca, I, *Il Medioevo*, Turin, 1927, p. 654, note 15, and works there cited, more particularly A. K. Porter's *Lombard Architecture*, I, 436, and III, 44. On Wiligelmo cf. Toesca, op. cit., p. 884, note 12. He has been claimed, as one might expect, by the Germans, but his Norman (or Breton ?) provenance would seem to be indubitable. Sig. Toesca offers no opinion on the source of the Arthurian figures sculped on the bas-relief, but it is almost certainly French. Miss Hutchings, discussing in a recent number of *Medium Aevum* (December 1932) the Isdernus figure, has come to the conclusion that the romance illustrated is not a romance of Gawain (most popular in Italy), but a romance of Yder and Guinevere. *Viderint sapientiores!*

[43] Toesca, op. cit., p. 1083.

out afresh every year. He then sent him back with presents for his master, the bishop, which were seen by many and by most admired for their *fabulosa novitas*, but in what their novelty consisted Gervase or his informants have not thought fit to reveal.[44]

Such then was the contribution of the Celtic races to the spiritual and intellectual enrichment of mankind. The Irish gave the feeling of communion and sympathy with nature, the sense of adventure, and compassion for the weak and defenceless; the Welsh, the wistful themes of their romances, with all that the word romance comports of mystery and pathos in the ever frustrate attempt to escape from the harsh realities of life under the spell of the remote and unattainable. The Celtic genius, rooted in spirituality, is prodigal of sentiment, but to be sentimental is to be ineffectual, and the children of this generation are wiser.

§ 5

The legends of the Mabinogion and the cycle of romances which revolves round the figure of Arthur seem to have slipped through the wicket of fancy into a world of enchantment. The knight, going forth to do battle with enemies of another world, giants and demons, was exposed to darts from invisible foes. He was counselled by sorcerers and allured by the smiles of women, unearthly, impalpable creatures who beckoned him on, beguiled him and vanished. Picking his way in solitude through an enchanted wood to a magic castle, he might at any moment espy "etins and elves and ogres" dancing by the side of his lonely path. Romance, illusion, and faerie are the stuff of the *matière de Bretagne*.

A world of difference divides these Celtic legends from the

[44] An analogous tale is told by Caesarius of Heisterbach in his *Dialogues* (*c*. 1240) as an episode in the conquest of Sicily by the Emperor Henry VI in 1194. Cf. the edition of J. Strange, Cologne, 1881, XII, 12, the essay by Graf on the legend 'Artù nell' Etna,' and the same author's interesting and detailed appendix in op. cit. II, 339, on 'References to Breton characters and legends in early Italian poetry.' The text was written unfortunately before the publication of Mr. E. G. Gardner's *The Arthurian Legend in Italian Literature*, London, 1932.

almost contemporary Carolingian romances known as the *chansons de geste*. It was formerly held with all the fervour attaching to a dogma, and the more tenaciously because it was indemonstrable, that the *chansons de geste* had been 'evolved' in some mysterious way out of *cantilènes* which everybody worshipped but which nobody had ever seen. The pious belief was shattered by the epoch-making work of M. Bédier,[45] who showed that the *matière de France* wrought into the *chansons de geste*—that great scholar has catalogued fifty-five historical characters—was the conscious product of monk and minstrel working together for the edification and entertainment of the pilgrims who thronged the great roads on their way to Santiago da Compostella, Rome and Jerusalem. The old Irish *peregrini*, who had set out merely for the love of Christ, had disappeared, their successors were practical men, and tramped along the great highways of Europe to make their devotions before the *pignora apostolorum* at the great shrines of Christendom. St. Guillaume du Désert, Ste. Marie Madeleine de Vézelay, and the abbey of St. Denis were lesser shrines improvised for those unable to make the longer journey, and round these and their relics the *chansons de geste* were composed. The monks supplied the minstrels with some elements of history, true or imagined, about the founder whom they had canonized, and the minstrels embroidered the theme for the glorification of the monastery to the great contentment of all parties. "The *chansons de geste* and the crusades"—M. Bédier describes his judgment as at once a tautology and a truism—"are works of the eleventh and twelfth century." They have the character of the time which begat them. Popular romances, deliberately composed for living men who took their part in crusade and pilgrimage, who crowded into the *parvis* before the church or stood gaping at the booths of the fair, they reflect the spirit of the naturally hierarchised

[45] *Les légendes épiques: recherches sur la formation des chansons de geste*, four vols., 2nd ed., Paris, 1914-21: "Ils [sc. the minstrels] n'ont pas pris la peine de se renseigner auprès des clercs instruits: ils se sont contentés de ce que disaient le frère hôtelier, le sacristain, les gens du pays. . . . Ces poètes sont restés 'peuple': ils se sont intéressés aux traditions des églises dans la mesure où s'y intéressaient autour d'eux les marchands, les chevaliers, les bourgeois, les pélerins qui venaient vers ces églises," Ibid. IV, p. 429.

feudal society, zeal for the Faith, loyalty to the sovereign lord, resistance to the arbitrary will of the local seigneur with whom the heroes, when they are not busily engaged fighting the *Paynim*, are at constant feud. Their women are not the eerie phantom figures of the Celtic imagination but living women of flesh and blood, faithful wives and devoted mothers.

The 'Niebelungenlied,' most familiar to a modern reader in Richard Wagner's 'Ring der Nibelungen,' provides yet another contrasting type of womanhood. Brunhilde and her sisters, the women of the northern cycle of romance, are more than women. Pagan goddesses, they, like their men, are inspired by malice, actuated by horrible motives of blood loyalty, and instigated by a passion for revenge. Grimhild lures her brothers to death to atone for the murder of Sigurd and her vengeance is repulsive in its savagery. The only joy in the dark German mind is 'Schadenfreude.' Deirdre and Isolde come out of another world.

§ 6

The Irish *peregrini* took the legends of their saints abroad with them on their wanderings and spread their fame wherever they settled; the Welsh on both sides of the Channel owed the diffusion of their romances to another means of communication, the tongue of their conquerors. Although the names of Arthurian romance had reached the Continent long before Geoffrey ever thought of setting pen to paper, and men were called Trystanus and Yvanus near Lake Constance in the eighth and ninth centuries, Artusius, Walvanus and Merlinus in the late eleventh and early twelfth centuries in Italy,[46] although the Welsh on both sides of the Channel had given stories to their neighbours, the English on the marches of Wales and the Normans on the borders of Brittany, the European renown of their legends had to wait for the coming of 'the little bullet-headed men' from Normandy, who, dominant and aggressive, combining the Latin sense of fact, which the Celts lacked, with the Roman talent for affairs, the Roman

[46] Chambers, op. cit., p. 72.

decisiveness in emergencies, carried the fame of their prowess from Greenland through Europe and the islands of the Mediterranean to Constantinople and beyond. The language they spoke was French, the most powerful language spoken in Europe at the time, and they administered their own laws wherever they went, in their own language. They were great builders, these Normans, and they built for permanence: their buildings endure, the castles and cathedrals of the eleventh and twelfth centuries. The world, in the words of a contemporary chronicler,[47] then seemed to have given itself a shake, to have renewed its youth and everywhere donned a radiant mantle of churches. All Europe at the time had been united in one ideal, the conquest of the Holy Sepulchre, and the laity were bound together for a moment as never before, and certainly never since, in a common intellectual understanding by a vulgar tongue. The Churchmen had their Latin. Between Paulinus of Nola or St. Augustine and St. Peter Damian or St. Thomas Aquinas, differences there may be, there is no separation. Sympathy and intercourse between the laity were quickened in the twelfth century by the prodigious flowering of new poetry in France, narrative verse in the North, the lyric in Provence. The fashion spread to Italy and Spain: it became the wear in the Germanies, in Scandinavia, even in Iceland, but the cut was determined by the Court. The old songs had been sung from generation to generation by bard and minstrel to the accompaniment of the harp; they were the simple history of the people, the commemoration of its heroes, and the expression of its hopes. The new verse was consciously artificial, deliberately based upon the science of music, composed for the entertainment of 'gentle' folk, self-consciously separated from the 'common' people by their

[47] "Erat enim instar ac si mundus ipse excutiendo semet, rejecta vetustate, passim candidam ecclesiarum vestem indueret. Tunc denique episcopalium sedium ecclesias pene universas ac cetera diversorum sanctorum monasteria seu minora villarum oratoria in meliora quique permutavere fideles," Radulfus Glaber, *Hist.*, III, IV, *P.L.*, CXLII, col. 651. The "villarum oratoria" were the original parish churches, round which the village, unknown before the eleventh century, grew and developed. The "oratoria per villas potentum" (Council of Chalon, 642, c. 14) were, however, ousted in Gaul and Switzerland, and, it is surmised, also in North Italy, by the Carolingian *cappella*.

ideal of chivalry and its expression in an elaborate and complicated game termed *l'amour courtois*. Courtesy, it is in danger of being forgotten, is the product of Courts. The laureate of the new school was the courtly maker *par excellence*, Chrétien de Troyes (*fl.* 1160-80), an accomplished exponent in the most captivating style of all the subtleties of emotion, especially love, and the very perfection of good breeding.[48] The note which Chrétien struck was 'sensibility,' and so 'the matter of Britain,' the stories of Tristan, who lived and loved in Cornwall, of Gawain, Perceval and Lancelot, became peculiarly associated with the sentimental romance so much in vogue in the great houses and polite society. In the *lais* (1165-67) of Marie de France the characters are mostly Breton and the action for the most part is laid in Brittany. In 1165 Maistre Wace, called Robert for no known reason, a Guernsey man by birth but long settled in Caen as *cler lisant* under the Henrys, wrote in French his *Geste des Bretons* or *Brut*, 15,000 lines in octosyllabic couplets, and dedicated it to Eleanor, the wife of Henry II. The Round Table makes its first appearance in this, the earliest full version of the story of Arthur. Wace was a canon of Bayeux when he died (*c.* 1175). *Brut* fell into the hands of Layamon, a simple, pious and patriotic priest, but a Saxon living on the banks of the Severn at Arley, near Bewdley. "It came to him in mind," he said, "and in his chief thought that he would tell the noble deeds of the English," and in order to do so adequately he doubled the length of the poem.

The Normans were fond of going on pilgrimages. As they were unconsciously responsible for the preservation and propagation of Celtic legends, the peculiar qualities of which they were so quick to appreciate, so it will be seen in Part II that, although devoted to their own saints, they could still adopt and propagate devotion to the saints of others. It is the Normans who are responsible for the widespread devotion in Italy to-day to the memory of an obscure sixth-century Irish *peregrinus*, St. Cathal of Taranto.

---

[48] Cf. Gustave Cohen: *Un grand romancier d'amour et d'aventure au XIIème siècle: Chrétien de Troyes et son œuvre*, Paris, Boivin, 1931.

CHAPTER VI

THE MARTYRDOM OF IRELAND

§ 1

ALTHOUGH strictly speaking foreign to the general purpose of this book, it would be impossible to conclude this first part without passing in rapid review the vicissitudes of Ireland's political fortunes from the Anglo-Norman invasion down to the present day; for these vicissitudes testify with the eloquence of facts and more effectively than a hundred dissertations to the generous characteristics of a race which has remained faithful in a heroic degree to the religion first implanted in its heart by St. Patrick and his disciples. The fruits of their labours are to be found, if anywhere, in the inflexible resistance of the nation to a pitiless martyrdom of four centuries' duration, in the course of which Ireland set the world such an example of fidelity to Christ and Rome as is without parallel in history. The *peregrini* of her golden age in missionary zeal spread the Faith in Europe: her exiles in the eighteenth and nineteenth centuries scattered the seeds of the Faith broadcast in the lands of their enforced sojourn, and unconsciously fulfilled a similar mission in America and Australia.

Christianity had had no martyrs in Ireland, but St. Patrick on more than one occasion expressed in his *Confessio* his readiness to give his blood for Christ: ". . . and if I should be found worthy, I am prepared [to lay down] my life without hesitation and very gladly for His name's sake" (§ 37). He ardently desired and would have welcomed eagerly the privilege which God had given others of His lovers of drinking from His cup (§ 57). "And if ever I have imitated any good thing because of my God Whom I love, I beg Him to allow me to shed my blood along with those proselytes and captives, even though I were to go without burial and my body to be horribly torn limb from limb by dogs or wild beasts or devoured by the birds of the air" (§ 59).

Patrick therefore implored the grace of martyrdom for Ireland. His prayer was heard, his wish granted, and the martyrdom was *red*.

The first phase of the *English* history of Ireland from the landing in Waterford in 1170 of Richard de Clare, Earl of Pembroke, to the accession to the throne in 1509 of Henry VIII, the second of the Tudor Kings of England, is distinguished by two main features—the failure of Irish arms and the triumph of Irish civilization. The central political authority of the old Irish State collapsed at the first onset of the invaders, but the local States were made of stronger stuff and showed more power of resistance. The Anglo-Normans, superior to the Irish in military equipment, political cunning, and the science of warfare, steadily pursued their practice of incastellation and, within seventy years, had brought three-fourths of the country under control. In Wales alone they erected 143 castles. The old Irish monastic churches were turned into fortresses and their fate was sealed. The Anglo-Normans seized the bishoprics and other benefices for their own candidates, so that the possibility of carrying further forward the reformation of the twelfth century and erecting a new ecclesiastical system upon the ruins of the old was destroyed. The new mendicant orders, however, though introduced as instruments of Anglo-Norman policy, remained to become *ipsis Hibernis Hiberniores* and in the event the chief ministers to the spiritual needs of the people. The Franciscans, especially, saved the soul of the nation. Towards the end of the thirteenth century the tide began to turn. National sentiment, slow to react in a loosely federated country to the sense of national oppression, was quickened by the introduction of a new element, the professional soldier. Bands of organized fighting men from the Norse Kingdom of Argyle and the Hebrides, the *gallóglaigh*, known to English writers by the 'uncouth name' of gallowglasses, and originally imported, it would appear, as mercenaries, furnished a model for the native Irish *buannadha*, 'buonies,' men on permanent military service, and ultimately repelled the advance of the feudal system.[1] The English had defined a Separatist policy at a parliament held in Kilkenny in 1367 under the presidency of Lionel, Duke of Clarence, who, by his marriage with the infant daughter of De Burgh, the ward of his father Edward III, had received the titular lordships of Connacht and Ulster, and a severe statute was passed, which, after reciting that the English had become 'mere' (i.e. pure) Irish in their language, names, apparel and manner of living, that they had allied themselves with the natives and adopted Irish laws, prohibited such deplorable approximations under penalties of high treason or at least the forfeiture of land.   Absorption, however, was inevitable, and steadily proceeded.   Resurgent Ireland continued to assimilate the foreigner and the growing consciousness of nationality found its highest and noblest and most typical expression in the two great festivals given in 1433 to '2,700 persons, besides gamesters and poor men,' by Margaret O'Connor, the wife of Calbach O'Connor, Prince of Offaly.[2]   The long civil Wars of the Roses in England consummated the ruin of English power in Ireland, and in 1500 the English authority, as distinct from the rule of the great Anglo-Irish nobles, had shrunk to the four counties in the Pale, Dublin, Louth, Meath and Kildare, in practice from Dublin to Dundalk and a day's ride inland.   The king's jurisdiction had diminished 'from a large forest to a narrow park.'   Two-thirds of the country was still in the possession, in defiance of the law which looked upon 'the wild Irish' as alien enemies, of the native race.

In 1603 the authority of the King of England had been everywhere established.   Absorbed in warfare with France, Scotland and Wales, the English monarchy throughout the Middle Ages had neither men nor money to spare for the reduction of Ireland.   Lambert Simnel had, indeed, been

---

[1] MacNeill, *Phases*, p. 326.

[2] 'Annals of An Dubhaltach Mac Fir-Bhisigh' in O'Donovan's ed. of the *Four Masters*, IV, 972-3, and cf. Mrs. A. S. Green, *The Old Irish World*, Dublin and London, 1912, chap. III.

crowned king in Dublin in 1487, and Perkin Warbeck royally entertained in Cork. The 'New Monarchy' bore these facts in mind. The national wealth of England had prodigiously increased in the interval, a new arm of warfare had been invented, gunpowder, and increasing experience in the use of artillery, a monopoly of the Crown, portended the doom of the castle and all that it stood for, the remnants of the feudal system. There were no guns in Ireland.

Henry VIII, an opportunist in policy, would have abandoned the medieval practice of keeping English and Irish separate and have united them wholly in one body, whereof he was to be 'the only head under God,'[3] but the 'circumspect and politic ways' he sought to employ were not such as were apt to win the sympathy of the Irish people. In 1534 the circulation of a report, later confirmed, that Garrett Oge, Lord Justice of Ireland and Earl of Kildare, the head of the great family of the Geraldines, who had been summoned to London to answer certain charges of suspicious approximation to the native Irish, had died in the Tower, drove his son 'Silken' Thomas to renounce his allegiance to the King of England and take up arms. The defeat of 'Silken' Thomas was effected by a combination of treachery and the new heavy artillery (23rd March, 1535), and when his stronghold at Maynooth had been destroyed, he and five of his uncles, some of them not concerned in the rebellion, were transported to London and 'attainted.' They were hanged, drawn and quartered at Tyburn on 3rd February, 1537.[4] One surviving child of ten, Gerald Fitzgerald, escaped to France, and, befriended on the Continent by his kinsman, Reginald Pole, *venerabile nomen*, received his education in Italy.[5] The destruction of this ancient house made a profound impression upon the nobles of Ireland.[6]

---

[3] Cf. An Act (28. Hen. VIII, c. 15) for the English Order, Habit and Language (*Irish Statutes*, 1786), I, 119-22.

[4] *Annals of the Four Masters*, V, 1419-45; *Letters and Papers, Henry VIII*, VII, no. 1682 (for the artillery); *State Papers, Henry VIII*, II, 236-7, 402-3, et passim.

[5] For an account of his adventures cf. J. Hogan, *Ireland in the European System*, London, 1920, chap. III.

[6] *Calendar of State Papers, Henry VIII*, II, 339.

§ 2

The religious revolution known as the Reformation first burst on Ireland in 1535, when a royal commission was appointed under the presidency of one George Browne, an apostate Augustinian friar, to persuade the nobility and gentry of the nation to acknowledge Henry VIII as the only Supreme Head on earth of the whole Church of Ireland. It was unsuccessful. George Cromer, Archbishop of Armagh and an Englishman, therefore, in sympathy, withdrew most of his suffragans and clergy. "He made a speech to them laying a curse on the people whosoever should own his Highness's supremacy saying that [this] isle—as it is in their Irish chronicles, 'Insula Sacra'—belongs to none but the Bishop of Rome [who] gave it to the King's ancestors."[7] But a Parliament was summoned in the Pale and various Acts were passed, the Act of the Supreme Head, the Act of Appeals, the Act of the First Fruits, an Act against the Authority of the Bishop of Rome, an Act for the Twentieth Part, an Act for the Suppression of Abbeys (28 *Henry VIII*, cc. 13, 14, 16, etc.), by which Henry became head of the Church. The proctors, who represented the clergy and sat in the Lower House, offered opposition to these measures, and a special Act (28 *Henry VIII*, c. 12) was passed depriving them of their votes. By the Act for the Suppression of Abbeys (1537) fourteen religious houses had been dissolved by name, and by the end of 1541 nearly all the religious houses in English districts had been dissolved, and their property, nominally vested in the king, in practice distributed, as in England and elsewhere as a matter of policy, among the great nobles. Desmond, Thomond, Clanrickarde, O'Neill and O'Donnell, English and Irish alike, all took their share of the spoil, and the citizens of Dublin were rewarded for their fidelity

[7] Cf. Browne's letter to his master Thomas Cromwell (4th December, 1535), printed in Cardinal Moran's *History of the Catholic Archbishops of Dublin*, p. 6. The " 'their' Irish chronicles" is significant. The obvious reference is to 'Laudabiliter'. The description 'Insula Sacra,' of which 'Insula Sanctorum' is merely an expansion, is as old as the Periplus of Himilco (sixth century B.C.) in Avienus, and the title, as Lingard has pointed out, would seem to be merely a case of confused etymology, the ancient name for Ireland having been regarded as cognate with the Greek *hieros* (Latin, *sacer*).

during the rebellion of 'Silken' Thomas by the grant of the Abbey of All Hallows.[8]   The Reformers in Ireland, as elsewhere, "broke down the monasteries and sold their roofs and bells, so that from Aran of the Saints to the Muir nIocht there was not one monastery that was not broken and shattered, with the exception of a few in Ireland, of which the English took no notice or heed.   They afterwards burned the images, shrines, and relics of the saints of Ireland and England; they likewise burned the celebrated image of Mary at Trim, which used to perform wonders and miracles . . . and the staff of Jesus, which was in Dublin, performing miracles, from the time of St. Patrick down to that time, and had been in the hands of Christ while He was among men."[9]   The few monasteries in Ireland of which the English took no notice or heed were without the Pale, and they continued in the exercise of their functions until the reign of James I,[10] but the outrage offered to the feelings of the people by the wanton destruction of objects venerable at the least for their ancient associations provoked riots in which several persons lost their lives.[11]   The state of religion reflected the disorder of the time.   The churches for the most

[8] They conveyed it in 1591 to the Council for the erection of a college of learning "dedicated to the Holy and Undivided Trinity, in which the Irish youth should be taught heresy by English teachers." Cf. in E. Hogan's *Ibernia Ignatiana, etc.* (1540-1607), pp. 36-7, a Latin petition to the Pope from Irish Catholics in exile. The first Chancellor was William Cecil, Lord Burghley, who derived his title from a confiscated nunnery, the first provost Adam Loftus, Protestant Archbishop of Armagh in 1563.

[9] *Annals of the Four Masters* (ed. and tr. O'Donovan), V, 1445-9.

[10] Irishmen, it will be remembered, were legally debarred by the Statute of Kilkenny (ed. Hardiman), XIII, XIV, from being received into English monastic houses in Ireland, and the Irish, not unnaturally, refused to admit Englishmen into theirs.

[11] The *Bachall Isa*, "per quem vulgari opinione sanctus Patricius venenosos ab insula vermes ejecit" (Giraldus Cambrensis, *Top. Hib.*, ed. cit., p. 180) and which St. Patrick was supposed to have received from the hands of Our Lord Himself, makes its first appearance in the ninth century original of Colgan's *Vita* III.   It was translated from Armagh to Dublin in Gerald's time and burned by Browne in 1536 as an object of superstition.   Henry's deputy, Lord Leonard Grey, "rased St. Patrick his church in Down and burned the monuments of Patrick, Brigid, and Colme, who are said to have been entombed there," and this, according to Stanyhurst, "lost him sundry harts in that country, always after detesting and abhorring his profane tyranny, as they did name it."   In Wales "the people looked on in sullen anger while the image of Dervel Gadarn was sacrilegiously torn from its shrine, and the altar of Dewi Sant was stripped for the benefit of a renegade bishop." Cf. *The Making of Modern Wales*, by W. Llewellyn Williams, London, 1919, p. 195.

part, at any rate within the counties of Kilkenny and Tipperary, "where there was like to be no more Christianity
than in the midst of Turkey," were in extreme decay; no
divine service was kept there.[12] In 1516 the cathedral at
Clonmacnoise of all places was reported to the Pope as
roofless; it had but one altar covered with thatch and a
small sacristy. The Cathedral of Ross was in the same
plight.[13] The prelates, being mostly either English or of
English sympathies, neglected their duties, the lower clergy
did not instruct or preach to the people, "saving the poor
friars beggars"; there appears to have been a deficiency of
schools.[14]

Henry VIII had been declared Head of the Irish Church
in 1536; in 1541 a Parliament was summoned in the Pale.
It met on the morrow after Trinity Sunday. The Earls of
Ormonde and Desmond, however, and many other lords of
Munster having not then come, the Solemn Mass of the Holy
Ghost was deferred till the Thursday following, being Corpus
Christi Day. Then one, Sir Thomas Cusack, Sheriff of
Meath, made "a right solemn proposition for the extirpation of the usurped power of the Bishop of Rome, a great
robber and destroyer of the realm, and the King of England
was declared King of Ireland. The whole House most
willingly and joyously consented and agreed to the same."
"The Saturday following, the same Bill was read in . . .
Parliament . . . and on Sunday all the lords and gentlemen
rode to the King's Church of Saint Patrick's, where there
was sung a solemn Mass by the Archbishop of Dublin, and
after the Mass, the said Act proclaimed there in presence of
2000 persons and *Te Deum* sung, with great joy and gladness
to all men." The 'great joy and gladness' were not destined
to endure, and it is probable that the people, apart from the
earls, viscounts, barons, archbishops and bishops, the
deputies assigned by the great O'Brien to be for him in the

[12] Cf. the Earl of Kildare's account of the 'Misdemeanour of the Earl of
Ormonde' (1525), *State Papers, Hen. VIII*, II, 120-3.

[13] Cf. Theiner's *Vetera Monumenta Hibernorum*, pp. 518, 521 and 529. The
annual incomes of some, perhaps most, of the sees were miserable. Of Ardagh,
e.g. 10 ducats; in 1674 the income of Cashel was £20, that of Waterford £30.

[14] Cf. *State Papers, Hen. VIII* (1534), II, passim.

Parliament, the great O'Reilly, the many other Irish captains, divers knights, and gentlemen of fair possessions who graced the notable assembly and took part in the revels, "great bonfires, wine set in the streets, great feastings in their houses with a goodly sort of guns,"[15] were unaware of what had taken place. They were soon to learn.

§ 3

Henry died on 28th January, 1547, and was succeeded by Edward VI (1547-53), the son of Jane Seymour, a sickly lad fostered in Zwinglianism. Under the Seymours the breach in discipline widened into a schism in dogma, and heresy, pure and simple, was established. The first Act of the new king's Parliament (1 *Edw. VI.*, c. 1) ordered the Sacrament of the altar to be administered in both kinds. In the following year (1548) the marriage of the clergy was declared lawful (2 and 3 *Edw. VI*, c. 21), but the new Communion Service, which had been devised to supersede the Mass, and the First and Second Prayer Books, composed in 1549 and 1552 respectively by Cranmer with the help of some French and Italian sectaries, and the new Creed of 42 Articles, the parents of the present 39, were deliberately not translated into Irish. The object of this singular omission was to compel the people to learn English; in practice it preserved them from being infected by the new doctrines.[16] Protestant bishops were established only where the English Government could protect them, and, as it was considered too dangerous to summon a parliament, the English liturgy was ordered by royal proclamation, and on Easter Day, 1551, read for the first time in Christ Church, Dublin. George Dowdall (1487-1558), Archbishop of Armagh and the successor of Cromer in the primacy of Ireland, vigorously

[15] Cf. Sir Anthony St. Leger, Lord Deputy to the King (26th June, 1541), *State Papers, Henry VIII*, III, 304-5.

[16] The first printing-press established in Ireland was not set up until 1561. The first printed book published in Ireland by one Humphrey Powell was *The Booke of the Common Prayer*. The first prayer book printed in Welsh appeared in 1567 and was followed in the same year by a New Testament, but it was not until 1630 that a vernacular Welsh Bible became available for the people and then at the expense of laymen.

opposed the king's command and energetically asserted the rights of the Church. He was deprived of his primacy for his pains. One, Hugh Goodacre, an English parson described as 'a wise and well-learned man,' was appointed by Cranmer to the see of Armagh (28th October, 1552); Dublin was bestowed on the eager Browne, and the wretched Dowdall, unable to stomach the affront, retired for a spell of voluntary exile to Brabant. A rebellion in Leinster, the countries of the O'Mores, O'Dempsies, O'Connors and others of the Irishry, led to a reduction of the districts called Leix and Offaly, which in the next reign were made shireland by the names of King's and Queen's County, appellations since happily abandoned; but the principles of the Reformation were neither established by law nor made any progress in the country.

The accession of Mary (1553-8) reversed, of course, what had been done, without, however, restoring any of the abbey lands to their original proprietors. The expectation of justice, if pitched too high in this world, is apt to be disappointed. Tranquillity was restored in ecclesiastical matters. Dowdall, re-established in his primacy, was promoted to the dignity of an Irish Privy Councillor, those of the clergy who had taken wives were ejected, and such of the persecuted Protestants as had fled for refuge to Ireland from the fires of Smithfield during the few short years of that unhappy woman's reign found shelter and were unmolested. In an age remarkable for the virulence of religious fanaticism Catholic Ireland thus offered the earliest example of that religious toleration which later distinguished the Catholic province of Maryland, founded as an asylum for refugees of any Christian denomination by Cecil Calvert, second Lord Baltimore, in 1634.[17]

The reign of Mary also saw one of the rare acts of restitution of confiscated property in the long story of English spoliation in Ireland, and the surviving Geraldine, through the interest of his patron Cardinal Pole, had his lands restored to him.

[17] The Maryland Assembly passed a Toleration Act in 1649 under which no man might be molested for his religious opinions, provided he were a Christian. During the Commonwealth the Puritans gained the upper hand and promptly proceeded to persecute everybody not one of the Saints.

Mary was succeeded by the Princess Elizabeth (1558-1603), the daughter of Henry VIII and Anne Boleyn, and the first care of her Government was to restore the constitution and liturgy of the Church by law established to nearly the same state as they had been left in by Edward VI at his death.

The same successive steps were taken in Ireland as in England. The Act of Supremacy (1559) revived the laws which had established the ecclesiastical supremacy of the Crown and offered the clergy the alternative of taking the prescribed Oath of Supremacy and Allegiance or being deposed from office.[18] The Act of Uniformity (1 *Eliz.*, *c.* 2) prescribed the use in Divine Service and in the administration of the Sacraments of the revised Book of Common Prayer, and punished all persons absenting themselves without lawful or reasonable excuse from their parish church on Sundays or holidays by ecclesiastical censures and a fine. These statutes were re-enacted in nearly the same words in Ireland, but no attempt was made to hold services in Irish or to preach in the language of the people. It was laid down instead that in districts where English was not spoken, and the minister had no knowledge of Irish, he might read the service in Latin. Everybody was bound under the same penalties to attend the Protestant Church and any other form of worship was prohibited ('Irish Statutes,' 2 *Eliz.*).

In 1567 Shane O'Neill of Tír Eoghain, who had defied all the attempts of the English to poison him, was hacked to death in the camp of the Scotch, with whom he had taken refuge, at the instance of an Englishman, Captain William Piers, "by whose devise this stratagem or rather tragedie was practised."[19] The territories which acknowledged Shane

[18] A cloud of obscurity hangs over the situation, but at the end of Henry VIII's reign, there were apparently at least 21 bishops who accepted the king's supremacy, and only some three or four who rejected it. For the rest, not half-a-dozen, there is no information. Cf. *The Reformation in Dublin* (1536-55), by Myles V. Ronan, London, 1926. 'Bloody' Mary continued to style herself 'Queen of England, France and Ireland, Defender of the Faith, and on earth Supreme Head of the Churches of England and Ireland,' *Calendar of Carew, MSS.*, III, xxi.

[19] Shane's head, "pickled in a pipkin," was sent to Sir Henry Sidney for the reward offered. It was stuck on a pole over Dublin Castle and there seen by

as suzerain, a large part of Down and Antrim, were forfeited to the Crown, and a natural son of Sir Thomas Smith, Secretary of State, was sent with a body of English to take possession of the district known as the Ards. He was attacked by the O'Neills of Claneboy in 1572 and lost his life.

'Silken' Thomas in his rebellion had boldly invoked the name of the Pope; now James Fitzmaurice, who, apprehensive of a government encroachment upon the power of the Desmonds in Munster, after plundering and burning Kilmallock in 1570, "not from a desire of its riches and various treasures, though its riches were immense, but because it had always been the rendezvous and sally-port of the English and Geraldines against him,"[20] had escaped to the Continent, made his way to Rome, and there professing the constant fidelity of Ireland to the Holy See, gained the sympathetic ear of Gregory XIII. The Pope interested himself in the cause and commissioned one of the most astonishing of the many astonishing adventurers of the Tudor era, who was hanging round his Court, to fit out a ship with men and munitions. This Sir Thomas Stuckley,[21] a reputed son of Henry VIII, a former slave trader, whose piracies on the high seas had made the English ambassador at Madrid 'hang his head for shame,' accepted 40,000 scudi from the Pope and on 4th March, 1577, set sail from Civitavecchia. On his way north he sold himself again to Sebastian, King of Portugal, then at war with the Moors, led his little force of

Campion in 1571. His character has been painted in the darkest colours by his enemies, as of a man gluttonous, licentious and only intermittently sober; but Campion, no friend of the Irish, remarking that the English courtiers, "noting his haughtiness and barbarity" (they, of course being paragons of modesty and refinement), devised his style thus: "O'Neill the Great, cousin to St. Patrick, friend to the Queen of England, enemy to all the world besides," also records that he "ordered the North so properly, that if any subject could approve the loss of money or goods within his precinct, he would assuredly either force the robber to restitution, or of his own cost redeem the harm to the loser's contention. . . . But the lords of Ulster and elsewhere, whom he yoked and spoiled at pleasure, abhorring his pride and extortion, craved assistance from the Deputy," etc. Cf. *History of Ireland* (ed. Ware, 1633), chap. x, and *Four Masters*, V, 1555.

[20] *Annals of the Four Masters*, V, 1653-5.

[21] He called himself 'Duke of Ireland' and enjoyed great credit at Rome under St. Pius V, perhaps because he had commanded three galleys at Lepanto (7th October, 1571) and acquitted himself with valour in that memorable fight. Cf. the index of *Calendar of State Papers from the Archives of Simancas* (1568-79).

six hundred men into battle at Alcazar, and on 4th August, 1578, along with his master, fell. Next year Fitzmaurice had collected an army and landed in Kerry, where he was joined later by seven hundred Italian and Spanish infantrymen with arms for five thousand volunteers, if so many should be forthcoming. He issued a proclamation that the war was undertaken "for the defence of the Catholic religion against the heretics . . . not against the lawful sceptre and honourable throne of England, but against a tyrant which refuseth to hear Christ speaking by His vicar,"[22] and set up a little fort 'ad Sanctae Mariae vicum [Smerwick] (Smerivic contracte vocant Hibernici).' On 11th November, 1579, "the fifth day, as they saw no succour coming from Spain and from Desmond, they raised the white flag and begged for a parley. This was refused. . . . The Deputy [Lord Grey], bitterly railing against the Pope of Rome, bade them surrender themselves without condition. And as they could obtain no other terms, they raised the white flag for the second time, crying 'misericordia, misericordia,' and delivered themselves over to the Deputy, who there and then consulted his officers what should be done with them . . . this was their conclusion (against the will of the Deputy, who wept thereat) that the leaders should be saved and all the rest put to the sword for an example [*in terrorem*] and that the Irish should be hanged; which was presently done. The Queen was vexed thereat. . . ."[23]

The English punished the rebellion in Munster with fearful cruelty and harried the whole province in a series of horrible campaigns, men and women being driven into barns and there burned. A dreadful famine ensued and "out of every corner of the woods and glens]the inhabitants] came creeping forth upon their hands, for their legs could not bear them; they looked like anatomies of death, they spake like ghosts crying out of their graves; they did eat of the dead carrions, happy were they if they could find them, yea . . .

[22] Cf. the text of the Proclamation in the *Calendar of the Carew Manuscripts*, eds. J. S. Brewer and W. Bullen, I, 400, and for a note on this collection by the Provost of Eton, *The English Historical Review*, 1927, pp. 261-7.

[23] Camden, *Annales rerum Anglicarum et Hibernicarum . . . ad annum salutis*, 1589, London, 1615, pp. 293-6.

and if they found a plot of watercresses or shamrocks, there they flocked as to a feast for the time, yet not able long to continue there withal; that in short space there were none almost left, and a most populous and plentiful country suddenly made void of man and beast."[24] Half a million acres of the most fertile soil in Ireland were confiscated and English settlers solicited to 'plant' in companies, in order not to sever too completely the ties which bound them to their native land. Parcels called seignories were apportioned among these gentlemen undertakers, it being provided that none should 'undertake' for himself a greater portion than 12,000 acres. Names famous in English history gave a shoddy lustre to the roll of those engaged in the unsavoury adventure. Sir Walter Raleigh obtained some 40,000 acres[25] in Waterford, Cork and Tipperary; Sir Christopher Hatton, a former Lord Chancellor, 11,000 in Waterford; Edmund Spenser, that effeminate little man, 3,028 acres in County Cork, including the old Desmond Castle of Kilcolman, where he wrote a portion of the *Faerie Queene*. There were others: Norris, Bourcher, Cuffe, Barkley and Courtney. Of some thirty undertakers, however, "only thirteen inhabited their properties in 1592 and they had only planted 245 English families on their lands."[26]

It would have been impossible in a half-conquered country to execute the penal laws in their full rigour, and Elizabeth herself, from motives of prudence, was disposed to be tolerant in matters of religion. It was not thought convenient that

[24] Edmund Spenser, *View of the Present State of Ireland*, *Works* (Globe ed.), p. 654. With this famous passage cp. the account of John Hooker (1526-1601) in the Epistle dedicatory to Sir W. Raleigh of the translation of Giraldus Cambrensis added by him to the second edition (1586-7), partly edited by him, of Raphael Holinshed's *Chronicles*. Hooker had been solicitor in Ireland to a ravenous adventurer from Devon, one Sir Peter Carew. The passage occurs on p. 104 of Vol. VI of the *Chronicles*, London, 1808.

[25] He sold the lot for £1,500 English to Sir Richard Boyle, the First and Great Earl of Cork, a typical adventurer, who, landing in Dublin penniless in 1588, twelve years later owned more land than anyone else in Ireland.

[26] Cf. W. F. T. Butler, *Confiscation in Irish History*, Dublin and London, 1917, p. 30. Sir William Herbert, another undertaker, was at least candid in his confession to Burghley, 20th October, 1588: "Our pretence . . . was to establish in these parts piety, justice, inhabitation and civility, with comfort and good example to the parts adjacent. Our drift now is, being here possessed of land, to extort, make the state of things turbulent and live by prey and by pay" (*Calendar of State Papers, Ireland*, p. 62).

'the gentlemen of the Pale' should be brought to compulsion against their conscience touching the refusal of the Oath of Supremacy, and the time was considered not ripe for severity.[27] The recusant Catholics of England flocked over to Ireland on the pretext of 'undertaking' Irish land and were left undisturbed in their refuge.[28] The situation changed when the Pope, St. Pius V, promulgated in 1570 his Bull, *Regnans in Excelsis*, against the Queen of England, released her subjects from their oath of allegiance, and invited the Catholic Sovereigns of Europe to unite in deposing her. The Catholic Sovereigns refused.

Elizabeth resumed the persecution. One of the first victims of the new temper was Padraig Ua Heilighe, whom the English called O'Hely. He was a Franciscan who had been appointed to the see of Mayo by Pope Gregory XIII in 1576. He sailed for Ireland in the same ship which bore Fitzmaurice, and landing in Kerry was hospitably received by the Countess of Desmond. Sped on his way to Limerick, he had no sooner reached the town than he was arrested by the English, duly apprised of his coming by the Countess, and taken to Kilmallock, where he was summarily tried, condemned, and forthwith hanged on 22nd August, 1578. Ua Heilighe was followed to the gallows by Diarmid Ua Hurthuile, whom the English called O'Hurley. He was a layman, 'the son of a gentleman,' who, after taking his degree in both the laws at Louvain and teaching for some years in Rheims, repaired to Rome, took Holy Orders, and at the age of sixty-two was appointed by the same Pope to the See of Cashel. He was arrested at Carrick-on-Suir in September 1583, whilst staying with Thomas Butler, Earl of Ormonde, and brought to Dublin. His papers had been captured by pirates on the voyage to Ireland and the English were thus fully apprised of his intentions. He refused to give any information and at Walsingham's suggestion was tortured. "His feet and legs were encased in top-boots . . . filled with a mixture of salt, bitumen, oil, tallow, pitch and

---

[27] Cf. Brady's *State Papers concerning the Irish Church*, Walsingham to the 'Archbishop' of Armagh (December, 1585), pp. 102-3, and *Calendar of State Papers (Ireland)*, March-October 1600, p. 274.

[28] Cf. *C.S.P., Ireland*, 1588-92, p. 494, et passim.

boiling water. The legs so booted were placed on iron bars, and horribly and cruelly roasted over a fire for a whole hour." He bore this excruciating ordeal with incredible patience and heroism, and, torture having failed, was brought back to prison. A little later they took him out again and hanged him 'for greater ignominy' with a halter made of plaited osiers before sunrise on 7th June, 1584.[29]

Grey was succeeded as Deputy by Sir John Perrott (1584-7), a natural son of Henry VIII. As Lord President of Munster, he had repressed disorder and enforced English laws by appointing sheriffs and hanging or killing some eight hundred rebels in the province, but he seems to have earned some respect in Ireland, in spite of the severity of his ordinances, for his departure was "lamented by the poor, the feeble, and the unwarlike of the country."[30] He warred in Ulster against the Scotch from the Hebrides, the MacDonnels of the Isles, and forced Somhairle Buidhe, whom he had failed to have assassinated, to renounce all his pretended right to the Castle of Dunluce, and to behave dutifully to her English Majesty in return for a free pardon, protection, letters patent of denization, and certain grants of land. But he was undone by a Court intrigue at home and sailed for England in July 1588, leaving behind him a memory, as the poet Spenser wailed, "of so hard usage and haughty demeanour among his associates especially of the English nation as never any before him had done." On his return, Perrot was incarcerated in the Tower, where he died in 1592.

The character of the struggle now began to change. England had become Protestant, Ireland and the Anglo-Norman families in the Pale remained Catholic, and the Pope was finally at issue with Elizabeth and English nationalism. The Catholic Church in Ireland and Wales, as later in Poland, became bound up, as never before, with the national cause. Protestantism in Ireland and Wales was an

[29] Cf. *Historiae Catholicae Iberniae Compendium*, by Philip O'Sullivan Beare (Lisbon, 1621), II, IV, c. 19, pt. translated by M. Byrne, *Ireland under Elizabeth*, Dublin, 1903, and the preface, pp. xiii-xlvi, to Cardinal Moran's edition (1884) of Dr. Rothe's *Analecta Sacra*, Cologne, 1617-19. *Ne obliviscatur.*
[30] *Four Masters*, V, 1665.

English, and therefore alien, innovation, importing strange doctrines and strange laws inculcated and administered by profligate and needy adventurers, unmindful of the traditions of the peoples they oppressed, unconcerned for their future, anxious only to enjoy and secure the plunder of the present. In Wales Catholicism, untended by Rome, simply withered, as the practice of religion ceased and the knowledge of it grew fainter with each succeeding generation; the heroic efforts of the Welsh priests to nourish the flickering flame of the faith through torture and imprisonment and martyrdom were gradually forgotten or credited to the general history of English Catholicism.[31] In Ireland the war in which the Tudor brigands engaged was transformed with the change in religion from an ordinary war of conquest, such as may be waged anywhere at any time on any pretext, into a holy war against Rome and Antichrist—a naked war of extirpation systematically waged, with all the fervour of fanaticism and all possible horror, against a nation which had the misfortune to possess land which its enemies coveted and was guilty of the crime of clinging to its own civilization and preferring the faith of its fathers.

Aodh Ó Néill, Prince of Tír-Eoghain, known to the English as Hugh, Earl of Tyrone, was formally declared a traitor in June 1595. He collected a force and in August 1598 destroyed some English troops under the command of his brother-in-law, Marshal Bagnal, at the Battle of the Yellow Ford, near Armagh. Ó Néill did not pursue his victory, and on 15th April, 1599, Robert Devereux, Earl of Essex, landed in Dublin with 18,000 men. He marched south, fought no battle because none was offered him, lost two-thirds of his army through disease, patched up a truce with Tyrone, and hurried back to England where ruin awaited him. He was succeeded by Sir Charles Blount, Lord Mountjoy.

In 1601 the Spaniards, who had been at regular war with the English for thirteen years, sent a belated force 5,000 strong under Don Juan del Aquila,[32] which landed at

[31] But cf. now The Catholic Martyrs of Wales, 1535-1680, by T. P. Ellis, London, 1933.
[32] For his proclamation which refers also to the Bull of St. Pius V cf. Stafford's Pacata Hibernia (1633), which would appear to have been written by Sir

Kinsale in September 1601, and was promptly invested by
Mountjoy both by land and sea. All through the autumn
and winter it was beseiged by the English, of whom a captain
of horse, a certain Oliver St. John, who, having killed his
man at home, had been forced to flee to Flanders, particularly
distinguished himself. Tyrone and O'Donnell marched
south to the relief of the Irish, against whom Tyrone had
fought during the rebellion in Munster, and surrounded the
English army. The Irish plan of attack on the night of 24th
December is alleged by some to have been betrayed by
Brian Oge MacMahon of Monaghan, and they were defeated
with heavy loss, the English "being tired with killing."
Those of the Irish that were taken prisoners, though they
offered ransom, were all hanged. On 2nd January, 1602, del
Aquila capitulated. O'Donnell fled to Spain, died of poison
at Simancas (1602) and was buried with great honour at
Valladolid; Tyrone returned to Ulster. The war was over.
The English were under no illusion as to the issues at stake
in the seige of Kinsale: "the honour and safety of Queen
Elizabeth, the reputation of the English nation, the cause of
religion, and the Crown of Ireland." Its successful resistance
portended the doom of the old Irish world. On 30th March,
1603, Tyrone, 'the tennis-ball of fortune,' made his penitent
submission to her Majesty's Lord Deputy Mountjoy at
Mellifont. Elizabeth had been dead for a week.

The state of the country after the conquest beggars description. The English, "using all means to famish them,"
destroyed and reaped the ripe and unripe crops with many
scythes and sickles, and carried away or burnt all the stores
of victuals in secret places, whither the rebels had conveyed
them, "and the consequence of this was that the inhabitants
fled";[33] famine followed, and starvation, so that "no spectacle
was more frequent in the ditches of towns, and especially in
wasted countries, than to see multitudes of these poor people
dead, with their mouths all coloured green by eating nettles,

George Carew, the father of Stafford, II, XII, 200-2, ed. O'Grady, Dublin, two
vols., 1896. The expedition was accompanied by Matthew de Oviedo, a
Spanish Franciscan, who acted as the chief intermediary between the Court of
Spain and the Irish Princes, and ultimately became Archbishop of Dublin.

[33] *Four Masters*, VI, 2179, 2187.

docks and all things they could rend above ground."[34] The
wolves came out of the woods and down from the mountains
and tore to pieces those whom hunger had disabled from
protecting themselves.[35] At the end of the reign "the area
of actual confiscation and colonization extended to about
half Queen's County, one-third of King's County, large and
scattered estates in Connacht, Leinster, Tipperary and
Clare. On paper there had been a great confiscation in
Ulster. . . ."[36]

§ 4

Elizabeth was succeeded by the son of Mary Stuart,
James I of England and VI of Scotland, a cowardly pedant
detested by the English because he was Scotch, but imposed
upon the nation by the will of Robert Cecil. His reign
opened in Ireland auspiciously. An Act of Oblivion was
passed, all offences against the Crown were pardoned and
all the Irishry were received into his Majesty's immediate
protection. The 'Flight of the Earls' changed the entire
situation.[37] On 14th September, 1607, Tyrone, Tyrconnel,
their wives and retainers, some ninety-nine persons in all,
"having little sea-store and being otherwise miserably accommodated," sailed at midnight from Rathmullan, "a town on
the west side of Lough Swilly." Abandoning a country which
they saw they no longer had the power to maintain, they left
it by their withdrawal completely at the mercy of King
James and his advisers. While they were received everywhere on the Continent, not as a "company of gypsies," as
Davis said they would be, but with honour, and ultimately

[34] Fynes Moryson, *Itinerary* (1617), II, III, 272; Glasgow, four vols., 1907-8.
This worthy was Mountjoy's secretary and thought it marvellous that "by
so barbarous inhabitants the ground should be so manured, the fields so
orderly fenced, the towns so frequently inhabited, and the highways and paths
so well beaten. . . . The reason whereof was that the Queen's forces during these
wars never till then came among them."
[35] O'Sullivan Beare, *Historiae Catholicae Compendium*, III, VIII, chap. 6.
[36] Butler, op. cit., p. 64.
[37] Cf. for the English official account, Sir John Davis to Salisbury (12th
September, 1607), *Caldendar of State Papers (Ireland)*, pp. 270-4; *Four Masters*,
VI, 2535-9; and the account of Tadhg Ó Cianáin (ed. and tr. Fr. Paul Walsh)
in *Archivium Hibernicum* (Catholic Record Soc. of Ireland), 1916, V.

found a refuge in Rome and are buried there in the Spanish Church of S. Pietro in Montorio, in Ireland they had left open a door "to bring in colonies of the English to plant both countries, to a great increase of His Majesty's revenues, and to settle the countries perpetually in the Crown, and besides to recompense many well-deserving servitors in the distribution."[38] The immediate consequence of the Flight of the Earls was a new confiscation sweeping in character and far-reaching in result—the Plantation of Ulster.

The formal process of Anglicization was carried on under James with the political and judicial organization of the country on English lines. Sheriffs were everywhere appointed, territorial divisions introduced, old customs determined by new judges of assize to be void, estates surrendered to, and received back from, the Crown, to be held thenceforth by some form of English legal tenure.

The six counties of Donegal, Tyrone, Armagh, Coleraine, Fermanagh, and Cavan were now confiscated and a series of three commissions was appointed to survey the land and determine the allotment to be made to each of the undertakers.[39] From a sense of the danger involved in granting any considerable area to any single person a division was made into parcels of 2,000, 1,500 and 1,000 English acres respectively and these offered to English and Scotch planters on condition (*inter alia*) that they built strong castles, took the Oath of Supremacy, and paid a fixed rent according to the size of their holdings. The City of London, invited to plant, at first received the invitation coldly, but its cupidity having been aroused by the attractions set forth in the Government prospectus, dispatched four agents to spy out the land. These returned with such glowing accounts that the City warmed to the enterprise and a company, later

[38] Cf. Fenton to Salisbury in *Calendar of State Papers (Ireland)*, 1608-10, p. liv. This Fenton had landed in Ireland in 1579 as penniless as his fellow-adventurer Boyle, to whom he gave both his daughter in marriage and notable assistance in his extortions. He was described as "a most apparent bribe-taker" and accumulated a very large fortune in a very short time.

[39] Cf. *Die englische Kolonisation in Irland* by M. J. Bonn. The eminent Jewish economist, writing in German, has concisely expressed the situation of the Irish under the Tudors and Stuarts: "Der Ire war sache, nichts mehr." For an account in English, cf. Butler's op. cit., the *State Papers (Ireland)*, pp. 409-10 and for Bacon's views, his *Life and Letters*, ed. Spedding, IV, 116-28, 205-7.

known as 'The Irish Society,' was formed to plant the modern county of Londonderry, part of Tyrone and adjoining districts in Donegal and Antrim, a little more than half a million acres.[40] They obtained more land, like everybody else, than they had originally bargained for, and by selling the timber of the woods, and retaining, in breach of their agreement, the Irish to work for them, became exceedingly prosperous. The rank and file of the planters were "able-bodied men, eighteen years old or upwards, born in England or the inland parts of Scotland," and if not "generally the scum of both nations," as one Steward (*c.* 1645-71), the son of a minister who came over to attend to the spiritual needs of such pious immigrants, described them, were, it may not unreasonably be assumed, not the most desirable elements of either. A backbone to the enterprise was provided by the lowland Scotch. They are reported to have been more frugal and industrious than their English neighbours; they brought with them the solidarity of their Presbyterian organization and impressed the settlement with the characteristics it still retains—an odd survival from the seventeenth century in a very changed world.

Some of the native Irish remained on to labour for their new English landlords, others, 'the swordmen,' were embarked and transported to Sweden to fight for Charles IX; others again drifted to Connacht, the remainder took to the woods as outlaws and preyed upon the settlers, until their last hope of regaining their lands was extinguished in 1690.

The Plantation of Ulster, it was observed, had far-reaching consequences. It cost Charles I, the son of its promoter, his head, and his grandson, James II his throne. The end is not yet.

In 1616 Oliver St. John, the victor of Kinsale, who, in 1608, had been one of the commissioners for the plantation of Ulster and himself undertook 1,500 acres in Ballymore, Co. Armagh, and another 1,000 in a place unidentified as 'Keernan,' was, through the interest of George Villiers,

---

[40] The total number of acres distributed in the six counties was about 100,000 less than 4,000,000. Cf. Bonn, op. cit., I, 324,335. The Irish who remained on were accommodated with 52,479 acres. Ibid., 331.

Duke of Buckingham, himself a planter in Upper Ossory, appointed Lord Deputy. He issued a proclamation[41] ordering all monks and friars educated abroad to quit the realm and committed the magistrates and chief citizens of Dublin to prison for refusing to attend the Protestant Church. The plantation of Longford in 1618 was followed by that of Leitrim, and the small landowners who protested found themselves transported to the new colony which had been founded in Virginia. St. John's remedy for the discontent in the island was to deport a hundred thousand native Irishmen for enlistment in foreign countries, but before this amiable project could be realized, he was recalled. His eminent services earned him a peerage and he became the first Viscount Grandison of Limerick in the peerage of Ireland.

He was succeeded by Sir Henry Cary, first Lord Falkland (1622-9), another nominee of Buckingham's. Bigoted in opinion and timid in practice, wavering constantly between two extremes, Falkland was at last spurred to action by the frenzied zeal of the learned Ussher, "that great luminary of the Irish [sic] Church," and issued yet another proclamation (21st January, 1623) banishing all priests from Ireland. This measure was at the least inexpedient while the negotiations for the Spanish marriage of the Prince Charles were still in being, and the Deputy was ordered to refrain from any more active steps than preventing the erection of religious houses and the congregation of 'illegal assemblies.' He it was who first laid before the nobles of Ireland the draft of certain concessions, later known as 'graces,' which Charles I promised to bestow in return for a contribution of £120,000 by equal payments spread over three years. His design to carry out further confiscations in Wicklow by trumping up charges against the O'Byrnes was frustrated as the result of

[41] The President and Council of Munster had issued a proclamation in 1604 (*Archiv. Hib.*, *C.R.S. of Ireland* (1914), III, 251-2) banishing all Jesuits, priests, and seminarists before the end of September of the following year. It had no effect. The Brussels Internuncio, Mgr. Bentivoglio, reporting to the Holy See on 6th April, 1613, remarked that greater learning and acquirements were desirable in many of the secular clergy, the best of whom were educated abroad, that there was a sufficiency of priests and that the English penal laws were not enforced (Ibid., 300). A different picture is painted three years later in the Memorial presented to Philip III by an Irish priest on behalf of the Irish Catholics (Ibid., 1917, VI, 48-54).

THE MARTYRDOM OF IRELAND

a Privy Council inquiry. The evidence alleged was found to be perjured. Falkland was excused on the pretext that his services were required in England, handed over his authority to the Lords Justices and on 10th August, 1629, took his departure.

In 1633 Thomas Wentworth, Earl of Strafford, the 'Black Tom Tyrant' of Irish tradition, landed in Ireland, and proceeded to coerce the country as it had never been coerced before. His motto was 'Thorough' and he did his best to live up to it. Strafford's letters[42] contain the best exposition of his policy. A conformity in religion, he explained to his master, was above all things principally to be intended, but it were too much to distemper the natives by bringing plantations upon them and disturbing them in the exercise of their religion, so long as it might be without scandal. Inspired by such Machiavellian conceptions of government, the new Deputy began his administration by reforming the Protestant Church. It had been established for less than a hundred years and its ministers, grown rich on the embezzled patrimony of the confiscated Catholic churches, were dissolute and ignorant, as careless to teach in a language which they did not want to learn as the people were predetermined not to listen to what they did not want to understand.[43]

[42] *Letters and correspondence*, ed. Knowles, 2 vols. London, 1739.
[43] In a much-quoted letter to Queen Elizabeth (28th April, 1576), Sir Henry Sydney, the Lord Deputy, reported that he had been "advertised" by the learned Bishop of Meath, one "Mr. Hugh Brady, a godly minister for the Gospel," who had succeeded the Catholic Bishop Walsh, a Cistercian who died at Alcalá in 1577, that out of 224 parish churches in his diocese 105 were impropriated . . . "no person or vicar resident upon any of them." Of the "simple or sorry" curates appointed to serve them, "only 18 were found able to speak English; the rest, Irish priests, or rather Irish rogues, having very little Latin, less learning, or civility. All these . . . were wont to live upon the gain of masses, dirges, shrivings and such like trumpery, goodly abolished by your Majesty, no one house standing for any of them to dwell in. . . ." A Collins, *Letters and Memorials of State* (1746), I, 112-3. Sir John Davis in a letter to Cecil (20th February, 1604) reported that the English churchmen for the most part could not read, even "if they should stand in need of the benefit of their clergy. . . . But for an example of pluralities, the Archbishop of Cashel is worthy to be remembered, having now in his hands four bishoprics, Cashel, Waterford, Lismore and Emly, and three score and seventeen spiritual livings besides. . . . The churches are ruined and fallen down. . . . There is no divine service, no christening of children, no receiving of the Sacrament, no Christian meeting or assembly, no, not once in a year; in a word, no more demonstration of religion than amongst Tartars or cannibals." *Calendar of S.P., Ireland*, p. 143. The first Protestant bishop of Derry, George Montgomery, who had received a rectory in Somersetshire from Queen Elizabeth and had been

He forced it to accept the Articles of the Church of England in place of a table of Calvinistic propositions drawn up by Ussher, and set himself to suppress the unpleasing Puritan practices which the Ulster settlers had imported from their native lowlands of Scotland. He conceived schemes for re-opening commerce with Spain, stimulated the growth and cultivation of flax, and encouraged industry with the object, however, of holding the Irish dependent upon the Crown "and not able to subsist without us." The manufacture of wools into cloth or stuff in Ireland was to be wholly laid aside, and the King of England made sole merchant of all salts in Ireland, so as to make the Irish dependent on England for their clothing, the improvement of all their native commodities, principally preserved by salt, and their victual itself. These measures their ingenious author held to be "strong ties and enforcements"[44] upon the allegiance of those who were the victims of them and secure safeguards of their obedience to His Majesty.

In pursuit of his objects Strafford determined to extend the plantation policy of the late reign to the western counties. Connacht was still free from the intrusion of English colonists, and the Irish there had complied with the usual conditions of surrendering their estates to the Crown to receive them back by a legal tenure, and paid large fees (£3,000) for this security. The grants, however, were not enrolled in Chancery, and the Council were not ashamed to propose, or the King to adopt, a scheme of declaring the whole country forfeited.

promoted later Dean of Norwich, held two other bishoprics as well, Clogher and Raphoe. He was ultimately appointed to Meath. In Wales, the degradation of the people after the Reformation was, if possible, even worse. Rome failed to fill vacant sees or to provide an ecclesiastical organisation. The Welsh had no friars to sustain their spiritual life, nobody to instruct them. They could not, for the most part, read their own language and they understood no English. As time went on, their condition steadily deteriorated and in 1631 it was reported that not a soul was to be seen in summer, "when the roads were driest and the weather mildest," in any one of the forty or sixty churches in every diocese in Wales. The 'hot gospellers' of Nonconformity, mostly simple enthusiasts, tinkers, tailors, shoemakers and labourers, took the redemption of their fellow-countrymen in hand, with the result that Wales to-day is as strongly evangelical as it was once fervently Catholic.

[44] Letter of 16th July, 1633, quoted in Mrs. Green's *The Making of Ireland and its Undoing*, London, 1908, p. 150. Cf. also C. Gill, *The Rise of the Irish Linen Industry*, Oxford, 1925.

Strafford went to Connacht in 1635. He proceeded to hold
an inquisition in each county and intimidated the jury into
finding upon such evidence as was laid before them a king's
title to all the lands. Only in Galway a jury showed some
spirit and refused. They and their sheriff were summoned
to Dublin. Each of the jurymen was fined £4,000, the
sheriff £1,000; all were forced to do penance on their knees
in open court for their temerity and imprisoned until the
fines were paid. The sheriff died in prison.

Strafford was recalled in 1640 and the administration of
the country entrusted to the Lords Justices Parsons and
Borlase, whose only object would appear to have been to
make peace impossible so that there should be plenty of
forfeited estates. The smouldering embers of disaffection,
fanned by the penal laws against recusants, which oppressed
the whole people, and the inquisition into titles, a systematic
iniquity which despoiled them of their possessions, burst
into a fire of revolt, the Great Rebellion of 1641. Confined
at first to Ulster, the flames rapidly spread and soon the
whole island was ablaze. The rebels repossessed themselves
of the lands from which they had been expropriated and the
planters were everywhere turned out of their homes. Large
numbers perished from cold, hunger and ill-treatment, but,
contrary to the reports which poured into England, there
was no general massacre. Excesses were committed—it
would have been a marvel had it been otherwise—but there
were also—what is happily for the honour of human nature,
never at any time an exhilarating object of contemplation,
not uncommon even in the most savage of civil wars—signal
examples of charity. Certain priests are recorded to have
concealed Protestant fugitives below their altars, and the
house in Cavan of Bishop Bedell, one of the few Protestant
prelates to earn the esteem of the Irish by his sympathy
and moderation, became an asylum of refuge for the
persecuted and was unmolested. As the rebellion grew
in strength, its character changed. It had ceased to be
a sudden outburst of wrath and became a war directed by
soldiers with the support of a nation eager to retrieve
centuries of wrong.

Charles, absent in Scotland at the time, wrote to his Parliament (8th April, 1642) that he would put himself at the head of an army and go into Ireland to suppress the rising, but the Parliament, mistrustful of the king's intentions, were determined to keep the conduct of operations in their own hands. They passed an Adventurers' Act, soliciting subscriptions wherewith to finance a private army and offering as security 2,500,000 acres of nationally forfeited Irish land. The original adventurers numbered 1,360 and included Oliver Cromwell, John Hampden, and Cromwell's nurse and servant, Elizabeth Austey. They subscribed a little over £43,000, of which the considerable sum of £200 was contributed by Mrs. Austey. The expeditionary force of the Adventurers, some 5,000 foot and 400 horse, recruited mainly in London, had mustered in Bristol ready to take ship for Munster, when, on 22nd August, 1642, Charles I unfurled his standard at Nottingham. It wheeled round and marched instead to Edgehill (23rd October).

In Ireland five[45] parties had taken the field: two Catholic, the old Irish and the Anglo-Irish, two Protestant, one Royalist, the other Puritan and Parliamentarian, the fifth Scotch Presbyterian, reinforced by some 10,000 of their covenanting brethren from Scotland, under the command of the savage Monroe. Owen Roe O'Neill, Don Eugenio,[46] a nephew of Tyrone, came over from Spain to lead the rebels, Irish 'swordmen' returned from France, and Richelieu meditated armed intervention. The Irish Parliament, known as the Confederation of Kilkenny (1642), established a regular government, got an army into the field in each of the four provinces, sent agents to Rome and to the Catholic powers, and, not least remarkable, established a printing-press. In 1645 the Pope, Innocent X, sent a Nuncio, Giovan

[45] Cox, in the preface to his *Hibernia Anglicana*, would make them six, "mere Irish, not an English Papist among them, commanded by the Bishop of Clogher," "mere English, all Papists, under General Preston," old Irish and English (Mount Garrett, Taaffe, etc.), new English (Ormonde, Inchiquin, etc.). Papists under the Nuncio, and an army of Protestants commanded by the Marquis of Ormonde.

[46] Luke Wadding sent him, by the hands of Massari, Dean of Fermo, who followed the archbishop to Ireland in 1647, the sword of his uncle Tyrone, "gladium duarum manuum quem Generali Don Eugenio destinavi."

Battista Rinuccini, Archbishop of Fermo,[47] to aid the Confederates with money and arms, and to compose the differences which divided the Irish and the Anglo-Irish. The Irish, counselled by the Nuncio, demanded the restoration of all lands confiscated in Ulster by James I, the restoration of the churches, complete religious freedom and a vigorous prosecution of the war. The Anglo-Irish were in favour of making peace on conditions which would give them security on their estates, relieve them from the more oppressive of the penal laws, and allow them to join forces with the King to overthrow the Parliament. Either course whole-heartedly pursued could not have failed to be successful: *dis aliter visum.* The fruits of a gallant victory over the Scotch at Benburb (1646) were lost when Ormonde, after making terms most excellent for himself, surrendered Dublin and other strong places to the Parliamentary General Jones. Charles, pressed by the increasing danger of his situation in England and eager for the help of an Irish army, conceded all that was asked and a peace was concluded on 17th January, 1649. A fortnight later the head of the Stuart king rolled from the block and the victorious Puritans were free to conquer Ireland in earnest.

§ 5

The effect produced in the island by the news of the king's execution was immense. Ormonde joined the Confederates; the Prince of Wales was proclaimed king by the title of Charles II; the Ulster Presbyterians declared for him to a man. The three nations for a moment marched as one. Charles at the Hague was invited to Ireland by Ormonde; he preferred to throw in his lot with the Scotch and the

[47] Cf. *The Mission of Rinuccini, Nuncio Extraordinary to Ireland,* 1645-1649, by Michael J. Hynes, Dublin, 1932. Two Irish Capuchins wrote an account in Latin of the war as seen by the Nuncio and his entourage in six volumes folio, 2,666 pages, now preserved in the Trivulzi Palace at Milan. The whole work, *Commentarius Rinuccianus de sedis apostolicae legatione ad Foederatos Hiberniae Catholicos per anno* 1645-9, is now in course of being edited by another Irish Capuchin for the Manuscripts Commission of the Irish Government. Only one volume, however, has so far appeared, bringing the story down to the arrival of the Nuncio in Ireland.

opportunity thus presented never recurred. On 25th February, 1649, Rinuccini sailed from Galway: on 25th July Oliver Cromwell landed in Dublin.

This great-great-grand nephew of the Thomas Cromwell who had grown rich on the loot of the plundered English monasteries came at the head of a rigorously disciplined and theoretically highly paid force of 20,000 men, 'prisoners, tinkers, pedlars, vagrants,' with several pieces of artillery, abundant stores, £200,000 in cash, a vast quantity of scythes and an immense supply of Bibles. A cavalry leader of genius —like Julius Cæsar, he was over forty when he took the field—and a fanatical Puritan by conviction—he had suffered the process known as 'conversion' in his youth—he began his campaign by the capture and sack of Drogheda (3rd September), where the indiscriminate slaughter continued uninterruptedly for five days. Three thousand persons were put to the sword: thirty survived and were shipped with other captives to the West Indies and sold as slaves to the planters. Owen Roe O'Neill, the most capable soldier in Ireland, died on 6th November, and with his death the heart went out of the Irish resistance. The campaign was carried on after Cromwell's departure (29th May, 1650) with equal rapidity and ferocity by his gloomy and fanatical son-in-law Ireton, the 'best prayer-maker and preacher in the army,' and peace was concluded only after, in the familiar Tacitean phrase, a wilderness had been created. Ireton, on his march to Limerick, passed through tracts of country where for thirty miles together there was not a human habitation or a living soul to be seen. About half the population of Ireland, some 600,000 men, women and children, are estimated to have perished by hunger or the sword, and, although the full weight of Cromwell's fist fell not on the mass of the people—extreme poverty has its compensations —but on the upper classes, the landed proprietors, the sufferings of the nation, in the opinion of Lord Clarendon, have never been surpassed but by those of the Jews in their destruction by Titus.

The conquest was followed (August 1652) by an Act for the Settling of Ireland. By clauses (i) and (iv) of this measure one hundred thousand Irishmen are considered to have been condemned to death and every Catholic landlord in Ireland, old Irish, Anglo-Irish or English, forfeited his estates. Some six and a half million acres were thus made available for division among Puritans of two classes: (i) the original adventurers who had hazarded their money in 1642 and who were now rewarded, their number having greatly increased, with parcels amounting in the aggregate to about half the forfeited land, and (ii) the troopers who, their pay being greatly in arrears, were given paper claims to allotments called 'debentures,' which their own officers bought from the ignorant and needy rank and file at shamefully low prices. Sir William Petty, the surveyor, bought up great tracts of land for a song, more particularly in Kerry, and grimly held on to them in the following reign. Only six of the adventurers founded families, so that, instead of Protestant yeomen being settled on the soil, an entirely new class of landlord came into being. On 30th November, 1654, a Declaration was published ordering all transplantable persons, i.e. landowners and their families and such of their former tenants as elected to share their fate,[48] to betake themselves to Connacht. The popular opinion that Connacht was selected because it was bleak, barren, and desolate, would appear to be ill-founded. These were characteristics of Ulster in the seventeenth century. Connacht was selected because of its situation. Secluded from the rest of the country by the lower Shannon and the Erne, fenced off by the woods, bogs and mountains of Leitrim, it made an ideal place of confinement in which to pen such as had survived hunger and the sword. Thither the landowners and their dependents made their painful way in the depth of winter; the vast majority of the poor, who alone could till the land and enable its new proprietors to live, remained on this side of the Shannon, a despised but indispensable class, forbidden to dwell in any walled town.

[48] By one of the pleasant ironies of which the history of Anglo-Irish relations is so full, the blow fell on the sons of some of the greediest of the English undertakers, and Brownes, Spensers, Fittons, Walshes, Thorntons and Raleighs, joined the trek to Connacht. They had married Irish women and become Catholics.

§ 6

The Restoration of Charles II (1660) found two peoples in Ireland, the old expropriated native owners and the new Cromwellian colonists installed in their stead, and three religions, the Catholic, the Presbyterian in Ulster and the Episcopalian wherever it was to be found. The latter two hated each other cordially, but merged their reciprocal animosities in a common detestation of the first. "Proprium humani ingenii est odisse quem laeseris." A Parliament containing not a single Catholic was assembled and proceeded to the task of settling the struggle between rival claimants to property on the basis of yet another redistribution of the soil. A Bill of Settlement, however, drafted by the English Privy Council in London, was transmitted to Ireland, and in May 1662 passed both Houses. This measure provided that the Adventurers *in primis* were to be confirmed in all the lands possessed by them on 7th May, 1659, and the soldiers in the estates already allotted for their pay, exception being made for Protestant church lands and some others. Innocent Papists, who had not been concerned in the rebellion, were to keep any lands allotted to them west of the Shannon, thus forfeiting all claim to their original properties, while those who had never sued out decrees for such lands were to have restored to them what they had been deprived of. It would have been quite impossible to carry out this Act if the Adventurers and the soldiers were to retain what they had acquired, and a clamour was raised that the Papist interest had prevailed. The discussion was adjourned to London and there the proposals sank to the bottom of a sea of jobbery and corruption.[49] The one

[49] Out of these dirty waters James, Duke of York, fished for himself an estate of, some say 120,000, others 95,000 acres in Tipperary, land which had actually belonged to men who had served under him abroad. The accounts differ as to whether he made any attempt at restitution, particular or general, and it is at least improbable. The question in any event has only an academic interest, for William III, after the Treaty of Limerick, bestowed the property on his favourite mistress, Elizabeth Villiers, Countess of Orkney, an intelligent woman, who, according to Swift, "squinted like a dragon." It was said to be worth £26,000 per annum, but was so burdened with rent-charges in favour of James's discarded mistresses and others that the income enjoyed by the Countess did not greatly exceed £5,000 per annum, say £15,000 gold. The English

tangible result of the Act of Settlement and its corollary, the Act of Explanation, was that, whereas in 1641 there is estimated to have been some 8,000 Catholic landowners in Ireland, in 1655 there were not more than 1,300.

The year 1678 was memorable in England for the popular frenzy aroused by the revelations of one Titus Oates, an ex-naval chaplain of infamous reputation, concerning a plot he professed to have discovered. The Catholics were to rise, the Protestants to be massacred, London to be burned, the king assassinated, and Ireland to be invaded by a French army. All London went mad with fear and rage. Two thousand Catholics were cast into prison and fifteen executed, including five Jesuits and the aged Viscount Stafford. The judicial Bench of England in the proceedings which followed "on charges as wild as Mother Goose's tales, on the testimony of wretches who proclaimed themselves to be spies and traitors," never sank so low in brutal manners and rancorous partiality. The Irish victim selected, Bl. Oliver Plunket (1629-81), Archbishop of Armagh, was not the least noble. Conveyed to London and there tried, if the word trial may be properly applied to judicial proceedings the issue of which was never in doubt, he was condemned to death after a quarter of an hour's deliberation by the jury, and on 1st July, 1681, hanged, drawn and quartered at Tyburn. "He was coolly and deliberately permitted to suffer death, lest the current of loyalty, still sensitive and suspicious upon the account of religion, might be somewhat checked in its course,"[50] and of his innocence, said Charles James Fox, "no doubt could be entertained." The martyred archbishop was beatified in 1920 by Pope Benedict XV.[51]

Parliament passed an Act of Resumption in 1699, but the Countess must have retained something, because in 1709 she emerged as a patron of letters and founded a school at Middleton, Co. Cork, for the teaching of English.

[50] Cf. *The Constitutional History of England* by Henry Hallam, 7th ed., London, 1854, II, p. 449. For a vivid picture of life in Ireland at the time, prelates ruling a diocese on £20 a year, going from hiding-place to hiding-place, with a price upon their heads, never eating a square meal, attempting to preserve order among priests who were farm-hands and cattle-dealers without churches, cf. 'A Bishop of the Penal Times' by P. Canon Power, *Irish Historical Documents*, No. 3, Cork University Press and London, Longmans, 1933.

[51] The *Book of Armagh* was in the hereditary keeping of a steward, the 'Maor na Canóine,' from which circumstance the family took their name of Mac Maoir or MacMoyre. The last steward, Florence Mac Moyre, whom the English

§ 7

James II came to the throne in 1685 determined to enforce religious toleration by suspending or annulling the penal laws against Catholics and Dissenters and to establish perfect religious equality. The means which he adopted for this purpose were such as the Whig oligarchy in the English Parliament had pronounced unconstitutional, and the equality proposed meant, in practice, it was apprehended, the substitution of Catholic for Protestant supremacy. The unsuccessful prosecution of the seven bishops (29th June, 1688), who, emboldened by the prospect of a revolution, had refused to read the king's proclamation of indulgence, precipitated a crisis. The nobles and clergy were already in communication with Holland; the loyalty of the army had been tampered with, the Court was honeycombed with treason, but James refused to retract his policy and rejected the offer of the French King, Louis XIV, to send him troops.

The Prince of Orange, his son-in-law, to whom Pope Innocent XI was bound by ties of amity,[52] landed at Torbay on 4th November, 1688, with a well-disciplined force of 15,000 veteran troops, Dutch and German mercenaries, whose pay was guaranteed by the promise of taxes to be levied on their victims. James attempted to bear up but was abandoned by everybody, his nearest and dearest, including his own daughter Anne—*est ce possible!*—his relations and favourites. Never was there a revolution in which so much ingratitude, meanness and selfishness distinguished the participants, but it succeeded, of course, to their immense enrichment. William's rapid and bloodless advance forced

called Wyre and whose signature, 'Florentinus Muire,' may still be seen on the book (fol. 104b), pawned it for five pounds to pay his expenses to London in order to give perjured evidence against the archbishop. Pressed by the Lord Chief Justice Pemberton at the trial, he did not deny that he was a Catholic. After the murder Mac Moire returned to Ireland and continued to live, but he never recovered the book.

[52] It would be difficult to prove that Innocent, although passionately denounced by Louis XIV for encouraging William to expel a Catholic king from the throne of England, had any personal knowledge that such was in fact the Dutchman's real design in spite of his professions. The letters of the Cardinal d'Estrées, if genuine, show that the intentions of the Prince were known to Count Cassoni, Papal Secretary of State, as early as 1687, though concealed by him from the knowledge of the Pontiff.

James to flee his kingdom and the conspirators declared that he had abdicated. On 18th December the Dutchman entered London, and one of the most sordid incidents in English history was over. It was called the 'Glorious Revolution.'

In Ireland the Earl of Tyrconnel had succeeded Lord Clarendon in 1686 as lord lieutenant, the first Catholic to occupy that post and the only one in the series with the exception of the last. The dispensing prerogative had set aside all the statutes, the army had been reconstructed, every means had been taken to give Catholics that share in the government of their own country to which their numbers entitled them, but the Protestant nobles, of course, joined the English conspiracy.

James landed at Kinsale on 12th March, 1689, and made a triumphal progress to Dublin. A proclamation was duly issued promising liberty of conscience, justice, and protection to all, and a parliament was summoned for 7th May. It met and sat for seventy-two days. It repealed the Act of Settlement, which was natural enough, and proceeded to commit a fatal mistake. It attainted two thousand persons by name, thus binding up their lives and interests with the success of William's cause. The Act of Attainder could not be enforced until it had been sanctioned by victory; then it would have been unnecessary. As it was, the only consequence was a war of three years' duration, waged by both sides for self-preservation, but of simple valour on the one side against a triple superiority on the other of military talents, resources and discipline. On 14th June, 1690, William landed at Carrickfergus; on 1st July, 1690, "a joyful day, excessive hot," he met James at the battle of the Boyne. The English king rode away before evening, and, after spending the night at Dublin Castle and throwing the blame for his disaster on the Irish soldiers who had fought for him, posted off to Waterford and thence made sail for Brest. He returned no more. The Irish fought on for two years longer, but could not ultimately prevail against the weight of numbers brought against them. Limerick, then the second most considerable town in Ireland and tolerably well fortified, was defended by an Irish soldier, Patrick Sarsfield, who had fought at the battle of Sedgemoor, and held out to the last. It capitulated on 3rd October, 1691, on conditions embodied in certain two-fold articles of agreement concluded between the Irish officers and Godart Van Ginckel, the Dutch commander. The Military Articles allowed "all persons without exception" to leave Ireland and settle anywhere abroad, except in England or Scotland, with their families and property, and provided for the free transport to France of such Irish officers and soldiers as desired to enter the French service. The Civil Articles provided (*inter alia*): (a) that the Roman Catholics of the kingdom should enjoy such privileges in the exercise of their religion as were consistent with the laws of Ireland or as they did enjoy in the reign of King Charles II, and their Majesties, as soon as their affairs would permit them to summon a parliament in Ireland, would endeavour to procure the said Roman Catholics such further security in that particular as might preserve them from any disturbance upon the account of their said religion; and (b) that all inhabitants of Limerick and other garrisons unsubmitted, and all officers and soldiers then in arms who should return to their Majesties' obedience, and all such as should be under their protection in the counties of Limerick, Kerry, Clare, Galway, and Mayo, should be secured in their estates and all their rights, privileges and immunities, which they held in the reign of Charles II free from all forfeitures or outlawries incurred by them.

The Articles were ratified by William and Mary on 24th February, 1692. The second Article was confirmed by statute some years later (9 *Will. III., c.* 2), but only as to the garrison of Limerick or other persons in arms. The first Article was passed over entirely.[53] The only result of the gallant defence and honourable surrender of Limerick, the last outpost held by the Irish on behalf of the popular monarchy of the English against an oligarchy alien in race and religion, was a broken treaty, the confiscation of yet another 1,060,792 acres of Irish soil, the withdrawal from

[53] It has often been observed that the drafting of this agreement reflects little credit on the Irish plenipotentiaries. Their unwisdom is severely criticised in his *Mémoires*, Paris, 1778, by the Duke of Berwick, who, it may be recalled, married Sarsfield's widow.

Ireland of some 12,000 Irish soldiers, and the imposition upon those who remained of a system of laws without parallel in European history.

§ 8

The Irish Brigade (four regiments) met their country's enemies again during the war of the Spanish Succession at Cremona in 1702, where O'Mahoney's exploit is one of the most memorable in military history, at Blenheim (1704), Ramillies (1706), Oudenarde (1708), and Malplaquet (1709), and during the war of the Austrian Succession at Fontenoy (1745). The Wild Geese, driven out of Ireland, flew over Europe. The Irish at home trod the mill of the penal laws, penal *par excellence*, "a machine of wise and elaborate contrivance, and as well fitted for the oppression, impoverishment and degradation of a people and the debasement in them of human nature itself as ever proceeded from the perverted ingenuity of man." [54] The ostensible object of the penal laws was the extirpation of Popery: in practice nothing was less desired than the conversion of the people to Protestantism. The real object of these tremendous statutes was the security of the victors by taking care that the land still owned by the conquered should never be increased, and should as far as possible be diminished, and by depriving the mass of the people of "all power which might come from the possession of property, education, political rights, social or official position, even special industrial skill, to reduce them into a helpless, hopeless mass of ignorant agricultural helots," [55] hewing wood and drawing water in a worse than Egyptian bondage. The Irish are not, as Aristotle might have said, by nature slaves, but the English Privy Council was determined to try to make them such. It was therefore enacted that intermarriage between persons of different religions and possessing any estate in Ireland was forbidden, and that the children, in the event of either parent being Protestant, were to be taken from the other and educated in

[54] Letter to Sir Hercules Langrishe, 3rd January, 1792, by Edmund Burke.
[55] Kenney, *Sources*, pp. 48-9.

that faith (9 *Will. III*, c. 3., 2 *Anne*, c. 6). The eldest son, being a Protestant, might turn his father's estate in fee simple into a tenancy for life and thus secure his own inheritance, but if the children kept their faith, the father's lands descended in gavelkind equally among them all. Papists were disabled from purchasing lands except for terms not exceeding thirty-one years at a rent of not less than two-thirds of the full value. If they acquired land by descent, devise or settlement, they were required to turn Protestant within six months on pain of forfeiture to the next Protestant heir, a provision which made it impossible for them to hold real property at all (ibid.). No Papist was allowed to keep a school or to teach in private houses any but the children of the family, and severe penalties punished such as should go themselves or send others beyond the seas for education in the ancestral religion. No Papist was permitted to retain any arms and search might be made at any time by two justices (7 *Will. III, cc.* 4 and 5). Priests and all who should come into the kingdom from foreign parts were banished on pain of transportation in case of neglecting to comply and of high treason if they returned from banishment. They were required to be registered and forbidden to leave their own parishes, while rewards were offered to informers who should detect any violation of these statutes to be levied on the Catholic inhabitants of the country (9 *Will. III, c.* 1; 2 *Anne, c.* 3, 7; 8 *Anne, c.* 3). No political privileges were left to a people thus dispossessed of the most elementary rights of civil society, and the elective franchise was taken away from the Catholics of Ireland in 1727.

The full force of this legislation fell mainly upon the wealthier families and in many cases these paid the price of national apostasy and conformed to the Protestant religion; such conversions, however, were not unnaturally suspect, and, to check the ardour of the new converts, a Bill was passed disabling them from practising at the Bar or as solicitors until they had attained five years' proficiency in their adopted religion. As a political body the Catholics were extinguished; but in spite of, or rather perhaps because of, the dreadful sanctions, the number of priests, instead of dwindling, actually increased, and Mass continued to be said in secret, in hidden places among the woods or in the hills, at midnight, always with the fear impending that informers would arrive accompanied by soldiers, and the blood of the celebrant not unfrequently stained the stones of the improvised altar.

One of the objects of the Catholic Confederates in the rebellion of 1641 had been the formal repeal of the Statute of Drogheda known by the name of Poyning's Law (1495). [56] This statute had enacted that all laws then lately made in England should be deemed good and effectual in Ireland, and, although it had been established subsequently that English statutes had no operation unless re-enacted by the Irish Parliament, Charles I had steadily refused his consent, until he was finally driven to refuse nothing. After the revolution the planters in the Irish Parliament acquiesced and even co-operated in a series of measures checking the development of manufactures and thwarting the growth of commerce for the benefit and advantage of what was called with irony and is still sometimes incongruously referred to, as 'the mother country.' The case of the wool industry is the most notorious. [57]

In 1698 the Irish Parliament agreed to a Bill imposing duties up to 20 per cent on all woollen goods, with the exception of frieze, for a limited period of three years from 25th March, 1699. The English Parliament went one step further by expressly forbidding the export of all wool and woollen goods except to England, and then proceeded to impose duties which were intended to be absolutely prohibitive. [58] Opposition to these pretensions began to develop about the middle of the eighteenth century, and the in-

[56] The most complete account of this legislation is contained in the chapter on the Acts of Poyning's Parliament contributed by Mr. Edmund Curtis to Miss Conway's *Henry VII's Relations with Scotland and Ireland* 1485-98, Cambridge University Press, 1932.

[57] But cf. also an article, not without a topical interest, on 'L'importation en France au XVIIIᵉ siècle du bœuf salé d'Irlande' in the *Revue historique*, September-October, 1928, pp. 79-85.

[58] Doubts as to the dependence of the Irish upon the English Parliament were formally resolved in 1721 by the passing of the English Declaratory Act (6 *George I*, c. 5), which in terms asserted the right of the English Parliament to legislate for Ireland.

P—i

habitants of Ireland, both original and imported, became
united in a common discontent, fanned by Jonathan Swift,
the Protestant Dean of St. Patrick's, Dublin, who had no
special love for the Irish, at the wretched English policy of
bestowing the chief posts in Church and State on strangers.
Two generations had passed, and the grandsons and great-
grandsons of the planters began to consider themselves Irish
and to chafe at their subjection to England. The murmurs
of revolt gradually swelled into audible complaints, and in
1753 the Irish House of Commons resolved to apply a
surplus revenue in liquidation of a debt. The Government
maintained that it belonged to the king and could not be
disposed of without his previous consent. The Crown
prevailed after a long and violent discussion, but the Irish
House of Commons took care by more particular applica-
tions of the revenue to prevent the recurrence of any such
undisposed surplus.

§ 9

George III came to the throne in 1760, and the Whigs,
Burke, Fox and the rest, began to show some sympathy for
the 'most unnatural condition' of the Irish. The popular
party in Ireland, led of course by Protestants, had steadily
grown and, under Henry Grattan (1746-1820) and Henry
Flood (1732-1791), began to agitate for free export, finally
conceded in 1779, in spite of the opposition of the English
manufacturers, by Lord North, and for such a reformation
of the Irish Parliament as would make it really representative.
It was a curious body this Irish Parliament. Nominally
elected by about one-fifth of the country it purported to
represent, it did not even represent that fifth. It was a
landlords' assembly. (One consequence of the penal laws
was a complete divorce between the owner of the soil and the
tiller of it, and in no country in Europe was the power of
the landlord so absolute as it was in Ireland.) It contained
not a single Catholic or so much as a Protestant merchant.
The landlords' nominees voted as the English Government,
through its representatives at Dublin Castle, directed.

Placemen and pensioners were half the whole effective strength, and the price of a seat was as familiar an object of discussion, and as nicely calculated, as the price of a sheep. Yet the leaders of this assembly, the venality of whose members passes belief, went to work to obtain the emancipation of their Catholic fellow-subjects. The revolt of the American colonies, the alliance between the American rebels and the French, and the consequent threat of invasion, gave them an opportunity, and in 1782 Grattan carried his resolution that the King of England and the Irish Parliament could alone make laws that would bind the Irish. Flood, although prepared to give complete religious toleration to Catholics in Ireland, consistently refused to give them any political power. Grattan, however, succeeded in having an Act passed to admit them to practise at the Bar, and then carried another actually enabling them to vote for Members of Parliament. He would have allowed them even to take their seats, but this was more than George III could stand, and these too sanguine hopes were disappointed.

In England the irrationality of imposing fetters on persons no longer suspected of disloyalty had long attracted the attention of liberal-minded statesmen, and in 1780 Sir George Savile introduced a Bill relieving Catholics from various pains and penalties. Priests were no longer subject to perpetual imprisonment for saying Mass, the prohibition on the purchase of landed property was removed, and a modified form of worship and education was permitted. Scotland was excluded from the proposals because a similar attempt to give a like measure of relief to Catholics there had been defeated by an outburst of religious fanaticism in Edinburgh. The frenzy spread to England. The Protestant zealots assembled in wrath and on 2nd June, 1780, some 50,000 stout fellows, decked with blue cockades and "ready," as Defoe is reported to have said of other such in his time, "to fight to the death against Popery, without knowing whether Popery was a man or a horse," marched in procession under the leadership of a madman named Lord George Gordon, who subsequently turned Jew, to the House of Commons, and petitioned for the withdrawal of the concessions.

After five days' dreadful rioting, in the course of which many Catholic chapels and private dwelling-houses were destroyed, the troops were called out by the king and killed or wounded 468 of the rioters. In 1791 another Bill was passed and in 1793 the most highly penal of the sanctions affecting Scotch Catholics were removed by the Statute, 33 *George III*, c. 44, which prescribed a form of oath and declaration on taking which Catholics were enabled to purchase or inherit landed property. These Acts were providential measures against the French Revolution and the consequent war with France which compelled priests, seminarians, and lay students in the English colleges there and in the Low Countries to return home.

In Ireland, however, the persistent repression of the agitation for Catholic relief and the spirit of discontent everywhere generated by the French Revolution combined to drive the Society of United Irishmen, a peaceful organization, formed and officered almost exclusively by Protestants to assist Grattan in carrying his reforms, to despair and open rebellion. Lord Edward Fitzgerald, an attractive young nobleman[59] and one of the society's most prominent members, had returned in 1798 from Bâle, where he had gone to confer with Hoche on a French invasion of Ireland. The rising was forced by horrors openly encouraged by the Government, but the plot had been betrayed. Lord Edward was seized after a desperate scuffle in Dublin, and some sixteen days later died of wounds (4th June, 1798). The rising was drowned in blood after some 30,000 people had been massacred.

The only result of the bloodshed was that the plan for the Union with England, secretly matured by Pitt in London, was openly announced in Dublin and warmly advocated by the Catholic Archbishop of Dublin, Dr. Troy. The voluntary association now proposed was commended by the refusal of all reforms—even of the outrageous system of collecting tithes or the removal of the disabilities affecting Catholics—and by

[59] He had had Cobbett as his sergeant-major in the 54th regiment of foot in New Brunswick and Cobbett described him to Pitt as the only really honest officer he had ever known.

the presence of 137,000 soldiers in the country. The Irish House of Commons was purged of opponents by the grant of fifty-four coronets and a host of minor pensions. The Press was bribed and doubters convinced by that most effective means of persuasion, gold, and, in spite of all Grattan's eloquence, the Irish Parliament, by whose cradle, he declared, he had sat and whose hearse he then followed, was united with the Parliament of Great Britain. Only seven of its members, it was reported, had not been bribed. For many years after the Union the Catholics of Ireland were forced to pay tithes for the maintenance of a State Church attended by a small minority of Protestants, and out of their own poverty to provide the means, but with unbounded devotion, to support their own clergy and to house in their own miserable chapels the Presence of Christ in the Blessed Sacrament.

§ 10

A young Irish student in the college at Douai, who had been driven home in 1793 by the French Revolution, made a mental vow, after the scenes of anarchy and carnage he had witnessed, to dedicate himself with all his energy to the good of his country, while adhering rigidly to the path of strict legality. "He who commits a crime adds strength to the enemy," and "No political change whatsoever is worth the shedding of a single drop of human blood," were favourite mottoes of Daniel O'Connell.

Lavish promises had commended the Act of Union, and the entrance into a Parliament in London, would, it was alleged, give Ireland "a power over the executive and general policy of the Empire which would far more than compensate her" for the loss of a simulacrum of independence. The threshold, however, was barred to Catholics by an oath which nobody who believed in Transubstantiation could conscientiously take. O'Connell set himself, therefore, to fan the flame of agitation kindled by sympathetic Protestant members for the emancipation of the Catholics. Grattan had died in 1820, Plunket had taken up his mantle, but once again the Lords threw out the Bill. In 1823 when Catholic hopes had sunk to their nadir, O'Connell, then a barrister in very large

practice and an orator of most magnetic appeal, organised
on a broad and popular basis 'The Catholic Association,'
and before the end of the year had brought many priests
into it, so that the movement for the first time became really
national and therefore irresistible. The English Government
in alarm brought in a Bill to suppress the association, but on
18th March, 1825, it dissolved itself. O'Connell next presented himself as a parliamentary candidate for Clare and
was elected amid enormous enthusiasm. On 15th May,
1829, he came to take his seat in the House of Commons, but
his claim was rejected. He went back to Clare and was
returned unopposed. He now formed a new society for
Repeal, 'The Friends of Ireland of all Religious Persuasion.'
It was quickly suppressed, only to be revived as immediately
under a succession of other names, until, finally, the English
Government yielded. Catholics were allowed to take their
seats in Parliament, the oath of abjuration was abolished,
that of supremacy modified, and the penal sanctions abro-
gated. England and Scotland also benefited by this measure.
The Act of Emancipation (10 *Geo. IV*, c. 7) received the
king's signature on 13th April, 1829, and the age-old conflict
conflict waged in Ireland for liberty of conscience came to an
end.

O'Connell, on his death-bed (1847), it may be recalled,
willed to leave his heart to the Pontiff, whose most devoted
subject he had ever been, and, although his body lies in the
Glasnevin Cemetery, Dublin, his heart is still preserved in
the Irish College in Rome. It was removed with the college
from S. Agata dei Goti to its new site in the Via Santi
Quattro.

§ 11

The Act of Emancipation brought the *religious* martyrdom of Ireland to an end. But the painful struggle was
continued through the great famine of 1846-7, when 729,000
people died of hunger, through the wholesale evictions
known as 'the great clearances,' when 482,000 families were
evicted between 1849 and 1882,[60] through the drain of

[60] Of these 119,000 were reinstated sooner or later. Cf. Mulhall, *Dictionary
of Statistics*, London, 1886, p. 175.

emigration which drew off some 4,976,462 persons between 1846 and 1901,[61] through the anti-Catholic riots in Belfast in 1864 and the Fenian insurrection in 1867, through Gladstone's campaign for the disestablishment and disendowment of the State Church in Ireland (1869) and the agrarian revolution effected by the Land Acts of 1870 and 1881, through the political obstruction and ceaseless agitation of the Parnellites, gradually preparing the way for a political emancipation, the substance of which was won, though not without fighting, after the convulsions of the World War, in 1921. An Irish Free State (*Saorstát Éireann*) has now been established, but includes only twenty-six counties of the country; the six counties in north-east Ulster of the Jacobean plantation have their own separate legislature and executive government and are incongruously described as 'Northern Ireland.'

The heroism of the Green Isle, clergy and people alike, from the time of Henry VIII onwards, becomes manifest in all its brilliance from the consideration of one single incontrovertible fact that, whereas in the countries of the North and England and Scotland, "the majority followed the example of the king or other governing power of the State and renounced the old faith and supremacy of the Pope . . . in Ireland, I do not hesitate to assert that not the tenth, nor the hundredth, no, nor the thousandth part, revolted from the faith of their fathers to the camp of the heretics."[62]

"Once upon a time," wrote Cardinal Moran,[63] "a devout person turned to the eminent Dr. Doyle,[64] Bishop of Kildare and Leighlin, in quest of a relic of some martyr of the Faith. The Prelate replied: 'Go to any graveyard in Ireland, the most remote in the island. Gather a handful of earth anywhere in that graveyard, and you will have the relic you seek.'"

[61] Cf. 'The Irish Migration of the 'Forties,' by F. Morehouse in *The American Historical Review*, April 1928, p. 591, and, more generally, *Ireland and Irish Emigration to the New World from 1815 to the Famine*, by W. F. Adams, Yale University Press, London, Milford, 1932. About 200,000 of the fugitives are estimated to have perished in the emigrant ships or immediately after landing in America.

[62] J. Lynch (1599 ? - 1673 ?), *Cambrensis Eversus* (1662), ed. and tr. M. Kelly (Celtic Society: Dublin, 1848-52), II, 613.

[63] *Ireland, the Island of the Saints*, p. 496.

[64] Cf. *The Irish Sketch Book of 1842*, by W. M. Thackeray, London, 1876, Vol. VII, p. 287.

PART II

THE IRISH SAINTS IN ITALY

CHAPTER VII

ST. PATRICK

§ I

THE main features in the life of the celebrated apostle of Ireland were sketched, however inadequately, in Chapter I, § 3; it now remains to add a few touches with special reference to Italy.

After hearing the call of the mysterious "voice of the Irish," Patrick went to the Gauls to educate himself and learn something of the traditional Christian teaching. Monasticism, a novelty in Western Europe at the time, attracted the curious from far and near, and Patrick made his way as far south as Lérins, a little island, one of a group off the coast of Provence, and the site of the famous monastery founded as recently as 410 by St. Honoratus.[1] "I had the fear of God to guide me in my journey through the Gauls[2] and Italy and to the islands of the Tyrrhene sea," he is reported to have said in an habitual *dictum* which the scribe Fer-domnach added to the Memoirs of Tirechán in the *Book of Armagh*. The islands of Lérins were, according to the geographical terminology of the time, Dom Gougaud observes, actually in the Tyrrhene sea.[3] But beyond Lérins the young traveller may also have visited several of those lonely islets, Capraja, Gorgona, Palmaria and Gallinaria, the haunt of cenobites and anchorites, which St. Ambrose (*Hexameron*, III, 5) gracefully likens to a necklace cast upon the sea, and to which also St. Martin of Tours had gone

---

[1] Cf. Gougaud, *Christianity in Celtic Lands*, pp. 35-6.

[2] He speaks of 'the Gauls' as he does of 'the Britains,' meaning the Roman provinces in Gaul and Britain, a form of expression sufficient in itself to exclude any suggestion that he could have been born about Dumbarton. There were four provinces in Gaul, the Narbonnese, Aquitaine, the Lyonnese, and Belgium (cf. *Strabo*, IV, 1). A fifth little province, the Maritime Alps, was administered by an imperial procurator.

[3] The island, formerly called Lerina, is now called Saint-Honorat.

between 356 and 360 to make his soul. Patrick says further that he went through Italy, and it is not impossible that from Lérins he travelled on to Milan to make contact with the community which St. Ambrose had founded there, and that from Milan he wandered down to the coast at Pisa, there to take ship for Capraja and Gorgona.[4] Rome and the southern part of the peninsula did not then form part of Italy proper,[5] and it would seem unlikely that on this occasion at least he went as far as the Eternal City. Bury[6] attributes the journey to Rome to A.D. 441, but even at that period it still remains extremely doubtful.[7] Some biographers having related that he had been ordained priest in the course of his wanderings throughout the Gauls and in Italy by a bishop named 'Senior' or 'Senator,' with an obscure reference to the see of the ordaining bishop, the early Bollandists hazarded the conjecture that the apostle of Ireland had been ordained in 410 by a bishop of Pisa. Gams and Zucchelli therefore included a 'Senior' or 'Senator' in the list of the bishops of Pisa. Mgr. Lanzoni, however, has not had the courage to follow them, as the Bollandist hypothesis can scarcely be sustained. Dom Gougaud thinks it more probable that the diaconate was conferred on Patrick by Amator, Bishop of Auxerre, who preceded St. Germanus and died in 418.[9] The Pelagian controversy, it is suggested, accounts for Patrick's presence at Auxerre.

His episcopal consecration, also, is a matter of some un-

[4] Cf. Ryan, *Irish Monasticism*, pp. 62 et seq. Some writers have imagined that he may have lived for some time among the solitaries on Monte Pisano (cf. Guerra-Guidi, *Compendio di storia ecclesiastica lucchese*, Lucca, 1924, p. 41).

[5] So when Ciaran of Saighir left Rome, which was in Latium, he went into Italy, originally the technical designation of the diocese of Milan. Cf. Duchesne, *Origines du culte chrétien*, pp. 31, 165, 193.

[6] Cf. *The Life of St. Patrick and His Place in History*, London, 1905, pp. 367-9.

[7] Cf. Gougaud, *Christianity in Celtic Lands*, p. 47; and for the arguments of those who maintain the journey to Rome, Mrs. Concannon's *St. Patrick: His Life and Mission*, Dublin and London, 1931, pp. 151 et seq.

[8] *Le Diocesi d' Italia*, Faenza, 1927, p. 585.

[9] Cf. *Christianity in Celtic Lands*, p. 37. The fact that Patrick had been ordained by Amator was vaguely remembered in the Irish tradition, but the fact that Amator was Bishop of Auxerre was completely forgotten. So Muir-chu has Patrick ordained 'ab Amatho rege,' the re-Latinized form of the Irish 'Amato-rig,' itself the Irish form of 'Amator.' The myth-makers then stepped in and 'Amatho rege' in their hands became 'Amatho ré Romanach' (King of the Romans), and from this it was but a step to have their hero ordained—'coram Teodosio imperatore.' Cf. Bury, *Life of St. Patrick*, p. 347, note 3.

certainty; but it may not unreasonably be assumed that he received it at the hands of St. Germanus himself at Auxerre.[10] The confused statements of Patrick's tenth century biographer Probus,[11] his startling variations of, and additions to, Muir-chu's life, have also had their repercussions upon the records of Italian bishops,[12] and some writers have taken it into their heads that he was consecrated by a bishop of Turin. Others—and this opinion received the support of Cardinal Moran[13]—by a bishop of Ivrea. Lanzoni refuses to countenance either hypothesis.

This eminent ecclesiastical historian, however, with reference to a certain Patricius named by a Bishop Lupercus in an inscription from Nola dated 786 after four other saints (Felix, Paulinus, Rufus and Laurentius), considered by local historians to have all been bishops of Nola, observes that a St. Patrick 'episcopus' was venerated at Nola on 17th March, i.e., the 'dies natalis' of the Irish St. Patrick, and concludes that Lupercus, when he came to compose his inscription, named first the two patrons of Nola, then two martyrs venerated in the Campania, and, lastly, St. Patrick of Ireland, as his own particular patron.[14]

§ 2

Among the liturgical feasts of the church in Genoa there is an entry under date 17th March,[15] according to the Diocesan Calendar for 1645, the oldest extant, as follows: "In Metropolitana S. Patritii Episc. et Conf., semid., ob reliquiam insignem manus sinistrae." The inventory of the metropolitan church, drawn up in 1386,[16] contains an item "manus Sancti Patritii munita argento."

[10] Cf. Gougaud, op. cit., p. 37.
[11] Colgan suggested that he might be Coeneachair, 'ard fer léiginn' in the school at Slane, who was burned to death by the Danes in A.D. 950.
[12] Cf. Savio, *Gli antichi vescovi d' Italia: il Piemonte*, Turin, Bocca, 1899, p. 294.
[13] Cf. *Analecta Bollandiana*, I, 1882, p. 554.
[14] Cf. for the connection between St. Patrick and Nola, Mrs. Concannon, op. cit., pp. 71-3.
[15] Cf. Cambiaso, *L'anno ecclesiastico e le feste dei santi in Genova*, Genoa. Soc. Lig. di Storia Patria, 1917, p. 23.
[16] Ibid., p. 453.

§ 3

Pavia, which certainly received many Irish scholars under the Lombards and the Carolingians, was once a lively centre of devotion to St. Patrick, St. Brigit, St. Columban, and even St. Brendan (cf. chapter V, § 2).

There was a church dedicated to St. Patrick in a suburb of Pavia which, until a few years ago, was appropriately called 'sobborgo S. Patrizio,' but has now had its name changed to 'sobborgo Piave.' Fr. Romuald Ghisoni[17] refers to a first very early church which stood on the site of that existing in his time, a site which was probably that of the residence of the mother of a certain Senator (a proper name), who founded a monastery for Benedictine nuns in the city in the eighth century under the Lombards. At all events the church was appropriately subject to the nuns of the Monastery of Senator who elected its rector. It is mentioned in the fourteenth century by De Canistris.[18] Restored in 1538, it was demolished in 1622 to make room for a more modern church, which was destroyed in its turn when the French besieged the city in 1655. It was rebuilt, however, and the new church was that seen by Ghisoni in 1699, the date of his writing. It has now ceased to exist, and all that remains is a fresco on the exterior wall of a house depicting Our Lady and the Child with St. Patrick kneeling.

§ 4

Near Vertova in the province of Bergamo there is a famous shrine of St. Patrick, the subject of a valuable monograph, with copious illustrations, by Don G. B. Baggi.[19]

The origin of the very ancient cult of St. Patrick in Vertova is uncertain, but it would seem to be connected with the manufacture of, and trade in, woollen cloth in the Valle Seriana.[20] The wool merchants, it should be observed,

[17] *Flavia Papia Sacra*, 1699.
[18] Cf. Gianani, *Opicino De Canistris*, Pavia, Fusi, 1927, pp. 56, 88 and 130.
[19] *S. Patrizio vescovo, speciale protettore di Vertova (Bergamo)*. Bergamo, Soc. Ed. S. Alessandro, 1928.
[20] Cf. Baggi, op. cit., pp. 137 et seq.

are also credited with having originated the cult of St. Pélerin d'Auxerre in the famous watering-place nearby of San Pellegrino. But the cult of the Irish saints in Lombardy must, it would seem, in general, be connected with monastic foundations in Italy and Rhaetia (St. Gall).

The shrine is pleasantly situated on the mule-path which leads from Vertova (Val Seriana) to Gorno (Valle del Riso). There was a so-called 'Tribuina' or 'Tribulina' there in former times, alongside which a precious little church was later erected (in the fourteenth century, perhaps), with frescoes, which may still be seen to this day, built into the imposing porch in front of the great shrine. The latter was built between 1581 and 1600, but not completed until about 1700. There is also a St. Patrick's Well.

The cult of the Irish saint is still very much alive among the Vertovesi, and found many graceful forms of expression during and after the World War. The elementary schools are closed to this day on 17th March, while the name Patrick, no less than Patricia, is not uncommon as a baptismal name in Vertovese families, as is also the surname Bernini, which, it has been suggested, derives from 'Hibernini' or 'Ibernini.'

§ 5

In the province of Ravenna (but in the diocese of Imola) there is a village called San Patrizio, which forms part of Conselice. The parish church is dedicated to the saint. The *Chartularium Imolense*, edited by Gaddoni and Zaccherini,[21] contains several references to the church of "S. Patritii or Patricii or Patrizii in Capite Silicis, Silyce plebs, Consilicis" (=Conselice) in documents ranging from 1092 (n. 732) to 1193 (n. 699) and always as a parish. Thereafter it appears either as a parish or as a deanery. The few inventories made in the eighteenth and nineteenth centuries disclose nothing having any reference to the origins of the church or the reasons for its dedication. A Benedictine monastery at Imola ('S. Mariae in Regula') appears from the Chartulary in question to have owned some estates in the

[21] Imola, Ongania, 1912.

parish of S. Patrizio and neighbourhood some centuries
before the year 1000, but by 1500 the church had already
yielded the primacy to the church at Conselice, where a
more prosperous quarter had gradually been growing up.
S. Patrizio in that century was merely a rectory, whereas
Conselice boasted an archpriest. S. Patrizio, however,
acquired an archpriest in 1705, and is still so governed. The
church faces east. It was last reconstructed *ex novo* in 1875,
and the archpriest's house has been transformed times
without number. The picture of the patron saint seems to
belong to the eighteenth century. St. Patrick stands in the
foreground on the left, with the Holy Trinity above, and
Melchisedech is depicted in mid-air making an offering of
bread and wine. The picture may have some connection
with a Confraternity of the Redemption which kept its
feast on Holy Trinity Sunday. A well stands in front of the
church but outside its boundaries: it belongs to the parish of
S. Patrizio and is a godsend in time of drought; the parapet
is built of marble from some old fountain.

The feast of the patron saint on 17th March is kept in
much the same way as other patronal feasts in neighbouring
parishes. An examination of the reports of pastoral visitations from the sixteenth century onwards seems to show a
lack of knowledge as to who precisely St. Patrick was.[22]

§ 6

The parish of Tirli in the commune of Firenzuola ('little
Florence' in the province and diocese of Florence) is likewise
dedicated to St. Patrick. Tirli was the last of the strongholds
in the 'Alpes Ubaldinorum' to fall into the hands (1373) of
the Florentines.[23] This stronghold would seem to have been
very extensive and, owing to its situation on the roads between
Santerno and Senio, of such great strategic importance that
even the Bolognese attempted to capture it in 1298. Having

[22] I am indebted for these particulars to the courtesy of the learned Fr.
Benv. Bughetti, O.F.M., who has been resident for some time in the Convent
of the Observance in Imola.
[23] Cf. Stefano Casini, *Dizionario biografico-geografico-storico del Comune di
Firenzuola*, 3 vols., Florence, Campolini, 1914, I, pp. 100 et seq.; II, p. 247.

extended their sway over the county of Imola, they attempted a *coup de main* on Tirli as well: but their plot failed. On 21st September, 1482, according to a parchment, the authenticity of which is guaranteed by the Archivio delle Riformagioni, the representatives of 'the commune of S. Patrizio,' together with those of S. Martino, Monti and Castiglioncello, betook themselves to Florence to negotiate and swear 'perpetuam fidelitatem' to the eminent people of Florence. The church of S. Patrizio at Tirli is recorded in the Campione Vecchio, the Register of Properties: in 1684, after the pastoral visitation, it was raised to the status of rural deanery of Camaggiore. The seventeenth century altar-piece depicting St. Patrick distributing Holy Communion is not without some value. The feast is kept on 17th March and the devotion of the people is remarkable.[24] As regards the origin of this cult, the comparative vicinity of Tirli to Imola and Conselice should be noted.

§ 7

I would here mention, as a possible clue in other investigations, that there is a picture by Spisanelli, which hangs above the altar in the sacristy of the Church of San Giovanni in Monte in Bologna, representing St. Patrick in the centre and above, on the left of the Virgin with the Child in glory, S. Guarino, a Bolognese saint of the twelfth century and a member of the Order of Canons Regular of the Lateran, who, until 1800, resided in that church.[25]

§ 8

In the diocese of Fermo (the province of Ascoli Piceno), between Montegiorgio and Montegranaro, is the commune of Torre San Patrizio, which once played a notable part in the life of the district. The name 'St. Patrick' seems to have been derived from the Benedictine monks who had impor-

[24] Cf. also with reference to this church, Santoni, *Raccolte di notizie, ecc.*, Florence, Mazzoni, 1847.
[25] Cf. *Bollettino Parrocchiale della Parrocchia di S. Giovanni in Monte* for 25th January, 1931, p. 5.

tant monasteries in the diocese of Fermo, and the suggestion derives some confirmation from the fact that the apostle of Ireland is joint patron of another place also in the archdiocese of Fermo, and, more precisely, of Campofilone, where the Benedictines once had a flourishing abbey. It should also be borne in mind that the edict issued by Lothair in 825 appointed Fermo to be the seat of one of the nine new schools of Italy (cf. Chap. III, § 4). Torre San Patrizio is certainly of great antiquity. It is included under the name 'Collis S. Patritii' in a list of places subject to the ordinary jurisdiction of the bishops of Fermo in the twelfth century.[26] The name 'Turris' must have been given to it some time later either because some tower stood on the spot or because such was the name bestowed in many cases on the less important castles.[27] There is record that about 1200 the fortress was also called 'Turris Patritia'; but later it is always 'Castrum Turris S. Patritii'; and the ancient Statute of Fermo in a classification of fortresses within the dependence of the city places 'Castrum S. Patritii' among the middle sort.

It belonged to Fermo, having been assigned to that city by King Manfred of Sicily in the year 1258 by a solemn deed reproduced by Fr. Adami, the historian of Fermo.[28] In 1301 it engaged in a contest with the Pope, but it was worsted by the Ruler of the Marches, the Pope's nephew, and condemned to pay a very heavy fine. In 1414 it was captured by Malatesta di Cesena, who aspired to control the Marches, and later sided with Francesco Sforza, who had become tyrant of Fermo and was at loggerheads with the Pope. In November 1443, however, it was attacked by the army of Paolo del Sangue, who happened to be in the

[26] Cf. G. Porti, *Tavole sinottiche delle cose più notabili della città di Fermo.*

[27] Cf. Palma, *Compendio della storia civile del Pretuzio*, Teramo, Marsili, 1856, p. 68. The word 'turris' is not uncommon as an adjunct of the 'villa' in the literature of the fourth century, and meant in practice an elegant country house, a sort of petit Trianon, like the modern French château, which is certainly not a fortress. The 'villa' only began to be fortified towards the middle of the fifth century (cf. the case of Pontius Leontius in Sidonius Apollinaris, *Carmina*, XXII), and then only against roving bands of marauders. It was not until well on in the tenth century that the 'turris' changed to a threatening aspect and began to develop into the medieval castle.

[28] *De rebus in civitate firmana gestis fragmentorum libri duo*, I, cap. 42.

Marches fighting the battles of the Church, and, despite the
heroic resistance of its inhabitants, it was stormed, sacked
and almost destroyed by fire. When fortune smiled on his
arms once more, Sforza gave the citizens of Fermo a week in
which to pay a special tax for the rebuilding of Torre S.
Patrizio, and the work of rebuilding the ruined fortress was
speedily begun at the instance of Sforza himself, who had
determined so to reward the fidelity of the Torresi.

On the final expulsion of the Sforzas in 1446, Torre San
Patrizio, still subject to Fermo, followed the fortunes of the
Papal States.

The archives of Fermo contain three parchments dated
1317 referring to Torre San Patrizio, but only of the slightest
and personal interest. [29]

The parish church of Torre San Patrizio is dedicated to
the Holy Saviour; but St. Patrick, the patron of the place,
has his own private chapel in which a relic (part of the
skull) has been preserved since 1653. It is the subject of a
pamphlet by B. Bonifazi, published in 1925. [30] A venerable
Confraternity of St. Patrick, long established there, keeps
his feast every year on 17th March with great devotion. A
picture, dating from 1599 and kept in the presbytery,
depicts Our Lady of the Assumption, the patron of the
diocese, with St. Patrick on one side, and, on the other, the
martyrs Hippolytus and Cassian.

§ 9

Everybody has heard of St. Patrick's Well in Orvieto: the
name is of comparatively recent invention and has no direct
connection with the saint, to whom no cult is paid in the
diocese. [31] It first occurs in an anonymous pamphlet published
at Orvieto in 1829. [32] The *Strenna Orvietana pel* 1848 [33] says on
page 32: " . . . it was called St. Patrick's Well from a simi-

[29] I am indebted for this particular to the courtesy of Mgr. Giov. Cicconi,
keeper of the municipal library of Fermo.
[30] Obligingly loaned to me by the present parish priest, Don Vinc. Leoni.
[31] Cf. Prof. Pericle Perali, *Orvieto*, Marsili, 1919, pp. 171, et seq.
[32] *Descrizione del Duomo d'Orvieto e del pozzo volgarmente detto di S. Patrizio, per
servire di guida al viaggiatore*, Orvieto, 1829, *chez* Sperandio Pompeo.
[33] Tosini, 1848.

larity in construction to a cavern in Ireland hollowed out in the rock by order of St. Patrick, who was sent there as bishop." A similar explanation is given by Fr. Pennachi.[34] Prof. Perali declares that the name owes its origin to English tourists in the beginning of the nineteenth century; before that strangers called it Pozzo d'Orvieto ('the Orvieto Well'), the citizens, Pozzo della Rocca ('Rock Well'); the same authority adds that, if it were desired to imagine some more ancient name, it might, perhaps, be sought for round about 1725, when the Gualterio family entertained the Stuarts and their little court in their villa at Crognolo.[35] A similar well, which, it has been suggested, was also called 'St. Patrick's Well,' has recently been discovered in the fort of Pisa, near the eastern corner next to the Arno.

§ 10

Lastly, the name 'St. Patrick's Well' has been given to a magnificent new stairway in the Vatican City. An article, 'Le nuove opera delle Città del Vaticano,' which appeared in the first number of *Illustrazione Vaticana* (25th December, 1930, p. 14), says: "Beside the Italian garden *fervet opus* for the new site of the Picture Gallery [opened in November 1932] and for the 'Pozzo di S. Patrizio,' a monumental undertaking opening the way into the Museums from the via Leone IV."

I would mention in conclusion that there is a modern church in Rome (in via Boncompagni) dedicated to St. Patrick[36] and belonging to the Irish Augustinians, and that the *Diario Romano e Vaticano* mentions a tooth[37] of the saint preserved in the church of S. Maria di Loreto beside the Forum of Trajan.

[34] *Cenni storici e Guida di Orvieto*, Tosini, 1873, p. 106.

[35] Op. cit., p. 273.

[36] On the occasion of the laying of the foundation stone of this church, the late Prof. Orazio Marucchi published a paper entitled 'La Chiesa di S. Patrizio d'Irlanda a Roma,' Rome, Tip. Propaganda, 1888, recalling the Christian associations that hung about the locality.

[37] The tooth, perhaps, to which the saint addressed himself in the fragment *A fir há* preserved in the *Vit. Trip.*, I, 140-1. As regards the relics of the saint mentioned in the text and the claims of various places to possess his remains, the prudent reader will bear in mind the passage in the *Book of Armagh*: "Ubi sunt ossa ejus nemo novit," one of the features in which Patrick was conceived to resemble Moses.

CHAPTER VIII

ST. BRIGIT OF CELL-DARA

§ 1

St. Brigit, Virgin of Cell-dara, 'thaumaturge,' was referred to in Chapter 1, § 5. She enjoys an immense popularity all over Western Europe, a popularity undoubtedly due to the intense propaganda made on behalf of their national saints by the Irish monks, missionaries and *peregrini* wherever they penetrated.[1] Her popularity, as will be seen presently, was just as great in Italy, but St. Brigit, the Virgin of Ireland (whose feast falls on 1st February), must be carefully distinguished from St. Bridget, the Widow of Sweden (1302-73, whose feast falls on 23rd July and 8th October), also very popular, but more particularly in central and southern Italy.

§ 2

In Piedmont St. Brigit Virgin is honoured either alone or together with the Irish St. Ursus of Aosta, whose feast also falls on 1st February. The cult of St. Brigit in the dioceses of Fossano, Mondovì, and Saluzzo, would seem to have been determined by the exceptional devotion paid to the Saint by the Blessed Oddino Barotti, the scion of a noble Fossanese family, in the fourteenth century. The territories of the three dioceses were under the jurisdiction at the time of the bishop of Turin. The Barotti family[2] numbered amongst their possessions near Fossano an oratory dedicated to St. Brigit, which has now disappeared, but in which they lodged the Capuchin Friars on their first coming to the place in 1569, and the Blessed Oddino persuaded the popu-

---

[1] Cf. Gougaud, *Gaelic Pioneers*, pp. 103-12, for particulars of the cult paid to the saint of Cell-dara in France, Belgium and Germany.

[2] Cf. Muratori, *Vita del b. Oddino Barotti*, 2nd ed., 1867, cc. X and XII.

lace to elect as patron of the countryside, then ravaged by hail and frost, "St. Brigit, venerated in Ireland next after the Virgin Mother of God, more than any other saint, and famous throughout the whole Latin Church." The Saint receives an official cult as joint patron of the city and diocese of Fossano, with a liturgical feast in the cathedral on 1st February and a devotional feast in the Church of St. Bernard close to the city.

St. Brigit is likewise joint patron of the city of Pinerolo and mentioned as such as early as 1318. I am informed by Mgr. Cuatto, Rector of the local Seminary, that there once was a church of St. Brigit in the neighbourhood of Pinerolo in the early fourteenth century; it was served by Augustinians, was destroyed and rebuilt a number of times, and is now a little country chapel.

The parish of Rocca Cigliè in the diocese of Mondovì and the province of Cuneo is dedicated to St. Brigit.

There is a chapel dedicated to her, and a popular festival held on 1st February, in the parish of Tarantasca, but a short distance from Fossano in the diocese of Saluzzo and the province of Cuneo. In the parish of Piasco (also in the diocese of Saluzzo) there is a chapel in honour of St. Brigit close to a chapel of St. Ursus (1st February), back to the mountains on the slopes of which is the parish of St. Columban (in the commune of Pagno), the first two on one side (Val Varaita), the latter on the other (valletta del torrente Bronda). At the present day it is St. Bridget of Sweden who is honoured in the chapel at Piasco, but the dedication of the chapel was certainly altered in ignorance at some more or less remote period, because it still retains a fresco depicting and naming the Saint which is earlier than the fourteenth century, earlier, i.e., than St. Bridget of Sweden.

Something similar must have occurred in the case of another chapel of St. Brigit in the parish of Villar S. Costanzo (again in the diocese of Saluzzo), near Dronero, where at the present day the Widow of Sweden is likewise honoured. The dedication may be presumed to have been altered from the great antiquity of the chapel and its proximity to the famous Abbey of Villar S. Costanzo.

The diocese of Aosta, which, as Canon Dondeynaz[3] observes, has always had a lively devotion to Irish saints, "always combines St. Brigit with St. Ursus."

St. Ursus and St. Brigit were the ancient patrons of the city of Ivrea[4] also; and there, close to the Abbey of St. Stephen, stood a church consecrated, according to Dondeynaz,[5] to the pair of them, but, so far as I have been able to discover, to St. Ursus alone.

St. Brigit is co-titular along with St. Ursus of the parish of Vallanzengo Biellese (in the diocese of Biella and the province of Vercelli).

Vercelli[6] had a church dedicated to St. Brigit and attached to a 'Scots' hospice' which, having been founded probably by one Bonfiglio, a priest of the Cathedral of St. Eusebius, was in existence as early as 1140, and seems to have been the oldest of the various hospices or hospitals in the city; it is cited as 'hospitale Scotorum' under date 1183 and 1184 in the charters of the Chapter Archives of Vercelli,[7] and served (according to a document dated 1305) "ad utilitatem omnium tam clericorum quam laicorum de Hybernia et Scotia transeuntium." This hospice was merged in 1343 into the hospital of St. Andrew, which was about a century old at the time and then greatly enlarged. The attached Church of St. Brigit appears from a document dated 1185 to have been a parish church. The parish ceases to appear in fourteenth-century documents, and the omission would suggest that it was suppressed when the Scots' hospice was absorbed by the St. Andrew's Hospital.[8]

§ 3

In Liguria also there is devotion to St. Brigit. "The holy patron of Ireland, who lived in the sixth century, received a

[3] Cf. Vie de Saint Ours, Aosta, Mensio, 1868, pp. 30 and 104.
[4] Cf. G. Saroglia, Eporedia sacra, Ivrea, Tomatis, 1887.
[5] Op. cit., p. 30.
[6] Cf. Carlo Dionisotti, Notizie biografiche dei Vercellesi illustri, Biella, 1862: Mgr. Riccardo Orsenigo, Vercelli Sacra, Como, 1909; and Mandelli, Il Comune di Vercelli nel M.E., Vercelli, 1858.
[7] Cf. vols. 70 and 71 of the Collana storica della Soc. Storica Subalpina, Torino.
[8] Cf. Savio, Gli antichi vescovi d'Italia: il Piemonte, pp. 483-4.

cult not only in Ireland but also in the Gauls and upper Italy.[9] But no mention of her is to be found in the Roman liturgical books. In Genoa her name occurs in the codices *C.M.V.*, with rite *sem.* and an *oratio propria*, 'Deus qui sanctarum virginum,' also found in the Ambrosian books. Her cult was promoted particularly by the Lateran Order: and the *Diarii* referred to contain this entry: 'The Lateran practice is to make the office of St. Brigit Virgin, their canoness, double." Dom Gougaud[10] has remarked upon the strange fact, "that ill-founded statement of late inventors," as Lanigan[11] described it, that the Canons Regular claim St. Patrick and St. Brigit as members of their order. I suggest as a possible explanation the important part played among the Canons Regular by those members of the Order who resided at St. Fridian's in Lucca and long made that city a centre of Irish influence (cf. Chap. II, § 9, and Chap. XVII, § 7).

There is an oratory dedicated to St. Brigit in the parish of Cervo Ligure (the diocese of Albenga and the province of Imperia).[12]

§ 4

Pavia once possessed a hospital of St. Brigit mentioned in the fourteenth century by Opicino de Canistris: it has disappeared without leaving any trace.[13]

It is not improbable that this hospital also, like those at Vercelli and Piacenza dedicated to the same saint, was a *hospitale Scottorum*. A relic of St. Brigit was formerly preserved in the cathedral at Pavia.[14]

[9] Cf. Cambiaso, *L'anno ecclesiastico in Genoa*, Genoa, 1917, p. 112; cf. also pp. 295 and 376.

[10] In *Gaelic Pioneers*, pp. 110-3, the only reference made by the learned Benedictine to the cult of St. Brigit in Italy.

[11] He also noted that the claim was vigorously opposed by the Order of Augustinian hermits who maintained that St. Patrick had been one of them. Colgan has a whole dissertation on the subject in *Tr. Th.*, pp. 237 et seq. Cf. also Fleury, *Instit.*, Part I, cap. 22.

[12] The statement in the *Annuario delle Diocesi e del Clero d'Italia*, 1904, p. 11* that SS. Reparata and Brigit are joint patrons of the parish of Aquila d' Arroscia (in the diocese of Albenga and the province of Imperia) is erroneous; the parish is dedicated to St. Reparata alone.

[13] Cf. Gianani, *Opicino de Canistris*, pp. 90 and 131.

[14] Cf. Romualdo Ghisoni, *Flavia Papia Sacra*, 1699, Part III, p. 2.

The Church of Ponzate, in the diocese of Como, raised to the status of a parish church in 1400, is dedicated to St. Brigit, a dedication which may be credibly attributed, as I am informed by Canon Giacinto Turazza of Como, to the Benedictines of St. Abbondio who owned property in the neighbourhood.

At Camerlata, also in the diocese of Como, there is another ancient Church of St. Brigit which may have been erected by a Bishop Amalric (844-65); it is traditionally celebrated and attracts a multitude of people, more particularly on 2nd February (the feast is kept in a number of places on 2nd instead of 1st February).

The Bergamasco has two parishes dedicated to St. Brigit: Lorentino, part of Calolzio (on the Adda), and Santa Brigida (in the upper Val Brembana, between Olmo al Brembo and Cusio). The church in Lorentino contains a stone bearing the following inscription: "D.O.M. Olim Dianae nunc B. Birgittae Virg.," and attracts a great multitude of people, especially on 1st February, when the relics are kissed as a remedy for sore eyes. Santa Brigida in Val Brembana is a village picturesquely situated and split up into different sections. Both parishes, once rural deaneries, now enjoy the privilege of being administered by archpriests, and belonging to the diocese of Milan, both observe the Ambrosian rite.[15]

§ 5

There is a parish church in Piacenza dedicated to St. Brigit of exceptional historical interest, which has been the subject of an original work by G. Tononi[16] and an ample monograph by Mgr. V. Pancotti.[17] It was built between 826 and 850 at his own expense by the Irish St. Donatus, bishop of Fiesole, in honour of St. Brigit, and presented by him as his own property on 20th August, 850, to the Monastery of St. Columban at Bobbio, together with all the build-

[15] Cf. Baggi, *S. Patrizio vescovo, protettore di Vèrtova, p.* 66.
[16] *S. Donato e la Chiesa di S. Brigida con ospizio pei pellegrini irlandesi a Piacenza,* Strenna Piacentina, 1891.
[17] *La Chiesa di S. Brigida,* Piacenza, Del Maino, 1929.

ings attached, and all the other property relating, thereto.
The deed of grant says: "Constat me Donatum sanctae
Vesulanae ecclesiae episcopum ex genere Scotorum jamdu-
dum contulisse, sicut et contuli, ecclesiam meam, quae est
constructa in honore sanctae Brigidae in civitate Placentiae,
monastero Bobii," etc.; and among the objects mentioned by
the donor it is specified that open house shall be kept for Irish
'pilgrims,' "si de gente mea aliquis peregrinus advenerit."
Mr. Mario Esposito has observed that the remarkable
diffusion of Latin *Vite* of St. Brigit in Italy is due in great
part to the activity of St. Donatus of Fiesole and that of
another Irish emigrant, 'Colman, bishop,' styled 'nepos
Cracavist,' who lived in Rome at the beginning of the
ninth century.[18] The hospice gradually declined in importance in course of time so far as achieving the object of its
foundation by Donatus was concerned, and the Church of
St. Brigit had early in the thirteenth century lost almost all
the possessions and properties with which it had been so
lavishly endowed by St. Donatus and other generous Irish
'pilgrims.' Pancotti (p. 21) maintains that the church
became a parish church in the first half of the eleventh
century, when the Monastery of St. Columban, then in full
tide of decay and torn by internal and external dissensions,
had abandoned the care of the Church and Convent of St.
Brigit, which then found themselves under the jurisdiction
of the bishop for the time being. In 1135 (ibid., p. 36)
St. Brigit's appears as a principal church (*prepositura*), and
in 1143 its incumbent is recorded as belonging to the congregation of urban parish priests.

On 21st January, 1185, the peace of Constance was
ratified and sworn by all the deputies of the Lombard League
in St. Brigit's, and in 1471 the Hospital of St. Brigit (ibid.,
p. 25) was annexed to the great hospital. From 1632 to 1806
the parish was administered by the Barnabite Fathers, and
after their expulsion by Napoleon, by spiritual superinten-
dents down to 1906, in which year its privileged status was

---

[18] Cf. "The poems of Colmanus, 'Nepos Cracavist,' and Dungalus 'praecipuus Scottorum' " in the *Journal of Theol. Studies*, XXXII, 1932, pp. 113 et
seq.

restored to it and it became a *prepositura* once more. The church was scheduled as a national monument in 1911. On 1st September, 1923, Cardinal Ehrle, the Papal Legate to the fourteenth centenary of St. Columban at Bobbio, said Mass in St. Brigit's in the presence of four Irish bishops and many pilgrims. St. Raymund Palmerio was born in the parish of St. Brigit and was accustomed to pray daily in the church before the Romanesque crucifix still preserved there. A clause in the ancient statutes of the Commune of Piacenza recognises the 1st February as a holiday dedicated to the patron of Ireland; all servile work was forbidden on that day *et forum silebat.* The Church of St. Brigit in Piacenza is referred to in Cipolla and Buzzi's *Codice diplomatico del Monastero di S. Colombano di Bobbio.*[19]

Parma also once had a church of St. Brigit which appears as an *ecclesia* in the tithe-rolls for 1230 and 1299, and in the rate-book for 1354.[20] In 1578 it was reduced to a mere oratory and the duties of the charge were transferred to S. Anastasio. It was later acquired and demolished in 1674 by Ranuccio II with the object of enlarging the College of the Nobles.[21]

I would also mention that between Minerbio and Granarolo dell' Emilia (Bologna) there is a suburb called Santa Brigida,[22] but I have been unable to ascertain whether it derives its name from the Irish saint or not.

§ 6

There are two parishes dedicated to our St. Brigit in the province of Trent: Don in the commune of Cavareno, and Romagnano in the commune of Mattarello, where 1st February is kept as a feast-day with much devotion. Fr. Teodorico Asson, O.F.M., has drawn my attention to a passage in Fr. Giangrisostomo Tovazzi's MS., *Notitia Ecclesiarum,* etc., *n.* 1164, p. 315 as follows: "Eccl. s. Brigittae virginis curata Romaniani plebis Pedescastellanae [Trent] de qua in 'Parochiali' *t.* 2, *c.* 135, *p.* 1386. Ibi festum tituli

[19] *Ist. St. It.*, Rome, I, pp. 165 and 167; II, pp. 230-1.
[20] Cf. A. Schiavi, *La Diocesi di Parma*, Parma, 1925, pp. 29, 44, 71, 89.
[21] Ibid, p. 160.
[22] Touring Club Map, sheet 19, A. I.

celebratur calendis febr. et festum dedicat. die 28 Octobris."
In the *Parrocchiale* the church is referred to as follows:
"Titularis (ecclesiae) ejus est S. Birgitta seu Brigitta vel
Brigida virgo scota monialis, cujus festum colitur calendis
februarii. . . . In ordine recitandi divinum officium juxta
ritum Eccl. abbat. S. Michaelis de Caudiana canonicorum
regul. S. Salvatoris Congr. Rhenanae Ordinis S. Augustini
pro anno 1777 ad 1 febr. habetur: Brigidae virg. semid.
canonissae regularis (*in margine:* In directorio nostrorum
Fratrum hibernorum Pragae commorantium[23] pro anno
1786 ad 1 febr. lego: S. Brigidae Virginis Hibern. Patronae
dup. 2 cl. or. et. lect. 2 noct. prop.)" This would suggest
that in the Trentino also the cult of St. Brigit was promoted
by the Canons Regular. It should, however, be borne in
mind that there was a Benedictine monastery at Piedicastello
(Trent), where the first Franciscan Friars lodged in 1221,
before building a convent of their own.

§ 7

The boundary between the area in which the cult of the
Irish saint is practised and that in which the cult of her
Swedish namesake begins has now been reached.

St. Bridget of Sweden is the dedicatee of a village, Santa
Brigida, part of Roncegno in the province of Trent, and of a
few St. Bridget chapels in Istria.

I have been unable to discover any trace of a cult of St.
Brigit of Cell-dara in central or southern Italy, but the
number of churches and chapels dedicated to St. Bridget of
Sweden is legion.

[23] For a list of the Irish scholars, Dominican, Cistercian, Benedictine and
Franciscan, who taught philosophy and theology in the archiepiscopal college
at Prague a hundred years earlier (1635-97) cf. Mrs. Green's *The Making of
Ireland and its Undoing*, London, 1908, pp. 454-8. The Franciscan establishment
is mentioned on pp. 442 and 445.

CHAPTER IX

ST. GALL

§ 1

THE more important events in the life of this companion of St. Columban, who, settling in Switzerland in 612, became the remote founder of the famous Abbey of St. Gall, whose importance in the history of medieval culture was certainly no less than that of the Bobbio monastery, were briefly mentioned in Chapter II, § 4.[1] The influence exercised by the monks of St. Gall on the origin and development of 'sequences' and the art of music was especially notable.[2] The Swiss monastery long maintained relations of various sorts with northern Italy, and, although the saint himself never penetrated south of the Alps, numerous traces may still be found of the cult with which he was once honoured even in Italy.[3]

---

[1] Cf. in addition to the bibliography given by Dom Gougaud in *Christianity in Celtic Lands* those given by Dom Bruno Albers in *Il monachismo primo di S. Benedetto* (pp. 109 and 116), Rome, 1916, and by Dom Ursmer Berlière in *L'ordre monastique des origines au XIIème siècle*, 3rd ed. Lille-Paris-Maredsous, 1924, pp. 183 et seq.

[2] Cf. Berlière, op. cit., pp. 133, 152, 158, and C. A. Cingria, *La civilisation de Saint Gall*, Geneva, Payot, 1929.

[3] Cf., for the connection between the Bobbio monastery and that at St. Gall (and with Switzerland in general), the *Cod. dipl. del. Mon. di S. Colombano di Bobbio*, edd. Cipolla and Buzzi, I, pp. 90 et seq., 159 et seq., 398 et seq., and 410, and, for the connection between the monastery at St. Gall and the *schola* of Eusebius at Vercelli, two important notes by Mons. R. Pastè: 'Di una lettera di Notkero Balbulo a Luitvardo vescovo di Vercelli' (in *Scuola Cattolica*, 1911, Vol. 21, pp. 91-95), and 'Sulle tracce dei monaci di S. Gallo' (ibid. 1913, Vol. 3, pp. 223-230); the latter refers also to the Irish influence in general upon the school at Vercelli. Cf. also Mons. E. Pasteris, 'Le prose ritmiche o sequenze di Attone di Vercelli,' in *Scuola Cattolica*, 1925, Vol. 6, pp. 295 and 340-346. That there were relations also between St. Gall and Como would appear from a document cited by Savio in *Gli antichi vescovi d'Italia, La Lombardia*, Pt. II, Vol. I. Bergamo, 1929, p. 309 à propos the bishop of Como, Luitvard I (888-905), whose death is recorded in the appendix to the book of the confraternity of St. Gall as follows (cf. *M.G.H., Libri confraternitatum*, p. 136): "VIII Kal. Julii (the 24th July) obitus Luitvardi Cumani episcopi. Cui dominus Salomo episcopus (Solomon III, bishop of Constance, 889-920) et cuncta congregatio S. Galli tales orationes concesserunt quales pro semetipsis agere consueverunt."

252

St. Gall died on 16th October, 646, and his feast is kept on that day in many countries of Europe, more particularly Switzerland, Alsace, the Germanies,[4] and—let it be added—Italy.

§ 2

In Piedmont the parish of Corneliano in the diocese of Alba and the province of Cuneo is dedicated to SS. Gall and Nicholas. The Monastery at Nonantola possessed vast estates in the county of Alba in the eleventh century, and there were at least two Benedictine monasteries also in the neighbourhood of Corneliano. Provost Don Vincenzo Calliano informs me that there is a document dated 1345 in the archives of the cathedral at Asti from which it appears that the parish of Corneliano was already then dedicated to SS. Gall and Nicholas.

Dondeynaz[5] states that St. Gall, along with St. Columban, had 'a distinct place' in the liturgy of the diocese of Aosta.

§ 3

As for Liguria, Mgr. D. Cambiaso[6] observes under date 16th October: "St. Gall ab. This is the famous companion of St. Columban, and it was only right that he should have been given a place in the liturgy of Liguria on account of St. Columban. In the codices referred to his rite is *sem.*, with the prayer *de communi*. He was venerated especially by Benedictine monks, as the seventeenth century diaries observe."[7]

§ 4

Lombardy at the present day has three parishes dedicated to St. Gall.

The first is Ponna inferiore in the diocese and province of Como, in the valleys running down to the Lake of Lugano,

---

[4] Cf. Gougaud, *Gaelic Pioneers*, pp. 121 et seq.
[5] *Vie de Saint Ours*, Aosta, 1868, p. 30.
[6] *L'anno ecclesiastico in Genova*, Genoa, 1917, p. 248.
[7] Cf. Ibid., and Gougaud, *Gaelic Pioneers*, p. 124.

in the *pieve* of Montronio (Castiglione d' Intelvi).   The
dedication to St. Gall may be due to the Cistercians of
Acqua Fredda who were great landowners in those valleys.

The second is Premadio in the diocese and province of
Sondrio in the upper Valtellina, that is to say, in the former
county of Bormio, once subject to the Bishop of Chur; the
title of St. Gall has been retained for the present parish
church built about the end of the fifteenth century on the
site of another church dedicated to St. Christopher; the old
church seems to have had a hospice attached for 'pilgrims.'
On the neighbouring mountain of Oga is a church dedicated
to St. Columban. Canon G. Turazza of Como states that the
titulars of these two churches were chosen, without any
direct monastic influence, from the *Proprium* of the diocese
of Chur, just as in the heart of the Valtellina there is a
church in the mountains dedicated to St. Lucius, [8] a second-
century saint, who is said to have been a king in Britain,
the first Bishop of Chur and a martyr.   His feast is kept on

[8] In the pontificate of Pope Eleutherus—i.e., between the years 177 and 181
—a British king, whose name has been preserved in the Latin form of Lucius
and who reigned, perhaps, in the neighbourhood of Llandaff, sent messengers
to the Bishop of Rome, with a request that he might be admitted into the
pale of Christianity. "He soon obtained his pious request and the Britons
preserved the faith which they had received uncorrupted and entire, in peace
and tranquillity, until the time of the Emperor Diocletian." (*Bede, H.E.*, I,
iv, Everyman edition, p. 9.) The earliest known source for this story is the adapt-
ation of the *Liber Pontificalis* known as the '*Catalogus Felicianus*' and attributed
to the year 530; Bede probably received it thence through his friend Nothelm
(cf. *Lib. Pont.*, ed. Duchesne, I, ccxxii f.). There is no mention of it in Gildas,
so that Dr. Plummer (Bede, *H.E.*, Vol. II, p. 14, Oxford, 1896) and other
scholars, e.g., Harnack, who argued, not very convincingly, that Lucius was
really a king of Edessa in *Sitzungsb. der Konigl. preussischen Akademie der Wissenschaft*,
1904, pp. 909-916 (Cf. also *D.C.B.*, articles 'Eleutherus' and 'Lucius'), have
pronounced it fabulous, but the tradition is there. Some corroboration of it
may be found in the fragment of Tertullian, *Adv. Judaeos*, VII, *P.L.*, II, 649-50,
quoted on p. 34 and attributed to *c.* A.D. 200-206.   Tertullian had visited
Rome and his words may well reflect the exultation felt there at the success
which had attended their early missionaries.

Malmesbury (*Ant. Glas.*, II) states that Lucius died A.D. 183 and was buried
in Glastonbury, but the legend only began to make progress under Geoffrey
of Monmouth (*Brit. Hist.* IV, v) and developed, until, finally, Lucius was
conceived to have abdicated his throne, become a priest, travelled through
France and the Germanies accompanied by his sister Emerita, and, after
enduring much hardship, to have settled at Chur, the capital of the Grisons,
which thus became the centre of his missionary labours. He was consecrated
Bishop of Chur and suffered martyrdom in the year 201, in the castle of
Martiola. The (eighth-century) cathedral at Chur is still dedicated to St.
Lucius.

3rd December, and he presents, it may be said in passing, great historical interest.

The third Lombard parish dedicated to St. Gall is to be found in a village appropriately called San Gallo in Val Brembana (Bergamo), near S. Giovanni Bianco. It would seem to have been formerly the site of a small Benedictine monastery, and part of the commune is still called Callabà, Casa dell' abate (abbot's house).[9] I am told by the parish priest that in the course of excavations made in 1908 in the piazza in front of the church coffins containing the remains of monks with fragments of their habits still clinging to them were discovered. The arms of the commune are a bear fleeing before a monastery.

There is another village in Lombardy also called San Gallo, part of the commune of Botticino sera in the diocese and province of Brescia, on the road from Brescia to Salò. A Benedictine monastery there once served as a country-house for the Benedictines of Brescia belonging to the monastery of SS. Faustin and Giovita, the patrons of the diocese. The name probably became attached to the district from the fact of their owning great estates there. The parish church is dedicated to St. Bartholomew the Apostle, but a side altar is dedicated to St. Gall.

The baptismal name 'Gall' is common in the parish.

§ 5

The famous Benedictine monastery of Val di Tolla in the diocese of Piacenza on the road traversed by pilgrims to Rome was dedicated to SS. Saviour and Gall. It has disappeared without leaving any trace,[10] but the dedication to SS. Saviour and Gall remains to the parish church of Monastero Valtolla (Lugagnano), whose parish priest still retains the title of abbot.

[9] Cf. Maironi Da Ponte, *Dizionario odeporico*, 1820, Vol. iii, p. 62.

[10] Cf. G. P. Bognetti, 'L'abbazia regia di San Salvatore di Tolla' in *Bollettino Stor. Piacentino*, 1929.

§ 6

The Veneto contains numerous traces of the cult of St. Gall. In the diocese and province of Padua is the old (thirteenth-century) parish church of the commune of Urbana, near Montagnana, which is dedicated to him. Part of the same commune known as S. Salvaro contains the remains of an ancient monastery.

The parish church of Pesina in the commune of Caprino Veronese (in the diocese and province of Verona) is likewise dedicated to St. Gall. Two convents, now suppressed, belonged to the territory of the parish which dates from 1460. The ancient church stood on the site of the present cemetery and the present church was built about 1760.

As for the Trentino, Fr. Tovazzi[11] refers to the churches dedicated to St. Gall at n. 310, p. 89, "Eccl. S. Galli de Egna in Athesia cujus meminit charta anni 1203" at Egna in val d' Adige, between Trent and Bolzano, and at n. 706 p. 206, "Eccl. S. Galli de Cagnodo plebis Revodi ad an. 1500," Cagnò in the *pieve* of Revò on the road to Anaunia, between Ponte di Mostizzolo and Cavareno (the commune containing the parish of Don already mentioned as being dedicated to St. Brigit). This St. Gall of Cagnò is a church perched upon an eminence round which hermits clustered from 1491 onwards.[12]

Another 'hermitage of St. Gall' stands on a magnificent site above Soligo in the province of Treviso and was founded apparently by a Friar Giles of Lombardy in 1430 on the ruins of a castle at Soligo belonging to the da Camino family, and destroyed towards the end of the fourteenth century by Rambaldo da Collalto on behalf of the Most Serene Republic of Venice. Friar Giles was determined to dedicate the church to the holy Abbot Gall in memory of the early years of his religious life which he had spent in the abbey of that name in Switzerland: the name survived and was applied to the whole mountain. He then invited another com-

[11] Cf. op. cit., *Notitia ecclesiarum*, etc.
[12] Cf. an interesting article on 'Gli eremiti nel Trentino' by Fr. Simone Weber in the *Rivista Tridentina* for December, 1912, which, on page 241, gives a list of the hermits who resided at S. Gallo di Cagnò from 1491 to 1729.

panion from Switzerland to join him, who had come in the train of men looking for some adventurer to hire their services. A few of them settled at Soligo and founded families which still exist in the village: Viezzers (Switzers) and Dorigos (from Zorigo, of the canton of Zurich).

The succession of pious hermits from Switzerland was maintained down to 1800: there is a hermit there at the present day, but he belongs to no congregation. A fresco in the church above the high altar depicts St. Gall and bears the date 1442. His feast is solemnly kept there on 16th October with a crowded attendance of the faithful from the whole district of the Piave and even from regions beyond: the intercession of St. Gall is particularly invoked to cure sick babies.[13]

§ 7

In the province of Udine is the abbey church of Moggio Udinese (Castrum Mosnicii, in German Mosburg), which has the name of St. Gall.[14] By a notarial deed or instrument usually assigned to the year 1084 or 1085, one Cacellino, a Count Palatine, granted his own inherited property in Carinthia and Friuli to his associate Federigo, patriarch of Aquileia, on condition that the castle on the freehold of Moggio should be demolished, a monastery built in its stead in honour of Our Lady and St. Gall, and the black monks invited to govern it.[15] The patriarch Federigo died in 1085, but his successor, Voldarico I, saw to the building of the monastery at Moggio, thus fulfilling the pious intention of Cacellino, and on 9th June, 1119, had it solemnly dedicated.

It may be that in dedicating it to St. Gall the patriarch was not so much giving exact expression to the wishes of the dead donor as being guided by feelings of gratitude of his own, he himself having governed the famous Benedictine

---

[13] I am indebted for these particulars to Mgr. Giovanni Pasin's admirable volume, *Soligo e la sua storia*, Venice, Libreria Emiliana Editrice, 1928, pp. 63 et seq.

[14] Cf. A. Battistella, *L'abbazia di Moggio*, Udine, Doretti, 1903, Mgr. P. Paschini in *Mem. Stor. Forogiuliese*, IX (1913), pp. 336 et seq., and Kehr, *Italia pontificia*, VII, Pars. I, p. 66.

[15] Battistella, op. cit., p. 10.

abbey in Switzerland. The consecration of the church and the various altars took place in August, and on this occasion Voldarico presented the monastery with much other property which he owned in Friuli and Carinthia. In that same year (1119), the name of one Bebulf is recorded as having been that of the first abbot. The abbot, although subject to the feudal supremacy of the patriarch, a supremacy confirmed to the see of Aquileia by Pope Innocent II on 29th June, 1132, was ecclesiastically dependent only on the Roman Curia, and voted among the prelates in the Parliament of the 'Patria' of Friuli. But power and wealth presently brought envy and invidious comparisons in their train, and the abbey, having grown to be a great feudal proprietor, found itself involved in manifold conflicts with its own dependents and the neighbouring barons (more particularly the families of Di Prampero and Mels and the commune of Venzone), and in such conflicts lost both its reputation and its influence.

The community in the thirteenth century numbered only some fifteen monks. The election of the abbot from 1184 to 1329 was made by the monks themselves. In 1329 the Pope himself (John XXII) and the consistory of cardinals took it in hand. Towards the end of the fourteenth century the abbey was financially in very low water and had been partially destroyed by fire. Early in the fifteenth century it became a *commenda*, like the other abbeys in Friuli at Sesto, Rosazzo, la Belligna, and Summaga. The temporal patriarchate of Aquileia foundered in the stormy waters of barren upheavals in 1420, and its disappearance hastened the decay of the abbey. In 1423 the abbot, submitting without protest to the new lordship of the Most Serene Republic, hastily appointed two procurators who resided in Venice. In October 1422 the patriarch Louis of Teck came down the valley of the Fella at the head of 4.000 Hungarians in order to recover his lost dominions, occupied the church, and, with the help of a traitor, burst into the monastery of Moggio and proceeded to sack it. Only the sudden intervention of the Venetian levies caused him to decamp, but not without dragging behind him a heavy train of plunder, codices, books and sacred vessels which his mercenaries sold by the way.

A commendatory abbot, Biagio Molin (1431-45), was the first of a series of twenty-one abbots, all commendatory. By a bull dated 6th March, 1561, Pius V conferred the abbey on Cardinal Charles Borromeo, who, five years later (1566), being desirous of devoting himself entirely to his church in Milan, renounced many benefices including also the Abbey of Moggio. He does not appear ever to have visited it. Borromeo was succeeded as abbot by the famous Bartolomeo di Porcia (1567-71), praised by Tasso alike for his eloquence, prudence and learning. The patriarchate of Aquileia was suppressed in 1751, and the two archbishoprics of Udine and Gorizia were created to take its place. This was another blow to the shattered edifice of the abbey at Moggio, inasmuch as it produced fresh and still more thorny difficulties in the matter of spiritual jurisdiction and left the abbot alone to contend with the Archbishop of Gorizia on the one hand and the imperial governors of Klagenfurt and Villach on the other.

In March 1762 Cardinal Delfino was succeeded as commendatory abbot by Count Felice Faustino Savorgnan, papal governor of Perugia, and the last abbot of Moggio. On his death in 1776 the abbatial jurisdiction of Moggio was abolished by a decree of the Senate of Venice passed on 2nd September, 1773. The ecclesiastical jurisdiction was transferred to the Archbishop of Udine so far as territories owing obedience to the Republic were concerned, and the fief, 'placed at the disposition of the public,' was sold by auction for 44,000 ducats to MM. Mangilli and Leoni, who, by a deed of investiture dated 4th February 1778, assumed the magnificent title of Marquis of St. Gall and arrogated to themselves the civil jurisdiction of first instance, the right of administering justice, the free choice of offices, and a vote (alternating annually between the two families) in the *magnifico Parlamento* of the 'Patria' of Friuli. The abbey church was converted into a parish church and became the mother of all the other churches in the Canal del Ferro, while the archpriest was given the status of a rural dean.

In September 1869, Pius IX gratified the wishes of the populace by reviving the title of abbey church and granted the vicar the insignia of a prelate.

Among the relics in the possession of the abbey of Moggio was the reputed head of St. Brigit (?) and a finger of St. Gall. During the pastoral visitation of 1565 it was discovered that the finger, which 'was of a greenish hue turning black' and preserved in a double box of silver and copper, was missing, and that two crumpled leaves of an old breviary had been substituted.

Prof. Battistella of the communal library at Udine informs me that the title of Marquis of St. Gall, which the Mangilli and the Leoni adopted in 1778, still survives in the Udinese family of Mangilli (as to the Leoni, who are not natives of Friuli, he has no information). They had it confirmed to them by Austria in December 1829, and were later inscribed in the Italian official Roll as of the nobility and marquises of S. Gallo di Moggio.

The feast of St. Gall is still kept on 16th October at the Abbey of Moggio and is attended by many of the faithful and all the priests of the Canal del Ferro (Val Fella).

§ 8

There was another church of St. Gall but without any connection with the abbey of Moggio, in the province of Udine and, more particularly, in the parish of Strassoldo, in the commune of Cervignano del Friuli. About two miles west of Strassoldo is a cluster of some thirty houses, nearly all separate, but together forming the unit still called San Gallo. Alongside one the ruins may be seen of an ancient church which fell to pieces through neglect about 1865. I am informed by Sig. Antonio Deluisa, school master at Strassoldo, that he has come across the name of the church in twelfth century documents and that a watercourse flowing alongside is called in fifteenth century documents "acqua di S. Gallo." There are traces, it would appear, under the apse, of a Roman temple, and the name 'Castra,' which still remains attached to another watercourse, flowing not

far from the ruins, gives rise to the suspicion that the site
was once occupied by a Roman camp: the via Postumia ran
only a few hundred yards away.

There is an ancient chapel dedicated to St. Gall near
Albona in Istria. Canon Don Silvio Zanoni of Albona
informs me that he has been unable to find in the parish
archives any document throwing light on the date of construction or the origin of the dedication. The chapel is very
small, stands in the open country, and is not served, but a
sung Mass is celebrated there every year on 16th October
with a considerable attendance of the faithful.

§ 9

The via San Gallo and the Porta San Gallo are familiar
to every visitor to Florence. Guccerelli[16] says with reference
to the via San Gallo: "The street ran from the centre of the
city to the Porta S. Gallo, built in 1294 to the designs of
Arnolfo. The locality has borne this name from the earliest
times, because on the exact site of the present parterre there
stood in 1218 a little church dedicated to St. Gall, surnamed
the Apostle of Switzerland. The Augustinians who served
the little church, made such adroit use of their influence upon
the munificence of Lorenzo il Magnifico that they succeeded
in obtaining his assistance towards the extension of their
church and convent.

"Giuliano di Francesco Giamberti, a famous architect
highly esteemed by the Magnifico, received the commission
for the work and erected a huge building, 90 cubits long and
imposing on account of the beauty of its structure, the
admirable lay-out of the cloisters, the refectory and the
hundreds of cells in the convent. And he was called Giuliano
da Sangallo because of the reputation he acquired through
that impressive achievement. Church and convent suc-
cumbed to the demolishing pick in the exigencies of the
siege during 1529-30, and the ruins were left derelict for
over two centuries."

[16] Stradario storico-biografico della Città di Firenze, Florence, 1929, pp. 414-5.

Vasari[17] gives a similar explanation of the surname Giuliano da San Gallo, but Milanesi suspects the truth of the story, because even before the date of the rebuilding of the monastery, and, more precisely, in 1485, Giamberti is already described as 'da San Gallo,'[18] and he declares that Giuliano and his brother were called 'da San Gallo' simply because they lived for many years outside the Porta San Gallo.[19]

Richa says (loc. cit.): "Outside the Porta San Gallo stood a hospital called after S. Maria del Popolo, founded, according to Leopoldo del Migliore, in the year 1218 by Guidalotto dell' Orco and Bernardesca, his wife, for the behoof of pilgrims and foundlings with an endowment entrusted to the care of the Augustinian Fathers; when Pope Pius II merged it in 1463 into the Ospedale degli Innocenti, then recently erected in the piazza della Nunziata, the Florentines having been goaded thereto by the long and learned harangues of Leonardo Aretino. . . . And so, the hospital of St. Gall having been suppressed, the state of those Augustinian Fathers in that place seemed pitiable indeed," when the Magnifico intervened on behalf of Padre Mariano. Richa also says (p. 165) that Giamberti "owing to the acclamation which greeted this building was called Giuliano da S. Gallo."

Let it be added that Boccaccio[20] refers to a "Lucifero da San Gallo" as a Lucifer that chewed and champed the

---

[17] Cf. *Le Vite dei più eccellenti pittori, scultori ed architetti*, with notes and commentary by Gaetano Milanesi, Florence, 1879, IV, 274. In Mrs. Jonathan Foster's translation, London, 1850-1885, cf. Vol. II, 1878, at p. 493.

[18] Arch. del Duomo di Firenze, Deliberaz. 1482-86, n. 107.

[19] Cf. for the Church of St. Gall, Gius. Richa; *Notizie istoriche delle chiese fiorentine*, Florence, 1754, Vol. I, pp. 264 et seq., and G. Carocci: 'Firenze illustrata. Fra la vecchia e la nuova cinta. Chiesa e convento di San Gallo' (in *Firenze Artistica*, an. III, 1874), and "Relazione e ragguaglio distintissimo della origine, fondazione e demolizione della chiesa e convento dei Frati di S. Gallo, esistente già fuori della città di Firenze, dalla quale chiesa fu presa la denominazione della Porta S. Gallo; colla notizia della sua erezione e del modo con cui pervenne nella Congregazione dei PP. Agostiniani Osservanti di Lombardia, del posto ottenuto di poi dai medesimi Religiosi in Firenze nel convento e Chiesa di S. Jacopo dei Fossi, e in qual maniera crebbe il culto e la divozione nella detta Città alla SS. imagine della Madonna della Tosse," Florence, Paperini, 1748, in 4to. None of these texts, unfortunately, goes back further than the thirteenth century.

[20] *Decameron*, VIIIth Day, Novel 9.

damned, and that Arturo Graf[21] observes that, according to Sansovino, quoted by Fanfani, the church of San Gallo in Florence contained a picture representing a devil with a number of mouths.[22].

It is interesting to observe that the cradle of Franciscanism in Florence lay close to the church of St. Gall.[23] When St. Francis went to Florence in 1211, "he received from certain devout citizens, who looked up to him as an admirable man, a little hospice next to the church of St. Gall, 'ad D.P. extra civitatem.' There he clothed a number, chief amongst whom was John Parenti of the town of Carmignano . . . who, after the death of St. Francis, was assumed to the high office of General." There he also clothed John Bonelli, Joseph Fiorentino ('the Florentine'), Michael de Albertis and many others. "They reposed in that first little convent of friars next to the Church of St. Gall amid the veneration of the populace. But when, many years later, the corpse of Friar Joseph was exhumed, it was found to be whole and uninjured, and the garment in which it was wrapped was unimpaired. Now the Florentines built a beautiful chapel in memory of the friars, and honourably laid their bodies therein, near the said church of St. Gall, which was much frequented and with great devotion by the people, until about the year 1482 (alias 1487) a certain Marianus, an Augustinian and a preacher of renown, obtained the Church of St. Gall from the Magnificent Lord Lorenzo dei Medici that he might build a convent beside it for his own. The said lord, however, determined to discharge the whole undertaking at his own expense, and, as the chapel aforesaid was in the way of the architect appointed by him, he had it taken down, but first he had the remains of the *Beati* removed. Our brethren, who had long since moved into the city, petitioned that the remains should be

---

[21] *Miti, leggende e superstizioni del Medio Evo*, 2 vols. Turin, Loescher, 1892-3, II, 94.

[22] The Lucifer in question was probably a representation of Leviathan (Job, XXXIX, 20; XLI, 4, 5, 10, 11, 12) in which the commentators beginning with S. Gregory the Great (*Moral in Job*, Migne, *P.L.*, LXXVI, 60), had early perceived a personification of Satan, a huge mouth belching forth flames with the Devil tossing in souls.

[23] Cf. Wadding *Annales minorum*, Vol. I, 113 and 114, xxiii.

handed over to them, but in vain, for the people of St. Gall protested and would not allow themselves to be deprived of such a treasure.   They promised, nevertheless, that they would erect a mausoleum for the holy men in the Church of St. Gall itself, but the deliberations entailed by the building of such an imposing structure were so long protracted and the expense so great that in the interval the remains were removed by stealth and became the property of someone else but whose I know not."

CHAPTER X

ST URSUS OF AOSTA

§ I

To clear the field of possible misunderstandings and to explain certain observations with regard to the Irish St. Ursus, it may be as well to begin by saying that other saints of the same name are venerated in Italy, including:

(i) A St. Ursus or Ursius, whose legend, recalling 'the story of Oedipus in all its gloomy horror,' resembles that of St. Julian the Hospitaller and other saints;[1] he is specially venerated in the province of Vicenza, where the commune of Sant' Orso or Santorso (feast, 3rd May) takes its name from him, and in Vejano, near Viterbo (feast, 29th January).[2]

(ii) A St. Ursus Martyr, an alleged disciple of St. Theonestus, whose feast falls on 21st June, and who is venerated together with two other martyrs (St. Alban, bishop, and St. Dominic, hermit), in Burano, near Venice.[3] Lanzoni, discussing the ancient Venetian diocese of Altinum to which Burano once belonged, writes as follows:[4] "The simple historical truth of this legend of itinerant saints, like so many others already considered, would seem to be just this, that when it was composed, a St. Alban martyr was venerated in Mainz, a St. Ursus martyr in Augusta della Vindelicia, and, in Altinum, a St. Theonestus martyr who is, perhaps, the same 'Theonestus martyr' as is venerated in Treviso, Vercelli and elsewhere."

(iii) A St. Ursus, Bishop of Ravenna in the fourth or fifth

[1] Cf. H. Delehaye, *Les legéndes hagiographiques*, Brussels, 1927, p. 60 (English trans., *The Legends of the Saints*, by Mrs. V. M. Crawford, London, 1907, p. 57), and Arturo Graf, *Miti, leggende e superstizioni del M.E.*, Turin, 1892, I, p. 288.

[2] Cf. D. Casalini, 'Studio giuridico-storico intorno a S. Orso' in *Scuola Cattolica*, 1900, vol. 19, pp. 124-143, 296-323, and 448-467.

[3] Cf. B. Verghetti, *Sei inni latini in onore dei SS. Martiri Albano, Domenico ed Orso, con cenni illustrativi intorno ai medesimi martiri per il sac. Frederico Longo di Murano*, Foligno, Artigianelli, 1893.

[4] *Le Diocesi d' Italia*, p. 907.

century (feast, 13th April), who built and consecrated the cathedral in Ravenna known as the Anastasis, and also described by the name of its builder as the Basilica Ursiana. At Ravenna, also, it should be observed, a martyr of similar name, S. Ursicino or S. Ursiano, is venerated, who is probably Ursicino, the martyr of Pannonia.

Such being the premises, Lanzoni's observations with regard to an alleged Ursus, Bishop of Aosta, become clear: "A *passio* of St. Theonestus of Altinum records a martyr named Ursus and places his death by error in Augusta in the province of Rhaetia instead of in Vindelicia under Theodosius (379-95); another *passio*, under King Hunneric (484). In these documents 'Augusta Vindeliciorum' has been confused (cf. *AA. SS.*, 1st February, 1, 99, 945) with 'Augusta Praetoria' with the result that the Ursus in question has been converted into a Bishop of Aosta (cf. Savio, op. cit., pp. 70-1), although the Altinum legend gives him no such episcopal status (cf. *M.G.H.*, *Scriptores*, *Rerum Merov.*, III, 31-2)."

It may be observed in passing that Saroglia,[5] in treating of St. Ursus, makes him die the death of a martyr, and, like other writers, concocts a fantastic brew out of ingredients borrowed from the legends of all the saints named Ursus, more particularly the Ursus of Vicenza.

§ 2

On St. Ursus of Aosta, whose feast is kept on 1st February, i.e., the same day as St. Brigit's, there is a volume (published anonymously) by Canon Dondeynaz,[6] which, although antiquated, still retains some value on account of the profound knowledge of the documents which informs it and the nice critical spirit which pervades it.

Ursus belonged to one of the earliest bands of Scots missionaries and seems to have come from Ireland to Italy early in the sixth century, after sojourning for a time in France in the neighbourhood of Meyronnes, now a hamlet

[5] *Eporedia sacra*, Ivrea, Tomatis, 1887, p. 169.
[6] *Vie de Saint Ours archidiacre d'Aoste*, Aosta, Mensio, 1868.

in the Basses Alpes, which still nourishes a lively devotion to him. He travelled thence down the Val d'Aosta combating the Arians on his way, became archdeacon of Aosta under a bishop named Jucundus, and shared the tribulations with which the Arians harassed the bishop and which were brought to an end only by the direct intervention of Theodoric.[7] Jucundus was succeeded on the episcopal throne of Aosta by one Plocean, who was either an Arian or imbued with Arian sympathies, and the troubles of the archdeacon broke out afresh. Ursus, however, unaffected by considerations of human prudence or personal fear, parted from the bishop who had been foisted upon him, and with great charity and energy saved the faith of his flock by withdrawing with a few canons of the cathedral outside the city to the church of St. Peter, and there laying the foundations of the famous collegiate church of SS. Peter and Ursus. This, it is presumed, was his headquarters in the campaign he waged for the defence and diffusion of orthodoxy, a campaign which he conducted so vigorously that he is still called the 'Apostle of the Valdostani.' The best known miracles attributed to him are of having stopped a threatened inundation of the Buthier in spate, of having made a spring gush out from a rock at Busseya (it is still called 'la fontana di S. Orso,' *fons S. Ursi*), and of having foretold the death of Plocean and of a servant (*ministerialis*) of his, to say nothing of his own, which duly took place in 529.[8]

§ 3

Savio transfers the death of St. Ursus to the second half of the sixth century, but adopts nearly all the arguments of Dondeynaz for placing it within that century. With regard to Plocean, he writes as follows:[9] "The name of this bishop, who is traditionally said to have been an Arian, has been preserved simply on account of its association with the

---

[7] Cf. Lanzoni, op. cit., p. 1055, nn. 3 and 4.

[8] Other miracles are recorded in op. cit., at pp. 89-92 and 101.

[9] Op. cit., pp. 79-81.

memory of St. Ursus, his archdeacon. Ughelli and Della
Chiesa say not a word about him. Besson placed Plocean
after 755 and declares that he was infected with iconoclastic
errors, but without producing any proof. As for St. Ursus,
some hagiographers conceived him to have been Bishop of
Aosta contemporaneously with St. Bernard of Menthon, the
famous founder of the hospice on the Great St. Bernard.
So in the breviary of the Canons Regular printed at Rome
in 1613 St. Bernard is said 'canonicum habitum ab Urso
ejus civitatis episcopo suscepisse.' This is an error due to
the misreading of the *Acta* of St. Bernard of Menthon, 'ad
ursum devotissimum episcopum' having been read instead
of 'ad virum devotissimum.' This is the suggestion made by
Papebrochius [the Bollandist Daniel Van Papenbroeck
(1628-1714)] in the legend of St. Bernard of Menthon on
15th June. Canon Gal (*Chart.* II, 29) has confirmed the
learned Bollandist's conjecture and proved its accuracy from
MSS. he has had under his eyes. The result is that he must
be considered to have been a simple priest and archdeacon
of the Church of Aosta, according to the account given in
his life. A St. Ursus is mentioned in the legend of St. Theonestus, but no reliance at all can be placed on this. In the
appendix to Vol. I for February, pp. 936-9, the Bollandists
have published an anonymous life much more deserving of
consideration. According to this account St. Ursus was a
priest in charge of the church of St. Peter in Aosta. It
depicts Plocean as a cruel and tyrannous usurper, but not
yet either an Arian or an iconoclast. . . . The Bollandists
did not investigate the question of the date of composition of
this life or express any opinion as to its value. It is certainly
earlier than the end of the eleventh century, as is proved by
the codices of that date which contain it, e.g., Codex cxxxiv,
alias 19, of the Capitular Archives of Vercelli. The sculpture
still to be seen above a pilaster in the cloister of St. Ursus
and depicting Plocean tortured by demons is a thirteenth
[twelfth (?)][10] century work and inspired by the Life.

[10] "The cloister of S. Orso d'Aosta has preserved from 1133 only the pillars
and the ornate capitals" (cf. P. Toesca, *Aosta*, Rome, 1911, p. 115). Sig.
Toesca, *Storia dell' arte italiana*, Turin, 1927, I, p. 766, thinks that the capitals
show a combination of Lombard and Burgundian influences. Cf. also p. 676,
n. 100.

On the other hand it is not much later than the eleventh century and a sufficient indication of this may be found in the use of the term *ministerialis*,[11] commonly employed in the eighth, ninth and tenth centuries to designate a vassal or a serf, but before then but little, if at all. Be this as it may, there is reason to believe that, although it may have been written about the year 1000, it was based upon more ancient and credible traditions. I am induced to this belief by the reference contained in it to SS. Severus and Julius. 'Migravit ad Christum,' says the Life narrating the death of St. Ursus, 'sociatusque et adjunctus sacerdotibus Christi Severo et Julio.' " Savio, supposing the St. Julius in question to be the St. Julius of the island of that same name in the lago d' Orta and St. Severus to be the saint of Ravenna, assigns St. Ursus and Plocean, but by a process of reasoning which cannot truthfully be described as very exacting, to the second half of the sixth century.

"If it is true that Plocean was an Arian," he continues on page 80, "as tradition insists, and 'there is no inherent improbability in the suggestion,' we are the more convinced in the belief that he occupied the see of Aosta in the sixth century at the time when the Arian Ostrogoths were still dominant in Italy (i.e, down to 553), or in the early years of the Lombard domination, for the Lombards also were Arians. I say in the early years of the Lombard domination, because, after the death of Clepho in 574, Aosta and its valley came under the sway of Guntrum, King of Burgundy, and remained under him and his successors and the Frankish kings down to the time of Charlemagne. And as Arianism ceased to find any foothold under either the Burgundian or the Frankish kings, it must necessarily be supposed that Plocean, if he was an Arian, was a bishop before 574. An additional argument may be derived from

[11] But Cf. Ducange, éd. Favre, Paris, 1885, Vol. V, s.v., *In Pacto Legis Salicae lit.*, II. § 6, "pro quovis famulo domestico. Glossae Isonis Magistri ad 2, Prudentii contra Symmachum: alumnos, nutritios, ministeriales, famulos," and, more generally, of the minor officials of kings, dukes, counts and feudal lords, 'villici,' i.e., bailiffs, 'seu villarum praefecti,' estate agents. The term 'ministerialis episcopi' occurs in an episcopal deed dated 1120: "si quis autem successorum sive ministerialium nostrorum contra hoc authoritatis nostrae privilegium aliquid calumpniae . . . . inferre temptaverit," etc.

the fact that the cult of St. Ursus was of great antiquity in Aosta as early as 923 [the year of the gift made by Bishop Anselmo I to the Chapter of St. Ursus], as the existence at that time of a church and a collegiate of canons named after him proves. It also appears from a decree by Bishop Gisus, *c.* 960, that even then one of the gates of the city was called 'porta di S. Orso'." [Savio reproduces the decree on page 85.]

Patrucco[12] inclines to assign Plocean to the Lombard epoch, 569-74.

Lanzoni,[13] while mistrusting the 'Life of St. Ursus' in *B.H.L.* 8453, writes with regard to Plocean that "it is difficult, nevertheless, to believe that its author can have invented the name of that bishop," and seems to share the opinion of Savio who "places him in the second half of the sixth century. Mgr. Duchesne [Fastes Episc. 1] does not mention him."

The admirable illustrated publication, *L'insigne collégiale d'Aoste*,[14] issued by the Academy of St. Anselm to commemorate the fourteenth centenary of St. Ursus, contained the text of the life of St. Ursus (printed by the Bollandists in their Appendix to Vol. I for February) according to an old legendary belonging to the Collegiate of St. Ursus. The authorship of the Life is there attributed to a Milanese or Vercellese hagiographer of *c.* 580 by reason of the anti-Arian statements it contains,[15] and the date of the death of St. Ursus is maintained to be very near to the traditional date of 529. Savio's arguments for transferring the date to the second half of the century do not appear very convincing, and Plocean may, perhaps, be given a place, with greater respect for tradition, intermediate between numbers four and five in Lanzoni's catalogue (page 1055), i.e., between 511 and 528.

Reasons for transferring St. Ursus along with St. Fridian to the second half of the sixth century had rather be sought, in my opinion, in Ireland than in Italy. It must be borne in

---

[12] 'Aosta dalle invasioni barbariche alla signoria sabauda,' in *Miscellanea valdostana* (Vol. XVII della *Bibl. della Soc. Stor. Subalpina*).
[13] Op. cit., p. 1056.
[14] Ivrea, Viassone, 1929.
[15] Cf. p. 24.

mind that the first half of the sixth century saw the death of St. Brigit, the foundation of the first great monasteries in Ireland, Cell-Lainne, Clúain-Iráird, Mag-Bile, Clúain-moccu-Nóis, that Colum-cille went off to found Iona only after the middle of the century, and that only towards its close did Columban set foot in Burgundy. The independent isolated activity in Italy in the first half of the sixth century of such as Ursus and Fridian is not an impossibility, but, even though they were to be assigned to the third quarter of the century, they would still have to be reckoned among the very earliest Scots *peregrini*.

§ 4

The memorials of St. Ursus in Aosta are, as might be expected, both numerous and important.

The Church of SS. Peter and Ursus and the attached Collegiate of St. Ursus contain precious memorials and veritable artistic treasures, copiously illustrated in the special publication before mentioned. On the site of the old Church of St. Peter, traces of which may still be seen in the crypt called the 'Confession of St. Ursus,' Bishop Anselm built in the tenth century the new Church of St. Ursus, which the Archdeacon Georges de Challant transformed, enlarged and embellished in the fifteenth century with arches, pictures, stalls, and stained-glass windows. He enlarged and embellished the Collegiate also. The cloister and the priory are most attractive: the campanile dates from the twelfth century: the reliquaries, which include a great coffin containing the body of St. Ursus, and the missals are of inestimable value. The Collegiate, under the shadow of which the Academy of St. Anselm sprang into being about a century ago, has always been an important centre of religious, intellectual, and social life (more particularly through the foundation of hospitals). No record[16] as to how the congregation instituted by St. Ursus spent the first three centuries of its existence has survived, the earliest historical data not going beyond 923. In 1184 it had within its dependence

[16] Cf. Dondeynaz, op. cit., pp. 108 et seq.

many parishes mentioned in a Bull of Lucius III and situate in different dioceses. In 1133 the canons of St. Ursus embraced the regular life under the rule of St. Augustine; in 1629 they were secularised by a Bull of Urban VIII. It was in this Collegiate[17] that Canon Boniface de Challant, together with the Bishop and other canons, courageously set Calvin at defiance in the sixteenth century and compelled him to abandon his propaganda and withdraw from the valle d' Aosta. The fidelity of this valley, originally evangelized by an Irishman, to the Church of Rome is remarkable.[18]

The Hospital of St. Ursus[19] in Aosta dates back probably to the seventh or eighth century; the earliest document to mention it is a deed of grant dated 1177. It is usually described as the hospital 'de porta Sancti Ursi' and in the official decrees of the thirteenth century is already referred to as 'vetus hospicium Sancti Ursi.' It was served from the beginning by religious lay-brothers and sisters ('conversi' or 'conversae hospitalis,' 'conversi' or 'conversae Sancti Ursi'), but it is impossible to say whether they formed part of the establishment of the Collegiate, where—as already mentioned—the religious life according to the Rule of St. Augustine had been introduced in 1133, or whether they belonged to the Hospitaller brothers and sisters of St. Anthony, who received the approval of Pope Urban II in 1095, or whether again they were merely persons who, making a present of their property to the house of St. Ursus, placed themselves at the disposal of the hospital without taking any regular vows. The hospital was certainly under the direction of a canon of the Collegiate called the Rector of the Hospital. Protected by the Pontiffs and the house of Savoy, helped by numerous legacies (of which the documents for the period 1177-1295 still subsist) from bishops, ecclesiastics, nobles and commons, the Hospital of St. Ursus became exceedingly

---

[17] Ibid., p. 123.

[18] For the history of the church and the collegiate of St. Ursus cf. also Savio, op. cit., p. 69 and p. 108.

[19] Cf. Dondeynaz, op. cit., p. 57 and M. Marguerettaz, 'Mémoire sur les hôpitaux anciens du Val d'Aoste,' in *Bulletin IX* of the Academy of St. Anselm, 1876, pp. 68-94.

prosperous. But in spite of the gifts lavished upon it, it fell, towards the end of the thirteenth century, into distress. Aymon de Challant, Bishop of Vercelli, commended it to the faithful of his diocese in 1285, and Nicholas I de Bersatoribus, Bishop of Aosta, was compelled, in order to provide for its maintenance, to unite it, with all its rights and property, in 1298 to the religious house of SS. Peter and Ursus of Aosta.

The hospital gradually fell into decay in the course of the following centuries: in the seventeenth, the buildings were reduced to a wretched condition and were further damaged by fire. This was made good, but in 1703 the building began, and continued, to be used as a barracks for passing troops. At the end of the eighteenth century it was sold by the Chapter together with various other properties, estates and precious objects, to make up the sum—an enormous amount for such a comparatively poor Chapter—of 170,000 francs levied as an extraordinary war tax by Edicts dated respectively 28th December, 1797, and 31st December, 1799. Charity, however, still continues to be practised, and a bank, absolutely distinct from the funds of the hospital, has been opened for the benefit of the poor and is carried on as a work of piety by the Collegiate.

The Porta di S. Orso has already been mentioned:[20] there were also in and around Aosta a 'Borgo di S. Orso,' a 'Fontana di S. Orso,' a 'Pietra di S. Orso,' and a 'Terra di S. Orso.' In the eleventh century, and even then of immemorial antiquity, there was a noble family 'De Porta Sancti Ursi,' which gave a bishop to Aosta. A lime tree called the 'Tiglio di S. Orso'[21] still flourishes beside the church, and under its shade the general Council of the Valley usually met to deliberate.

Marguerettaz[22] relates the following curious little item of folklore: one form of charity practised by St. Ursus was the distribution of wooden shoes, *sabots*, to the poor, and he was portrayed in the performance of this duty on a bas-relief in

[20] Cf. Dondeynaz, op. cit., pp. 57, 74 and 98.
[21] Cf. Vaccari, *Come vivono le piante*, Torino, Lattes, 1930, fig. 286 on p. 155.
[22] Op. cit., pp. 68 et seq.

s—i

the parish church of S. Cristoforo. A similar custom was kept up for many centuries as a tribute to his memory by the Collegiate which he had founded, and is said to have given rise to the market in wooden implements and utensils still held on the eve of St. Ursus in front of the house where once stood the ancient hospital, and the adjacent houses. No such market is held anywhere else than in the *borgo* of St. Ursus in Aosta and at Donnaz, where also the Collegiate had a hospital from time immemorial.[23]

§ 5

The valley of Cogne, the scene of his zealous missionary labours, preserves many memorials of St. Ursus, and the parish church is dedicated to him.[24] The original church was on the Cret: in 1202 a new church of St. Ursus was built in the place called Villa, the site of the present parish church (the deed relating thereto is still in existence); it was reconstructed *ex novo* in 1642. References to a church of St. Ursus of Cogne are to be found in the before-mentioned brief of Lucius III, dated 1184: but it would seem to have been some other church, not that on the Cret. The name 'Prato di S. Orso' is given to a large tract of meadow-land in Cogne where the saint is traditionally supposed to have preached.

The parishes of Derby, Jovençan and Donnaz[25] in the diocese of Aosta all have a lively devotion to St. Ursus, and in Jovençan he is the titular.

A Bull of Alexander III dated 1176 mentions the parish of SS. Peter and Ursus at Donnaz,[26] now entitled St. Peter-in-Chains. It was in consequence, no doubt, of a disastrous inundation in 1177 that the chapel of St. Ursus was built overlooking the *borgo* of Donnaz on the rock jutting towards

[23] In my inquiries into the memorials of St. Ursus in Aosta I have received the kindest assistance from Canon Pantaleone Micheletto, Prior of the Collegiate Church of St. Ursus and Rector of the Great Seminary.

[24] Cf. Dondeynaz, op. cit., pp. 61-64, Mgr. Duc, *Histoire de l'Eglise d'Aoste*, Aosta, Imprimerie Catholique, 1901, I, 105, and Pietro Giacosa, *Cogne*, Ivrea, Viassone, 1925, pp. 66, 234 et seq.

[25] Cf. Dondeynaz, op. cit. pp. 68 and 99.

[26] Ibid., p. 99.

the Dora, south of the great Roman road; and that with the object either of erecting a building in honour of St. Ursus who until then had been the patron of the parish, or invoking his protection against the dreaded inundations of the Dora. Donnaz had a hospital ('Hospitale, hospicium pauperum de Donacio') which was a dependence from the Collegiate of SS. Peter and Ursus in Aosta.[27]

§ 6

It is probable that the cult of St. Ursus passed into the Valsoana ('Vallis Soquanae'), in the diocese of Ivrea, from the valley of Cogne with which it was intimately associated.[28] He is the titular of the parish of Campiglia, the first parish to be met in the Valsoana on the road out from Cogne: the 'Piazza di S. Orso in Valsoana' is mentioned in a deed dated 1281. The Church of Campiglia, the oldest and the mother of all the churches in the valley, has, as a result of the successive formation of the parishes of Ronco, Valprato Corsonera, Ingria and Valprato Pianetto, suffered the common fate of mother churches and remained the smallest.

The city of Ivrea, of which St. Ursus was one of the patrons,[29] once had a church dedicated to him. Benvenuti,[30] under the heading 'Churches gone out of existence,' says: "The Church of St. Ursus, archdeacon of Aosta, was built about the beginning of the twelfth century in the round which used to be described as 'ad petram mali consilii': for this reason the street leading to the former palazzo of Count Perrone was called down to the beginning of this present [the eighteenth] century in cadasters and other instruments 'Ruca S. Ursi.' The Ursus in question was the Ursus who, together with St. Brigit, was one of the patrons of the city, and his feast was kept as of obligation 'maxime intra civitatem Epor.' [Eporedia=Ivrea] on 2nd February in accor-

[27] Cf., Marguerettaz, mem. cit., *Xth Bulletin*, 1879, p. 242.
[28] Cf. Dondeynaz, op. cit., pp. 64 and 103, Saroglia, *Eporedia sacra*, p. 98.
[29] Cf., Dondeynaz, p. 103.
[30] 'Istoria dell' antica Città d'Ivrea dalla sua fondazione alla fine del sec. XVIII' (an unpublished MS. in the possession of Cav. Avv. Mario Rossi d'Ivrea), p. 317.

dance with the ancient statutes confirmed by the bishops. The church was probably destroyed when work was begun on the Naviglio [a canal to irrigate the 'Agro Vercellese,' drawn from the Dora Baltea at Ivrea, and cut between 1433 and 1468]." Carandini[31] explains the situation of the 'Ruca S. Ursi' (it is now known as the via Perrone) and recalls that it is mentioned in the deed of 1075 confirming the possessions and privileges of the Monastery of St. Stephen.[32]

There was a hospital of great antiquity maintained by the Canons Regular of St. Ursus of Aosta between Donnaz and the city of Ivrea, almost at the gates of the city. Its chapel went under the name of St. Anthony,[33] and it was itself known as the Hospital of the XXI, according to some accounts, because of the twenty-one beds or places which it kept for the use of pilgrims: it would seem to have been founded about the year 1000 by the patrician families of Challant and Solerio. It was handed over to the house of St. Ursus of Aosta by Albert, Bishop of Ivrea, in 1310, and accepted by the prior Guillaume de Lydes the elder, "intendentes illud, licet nunc modicum hospitale, multis ampliare bonis cum Omnipotentis auxilio, sicque hospitalitas perfecta servetur ibidem et divinus cultus multipliciter augeatur."

The future proved how just and well founded were the high hopes entertained by Bishop Albert. The chapel of the Hospital of the XXI became a station of devotion to which the confraternities of the city of Ivrea betook themselves in solemn procession. We shall meet this hospital again at the end of our pilgrimage throughout the provinces of Italy in quest of Irish Saints. It was destroyed in 1544 during the Franco-Spanish war, but the walls remain. The church was reconstructed on its present site under the title of St. Anthony Abbot. Cardinal Richelmy, to welcome the sons of Don Bosco to Ivrea, persuaded his mother to make over to them the considerable neighbouring property of the villa di S. Antonio.

[31] *Vecchia Ivrea*, second edition, Ivrea, Viassone, 1927, p. 528.
[32] Cf. Barelli, *Cartario dell' Abbazia di. S. Stefano d'Ivrea*, Pinerolo, 1902, p. 285.
[33] Cf. Marguerettaz, *Xth Bulletin*, p. 285.

Canon Giacomo Boggio [34] mentions a chaplaincy of St.
Ursus, founded by Bertolino de Lance in 1361, which,
though still in existence in 1477, had disappeared when the
parish of St. Maurice was transferred to the Dominicans,
although the altar still stood beside the choir at the time of
the visitation by Cesare Ferreri on 12th April, 1584. This
may be the benefice which Dondeynaz says existed in Ivrea
under the name of St. Ursus, but the benefice which he does
mention is in the names of St. Ursus and St. Brigit.

Guido, Bishop of Ivrea and a former Canon of St. Ursus in
Aosta, a scion, also, in all probability, of the noble Val-
dostan family of Quart, by deed dated 1136, granted [35] to
the Canons of St. Ursus of Aosta the churches situate in
Pavone, a district some two and a half miles from Ivrea. [36]

§ 7

A church of St. Ursus in the parish of Piasco in the diocese
of Saluzzo has been mentioned before with reference to St.
Brigit. Piasco was under the jurisdiction of the Bishop of
Turin until the constitution of the diocese of Saluzzo (1511),
and the church of St. Ursus, although transformed out of
recognition at the present day, is undoubtedly of great
antiquity. By a deed dated 26th May, 1075, Cunibert,
Bishop of Turin, is expressed to have ceded to Marinus,
Abbot of S. Maria di Cavour, "ecclesiam sancti Ursi quae
est sita in erpiascho (Piasco) et illum montem qui est inter
duos rivos et ex alia parte illud totum quod est usque ad
viam que est ad radicem montis cum sediminibus et vineis,
cultis et incultis, quae ibidem sunt." [37]

In the diocese of Turin the office of St. Ursus has been
recited from time immemorial on 1st February as at Aosta,
but as of a pontifical confessor, in the erroneous belief,

[34] *I rettori della parrocchia di S. Maurizio d'Ivrea*, Ivrea, Viassone, 1911, p. 7.

[35] Cf. Gabotto: *Documenti e studi sulla storia d'Ivrea, Le carte dell' Archivio vescovile d' Ivrea fino al 1313*, I, pp. 16-17.

[36] In my investigations into the memorials of St. Ursus in Ivrea I have had inestimable help from the Marchese Francesco Carandini and Avv. Galileo Pinoli.

[37] Cf. Can. C. F. Savio, *L'antica chiesa di S. Giovanni Battista in Piasco*, Saluzzo, Tip. Vescovile, 1899, p. 16.

already explained, that he was a bishop. As such he appears in the ancient picture which hangs above an altar raised in his honour in the left lateral nave of the cathedral.[38] St. Ursus in Turin was once the patron of tanners. In the diocese of Novara (beginning with the celebrated Collegiate of St. Gaudentius), and in that of Vercelli, the cult of St. Ursus has existed as long as man can remember.

As regards Vercelli, Dondeynaz slips into error in saying that "a convent of St. Ursus, sometimes called the Irish Hospital (i.e. *degli Scoti*) and at other times the convent of St. Ursus and St. Brigit, his inseparable companion, stood outside the walls of the city as early as the thirteenth century." There were in fact two separate and distinct hospitals, each with a church attached: the Irish Hospital, with its Church of St. Brigit, already referred to apropos that saint; and a Hospital of St. Ursus with a Church of St. Paul. The Hospital of St. Ursus had been endowed with various properties and rights as early as the twelfth century. In the year 1173 "religiosissimus prior de Augusta (Aosta) Guillelmus suo nomine cum fratribus suis" besought the bishop, Guala Bondoni, to grant them "ecclesiam S. Pauli quae est supra Sicidellam (a tributary of the river Sesia) cum hospitali ibidem constructo." He obtained the concession craved, and the church and hospital were thereafter called of SS. Paul and Ursus. The hospital does not seem to have lasted much beyond the thirteenth century; the church passed into the hands of the Dominicans in 1234.[39]

In the diocese of Vercelli the parish church of Rongio, near Masserano, is dedicated to St. Ursus. And in the province of Vercelli, the parish church of Vallanzengo, although belonging to the diocese of Biella, is also dedicated to him.[40]

---

[38] Cf. Dondeynaz pp. 35 et seq., and also Gallizia, *Atti dei santi che fiorirono nei domini della Real Casa di Savoia*, Turin, R. Stamperia, 1756, vol. III, p. 226.

[39] Cf. Savio, op. cit., pp. 483 et seq., with reference to Bishop Guala (1170-82).

[40] Cf. S. Lesna, *Vita popolare di S. Orso*, Varallo Sesia, Unione tip. valsesiana, 1916.

§ 8

The cult of St. Ursus has also spread outside Italy into France and Switzerland.[41] At Meyronnes in the Basses Alpes, in the diocese of Digne, close by the Col de la Madeleine in the Val di Stura, is a famous Sanctuaire de Saint Ours, which attracts great crowds of pilgrims from various valleys and dioceses and even from Piedmont. The old St. Ours having fallen into ruins early in the seventeenth century, the church was rebuilt about half a mile away in the Plan St. Ours and became the parish church of St. Ours, a hamlet detached from Meyronnes in 1855.[42] The feast is kept there on 17th June and miracles are reported to have taken place in the chapel of St. Ours at Meyronnes.

St. Ursus is also honoured in France at Barcellonnette, at Guillestre (Hautes-Alpes), where there is a chapel dedicated to St. Ours, and his feast is kept on 17th June as at Meyronnes, at Montbar in the diocese of Langres (Burgundy), which boasts a church of St. Ours and relics, at Bernex and Vacheresse in Savoy, where the two parish churches are dedicated to him, and in the parish of La Thuile, also in the diocese of Annecy.

There is a cult of St. Ursus in Switzerland, at Sion in the Valais: there he already figured in an eighteenth-century missal on 1st February as at Aosta. St. Ursus is specially invoked in Sion against damage from inundations and hailstorms.

[41] Cf. Dondeynaz, pp. 31, 68, 79, et seq., 94, 100 and 103, and Burlet, *Le culte de Dieu, de la Sainte Vierge et des saints en Savoie avant la révolution*, Chambéry, Librairie cath., 1916.

[42] Cf. 'St. Ours' and 'Rochers de St. Ours' on sheet 14, B3, of the Italian Touring Club map.

CHAPTER XI

§ I

ST. GUNIFORT, whose body, accoutred in the uniform of a soldier, pierced with arrows, and enclosed in a superb urn, is venerated in Pavia in the Church of SS. Gervase and Protasus, a dependence from the parish church of the Carmine, is, like St. Emilian of Faenza and S. Pellegrino of Garfagnana, a most puzzling figure.

His legend is the following:

He and his brother Gunibald, 'genere Scoti,' were of noble blood; they had two sisters whose names are given in one text as Pusillana and Favilla. A fierce persecution having broken out 'in regno Scotie' against the faithful of Christ, all four decided for the love of God 'parentibus et patrie renuntiare et crucem Christi nudam portare.' They stole away from their country and betook themselves to the Germanies, 'ad nequissimos teuthonicos.' But their efforts at evangelization encountered the most formidable hostility and they were thrown into prison and tortured. Pusillana and Favilla were condemned to death and duly decapitated. "Crudelis Scotia, sed crudelior Teuthonica; Scotia mater fuit, Teutonica noverca." Gunifort and Gunibald were released and decided to leave the Germanies. They crossed the Alps and came to Como, where, unfortunately, Christians were being slaughtered daily: "ubi quotidie christianum nomen se habere confitentes jugulabantur." There they began to preach the Gospel with excellent results, until they were denounced to the 'princeps civitatis,' who had them arrested and interrogated: "Scoti sumus genere," they replied, "sed christiani professione." They were both condemned to death, but, in the event, and in the hope that the execution of one brother would induce the other in panic to abandon the Faith, only Gunibald was decapitated and his body buried secretly the following night by the Christians of Como. Gunifort was set free. Making his way to Milan, he there preached the name of Christ unwearyingly 'et multorum errores conculcavit.'

Invited but in vain to offer sacrifice to the idols, he was denounced to the 'tyrannus' and condemned to be decapitated outside the city walls, but, as a preliminary to his execution, he was shot at with arrows and scourged with iron rods along the way. He was indeed so tortured by the cruelty 'hereticorum' that, before arriving at the place of execution outside the gates of Milan all covered with blood and exhausted by many wounds, he fell to the ground inanimate. His persecutors, believing him to be dead, left him where he lay without carrying out the capital sentence. Gunifort, however, revived after an interval seemingly none the worse for his unfortunate experiences, rose, and made his way to Pavia.

There he fell in with a devout and pious matron who, perceiving the miserable plight of the holy man, brought him with all respect and charity to her own house 'juxta ecclesiam Scoti Romani,' and with great devotion tended him; but the third day, a 22nd August, had scarcely dawned when Gunifort returned his soul to God, while the bells of Pavia rang a merry peal of their own accord. He was buried in the Church of S. Maria by the side of S. Romano.

§ 2

The legend was first published in the fifteenth century by B. Mombrizio,[1] a Milanese, republished by Tatti,[2] and again for the third time by the Bollandists (G. Cuperus)[3] according to the original text of Mombrizio, which may have been derived from a Lateran Passionary or a fifteenth-century codex preserved in the Archives of the Fabbriceria

[1] *Sanctuarium seu Vitae Sanctorum*, I, 338-40.
[2] *Annali sacri della città di Como*, 1663, I, 903.
[3] *Acta Sanctorum*, Vol. IV, for the month of August, pp. 524-30.

del Carmine in Pavia.[4] The Carmine codex, once the property of Sinibaldo Mezzabarba (1350-1441) of Pavia, contains, in addition to the text of Mombrizio, an account of the miracles attributed to the martyr and ends with some historico-liturgical particulars concerning the feasts of St. Gunifort at Pavia (22nd August), St. Gunibald at Como (13th October), and the sisters, whose names are given, in *Alamania* (9th January). It adds that the bodies of SS. Gunibald, Pusillana and Favilla are buried at Como in the church of S. Carpoforo outside the walls of the city.

The martyrdom of St. Gunifort has been attributed—in view of the uncertainties of the text—by some hagiologists to the pagans, by others to the Arians. His date has been fixed by F. Ferrari[5] in the reign of the Emperor Constantius (337-60); Dempster[6] 'with his usual effrontery' naturally made him Scotch and has unfortunately been followed in this respect by many later writers down to Majocchi. 'Floruit,' according to Dempster, 'anno 417 aut circiter.' Tatti,[7] the Bollandists[8], Padre Severino Capsoni, Guiseppe Robolini, and Majocchi, all incline to 303, i.e., to the time of the great persecution under Maximian and Diocletian.

§ 3

It may be well to consider carefully the historical value of the legend which is manifestly a very late compilation (thirteenth or fourteenth century).

It must be observed in the first place that in the time of Imperial Rome there was no kingdom of Scotland or any Scotland, and that no severe persecutions were ever directed against the Christians either in Great Britain or in Ireland. In spite of what the pamphleteer Gildas, who wrote in the

---

[4] Cf., Mgr. R. Maiocchi: *La leggenda e il culto di S. Guniforto mart. in Pavia*, Pavia, Artigianelli, 1917, p. 12.

[5] *Catal. Sanct. Italiae*, Milan, 1613.

[6] To be quite fair to Dempster, he merely reports, or professes to report, popular rumour. Chambers gives the 29th October as the feast-day (Cf. *De Scotorum fortitudine etc.*, Paris, 1631, *sub die*) and his authorities: 'Vide Tabulas Ticinenses Jacobum Guallum J-C.,' in *Sanctuario Papiae et alias*.

[7] Op. cit.

[8] Cf. *AA. SS.*, August, IV, pp. 534 et seq.

sixth century, relates,[9] the Diocletian persecution did not
extend across the Channel owing to the efforts of Constantius Chlorus, the father of Constantine, while doubts
have been expressed as to the preceding martyrdoms of St.
Alban at Verulamium and SS. Aaron and Julius at Caerleon-
on-Usk (286 or 287), who, in any event, would be the sole
martyrs of the conversion of the islands to Christianity.[10]
The Church of S. Romano in Pavia was not yet in existence;
the first reference to it occurs in the seventh century, and in
476 there were only two churches in Pavia, those of St.
Gervase and St. Inventius.[11] No trace of the martyrdom or
of any cult of the two sisters is to be found either in the
Germanies or in Switzerland (in the canton of the Grisons),
or at Como, and at Como itself there is no trace of any
Gunibald, although the Church of St. Carpoforo is still in
existence and its history is well known.[12] Père Delehaye, in
Chapter VII of his *Les Origines du culte des martyrs*,[13] gives a list
of the authentic Italian martyrs,[14] but makes no mention of
any St. Gunifort.

The fact that the four names (those of the two sisters are
certainly spurious) have not a Celtic appearance does not

[9] Cf. 'De Excidio Britanniae Liber querulus' in Migne, *P.L.*, LXIX, Cap.
Vii, col. 337.
[10] The date 283 is the date given in the Anglo-Saxon Chronicle and the
Book of Llandaff. Gildas, op. cit., cap. x, says: "Sanctum Albanum Verola-
miensen, Aaron et Julium Legionum urbis cives et caeteras utriusque sexus
diversis in locis summa magnanimitate in acie Christi praestantes dico"; and
the fact remains that, when St. Germanus came to Britain in 429, he visited
his relics, presumably at Verulamium (Constant. in *V.S. Germani*, written *c.*
473-482), and took a handful of dust from the grave to place in a new church
at Auxerre which he afterwards dedicated to the British proto-martyr (Bede,
H.E., I, c. 18). Cf. also Père Hippolyte Delehaye's paper: 'In Britannia dans
le Martyrologe Hieronymien' in *Proceedings of the British Academy*, XVII, 1932.
[11] Cf. Majocchi, op. cit., p. 26.
[12] Ibid., pp. 32-35 and 176. A characteristic example of Dempster's methods
may here be cited in passing. In his *Apparatus de Religione*, II, cap. ii, he
invented a church and monastery erected in Como in honour of St. Gunibald
"which have been in the possession of the Scotch for a very considerable time."
—Lanigan (*Eccl. Hist.*, Dublin, 1822, I, p. 9) commented that Dempster's
nonsense concerning the saints having suffered martyrdom during the reign
of the great and pious Theodosius "had been well exposed by Ussher," and
with his usual shrewdness made the acute suggestion that instead of 'Como'
the reading in the text 'Camara' should be taken to mean 'Camariano,' "a
place near the north side of the Po in the ancient Insubria, mentioned by
Alberti (*Descrittione di tutta Italia*, p. 394)."
[13] Brussels, 1912.
[14] Cf. Lanzoni, op. cit., p. 70.

mean very much, for the Scots *peregrini* often changed their names or had new names given them, and Canon O'Hanlon[15] declares that many account a Cunibald or Chunibald, a missionary companion of St. Rupert in Bavaria, as an Irishman.[16] The foregoing considerations are sufficient in any event to make it probable that the legend of St. Gunifort is one of those 'centos' which, in Père Delehaye's lapidary words,[17] bear about as much resemblance to an historical narrative as an industrial product to an artist's masterpiece.[18]

The earliest liturgical record of St. Gunifort occurs in the Litanies of the Saints formerly sung at Pavia in the procession *delle Crocette*, which dates back to the tenth century. The surviving text of the Litanies includes his name among the pontifical martyrs, contains also the names of St. Lanfranc, St. Thomas Aquinas and St. Roch, and is a fourteenth-century compilation; it cannot therefore be said that the name of St. Gunifort was included in the primitive text of such litanies.[19]

The earliest historical record of Gunifort is contained in the *Catalogo Rodobaldino dei Corpi santi di Pavia*,[20] an account of the visitation made of the churches of the city in 1236 by Rodobald II, Bishop of Pavia (1230-54), who found the 'corpus S. Guinifortis martiris' preserved in the 'ecclesia sancte Mariae apud sanctum Romanum majorem.'

Lanzoni in the introduction to his *Le Diocesi d'Italia* deals admirably with the formation and value of *Gesta* and *Passiones* in which the writers have "drawn on their imaginations" (p. 52) to describe the various stages traversed by these "itinerant martyrs" (p. 56), and in some cases have even "passed off as martyrs persons who were never such" (p. 62), describing "simple confessors, either in the ancient or in the more modern sense, as martyrs" (p. 65), and

---

[15] *Lives of the Irish Saints*, Dublin (1875-1903), Vol. VIII, p. 322.
[16] Ibid., Vol. IX, p. 536 on the 24th September.
[17] *Les passions des martyrs*, Brussels, 1921, p. 236.
[18] Lanigan (*Eccles. Hist.* I, p. 8, note) makes the suggestion here repeated for what it is worth that the words 'Scotica gente' have by mistake been substituted for 'Scythica gente.'
[19] Cf. Majocchi, op. cit., pp. 37-43.
[20] Cf., the edition by Boni and Majocchi, Pavia, Fusi, 1901.

occasionally creating even martyr-bishops (pp. 75 et seq.). The case of St. Gunifort is nevertheless a perplexing one; there would seem to be little doubt that he was a *Scot* and his apostolic pilgrimage bears a curious resemblance to the itinerary of St. Columban.

§ 4

His body, it has been said, was venerated in 1236 in the Church of S. Maria *presso* S. Romano. There the Anonimo Ticinese also found it in 1330,[21] when a chapel had been built and dedicated to him; in the fourteenth century the church began to be called St. Gunifort's. In 1443 a community of Canonesses Regular or Rocchetines settled beside the Church of St. Gunifort in a convent called S. Maria di Giosafat or the New Convent, and succeeded in building a church of their own adjoining and communicating with the Church of St. Gunifort. The latter was transferred to them in 1511, but gradually fell into decay; in 1650 the body of the saint was transported into their new church appropriately called S. Maria di Giosafat. The community fell into very low water financially and was suppressed in 1768, when the remains were transferred to the parish church of S. Maria Gualtieri. In 1769-70 the body was recomposed and dressed in its present state. When the parish of S. Maria Gualtieri was abolished in 1789, St. Gunifort was conveyed on the night of 7th January, 1790, to the Church of St. Gervase, where the body now lies. By a Decree of the Sacred Congregation of Rites dated 21st October, 1914, the feast of the saint is kept on 26th August, the 22nd being the octave of the Assumption.

§ 5

When the plague of 1373-4 had lost its virulence, Galeazzo Visconti established in Pavia an annual votive feast at the Church of St. Gunifort, to which the guilds of arts and crafts

[21] Cf., Majocchi, op. cit., pp. 49-51, and Gianani, *Opicino de Canistris*, pp. 54, 79, and 124.

all repaired in procession.[22]   The most potent influence, however, in the establishment of the cult of the saint in the fourteenth and fifteenth centuries was that of Stefano Mezzabarba who was responsible for the transcription of the Carmine codex containing his legend.   He was the custodian of the Church of St. Gunifort and in 1415 he persuaded Filippo Maria Visconti to assign to him all the revenue from the communal weighing machine at Pavia, and, in 1424, himself assumed the contract for the communal weights and measures; in 1416 he persuaded the College of Jurists to establish an annual feast and make an annual offering to the saint as to its other saintly patrons and persuaded Martin V, by a Bull dated from Mantua on 7th January, 1419, to grant special indulgences to the faithful who visited the church. In 1423 Mezzabarba himself undertook to defray the expense of the necessary repairs.

Between 1374 and 1396 a Confraternity, founded in 1216, took up its quarters in the Church of St. Gunifort and retained even after 1396 its name of the Confraternity of the Penitents of St. Gunifort.

One of the most resounding miracles performed by the saint is associated with the financial fortunes of the wealthy Pavese family Da Morzano in the thirteenth century, while on another occasion he was the means of saving from a watery grave a Genoese merchant, a certain Francesco Pastecca, who had the misfortune to fall into the sea in the harbour of Pera (Constantinople) in 1430, a miracle which would suggest the existence of some sort of cult of St. Gunifort in Genoa.

The name Gunifort was a common baptismal name in the provinces of Pavia and Milan from the fourteenth to the sixteenth century.   Majocchi gives many examples ranging from 1372 to 1525, to which may be added 'Gunifortis de Canibus de Papia,' Abbot of St. Columban of Bobbio from 1390 to 1408, and 'Gunifortis de Papia prior.'[23]   In the Milanese, it should be observed, the name is often transformed into Bonifort.

[22] Cf., Majocchi, pp. 54-57.
[23] Cf., Cipolla and Buzzi, *Cod. Dipl. di S. Colombano di Bobbio*, I, 33 and 51.

§ 6

Although the Ambrosian Liturgy contains no reference to St. Gunifort, a Milanese, Giacomo Manzoli, is found building and endowing in 1446 a little church dedicated to SS. James and Gunifort at Porta Ticinese on the Naviglio, i.e., right on the road to Pavia; the chapel is described as "of St. Bonifort on the Naviglio" in a deed of 1564,[24] and as the Oratory 'S. Boniforti super ripam Magni Navigii foris Mediolani' in an instrument dated in 1580 and preserved in the archiepiscopal archives of Milan, whereby St. Charles Borromeo ceded the said oratory in a derelict condition at the time to the Confraternity of S. Maria di Naviglio, which had it unconsecrated and then converted it into a school of Christian doctrine.

Two parishes are still dedicated to St. Gunifort at the present day: Nosate in the diocese and province of Milan, and Casatisma in the province of Pavia and the diocese of Tortona.

The church at Nosate, a district on the banks of the Ticino, has been the subject of a treatise by a parish priest,[25] according to which the church was built by Filippo Maria Visconti and raised to the dignity of a parish church by Cardinal the Archbishop Federico Borromeo; Majocchi, however, has his doubts about these statements in the absence of documentary evidence. The parish boasts a relic of the saint presented in 1726 by D. Giulio Buonsignori, Abbot of St. Epiphanius. Don Sironi records as current in Pavia the curious adage: "The client of St. Gunifort's in three days lives or turns a corpse." In a pamphlet on the saint, without cover or date (but evidently printed at Pavia after 1865),[26] the explanation is given that when any member of a family among the people falls seriously ill, it is customary in the last resort to send a garment to be blessed upon the coffin of the saint, and then to make the patient put it on in deference to the adage. A belief in a decision

---

[24] Cf., *Arch. Stor. Lombardo* for July, 1916, p. 141.
[25] E. Sironi, *Vita di S. Guniforte Martire che si venera in Nosate*, Milan, 1855.
[26] Obligingly loaned to the writer by the present incumbent, D. Enrico Aspesi.

after three days in cases of serious illness is also current in Aquila, where the sick have the sign of the cross made on their foreheads with a stick which forme·ly belonged to St. Bernardino.

In the parish of Casatisma the cult of St. Gunifort is again due to the Mezzabarba family which owned considerable estates in the neighbourhood. When the family became extinct towards the end of the eighteenth century, the property passed by way of inheritance to the d'Adda and Borromeo families. A relic of the saint had been given with the object of maintaining the cult to the Count Mezzabarba in 1670 by the then vicar, Barusio.[27] A street in Casatisma is called after St. Gunifort to this day.

Relics of him are to be found in the parish church of Villalbese in the diocese of Milan and in the following parishes of the diocese of Pavia: Monticelli, Borgarello, Torriano, Torre d' Arese, Mirabello, Villanterio and Zerbo. A parish in France, Méoties in Normandy, boasts some, while others are in the possession of private individuals.

In 1916 the Bishop of Pavia ordered a formal examination to be made of the remains of St. Gunifort, martyr, an account of which is given by Majocchi in an appendix.

[27] Cf., Majocchi, p. 148.

CHAPTER XII

ST. COLUMBAN OF BOBBIO

§ 1

THE more prominent features in the life of this gigantic Irish saint (540?—23rd November, 615), who made such a profound impression in the history of missionary activity and monasticism, of culture and piety, were briefly sketched in Chapter II, § 4. H. H. Pope Pius XI in his letter to the Most Eminent Cardinal F. Ehrle, papal legate to the celebrations held at Bobbio in 1923,[1] has admirably pictured the character and described the achievement of the man.

The literature relating to the founder of the abbey at Bobbio (614)—the Monte Cassino of northern Italy—is vast, and Columban is certainly the best known of the saints who form the subject of this book. This is not the place for an exhaustive study of the man and his work, and it may be sufficient, perhaps, to give a bare list in chronological order of the more important Italian publications concerning Columban and his monastery as an introduction for the reader to the complete bibliography:

(i) Benedetto Rossetti: *Bobbio illustrato*, Turin, 1795.

(ii) Antonio Gianelli: *Vita di S. Colombano abate, irlandese, protettore della città e diocesi di Bobbio*, Turin, 1844; second edition, 1894.

(iii) D. Bertacchi: *Monografia di Bobbio*, Pinerolo, 1859.

(iv) F. Novati: 'Due vetustissime testimonianze dell' esistenza del volgare nelle Gallie e nell' Italia esaminate e discusse (La vita di S. Mammolino e L'epistola di S. Colombano a Bonifacio IV),' Milan, 1900, an extract from the *Rendiconti del R. Istituto Lombardo di Scienze e Lettere*.

(v) Achille Ratti: *Le ultime vicende della Biblioteca e dell' Archivio di S. Colombano di Bobbio*, Milan, Hoepli, 1901.

[1] Cf. *Civiltà Cattolica*, 1923.

(vi) Achille Ratti: 'Reliquie di antico codice bobbiese ritrovate,' in *Miscellanea Ceriani*, Milan, Hoepli, 1910.

(vii) Dom Placido Lugano, O.S.B. : 'S. Gregorio Magno e S. Colombano nella storia della cultura latina,' in *Riv. Storica Benedettina*, 1915, pp. 161-5.

(viii) Dom Placido Lugano, O.S.B. : 'S. Colombano, monaco e scrittore,' in *Riv. Storica Benedettina*, July, 1916 (pp. 5-47). The December number (1920) of the same review contains (pp. 185-202) the texts of the *Regula Monachorum*, the *Ordo de vita et actione monachorum* and the *Oratio*.

(ix) Dom Bruno Albers, O.S.B.: 'Aforismi di storia monastica,' Rome, 1916, an extract from the *Riv. Storica Benedettina* (pp. 108-24).

(x) D. Cambiaso: 'S. Colombano. Sua opera e suo culto in Liguria,' in *Riv. Diocesana Genovese*, 1916, p. 121.

(xi) G. Domenici: 'S. Colombano,' Rome, *Civilta Cattolica*, 1916.

(xii) D. Cambiaso: *L'anno ecclesiastico e le feste dei santi in Genova nel loro svolgimento storico*, Genoa, Olivieri, 1917.

(xiii) C. Cipolla and G. Buzzi: *Codice diplomatico del monastero di S. Colombano di Bobbio fino all'anno MCCVIII*, three volumes, Rome, Istit. Stor. Italiano, 1918. The article by Dom Pl. Lugano, 'Il Cod. dipl. del Mon. di S. Colombano di Bobbio' in *Riv. St. Bened.*, December, 1920, pp. 173 et seq., is a useful introduction to this important collection.

(xiv) G. Micheli: 'Le carte bobbiesi dell' Archivio Doria di Roma,' in *Arch. stor. per le prov. Parmensi*, 1923, pp. 375 et seq.

(xv) G. B. Curti-Pasini, *Il culto di S. Colombano in S. Colombano al Lambro*, Lodi, Bosini-Abbiati, 1923.

(xvi) Mgr. P. Calchi-Novati, Bishop and Count of Bobbio: *Lettera pastorale al clero e popolo della diocesi di Bobbio per la quaresima del 1923*, Bobbio, Baldini and Foppiani, 1923.

(xvii) M. Cordovani: 'Il XIII Centenario di S. Colombano e l'Apostolato Internazionale della Chiesa,' in *Scuola Cattolica*, 1923.

(xviii) A. Pellizzari: 'S. Colombano e le lettere,' ibid.

(xix) L. Grammatica: 'La Biblioteca di Bobbio,' ibid.

(xx) G. Celi: 'Cimeli bobbiesi,' Rome, in *Civiltà Cattolica*, 1923.

(xxi) C. G. Mor: 'Bobbio, Pavia e gli "Excerpta bobiensia"' in *Contributi alla storia dell' Università di Pavia*, Pavia, Tip. Co-operativa, 1925.

(xxii) I. Reposi: *Pagine di storia bobbiese*, Piacenza, Del Maino, 1927.

(xxiii) S. Rebolini: 'S. Colombano di Bobbio,' in the December (1928) number of the series 'I Santuari d'Italia illustrati' or supplement in *Pro Famiglia*, Milan, 10, Via Broggi.

(xxiv) Maria Massani: 'S. Colombano di Bobbio, nella storia, nella letteratura, nell'arte,' in *Didaskaleion*, Turin, Soc. Ed. Intern., VI, 1928.

(xxv) E. Nasalli Rocca: *Bobbio e i suoi Statuti*, Arch. Stor. Lombardo, November, 1929, and March, 1930.

(xxvi) E. Nasalli Rocca: *Pievi della montagna piacentina*, Parma, La Giovane Montagna, 1930.

(xxvii) E. Nasalli Rocca: 'Le giurisdizioni territoriali delle Pievi piacentine secondo gli studi di A. Wolf,' in *Arch. stor. per le prov. Parm*, 1930, p. 117.

(xxviii) N. Grimaldi: 'San Colombano ed Agilulfo,' in *Archiv. stor. per le prov. Parm*. 1930, p. 79.

(xxix) A. Maestri: 'Il nome di S. Colombano al Lambro,' in *Arch. stor. lodigiano*, Lodi, 1932, pp. 83-106.[2]

---

[2] The following newspapers may also be mentioned:

(1) *La Trebbia*, Bobbio, 9th September, 1923, for an account of the festivities on the occasion of the thirteenth centenary.

(2) *La Trebbia*, Bobbio, 7th September, 1930, for 'Il Millenario della traslazione di S. Colombano celebrato a S. Colombano al Lambro.'

(3) *Il Cittadino*, Lodi, 21st August, 1930, for 'Il Millenario della traslazione di S. Colombano (930-1930).'

(4) *L'Italia*, Milan, 14th September, 1930, for an important article by Mgr. Gianani on the 'Traslazione di S. Colombano.'

(5) *La Trebbia*, Bobbio, 5th December, 1931, for 'Il Culto di S. Colombano nella Diocesi di Lodi' by Don A. Maestri.

(6) Do., 11th December, 1931, for 'Le Idrie di Cana,' review of an article thereon by Corrado Ricci which appeared in *Felix Ravenna* (1931, No. 2).

§ 2

In addition to the great saint of Bobbio, a number of other saints of the name are honoured by the Church, including a Columban 'junior,' one of the original twelve companions of the great Columban during his peregrination mentioned by his biographer Jonas, who also tells the story of his death,[3] and a tenth century S. Columban, also an Irishman, who lived the life of a recluse close to the church of Saint Bavon in Ghent, and who is commemorated on 2nd February.

Italy has a St. Columban, penitent and hermit, who lived and died in an age unknown, but remote, in the province of Forlì, in the diocese of Bertinoro and the commune of Meldola, in a part called S. Colombano[4] where his body is preserved.[5] He is said to have established a number of hospices for pilgrims in the valley of the Bidente. Mgr. Pasini of Forlì[6] mentions as attributable to him a little hospice of St. Columban dating traditionally as far back as the fourteenth century, in the Pianta suburb of Forlì in a locality still called Ospedaletto. Near Forlì, outside the Porta Ravaldino (now called Diaz), in a locality called S. Colombano, there is a church dedicated to St. Columban the Hermit which was formerly the family chapel of the Marchesi Colombani of Forlì. I am informed by Don Z. Francesconi that another church dedicated to St. Columban the Hermit is to be found in the neighbourhood of Ravenna.

There is also an Italian St. Columban Martyr (a relic of whom is in the possession of the church of St. Columban al

[3] ". . . . 'febre correptus atque in extremis positus,' he would fain have died, but his abbot kept praying for him. When Columban came to visit the sick man, 'cur me, inquit, tuis orationibus in hac aerumnosa vita detines? Nam adsunt qui me ducere volunt si tuis fletibus et precibus non praepedirentur. Retentationis, quaeso, solve obstacula ut mihi jam pateant coelestia regna.' Tum metu Columbanus percussus . . . corpus Christi abeunti de hac vita viaticum praebuit et post extrema oscula defunctionis cantum implevit. Erat enim ex eodem genere quo et B. Columbanus unoque comitatu et nomine ex Hibernia processerant.' " Vita. Col. 29, Migne, P.L., LXXX, col. 1028. Mabillon notes that this Columban in Martyrol. Bened. X Kal. Decamb. memoratur.

[4] Italian Touring Club map, sheet 19, D. 4.

[5] I am indebted to the Prior of S. Pietro in St. Colombano, through the intermediary of Don Z. Francesconi, for a pamphlet recently published at Castelnuovo, but without name of author or date, and containing "Brevi notizie sulla vita e culto di S. Colombano Eremita."

[6] Cf. La Madonna del Fuoco, March 1920, and Il Momento, 24th May, 1930.

Lambro) who is venerated in the parish church of S. Andrea at Mosciano, near Florence, where his body, clad in the uniform of a Roman soldier, lies in a gilt urn below the High Altar. It is said to have come from the Catacombs and to have been presented by Cardinal Guadagni *c.* 1810 to the missionaries of the Society of St. Vincent de Paul in S. Jacopo Soprarno, the patrons at the time of the church in Mosciano. His feast is kept on the first Sunday in September.[7]

§ 3

In the search for traces of the great Irish saint, it were best to proceed, as usual, through the provinces serially and to begin with Piedmont.

In the province of Alessandria, the nearest to Bobbio, the parish of Variana, part of Grondona, in the diocese of Tortona, is dedicated to St. Columban.

Buzzi[8] mentions as part of the *mensa* of the Abbot of St. Columban an "Ecclesia Sancti Columbani de Monteclaro cum pertinentiis suis, S. Columbani de Monte Claro Albensis diocesis." The administrative centre of the estates belonging to the monastery in the Astigiano was Camariano (Camerano Casasco) in the civil district of Montechiaro d' Asti in the province of Alessandria.

The parish of Pezzolo (Valle Uzzone) in the diocese of Alba and the province of Cuneo is dedicated to St. Columban at the present day.

In the province of Cuneo, but in the diocese of Mondovi, there is a chapel dedicated to St. Columban in the parish of

---

[7] Yet another St. Columban may be mentioned of whom nothing apparently is known beyond the fact that he was Abbot of St. Trond. He was believed to have been a contemporary of Charlemagne and was credited with the composition of a dirge "Carmen lugubre de obitu Regis Caroli Magni," twenty rather rough couplets, each ending with the refrain 'Heu mihi misero!' and the whole concluding with the prayer "In sancta sede cum tuis apostolis, Suscipe pium, o tu Christe, Carolum. Heu mihi misero!" (Migne, *P.L.*, CVI, 1257 et seq.). It is now attributed to a monk of Bobbio, believed by some, but improbably, to have been an Irishman. Cf. Dümmler in *Neues Archiv. etc.*, IV (1879), p. 151.

[8] *Codice diplomatico di S. Col. di Bobbio*, III, pp. 136-7.

Monasterolo-Casotto, where there once was a monastery of Cistercian nuns. His feast is still kept there.[9]

The parish of the commune of Pagno, still in the province of Cuneo but in the diocese of Saluzzo, is dedicated to St. Columban; it was once the site of a famous abbey founded by Astulf, and the Bishop of Saluzzo still retains the title of perpetual Prior Commendatory of St. Columban, Lord of Pagno. The chapels of St. Brigit and St. Ursus, mentioned in preceding chapters, are, it will be remembered, behind the mountain on the slopes of which stands the Church of St. Columban.

Lastly, in the province of Cuneo but in the diocese of Fossano, the feast of St. Columban is kept in the parish of S. Biagio (St. Blaise), part of Centallo.

In the province of Turin the name San Colombano is borne by part of the commune of Exilles in the valley of the Dora Riparia (in the diocese of Susa, where Jonas, his biographer, was born). The name seems to have been derived from the ancient Benedictine monastery of the Losa. In the same province of Turin a Monte Colombano (5,000 feet high), south-east of Viù, towers above the valley of the Mortiera and divides it from the valley of the Stura di Viù.[10]

Dondeynaz[11] declares that the Collegiate Church of St. Ursus in Aosta has some relics of St. Columban in its treasury, and that St. Columban and St. Gall were honourably remembered in the ancient liturgy of the church in Aosta. The province of Aosta has a village called San Colombano Belmonte, part of Cuorgnè with a church (a parish church since 1822) dedicated to St. Gratus.

Curti-Pasini declares that there is a village of S. Colombano near Gattinara, in the province of Vercelli, but it does not figure in the maps or in the 'Annual of the Italian Touring Club.' Not far from Gattinara is Masserano, before mentioned, with the parish of Rongio dedicated to St. Ursus.

In the province of Novara, but in the diocese of Vercelli,

---

[9] Cf. Curti-Pasini, op. cit., p. 10.
[10] Cf. Italian Touring Club map, sheet 8, C. 6.
[11] *Vie de Saint Ours*, p. 30.

the parish of Biandrate is dedicated to St. Columban. Mgr. Pastè[12] writes as follows: "I notice in the ancient liturgical calendar of Vercelli that the great Bishop Patrick and the Abbot Gall are venerated among the Irish saints in a place where the name of St. Columban is not even mentioned and that is the Church of Eusebius: and yet it had days set apart to commemorate other saints from over the mountains, such as Brice, Amandus, Armandus, Gothard and Leodegair. So also none of our codices makes any reference to St. Columban, and yet his cult must certainly have been widespread throughout the diocese, and, more particularly, in the neighbourhood of Caresana and in the deanery of Biandrate.

"The earliest extant document is dated the 18th April, 996 (cf. *Carte dell' Arch. Capit. di Vercelli*, S.S.S. Vercelli, Unione Tipogr. Vesc., 1911). 'Domna Adelegida Impcratris' thereby conveyed to the Canons of St. Eusebius 'corte[13] una domui cortile que vocatur carisiana cum castro inibi abente et cum capella foris [of St. Matthew] et com porto sicide [Sesia] cum omnibus alueis suis de capella sancti Columbani usque in fluvio pado.' But where precisely the Chapel of St. Columban was situate is not very clear.

"But there are three other documents relating to the church at Biandrate which was later raised to a deanery. In a parchment from the same Capitular Archives belonging to the year 1174 and relating to the Abbey 'S. Nazarii de Biandrate' mention is made at the end of the *Ecclesia Sancti Columbani*. An agreement dated 1217 and made between Novara and Vercelli also proves the existence of a Church of St. Columban at Biandrate served by monks (cf. Viglio, *Ricordo storico*, etc.). In the 'Necrology of St. Eusebius,' No. 155 (cf. *Bollettino stor. bibliografico subalp.*) under date the 2nd March, 1217, there is an entry that the Archdeacon Guidalard presented the Church of St. Eusebius with a house which he had acquired from the Monastery of St. Columban

---

[12] Cf. 'Sulle traccie dei monaci di San Gallo,' in *Scuola Cattolica*, 1913, Vol. III, pp. 223-30.

[13] The word 'chors' in the classical Latin writers, e.g., Varro, Columella, and Vitruvius, meant a large courtyard: it gradually (fourth century onwards) became corrupted into 'curtis' and meant a property or landed estate (Cf. *Vita Placidi*, 16-18, in Mabillon, *AA. SS.*, I, 52-53), in nearly every case with a proper name attached.

at Biandrate 'in hora (*sic*) Sancti Eusebii apud portam araldi,' i.e., close to St. Andrea."

The very ancient Church of St. Columban at Biandrate has been treated at length by Mgr. G. Borgomanero in a biography of St. Serenus, Bishop of Marseilles in the sixth century, whose body is preserved there.[14] It is doubtful whether it derives its titular name from the Benedictines, who were certainly established in the neighbouring Abbey of S. Nazaro before the ninth century, or from the fact that it was a daughter house directly descended from Bobbio.[15]

§ 4

Cambiaso,[16] discussing the rapid growth of the influence of the Bobbio Monastery over Ligurian territory, says: "A diploma of Charlemagne dated the 5th June, 774[17] confirmed the Monastery of Bobbio in the possession of a vast tract of land reaching down from the Valle d'Aveto to the sea. Other similar documents, ranging from the eighth to the tenth century, mention many localities situate in those regions or in the neighbourhood as within the dependence of that monastery, with churches and small monastic houses, 'oratoria,' 'cellae,' ecclesiae,' 'plebes,' many of which were dedicated to St. Columban. Within the former ambit of our own diocese his name was borne by the churches of Moranego, Certenoli, Costa, Noano, Piazza (near Framura), and the church in Genoa near the Hospital for Incurables. Near this last stood the famous monastery, later an urban

---

[14] Cf. *San Sereno, Vescovo di Marsiglia e Protettore di Biandrate*, Grottaferrata, Tip. S. Nilo, 1911. This St. Serenus, be it observed, was the bishop to whose good offices Pope Gregory commended St. Augustine on his way to England in 596 (Migne, *P.L.*, LXXVII, 836), and, three years later, the monks who were dispatched to help him (ibid., 1176).

[15] Ibid., pp. 71 and 130-1.

[16] Cf. *L'anno ecclesiastico in Genova*, p. 262.

[17] It may be read in Migne, *P.L.*, XCVII, 1,000. The head-note runs: "Donatio sylvae et curtis de Monte Longo a Carolo Magno facto monasterio Bobiensi ejusque abbati Guinibaldo anno 774." The texts of two other charters, the first of which purports to be the grant of Bobbio to Columban by King Agilulf in 598 (*sic*), and the second the grant of the monastery by Columban to the Pope are preserved in *P.L.*, LXXX, 321-3. Neither can be regarded as genuine.

parish, of S. Stefano, another dependence from Bobbio, with a crypt said to date back to the eighth century, while in the most central part of the old city the Church of S. Pietro in Banchi is referred to as early as 972 as a foundation from Bobbio: 'Ecclesia sancti Petri que est sita in civitate Janue' (cf. Grassi, *Vescovi di Genova*, pp. 12-13).

"A perusal of these documents shows that the labours of St. Columban and his sons had extended in the eighth-ninth centuries from Bobbio to Genoa and over a very wide area in between. But we must not stop there. When discussing the work of St. Benedict, we observed that his order was, from the earliest days of its institution, very far spread throughout Liguria, and we referred to many monasteries, such as Portovenere, S. Andrea di Sestri, S. Fruttuoso di Capodimonte, S. Stefano and S. Siro in Genoa, S. Siro in Struppa, S. Gregorio and S. Maria del Porale on the slopes of the Apennines, S. Clemente near Gordena, S. Maria del Tiglietto near l' Olba, S. Pietro di Savignone and S. Pietro di Precipiano in the valle Scrivia, S. Giustina di Sezzè and Giusvalla in the val Bormida, S. Marziano and Vindersi in the val Borbera, S. Maria in Val di Taro, S. Onorato di Patrania, S. Andrea di Borzone, etc., some of which have authentic documents of the sixth and seventh centuries and others later, but historians are unanimous in attributing the foundation of them all to the Lombard and Carolingian epochs, although the majority of them have been rebuilt, after having been laid waste by the Saracen invaders of the tenth century, in more recent times.

"Now the labours of the monks of Bobbio cannot have been for nothing in such a fruitful crop of monastic foundations. It is common knowledge that after the death of St. Columban they adopted the rule of St. Benedict . . . and supplied the largest number of recruits to the Benedictine Order in Liguria: so that their monastery at Bobbio must be regarded as the principal centre from which the religious and monastic life was spread amongst us. And to their efforts also must partly be attributed the conversion of the natives of the Apennines, who were still largely addicted to pagan practices at the coming of St. Columban.

"Along with the work of St. Columban and his monks went a veneration and regard for the saint himself no less far-reaching amongst the peoples in whose midst they laboured, and a corresponding concern for the celebration of his feast. It is found established at a very early date . . . in northern Italy, where it is included in the liturgical calendars of Mantua, Brescia, and Verona, to name but a few, whereas it is totally absent from the Roman liturgy.

"In Liguria also it is of great antiquity.

"In fact, it is not only to be found in all our earliest liturgical books with a proper prayer, 'Deus qui nos beati Columbani,' but is also mentioned among the civil and ecclesiastical holidays in the list for 1375, the oldest extant, and not in succeeding lists, which shows that the importance of the feast declined in course of time. Even the liturgical feast disappeared from the Genoese calendar. A simple commemoration still survived in the gradual of S. Matteo in 1412, but this too disappeared in course of time, and the only reference in the Diocesan Calendar for 1645 is the bare indication on 21st November: 'Dies S. Columbani.' There is no mention of him in the office, which is solely concerned with the Presentation B. V. M., an omission which shows that the feast of St. Columban had ceased to be other than a memory. Its transference to the day of the Presentation, a day of great devotion among the Genoese, facilitated its complete disappearance.

"It has been observed, and justly (cf. *Analecta Bollandiana*, 1906, p. 119, and Martin, op. cit., p. 19) that St. Columban does not occupy, either in the liturgy or in the memory of the faithful, the place to which his labours and his influence upon the monastic and religious movement of the seventh century would seem to entitle him."[18]

Cambiaso attributes (p. 441, *Exempti*) the Church of St. Columban in Genoa to the thirteenth century and the neighbouring Monastery of S. Stefano (p. 430) to the eighth.

The parish of Moranego near Davagna (in the diocese and province of Genoa) on the hill called della Scóffera, on the

[18] Cf. also for the cult of St. Columban, Cambiaso, op. cit., pp. 12, 14, and 395.

road from Bobbio to Genoa, is dedicated to St. Columban to this day. "There is a tradition, unfortunately devoid of documentary support," says Cambiaso at page 262, "of a journey which the saint is said to have made from Bobbio to S. Fruttuoso di Capodimonte on the promontory of Portofino, and of a little cross (still preserved) that he left there as a souvenir. In memory of his passage and at the request, as it is said, of the saint himself, the population of Moranego and neighbourhood used in the past to go every year in procession to S. Fruttuoso di Capodimonte (cf. Remondini, *Parrocchie dell' Archidioc. di Genova*, Reg. X, p. 55)."

The valleys facing the torrent Entella on the way down to Chiavari are all full of memories of Columban. There, almost opposite one another, are the two parishes of S. Colombano di Vignale and S. Colombano della Costa, both very ancient foundations from Bobbio; up the valle Sturla is Caregli di Borzonasca, the centre of the famous *corte* of Carelius which once belonged to the Bobbio Monastery[19] and had an abbey at Borzone or Bresone. Gomorga, near S. Colombano di Vignale, was the administrative centre for all the estates owned by the monastery in the civil districts of Chiavari, Lavagna, Ne, Sestri Levante, and those scattered about Tuscia Marittima. Graveglia, near Ne, also had a *corte* with a monastery and a church.

The parish church of S. Colombano della Costa, which dates back to 1207, stands at Costa S. Salvatore, near Cogorno, above Lavagna. That of S. Colombano di Vignale, which dates from 1142, has, together with the part known as Certenoli, given its name to the commune of S. Colombano-Certenoli, just where the valley of Fontanabuona begins. There the monastery owned the 'curtis Vignalis,' and the place was also called Bembelia or Benbelia or Binbegia.[20]

Devotion to St. Columban in these Ligurian valleys is still lively and the feasts held in his honour, more particularly at Vignale, are kept by crowds of people and generously

---

[19] Cf. Cipolla and Buzzi, op. cit., III, p. 92.

[20] Cf., for the history of these churches, A. Ferretto, 'Le pievi battesimali e le chiese minori,' *Atti. Soc. Lig. di Stor. Patria*, vol. XXXIX.

supported with their offerings by the sons and daughters of
the village who have emigrated to America.[21] Cambiaso
has unearthed a reference to these two parishes in the
Registrum talee omnium ecclesiarum Januensis diocesis for 1360
by the names 'S. Columbani de Costa' and 'S. Columbani
de Bombelio.' The Church 'S. Columbani de Noano,'
founded in 1190, also figures there as in the territory of 'Sigestro' (Sestri Levante), between the churches of Casarza and
Velici and those of Loto and Montedonico. The parish of
Piazza, near Framura, in the diocese of Chiavari, the
commune of Deiva and the province of Spezia, is now
dedicated to the Blessed Virgin.

In the province of Spezia the parish of Cornice, near
Godano in the diocese of Luni-Sarzana, not far from the
Passo del Bracco, is still dedicated to St. Columban.

Brugnato in the val di Vara, close by, was the site of an
important Benedictine abbey founded in the time of Liutprand and, perhaps, by Liutprand himself, which was
entitled after SS. Peter, Lawrence and Columban.[22] It was
raised to the dignity of an episcopal see by Pope Innocent II
in 1133 and placed within the dependence of the see of
Genoa, which the same Pope raised to metropolitan status,
granting it at the same time three suffragan sees in Corsica,
viz., Mariana, Nebbio and Accia, and the bishopric of Bobbio.
The diocese of Brugnato continued its independent existence
down to 1820, when it was united to the diocese of Luni-
Sarzana.[23]

West of Genoa, in the province of Imperia and the diocese
of Albenga, the parish of Gavenola, part of Borghetto d'
Arroscia, is dedicated to St. Columban.

Curti-Pasini mentions a San Colombano, part of
Lodisio, in the province of Savona. There is, in the province
of Savona a Lodisio, part of the commune of Santa Giulia

[21] Cf. a pamphlet entitled *Solenni feste celebrate per il XIII centenario di S.
Colombano a Vignale*, Chiavari, Artigianelli, 1920.
[22] Cf. Lubin, *Abbatiarum Italiae brevis notitia*, p. 64, and Cipolla and Buzzi,
Cod. dip., II, pp. 13 et seq.
[23] Luni (Latin *Luna*), an old Roman town, some nine or ten miles south-east
of Spezia, is too important to be overlooked. It was the point of junction for
the pilgrims who had come across the Monte Bardone and those who came by
sea from St. James of Compostella.

(with a parish dedicated to St. Columban and the Guardian Angel, in the diocese of Acqui) on the hills dividing the valley of the Bormida di Spigno from the valley of the Uzzone, i.e., quite close to the parish of Pezzolo in the province of Cuneo which has already been found dedicated to St. Columban.

§ 5

To cross over now into Lombardy and to begin with the province of Milan.

The traveller on the railway from Pavia to Casalpusterlengo will be struck near the station of Miradolo by a curious hill, clad with vineyards, which rises in lonely eminence some 210 feet above the great plain; this is the collina di S. Colombano. Behind the hill is the village of San Colombano al Lambro (in the circumscription of Lodi), with a castle which, formerly the property of Barbarossa, passed into the possession of the Visconti, and has now been restored by the Barbiano family of Belgiojoso. The frescoes, which had been painted in the now demolished chapel by Bernardino Campi, were removed to the parish church dedicated to St. Columban. The place was formerly called Mombrione or Mombrone or Brioni[24] and is first found mentioned under its new name in a deed of donation made by Aribert in 1034. An ancient tradition has it that the saint passed that way in the course of his journey from Milan to Bobbio, that he converted the pagan or heretical inhabitants, that he taught them the cultivation of the vine and so left his name to the locality. Redi refers in his *Bacco in Toscana* to that:

> " . . . bel colle,
> cui bacia il Lambro il piede
> ed a cui Colombano il nome diede."[25]

[24] Cf. Cipolla and Buzzi, op. cit., III, 92.

[25]   " . . . that fair hill
      whose foot the Lambro kisses
      and to which Columban gave his name."

Francesco Redi of Arezzo (1626-98), naturalist, Greek scholar, professor of rhetoric and physician to the grand-dukes of Tuscany, is remembered only, in spite of his scientific works, by this dithyramb sung by Bacchus in praise of the excellent vintages of Tuscany. Selections from it have made their way into all anthologies of Italian verse.

Don A. Maestri,[26] however, has recently shown that the name of the village and the local cultivation of the vine may be explained by the simple fact that the Bobbio monastery owned considerable estates in the neighbourhood.

Devotion to St. Columban among the *banini* is very lively: the feast of the patron is kept on 21st November and on 30th July the feast of the Translation, to be mentioned presently.

The parish of Fombio, also in the circumscription of Lodi, is said by Curti-Pasini (p. 9) to be dedicated to SS. Peter and Columban. The official dedication, however, would appear to be to SS. Peter and Paul. Agnelli[27] mentions a church which the saint had there, built by King Liutprand.[28]

The little Romanesque Church of St. Columban (eleventh or twelfth century) at Vaprio d' Adda (at the confluence of the Brembo and the Adda, in the province and diocese of Milan) is important in the history of art. Built throughout of hewn stone, it has only one nave and a tripartite vaulted choir. The original but primitive sculptures on the porch are decorated with a fleur-de-lis, the mark of the masons who built it, rare in Lombardy but not uncommon in Romanesque buildings in Provence. The four pictures of the saint in the church are of considerable interest for the iconography of St. Columban, more particularly one painted on wood 'in cornu evangelii' on the triptych above the altar. The church stands on the edge of the village facing a tiny square, and would seem to have belonged once upon a time to a convent; adjacent to it is a commodious building now occupied by the families of agricultural labourers.[29]

The cult of St. Columban in Pavia seems to have arisen on the occasion of his Translation.[30] The story goes that Hugo, King of Italy, suggested to the Abbot of Bobbio, who

[26] *Il nome di S. Colombano al Lambro*, Lodi, 1932, and *Origini del culto pel patrono a S. Colombano al Lambro*, Lodi, 1933.

[27] Cf. *Lodi e il suo territorio*.

[28] Cf. with reference to the cult of St. Columban in the diocese of Lodi, the before mentioned article by Don A. Maestri in *La Trebbia* for 5th December, 1931.

[29] Cf. P. Toesca, *Storia dell' Arte Italiana*, V.T.E.T., Turin, 1927, I, pp. 514 and 888, and the Italian Touring Club's publication *Attraverso l' Italia*, Part I, Milan, 1931, p. 120, which contains a reproduction of the porch.

[30] Cf. Mabillon, *Annales Ord. S. Ben.*, sec. II.

was bewailing the fact that property belonging to the abbey was being usurped by various feudal lords, that he should ask the saint himself to have it returned, by solemnly transporting his body to Pavia on the occasion of the assembly of the royal council to be held there in 930. The saint's remains were in fact borne in solemn procession to the basilica of St. Michael in Pavia, and the feudal lords were so affected by the miracles which took place during the journey, and while the body rested at Pavia, that they not only suffered a change of heart and agreed to restore the stolen property, but Hugo also granted the abbey fresh privileges over and above those granted by preceding sovereigns. The return of the body to Bobbio was made the occasion for another solemn procession and ever afterwards commemorated by the monks of Bobbio in a feast celebrated on 30th July. The feast and the date were officially recognized by a decree of the Sacred Congregation of Rites dated 27th August, 1836.[31]

The consequence of these events was the erection in Pavia of two churches dedicated to St. Columban, a 'major' and a 'minor.'[32] The Church of St. Columban 'major' (also called S. Colombanino) is now derelict, and, though degraded to the lowly condition of a carpenter's workshop, is still extremely interesting as a specimen of Lombard architecture: it stood in the street called to this day S. Colombano.[33] The Church of St. Columban 'minor' (also called S. Columbani de Cellanova) stood, perhaps, at the corner where the present via Roma runs into the via XX Settembre; the last remnant of it may have been the oratory of the old orphanage which was demolished when all such institutions were concentrated in the Monastery of S. Felice.

In Pavia the Bobbio Monastery owned a *xenodochium* as early as 862[34] described in a diploma dated 893 as a "xenodo-

[31] Cf. Curti-Pasini, op. cit., pp. 26 and 36.

[32] Cf. Mgr. Gianani, *Opicino de Canistris*, p. 57, for the 'major' pp. 80 and 125, and for the 'minor' pp. 79 and 124. Cf. also P. Romualdo Ghisoni, *Flavia Papia Sacra*, I, pp. 61 and 73, and Mgr. Maiocchi, *Le Chiese di Pavia*, pp. 138.

[33] An account of all that now remains of this church may be found in the before-mentioned memoir by C. G. Mor, *Bobbio, Pavia e gli 'Excerpta bobiensia,'* Pavia, 1923, p. 34.

[34] Cf. Cipolla and Buzzi, III, pp. 248.

chium cum ecclesia," but Cipolla apprehends that the words "cum ecclesia," lacking in the corresponding place in diplomata dated respectively 888, 896 and 903, may be a copyist's error.

A dairy-farm called S. Colombanino is marked in the Italian Touring Club map (sheet 10, C. 5) near Carpignano (Certosa di Pavia).

Five parishes are still dedicated to St. Columban in the Pavese region beyond the Po, where the Bobbio Monastery owned many estates: three in the diocese of Tortona, viz., Corbesassi (in val Trebbia, south of Bobbio), Santa Giulietta (between Stradella and Voghera), and Torre Menapace (north of Voghera), and two in the diocese of Bobbio, viz., Monteforte (near Varzi in val Staffora) and Ottone soprano (in val Trebbia). The church at Monteforte (Varzi) is mentioned in Cipolla and Buzzi as "Ecclesia S. Columbani de Monteforte," as is a neighbouring "Ecclesia S. Columbani de Caxasco," near Menconico, south-west of the Passo del Penice. Curti-Pasini cites (p. 10) a "Columbano, part of Cicognola (Voghera)," but the Italian Touring Club map (sheet 10, D. 5) designates the place near Cicognola (on the hills between Santa Giulietta and Stradella) as Colombarone.

At Como there was an ancient monastery of Benedictine nuns with a church dedicated to St. Columban and reputed to have been founded by Amalric (844-65), who, even as Bishop of Como, retained the title, and continued to exercise the functions of Abbot of Bobbio.[35] Lubin mentions the "abbatia sive monasterium tituli Sancti Columbani Cumanae [i.e., of Como] dioec. unitum abbatiae S. Victoris extra muros Mediolanenses sitae, per litteras Leonis Papae X Pontificatus anno 9, ita Codex Taxarum Camerae Apostolicae anno salutis 1521 in Lombardia."[36] There was a monastery with a Church of St. Columban, which may have dated from the seventh century, in Mantello sopra Dubino (in the lower Valtellina), which passed into the hands of the Cluniacs, who thence proceeded to build the imposing Abbey and Church of St. Peter in Vallate on the ruins of

[35] Cf. Cipolla and Buzzi, III, p. 185.
[36] Cf. *Abb. Italiae br. not.*, p. 107.

the castle of Cosio which had been destroyed in 1304. There is still a church nearby dedicated to St. Columban, the Church of Campo, near Novate Mezzola, on the lake of Mezzola, in the diocese of Como, but in the province of Sondrio, which was raised to the dignity of a parish church in 1704. It was erected when the counties of Chiavenna and the Valtellina were subject to Chur. The pass between Val di Fraina and the Valle del Bitto in Gerola, north of the Pizzo dei Tre Signori (cf. the Italian Touring Club map, sheet 4, D. 1), is still called Bocchetta della Colombana.

In the upper Valtellina, in the county of Bormio, formerly subject to the supremacy of the Bishop of Chur, is the Corno di S. Colombano, over 9,000 feet high, in the group of peaks called la Cima di Piazzi, with a chapel dedicated to the saint on the path leading to the Valle Viola Bormina. The parish church of Oga in those parts is still dedicated to St. Columban, while that of Premadio, close by, is dedicated to St. Gall.

Two parishes in the province of Bergamo are dedicated to St. Columban, viz., Valtesse, a village immediately to the north of Bergamo in val Morla, and Parzanica, on the Bergamasque shore of the lago d' Iseo: the former, which dates back to the eleventh century and used to be known as S. Colombani de Tegete, was once the seat of a monastery of Benedictines (Celestines), while the archives of the latter were completely destroyed in 1700. The feast is kept at Valtesse on 21st November, at Parzanica on 7th November,[37] as at S. Colombano al Lambro.

In the province and diocese of Brescia the parish of S. Colombano, part of Collio in the upper Mella, is dedicated to St. Columban; and in the province and diocese of Mantua that of Riva di Suzzara on the right bank of the Po.

§ 6

The province of Piacenza contains the shrine and the Monastery of Bobbio ("Bobio, Aebobium, Ebobium, Ebovium, Popium"), which the great monk founded, a year

[37] Cf. Curti-Pasini, pp. 8 and 32.

U—i

before his death in 614, in a then wild and derelict tract in
the Val Trebbia beside the ruins of a church once dedicated
to St. Peter, which he restored and enlarged with the help
of his few companions. There his bones have lain for thirteen
centuries. Monte Cassino, it may be recalled, which had
been founded in 529, was reduced to ashes by the fury of the
Lombards in 581 and did not rise again until c. 717. Its
monks in the interval had found shelter in Rome, in the
Lateran itself. There is no need to describe the shrine at
Bobbio, and the reader is referred to the books already
cited, more particularly that by Rebolini, which is copiously
illustrated and easily procurable, and Miss Stokes's *Six
Months in the Apennines*, which describes (pp. 109-200) everything relating to the saint to be found in Bobbio and neighbourhood, La Spanna, Coli, etc.[38] A great part of the land
about Bobbio formerly belonged to the monastery, whose
estates stretched far and wide all over the Piacentino. The
name 'Monte Colombano' is still given to a mountain
between the val Trebbia and the val Tidone, north of
Monteventano (cf. the Italian Touring Club map, sheet
11, E. 1), which is mentioned also by Nasalli-Rocca[39] with
reference to the parish of Momeliano from which a church of
St. Columban depended.[40]

The province of Piacenza has four parishes still dedicated
to St. Columban, viz., Vicobarone, part of Ziano Piacentino,
north-west of Pianello Val Tidone; Muradello, part of
Pontenure, towards the Po; Lusurasco, part of Alseno, near
the Arda, between Fiorenzuola and Castellarquato; and
Vernasca, a commune in the val d' Arda, south of Lugagnano d' Arda.

Schiavi[41] mentioned an "Oratorio di San Colombano" in
Parma referred to in the life of St. John the First Abbot.
Cipolla and Buzzi mention an "ecclesia Sancti Columbani"
in the val di Taro, which in 1204 was placed within the

---

[38] As to these last cf. also the article by Dom Gougaud, 'Archéologie de
Saint Colomban,' in the *Dictionnaire d'archéologie chrétienne*, col. 2196, and *Gaelic
Pioneers*, pp. 122 et seq.

[39] *Pievi della montagna piacentina*, p. 7.

[40] Cf. Campi, *Storia eccl. di Piacenza*, Vol. III, pp. 84 and 134.

[41] Cf. *La Diocesi di Parma*, Parma, 1925, p. 158.

jurisdiction of the archpriest of the parish of S. Giorgio in the val di Taro.

In the province of Reggio Emilia the parish of Fogliano, part of Reggio Emilia to the south-east of the city on the road to Scandiano, is still dedicated to St. Columban. As regards the Modenese, Don Emilio Benti, referring in § IV of the chapter entitled 'Vicende e condizioni ecclesiastiche' in *L'Apennino modenese*,[42] the work of a number of contributors, to the very ancient parish of Fanano on the slopes of Monte Cimone, says: "There was once there [in the territory of Fanano] a pilgrims' hospice dedicated to St. James, and itself a dependence from the Hospital of Val di Lámola with a church dedicated to St. Columban and situate on the crest of the mountains." At the present moment, I am informed by Don Camillo Bullarini, the rector of the church of St. Columban in Bologna, nothing of the sort has survived, and the hospital of val di Lámola is now a little parish high up in the mountains canonically established in 1559 with a church dedicated to St. James. The territory of Fanano had been granted by Astulf to the Abbot of Nonantola.

An ancient church of St. Columban, as mentioned above, still stands in Bologna, via Parigi.[43] It dates back apparently to the seventh century,[44] and would seem to have been served first by Benedictines of the St. Gall Congregation, who, in 1144, were succeeded by Cluniacs. A campanile, the first in Bologna, is said to have been erected about that time. In 1073 Gregory VII, in a deed confirming to Lambert, Bishop of Bologna, the rights of the Church, refers to a "Monasterium S. Columbani." Towards the end of the twelfth century the Monastery of St. Columban was ceded to the nuns of S. Clemente who remained there until the fourteenth century, i.e., until 1332, when the Legate Bertrand suppressed this and other convents and established instead a

[42] Rocca S. Casciano, Cappelli, 1895.

[43] Cf. Guidicini, *Cose notabili della Città di Bologna*, Bologna, Vitali, 1868, IV, pp. 47-9, and the same writer's *Miscellanea storico-patria bolognese*, Bologna, Monti, 1872, p. 279.

[44] Lubin, op. cit., p. 58, says: "Abbatia sive Monast. tit. S. Columbani confessoris a Petro Bononiensi episcopo constructum qui sedit anno 616."

collegiate church of canons, consisting of a prior, a dean, and five canons, one of four collegiate churches in the four quarters of the city, viz., St. Columban, St. James de' Carbonesi, St. Sigismund, and St. Michael dei Leprosetti.

In 1334, under the pontificate of Benedict XII, the sisters recovered their convent, but in 1347 Cardinal E. Albornoz, the Legate of Pope Clement VI, suppressed it again as a convent and, reinstating the canons, revived the collegiate church with cure of souls, and appointed the vicar prior.

In 1595 the parish of St. Columban was suppressed by Clement VIII and the parishioners distributed among the neighbouring parishes. In 1597 the priory of St. Columban was acquired by Padre Giovanni Califani, as attorney and mandatory of St. Camillus of Lellis, for the purpose of establishing in Bologna a convent for the Servants of the Sick.

The Camillines ceded the church in 1679 to the college of St. Thomas Aquinas, which later leased it to the Brethren of Our Lady of Humility; the convent was subsequently acquired by the Republic of Lucca, which converted it into a school. The school was suppressed in 1788, when the building was sold to the owner of the adjacent palazzo. The church was granted in 1704 to the Congregation of the Guardian Angel, which became extinct in 1798. It was used as a parish church by the former parishioners of SS. Fabian and Sebastian (a parish abolished in 1797) down to 1805, and from 1808 to 1820 it remained closed. It was re-opened in 1820 for religious services by the Confraternity of Our Lady of Mercy to whom it still belongs.[45]

§ 7

The Bobbio Monastery owned vast and lucrative estates in the Veronese which made up the *corte* of Garda.[46] An "ecclesia sancti Columbani de Bardolino" and a "prioratus sancti Columbani de Bardolino" are recorded: the "ecclesia

[45] Cf. also an illustrated article by Don Cam. Bullarini in a publication to commemorate the golden jubilee of Mgr. Giovanni Nardi, Tipogr. Luigi Parma, Bologna, 1929.
[46] Cf. Cipolla and Buzzi, op. cit., III, 98.

S. Columbani in Corte," "in Costa" would also seem to have been close to Bardolino. Garda had two chapels —one the "ecclesia S. Columbani in Garda," the other, name unknown, situate, perhaps, in the "sors de Sigebaldo," Sigebald's allotment or estate.

In the Trentino, along the road from Rovereto to Pian delle Fugazze, about a mile and a half from Rovereto, the Ponte di S. Colombano bridges the deep ravine down which the Leno of Terragnolo flows into the Leno of the Vallarsa. Almost facing the bridge, to the left of the Vallarsa, stands the ancient little shrine of St. Columban recorded as early as 1319 in a testament of Guglielmo di Castelbarco.[47] It is picturesquely and perilously poised on the sheer rock with a hut attached for its hermit custodian. Weber gives a list of the hermits who lived there from 1698 to 1740.[48]

A locality called Colombano is indicated on the Italian Touring Club map (Sheet 13, D. 1) near Badia Polesine in the province of Rovigo.

In the province of Treviso, the parish of Pero, part of the commune of Breda di Piave, between Maserada and S. Biagio di Callalta, is dedicated to St. Columban. The old church was demolished in 1899 to make room for a larger one. The parish of Pero, like the neighbouring parishes of Breda and S. Biagio di Callalta, owes its origin apparently to the Benedictines who had a priory in Pero. The great Abbey of Monastier, the fabric of which still stands, was built later on some six miles away. The present titular of the parish church of Monastier is Our Lady of the Assumption 'de Pyro,' and the suggestion is that this is due to the fact that the priory of Pero, whose church had St. Columban for titular, was transferred at the time of the new building.

§ 8

Further traces of St. Columban must be sought in Tuscany, where they are connected with those discovered in Liguria in the diocese of Luni-Sarzana.

[47] Cf. P. Tovazzi, *Notitia ecclesiarum*, etc., vol. 35, s.n. 22, p. 24, and vol. 37, I, c. 65, p. 809.

[48] *Gli eremiti nel Trentino*, Rivista Tridentina, December 1912, p. 244.

In the province of Massa-Carrara there is a parish dedicated to SS. John and Columban at Pontremoli di val di Magra, between Parma and Sarzana, on the road through the Cisa. In the same province and still in the diocese of Pontremoli, the parish of Canneto is dedicated to SS. Columban and Martin, and the parish of Posara to St. Columban alone; Canneto and Posara are both constituents of Fivizzano in the valle Rosaro, between Reggio Emilia and Sarzana on the road through the Cerreto.

In the province of Lucca, just where the Serchio, flowing down from Garfagnana, emerges into the plain, is the village of S. Colombano, part of Capannori, lying in the hills to the east of Marlia. The parish church, built apparently in the eleventh century, is dedicated to the saint, and the Archbishop of Lucca has his country seat in the village.

The city of Lucca once boasted a church dedicated to St. Columban.[49] A document dated 730 mentions a church or deanery of St. Columban, which the archpriest Sigismund, brother of the then reigning Bishop Thalesperian, and other prominent citizens undertook to erect and endow "in susceptionem peregrinorum."[50] It was the third hospice to be built in the eighth century outside and close to the porta S. Pietro. The actual building was begun under Thalesperian but suffered various delays. Bishop Walprand, who died in 755, disposed by will that the income from one-fourth of his property should be applied for the benefit of the hospice of St. Columban, founded—in the words of his testament—by his predecessors. Walprand was succeeded as Bishop of Lucca by one Peredeus who lived to see the completion of the important edifice and consecrated the new church. He died in 779 and he, too, bequeathed part of his property to the hospice of St. Columban, increasing by twelve the number of poor folk to be fed there weekly.[51] A bastion in the present

---

[49] Cf. Bertini, Vol. IV of *Memorie e documenti per servire alla storia di Lucca*, published by the Royal Academy of Lucca.

[50] The date usually assigned to the document is 729 which Mgr. Guidi has corrected to 730. Cf. Guerra and Guidi, *Compendio di storia ecclesiastica lucchese*, Lucca, Co-op. Tip. Editrice, 1924, p. 70.

[51] Cf. Guerra and Guidi, op. cit., pp. 64-5, 70, 75, 85.

sixteenth century south wall of the city stands on the site of the old church and hospice of St. Columban and is called the Baluardo S. Colombano.

Two parishes are dedicated to St. Columban in the province and diocese of Florence: S. Colombano at Settimo and S. Colombano at Bibbione.

S. Colombano at Settimo, part of the commune of Casellina and Torri, lies about six miles west of Florence, a short distance from the Arno, near Badia a Settimo. It was an eleventh century Benedictine foundation (the Abbey of S. Salvatore of Settimo), which, in the thirteenth century, passed into the hands of the Cistercians and, after playing a conspicuous part in the history of Florence down to 1782, is now in private ownership. The monks of S. Salvatore were undoubtedly responsible for the local devotion to St. Columban and for the dedication of this ancient church, which also must have been one of their foundations. S. Colombano was the home of the Gozzoli family, whose most distinguished member, Benozzo, came from there.[52] The feast is kept on 21st November, as at S. Colombano a Bibbione.

The Church of St. Columban a Bibbione, also called S. Columbano alla collina (on the hill), stands about twelve miles south of Florence in the commune of S. Casciano in val di Pesa on the road to Siena. It dates back to the eleventh century, but all that remains of the ancient building is the apse. Devotion to St. Columban, still lively, derives probably from the neighbouring ancient Abbey of St Michael the Archangel at Passignano in the val di Pesa, belonging to the Benedictines of Vallombrosa, where the body of S. Giovanni Gualberto rests since 1073.[53]

A Benedictine 'monasterium S. Columbani,' near Castro, is cited by Kehr as in existence as early as 1027.[54]

§ 9

Mention should also be made of a village called St. Columban in France, near Nice, in the valley of La Vésubie, near

[52] Cf. Carocci, *I dintorni di Firenze*, Florence, 1907, II, 448.
[53] Cf. with reference to this abbey, Lugano, *L'Italia benedettina*, Rome, Ferrari, 1929, p. 357. [54] *Italia Pontificia*, II, Latium, p. 218.

Lantosque, and of Saint-Colomban-des-Villars, near St.
Jean de Maurienne, in Savoy,[55] but it is in Corsica, above
all, that the name of St. Columban most frequently recurs.[56]
The traveller along the road from Ponte Leccia to Calvi is
not long before coming to a 'Rio di S. Colombano,' a 'Passo
di S. Colombano,' a 'Monte di S. Colombano,' and a ruined
'Torre di S. Colombano.' G. Cambiagi[57] recalls that Gregory
VI, in an attempt to pacify the island in 1045, when it was
rent by factions whose respective headquarters were at Pisa
and Genoa, sent the Marquis di Massa di Maremma there,
and that he, with a view to curbing the high-flown insolence
of the Amondaschi and Pinaschi families, built a castle named
after St. Columban "in the parish of Giussani (which
consists of six villages and marches with the parish of Ostriconi in the province of Balagna)." In 1133 Innocent II,
having succeeded in restoring peace between Pisa and Genoa,
placed under Genoa—as already mentioned in § 4 apropos
the Abbey of Brugnato—the three Corsican bishoprics of
Mariana, Nebbio and Accia, together with the bishopric
of Bobbio. In 1267 one of the Marchesi di S. Colombano is
found in the camp of Giudice, and another in that of his
adversary Giovanninello. Besides this castle in the heart
of the island, to which the topographical names above-
mentioned all refer, there was still another 'Castello di S.
Colombano' in Corsica, and more precisely, in the Capocorso, which offered a stout resistance to the Genoese but was
ultimately stormed and razed to the ground in 1554: out of
its ruins rose Rogliano.[58] This castle in the Capocorso is
described in the *Cronica corsa di Pietro Cirneo*[59] as the "Sancti
Columbani civitas," and Giacomo Mari, the son of Simone,
Lord of the Capocorso and husband of a Pallavicino of

---

[55] Cf. as to this last Curti-Pasini, p. 6.
[56] Cf. the Italian Touring Club map, sheet 25 trs., A. 3, and its Guide,
Sardegna e Corsica, 1929, p. 425.
[57] *Istoria del Regno di Corsica*, 4 vols., 1770-2, vol. I, p. 92.
[58] Ibid., II, p. 51, Cf. as to this second castle, also Vol. I, pp. 287, 302,
329, Vol. II, p. 11. Reference is made in Vol. IV, p. 7, to an Angelo Colombani,
who, in 1755, engaged in operations against Paoli, the Paoli whom 'Corsica'
Boswell on the evening of 10th October, 1769, presented to Dr. Johnson, and
in Vol. IV, p. 229, to a Pietro Maria Colombani, a deputy of the Third Estate
in 1770.
[59] Published by Letteron, Bastia; 1884, p. 17.

Genoa, is described (p. 367) as "Sancti Columbani princeps."

§ 10

The foregoing exposition will have shown how numerous are the traces of St. Columban still surviving in Italy. The number of parishes alone dedicated to him to-day amounts to thirty-four: which means that there are still thirty-four centres of life in Italy where the people are taught to know, honour, pray and offer thanks to, the great Irishman. The office of St. Columban is recited to-day not only in the parishes called after him but also in the diocesan propers of Bobbio, Lodi, Tortona, and Saluzzo, and in the Benedictine Order; until the reformation of the breviary it appeared also in the diocesan propers of Piacenza and Chiavari. It is included also, as already mentioned in § 4, in the liturgical calendars of Mantua, Brescia and Verona.

A complete and exhaustive account of the origins of all the churches and foundations named after St. Columban would be matter enough for a book in itself. Don A. Maestri of S. Columbano al Lambro has recently announced a volume on devotion to St. Columban in Italy.

There can be no doubt that Bobbio was the chief centre from which the cult of St. Columban radiated over Italy. The influence of Bobbio made itself felt in three ways: through the monastic foundations deriving directly from it (Biandrate, for instance, may be a case in point) during the brief period in which the Rule of St. Columban was supreme and unchallenged;[60] through Benedictine monastic foundations after it had become a Benedictine abbey (the abbeys in the Piedmontese Alps, that at Pero near Treviso, those in the diocese of Florence, that at Castro, etc., may be cases in point), and through its territorial possessions (as in the case of the churches in Liguria, the Tortonese and the Veronese). It is well to remember that the "ecclesiae sancti Columbani" mentioned in the *Codice diplomatico*,[61] and including Bobbio,

[60] Cf. Cipolla and Buzzi, I, 88.
[61] Ibid III, 207.

number only eight; the *Codice diplomatico*, however, comes down only to 1208. The territorial possessions of the Bobbio Monastery from the ninth to the twelfth century are considered by Buzzi in Vol. III, pp. 77-141. The alphabetical list of the *corti* in 1014, when the monastery was raised to the status of a bishopric, is given on pp. 85-115 inclusive. They are extensive and situate in the region round Bobbio (Pavia, Voghera, Tortona, Asti, Alba, Piacenza, Parma, Genoa and Chiavari); but they are to be found also—as we have had occasion partly to point out—in the Comasco, the Cremonese, the Lodigiano, the Mantovano, the Veronese, at Comacchio, at Marradi and in the Casentino. Buzzi gives on pp. 117-34 inclusive a schedule of the properties which made up the episcopal *mensa* as it was constituted in 1014, properties which reverted to the monastery once the bishopric became detached, and on pp. 134-41 a schedule of the estates which made up the patrimony of the conventual *mensa* and the various houses in its obedience.

But if Bobbio was the chief centre from which devotion to St. Columban spread over Italy, that is not to say that it was the only one. It is probable that the Abbey of St. Gall in Switzerland made its contribution too, directly or indirectly, through the churches in the Valtellina and its own church in Bologna, while the canons of St. Fridian of Lucca also, no doubt, made their contribution as regards the churches in Lucchesia.

Unfortunately the complete list of the monasteries of Italy from the seventh to the thirteenth century still remains to be drawn up.

CHAPTER XIII

S. CUMMIAN OF BOBBIO

§ 1

THE crypt in the basilica of St. Columban at Bobbio was completely renovated—with much devotion, an admirable sense of history and great artistic taste—in 1910 at the express wish of Cardinal Logue, Archbishop of Armagh, and with the offerings of the Catholic people of Ireland. The body of St. Columban was replaced in the beautiful fifteenth century, storied and many-coloured sarcophagus designed by Giovanni dei Patriarchi, and the two seventh century coffins, containing respectively the bodies of St. Athala the Burgundian, the second abbot (615-c. 620), and St. Bertulf, the third abbot (c. 626-40) and the blood relation of Arnulf, Bishop of Metz, were left beside the tomb of the founder backed against the wall. The bones of some twenty other Bobbiese saints, the successors or disciples of St. Columban, including those of St. Bobulenus of Luxeuil, the fourth abbot and of the Irish St. Cummian, were reverently assembled under the new marble altar.

The tombstone of St. Cummian and the fragments of a coffin containing his and other remains and of a console which supported the coffin were removed, together with other important debris, to a part of the crypt railed off by the superb fifteenth century wrought iron lattice which originally enclosed the tomb of St. Columban, and a sort of small lapidary museum was thus constituted.[1]

§ 2

Who was this St. Cummian?

Ughelli[2] gives a few meagre historical details which he

---

[1] Cf. Rebolini, 'S. Colombano di Bobbio' in the series *Santuari d'Italia illustrati*, and Cipolla and Buzzi, *Cod. dipl.*, I, 118 et seq., and 132 et seq.

[2] *Italia sacra*, second edition, Venice, 1719, IV, pp. 959-60.

declares to have been derived from the *Chronicon Bobiense quod extat in bibliotheca Aniciana*; but the only positive data —which, moreover, are in substantial agreement with the information given by Ughelli—are such as are to be gathered from the inscription on the tombstone itself. It has been published several times more or less accurately, and is given below according to the critical text established by Cipolla:[3]

 † Hic sacra beati   membra Cumiani solvuntur.
 Cuius caelum penetrans anima c(um) angelis gaudet.
 Iste fuit magnus   dignitate, genere, forma.
 Hunc misit Scothia   fines ad Italicos senem.
 Locatur Ebovio   D(omi)ni constrictus amore.
 Ubi, venerandi   dogma Columbani servando
 Vigilans, ieiunans   indefessus, sidule orans
 Olimpiadis quattuor   uniusque circolo anni.
 Sic vixit feliciter   ut felix modo credatur.
 Mitis, prudens, pius   fratr[i]bus, paceficus cunctis.
 Huic aetatis anni   fuerunt novies deni
 Lustrun quoque unum, mensesque quattuor simul.
 At pater egregie   potens intercessor exsiste
 Pro gloriosissimo   Liutprando rege qui tuum
 Praetioso lapide   tymbum decoravit devotus
 Sit ut manifestum   almum ubi tegitur corpus.

 D(e)p(ositus) est hic d(o)m(inu)s Cumianus ep(iscopu)s. xiiii. k(a)l(endas) s(e)pt(em)b(ri)s.

 Fecit † Iohannes magister.

From this we learn that St. Cummian was an Irish bishop who left Ireland when he was already well on in years, that he came to Bobbio to live according to the Rule of St. Columban, that he lived there for seventeen or twenty-one years, according as an olympiad is reckoned at four or five years,[4] and that he died there at the age of ninety-five years

---

[3] *Cod. dipl.*, I, 122.

[4] Cf. Ussher, *Whole Works*, IV, Dublin, 1862, p. 420, apropos the chronology of St. Columban himself. In the hexameters appended to the 159 Adonic lines addressed 'Fidolio fratri suo' he gives his age: 'Nunc ad olympiadis ter senae venimus annos.' Mabillon and Krusch, following him, took an 'olympias' as the equivalent of a 'lustrum,' founding on a line in which Ausonius (XXII, 4, 6) gives his father's age 'Undecies binas vixit Olympiadas'—22 times four years, although Ausonius in another passage (III, 4, 61) makes his father say

and four months one 19th August, in the reign of King Liutprand, i.e., some time between 712 and 744. He was therefore certainly born in the seventh century and died in the first half of the eighth.

The tombstone is of great interest on account of the lettering of the inscription and the decorations *opere pampinaceo* surrounding it. It has been described by Miss Stokes[5] following Remondini[6] and considered more fully by Cipolla.[7] When the stone was removed in 1910 to be placed in the museum, the pleasing discovery was made that the reverse was also elaborately decorated in an intricate ribbon pattern divided into ten panels. Both sides of the stone are reproduced by Rebolini in the number of the *Santuari d'Italia illustrati* before referred to.

Also very important—although it contains no reference to the saint—is a puzzling eighth century inscription carved on fragments of the console which supported the coffin of St. Cummian. It alludes to a King of the Frisons.[8]

The name Cummian, also written Cumin and Cumman, appears in Latin in the various forms *Cumianus*, *Commeanus*, *Cuminus*, and a number of Irishmen are recorded under the name, all of whom must be carefully distinguished. In addition to the Bobbio saint, Dom Gougaud[9] mentions a Cummian, the author, *c.* 632, of a famous letter 'De controversia Paschali' (Migne, *P.L.*, LXXXVII, 969 et seq., a reprint of the text first published by Ussher in *Veterum Epistolarum*

'Nonaginta annos . . . Exegi.' Poets are not tied to rigour of definition. Cf. also note 69 to chapter XIII of Lanigan's *Ecclesiastical History of Ireland* and the Abbé Martin's *St. Colomban*, p. 12 n.

[5] *Six months in the Apennines*, pp. 170 et seq.

[6] 'Iscrizioni medioevali della Liguria' in *Atti della Soc. Lig. di St. Patria*, 1887.

[7] Op. cit., I, pp. 118-23.

[8] Noticed rather inadequately by Miss Stokes, op. cit., pp. 167 et seq., it has now been exhaustively considered by Cipolla, op. cit., I, pp. 132-34. The '*Johannes magister*,' it may be added, who '*fecit*' the inscription to Cummian, was probably the 'master' stonemason under whose direction the other *muratori*, *collegae*, *consortes*, worked. The words 'magister comacinus,' sc., of or from Como, occur for the first time in an edict of Rothair, *c.* 643, and reappear in the laws of Liutprand and occasionally in eighth century decrees. Cf. Pietro Toesca, 'Storia dell'arte italiana,' I, *Il Medioevo*, Turin, 1927, p. 149, n. 106. Sgr. Toesca thinks that the original pattern on the Bobbio stone was practically effaced to receive the epitaph and that the stonecutter huddled his letters together regardless of the run of the design upon which he was carving.

[9] Cf. *Christianity in Celtic Lands*, pp. 190-3 et alias.

Hibernicarum Sylloge, Whole Works IV, pp. 432-43), to Segene, fifth Abbot of Iona (623-52), pleading with the Irish to conform with the rest of Christendom in the matter of keeping the Easter celebration, and, incidentally, making the first extant allusion to 'sanctus Patricius papa noster' as having made and imported a variant cycle, and another[10] to be distinguished as Cummean, the compiler of a very learned abridgement of the ancient penitential canons, a typical early 'doom-book,' *De poenitentiarum mensura,* known as the Penitential of Cummean (Migne, *P.L.,* ibid, 988) and discovered by Fleming in the Monastery of St. Gall, the date of which (*c.* 650) would make its attribution to St. Cuimine *fota,* Abbot of Clúain ferta-Brénaind (592-662), reasonably certain. Miss Stokes mentions a Bishop Cumin, born in 592, the son of Fiachna, King of West Munster, whom Ughelli wrongly identified with the Cummian in question, and who is none other than St. Cuimine *fota,* a member, according to the genealogists, of the royal family of the Eoganacht of Loch-Lém, which dwelt around the lakes of Killarney, and still another Cummian, Bishop of Nendrum, who died in 658, and with whom Colgan[11] was inclined to identify the saint of Bobbio.

As to the date of the saint's feast, Cipolla observes: "In the parish archives of St. Columban at Bobbio I saw an eighteenth century document containing a transcription [of Cummian's epitaph] with the following note appended: 'In calendariis antiquis legitur ejus festum quinto idus julii. In codice signato N † ad diem 9 iulii legitur S. Cumiani.' Rossetti, III, 58, also reproducing the inscription, quotes Codex N †, but says that the name of St. Cummian was included under 9th June. Codex N † is scheduled in the eighteenth century catalogue attributed to the Abbot Charisius under the following description: 'Psalterium et Kalendarium utrumque pervetustum, in fol., ex membr.' The codex has never been identified, and may, therefore, be reasonably considered lost. I would add that a much earlier

[10] Ibid., pp. 237, 284-5, 327 and 360. Cf. also in regard to each M. Esposito 'Notes on Latin-learning,' etc., in *Hermathena.*

[11] Cf. *AA. SS. Hib.,* p. 58.

text of this catalogue of Charisius is in existence, that belonging to Giovanni Antonio de Cantellis and dated 1722. It was first brought to my notice by the lamented Canon A. Civardi of Bobbio and is recorded in the *Inventario dei codici e delle carte bobbiesi* in the possession of H.E. the Marquis Obizzo Malaspina. . . . The feast of St. Cummian is still kept at Bobbio on 9th July." A seventeenth century liturgical fragment[12] contains a list of the feasts customarily kept at Bobbio in honour of its own particular saints, and reads: "Die XII ianuarii, in monasterio Bobiensi, S. Cumiani sive Cumini episcopi, Iberni patria, qui pro . . . eius corpus est in ecclesia S. Columbani in tugurio (tiburio?) Bob." Some hagiographical dictionaries[13] give the date of his death as 19th August. O'Hanlon[14] and the Bollandists treat of St. Cummian on 9th June.

I have found no traces of any cult of St. Cummian outside Bobbio.

[12] From cover No. 70, cat. IV, Miscellanea in the *Archives of the Abbey of Bobbio*, cf. Cipolla Cod. dipl. I, p. 123.

[13] e.g., the *Dictionnaire d'hagiographie*, by Dom Baudot, Paris, Bloud et Gay, 1925.

[14] *Lives of the Irish Saints*, VI, 605.

CHAPTER XIV

S. FULCO DI PIACENZA "EX GENTE SCOTA"

§ 1

LET it be said at once that S. Fulco is not an Irishman in the sense of having been born in Ireland. "A multis dicitur S. Fulcus natione Scotus fuisse, sed certissime Placentiae natus est."[1] It will, nevertheless, be seen that he makes a very natural and appropriate starting-off place for an historical digression not without interest upon the subject of the Scots' emigration to Italy and, more generally, to Europe, during the early Middle Ages.

Every work dealing with the civil and ecclesiastical history of Piacenza and Pavia[2] tells the story of a S. Fulco born in Piacenza in 1164 of an impoverished branch of the *Scotti* family, which by that time had grown and ramified extensively all over the city. Fulco joined the Order of the Canons Regular of St. Euphemia in 1185 and was sent to complete his studies in Paris. Returning home *c.* 1192, he was shortly afterwards ordained priest, and in 1194 appointed Provost of St. Euphemia. During the troublous times which followed the interdiction of Piacenza between 1203 and 1207, he sought refuge with his friend, Bishop Grimerio, at Castellarquato. On his return to the city, he took part in the diocesan synod of 1208, was appointed canon, and, very soon after, archpriest at the cathedral. Grimerio died in 1210 and Fulco was elected Bishop of Piacenza. By some accounts he is alleged to have taken part in the Lateran Council held by Innocent III in 1215, but there is no certainty in the matter.[3] When the Bishop of Pavia died in 1216, Fulco was

---

[1] *AA. SS.*, October, XII, p. 3.
[2] Cf. e.g.: Campi, *Dell' historia ecclesiastica di Piacenza;* Poggiali, *Memorie storiche di Piacenza;* Magani, *Cronotassi dei vescovi di Pavia;* and more particularly, C. Molinari, *Compendio della vita di San Fulco vescovo*, Piacenza, Tononi, 1901.
[3] Cf. *AA. SS.*, loc. cit., p. 14.

appointed Bishop of Pavia, and, after devoting himself with much charity and considerable talent to the task of composing the differences between the Piacentini and the Pavesi, and restoring peace among the various factions in both cities, died there on 26th October, 1229, according to the generally accepted opinion.

He was buried in the Cathedral of Pavia near the altar of St. Simon, and in 1579 his body was placed below the high altar together with those of St. Syrus and other Bishops of Pavia. A number of miracles is attributed to him. His feast was fixed on 26th October, and his cult, originally rather restricted in Pavia, began to spread after 1579, and in Piacenza would seem to be due largely to the activities of Campi.

Another St. Fulco, it should be observed, is venerated exclusively in the parish of Saletto (S. Maria in Duno) in the diocese of Bologna, and Ferrari, on the analogy of S. Fulco of Piacenza, has placed him under the same date. He may belong to the eleventh century, but, according to the Bollandists,[4] his "res gestae ignorantur. Quae de eo circumferuntur partim falsa aperte sunt, partim valde dubia."

§ 2

The reader may wonder what connection there is between S. Fulco of Piacenza and Ireland. Some writers have attempted to connect them by devious ways: I propose to do so directly, but remotely.

In chapter VIII it was related that Donatus of Fiesole 'de genere Scotorum' presented the Bobbio Monastery with a church dedicated to St. Brigit and a hospice attached which he had built in Piacenza. A passage in Pancotti's memoir *La Chiesa di S. Brigida*[5] merits reproduction in its entirety:

"But some attempt must be made to resolve a doubt which the document above referred to still leaves subsisting.

[4] Cf. *AA. SS.*, Oct., XI, p. 1039.
[5] Piacenza, Del Maino, 1928, pp. 13 et seq.

The document states that this Donatus, Bishop of Fiesole,
was 'de genere Scotorum.' It should be pointed out meanwhile that Sansovino errs in stating ('Della origine et de'
fatti delle Famiglie illustri d' Italia,' Vinegia, Altobello
Salicato, 1582, I, 3, *De Familia Scota*) that the founder of S.
Brigida was Bishop of Bobbio; the document, on this point,
is as explicit as it can be. How are the words 'ex genere
Scotorum' to be understood? Do they merely mean that
Donatus was Scotch by origin, according to some accounts,
or, according to others, do they indicate that Donatus
belonged to the Scotti family? Cristoforo Poggiali (*Memorie
storiche di Piacenza*) rejects the descent of this Donatus from
the Scotti family and taxes Sansovino with romancing for
alleging it. As the question concerns one of the most distinguished families in Piacenza, which could boast of having
produced another saintly bishop as well, Fulco Scotti, it is of
the highest local interest and not to be lightly passed over.

"It would appear from the testimony of the chronicles
cited by Campi [*Dell' hist. eccl. di Piacenza, I*, 215: *Anno
Domini DCCCLXVIII: Donatus Episcopus, qui fuit de Scotis* (*ut
aliqui dicunt*) *aedificavit*, etc.] that the founder of the Church
of S. Brigida was a Scotti and, more precisely, Donatus
Scotti, Bishop of Fiesole, the son of William I. There is
reproduced opposite for the benefit of amateurs of genealogies
a genealogical table of the Counts Douglas-Scotti (Italian
branch) showing the alleged founder of the church.

"This genealogical table is derived from the *Giornale
Araldico genealogico-diplomatico*, published by the Royal
Italian College of Heraldry, and edited by Crollalanza (cf.
Vol. XI, Pisa, 1864, p. 126, Table I). No genealogy beyond
the year 1000, and this one goes back to the year A.D. 700,
offers any trustworthy guarantee of authenticity. Reasons
for doubting its veracity are not far to seek. It has no ad-
mittedly genuine documentary evidence to produce in its
favour and, as a rule, is made up out of vague traditions, the
sole origin of which in the majority of cases is the ambition
of families. Other books which I have consulted on the
matter begin very much later. An interesting memorial on
this family entitled *Notizie genealogiche relative alle famiglie*

SHOLTO DOUGLAS
comes at the head of his vassals to the help of Solvatius, King of Scotland, in 767.

HUGH
The founder of the great Scotch family which ramified first in France and later over other nations in Europe.

WILLIAM
A Scotch captain, dispatched by the King of Scotland to the assistance of Charlemagne, accompanies the great Emperor to Italy but, after the defeat of Desiderius, instead of returning home, settled in Piacenza, takes to wife the daughter of Antonio Spettini and founds the Italian family called Scotti because of its descent from a Scotchman.

ST. DONATUS,
Bishop of Fiesole.
The founder in 868 of the Church of St. Brigit.

GIOVANNI
David surnamed il Vecchio, the elder.
Married Eugenia Paleologa and makes his will the 6th November, 997.

LEONARDO   PIETRO   TADONE I   GIOVANNI   BRADAMANTE   BRISEIDE
Vicar Imperial in Ravenna (1017)

TADONE II
Imperial Judge in Ravenna and elsewhere

REGINALDO
Vicar Imperial in various cities and later in Piacenza, along with his father takes a hand in the administration of the Monastery of St. Brigit (1044)

GUIDO SCOTTI
(1164).

MANFREDO DE' SCOTTI
goes warring with Rainaldo d' Este (1162).

David Junior.

S. FULCO ex gente SCOTA
b. 1164. Canon Regular of St. Euphemia: Bishop elect of Piacenza (1210). Consecrated Bishop of Pavia (1216) † 1229.

---

dei nobili signori conti Douglas Scotti di Vigoleno, Sarmato e Fombio, Piacenza, Tip. Tedeschi, 1859, contains the genealogical table of the Scotti family of Vigoleno, which it dates back to 1200. The founder would appear to have been a David Scotti, who lived towards the end of the twelfth century, and the author of this memorial declares that this David is to be regarded as the head of all the Scotti families. The genealogical synopsis of the Scotti family in the possession of Count Dionigi Barattieri, a high authority in such matters, which I consulted, leads to the same conclusion.

"Canon Balduzzi deals with this St. Donatus at some length in his book, *I Douglas e gli Scotti Douglas* (published at Pisa by the comptrollers of the Giornale Araldico in 1883). He also makes the family begin with a Sholto de Douglas in the eighth century. This Sholto was the father of Hugo, and Hugo, the father of William, who was appointed Governor of Lombardy by Charlemagne. He came to settle in Piacenza in the first thirty years of the eighth century and was the father of Donatus, who later became Bishop of Fiesole and was the founder of our church. Balduzzi himself, however, expresses many doubts on the subject.

"This is what he says: 'Some writers have very confidently asserted that this William had two sons, Donatus and John, the former of whom, the Bishop of Fiesole and a saint, built a church near Piacenza in honour of St. Brigit, a Scotch nun, and endowed it with considerable property. Candidly, such confidence in asserting St. Donatus and John to be the sons of William seems to me excessive, and excessive it seemed also to Frederick Scotti, a jurisconsult, orator and poet of renown, who openly admitted that from the first William down to 1200 there were no authentic data upon which any continuous genealogical table of his descendants could be based. All that the Roman Martyrology has to say of this St. Donatus is, on 22nd October: 'In Tuscia Sancti Donati Scoti episcopi Fesulani' (?). I am precluded from sharing these doubts that the Bishop Donatus belonged to the Scotti family by the reflection that this family *ab antiquo* maintained the closest relations with the church and monastery referred to, had estates from it in emphyteusis, and was regarded as a joint patron of it together with the Bobbio Monastery. And would not the propaganda made by Donatus to spread the cult of, and devotion to, a Scotch saint be some confirmation of what has been said about the Scotch origin of the family and the relation of Donatus to the Scotti family? (Balduzzi, op. cit., p. 31).' From which last observation the reader will gather that Balduzzi, while oscillating between the two opinions, is inclined to the affirmative.

"The question, as far as we are concerned, is only of secondary importance. What concerns us primarily is to establish the fact that the Church of St. Brigit must have been founded, if not by Donatus Scotti, at any rate by an Irishman or Irishmen who wanted to have in Piacenza a nodal point of the utmost importance for their pilgrims' ways, a hospice and a rest house."

§ 3

Thus far Pancotti. It has been thought proper to reproduce his observations at length so that the reader may see what a tissue of errors and absurdities has been woven by the confusion—both in good faith and bad—between the Scots and the Scotch. The figure of St. Donatus stands out quite clearly in history, and it would seem incredible that such suppositions as those of Sansovino and Balduzzi could ever have been made in this connection.

The whole genealogy of the Scotti family of Piacenza, no branch of which deserves serious historical consideration before 1190, is tainted by the tardy ambition to derive it from Scotland.

F. Alessio,[6] referring to a book[7] by David Hume of Godscroft, repeats the legend of the eighth century Scotch origin of the Piacentine Scotti. The founder according to this account was one Sholto [the family motto 'Sholto du Glasse,' is supposed to mean in ancient Scotch, 'Behold that dark gray man'], who is alleged to have saved King Solvatius (767) from an attack by a certain Donald Bane. This Sholto had two sons: Hugo and William. William, by order of Achaius, King of Scotland, the successor of Solvatius, went with four thousand men to the help of Charlemagne in his expedition into Italy (773) against Desiderius. On his way back from Rome, William fell ill at Piacenza, stopped there, took to wife a young Piacentine woman called Spettino, and founded a family which called itself Scotti because William was Scotch. Crollalanza's genealogy, as given by

---

[6] *Rezzanello, monografia storica*, Piacenza, Del Maino, 1883.
[7] *The History of the House and Race of Douglas and Angus*, Edinburgh, 1644. Alessio is really quoting from the edition reprinted in 1743.

Pancotti, derives, it will be observed, from Hume: and Hume, perhaps, borrows from Crescenzi.

For Crescenzi[8] goes back as far as the four thousand warriors of William, the Scotch noble, and adds: "Writers of the utmost sobriety state that these same soldiers of William were the progenitors of the Scoti of Piacenza, the Mariscotti of Bologna and Siena, the Biarii of Savona, the Scozia family of Mantua, the Paparoni of Rome, the Schizzi of Mantua, Cremona and Verona, and countless others."

Naldi[9] considers David junior of Manfredo to be the certain founder of the family, because—according to his own account—his name appears in the will of Count Albert II Scotti (Rog. Lodovico Ciceri, Not. Milanese, 6th December, 1429) and the will of Count Francesco (Rog. Giacomo Carasi, Not. Piacentino, 9th July, 1464). A son of David, Lanfranc, appears as legate of the commune of Piacenza in 1222, and from David, according to Naldi, all the Scotti descend.

U. Locati[10] cites the earliest documents apparently in which the surname Douglas appears, viz., a diploma of the Emperor Sigismund dated 12th February, 1414, and other diplomata of the same Emperor dated in the same year, all attributing that title to Counts Peter and Albert II Scotti (the latter the Count Albert whose will, dated 1429, is referred to by Naldi, and who was an imperial counsellor, a man of letters, and a Maecenas who died in 1462), who were both receiving at the time many feudal estates near Piacenza. The claim to the surname Douglas and its addition to the name Scotti: Scotti Douglas, dates, according to Locati, from that year. As a matter of fact Boehmer[11] has a reference to a diploma (No. 863) granted by Sigismund at Cremona, under date 12th January, 1414, and appointing Albert de Scottis, Count of Duglessum (?) and Vigoleno, to

---

[8] *Corona della nobiltà italiana*, Bologna, 1639.

[9] *Notizie genealogiche delle Famiglie Scotti, etc.*, Piacenza, 1859.

[10] *De placentinae urbis origine*, 1564.

[11] Cf. 'Regesta Imperii XI' (W. Altmann, *Die Urkunden Kaiser Sigmunds, I Band* (1410-24), Innsbruck, 1896-97, p. 51).

be his counsellor and 'familiaris,' and Pietro and Giovanni de Scottis to be his 'familiares.'[12]

The probability is that, when the family was invited by the Italian College of Heralds to furnish an account of its origin, it declared that it hailed from Scotland, that its real name was Douglas, and that the name Scotti was a sort of surname added in Italy to indicate its Scotch provenance (Hume's theory). The family was unable to produce any documentary evidence in support of this statement, but as it was an ancient family established in Piacenza since the thirteenth century, and there was no document in flagrant contradiction of such a tradition, the College accepted it until proof to the contrary should be forthcoming.

§ 4

As regards the tradition itself and its various supporters, certain observations fall to be made.

In the first place it should be observed that the house of Douglas in Scotland does not go back to the Carolingian epoch. The *Encyclopædia Britannica*[13] *s.v.* 'Douglas,' says: "The first member of the family to emerge with any distinctness was William de Douglas or Dufglas, whose name

[12] Other documents (nn. 947-52) relating to this same Scotti family of Piacenza may be found on p. 35 under date 10th February, 1414. They are said to be preserved in the Viennese State and Court Archives among the *Reichs-Registraturbuecher Sigmunds*, Vol. E, 69, V. The authenticity of, or at any rate the circumstances surrounding, these diplomata, would seem to require searching examination. Campi, but at the instance of Locati, refers to them with a deliberate ambiguity of expression: "King Sigismund is said to have dispatched," etc., Poggiali, who criticises in Vol. II, pp. 259-84, with much asperity the alleged descent of the Scotti from William in the time of Charlemagne (describing it as a legend, a yarn) skims over the Douglas question without pronouncing any opinion, possibly out of a feeling of regard for the distinguished Piacentine family. Boselli (*Storie Piacentine*, 1804, Vol. II), who made extensive use of the archives of the Counts Scotti of Agazzano, states that he saw a diploma of Sigismund dated 21st February, 1414 and granting Castelnuovo Terzi to the Scotti and a dispatch by the same referring to Vigoleno, but all that he says with reference to the diploma of 12 January relating to the surname Douglas is: "I know that it did exist," but that he never saw it. Count Emilio Nasalli Rocca, who carried out on my behalf, with his well-known competence and a courtesy befitting his estate, these researches into Piacentine history, has since informed me that the descendants of the family, Count Riccardo Douglas Scotti of Vigoleno and Count Anguissola Scotti, have told him in answer to his inquiries that there are no diplomata of Sigismund's in their family archives.

[13] Cf. the 14th edition, Vol. VII, pp. 550 et seq.

frequently appears on charters from 1075-1213": that is to say, the noble Scotch house blossoms into history contemporaneously with the noble house of Piacenza. In the second place it should be observed that neither the name Sholto nor any similar name is to be found among the Scotch Douglases. The names which appear in the twelfth, thirteenth and fourteenth centuries are William, Freskin, Brice, Archibald and James; the name Sholto du Glasse was probably invented in Italy by somebody who wanted something which sounded like Scotti Douglas.[14] In the third place it should be said that David Hume of Godscroft (1560-1630), secretary to Archibald Douglas, eighth Earl of Angus, does not enjoy the best of reputations: "He was a partial historian and his account can only be accepted with caution."[15]

One step more. It has been seen that Crescenzi (1639) stated that "writers of the utmost sobriety" derive the Scotti of Piacenza and other Italian families of similar name from William's famous warriors. But, the reader may inquire, who are these writers of the utmost sobriety? Professor Giulio Scotti of Milan[16] is at hand to tell him. "The pity of it is that these 'writers of the utmost sobriety' are [John] Lesley, Dempster,[17] and [George] Conn, all belonging to

[14] As to the etymology of the word Doughlas, the *Ency. Brit.* says: "The name represented the Gaelic *dubh glas*, dark water."

[15] Ibid. It has not been found possible to refer to the modern sources quoted by the writer of the article in the *Ency. Brit.*, viz., Sir William Frazer, *The Douglas Book*, 4 vols., Edinburgh, 1885; Sir A. Maxwell, *History of the House of Douglas*, 2 vols., 1902; G. E. Cokaine's *Peerage*, and Douglas's *Scots Peerage*.

[16] Cf. *L'antica famiglia Varennate degli Scotti*, Como, 1916, p. 10. The author expresses his grateful acknowledgements for the extreme kindness with which he has placed his notes at his disposal. Professor Scotti, however, is not quite fair to Lesley, who, with more sense than one would expect, considering his earlier performance, says quite simply (*De Origine, etc.*, p. 230): "Ab hoc Jacobo [sc. the good Sir James of Douglas, 'the Black Douglas,' familiar to everyone as Bruce's greatest captain in the long War of Independence] clarissima Douglasiorum familia primum nobilitatis nomen accepisse perhibetur." This seems to have annoyed Dempster, who, after giving his own fabulous account of the descent 'ex Mordaco rege de anno 767,' declares (*Historia Ecclesiastica*, bk. IV of Bannatyne Club reprint, pp. 218-9): "Ex hoc patet quam parum consulto Joannes Leslaeus lib VII sub initio scribat hanc Douglasiorum familiam sub Roberto Brucio rege anno MCCCV ortam." And Dempster on this occasion does give his authority: "Haec quidem omnia liber habebat MS. . . . quo utebatur Alexander Duffus Tillisaulae prope Strathbolgiam." Whether such a manuscript ever did exist is another matter.

[17] It was only to be expected that he should be found fishing in these troubled waters, but it has not been possible to ascertain if, as may well be suspected,

the sixteenth century and therefore comparatively recent, and they do not quote the sources in support of their statements. It is also notorious how easy plagiary was at the time in making up the genealogical tables of illustrious and powerful families. The *Historia ecclesiastica gentis Scotorum*, moreover, is dedicated by Dempster to a Piacentine Scotti: 'Illustrissimo viro Fabio Scoto Plac°. Niceni Com'.

Extreme suspicion also attaches to the two sources cited by Balduzzi, to wit, a *Sunto storico* or précis of history (probably in manuscript) written about the family, *c.* 1745, on behalf of the Marchese Annibale Scotti, who was anxious to secure the French decoration of the Saint Esprit, and a *Chartier français* concerning whom he gives no further information.

It seems clear from all this that the traditional genealogy of the Scotti family is a late fabrication, concocted in all probability no earlier than the fifteenth century (Albert II Scotti), i.e., at a time when it had been forgotten, or it was desired to forget, that *Scotus* down to the twelfth century meant simply *Irish,* and that the Scotch in the time of Charlemagne *had no existence* as such.

§ 5

Hitherto we have been engaged in demolishing: we must now make an attempt at reconstruction.

The one historically certain fact is the presence in Piacenza in the twelfth century of a notable family of Scotti. I have made no investigations regarding the wills cited by Naldi and purporting to give David junior as the founder of the family, but, even though one of the wills should turn out to have been made by that same Albert II who claimed the surname Douglas, there are no *a priori* reasons for denying their existence. Campi cites (II, 16) a Manfred Scotti in the train of Rinaldo d' Este in 1162, and (II, 75) a Guido Scotti among the members of the Community of Piacenza in 1194, i.e., at the time of St. Fulco, and among the earliest Piacentines found using the word Scotti as a proper name.

Crescenzi derives from him. What contribution George Conn could have made to the tangled story is not so clear.

It was a family which had already attained a position of some eminence and produced in the thirteenth century a certain Albert Scotti, surnamed 'the Great,' who, while head of an important and wealthy company of *mercatores*, also played a considerable part in politics, lording it over Piacenza as a Guelph and fighting against Galeazzo Visconti.

Tononi[18] records that the Society of the Piacentine Scotti ('Societas Scotorum') made loans to the crusaders in the days of Louis, King of France (1256-66), and that a Bernard Scotti of Piacenza was employed by Gregory IX to raise funds in various parts of Christendom. The Scotti had agents in Famagusta in 1301, and were acknowledged as wealthy Piacentine merchants in the documents published by Belgrano (1238-67). Their company loaned a considerable sum of money to the Pope in 1272, and Bernard Scotti was employed by Philip III to settle his account with the Pope. In the time of Gregory X the Scotti included among the members of their society Guglielmo della Vecchia, Opizzone di Farignano and Rolando di Ripalta, all three belonging to the household of the Pope. There are recorded as members of their company in accounts and payments Ferrante di Ferrara, and Erode (1228), Bernard Espi (1292), Francesco (1296), Giovanni (1298), Giovanni Miquitin (Michelino perhaps, 1299). The seal of the society still exists, a shield with an eight-rayed star above a crescent and the legend † *S. Escot: drapier.*

In the accounts of the Treasury of the Louvre (1296) there is record of a contract made by "Alpicio Dyan de Societate Scotorum de Placentia," and in the National Archives of France, the receipts given by the Lombards to Queen Blanche include one by a Scotto *drapier* dated in 1249. Ferrato de Ferrari and Erode of the Society of the Scotti figure in the records of the financial operations of the Templars as having repaid a loan in 1285.[19]

Now it is obvious that the emergence of this family in numbers and importance so early as the end of the twelfth

---

[18] *I mercanti piacentini in Francia*, Strenna Piacentina, 1894.

[19] Tononi has based his account on C. Piton: *Les Lombards en France et à Paris*, Champion, 1892, pp. 76 et seq., used also by Pancotti in his recent work *I paratici piacentini e i loro statuti*, Piacenza, Del Maino, 3 vols., 1925-30, I, pp. 106 et seq.

century must have been preceded by a prolonged period of preliminary preparation in obscurity, and that tradition, in dating the origin of the family back to the eighth century, is not so very far away from truth. But if we have to go so very far back to the time when the word *Scoti* meant indubitably only Irish, the inevitable consequence is that the family must have been of Irish origin. There is nothing more probable than that some Irishman stopped and settled in Piacenza, a city of passage very close to Bobbio, and possessing a rendezvous for Irishmen set up by Donatus of Fiesole under the shadow of the Church of St. Brigit. Considered from this angle, the old tradition becomes illuminated with fresh light. Many of the overhanging clouds can be dispersed once the arguments improperly employed by the beforementioned writers in support of erroneous theses can be converted in support of the thesis now put forward. To take an example: The fact noted by Balduzzi of the intimate relations maintained *ab antiquo* by the Scotti family with the Church and Monastery of St. Brigit, so far from showing that St. Donatus was a member of that family, may simply be evidence of a devotion on the part of the Scotti to the saintly patron of their mother country, and of a natural attachment to their compatriots who gathered about her church.

Alessio quotes De Mussi[20] but with a note of interrogation: it may be well, therefore, to scan a little closely what De Mussi, a Piacentine chronicler who wrote between the thirteenth and the fourteenth century from sources still comparatively unsullied in local traditions, has to say. This is the passage: "Cum rege Carolo venit miles quidam Scotus, in armis probissimus, et ex casu cujusdam aegritudinis Placentiae remanens, sanatus in civitate domum emit, et uxorem accepit, quae fuit illorum de Spetinis, habuitque possessiones ultra Padum, et filios quam plures generavit. Qui longo tempore fuerunt egregii mercatores, et cives peroptimi. Et ex istis postea descendit anno Christi MCCXC. Dominus Albertus Scotus."

There is nothing in the least improbable in the story. It may well be the most precise statement in our possession

[20] Appendix to the *Chronicon Placentinum, RR. II. SS.*, Vol. XVI.

as regards the origin of the Scotti family: it is quite possible
that an Irish soldier settled in Piacenza some time towards
the end of the eighth century, that he there made an excellent match with a Da Spettine, an old Piacentine family
even then, and that from him gradually (*longo tempore*)
derived the family of *mercatores* which took the stage of
history in the thirteenth century.

The Church of St. Brigit—the Church of the Borgo—is
situate, it should be observed, in the immediate neighbourhood of, and is almost indistinguishable from, the mercantile
centre of the city, the 'Collegium Nuxii,' right in the main
arterial way, known in the thirteenth century as Guasto
degli Scotti and the permanent site of the palaces belonging
to the family.[21]

Alessio quotes also Einhard,[22] but tendenciously. And what
does Einhard say? "Auxit etiam gloriam regni sui quibusdam
regibus ac gentibus per amicitiam sibi consiliatis . . . Scotorum quoque reges sic habuit ad suam voluntatem per
suam munificentiam inclinatos, ut eum nunquam aliter
nisi Dominum, seque subditos ac servos ejus, pronuntiarent.
Extant Epistulae ab eis ad illum missae quibus huiusmodi
affectus eorum erga illum indicatur." Lesley had taken this
passage as evidence of the expedition of the four thousand
Scotch warriors despatched by King Achaius, but all that
Einhard's text goes to show is Charlemagne's hospitable
disposition towards the Irish, familiar also from other texts
cited, e.g., by Dom Gougaud.[23] This sympathy on the part
of the great Emperor makes it all the more probable that some
Irish captain or soldier of fortune (*miles Scotus*) accompanied
him on his expedition against Desiderius in support of the
Roman Church.

Moreover, even if the establishment of the first *Scotus* in

[21] Cf. E. Nasalli Rocca, 'Notizie di agiografia piacentina, etc., in *Bollettino
Storico Piacentino*, 1933, p. 25, and 'Le Origini detta famiglia Scotti,' in *La Scure*
of Piacenza, 12th March, 1933.

[22] *De vita et gestis Caroli Magni, cum commentario Besselii et Bollandi*, 1711, c. XVI,
p. 79; in Migne, *P.L.*, XCVII, 40. This text is the basis of the statement made
by Innes, op. cit., p. 172, that "there are proofs that Charlemagne entertained
friendship with the King of Scots as he did with other neighbouring princes."
But for some penetrating criticism of Einhard cf. L. Halphen: *Études critiques sur
l'histoire de Charlemagne*, Paris, 1921, pp. 60-103.

[23] Cf. *Christianity in Celtic Lands*, p. 166.

Piacenza is to be assigned to the ninth or tenth century instead of to the eighth, i.e., the time of the Danish invasions, this would not in any way invalidate the argument. The preceding examination, summary though it be, seems to me sufficiently conclusive of the Irish origin of the Scotti family of Piacenza.

§ 6

This case, considered within the ambit of Piacenza, is but a single instance, however, of a much more extensive and imposing phenomenon. About the end of the twelfth century, families of Scotti begin to emerge in very many parts of Italy, more particularly along the roads leading from the Gauls and Switzerland to Rome. There was, therefore, something profoundly true and interesting in the connection between the various Italian families which Crescenzi sought to establish in 1639, although he erroneously assigned them all to one common founder in the person of the Scotchman William. One scholar to perceive the importance of this fact and to attribute it to its proper cause in Scots, i.e., Irish, migrations, is Professor G. Scotti of Milan, who first proposed it in a pamphlet published in 1916 and already quoted, and amplified it in a subsequent essay. [24] The name Scotti is found written in Italian documents of the twelfth and thirteenth centuries in very various forms as follows: 'scotus,' 'scottus,' 'schotus,' 'scoto,' 'scotto,' 'schoto,' 'scota,' 'scotta,' 'schotta,' 'scoti,' 'de scotis,' 'de scottis,' 'de schottis,' and other.

"From the last quarter of the twelfth down to and all through the eighteenth century," writes Professor Scotti in the second essay mentioned, "Varenna always had a number of families of this name, all very probably derived from one common stock. The oldest extant document of which we have knowledge brings us down to a *ser Anselmus de Scottis vel de Scotta fil. q. Andreae*, who, on 5th May, 1278, attested a notarial deed in the Isola Comacina, and, on the 16th of the

[24] 'Famiglia Scotti di Varenna,' in Col. V. Adami's volume *Cenni genealogici sulle famiglie di Varenna e del Monte di Varenna*, Milan, Co-op. Tip. Ed., 1923.

same month and year, acquired property in Varenna from the de Pino family. Where he came from is uncertain: but as to this there are two curious pieces of information, each contradicting the other, which come to us in the early years of the sixteenth century from two well-known historians of the Comasco, the brothers Benedict and Paul Giovius. The former in the course of a letter to Giovanni Maria Scoto congratulates himself and his friend on their common, though distant, origin from the patrician families in the Isola Comacina, the boast of the brothers Giovius.

Brother Paul, however, who was also a friend of Scoto, in his *Descriptio Larii Lacus* (Venice, 1559) blurts out the categorical statement with reference to Varenna: "Negat se ortum ab Insulanis, quum genus suum altius deducat, Joannes Maria Scotus, jurisconsultus inter Varenates facile princeps." These words look as though they were a rather contemptuous denial by Scoto of what Benedict Giovius had said. And, as a matter of fact, none of the numerous documents from the Island in the twelfth and thirteenth centuries shows that the Scotti either lived or owned property there before they migrated to Varenna. There is, however, another 'Anselmo de Scoto' to be found in the Island (the grandfather, perhaps of the Anselmo quoted above), first in 1173, afterwards at Chiavenna in 1176, while an 'Obertus Scoto,' also at Chiavenna, shows up in 1163, but they all appear simply as witnesses, which might only imply a temporary residence, not a permanent domicile. It is curious to find even in Rivoli (Piedmont) between 1190 and 1195 another (or is it perhaps the same?) 'Anselmus mediolanensis scota,' who seems to have been resident there (Rossano, *Cartario di Rivalta*).

"Be that as it may, the Scotti cannot reckon themselves, like the Caginosa family, their relations, or like the other families of de Pino, de Conca, de Murofracto and Giovio, among the number of those nobles from the Island who migrated to Varenna after 1169, when the Island was wrested from the Comaschi and its inhabitants driven out. These were almost certainly of Milanese origin, for three of the name Caginosa are found among the consuls of the twelfth and thirteenth centuries. Nor can it be thought that the Scoti came from Como or the 'agro comasco,' where they do not make an appearance until comparatively late, as it is not until well on in the fourteenth century that the slightest trace of them is to be found in the documents pertaining to that region. What then was that "more distant place of origin" to which Scoto, as reported by Paul Giovius, referred? As a protracted inquiry into the matter is here out of place, it may be sufficient to produce a few of the most ancient specimens of Milanese and Monzese Scotti, who are probably connected with the Scotti of Varenna:

(i) 1130-57, in Milan: "Scotus not. iudex ac missus Domini secundi Chunradi regis" (Bonomi MSS. in the Ambrosiana, vols. 20 and 23).

(ii) 1145-52, in Morimondo, in the Milanese: "Lanfrancus de Scota" (*Codex Monti*, in the Ambrosiana).

(iii) 1146: "Scoto qui dicitur Bacco de civit. Mediol. decanus de schola S. Michaelis" (ibid.).

(iv) A.D. 1207, "Johane qui dicor Scoto not. Dom Henrici Regis, in loco Gradi" (Agrate?). This "Johannes Scoto," the son or kinsman of the Scotus here referred to *sub annis* 1130-57, should be compared with a "Scotus imp. not. scriptor de Placentia" (sic), who in 1200 attested two notarial instruments in the Isola Comacina (the Pagensi papers in the Ambrosiana).

"In a district still nearer to Varenna, sc. Monza, we find Scotti certainly connected by bonds of kinship with the Milanese Scotti (cf. Gius. Trivulzio Manzoni, *Memorie intorno ai Gallarati Scotti*, Milan, Artigianelli, 1897, last table). A *scotus* was living in Monza as early as 1132, and there were also a 'Scotti de Morgora' (1148), a 'Ugo de Scota' (1175), a 'Scotti de Caponago' (1176) and an 'Arnulphus de Scoto' (1198).

"The most important, however, in the present investigation is a 'Petrus de Scoto,' who owned property *prope Cixinusculum* and appears among the Decumans or Canons Minor of the Basilica at Monza between 1208 and 1220 (Parchments from the Chapter of Monza in the State Archives, Milan). The mind jumps to a probable connection between the Scotti in Milan, Monza, and Varenna, remembering that the church in Varenna dedicated to St. John the Baptist, founded by, and with a right of presentation reserved to, the Scotti, appears as early as 1143 among the churches dependent from the Basilica at Monza (Archiepiscopal Archives of Milan, *Pievi lacuali*, Vol. X. Case against the Serponti, who usurped the right of presentation to the damage of the Scotti)."

Professor Scotti has found Scotti as early as the twelfth century in Piedmont, at Rivoli, Saluzzo and Agliè, at Casal Monferrato, Asti and Ivrea, etc.; but principally at Vercelli, where the well-known *hospitale Scottorum* was (cf. Chapter VIII, § 2), and where we also find 'Anricus Scotus' (1176), 'Scotus Sartor' (1186), 'Petrus Scoto,' notary and canon (1221), 'Dominus Jacob de Scoto de alice, judex et consul justitiae' (1252), followed by others. In the *Cartulary of Oulx* (Susa), edited by Giovanni Collino,[25] he has found traces of a *scoto*, who represents as it were a transitionary period, the description oscillating between the adjective indicative of place of origin and the surname true and proper; in a *breve recordacionis* of agreements with the Canons of Oulx (in some year between 1050 and 1079) the following names of witnesses appear: 'Guigone de Torrenco,' 'Wilelmo rupho,' 'Guigone de valle Bonisio,' 'Wilelmo de Cuneolo,' 'Petro Scoto,' 'Petro heron.,' 'Arnaldo gubiano,' 'Guidone forti.'

In Genoa also the Scotti date very far back. According to N. Battilano[26] they were there divided as early as 1190 into two branches: (i) of Gerard and Ogerio, the latter of whom was making notarial deeds in 1214 and well advanced in years at the time; and (ii) of Hugo. Among the notarial instruments drawn up by Giovanni, the scrivener, in the year 1158, there is an agreement made between Hugo Scotto, the son of *quondam* Ido, and Lambert, the son of Lambert.[27] Professor Scotti has drawn my attention to a MS. in the

---

[25] *Cartario di Oulx*, Pinerolo, 1908, pp. 4, 5.

[26] *Genealogie delle famiglie nobili di Genova*, Genoa, 1825, Vol. I.

[27] Cf. also Buonarroti, *Genealogie genovesi*.

municipal library of Genoa, *Origine e fasti delle nobili famiglie di Genova*, by Girolamo Giscardi, a friar (*c.* 1774), which in Vol. IV, p. 1813, reads as follows: "Scotti, noble citizens of Genoa, derive their origin from Scotland and thence settled in Albenga and Lombardy: some of them had themselves called 'Salvaghi' and other 'Centurioni' . . . there are also some called Colonne Scotti. Gherardo Scotto was consul of Genoa in the year 1127, and banished as one of the ringleaders in the civil disturbances for which he was put to death in 1130." He then cites an 'Ingono Scotto' (1170-72) who captured a galley from the Pisans in 1175, an 'Odo Scotto' who "was with the army at the taking of Almeria in 1127," then a 'Balduino' and an 'Ogerio.' Elsewhere he says: "About the middle of the fifteenth century the *Albergo* Centurione was founded in Genoa and was composed of five families belonging to the Gibellini faction of nobles, and they were Cantelli, Becchignoni, Bestagni, Oltremarini and Scotti, and they pooled all their interests and took one name in common . . . the only one of them of great antiquity was the Scotti."[28]

Seven members of the Scotti family are mentioned in the obituary inserted in the Book of Collects of the Metropolitan Church of Genoa, edited by Cambiaso, but they probably belong to the fourteenth and fifteenth centuries. With reference to the Scotti of Genoa, it is pleasant to recall[29] that the great woman saint of the Dominican Order was entertained in Genoa in the house of the devout Monna Orietta Scotti in the palazzo Scotti, later Centurioni, situate near the harbour at number 44 via del Canneto.

Gregorovius[30] gives some particulars of the Scotti in Rome. "Claricia, the mother of Innocent III, was a Roman member of the family of Romanus de Scotta." The note 2 to page 6 of Vol. V, Part I, reads: "A Romanus de Scotto in 1109 [found attesting a deed, cf. Vol. IV, p. 327, *n.*]; a Senator Bobo Donnae Scottae, anno 1118 (ibid). Grimaldi,

---

[28] Cf. as to the Albergo Centurione with particular reference to Becchignoni and Bestagni, V. Spreti, *Enciclopedia storico-nobiliare italiana*, Milan, 1929, Vol. II.
[29] Cf. G. Joergensen, *Santa Caterina da Siena*, Rome, Ferrari, 1921, 325 s.
[30] *History of the City of Rome in the Middle Ages* (tr. Hamilton), Vol. V, Part I, London, 1897.

Liber canonicorum sanctae Vaticanae Basilicae (MSS. Vat. 6437), says that the Scotti dwelt in the Reg. Arenula near S. Benedicti Scottorum, the present S. Trinitatis Peregrinorum." They were a numerous family and in the twelfth century were amongst the most highly reputed patrician houses in Rome. "At the time that Innocent III ascended the throne, Scotto Paparone, a noble Roman of ancient family, probably related to the Pope on his mother's side, was senator," while another member, Goffredo Scotti, as syndic of the people, held a globe as symbol of the world before the tribune Cola di Rienzo.

A sound and exhaustive study of the *Scoti* in Rome, as suggested in Chapter II, § 9 à propos the *ecclesiae Scottorum* in Rome, might, it is conceived, be productive of some interesting and surprising results, and it is strange that nobody has so far thought of undertaking it. Amayden[31] gives only the following meagre and inexact particulars with reference to the Scotti: "From the fifteenth century onwards, some members of the noble Scotti family of Piacenza settled in Rome, and in 1432 Dominus Gottifridus de Scotis de regione Arenulae died and was buried in the Church of S. Salvatore in Campo. In 1593 Bernardino Scotti was Conservator of Rome. The surname still survives."

Professor Scotti has discovered some Scotti in Orvieto among the consuls of the twelfth century and at Benevento in the fourteenth. I would add that a *Scotus* was the last heroic *podestà* of Semifonte, a famous little city in the Val d'Elsa, destroyed by the Florentines in 1202.[32]

It may safely be said that there is not a chronicle or cartulary in Italy but contains the name of some *Scotus*. A few instances which have fallen casually under my eyes are set out below:

(i) Cipolla and Buzzi, *Codice diplomatico di S. Colombano di Bobbio*, II, 309, A.D. 1203: "terram quam filii scoti ibi tenent."

(ii) Gaddoni and Zaccherini, *Chartularium Imolense*: p.

---

[31] *La storia delle famiglie romane*, Bertini, Vol. II, p. 191.
[32] Cf. R. Davidsohn, *Storia di Firenze le origini*, Florence, Sansoni, 1909, Vol. II, p. 982.

559, a "scottolus" in 1143; p. 619, a "Scotia," a nun in the monastery of S. Stefano in 1163; pp. 637-9, a "Scottolinus Mariscotti," the brother of one Rudolph in 1169; p. 687, a "Scottus" in 1189.

(iii) Guidicini, *Cose notabili della città di Bologna*, I, pp. 228-37, "Caterina, daughter of Roberto di Scozia, shoemaker, deceased," in 1522.

(iv) Nicolli, *Della etimologia dei nomi di luogo degli Stati Ducali di Parma Piacenza e Guastalla*, two volumes, Piacenza, Tedeschi, 1833, II, 185, a "scotolinus" in 1180. In Nicolli also two indications of place have been noticed:(i) 257, "Paule de Scotis" (*c.* 1494) and on p. 258 (*a.* 1320 and 1333) "habitant ad Paulle Scotorum" (Kehr, *Italia Pont*, VI, Pars. I, Lombardia, p. 256, mentions a monastery at Paullo near Lodi); (ii) 214 (thirteenth century) "prope molendinum coheret scotorum."[33]

§ 7

A systematic investigation, embracing also similar surnames such as Marescotti and others, would complete the picture; but the foregoing considerations may be sufficient to show that *Scoti* appear from the beginning of the twelfth century in the position of judges and notaries (1120 Isola Comacina, 1130 Milan), consuls (1127 Genoa), *podestà* (1202 Semifonte), canons (1208 Monza, 1221 Vercelli), seacaptains (1127, 1170 Genoa) contemporaneously in quite a number of places in northern and central Italy; that to have attained such eminent positions they must have been settled for some time in the country; that their Irish origin

[33] Apropos the Italian Scotti, attention may be drawn to a note 'Gli Scotti di Monza tipografi editori in Venezia' in *Archivio Storico Lombardo*, 1932, p. 365. In Milan also a number of painters surnamed Scotti are found working in the Duomo in the fifteenth and sixteenth centuries, some native Milanese, others from Piacenza and the Valtellina. Traces are to be found of a Balzarino Scotti between 1409 and 1451: of a Baldassare in 1410: of a Marchione in the period 1415-30: of a Magrone in 1427: of a Piacentine Gottardo Scotti, a triptych by whom is preserved in the Poldi-Pezzoli Museum, in the period 1457-85: of Giacomo Scotti in 1487: of the brothers Bernardino and Stefano in the years 1487, 1489, and 1520, and of Gian Paolo in the years 1535 and 1543. Cf. L. Ambiveri, 'Supplemento alla Cronaca degli Artisti Piacentini' in *Strenna Piacentina*, 1885, and 'Notizie intorno ad alcuni artisti piacentini' in *Indicatore Commerciale Ziliani*, Piacenza, 1888.

—considering the dates—would seem to be beyond doubt. Something similar must have happened also in Belgium, France, and the Germanies when the names Schott, Schotte, L'Escot, Lescot are still as common as the names Scot and Scott in England, Scotland and North America. In Holland, too, there is the form Schotanus.

As the change over in meaning of the word *scotus* from the geographical signification 'Irish' to the national appellation 'Scotch' took place precisely at the time when the adjectival form in nomenclature, indicative of nationality or country of origin, was becoming stereotyped as a surname, there is always the possibility that the cases cited may in some belated instances indicate a Scotch origin, but in the great majority, where it can be established that the expatriation took place before the twelfth century, it may be taken as well-nigh certain that an Irish origin is indicated.

This very important emigration of the Scotic 'laity' to Europe, the counterpart of the ecclesiastical (apostolic and cultural) touched on in Part I, must date back, in my opinion, on the whole, to the time of the Danish invasions (ninth and tenth centuries), which wrought such havoc in poor Ireland and compelled so many people to seek safety in flight. The possibility, however, that it may be to some extent earlier than, and independent of, the Danish invasions, that it may have taken place in the eighth century, should always be borne in mind. It is moreover perfectly consonant with the character of the Irish, who, as they have produced great saints, so also have produced great soldiers, fighting men like the 'Irish Brigade,' and generals such as O'Mahony, Sarsfield and Macmahon of Magenta. This would seem to be rather an interesting conclusion on a subject which does not appear to have received the attention it deserves, and brings me to the end of the chapter, in which I hope that I have kept the promise of the beginning to prove that St. Fulco may be included among the saints who look back, from howsoever great a distance, to the green hills of Ireland.

CHAPTER XV

ST. EMILIAN OF FAENZA

§ 1

THIS saint has been the subject of an exhaustive study by Mgr. Francesco Lanzoni,[1] the distinguished historian of Faenza, and the work of the Bollandists is also comparatively recent.[2]

He was an Irish bishop, travelling as usual under a latinized name—his own, it is suggested, was Emmian—who returning from a pilgrimage to Rome died, according to the legend, in Faenza about the end of the seventh or the beginning of the eighth century. His body was buried in the Church of St. Clement, which prior to the extension of the walls in the fifteenth century stood outside the city, close to the so-called *porta del Conte*, the Porta Comitis.[3] Faenza was more or less completely destroyed under Liutprand in 740, when all trace of the grave was lost. Between the ninth and tenth centuries, under the government of the 'Counts,' it was re-discovered by chance in a most extraordinary way. Two men, unaware of the holy ground on which they stood, were engaged in heaping up hay, gossiping together the while. One of them suddenly received a blow, and, there being no other present, not unnaturally upbraided his companion. The latter vigorously repudiated the suggestion, but the words were scarcely out of his mouth when he too received a blow still more violent and no less mysterious.

Panic-stricken, the pair took to their heels. They ran to

[1] 'Le "Vite" dei quattro santi protettori della Città di Faenza' (St. Terence, St. Savinus, St. Emilian and St. Peter Damian) in the Appendix to Vol. XXVIII of the new edition (Bologna, Zanichelli, 1921) of the *RR. II. SS.*, pp. 285-395.

[2] Cf. *AA. SS.*, Vol. III (November), pp. 291 et seq.

[3] This church has been reconstructed and transformed out of recognition, but still exists, unconsecrated, in Via Naviglio, No. 39, directly opposite the barracks of S. Chiara. Cf. Lanzoni, op. cit., p. 327.

the Count and told him their story. The Count promptly
ordered the place to be excavated. They prised up a stone
and discovered the tomb, which, once opened, exhaled a
most fragrant odour. The sacred body was laid upon a
wagon drawn by oxen and driven by order of the Count and
Countess into the city to the Church of S. Maria beside the
praetorium consulis (S. Maria del Conte, *S. Maria Comitis*).
Presently the oxen drew up, grew obdurate, and refused to
budge.

Husband and wife realised that the saint was unwilling
to enter the church without a dowry, and immediately
bestowed upon him *mansi* or farms. The oxen then moved on
and continued their journey, and the body was borne in
triumph into the church. After receiving the saint the
Church of S. Maria del Conte, as often happens in similar
cases, was called also of St. Emilian, and later exclusively of
St. Emilian, under which name it appears in the twelfth
century. The parish church of St. Emilian[4] was at the top of
the St. Emilian quarter or the *Rione Rosso*, and the *Congregatio S. Aemiliani* included in 1192 nine parishes situate in
the north-west part of the city.

§ 2

The earliest surviving document relative to the cult of St.
Emilian is a deed of donation dated 15th February, 1139, in
favour of Farulph, archdeacon of the cathedral, one of the
witnesses being "presbiter Ugo Sancti Emiliani," the same
"presbiter Ugo ecclesiae Sancti Miliani," perhaps, who
appears in another deed of the Cathedral Chapter dated
10th July, 1147, and again in a third dated 8th December,
1159. A "regio Sancti Emiliani" is also recorded in an
instrument dated 29th August, 1182, in the Chapter Archives
of Faenza, while on 21st September, 1191, occurs a bequest
in favour of the "ecclesia sancti Emiliani."

Citizens of Faenza are found in thirteenth century docu-

----

[4] It is now unconsecrated but still stands at No. 5 Via Naviglio facing the
vicolo Ugolino d'Azzo Ubaldini, about one hundred and fifty yards from S.
Clemente. Cf. Lanzoni, op. cit., p. 327.

ments, and even earlier, bearing the names Emilianus and Milianus or Millianus.

A diocesan synod held in 1321 ordered the feasts of St. Emilian bishop and St. Terence deacon to be celebrated in the city and suburbs, because the tomb of each in their respective churches was the scene of daily recurrent prodigies.

Ever since then the name of one or other of the saints and sometimes both together appear frequently among the holy patrons of the city. A Faentine calendar of the first half of the fifteenth century shows that the feast of St. Emilian fell on 6th November, as it does to-day.

In 1468, on the occasion, perhaps, of a restoration or reconstruction of the church, the bones of the saint were translated into a new urn, according to an inscription carved on the pedestal, probably, of the urn, but which has now disappeared: "Nova translatione in hoc tumulo Sancti Emiliani episcopi et confessoris ossa quiescunt, 1468, 24 Aprilis." In 1782 this urn was opened, and two strips of lead were found within, one bearing the inscription: "Corpus sancti Emiliani episcopi," but on the other it was impossible to make out a thing.

In 1512 the citizens of Faenza, hearing of the frightful devastation of Ravenna by the French troops under the command of Gaston de Foix, made a vow to keep the days of devotion to the memory of their four saints, Emilian, Terence, Savinus and Peter Damian, as holy days of obligation, if the Providence of God spared their city from carnage, sack and fire. The city of Faenza succeeded in coming to an arrangement with the French *condottiere* and so escaped being sacked with the result that devotion to the four saints increased. They have been constantly invoked together from 1524 onwards as the four patrons of the city, even as "the four patrons" *tout court*, and to the exclusion almost of any other.

The parish church of St. Emilian was suppressed by the notorious Napoleonic decrees, unconsecrated, and sold to a private individual in 1809, when the body of St. Emilian was transferred to the cathedral and placed in a chapel dedicated to him. Three sculptures from the pedestal on the fifteenth century urn were brought there along with it, while others finally found shelter in the Musée Jacquemart André in Paris, and another fragment went amissing.[5]

Faenza is the only place where there is any cult of this St. Emilian. In the sixteenth century there was also a little church dedicated to him in the hills around Pergola close to the city.

The miracles attributed to him are all cures of cases of demoniac possession with the exception of one case of paralysis and a saving from shipwreck.

§ 3

The historical sources for the legend of St. Emilian are as follows:

(a) Fra Pietro Calo da Chioggia, a Dominican († 1348), whose book, *Legendae de sanctis*, compiled *c.* 1340, contains a chapter, 'De sancto Emiliano' (the *Vita prima*), which the Bollandists attribute to Calo himself, but which Lanzoni considers to be the work of some thirteenth or fourteenth century citizen of Faenza.

(b) Fra Pietro Natali, who in his *Catalogus Sanctorum*, composed between 1369 and 1372, summarised the *Legendae* of his confrère Pietro Calo.[6]

(c) Giovanni Antonio Flaminio, a humanist of Imola († 1536), who, between 1526 and 1534, composed the Lives of the four holy patrons of Faenza.

(d) Ser Bernadino Azzurrini, notary of Faenza († 1620), who composed in 1609-10 a *Compendium* or *Summarium* of the Lives of the four saints which he transcribed into his *Liber Rubeus*.

The most delicate point in the story of St. Emilian is how the Faentines, after the fortuitous invention of the tomb between the tenth and eleventh century, came to know that

[5] Cf., Lanzoni, op. cit., pp. 310-11.
[6] Ibid., p. 332—Chambers (*De Scotorum fortitudine*, p. 198) cites Fra Natali as his authority, but his statement is commendably brief: "12 August, Sanctus Aemilianus Episcopus Faventinus qui Domino a puerilibus annis militavit. Ejus vitam habet Petrus de Natalibus. Alii ejus festum ponunt 21 Novembris."

that particular grave contained the body of a Scots bishop
called Emilian who died in Faenza on his way back from a
pilgrimage to Rome. Fra Pietro Natali relates that the
Count of Faenza found the body of St. Emilian "cum
epitaphio in quo praedicta continebantur." The Bollandists
think that Natali derived this piece of information, un-
mentioned in any of the other sources, from another recension
of the Life than that used by Calo.

Lanzoni does not share this opinion. He thinks there is a
possibility that, although trace of the grave had been lost
before the *inventio*, the citizens still retained the recollection
of a Scots Bishop Emilian having been buried there in days
gone by. But he cannot dismiss altogether the suspicion
that the medieval writer, confronted with the task of writing
the life of a saint who was either unknown or *inventus*, passed
him off as a Scot, simply because such a device was a common
practice among certain hagiographers at the time. There is,
in my opinion, no ground for such a suspicion, and it would
be more natural, I suggest, to adhere to the Bollandists'
hypothesis or to Lanzoni's first suggestion.

Lanzoni has also published the text of a 'Praise in honour
of St. Emilian,' contained in a codex in the Vatican,
written in 1426.

CHAPTER XVI

S. PELLEGRINO DELLE ALPI DI GARFAGNANA

§ 1

THE road leading from the Garfagnana to Pievepelago, Frignano and Modena crosses the chain of the Apennines at a pass called Foce delle Radici, some 4,584 feet above sea-level. A road south from the pass and almost on the level for a couple of miles brings the traveller to the very ancient shrine of S. Pellegrino.

This saint[1] has recently been the subject of a work by the eminent Mgr. Angelo Mercati,[2] and our task in his regard has therefore been greatly facilitated.

The legend may be summarized as follows: Pellegrino, 'Pilgrim,' was born in *Scotia*, the son of a king named Romanus, who had already been converted to Christianity; in the full vigour of youth, he renounced his right of succession to the throne, distributed his substance to the poor, and set off incognito for Palestine; after making the round of the holy places, he remained for forty years in the desert where Our Lord kept His long fast, and then betook himself to preach at the court of the Sultan. There he was scourged, loaded with chains, and thrown into prison; miraculously set free, he suffered ordeal by fire and emerged unscathed. A prompting from Heaven then directed his course towards Italy: he was thrown into the sea by a ruffianly crew during a storm, but with great presence of mind converted his cloak into a raft, his stick into a mast, his wallet into a sail, and seven days later floated into Ancona. He then visited the tombs of the Apostles in Rome and St. Nicholas in Bari and the shrine of St. Michael in the Gargano. Another heavenly prompting then came to him and, under the guidance of a star, he went

[1] Cf. *AA. SS.*, for August, I, pp. 77 et seq., *B.H.L.*, n. 6630.
[2] *S. Pellegrino delle Alpi in Garfagnana*, Rome, Tip. Vat., 1926.

up into the wildest district of the Apennines and settled in a wood which he afterwards called Romanesca.

After twelve years of terrifying ordeals he succeeded in clearing the wood of evil spirits and retired to live in a cave on a diet of herbs and dew with only the wild beasts of the neighbourhood for company. After living this life for a number of years 'Pilgrim' quitted his cavern to discover in a place called 'Thermae salonis' a stately age-old tree with a hollow trunk. He clambered in and made his home there for the next seven years. Finally at the age of ninety-seven years, nine months and twenty-three days he departed this life.

A certain Peter, who lived with his wife Adelgrada in a village in the neighbouring country of Frignano, had a revelation of the death of the holy anchorite. Husband and wife, with the assistance of an angel, climbed the mountain together, came upon the body, learned the history of the saint from a parchment held fast in his hand, and gave the corpse an honourable burial. The news of the precious discovery spread on both sides of the Apennines, and Tuscans and Lombards together climbed the hill to possess themselves of the remains. A riot would have broken out had not the bishops present suggested that the body should be placed upon a cart, the cart yoked to a pair of wild oxen, one Tuscan the other Lombard, and the oxen allowed to go as their fancy dictated. The suggestion was greeted with applause and forthwith carried into effect. The oxen departed so quietly as to give the impression that they were tame and came to a halt on the border between Tuscany and Lombardy, more precisely at 'Thermae salonis'. The building of a basilica in honour of the saint was forthwith taken in hand, and the canonisation and translation took place simultaneously with the dedication of the basilica on 1st August, 643. God immediately began to perform countless miracles through 'Pilgrim's' intercession, and such was the affluence of the faithful that a hospice had to be erected for their accommodation near the church. The first persons to render assistance to those who undertook the pious journey were Peter and Adelgrada. The feast has been fixed ever since on 1st August.

§ 2

This legend has clearly no historical value,[3] and, critically considered, bears all the appearance of having been put together no earlier than the first half of the fourteenth century. As the solitary codex containing it is a fifteenth century codex, No. 1061 in the Lucca State Library, Mercati conjectures that it is the work of a certain Lionello de Nobili, who will be mentioned presently and who took a great interest in the shrine.[4] "The earliest certain record of S. Pellegrino and his church," Mercati concludes on page 31, "is dated 1110; now a fourteenth or possibly fifteenth century compiler, who weaves together a tissue of chronological and historical errors, who even distorts other known facts of history, deserves no sort of credit and leaves his reader in the greatest uncertainty as to what may have been the real historical basis of his legend, which, like so many others, may contain a kernel of truth. If 'Pilgrim' was not a baptismal name but merely one bestowed on some unknown wanderer who came to settle in the Tuscan Emilian Apennines, and, because he led a holy eremitical life, was therefore called 'Pellegrino,' he may not unreasonably have been supposed to have been one of those numerous Irish, called 'Scotti' after their native land, who, from the sixth century onwards, actuated almost exclusively by ascetic and missionary impulses . . . [as] voluntary exiles, pledged themselves not to return to their native land for a considerable period or indeed, in most cases, for the rest of their life, whether or not they undertook the duties of the missionary as well." (Cf. Gougaud, 'L'oeuvre des Scotti' in *Revue d'hist. ecc.*, IX, 1908.)[5]

[3] Cf. Mercati, op. cit., pp. 26-31 and 66.

[4] Dempster, for once making use of his critical wits, attributes it (*Historia Ecclesiastica*, II, p. 530) to an 'anonymous and unlearned Italian'; "*mihi est jure suspecta quod anilibus fabulis sit refecta nec quicquam bonae frugis contineat.*" Despite these old wives' tales "constat tamen magnae sanctitatis virum fuisse et piae vitae anachoretis unicum exemplar." The holy anchorite, according to this authority, composed a book of prayers and another book of 'Meditations,' "which, they say, were written with his own hand on the bark of trees and are still preserved to this day. . . . He died in the year 464 and 1st August is kept as his *natalis dies* by the inhabitants of Bologna, Modena and Lucca, *aliique Italiae populi.*"

[5] Cf. *Christianity in Celtic Lands*, p. 130.

In this sense they were called pilgrims, *peregrini*, a description which "became practically a technical word on the Continent to denote an Irish missionary (cf. Ch. Plummer, *Vitae Sanctorum Hiberniae*, I, Oxonii, 1910, p. cxxiii, *n.* 2). And the name may have induced the compiler to make the holy hermit a professional *peregrinus* and to devise various peregrinations for him. . . . The presence of the body, assuming it to be genuine—and nothing has occurred since the original certification in 1255 to make one doubt it— precludes this *peregrinus* from being identified with other saints of the same name honoured elsewhere and on different days. . . . As to the time when S. Pellegrino lived and died, there is nothing to be said except that he was already venerated in 1110, the church in the Tuscan Emilian Apennines being named after him. Any investigation would have to go beyond that date, but just how far, in the absence of any positive basis to work upon, it is impossible to say." Mercati, possibly because of the peculiarity of the name, does not refer to the suggestion mooted, e.g., by Lanzoni with regard to St. Emilian, of a latinized or accommodation name.[6] S. Pellegrino has constantly been reckoned among the Irish saints of the seventh or eighth century.[7]

§ 3

The first certain mention of the present S. Pellegrino occurs, as already observed, in a document dated 6th August, 1110, in the archiepiscopal archives of Lucca, which refers to an "ecclesia sancti Pelegrini" and a "casa quod est ispetale qui est positam in loco et finibus, ubi dicitur Terme saloni" (sic).[8]

Alexander III, by a deed dated 1168 and confirmatory of the possessions and privileges of the parish 'de Foxiano' (*sc.* Pieve a Fosciana), enumerates among the former "Hos-

---

[6] Cf. *Le Vite dei Quattro SS. Protettori di Faenza*, pp. 332 et seq.
[7] Cf. O'Hanlon, *Lives of the Irish Saints*, VIII, p. 20. On Dempster cf. Mercati, op. cit., pp. 9, 27 and 31 and Banorri, *S. Pellegrino in Alpe*, Modena, 1915, p. 15.
[8] Cf. Mercati, op. cit., p. 36.

pitale S. Peregrini de Alpibus." In 1254 Innocent IV decided
in favour of the incumbent of Fosciana a question at issue
between him "et magistrum et fratres hospitalis sancti
Peregrini de Alpibus eiusdem dioecesis [sc. of Lucca] super
subjectione dicti hospitalis."

The first mention of the body of the saint and of the graces
to be obtained at his shrine is contained in a letter addressed
by Alexander IV from Anagni in 1255: "rectori et fratribus
sancti Peregrini de Alpibus inter Tusciam et Lombardiam in
confinis Lucane, Regine et Mutinensis dioecesium existentis,"
in which, because of the charitable work there practised, the
Pope takes the hospital, church, staff and property, "sub
speciali beati Petri Apostolorum principis protectione," and
exempts them from all and every jurisdiction and superiority
of anybody, ecclesiastical or secular. But S. Pellegrino being
in a border district, its immediate subjection to the Holy See
was soon lost sight of, and the bishops of Reggio and Modena
occasionally interfered in its affairs, according as the vigilance
of the bishops of Lucca, to whose diocese, ecclesiastically
speaking, it belonged, was alert or relaxed.

By three diplomata dated respectively 1187, 1191 and
1197, the Emperor Henry VI granted the hospital special
concessions which his son Frederick II confirmed and
increased in 1239. The 1197 diploma refers to the alms
collected by the mendicant brethren of the hospital in the
dioceses and territories of Lucca, Pisa, Volterra, Pistoja,
Luni, Parma, Reggio, Modena, Mantua and Bologna,
which explains how the hospital of S. Pellegrino came to be
known over such a widespread area and was able to give rise
to other distant foundations, such as S. Pellegrino near
Moena in the Trentino, which will be mentioned presently.
The Order of S. Pellegrino dell' Alpe was not an Order by
itself but a congregation of religious professing the rule of St.
Augustine, like most of the congregations then devoted to
the care of the sick and the poor, and took its name from the
place where it worked.[9] When precisely this community
was founded is not known. It was flourishing in the thirteenth

[9] Ibid. For the office of the saint recited by these religious Cf. Banorri,
op. cit., p. 22, and Bindoli, *Una gita a S. Pellegrino in Alpe*, Lucca, 1925, p. 24.

century with twenty religious, but after 1379 all trace of it
is lost.[10]

In 1290 Nicholas IV placed the hospital of S. Giacomo de
Ponte populi, at Loppia, near Barga, under S. Pellegrino.[11]

A great change came over the fortunes of the hospital in
the fifteenth century.

During the pontificate of Nicholas V (1447-55) a certain
Lionello de Nobili, a kinsman of the Pope,[12] was appointed
Commendatory of the Hospital of S. Pellegrino and Abbot
of Frassinoro; and in 1461 Pius II granted the de Nobili
family the "jus patronatus in dicto hospitali ac presentandi
personam ydoneam quotiens ipsum vacare contigerit" (ib.
49-50). The administration of S. Pellegrino thereafter
became practically a monopoly of the de Nobili family with
the result that the property of the hospital came to a deplorable end through the rapacity and litigiosity of the bene-
ficiaries.[13]

Lionello did indeed restore and add considerably to the
buildings of S. Pellegrino, and Mercati suspects, as already
observed, that he was responsible for the compilation of the
legend and the Lucca codex containing it with the Mass and
office proper of the Saint.

Lionello was succeeded in 1473 by his nephew, Giacomo,
who had the elegant *tempietto*, the undoubted work of Matteo
Civitali, erected in the middle of the church to contain the
sacred bodies. It was built very slowly. The marble urn was
finished in 1475, but in 1484 the remainder had not yet been
completed. The words "sacred bodies" were used because
another saint, S. Bianco, of whom nothing is known, lies by
the side of S. Pellegrino. He is said to have been a companion
or disciple of the latter, and his feast is kept on 3rd March.
The first mention of the body of S. Bianco occurs in a description which Ludovico Parisetti the younger, the Reggio
humanist (1503-70), wrote of a pious pilgrimage he made to
the place. Another reference is found in the holy visit of
1659.

[10] Cf. Banorri, p. 42 and Bindoli, pp. 24 et seq.
[11] Cf. Kehr, *It. Pont.*, III, pp. 465 et seq.
[12] Cf. Mercati, op. cit., pp. 46-7.
[13] Cf. Banorri, op. cit., p. 44 and Bindoli, op. cit., p. 23.

Ippolito de Nobili, who became Rector of S. Pellegrino in 1663, determined to have an examination made of the two sacred bodies and to change their positions. The examination took place in 1666 in the presence of representatives of the Bishop of Lucca, and was conducted by Girolamo Cremona, "one of the first anatomists in Lucca," who first "according to his custom assembled" the bodies, placing all fragments and ashes "in the hollow of the belly of each"; he then embalmed and richly dressed them, and placed them side by side, just as they may be seen to this day. (Cremona, as will be seen in its proper place, also recomposed the bodies of St. Fridian and St. Silaus.) On this occasion Civitali's shrine was moved from the middle of the church into the choir behind the high altar; the 1475 urn, by this time empty, was attached to the back wall of the choir itself with brackets in support, and the two bodies, recomposed, were replaced in the shrine but in a more commodious coffin of wood and glass, which has recently given place to a marble urn designed by an architect, Sig. Collamarini.

The Garfagnana and S. Pellegrino were together transferred early in the nineteenth century from the diocese of Lucca to the newly constituted diocese of Massa Carrara, but the de Nobili family continued to enjoy its privileges until 1897, when the Bishop of Massa Carrara entrusted the custody of the shrine to the provost of Piandelagotti. In 1908 S. Pellegrino was raised to the status of a parish, and in 1913 the parish priest was gratified with the title of archpriest. As regards civil jurisdiction, the *borgo* of S. Pellegrino belongs partly to the commune of Frassinoro (in the province of Modena), and partly to the commune of Castiglione di Garfagnana (in the province of Massa Carrara).[14]

§ 4

It is not easy to determine with certainty the places in which this S. Pellegrino is venerated, many other saints of

[14] Cf. Bindoli, op. cit., p. 27. On the two ancient hospitals in the neighbourhood, S. Bartolomeo di Cicerana or *Saltello* and S. Geminiano *De Alpibus* cf. respectively Banorri, op. cit., pp. 73 et seq., and Bucciardi: *La Pieve di Rubbiano nell'Appennino Modenese*, Parma, La Giovane Montagna, 1930, pp. 12 et seq.

the same name being honoured in Italy, even on the same days. Thirty-four saints of the name Peregrinus, of whom twenty-five are anterior to the year 1000, are enumerated in Stadler and Gindl's Dictionary.[15] Rigollot[16] reckons twenty-three discussed or cited in the first ten months by the Bollandists, and another four awaiting discussion.[17] "The question of saints named Pellegrino venerated in every province of Italy from the Alps to the Lilybaeum would be worth studying," writes Lanzoni,[18] and all that can be done at the moment is but to record and recommend the suggestion of the lamented historian of Faenza. St. Pélerin d'Auxerre has been the titular of the little church beside St. Peter's in the Vatican ever since the time of Leo III (795-816), and has also given his name to the well-known watering-place in the Val Brembana and the parish thereof, where the cult would seem to have been introduced in the fourteenth century by weavers from Piazzo Basso whose business took them frequently to France, and to the parish of Navarons in the commune of Meduno (Udine). St.Pélerin d'Auxerre is also apparently the saint venerated in Terni, Ancona, Gualdo Tadino, Nocera Umbra and S. Pellegrino di Norcia, in spite of the distortions of local legends.[19] Bindoli mentions a S. Pellegrino, whose feast is kept in Piacenza on 10th February, while a S. Pellegrino martyr is venerated in Siena on 25th August in the parish of S. Pellegrino alla Sapienza. Another S. Pellegrino martyr is found in the diocese of Amiterno,[20] and a third Pellegrino, a third century martyr, the disciple and contemporary of Marcian, is found in the dioceses of Taormina, Girgenti, and Tricola, near Caltabellotta, in Sicily. Mazochius[21] identifies the Caltabellotta Pellegrino with his namesake venerated in Naples, while the legend of the Neapolitan Pellegrino in its turn

---

[15] *Vollständiges Heiligen-Lexicon,* IV, pp. 761 et seq.

[16] *Ad Acta Sanctorum Supplementum.*

[17] Cf. Mercati, op. cit., p. 32.

[18] *Le diocesi d'Italia,* p. 384.

[19] Cf. Lanzoni, pp. 384, 406 and 454.

[20] Cf. Lanzoni, op. cit., p. 363.

[21] *In vetus marmoreum sanctae Neapolit. eccl. Kalendarium commentarium,* Naples, 1744. Cf. Mercati, op. cit., p. 35.

bears a close resemblance to that of S. Pellegrino delle Alpi.[22] A S. Pellegrino Laziosi, a Servite, is venerated at Forli. Pope Gregory the Great in his *Dialogues*, II, c. xxvii,[23] mentions a Pellegrinus as his authority (*narrare consueverat*) for one of the miracles he relates of the blessed Benedict. This Peregrinus was a disciple of St. Benedict.

Such being the multiplicity of homonymous saints, the particulars which follow with reference to the cult of the present S. Pellegrino may include some relating to namesakes or exclude some relating to him, although every care has been taken to sift the information received.

§ 5

He is certainly the titular of the neighbouring parishes of S. Pellegrino al Cassero in the commune of Sambuca Pistoiese and of Cascianella, in the commune of Camporgiano. Two parishes of S. Pellegrino and S. Pellegrinetto are to be found in Pariana, part of the commune of Massa.

"It is not improbable that the Church of S. Pellegrino in Lucca, mentioned as early as 1078, and the starting point some centuries later of a pilgrimage made by a confraternity once every three years to S. Pellegrino delle Alpi, was dedicated to our saint."[24] The confraternity in question is still flourishing and turned up again at the shrine in 1926.

There is a village S. Pellegrinetto on the mountain Bicocca, near Trassilico, above Gallicano (Lucca). The names Gallicano, Pieve a Fosciana and Loppia are found among the parishes established by St. Fridian.

§ 6

There is a quarter called S. Pellegrino near Parma on the road to Fornovo.

In the suburbs of Reggio Emilia an oratory dedicated to

[22] Cf. Mercati, op. cit., pp. 32 et seq., Banorri, op. cit., pp. 81 et seq.; Bindoli, op. cit., pp. 30, et seq.

[23] Cf. Migne, *P.L.*, LXVI, 134.

[24] Mercati, op. cit., p. 35. Cf. Banorri, p. 23 and Guerra and Guidi: *Compendio di stor. eccl. lucchese*, pp. 68 et seq.

S. Pellegrino was in existence as early as 857, as appears from
a document published by Tiraboschi; it was reconstructed a
number of times, raised to the status of a parish in 1787, and
still keeps the saint's feast on 1st August. A ninth-eleventh
century bas-relief of the greatest interest but difficult to
decipher, had been worked into the stones of the façade, but
is now preserved in the sacristy. I do not understand why
Mercati, running counter to the common opinion and the
accepted tradition (the first *Life of S. Pellegrino* ever printed, [25]
that by Isachi, was printed at Reggio in 1586), should think
it out of the question to consider that oratory as having been
dedicated to the present S. Pellegrino, while admitting that
the date 857 would offer an important terminus *ante quem* for
the chronology of the saint. [26] Banorri adds that three or
four other oratories in the diocese of Reggio were dedicated
to the saint. I would draw attention to the parish of Ceredolo
in the commune of Ciano d'Enza.

§ 7

"A catalogue of the churches in Modena, drawn up towards
the end of the fifteenth century," writes Banorri, "mentions
an oratory dedicated to S. Pellegrino and situate on the road
from Modena to Carpi. A chapel in the parish church of
Semelano (Modena) is dedicated to S. Pellegrino and a bell
in the parish bears his name. The parish church of Monte-
corone (Modena) has an altar dedicated to S. Pellegrino
and there are pictures of the saint in various churches and
oratories in the dioceses of Modena and Nonantola, among
which particular mention may be made of the wall painting
in the Oratory della Riva near Maserno." I would add the
chapel of S. Pellegrinetto along the road from Prignano to
Monfestino in Serra Mazzoni, the *borgo* of S. Pellegrino near
Spilamberto, the chapel between Frignano and Montepiccolo, and the quarter Ponte di S. Pellegrino, north of S.
Felice on the Panaro and east of Mirandola.

[25] Dempster, *loc. cit.*, attributes the first printed life to a certain Peregrinus
Carpius of Reggio, but gives no date.
[26] Cf. Mercati, p. 35 and Banorri, pp. 21 and 33.

At Sestola (Nonantola) the cult is evidenced by documents dated 1630. The villagers of Piandelagotti (Modena) go up to the shrine on 1st August, those of Riccovolto (Modena) on the second Sunday in August.

§ 8

The district round Bologna also has always had a veneration for S. Pellegrino, has dedicated altars and oratories to him, and sent him its contingent of pilgrims. In the city of Bologna, according to Banorri, there is an institution with an oratory containing the inscription, "S. Peregrino de Alpibus." Guidicini[27] gives particulars of a "church and a confraternity of the Stigmata of St. Francis called after S. Pellegrino, which arose in 1518 where the porta S. Isaia now stands." I cannot think that this is our saint.

The parish church of Casacalistri (Bologna, in the commune of Granaglione) is dedicated to S. Pellegrino and high festival kept there on 1st August.

§ 9

On the road from Imola to Florence along the valley of the Santerno, there is a *borgo* called S. Pellegrino, part of the commune of Firenzuola, 'little Florence.' This *borgo* takes its name from an ancient church which had a hospice attached for wayfarers, was well endowed, and stood formerly on the bank of the river: "ecclesia S. Peregrini juxta Salternum."[28] The reader may remember that the adjoining parish of Tirli is dedicated to St. Patrick.

§ 10

No trace of our saint is to be discovered in the diocese of Genoa.[29] But in the diocese of Chiavari, i.e., in that part of

---

[27] *Cose notabili della Città di Bologna*, II, p. 303.
[28] Cf. Kehr, *It. Pont.*, III, p. 71, and Casini, *Dizionario biogr. geogr. stor. del Comune di Firenzuola*, I, pp. 98 et seq., and Repetti, *Dizion. geografico della Toscana*, *s.v.* "S. Pellegrino."
[29] Cf. Cambiaso, op. cit.

Liguria where the estates of the Bobbio monastery were found to be so numerous and the cult of St. Columban so widespread, devotion to S. Pellegrino is also widespread. It is of very ancient date in S. Maria di Sturla, part of Carasco (Chiavari); there the church boasts a fine altar with a wooden statue dedicated to the holy anchorite, while an old-established confraternity bears his name. There is great devotion and even at the present time his feast-day, the second Sunday in August, is attended by crowds from the neighbourhood, more particularly Rapallo, S. Michele di Pagana, and Santa Margherita Ligure.[30] S. Pellegrino is also venerated in the following parishes,[31] the geographical distribution of which makes an interesting study:

(i) Porcile, in the diocese of Chiavari and the commune of Borzonasca;

(ii) Pontegiacomo di Foce: diocese of Chiavari, commune of Mezzanego;

(iii) Semorile: diocese of Chiavari, commune of Zoagli;

(iv) Monticelli: diocese of Chiavari, commune of Cogorno;

(v) Breccanecca: diocese of Chiavari, commune of Cogorno;

(vi) Cembrano: diocese of Chiavari, commune of Maissana;

(vii) Pavareto di Carro: diocese of Chiavari, commune of Carro;

(viii) Priosa di Scorbò: diocese of Bobbio, commune of Rezzoaglio;

to which may be added Villafranca di Lunigiana in the diocese of Pontremoli, where a grand fair is also held on the feast-day.

§ 11

Finally I would mention that the very ancient Church of S. Pellegrino in Viterbo, which stands in the little piazza so-called in the well-known quarter of the city which has

[30] Cf. P. Castellini, *S. Pellegrino in Val di Sturla*, Chiavari, 1903, and Banorri, op. cit., p. 24. [31] Cf. Banorri, *loc. cit.*

best retained its medieval character, is dedicated to our
saint, and his feast is kept there, as I am kindly informed by
the Rector of Viterbo inter-diocesan Seminary, on 8th
August.

§ 12

An undoubted dependence from S. Pellegrino delle Alpi
is S. Pellegrino del Trentino. The name Valle di S. Pellegrino is given to a valley, which, beginning at Moena di
Fiemme, continues in an easterly direction for a good three
hours' walk until it merges into a pass, also called S. Pellegrino, and thence proceeds down into the Canal d'Agordo.
Near the pass, some 5,760 feet above sea-level, are a little
lake, a church, a hospice and a hotel, all called after S.
Pellegrino. Here in the Middle Ages ran one of the direct
roads connecting Italy with Bolzano and the Germanies.

The history of this church and hospice was investigated
by Padre Giangrisostomo Tovazzi, O.F.M., deservedly
called "the Muratori of the Trentino," whose acquaintance
we have already made and whose numerous manuscripts
are preserved in the archives of the Convent of S. Bernardino
in Trent. In a memoir dated 1794 and entitled 'Documenti
antichi dell' Ospizio di S. Pellegrino appresso Moena in
Fiemme,' Padre Tovazzi transcribed and prefaced with a
learned introduction sixteen parchments still preserved in
the communal archives of Moena, and ranging from 1358
(the foundation charter of the hospice) to 1577 (a testament
and legacy in its favour). Don Lorenzo Felicetti of Predazzo[32] has written an interesting and exhaustive monograph on the subject, and refers to it more succinctly in his
Racconti e Leggende del Trentino.[33]

Padre Tovazzi states in his preface that the S. Pellegrino
to whom this hospice is dedicated is not the S. Pellegrino
Laziosi of Forli, "or any other of those recorded in the Roman
Martyrology, but he who on 1st August is described in the
Bologna Calendar of the year 1761 as 'S. Pellegrino Re'
(the king); in another Bologna Calendar of 1777 as 'S.

[32] *L'Ospizio di S. Pellegrino presso Moena nel Trentino*, Cavalese, Tabarelli, 1906.
[33] Third Edition, Zordan, Valdagno.

Pellegrino, believed to have been a king of Scotland'; in a third Bologna Calendar (1782) as 'S. Pellegrino, King of Scotland'; and in a Parma Calendar for 1787 as 'S. Pellegrino Confessor,' because his feast is also kept on the first day of August as by the Moenati."

By the deed dated 14th June, 1358, the men of the 'Regola,' i.e., the commune of Moena, assembled on Mt. Aloch (a meadow in the valley later called after S. Pellegrino), granted to a certain "Friar Gualtiero of the Order of S. Pellegrino delle Alpi in the name and on behalf of the hospital of S. Pellegrino delle Alpi," a piece of meadow-land with a wood in those parts to build thereon "a hospital in honour of S. Pellegrino, to the end that wayfarers crossing that mountain might be hospitably entertained there" and so forth. It was expressly agreed that, if for any reason the future hospice should not continue, all its goods and chattels should revert to the 'Regola' of Moena. This was a providential reservation, for when the hospice, like many another convent (e.g., that of S. Martino di Castrozza), was suppressed, *c.* 1420, as a result of the Council of Constance in 1418, its property reverted to the men of Moena who own it to this day, whereas property elsewhere fell into the hands of the feudal nobles and remained there. After 1420 the prior of the hospice was appointed from among the candidates from Moena by a majority of the votes cast by the heads of families and paid an annual rent for the 'malghe,' the hotel and the meadows. At the present day the priory is leased by the commune to the highest bidder. The prior was under obligation to ring the bell in winter evenings to direct any traveller who might have lost his way, to keep a dog ready to go out and track him, to give free board and lodging to the poor for three days, and to plant long poles to indicate the road when it was covered with snow.

On 24th May, 1915, on the declaration of war, the Austrians burned the church, the hospice and the inn; all were rebuilt after the war. I believe that very few of the holiday-makers who spend the summer in that delightful spot ever give a thought to the Irish hermit of the Tuscan-Emilian Apennines after whom the place itself is named.

CHAPTER XVII

ST. FRIDIAN OF LUCCA

§ 1

WITH St. Fridian we return to the plain of history. The main features of his character can be restored sufficiently clearly for us to perceive him a tower of strength in piety, apostolic zeal and practical activity throughout the hurricane which swept the Church in the sixth century, the storm of the Ostro-Gothic wars and the waves of the Lombard invasion. The Roman Church was likened by its pilot to an old and shattered ship with the water pouring in on all sides, its timbers rotten, shivered by daily tempests, a hulk drifting on to the rocks, and all the skill of Gregory the Great was needed to bring it safely into port. Gregory, in the words of his biographer, John the Deacon, was an "athlete of Christ," and "the sweat poured off his brawny muscles as he strove like a man in the gymnasium of Holy Church."[1]

And St. Gregory the Great also refers to our St. Fridian: he tells in his *Dialogues* (III, 9)[2] how he heard Venantius, Bishop of Luni, a close neighbour, relate the story of a marvel performed by "Frigdian," Bishop of Lucca, then some time dead: "fuisse mirae virtutis virum, Frigdianum nomine narravit, episcopum." It was a comparatively recent occurrence: for the saintly doctor has proposed a little earlier to give over talking about events in the remote past (τὰ ἀρχαῖα) and to discuss instead the events of his own time, "sed oportet jam ut priora taceamus: ad ea quae diebus nostris sunt gesta veniamus." The full import of this lauda-

---

[1] *In vit. S. Gregor.*, Migne, *P.L.*, LXXV., col. 87. Cf. the 'Antiphonary of Bendchor' (Muratori, *Anecd.*, IV, pp. 121 et seq.), ibid,. LXXII, col. 593, in the hymn of St.Comgall "our abbot": *Audite πάντες τὰ ἔργα Allati ad angelica Athletae Dei abdita A juventute florida.* The simile seems to have been a favourite and St. Bernard applied it to his hero St. Malachy. "Quid faceret athleta Domini?" Ibid., CLXXXII, col. 1084.

[2] "Dialogorum libri IV de vita et miraculis Patrum Italicorum et de aeternitate animarum," in Migne, *P.L.*, LXXVII, col. 233.

tory reference to St. Fridian can only be realised if the
circumstances in which Gregory wrote his *Dialogues* are
born in mind.

"Gregory's unwearying zeal," writes Fr. Grisar,[3] "to
renew the spirit of Christian piety in the flock committed to
his care, inspired him with the design of writing his book of
Dialogues. The saintly pontiff began this work in 593 and
completed it, as we should say, at a sitting; so spontaneous
is it in invention, so effective in the choice of matter for
argument, so sincere and indescribably limpid in style . . .
Peter the Deacon, the confidant and interlocutor of Gregory
in the *Dialogues*, expresses the fundamental intention of the
book in these words: 'Our experience is that every day we
see the fulfilment of those words of Truth which say: "Pater
meus usque modo operatur et ego operor" ' (John v, 17).
Readers of the *Dialogues* should therefore vividly appreciate
that Italy of the time, however disastrously ravaged by storms,
had not yet been utterly abandoned by God, and have an
abundance of palpable evidence to show the working of the
divine power on behalf of the country. The ecclesiastical
history of ages similar to that which we have undertaken to
describe chronicles in nearly every case many events testifying to the intervention of such a divine power. No conversion
of a barbarous people was ever achieved in the Middle Ages,
but we have the testimony of unimpeachable witnesses to
miracles performed to help and comfort the infant churches;
for the struggle between Christian civilisation and pagan
superstition everywhere produced men as remarkable for the
sanctity of their lives, as for their gifts of supernatural energy
and grace."

St. Fridian was one of the examples proposed by Gregory
to the faithful at a time of universal sadness and despair for
their edification and encouragement.

§ 2

Fridian, then, according to the legend, was born of royal
blood in Ireland: "beatus igitur Frigianus sicut prisci catho-

---

[3] *San Gregorio Magno*, Rome, Desclée, 1928, p. 62.

lici tradiderunt ex Ybernia insula Scotiae partibus oriundus extitit."[4] Some go further and declare that he was the son of a king of the Ulaid in modern Ulster. He embraced the Christian religion in his youth, converted his parents, and, as he grew in years, so also he increased in virtue. He became the love and admiration of his people, and God distinguished him by the gift of miracles. But the honours of the world came to pall, and, longing for a life of mortification, Fridian forsook his country and betook himself to Italy. Settling there, he led the hermit life in one of the fastnesses of the anchorites on the Monte Pisano, near Lucca, which had risen to fame through the sojourn which St. Augustine, and as was mentioned above, St. Patrick also, were reputed to have made there.[5] But "fama de eo boni operis circumquaque crebescente, a populo lucane civitatis heremum deserere coactus est": and on the death of the venerable Obsequentius, Bishop of Lucca, "consentientibus civibus omnibus, beatus Frigianus cathedram pontificalem Lucanae civitatis suscepit," *c.* 560; and held it for twenty-eight years. He occupied the see in the anxious times which followed the Lombard invasion. "The barbarians had sown discord and terror everywhere, and St. Fridian spoke of brotherly love and peace; the barbarians had persecuted and slaughtered priests and virgins consecrated to God, and Fridian sought to recruit them afresh; the barbarians had destroyed churches, and Fridian rebuilt them."[6] He strove hard and with excellent results to convert the Arian conquerors to orthodoxy.

The following twenty-eight *plebes baptismales* (the number corresponds to the years of his episcopacy) are said to have been founded or restored by him, three in the city of Lucca and twenty-five in the country:

(i) The suburban Church of S. Vincenzo in Lucca, also called of the Three Levites, where Fridian himself was buried and which was therefore also known as the basilica of S. Frediano;

[4] Cod. Ambr. B 55 Inf. Fol. 228 r, of the eleventh century.
[5] Cf. Miss Stokes, *Six Months in the Apennines*, pp. 50-62; on Rupecava or rather Lupocava; cf. also Guerra and Guidi, *Comp. di storia eccl. lucchese.*, p. 193.
[6] Cf. Guerra and Guidi, op. cit., p. 48.

(ii) the Church of S. Giovanni Battista in Lucca, a most ancient city parish;

(iii) the urban Church of S. Martino, which, down to the eighteenth century, had above the altar of S. Stephen the inscription "Disponente episcopo Fric, iano valerianus, presbyter altare cum columellis suis fecit," and a jewelled cross, commemorating the consecration of the altar, faithful reproductions of which have been preserved and present all the characteristic features of sixth century art.[7] This church became the Cathedral of Lucca and absorbed the Chapel of S. Maria ad praesepe placed within it;

(iv) the parish of Lunata, dedicated to St. John the Baptist, but now known as San Frediano di Lunata;[8]

(v) the parish of Lammari, now dedicated to SS. James the Apostle and Christopher;[9]

(vi) the parish of Segromigno, dedicated to St. Lawrence;

(vii) the parish of Villa Basilica, dedicated to Our Lady of the Assumption;

(viii) the parish of S. Gennaro;

(ix) the parish at Compito;

(x) the parish of St. John the Baptist at Camajore;

(xi) the parish of Diecimo, dedicated to Our Lady of the Assumption;

(xii) the parish of Gallicano, dedicated to St. John the Baptist;

(xiii) the parish of Controne, dedicated to St. John the Baptist;

(xiv) the parish of Sesto a Moriano, now dedicated to Our Lady of the Assumption;

(xv) the parish of Monsagrati, dedicated to St. John the Baptist;

(xvi) the parish of Brancoli, dedicated to St. George;

(xvii) the parish at Ilice, dedicated to St. Pantaleone;

(xviii) the parish of Arliano, dedicated to St. John the Baptist;

[7] Cf. Guerra and Guidi, p. 54*.
[8] Cf. Miss Stokes, op. cit., p. 92.
[9] Ibid, p. 93, who gives a drawing of the primitive baptismal font.

(xix) the parish of Our Lady of the Assumption, later the cathedral of the city of Pescia and capital of the province of the Val di Nievole;

(xx) the parish of S. Ginese of Vico-Vallari, the capital of the province of the lower Valdarno in the diocese of Lucca, but now joined to the Cathedral of St. Miniato al Tedesco;[10]

(xxi) the parish of the Valle Ariana, formerly dedicated to St. John the Baptist, afterwards to St. Thomas the Apostle and to St. Ansan, and now in the diocese of Pescia;

(xxii) the parish of S. Pietro in Campo, now one with the Church of St. Andrew, the deanery of Monte Carlo;

(xxiii) the parish of Massa Buggianese;

(xxiv) the parish of Montecatini in Val di Nievole;

(xxv) the parish of S. Maria in Monte, now in the diocese of San Miniato;

(xxvi) the parish at Fosciana, then chief of all the Lucchese churches in the Garfagnana;

(xxvii) the parish of Loppia, now one with the parish of Barga;

(xxviii) the parish of St. John the Baptist in Val di Castello and Capezzano, later called the parish of St. Felicity in the Versilia, district of Pietrasanta.

Two of the four miracles performed by St. Fridian during his lifetime took place in course of the construction of the Church of S. Vincenzo (San Frediano); an enormous block of stone was prodigiously transported from Vaccoli to Lucca, and the purse of a rich man who had refused an alms to a beggar, after having been lost in the water, was found in the mouth of a fish. The saint refused to give it back to its owner, but addressed him instead a few suitable and edifying observations.[11]

St. Fridian had a great devotion to S. Miniato the martyr: "consuetudo fuerat beato Frediano ecclesiam S. Miniati martiris, que non longe a Florentina urbe distare videtur,

---

[10] Cf. Guerra and Guidi, pp. 134* et seq.
[11] Ibid, pp. 49-50.

annis singulis debita veneratione visitare":[12] one year, when the Arno was in spate, the saint found himself unable to cross it, but, undeterred, performed his third miracle. He espied a boat on the other side, but the boatman had not the courage to launch out on the flood when, hey presto! boat and boatman found themselves at the other side ready to take the saint over. This tale, not found, however, in Codex C (cart. 103) of the Lucca Chapter Library,[13] contributed greatly to the popularity of St. Fridian in Florence.[14]

The last miracle, universally known, is that related by St. Gregory the Great,[15] the deviation of the river Auser, which St. Fridian made to flow straight into the sea, whereas, until he appeared on the scene, it had flowed into the Arno.[16] It has been historically proved that this deviation, a real boon to the country round Lucca, did in fact take place during the time of the saint.[17]

Shortly after performing this feat he retired to Lunata through love of solitude. But there he was outraged and maltreated by the peasants, who may perhaps have suffered loss through being no longer able to fish in the formerly neighbouring stream, and, returning to Lucca, departed this life, on an 18th March in a year which tradition—which cannot be very far out, as we shall presently see—maintains to have been 588.

§ 3

The Life of the saint has come down to us in at least three different redactions anterior to the thirteenth century and

[12] Cf. Lanzoni. *Le Diocesi d'Italia*, p. 575.
[13] Cf. Lanzoni, ibid. By an obvious misprint the codex is said by the writer to be earlier than the eighth century: for 'eighth' read 'thirteenth.' The codex belongs either to the eleventh or to the early years of the twelfth century.
[14] Cf. Guerra and Guidi, pp. 39* and 58*.
[15] "quod Auseris fluvius . . . saepe inundatione facta . . . per agros diffundi consueverat. . . . Sed quamvis diutius laboratum fuisset, a proprio alveo deflecti non potuit. Tunc vir Domini Frigdianus rastrum sibi parvulum fecit, ad alveum fluminis accessit et solus orationi incubuit: atque eidem flumini praecipiens ut se sequeretur, per loca quaeque ei visa sunt rastrum per terram traxit. Quem relicto alveo proprio tota fluminis aqua secuta est ita ut . . . quaeque essent alimentis hominum profutura sato vel plantata ultra non laederet." Gregor. Pap. *Dial. lib.* III, cap. IX, loc. cit. ante.
[16] The abandoned bed, or rather one of the abandoned beds, retained the name *Auser*, Ozzeri. The new bed was called *Auserculus*, whence Serchio.
[17] Cf. Guerra and Guidi, op. cit., pp. 50 and 59*.

contained in a number of eleventh, twelfth and thirteenth century codices preserved in Lucca and other Italian cities. These various redactions are not conflicting but distinguishable merely by their varying lengths, more particularly as regards the miracles.[18] Although no codices certainly anterior to the eleventh century have, so far as is known, survived, that there must have been some in existence— Mgr. Guidi observes—may not unreasonably be inferred from the number of those which have survived from the eleventh century,[19] and the inference finds support in a ninth-tenth century inventory of books belonging to the bishopric of Lucca and including (*inter alia*) *Vita S. Laurentii cum memoria sancti Fridiani.*[20]

St. Fridian naturally finds a place in all works treating of the ecclesiastical history of Lucca. Fanucchi,[21] though antiquated and uncritical, is a mine of information as regards his cult.

§ 4

The chronology of St. Fridian has been the subject of discussion. Even in recent times some writers have proposed to date him further back, as far back as the third century;[22] but the discussion has served only to confirm his traditional attribution to the sixth.[23] The reasons which have motivated the discussion are essentially four:

(*a*) The non-chronological order in which the first bishops of Lucca are set out in two catalogues not reaching beyond the sixth century and contained in Cod. Capitol. 124, a codex written in a hand belonging to the second half of the twelfth century, but itself probably a transcription from very much older documents;

[18] Cf. Guerra and Guidi, op. cit., p. 43*.
[19] Mgr. Guidi, loc. cit., indicates an eleventh century codex at Lucca, two in Rome, one in Milan, one in Naples and no less than seven in Florence.
[20] Cf. Guidi and Pellegrinetti: 'Inventari del Vescovato della Cattedrale e di altre chiese di Lucca,' Rome, 1921, p. 14 in *Studi e Testi*, published by the staff of the Vatican Library.
[21] Cf. *Vita di S. Frediano*, Lucca, Landi, 1870.
[22] A. Pedemonte, *I primi vescovi della Paroecia Lucensis*, Lucca, 1915.
[23] Cf. Guerra and Guidi, op. cit., Appendix III.

(*b*) the erroneous statement in the *Chronicles* of Giovanni Villani, I, 49, that St. Fridian was the first Bishop of Lucca;

(*c*) the doubtful meaning of the words 'diebus nostris' in the *Dialogues* of St. Gregory, who in the same book cites, besides eleven sixth-century saints, one belonging to the fifth and one belonging perhaps to the fourth century;[24]

(*d*) the comparison drawn, but only, in point of fact, as regards the apostolic spirit informing each, between St. Fridian and St. Martin (who died in the year 400) in certain verses attributed to Rangerius, Bishop of Lucca (1097-1112), described as a former disciple of St. Bruno.[25]
The question, however, may now be considered settled, and there is no longer any doubt that the saint belongs to the sixth century, although it is impossible to determine the years in which he exercised his activity and when precisely he died.

§ 5

That he came from Ireland[26] is the concordant testimony of all the texts. Guidi considers his name to be a Latin or latinized form assumed in Italy, on the origin of which the last word has not yet been said, for we are still very much in the dark as to its true primitive form in writing. There is considerable variation in the forms which have come down to us: 'Frigidianus,' 'Frigdianus,' 'Fricdianus,' 'Frigianus,' 'Fricianus,' 'Fridianus, 'Fredianus,' with the initial 'F' often changed into 'Ph' and the first 'i' into 'y.' Many Irish hagiographers, beginning with Colgan,[27] have identified him with St. Finnian, Findian or Findbar of Mag-Bile, who may have introduced into Ireland one of the first copies there known of St. Jerome's Vulgate[28] and who also flourished in the sixth century; but the Bollandists,

---

[24] Cf. Guerra and Guidi, op. cit., p. 37*.
[25] Cf. *Sancti Anselmi Lucensis episcopi Vita*, De la Fuente, Madrid, 1870, p. 153. Guerra and Guidi, op. cit., p. 41* and Migne, P.L., CLII, col. 556: "vir venerabilis Brunonis quondam discipulus."
[26] Cf. Guerra and Guidi, p. 47*.
[27] *Acta Sanctorum Hiberniae*, I, p. 642.
[28] Cf. Gougaud, *Christianity in Celtic Lands*, p. 260.

beginning with Svyskens,[29] O'Hanlon,[30] Guerra and
Guidi, and Dom Gougaud,[31] all protest that such an
identification is inadmissible. The ancient life of St. Fridian
is as distinctively Lucchese as that of S. Finnian, compiled
by John of Tynemouth in the first half of the fourteenth
century from Welsh sources, is distinctively Irish. The
narrative of miracles performed in Ireland forms no part
of the ancient texts of the Legend of St. Fridian. Ireland
down to the fourteenth century at least had no knowledge
of St. Finian's activities in Lucca, while Lucca was as
absolutely ignorant of the activities of St. Fridian in Ireland.
The confusion, then created, passed into the hagiographical
treatises broadcast by the printing-press in the sixteenth-
nineteenth centuries.[32]

Dom Gougaud,[33] founding on Dr. Kenney,[34] has recently
included St. Fridian in a class of "doubtful and pseudo-
Irishmen." Dr. Kenney's observation that the earliest of the
Lives, "late compositions," is "posterior to 1171," is, however,
not quite exact. Codices belonging to the eleventh century
are, as already observed, fairly numerous, and traces of a
Life may be found in ninth-tenth century documents. The
date suggested, as already mentioned apropos of St. Ursus,
brings us to an era earlier than that of St. Columban,
but in the case of St. Fridian may be of importance
as evidence that some isolated Irish *peregrini* had already
taken the road to Italy[35] and settled there permanently
before the arrival of the founder of Bobbio. The eleventh
century codex in the Ambrosiana referred to in § 2, in
recording that Fridian was an Irishman, "sicut prisci Catho-
lici tradiderunt," merely repeats an ancient and constant
tradition concerning moreover a perfectly historical character, a bishop who was a founder of parishes and received his
meed of praise a few years after his death from St. Gregory,

[29] *AA. SS., s. d.*, 25 September.
[30] Cf. *Lives of the Irish Saints*, IX, 254 loc. cit., pp. 44 et seq.
[31] Cf. Gougaud, loc. cit.
[32] Cf. Guerra and Guidi, pp. 45* and 46*.
[33] "Les surnuméraires de l'émigration scottique" in *Revue bénédictine*, 1931,
pp. 296 et seq.
[34] Cf. *Sources*, etc., I, pp. 184-5.
[35] Cf. Kenney, op. cit., p. 183.

and from the public the tribute of an immediate and spontaneous cult (cf. the diploma of Cunibert dated 686 and to be referred to presently). It is important also to remember that a cult was paid to a number of other Irish saints in Lucca and its territory, more particularly to St. Columban (as early as the eighth century), to St. Peregrinus, to St. Silaus and to St. Cathal, and that all through the Middle Ages the city of St. Fridian was an important centre of Scotic influence in Tuscany (cf. Ch. II, § 9). This was no doubt partly due to the political importance of Lucca, as the capital of the Lombard kingdom in Tuscany, partly to the further fact that through Lucca ran one of the great arterial ways, the 'strada francigena peregrinorum,' one of the roads trodden by the '*romei*,' the terminus of which was Rome, the *limina Apostolorum*. Luigi Schiaparelli[36] has demonstrated the existence of a school of writing in Lucca towards the end of the eighth century in which pupils were taught foreign, i.e., non-Italian, handwriting by masters from abroad who had settled in the city, and maintains that the oldest foreign influence appears to have been that of the Irish masters.

§ 6

The cult of St. Fridian spread rapidly all over Tuscany and extended into other regions of Italy. The body of the saint enclosed in a marble coffin was jealously buried underground in the church which, as already mentioned, bears his name. The story of the miraculous re-discovery of the coffin, the exact situation of which had been forgotten, some two centuries later, is well-known. One day when they were about to bury the body of a girl in the church and a tomb had been excavated for the purpose, the lass came back to life for a moment and exclaimed: "Be careful! Don't place my despicable body above the body of the most blessed

[36] In an article entitled "Codex 490 of the Chapter Library at Lucca and the Lucca School of Writing (eighth-ninth century)" in *Studi e Testi*, No. 36, Rome, 1924, p. 107. The codex in question, begun apparently between 787 and 796 and finished in 816, includes documents written by over forty different hands. Cf. also Sig. Schiaparelli's very important contribution to *Archiv. Str. Ital.*, Vol. II, Florence, 1917, on the origin and characteristic features of, and, more particularly, the system of abbreviation practised in, Irish writing.

Fridian!" A great stone was removed, and behold the bones of St. Fridian appeared. They were reverently collected and transferred to an exalted place protected by a lattice, and an altar was erected above them. On this occasion the Feast of the Translation was fixed on 18th November and has since rather eclipsed that of the *dies natalis* (18th March). Some writers, including Guerra, have attributed the translation to Bishop John II (eleventh century), but Guidi has shown that it took place (in accordance with current tradition which attributed it to 782) under Bishop John I (780-800), who, in 781, translated the body of St. Regulus, bishop and martyr, from Gualdo di Populonia to Lucca, and in 782 enriched Lucca with the famous cedarwood crucifix known as 'Il Volto Santo.'[37] That John I was responsible and not John II is clear—to say nothing of various other arguments—from a document dated 857 and already containing a reference to "festivitate S. Fridiani, quod sunt in mense novembrio" (sic.).[38] A second translation from the marble coffin into one of glass took place in 1152 and a third in 1566. The fourth and last occurred in 1652 when the bones were regularly examined and recomposed by the famous anatomist Gerolamo Cremona, whose acquaintance we have already made, into a body which, vested in ponti-ficals, was placed below the high altar in a new coffin of cypress-wood and glass. There it may be seen to this day.[39]

§ 7

Mention should also be made of the fact that St. Fridian established beside the church which bears his name a

[37] On the Volto Santo cf. the article "Le Saint Vou de Lucques," by W. Förster in *Romanische Forschungen* (*Mélanges Chabaneau*), Vol. XXIII, 1906. "Par le volt de Luche" was the favourite oath, according to Eadmer (*Historia novorum in Anglia*, Migne, *P.L.*, CLIX, col. 364), of William the Conqueror, "per sanctum vultum de Luca sic enim jurare consueverat." It is a Byzantine work and was probably imported into Lucca about two centuries later than the traditional date of 782. On the charming legend of the slipper kicked by the crucified Christ to the hungry jongleur and the attribution of the incident to St. Genesius, the Roman actor martyr (*c.* A.D. 285), and the hero of M. Henri Ghéon's beautiful play *Le comédien et la grâce*, merely because San Genesio happened to be on the *via francigena peregrinorum* and his legend was familiar, cf. M. Bédier's *Les légendes épiques*, Paris, 1917, Vol. II, pp. 221-229.

[38] Cf. Guerra and Guidi, Appendix VI, p. 112*.

[39] Cf. Fanucchi, op. cit., pp. 193 et seq.

monastery of monks under the regular government of an abbot, which was much frequented by other religious and may also have sheltered the saint himself. The existence of the monastery appears from two important charters dated respectively 685 and 686, by the former of which the bishop, Felix, granted the monastery extensive privileges and by the latter of which King Cunibert confirmed the immunities granted by Felix and the gifts made by his own mayor of the palace, Faulo.[40] A document of the kind may be described in the words of Guerra and Guidi as "a summary of an ancient glorious history and a mirror reflecting far-distant horizons for the future. As a last testimony of a whole long past, it echoes Latin names in its list of the bishop and his clergy. The Lombard element scarcely appears and yet it will presently emerge proudly triumphant either in all the names attached or in the latinized terminations of Lombard roots or in the Lombardized terminations of Latin roots. So the series of bishops, which nearly all through the seventh century retained the Latin form of its names, becomes definitely Lombard just as the seventh century turns into the eighth, and continues so for a number of decades; and a Lombard clergy comes to crown the Lombard bishop. Such a document tells us also of the once considerable cult paid to a great saint of ours and of a 'monastery' not then founded but restored, of a special liturgy 'long since' in use, of a clergy 'long accustomed' to repair to that monastery." The monastery, the oldest, perhaps, in Lucca, became extinct in the eighth century. In Bishop Walprand's time (737-55) it had ceased to have any monks, and the church with all the property appurtenant had passed into the hands of the bishop.[41]

But there arose later beside the tomb of St. Fridian another famous institution, 'the Canons Regular of St. Fridian.' To combat the incontinence and simony which were so rife

---

[40] Cunibert's charter is printed by Mabillon in the appendix to Vol. I of *Annal. Bened.*, p. 707, and attributed by him in error to A.D. 700. By the deed dated XII. Kal. Febr. 685, Felix, Bishop of Lucca, confirmed to Balbinus, Abbot of St. Fridian, the donations made by Faulo "ac futuras oblationes eidem concessit." Cf. Migne, *P.L.*, LXXXVII, col. 1347.

[41] Cf. Guerra and Guidi, op. cit., pp. 56 and 105.

among the clergy of the eleventh century, many bishops, including also those of Lucca, conceived the plan of grouping their clergy in colleges where they could live together under a discreet and tempered rule and be provided with the means for leading a decorous life. Bishop John II made a first experiment at Lucca as early as 1025 in the parish church of S. Maria a Monte. Communal life is next found in practice in 1041 in the Church of S. Maria Forisportam, in 1063 in the Church of St. Donatus, and later in that of SS. John and Reparata. "But it was in this respect that the priests and clerks of the parish church of S. Fridian chiefly distinguished themselves among the clergy of Lucca. The communal life was practised, if not by all the clergy of that church, at any rate by a great majority as early as 1039, and that at the instance, not of St. Anselm, as some have declared, but of Bishop John, his predecessor. There began the reform which ade the canons or clergy of St. Fridian so famous in the Church and endeared them so much to the Supreme Pontiffs."[42] When Paschal II visited Lucca in 1105, he had an opportunity of admiring the saintly life they led and besides lavishing praise upon, and granting them various privileges, he invited them to Rome to reform the clergy of the Lateran Church according to their model, with the result that the Order later took the name of the Lateran Canons of St. Fridian.[43] Kehr[44] gives the following list of churches entrusted by other pontiffs to their care: S. Petri juxta Pistorium (by Honorius II), S. Joannis in Capite burgi (1135), S. Pantaleonis de Luca (1137), S. Salvatoris in Mustiolo (1140), S. Mariae Novae de urbe (1140-42), S. Mariae de Montebello, in the diocese of Bologna (1150), S. Andreae de Carraria, in the diocese of Luni (1151), S. Crucis in Hierusalem (1166), S. Salvatoris de Ficarolo, in the diocese

---

[42] Cf. Guerra and Guidi, op. cit., p. 138—St. Bruno died in 1101. On that occasion the Canons of St. Fridian despatched the following message: "Nos humiles Sancti Frigiani Lucensis ecclesiae fratres pro tanto viro et tam glorioso voluntarie officium commemorationis impendimus credentes nos apud Deum ejus sanctis commendari meritis." Cf. Migne, *P.L.*, CLII, col. 557.

[43] Alexander II, by a privilege granted in 1065, placed the property of the canons of St. Fridian in the Maremme under the protection of the Holy See. The text is printed in Migne, *P.L.*, CXLVI, col. 1346, from *Memorie e documere, per servire all' istoria del principato Lucchese*, Lucca, 1813, II, p. 144.

[44] *Italia Pontificia*, III, p. 412.

of Ferrara (1181), S. Martini Senarum (1182), SS. Quadraginta de Tarvisio, S. Bartholomei de Monte Scalocchio, Canonica S. Floridi Castellana (Città di Castello) "quarum priorem ecclesiam S. Fridiani Lucanam ejusque priorem velut caput et priorem generalem totius congregationis recolebant. Ita S. Fridiani congregatio floruit usque ad a. 1517, quando cum Lateranensi congregatione unita est."[45] The community of the Canons of St. Fridian of Lucca was suppressed by Pius VI on 19th July, 1780.

It may be taken as certain that both the first monastery founded by St. Fridian and the later congregation of the Canons of St. Fridian were centres of assembly for Scots *peregrini* and so, as already observed in Ch. II, § 9, of the diffusion of devotion to the Irish saints.

§ 8

Reference has been made to the foundation of the Church of St. Fridian in Lucca under the name of the Church of St. Vincent, and to the diploma of King Cunibert (686) relative thereto. Bishop Walprand († 755), who by will disposed in favour of the Church of St. Columban, also disposed in favour of the Church of St. Fridian. It contains many bodies of saints, including St. Richard, King of the West Saxons and the father of SS. Willibald, Wunibald and Walburga, who died in Lucca in the eighth century.[46] In the eighth

[45] Cf. also Widloecher: *La Congregazione dei Canonici regolari lateranensi:periodo di formazione*, Gubbio, Oderici, 1929.
[46] Cf. Guerra and Guidi, op. cit., pp. 66 et seq. Dempster 'with his usual effrontery' makes them all Scotch, but drags in John Trithemius and gives references which, unfortunately, it has not been possible to check. As regards St. Willibald he says: "Anglum facit impius Balaeus, ut solet, nullo argumento, ut et maledicus et indoctissimus Capgravius. . . . (These epithets from so scrupulous an authority as Dempster are good). . . . Ego Scotum fuisse bonis testibus aio." *Joann. Trithemius de Scriptor. Ecclesiast.*, p. CCXLIX: "Willibaldus primus episcopus Eistetensis [i.e., Eichstadt in Bavaria] natione Scotus, frater S. Walpurgae virginis, abbatissae Heidenhemensis, monachus ac discipulus S. Bonifacii martyris ordinis S. Benedicti [John made S. Columban also a Benedictine], vir doctus atque sanctissimus, ingenio et eloquio clarus." Of St. Walpurga he gives the following account: "Errant qui hanc Anglam existimant cum fratris sint Scoti . . . et imperiti ad Anglorum gloriam id trahentes Richardi regis filiam esse volunt qui Lucae conditus: sed ego verius puto eam Malduini fuisse qui LV apud Scotos regnavit extinctus anno DCLXXXV nec tamen certo affirmarim. . . . Floruit cum fratribus anno DCCL Trithemio teste." *Historia Ecclesiastica*, Vol. II, pp. 640-5. Mabillon

century also the blessed Bishop John was buried there. Thither in the ninth century the bodies of SS. Cassius, Juvenal and Fausta were brought from Narni, and there in the tenth century was buried the blessed Bishop Conrad, and in the twelfth St. Zita. The church also boasts an important collection of relics.[47] It had fallen into decay in the twelfth century and was begun to be rebuilt in 1112 by the prior Roto. In 1147 the new church was consecrated by Eugenius III. In 1220 it had a graveyard attached to it with a chapel dedicated to St. Catherine, of which now only a few stones remain. The numerous side chapels in the Basilica were built in later centuries. Miss Stokes gives an ample description of San Frediano with illustrations.

The bastion of the walls of Lucca nearest to the church is called the Baluardo S. Frediano.

The name 'Frediano' is common in Lucchese nomenclature from the seventh and eighth centuries onwards.

§ 9

The parish church of St. Fridian in Florence on the south side of the Arno was built apparently in the eighth century.[48] The saint enjoyed a high reputation in Florence and gave his name to the Borgo S. Frediano and the Porta S. Frediano. The patronage of the church belonged to the monastery of Nonantola,[49] but in 1190 was assigned to the convent of Settimo which transferred its principal seat there. The dome by Ferri (1680-9) is famous.

Pisa also boasts a very ancient Church of St. Fridian in a little piazza situated between the Lungarno and the Piazza dei Cavalieri, and the diocese of Pisa was among the first to offer its tribute of devotion to St. Fridian on 18th March. Kehr[50] mentions a "monasterium S. Martini et S. Fridiani"

has edited the anonymous "Odoeporicon" in *Acta SS. o. s. B.*, sec. III. pt. 2. Cf. also his edition of the Life of St. Boniface in Migne, *P.L.*, LXXXIX, col. 599, and the Martyrologium of Notker Balbulus, ibid., CXXXI, col. 1099, for the martyrs who died along with St. Boniface.

[47] Cf. Guerra and Guidi, p. 194.
[48] Cf. Lami, *Mon. Eccl. Florent.*, III, p. 587.
[49] Cf. Davidsohn, *Storia di Firenze*, p. 103.
[50] *Italia Pont.*, III, p. 346.

in Pisa, which in 1077 passed into the hands of the Camaldolese, having been granted by Binia, a widowed lady, to
the blessed Rudolph, fourth prior of the hermitage of Camaldoli and the compiler of the first Constitutions (1080) of
those hermits.[51]

Part of the commune of Cascina in the province of Pisa
is called S. Frediano a Settimo.

A locality S. Frediano is marked on the Italian Touring
Club map (Sheet 22, A. 1), north of St. Ermo, between Bagni
di Casciana and Fauglia, and some houses, 'Case S. Frediano'
(Sheet 22, D. 2), are shown north of the halt at Vignale,
between Campiglia and Follonica.

Guidicini[52] mentions a church of St. Fridian in Bologna,
outside the Porta S. Mamolo; it would seem to have belonged once upon a time to the convent of the Brethren of
Penance of Jesus Christ, also called 'del Sacco,' and later to
have passed into the hands of the Canons of St. Fridian of
Lucca.

§ 10

An excellent idea of the still-living devotion to St. Fridian
all over Tuscany may be gained from the number of parishes
still dedicated to him. There are twenty-three, as follows:

(a) Eleven in the diocese of Lucca; Aramo in the
commune of Pescia (formerly Villabasilica), Arsina in the
commune of Lucca, Chifenti in the commune of Borgo a
Mozzano, Compignano in the commune of Massarosa,
Crasciana in the commune of Bagni di Lucca (where the
dedication is to SS. James and Fridian), Deccio in the
commune of Lucca, Lunata in the commune of Capannori, Montefegatesi in the commune of Bagni di Lucca,
Piazzano in the commune of Lucca, Valgiano in the
commune of Capannori, St. Fridian in Lucca;

(b) two in the diocese of S. Miniato: Camugliano in the
commune of Ponsacco, and Forcoli in the commune of
Palaja;

---

[51] Cf. Lugano, *Italia Benedettina*, p. 236, and Lubin, *Abb. It. br. not.*, p. 150.
[52] *Cose notabili della Città di Bologna*, III, pp. 88-9.

(c) two in the diocese of Pistoia, Burgianico in the commune of Pistoia, and Pavana in the commune of Sambuca Pistoiese;

(d) Four in the diocese of Pisa: St. Fridian in Pisa, St. Fridian at Settimo in the commune of Cascina, Sommocolonia in the commune of Barga, and Vecchiano in the commune of Vecchiano;

(e) two in the diocese of Florence: St. Fridian in Florence and Nebbiano in the commune of Montespertoli;

(f) one in the diocese of Volterra: Montignoso in the commune of Montajone; and

(g) one in the diocese of Massa Carrara: Sassi in the commune of Molazzana.

Only three or four of these names are to be found in the list of the twenty-eight parishes founded by St. Fridian and dedicated by him naturally to other saints: on the other hand, it is noticeable that some of these twenty-eight parishes were also centres of devotion to S. Pellegrino, just as in the diocese of Chiavari we have seen many cases of the cult of St. Columban combined with that of S. Pellegrino.

§ 11

"There are many other churches dedicated to St. Fridian," says Fanucchi, "which have existed in our diocese [sc. Lucca] from immemorial antiquity, and in other dioceses also, such as those of Pescia, Pistoia, Volterra, S. Miniato and others too numerous to mention. The name of St. Fridian was invoked in the Litanies used in the churches of Florence, Siena, and Lucca in the eleventh and twelfth centuries, to say nothing of the office and proper Mass once celebrated and described in various codices and rituals of different dioceses. The Roman Martyrology refers to St. Fridian on 18th March in the following terms: "Lucae in Tuscia natalis S. Frigiani Episcopi virtute miraculorum illustris cujus festivitas XIV Kalendas decembris, quando ejus corpus translatum fuit, recolitur." And the very ancient Martyrology published by Fiorentini mentions our saint on 18th November as follows:

"In Tusciae Luca civitate, depositio [i.e., as Fiorentini himself observes, *translatio*] S. Fridiani Episcopi." He describes him as "in aquis Thaumaturgum."

I would add that Fanucchi declares there is a Church of St. Fridian in Sartene in the island of Corsica, where devotion to our saint is apparently widespread.

The powerful personality of this most active and holy bishop—a true brother of Ursus and Columban—has undoubtedly made a profound impression on the ecclesiastical history of the Tuscan countryside, and constitutes one of the most unsullied glories of the Irish expansion.

CHAPTER XVIII

ST. SILAUS OF LUCCA

§ I

SILAUS, Sillan or Sillao (in Italian), was born in Ireland, naturally "of royal blood,"[1] and, after receiving, together with his sister Hermengarda, Mingarda or Mionghar, a Christian education, embraced the ecclesiastical career and became a priest; then seized with a desire for greater perfection, he distributed his substance among the poor, retired into a monastery called after St. Brendan and shortly afterwards became its abbot. An important episcopal see in Ireland falling vacant—the legend does not specify which—Silaus was elected bishop by clergy and people; but he refused to accept until he had travelled to Rome and laid the case before Gregory VII,[2] who consecrated him with his own hands. Shortly after her brother's return Hermengarda also went off on a pious pilgrimage to Rome. She stopped on the way at Lucca, where a sprig of nobility, a certain Suffred, a widower with one son, fell in love with her, and waylaying her on her way back from Rome, carried her off and imprisoned her in his castle at Chiatri. The consuls of Lucca laid seige to the castle with the intent to punish a course of

---

[1] The constant exalted lineage of the hagiographers' hero is, considering the date of composition of the Irish *Vitae Sanctorum*, susceptible of three strands of explanation: (a) the aristocratic sentiment of the people and the consequent importance they attach to pedigree. Ciaran, e.g., was admonished not to quarrel with the great Colum-cille, because whereas all that Ciaran had given up for God were the tools of his father's trade, his father having been merely a humble wright or carpenter, Colum-cille had given up the kingship of Ireland; (b) the fact that the great Frankish bishops, who exercised such immense power, had in nearly every case been important officials at Court, *nutriti regis*, before their episcopal appointment by the king; and (c) the natural desire of the disciple to make out the best case he can for his master in order to distinguish him from the common herd.

[2] The name 'Gregory' in Irish hagiography is a stock name for the Pope, and its retention by the Italian twelfth century composer of the *n*th redaction of the fabulous 'Life' of St. Sillan would suggest that the prototype had some core of substance in an Irish tradition.

conduct which disgraced the whole city, and a bitter civil
war ensued: but the lady, being of a peace-loving disposition,
ultimately condescended to marry her ardent wooer, Suffred.
She lived with him for nine years without children, and then
retired from the world, with his consent, to the Convent of
S. Giustina, where she ended her days. All this time Silaus
in Ireland, while seeking to discharge the duties of his episcopal office, was the victim of the most abominable impositions at the hands of the civil authorities, and, every other
expedient having failed, was driven in the end to have
recourse to Rome for assistance and advice. At Lucca he
learned from Suffred the news of his sister's death. On his
way back he stopped in his brother-in-law's palace again,
but on this occasion he fell ill, and, feeling that the hand of
death was upon him, preferred to end his days in a poor cell
rather than in a sumptuous apartment; so he had himself
carried to a little room above the sacristy in the Convent of
St. Giustina, and there on 21st May, about the year 1100,
when the Sunday after the Octave of the Ascension falls on
that date, Silaus breathed his last.

§ 2

The earliest twelfth century text of this part of the legend[3]
has tacked on to it another part, absolutely contradictory,
which brings us back to the fifth century and makes St.
Silaus a disciple of St. Patrick.

The second part must, in the opinion of the Bollandists
themselves, be regarded as absolutely spurious, while the
first part is not to be accepted without very considerable
reserve. The historians of Lucca are unanimous in assigning
Hermengarda and Silaus to the eleventh century.[4] As to
the exact date of his death, the Bollandists,[5] founding on the

---

[3] Cf. the Bollandist *AA. SS.*, May, V, 21 May, and *B.H.L.*, II, 1118; O'Hanlon,
Lives of the Irish Saints, V, 528; Stokes, *Six months in the Apennines*, pp. 97 et seq.;
F. M. Fiorentini, *Vita di S. Silao*, Lucca, Paci, 1662; R. Salvetti, *Vita di S.
Silao*, Lucca, Landi, 1903; and G. Bindoli, *Brevi notizie sul paese di Chiatri*,
Lucca, Landi, 1902.

[4] Cf. Salvetti, op. cit., pp. 15 et seq.; Guerra-Guidi, *Comp. di storia eccl. lucchese*,
p. 202.

[5] Cf. *AA. SS.*, vol. cit., pp. 62-68.

circumstance mentioned in the legend of the coincidence between 21st May and the Sunday within the Octave of the Ascension, place it either in 1094 or in 1105; there is nothing to choose between the two dates.[6]

§ 3

The cult of St. Silaus is closely bound up with the history of the monastery of S. Giustina which Salvetti sets out in detail.[7] This monastery was founded in the eighth century by Duke Allo in honour "Domini et Salvatoris"; from the eighth down to and throughout the tenth century it appears in documents with the single name of S. Salvatore. About the middle of the eleventh century the added title of S. Giustina appears, at first together with the preceding S. Salvatore, but in succeeding centuries always alone. The abbess enjoyed as early as the tenth century the right to carry the pastoral staff at such solemn functions as clothings, professions and giving the nuns the sacred veil,[8] and to wear the imperial mantle tipped with ermine.

St. Silaus performed so many prodigies that offerings poured into the Church of S. Giustina. Suffred under specious pretexts laid claim to a share, and the nuns, in order not to antagonise so powerful a personage, were compelled to allow him a third of the takings. This graceless bargain was no sooner concluded than the miracles ceased, devotion cooled in consequence, and the memory of the exact spot in which the sacred body lay gradually faded from the minds of the community. Eighty years later the nuns, proceeding to investigate, on 3rd December, 1180,[9] discovered the coffin intact with the following inscription: "Divi Sylai corpus qui in Hibernia episcopus fuit summa veneratione hoc sepulcro conditum ob praecipua miracula religiosissime custoditur." A surviving nephew of Suffred, one Lothair, renounced whatever rights he might have had, the fame of the saint shone forth as resplendent as ever, and

[6] Cf. Salvetti, p. 55.
[7] pp. 56-83; cf. also Guerra-Guidi, op. cit., p. 92.
[8] Cf. Salvetti, p. 78.
[9] Cf., as to the date, Salvetti, p. 91.

Lucius III, a Lucchese Pope, passing through his native city in 1183, authorised the cult of St. Silaus.[10]

In the sixteenth century the nuns placed upon the sarcophagus a recumbent figure of the saint sculped in marble, an estimable work of the school of Civitali, now to be seen in the Picture Gallery on the first floor of the Palazzo Publico at Lucca.

In 1662 the remains of St. Silaus were recomposed and redressed by Dr. Girolamo Cremona.

When the Napoleonic decrees suppressing their convent and others were issued in 1806, the nuns of S. Giustina together with the 'Gesuate' of St. Joseph were compelled to transfer to the monastery of S. Ponziano, whither the body of St. Silaus also was transported on 31st August, 1808.

The famous original monastery of S. Giustina was demolished only a few years ago to make room for new wings of the civic hospital, and nothing now remains to commemorate it but the name of the street which formerly lea up to it and now leads up to the hospital.

After the decree of 1811, which ordered the closing of all monasteries within two months from the date of promulgation, St. Silaus was removed from S. Ponziano in April of that year to a chapel specially prepared for the purpose in his Palazzo by the Marquis G. Sardini, the brother of the abbess.

After the fall of Napoleon, in 1817, the sacred body unexpectedly returned to public devotion in the parish church of S. Maria Corte-Orlandini: but once the nuns of S. Giustina had reconstituted their community and obtained from Pope Pius VII the former Servite monastery with the adjoining Church of S. Lorenzo ai Servi, the sarcophagus containing the remains of the saint was transferred, on 12th May, 1825, to that church and placed under the high altar.

When the Benedictine community of S. Giustina was being reconstituted, five nuns broke away and, instead of going to S. Lorenzo ai Servi, founded the convent of the reformed Benedictines at la Zecca.

The nuns of S. Giustina remained at S. Lorenzo with the

[10] Cf. Guerra and Guidi, p. 202.

body of St. Silaus down to 26th July, 1912, when, their number having fallen below the six prescribed by law, they were forced to leave their convent to the municipality of Lucca which turned it into an old men's home in charge of the Sisters of Charity. The nuns of S. Giustina then withdrew to the monastery of the Capucine Mothers and remained there until 5th August, 1915, when they succeeded in securing the Monastery of S. Scolastica at Buggiano Alto in the diocese of Pescia, which formerly belonged to the Franciscans.

When the nuns quitted the Servite Convent, the body of St. Silaus was provisionally placed with the reformed Benedictines at la Zecca in a room behind the high altar, and there it still remains, or did in November, 1931.

§ 4

As for the cult of the saint, Salvetti writes as follows: "The holy bishop did not receive the veneration of the faithful only in the Church of S. Giustina, but he was invoked as a saint also in public processions from the cathedral. He had an office to himself printed at Lucca in 1527, which used to be recited on the day of his feast, until its continued use was suspended by a general decree of the Holy See. His feast, as already mentioned, was inserted in the Diocesan Calendar on 21st May in red letters, as other feast-days also were printed. In bygone ages, Fiorentini observes, St. Silaus was also publicly invoked in the processions held on rogation days, as may be seen from a manuscript *rituale* preserved in the sacristy of the cathedral and entitled 'Ordo litaniarum . . .' So also in a missal, 'secundum consuetudinem sanctae Romanae Ecclesiae,' printed in Lucca in 1561, a fragment of which is preserved in the State Archives owing to the rarity of the edition, St. Silaus is invoked in the litanies which used to be recited after the blessing of the font, next after SS. Fridian and Theodore."

CHAPTER XIX

ST. DONATUS OF FIESOLE

§ 1

HE has already been encountered twice in passing: once as
the donor of the church of St. Brigit in Piacenza to the
Bobbio monastery, and again as the alleged relative of St.
Fulco Scotti. The time has now come to exhibit in clear light
the real features of this Irish bishop, who occupied the see of
Fiesole for nearly half a century, from 829 to 876, amid all
the difficulties peculiar to the Carolingian epoch, and left
behind him a great reputation, both as a statesman and a
man of letters. Donatus, unlike Ursus, Fridian and Columban, was not confronted with the task of converting Arians,
but he was confronted with the duty of defending the property
of his church from many assaults.

In the welter of corruption and anarchy in which the
successors of Charlemagne carried on their domestic feuds,
the episcopal office was as difficult as it was insecure. It may
be sufficient to recall the fate which, but a few years earlier,
befell Alexander, another Bishop of Fiesole. This prelate
had gone to Pavia in 823 to prefer a complaint at the court of
Lothair against certain feudal barons who had seized some
of the property of the bishopric. There he had been successful
in securing not only confirmation of the property in question,
but other concessions also of importance for the future
fortunes of the see and its relations with Florence, to wit, the
citadel of Fiesole, the impregnable stronghold of Etruscan
times, the possession of which made the bishops lords of the
district, and the fortified castle of Monteloro dominating the
Val di Sieci, some three or four miles away.[1] The news of the
bishop's diplomatic triumph was so far from pleasing to the

[1] Cf. Davidsohn, *Forschungen zur älteren Gesch. von Florenz*, Berlin, Mittler,
1896, pp. 26 et seq., *Die Bischöfe Alexander und Donatus von Fiesole*, and
Davidsohn, *Storia di Firenze*, Florence, Sansoni, p. 119.

feudal barons when it reached their ears, that a number of them hastened to go and meet him on the pretext of doing him honour and as a demonstration of loyalty, but with the secret intention of seizing a favourable opportunity to put him out of the way.

As it happened, while they were crossing the Reno near Bologna, the barons pounced on the unfortunate bishop and drowned him. They escaped scot free, and the bishop was buried in Fiesole in the church, now named after him, but which then stood within the strong walls of the fortress. But not even in the tomb was he allowed to rest, and his grave was despoiled by marauders.[2]

The task facing Donatus, difficult enough on account of the internal circumstances of administration mentioned, was rendered doubly difficult by events outside. In the ninth century the civil life of the peninsula, Tuscany included, was continually exposed to the danger of two formidable menaces from the sea: the Saracens and the Northmen. The menace of the Northmen had taken concrete shape in 825 in a lightning and terrifying raid which caused particular damage to the church in Fiesole. The cathedral of Fiesole, it should be remembered, stood in the ninth century outside the fortified walls of the city, according to the custom of the time, in the open country below, more particularly, on the present site of the Badia Fiesolana (dedicated to St. Bartholomew), not far from S. Domenico.[3] In 825 the Northmen had suddenly sailed up the Arno in their lightly handled craft beyond the city of Florence, and, disembarking, spread fire and slaughter over the countryside below Fiesole. While the panic-stricken population sought safety within the stout walls of the city, the episcopal palace at Fiesole was sacked from floor to ceiling by the Northern pirates. The loss of the documents in his archives aggravated the difficulties of the bishop in the defence of his legitimate interests: "Tempore

[2] Cf. *AA. SS.*, 1 June, 749 et seq.

[3] It was not until 1028 that Jacopo Bavaro (James the Bavarian), Bishop of Fiesole, after a fresh outbreak of those acts of hostility on the part of the Florentines (cf. Davidsohn, *Storia di Firenze*, p. 195) which were destined to lead about a century later to the destruction of the city (1125), built the present cathedral on the top of the hill. Cf. also: V. Viti, *La Badia Fiesolana, Pagine di storia e arte*, Florence, Tip. Giuntina, 1926.

. . . illo," says the "Vita S. Donati,"[4] "contra praedictam Fesulensem ecclesiam in rebus facultatibusque suis multae olim factae fuerant invasiones per praecepta imperatorum et chartularum amissionem, quae ob devastationem crude-lissimae gentis Normannorum acciderat. Unde aliquantis ecclesia solimata fuerat, et pro huiusmodi facultatibus redimendis multum angebatur."

Besides the political activity which Donatus, as a bishop and feudal dignitary of the empire, was forced to display and in such peculiarly trying circumstances did display, the activity which he manifested as a man of letters, and as a characteristically Irish man of letters, was of no less impor-tance. Lothair, alarmed at the general decline of culture, had, as already mentioned, promulgated in 825 the famous edict establishing a school in each of nine Italian cities for young men anxious to embrace the ecclesiastical career. Dungal, the Irishman from St. Denis, had been invited to take charge of the school in Pavia. In Tuscany, the city chosen for the new seat of learning was Florence. There is no direct proof, but many indications including, and not least, the closing lines of his epitaph, tend to show that Donatus must have been *pars magna* of that school and have succeeded in introducing there the entirely Irish love of the classical culture. "He knew and he taught the knowledge of Virgil," says Davidsohn,[5] " . . . In the lines which he prefixed to the biography of St. Brigit, his compatriot, he mentions Democritus and Hesiod; and his poetical works after the lapse of several centuries were still held in great esteem; the busy zeal, as a teacher, of this Irish bishop must have had a considerable influence, even if only indirectly, on many later manifestations of intellectual life."

The Bollandists[6] print the *Vita Sancti Donati episcopi, Christi familiaris, ex MS. Minervae, Plut.* XXVII (in the Lau-rentiana at Florence), *collato cum MS. Chronicae Fesulanae et altero MS. Card. Strozzi* (Cod. Strozzianus II). A text had previously been published by Ozanam,[7] who strenuously

---

[4] Cf. *AA. SS.*, October, IX, p. 657.   [5] Cf. *Storia di Firenze*, p. 122.

[6] Cf. *AA. SS.*, October, IX, for the 22 October, pp. 648 et seq.

[7] Cf. *Documents inédits pour servir à l'histoire littéraire de l'Italie depuis le VIIIeme siècle jusqu'au XIIIeme*, Paris, Lecoffre, 1850.

endeavoured to draw attention to the saint's merits as head
of a school. Miss Stokes[8] deals with him at some length but,
as usual, in no very critical spirit. G. Tononi[9] gives some
precise biographical particulars, while some other items of
information may be gleaned from the 'Vita S. Andreae,'
his archdeacon, who will presently engage our attention.

§ 2

Donatus was born in the closing years of the eighth or
early in the ninth century and must have received a sound
education in one of the best schools of his native island.
Inis-Celtra, 'Church Island,' in Lough Derg, has been mentioned, and there, it is said, he may have taught and made the
acquaintance, perhaps, of his pupil Andrew, who afterwards
became his faithful follower and never left him until death.
Donatus and Andrew set off one day to make the journey
to Italy, determined to see all the holy places and to visit
the tombs of martyrs, monasteries and hermitages. On their
way through Fiesole, they were accosted by a multitude of
the faithful mysteriously assembled in front of the church
and on tip-toe with a no less mysterious suspense. The
see happened to be vacant at the time, and the crowd,
scarcely taking time to ask the two strangers their names,
suddenly chose Donatus to be their bishop. Protest was
unavailing: "Christus eum adduxit ex occiduis; eligamus nos
in Fesulis. Et ecce nunc Domino dignum a Christo demon-
stratum, a Domino Donatum; ad sedem nunc perducatur,
ut nobis a Domino datus sit pater Donatus; si est voluntas
resistendi, fiat vis eligendi."[10]

8 Cf. *Six Months in the Apennines*, pp. 227 et seq. and the appendices.
9 Cf. *S. Donato e la Chiesa di S. Brigida*, Strenna Piacentina, 1891.
10 Cf. *AA. SS.*, pp. 656-7. It would be an error to regard this anecdote as
other than a slight exaggeration of actual fact. The story of Ambrose, who,
in his own words, was "raptus a tribunalibus ad sacerdotium" (*De Officiis*,
i, iv) and acclaimed to the see of Milan through the voice of a child, is familiar
to everyone. Gregory of Tours tells a somewhat similar tale of the election
to the see of Auvergne. Venerandus, the bishop, had died, and the other
bishops of the province had assembled in the city on a Sunday, but waited
for the populace to give them a lead. The populace was divided, there was
a number of candidates and the bishops were afraid to make a decision.
"Subito Rusticus advenit [an obscure priest]. Quo viso, mulier ait: En ipsum

The public life of Donatus began with this election which dates back to 829. Only five fragmentary pieces of information have survived with reference to the forty-seven years of his episcopate ("octonis lustris septenis insuper annis"), but, such as they are, they show him in constant accord with the various sovereigns of Italy, and confirm the exactness of the verses in his epitaph:

> "Regibus Italicis servivi pluribus annis,
> Lothario magno, Ludovicoque bono."

In 840 or thereabouts Donatus is found, along with many other Italian bishops, and certainly at the head of his own vassals, taking an active part in the military expedition which Lothair had entrusted to the command of his son Louis.[11]

A little later, in 844, Donatus was in Rome with the Bishop of Florence, a guest at the coronation of Louis as King of the Lombards by the hands of Sergius II,[12] and they sat together on the bench, along with the Pope and the Emperor, to hear a long-standing dispute between the bishops of Arezzo and Siena, which on this occasion was decided in favour of Siena.

In 862 he attended the Council of Rome which Pope Nicholas I had convened against John, the Archbishop of Ravenna.

In 866 he had taken the field again at the head of his vassals to support Louis II in the campaign which the latter, after the death of Lothair, had launched against the Saracens

---

quem elegit Dominus: hic ordinetur episcopus. Omnis populus clamavit dignum ac justum esse. Qui in cathedra positus pontificatus honorem populo gaudente suscepit." *Hist. Franc.*, II, 13.

[11] Cf. Davidsohn, p. 123.

[12] "Almificus pontifex manibus suis Ludovicum, Lotharii imperatoris filium, oleo sancto perungens, regali et pretiosissima coronavit corona regemque Longobardis praefecit." Masses were then celebrated, and the prelates "omnes cum rege laetantes regressi sunt." Last on the list, "Donatus episcopus Ecclesiae Fesolane et caeteri." Anastasii Bibliothecarii *Historia de vitis Rom. Pont.*—*Sergius II*, in Migne, *P.L.*, CXXVIII, col. 1298, 486, and cf. Duchesne's edition, *Liber Pontificalis*, II, 90.—*Quo anno* (i.e., 846), say the *Ann. S. Germani minores* (M.G.H., SS., III, 2): "Saraceni basilicam sancti Petri et Pauli vastaverunt," and carried off the altar above the tomb of the apostle. The invaders were repulsed beside the basilica of St. Paul *fuori le mura* and took to their ships again. For the importance of this incident in the composition of the *chanson de geste* Fierabras, or rather its parent Balan, cf. M. Bédier's *Les Légendes épiques*, Paris, second edition, 1927, II, pp. 256-265.

in south Italy. Under the walls of Capua, Donatus, who had already taken the precaution of having reconfirmed to himself the old concessions which had cost his predecessor Alexander his life, succeeded in having his episcopal territories raised to the status of immunity and so not only made himself independent of the royal officials, but also acquired the rights to impose his own taxes and to hold his own courts.[13]

In 876, early in February, before Piacenza, Donatus received from Charles the Bald, to whom he had gone to pay his respects, confirmation of the above-mentioned immunities. He does not seem to have been present at the synod of Pavia which nominated Charles the Bald King of Italy.

In addition to these five incidents of his public career, we may recall the grant, made on 20th August, 850,[14] of the church of St. Brigit in Piacenza to the monastery at Bobbio. The text of the deed of donation is interesting on account of the Irish spirit pervading it, the devotion manifest to S. Brigit, the affection displayed for the blessed Columban and his monks, the charity shown towards pilgrims from his own country and, not least, the generosity with which St. Donatus endowed his own pious foundation in Piacenza. No less characteristically Irish was the encouragement he gave St. Andrew, his archdeacon, to restore the Church of St. Martin at Mensola.

The death of Donatus certainly took place on 22nd October 876, because in 877 a certain Zenobius is found mentioned as bishop.

§ 3

He is credited with having performed a number of miracles in the course of his life. He snatched a baby from the jaws of a wolf, he converted a plunderer of church property, he turned a mountain into a barren wilderness and then made it fertile again through his prayers, he himself recovered from a disease of the feet through a few drops of oil let fall from

---

[13] Cf. Davidsohn, pp. 127 et seq. and p. 540.
[14] Cf. Chapter VIII, § 5, and Tononi, op. cit.

her lamp by St. Brigit during an apparition; he traversed a violent storm of rain without getting wet. . . . The following miracle also is related as having taken place after his death: Drops of rain kept falling one night through leaks in the roof pitter-patter on the stone urn containing his body. Donatus appeared to a clerk and besought him with insistence to remove the stillicide; he besought him a second time, but the obdurate clerk refused to budge; the third time "apparuit et inter verba addidit et verbera." The clerk then "surrexit et paruit: verba annunciavit et vulnera declaravit."

§ 4

Of the literary activity of Donatus three specimens have survived in the 'Vita Donati' published by the Bollandists, who quote Lanigan's observation on Dempster[15]: "consueta sua impudentia effinxit titulos operum quae a sancto viro composita somniaverat. Confer Biographiam universalem"[16] —the Bollandists add—"ubi nihilo mitius vapulat Dempsterus, et quidem jure merito." The three specimens are: (i) a metrical *Credo*, said to have been recited among his friends and disciples shortly before his death; (ii) an epitaph dictated by him for his own headstone; and (iii) a well known description in verse of Ireland.

The *Credo* runs as follows:

1. Christe Dei virtus, splendor, sapientia Patris,
   in genitore manens genitus sine tempore, et ante
   saecula, qui nostram natus de Virgine formam
   sumpsit; nutritus, lactatus ab ubere matris;

[15] The Bollandists are careless. Lanigan's observation (*An Ecclesiastical History of Ireland*, III, p. 281) that "Dempster with his usual effrontery has forged the name of certain tracts as if written by this saint (Cf. *Ware and Harris* at *Andrew)*" refers to St. Andrew of Fiesole. As to Dempster and St. Donatus, Lanigan merely remarks (III, p. 283) that "Dempster has made up some tracts for him which are mentioned by Ware (*Writers* at *Donat*) merely on his authority: yet it is certain that he composed some works."

[16] The *Nouvelle biographie générale*, Paris, 1854, quotes (Vol. XIII, p. 627) the judgment on Dempster of Baillet (1649-1706): "Quoique Dempster fut habile d'ailleurs, il n'en avait ni le sens plus droit, ni le jugement plus solide, ni la conscience meilleure. Il eût voulu que tous les savants fussent Ecossais; il a forgé des titres de livres qui n'ont jamais été mis au monde pour relever la gloire de sa patrie, et il a commis diverses autres fourberies qui l'ont décrié parmi les gens de lettres."

5. qui sancto nostras mundans baptismate culpas,
  nunc nova progenies coelo deducitur alto;
  noxia qui vetiti dissolvit prandia ligni,
  vulnera quique suo curavit sanguine nostra,
  qui moriendo dedid vitam, nos morte redemit;
10. cumque sepultus erat, mutavit jura sepulchri,
  surgens a morte, et mortem damnavit acerbam;
  Tartara qui quodam, qui nigri limina Ditis
  destruxit, scatebras superans acherontis avari,
  qui hostem nigrum tortorem detorsit in imo;
15. ascendit; duxit captivum dextera Patris;
  laudant virtutes victorem millia mille.
  Tu quoque, qui tantas pro nobis sumere poenas
  dignatus, miseris coelestia regna dedisti;
  da mihi praecelsas paradisi scandere scalas;
20. fac bene pulsanti portas mihi pandere vitae.
  Non mihi perveniat tumidus, non hostis avarus,
  nec me externa manus tangat, nec praemia tollat;
  sed me, Christe, tuum miserum nunc suscipe servum,
  ut merear pavidus convivas visere claros,
25. qui tecum gaudent, videam convivia Sancti,
  qui cum Patre manes regnans per saecula semper.
  Spiritus et Sanctus. Numero Deus impare gaudet.

The sixth verse of this *Credo* is notable for the palpable echo of lines 5-7 in Virgil's famous IVth Eclogue, remarked by Ozanam and also by Comparetti.[17] Dante, as all the world knows, "paid the Eclogue of the Mantuan poet the honour of predicting exactly not only the coming of Christ, but also of converting to Christianity some of the choice wits of imperial Rome.

> "Quando dicesti: Secol si rinnova,
>   torna giustizia e primo tempo umano,
>   e progenïe scende dal ciel nuova,
>   per te poeta fui, per te cristiano."[18]

               (*Purg.* XXII, 70-3).

[17] Cf. *Virgilio nel medio evo*, 2 vols., Leghorn, Vigo, 1872, I, 137, and a very recent study of the question: "Il Messianismo ebraico e la IV Egloga di Virgilio," in *Civiltà Cattolica*, 4th and 8th April, 1931.

[18] "When thou saidst 'The ages are renewed: Justice returns, and the primeval time of man, and a new progeny descends from Heaven.' Through

The epitaph dictated by St. Donatus for his headstone runs as follows:

"Hic ego Donatus, Scotorum sanguine cretus,
solus in hoc tumulo, pulvere, verme, voror.
Regibus Italicis servivi pluribus annis,
Lothario magno, Ludovicoque bono,
Octenis lustris septenis insuper annis,
post Fesulana praesul in urbe fui.
Grammata discipulis dictabam scripta libellis;
schemmata metrorum, dicta beata senum.
Posco, viator, adis quisquis pro munere Christi,
te, modo, non pigeat cernere busta mea,
atque precare Deum, regit qui culmina caeli,
ut mihi concedat regna beata sua."

It is notable for the biographical and chronological particulars which it contains and, more particularly, for its reference to his activity as a teacher.

The description of Ireland runs as follows:

"Finibus occiduis describitur optima tellus,
nomine et antiquis Scotia scripta libris.
Dives opum, argenti, gemmarum, vestis et auri;
commoda terrigenis corporibus aere, putre, solo.
Melle fluit pulchris et lacte Scotia campis,
vestibus atque armis, frugibus, arte, viris.
Ursorum rabies nulla est ibi, saeva leonum
semina nec unquam Scottica terra tulit;
nulla venena nocent, nec serpens serpit in herba,
nec conquesta canit garrula rana lacu,
in qua Scotorum gentes habitare merentur,
inclita gens hominum, milite, pace, fide."

Both the *Credo* and the description of Ireland belong to a metrical *Vita Brigidae* composed by St. Donatus, who, as already mentioned in Chapter VIII, § 5, was greatly devoted

thee I became a poet, through thee a Christian." Charles Eliot Norton's translation. London, 1891, p. 142.

to the saintly patron of Ireland. Mr. Mario Esposito[19] gives a list of the MSS. of this metrical life, but, owing to the lack of a sufficiently critical text, has deferred consideration of it until later. It begins as follows:

> "Has ego Donatus virtutes sanguine Scottus
> Bricte descripsi presul et exiguus
> Virginis indocto carptim sermone repertas
> pangere presumpsi carmine dactilico . . ."

and after twenty-eight such verses continues in hexameters.

The whole composition is dedicated to one described by the author as 'magne poeta' and 'sancte pater doctissime.'

In addition to this metrical *Vita*, Donatus has left a prose 'Life of St. Brigit' contained in a MS. of the *Biblioteca Casanatense* 726 of the eleventh or twelfth century, and prefaced by the following introduction in elegiac verses: "Incipit Prologus Sancti Donati Episcopi in Vita Sancte Brigide."

> "Presul ego dictus Donatus sanguine Scottus
> Virtutes scripsi virginis eximie
> Quas primus inculto didici sermone notatas
> Has ego disposui pandere lucidius. . . ."

Mr. Esposito suggests that Donatus composed his new Life in prose because he was dissatisfied in later life with his earlier metrical *Vita*, which "in fact betrays numerous signs of hasty and careless compilation." The metrical *Vita*, in his opinion, is dedicated to Dungal (cf. Chapter III, § 4) as was presumably another poem published by Karl Strecker,[20] and entitled probably, because the title has been partially effaced, "[Versus Donati] Praesulis Dungalo Abbati." Mr. Esposito attributes this latter poem to Donatus for the following reasons: that it contains a number of verses taken almost literally from the metrical *Vita*, that the author refers to himself therein as *Praesul*, as Donatus does in the two prologues above mentioned, and that the addressee is

---

[19] Cf. "The poems of Colmanus, 'nepos Cracavist' and Dungalus, 'praecipuus Scottorum,' " in the *Journal of Theological Studies*, Vol. XXXIII, January 1932, p. 129.

[20] Cf. *Zeitschrift für romanische Philologie*, 1921, pp. 566-573.

described in verse 5 as "illustris magister," a compliment reminiscent of the previous invocations to the addressee of the metrical *Vita*. These very possible relations between Donatus and Dungal, who may well have been at Bobbio when the verses were sent to him, deserve serious consideration, and the further studies which Mr. Esposito has promised on the literary productions of Donatus as a whole are eagerly looked forward to.

Ozanam drew attention to a number of Greek expressions in the *Vita Donati*: e.g., in the tale of the miracle of the wolf there is an invocation "Theologo et Pneumati" (to the Word, θεοῦ λόγος, and to the Holy Ghost, πνεῦμα), followed a little later by the words "multa mox in *doxa* Patris cecinit populus." His conclusion was that there was some knowledge of Greek in Fiesole in the ninth century, that the language was held in high estimation as the language of the New Testament and the Greek Fathers and was readily quoted as imparting a flavour of mystery and an air of solemnity to the discourse.

§ 5

St. Donatus was buried in the cathedral which, as has been said, stood upon the site of the present Badia Fiesolana, and there his remains lay even when after the church had been deprived of its status of cathedral in the eleventh century there were erected in its proximity, first a Benedictine abbey and, later, in the fifteenth century, a monastery of Lateran canons, surnamed Rocchetines, who were on the friendliest terms with the Medici. This monastery was suppressed in 1778.

The Bishop of Fiesole, Ranieri Mancini, conceived the project, in spite of the distresses of the Napoleonic era, of removing the sacred remains (which he had had regularly examined in 1810), so that they should lie beside the remains of the other great bishops of Fiesole in the new cathedral, and with this intention had an altar erected there and dedicated to St. Donatus in the last chapel on the right behind the high altar. The transference of the remains took place on St. Peter's Day, in 1817, but by that time the bishop was dead.[21]

The tombstone bearing the inscription dictated by St. Donatus himself has been lost.

The head of the saint, enclosed in an interesting bust of gilt bronze representing St. Donatus, a valuable specimen of metal work in the material executed in 1546 by a Maestro Niccolo Guascone, is now in the possession of an ancient Confraternity of St. Donatus of Scotland which had its headquarters from the earliest times in the Badia Fiesolana. When the abbey was suppressed, the Confraternity moved to S. Domenico and in 1792 built itself a new oratory by the side of that church. The bust is preserved in the Oratory which still belongs to the Confraternity.

I have made enquiries,[22] but there appear to be no parishes dedicated to St. Donatus. There is, however, a benefice founded in the Cathedral of Fiesole and in the patronage of the Bocchi family of Florence for 104 ferial Masses.

[21] Cf. *AA. SS.*, p. 662 and Miss Stokes, op. cit., pp. 258 et seq.
[22] The information was kindly given me by Mgr. Luigi Turini, chancellor of the episcopal curia of Fiesole.

CHAPTER XX

§ I

ANDREW, born of noble parents in Ireland in the early years
of the ninth century, had the good fortune to meet in his
youth the Donatus who later became Bishop of Fiesole,
and became so attached to him by bonds of such lively
affection and sympathy that he never parted from him
again. When they decided to make together the pilgrimage
to Italy, great was Andrew's grief at having to leave his
sister Brigit behind.

The *Lives* of Andrew relate the arrival of the two pilgrims
at Fiesole and the election of Donatus as bishop in terms
very similar to those employed by the biographers of
Donatus. Andrew, it appears, was ordained priest by the
new bishop and carried out many confidential missions on
his behalf. One day a noble of Fiesole, whose daughter
was paralysed, asked Donatus to intercede with the Lord
for her cure. Donatus dispatched Andrew to the sick-bed,
and the envoy, after offering fervent prayers, made the
sign of the cross on the girl's forehead, with the result that
she miraculously recovered. The report of such a prodigy
increased the affection of the Fiesolani for the saintly
companion of Donatus. The latter appointed him archdeacon of the cathedral and made great use of him in
reducing the clergy and people to an exemplary manner of
life. One day, as the two prelates were taking a walk
together in the country round Settignano, they climbed
up a hill and came upon a little ruined church which had
once been dedicated to St. Martin of Tours. Donatus was
so afflicted at the spectacle of such dereliction that Andrew
forthwith suggested that he should devote himself to rebuilding the abandoned house of God, and with the per-

mission of Donatus, once the restoration was complete, proceeded to build a monastery beside the little church so that there should always be somebody to look after it: the better to attain his object he himself retired to live among the monks in his foundation.

Shortly after the death of Donatus in 876, Andrew himself fell ill. As he lay on his deathbed surrounded by his brethren, he felt a longing to see once again his sister Brigit whom he had left nearly ten lustres ago in his own country; and, lo! she, who was sitting quietly at home in Ireland, intent on a frugal repast of herbs and little fishes, suddenly found herself miraculously transported, table and all, to her brother's cell in St. Martin's at Mensola. The surprise was mutual, and the saintly archdeacon, having died happy in the gratification of his wish by Heaven, was buried in the centre of the church.

§ 2

Some time afterwards not a monk was left in the monastery, and it was handed over *c.* 1050 to a community of Benedictine nuns who had a house at St. Andrew's in the Mercato Vecchio at Florence. In 1285 they rediscovered the sacred body as follows: a girl "famosae pulchritudinis et praecipuae vanitatis"[1] having been buried in the church, the saint appeared one night to the nuns' chaplain and ordered him to remove his body some distance from the maiden's. The chaplain having failed to comply, the saint reappeared the following night and the chaplain persisting in his dis- obedience, reappeared on the third night "minari verbo primum, et asperrimo deinde flagello percussit." This miracle is conspicuously like that told of Donatus. (Ch. XIX, § 3.)

A search was then made for the sacred body which was deposited when found in a marble urn under the high altar, God taking advantage of the translation to work a number of miracles, including the instantaneous healing of a member of the Filicaja family. In the fifteenth century

[1] Cf. *AA. SS.*, August, IV, 539 et seq.

when St. Antonino was Archbishop of Florence, the nuns were transferred to other quarters, and St. Martin's at Mensola, restored at the expense of the Gherardi family, passed into the possession of the Benedictine monks of the Badia of Florence, who, when their monastery was suppressed in 1451 by Nicholas V, ceded a portion of the buildings to the parish priest and leased the remainder. In 1611 the saint was again translated to a new altar erected by the Abbot of the Badia, Dom Luca Bartolini da Buggiano, and consecrated by Mgr. Borghi, Bishop of Borgo S. Sepolcro.

A silver bust containing the head of the saint and presented to the nuns in 1380 by the Filicaja family was kept for safety in the Badia at Florence and exposed there above the high altar on 22nd August.

St. Andrew is mentioned in Vespucci's Florentine Martyrology under date the 22nd August: "XI Kalendas septembris Sancti Andreae diaconi et ministri Sancti Donati de Scotia episcopi fesulani cujus corpus honorifice sepultum est ecclesia S. Martini de Mensola, in territorio Florentino."

A venerable Guild of St. Andrew of Scotland dating from time immemorial still has its headquarters in the church of St. Martin of Mensola. According to the Bollandists, on the dissolution of the most ancient congregation, another was formed in 1473, with sections for men and women, on the initiative of the Badia in Florence, which also reorganised it in 1600.

§ 3

Some biographical details are to be found in the *Vita ed actioni del B. Andrea di Scotia*, etc., by Puccinelli, Benedictine Abbot of the Badia of Florence, Milan, 1645, and Florence, 1676. Brocchi[2] mentions an old Passionary, still preserved in the Capitular Archives of Fiesole and giving an account differing only in a few particulars from that given by Puccinelli.[3] Miss Stokes refers to St. Andrew on pp. 264

[2] *Vite dei Santi e Beati Fiorentini*, 1752, Part II, p. 120.
[3] Cf. in addition to the Bollandist reference already given, *B.H.L.*, I, 74, II, 314, and *Supplt.* 21.

et seq., of *Six Months in the Apennines, etc.*, and on p. 269 mentions a church of St. Martin supposed to have been built by Andrew in the via dei Magazzini in Florence in 786. [4]

[4] Cf. also Carocci, *I dintorni di Firenze*, 1907, I, pp. 54-6. In Vol. II, p. 114, the author writes: "Down the via Chiantigiana at the corner of the via del Paradiso there is a handsome Tabernacle or *maestà*, which retains its original fifteenth century structure almost unimpaired. Both inside and outside the building the remains of valuable fifteenth century frescoes may be seen. The frescoes within depict the Madonna enthroned with the Infant Jesus between St. Brigit and St. Andrew of Scotland; those without, badly faded through exposure to the elements, depict the Annunciation and two saints. The tabernacle was built by the nuns in the via del Paradiso against the wall of a property of theirs."

It is strange to find St. Andrew of Scotland venerated by the monastery of SS. Saviour and Brigit at Paradiso, founded in 1390 by Antonio degli Alberti for the new religious order created by St. Bridget of Sweden.

CHAPTER XXI

ST. BRIGIT AT OPACO

§ I

THE attractive figure of the solitary Irish woman saint whose bones rest under the Italian sky is already familiar to us through the Lives of Donatus and Andrew, to which the reader is referred.[1]

Nothing is known of her youth, except the fact that she loved her brother tenderly and that to part from him when he went to Italy with his master Donatus was a great sorrow to her. Some authorities allege that she became a nun in Ireland, but there is no certainty in the matter. We make her acquaintance only towards the end of her life, when, transported miraculously on the wings of an argel, she came to visit on his death-bed at St. Martin's in Mensola the brother who ardently desired to see her again. John Bolland, who wrote of this St. Brigit himself,[2] added:[3] "Probabilius est fortasse, quod idem tradit Lahierius, divinitus edoctam fratrem propediem migraturum e vita, illico ejus visendi studio profectam e patria, summaque usam celeritate, Faesulas tempori appulisse, ut morienti adesset." At all events, we do know that she brought this much consolation to her brother, and that, immediately after his death, she disappeared from St. Martin's at Mensola and went into retirement in a remote part of the Val di Sieci, where amid the slender grace of the cypress trees of Tuscany the ancient parish church of St. Martin at Opaco now stands. Some hagiographers, including Dempster, allege that she there founded a monastery appropriately dedicated to the Saint of Tours. But Bolland, criticising the inaccuracies and erroneous quotations of Dempster, *secum ipso pugnantis*, says: "Monasterii a S. Brigida conditi nulla usquam mentio."

[1] Cf. Chapters XIX and XX.
[2] In *AA. SS.*, February, I, pp. 243 et seq.
[3] Ibid., p. 247.

She removed thence, according to the legend, a few miles further away along the left bank of the valley which slopes gently down to the Arno, in order to live a still more secluded life of penance in a cave yet visible and still venerated, below the church of the hamlet which has taken her name: "Santa Brigida a Opaco." It is pleasant to think of that dear old woman come from distant Ireland to console her saintly brother and thereafter remaining in Italy to set an example of mortification, self-sacrifice, and ardent devotion, in the solitude of the Val di Sieci. There she passed away when almost a hundred years old, about the end of the ninth century on a 1st February, the anniversary of the death of the great patron of Ireland, the virgin of Cell-dara. She was buried where she died, and the church, erected there in her honour, is still called after her, although all search for the remains of her mortal coil has hitherto proved fruitless.

Miss Stokes, *Six Months in the Apennines*, reproduces on page 275 a photograph of the cave of St. Brigit, and on pp. 271 and 274 respectively, drawings of the two little churches of St. Martin at Opaco and St. Brigit at Opaco.

CHAPTER XXII

ST. CATHAL OF TARANTO

§ 1

No other Irish saint, perhaps, not even St. Columban, is the object of a cult so widespread over Italy as St. Cathal, venerated under the name of San Cataldo as a prodigious wonderworker throughout the country from Lombardy to Sicily. The historical figure of the man has until recently been wrapt in mist, but now, largely owing to the happy intuition of Mgr. G. Blandamura,[1] who realized the importance for the chronology of the saint of ascertaining, so far as might be, the approximate date of a little gold cross found in his sarcophagus in 1071, and the necessity no less of linking Tarantine tradition with the tradition of the Church in Ireland, which many Italian hagiographers in the past had completely neglected, some characteristic features may be discerned more or less clearly. Recent investigations into the rolls of Italian bishops in the early Middle Ages[2] enable the student to fill in to some extent the historical picture.[3]

§ 2

Cathal was born in Ireland, in Munster, early in the seventh century, at Canty perhaps (in the diocese of Water-

[1] *Un cimelio del secolo VII esistente nel Duomo di Taranto*, Lecce, Spacciante, 1917.
[2] Lanzoni, *Le diocesi d'Italia*.
[3] Cf. for the 'Legend of St. Cathal,' *AA. SS. Maii.* II, pp. 569 et seq.; Butler, *Lives of the Irish Saints*, IV, p. 610; O'Hanlon, *Lives of the Irish Saints*, V, p. 196; O'Riordan, *St. Cathal of Lismore*; Cassinelli, *Vita e memorie di S. Cataldo vescovo di Taranto*, Naples, Nosca, 1717; *Vita e Miracoli di S. Cataldo* (an Italian translation of the *Cataldiados*, six books of Latin hexameters composed in 1614 by Bonoventura Morone, and supplemented by the *Vita et Miracula S. Cataldi episcopi* of his brother Bartolomeo, Rome, 1614), Naples, Migliaccio, 1779. A recent Italian publication *Vita di S. Cataldo, Vescovo e protettore di Taranto*, by Don Andrea Martini, S.T.A.T., Taranto, 1932, is historically worthless. It assigns Cathal to the fifth century.

ford), some seven miles from Liss-mor.[4]   He learned his
elements and later taught in the famous monastery at
Liss-mor, which had been founded by St. Carthach (Mo-
Chuta), its first abbot, who died there in 637.   This school
attracted students from all parts of Europe and the legendary
St. Cadoc of Llan-Carvan, the great saint of Wales, who was
such a passionate admirer of Virgil, spent three years there
"until he had acquired the complete knowledge of the
West."[5] Some writers have imagined that Cathal taught there
until about 665, even when he was already bishop, a dignity
to which he had been promoted in an exceptional way.
When his parents died, he had generously distributed his
patrimony among the poor, had himself ordained priest and
performed a few miracles, including a resurrection from the
dead.   These activities resulted in his being denounced to the
King of Munster by Meltrid,[6] King of the Desi, for practising the art of magic, and Cathal found himself in gaol.   The
sudden death of Meltrid, however, and the nocturnal
apparition of two angels to the king brought about not only
the release of the saint but also his appointment to the
bishopric of Rachau, the episcopal *mensa* of which the king
generously endowed with the revenues from the deceased
Meltrid's estates.

Cathal governed his diocese for some years, and then went
off (according to some authorities about 666) on a pilgrimage
to the Holy Land.   On his way back he again performed a
few miracles, such as resuscitating a sailor who had had the
misfortune to fall from the mast of a ship and be killed, and
stilling a tempest.   Some say that he landed quietly on the
Adriatic coast "ad portum Hydrunti," the modern Otranto,[7]
or at the place now called Rada di San Cataldo near Lecce:[8]
others that he was wrecked in the gulf of Taranto itself after
rounding Cape Santa Maria di Leuca.[9]   He set out on foot
for Taranto, curing by the way a deaf and dumb shepherd-

---

[4] Cf. Blandamura, op. cit., pp. 30 et seq., and O'Riordan, op. cit., pp. 4
et seq.

[5] Lifris, *Vita Cadoci* in *AA. SS. Boll.*, January III, 217-20, c. 7.

[6] An attempt, presumably, to render the Irish name Moelochtrid.   The
'miracles' mentioned in the text appear to have been invented by one or other
of the brothers Morone.   [7] e.g. the Bollandists, p. 578.

[8] Cf. O'Riordan, op. cit., p. 10.   [9] Cf. Blandamura, p. 35.

girl, and baptizing, as he entered the city, a blind beggar whose sight he also restored. At the request of the Tarantines, who happened to be without a bishop at the time, he agreed to mount the episcopal throne and immediately devoted himself with great zeal to preaching and reforming the morals of clergy and laity, reviving the liturgy, more particularly, the recitation of the Office, and building new churches. After governing the church at Taranto for about fifteen years, "in Domino obdormivit saeculo septimo ad finem vergente" on an 8th of March, not, however, before delivering a most edifying discourse to those by his bedside. He was buried under the pavement of the cathedral.

§ 3

Taranto, as is commonly known, was destroyed by the Saracens after a massacre of its inhabitants in 927, and, reduced to a heap of ruins, lay derelict for forty years, when the natives began to return very gradually and set to rebuilding their city. In such circumstances the memory of Cathal's burial place was lost. In 1071 when one Drogo, who rebuilt the cathedral of Taranto, was bishop, the body of St. Cathal was discovered on 10th May in the chapel of S. Giovanni in Galilea, which corresponds to the present baptistery,[10] and placed by the bishop with every circumstance of honour in its original urn below the high altar in the new cathedral. The occasion was made memorable by the occurrence of four great miraculous cures. In 1107 Bishop Rainald had an examination made of the remains and transferred them into another urn, but still under the high altar. In 1151 the bones of the saint were translated from the high altar to a chapel specially built by the Archbishop Gerald "in cornu epistolae" of the transept, a chapel corresponding to the vestry of the present *cappellone*, and this event also was signalised by numerous miraculous cures of sundry cases of paralysis, blindness, demoniacal possession, epilepsy and scrofula. The urn containing the bones was

[10] Cf. Blandamura, *Il Duomo di Taranto*, Taranto, Tip. Arcivescovile, 1923, pp. 119-23.

re-opened and the remains placed in a new silver urn inlaid with a gold cross richly studded with jewels. It was on this occasion apparently that the *crocetta aurea* to which reference has been made was removed from the urn.[11] In 1598 Mgr. Vignati, Vicar Apostolic in Taranto, conceived the idea of transforming the chapel of St. Cathal completely and obtained the authorisation of Clement VIII for the purpose. The chapel reconstructed by Mgr. Vignati lasted until 1657, when Mgr. Caracciolo undertook the building at enormous expense of the gorgeous *cappellone* so dear to the heart of the Tarantines, the decoration of which was not completed until early in the nineteenth century.[12]

§ 4

Such is the Legend of the saint, the story of his invention and his various translations. The Irish hagiographers never had any doubt that St. Cathal was properly to be assigned to the seventh or the early eighth century at latest, but their Italian confrères reposed in no such certainty and, lacking any foundation to build on, made him alternate between the second century and the tenth. The first Italian writer to place the question of St. Cathal on solid ground was, as already mentioned, Blandamura, who pointed out that the earliest historical documents at all bearing on the saint were such scraps of information as had been supplied by a certain Berlingiero, a deacon of Taranto, in the eleventh century, contemporaneously or nearly so with the rediscovery of his remains. According to this authority there was discovered along with the body a "crux aurea nomen sancti in litteris latinis designans,"[13] which golden cross Blandamura submitted to the scrutiny of the very learned Mgr. Cosimo Stornaiolo, of the staff of the Vatican Library. The cross is of the kind known as benedictional, because such crosses

---

[11] Cf. Blandamura, *Un Cimelio, etc.*, p. 18.

[12] Cf. for a detailed description of the edifice and full particulars of the relics, Blandamura, *Il Duomo di Taranto*, pp. 155-211.

[13] Cf. also A. Hofmeister, "Der Sermo de inventione Sancti Kataldi," Münchener Museum, IV, pp. 104-14, cited in *Analecta Bollandiana*, XXXIX, 1921, p. 364.

were inserted in a pastoral staff or wand, which the bishops of the time were wont to carry in the left hand, while they gave the blessing with the right.[14]

One side of the little cross is inscribed "Cataldus Rachau." The examination made by Prof. Stornaiolo and other archæologists and palæographers consulted by him has resulted in the unanimous attribution of the engraving of the word 'Cataldus' to the seventh or eighth century. The name may have been engraved on the cross, during the lifetime of Cathal, as a sign of ownership, or have been engraved on the occasion of his burial, as a mark of identity. The initial 'Ra' of the traditional appellation 'Rachau' was probably added when the discovery was made in 1071: and the terminal 'chau' on the occasion either of the examination in 1107 or of the translation in 1151. At all events, the death of Cathal at the end of the seventh or the beginning of the eighth century is one more or less certainly established fact.

It may be observed in passing that Dempster made Cathal a native of Scotland, "natus in Scotiae montanis quae Hiberniae nomen habuerunt," assigned him to the fourth century, and succeeded in determining the date of his death: 361; "qui annus est, ut puto, depositionis."[15] Costanzi, after referring to his elucubrations, observes: "This industrious rhapsodist did not notice how many facts mutually contradicting each other and the simple truth he had collected in this astonishing farrago. Leaving out of account Dempster's good faith in this as in all other passages, it may be doubted, etc. . . ."

§ 5

Two points, however, still remained to be elucidated even after the labours of Blandamura: the approximate dates of the episcopate of Cathal at Rachau and his episcopate at Taranto.

[14] Cf. Blandamura, *Un cimelio, etc.,* p. 14.
[15] He continues "Dicere autem eum Hibernum ortu est omni historicae ecclesiasticae luce destitueri, nam nec tunc quidem nec centum triginta annos postea ullus Catholicae fidei Hirlandiae radius illuxit." *H.E.,* III, p. 163, Edinburgh, 1829.

The Irish hagiographers, beginning with Colgan,[16] are in general agreed that Cathal occupied the 'episcopatum Rachau,' but, there being no place now called Rachau in Ireland, have been driven to make various conjectures. Colgan, observing that in his day there were various places called Rathan and Rathen, originally suggested that Rachau might be a corruption of Rathan.[17] This is the current opinion. Blandamura declares that Dr. Fogarty, Bishop of Killaloe, informed him in 1913 that the native name Rath-Cua became gradually corrupted into Rachau, Rachan, Rathan, Sen Raghan, and, finally, Shanrahan, i.e., old Rachan. O'Riordan writes as follows: "But where is Rachau? Dr. Lanigan [*Ecclesiastical History of Ireland*, III, 125] and Canon O'Hanlon [*Lives of the Irish Saints*, V, 194] seem inclined to identify it with Shanraghan, a townland lying a little west of Clogheen, in South Tipperary, and just outside the borders of Waterford and Cork. The ruins of an old church and monastery still remain there, and in pieces of masonry lying near can be discerned the traces of still older buildings. [Cf. an article by the Rev. P. Lonergan in the *Irish Ecclesiastical Record* for May, 1896]. . . . No such diocese as Raghan exists at present, but it might have existed at one time. When Lismore was in its glory, it is said that Raghan was a place of importance, but it has passed through its decline and has become the name of a townland.[18] The lapse of centuries might have done with the diocese of Raghan what time is gradually doing with the dioceses of Emly, Aghadoe, Ardfert, Kilmacduagh and Clonmacnoise. These have become merged in Cashel, Kerry, Galway and Ardagh, and are gradually fading from the knowledge and memory of the people. Besides, a redistribution of ecclesiastical Ireland was made in the pontificate of Eugenius III [in the

[16] *AA. SS. Hiberniae*, 1645, II, 555.
[17] Now Rahan, near Tullamore, in Offaly.
[18] It may perhaps be not improper to recall the ingenious suggestion first made by Dr. Reeves that Mo-Chuta, St. Carthach, Abbot of Rahan early in the seventh century, and expelled, according to Tighernach, in *Diebus Paschalibus*, as a result of the Paschal controversy, was expelled because of his sympathies with the "Roman" party. There is no hint of this either in the Irish or the Latin sources, but Dr. Plummer, cf. *VV. S. H.*, Oxford, 1910, I, p. xlvi, thinks it may nevertheless be true. Mo-Chuta went into the land of the Dési and founded Liss-mor.

twelfth century; cf. Dom Gougaud's *Christianity in Celtic Lands*, Ch. XI, § IV, pp. 398-409] and in the change Raghan might have disappeared as a diocese. Or it may be that Cathal was head of a monastery and became what is known in canon law as an 'episcopus nullius,' such as is the Abbot of Montecassino at present . . . . All this, however, is but mere speculation; historical certainty is out of the question."[19] It would be impossible to come to a more exact conclusion, and yet the fact remains that the old Irish tradition is unanimous in assigning the bishopric of Rachau to Cathal.

§ 6

As for the episcopate at Taranto, it is rejected absolutely by modern criticism. Blandamura declares that Cathal "must have governed the church at Taranto" in the interval between Bishop Germanus (680) and Bishop Caesarius (743), but admits that "there is no documentary evidence yet available of an episode of such interest to the history of Taranto." Lanzoni,[20] discussing the episcopal rolls of the city, expunges the name of Cathal.

He begins (p. 79) his examination of the alleged apostolic or Petrine origin of many Italian dioceses and observes that the legend of Cathal's missionary activities at Taranto (*B.H.L.*, 1652) dates back no further than the twelfth century. Four cities contend for the first landing of St. Peter in the peninsula—Pisa, Pozzuoli, Gallipoli and Taranto. As regards the claims of Taranto, the curious reader is referred to the chapter entitled 'The Legend of St. Peter in Taranto,' in Blandamura's book, *Choerades Insulae*,[21] where the learned archdeacon attempts to defend the tradition. Lanzoni, however, will have none of it: "The city of Taranto also"— he writes on p. 315—"boasts of having welcomed in its harbour the prince of the Apostles, accompanied by the

[19] The Bollandists, while admitting that every circumstance tended to show that Cataldus was a native of Ireland, "yet, as if to display their ingenuity," annoyed Lanigan by throwing out "a conjecture that he might have been from Ragusa(!)" (*Hist. Irel.* III, p. 124).
[20] *Le Diocesi d'Italia.*
[21] Taranto, Tip. Arcivesc., 1925, pp. 139-66.

evangelist St. Mark, on the first occasion of his setting foot in Italy.

"A document (*B.H.L.*, 1652-3), composed in the twelfth or thirteenth century, and as stuffed with fabulous details as the Pisa document, relates that St. Peter, on his arrival from Antioch in Italy in the year A.D. 45, landed at Taranto, cured a market gardener named Amasianus, and converted the Tarantines to the Christian faith through the agency of St. Mark the Evangelist. This legend, which may be still more ancient than its presumptive date, does not state that Amasianus became Bishop of Taranto, but the Tarantines in course of time came to believe that the Amasianus of the legend had been their first bishop, although only for a very short period. Another Tarantine legend (*B.H.L.*, 6679), however, later in date probably than the former, states that St. Peter, after landing at Taranto with St. Mark, nominated and consecrated a St. Cathal Bishop of Taranto. Gams (p. 929) naturally realised that he had to decide for one or the other, for Amasianus or Cathal, as the first bishop, and came to the conclusion that the easiest way out of the difficulty was to put the former in brackets and the latter in italics. But the early Bollandists had already perceived (*AA. SS.*, May, II, 569-73) that the tale of the apostolic consecration of St. Cathal was historically untenable. This St. Cathal, venerated, as a matter of fact, at Taranto, was undoubtedly a seventh century Irish bishop from Rachau, who died at Taranto as he was about to embark for the Holy Land or shortly after his return from the journey. The Tarantines piously buried him in their cathedral and, after its destruction by the Saracens in 927, discovered in 1094 among the ruins a body with a little gold cross engraved with the name of an Irish bishop and his see (cf. Blandamura and *Ana. Boll.*, 1921, p. 368).

"They went further. The Tarantines, who, in 1094, discovered the tomb of St. Cathal in the old cathedral, thought that he had been a bishop of Taranto and found no difficulty in connecting him with the landing of St. Peter and St Mark in their port. When in course of time the real *floruit* of the Bishop of Rachau came to be known, they had not the courage to abandon a legend which by that time had taken firm root in Taranto, and so they placed a Cataldus I in the first century and a Cataldus II in the sixth century (really the seventh and eighth). Facing the Mare Grande [Taranto is situated on a rocky island which divides the deep inlet into the Mare Piccolo and the Mare Grande] are two low-lying islands (the Cheradi), the larger on the right called S. Pietro and the lesser on the left very close to its neighbour, called S. Paolo, which have played a considerable part in the development of the Tarantine legend. Now it is not improbable that there was a little church dedicated from the earliest times to the fisherman of Genesareth on the island of S. Pietro." And with regard to Cataldus II, whom Cappelletti (XXI, 132) and others assign to the sixth century, he states quite definitely on p. 316 that "the authentic Tarantine catalogue includes neither a Cathal I in the first century nor a Cathal II in the sixth, for the simple reason that St Cathal was an Irish bishop of the seventh or eighth century buried in the ancient cathedral of Taranto. And it is not known that he ever held the episcopal see of Taranto."

In other words the case of St. Cathal comes within the class described by Lanzoni on p. 11: "It happens very much oftener than one would believe with regard to quite a number of dioceses that saints venerated in the episcopal city or elsewhere in the diocese come to be considered or believed to have been local bishops and are lumped together among, and included in the list of, such, although in fact they have never been such and in some cases have never even been bishops at all. In dioceses where the diptychs, that is to say, the complete and authentic rolls of the ancient bishops of the place, had gone amissing and were subsequently discovered (as was the case in Verona), we can be perfectly certain that confusions of the sort occurred very frequently and that the local episcopal rolls have been considerably tampered with; this was the case nearly everywhere, although in dioceses where there are no diptychs available as a check the certainty of such intromissions cannot in every case be established by evidence, only the probability. There is nothing surprising in such blundering or confusion. When a saint, more particularly a saint invested with episcopal dignity, had been venerated from time immemorial in a church in some city or diocese, more especially in a cathedral church, and had been, or was believed to have been, buried in it, when his remains, real or imagined, were preserved in that church along with those of other bishops of the diocese, actual or presumptive, when the saint was either titular of the cathedral or a co-titular together with other episcopal saints of the locality, when the story of the saint and of the origins of his cult in the district had been a familiar tradition with the townspeople or countryfolk for years, and even centuries, and the authentic records of the bishops of the diocese had either been lost altogether or lay mouldering in the dust of some archives, so that it was impossible or nearly so to check them, it was easy for the belief that the saint in question had been bishop of the place, especially if first given currency by men esteemed on account of their authority, virtue, and whatever smattering of education they may have possessed, to insinuate itself and take firm root in the minds of a people ignorant on the one hand and on the other anxious to learn the history of the saint, and for this individual or particular belief to grow into a universal conviction and be transmitted as certain beyond the possibility of doubt."[22]

§ 7

Another point lacking the support of any secure historical basis is the existence of an alleged St. Donatus, Bishop of Lecce, the brother of St. Cathal, who is mentioned, e.g., also by Miss Stokes.[23] Blandamura declares that, according to Infantino, "when St. Cathal came from Hibernia with his

[22] Agnellus of Ravenna, writing to his brethren, c. 842, "had no hesitation in propounding in bare words the theory which so many hagiographers before and since his day have followed without explaining their methods: 'Lest there should be gaps in our account of the succession of bishops, by the help of your prayers, I have composed the lives of them all; and I do not think I have told falsehood herein, for they were all men of prayer, and chaste, and lovers of almsgiving, and fishers of men.'" Edmund Bishop, *Liturgica Historica*, Oxford, 1918, p. 377. Agnellus took comfort from the example of Moses "[qui] preexcellentissimus vir, inspirante Deo, Genesis librum descripsit." Cf. Migne, *P.L.*, CVI, col. 459.

[23] *Six Months in the Apennines*, p. 202.

brother, who was called Donatus and later became Bishop of Lecce, they disembarked on our shores in the present harbour of Lecce, now called S. Cataldo in memory of that very saint: they built a chapel there, still standing, in the shape of a little grotto in which they lived as hermits for fourteen years. When the Bishop of Taranto of the time came to die, the Tarantines at the request of the Leccesi made him their pastor." Blandamura adds that Galateo and Marciano tell the same story and are "rightly contradicted" by Lenormant.[24]

There never was in fact either a saint or a bishop of Lecce called Donatus. There is a district, S. Donato di Lecce, south of Lecce, but its patron is St. Donatus of Arezzo, whose feast is kept there regularly on 7th August; so also, near Taranto, about two miles to the east, there is a wide stretch of country called S. Donato with a commodious country chapel where Mass used once to be said on holidays: but this chapel, also, as may be inferred from the picture hanging above the altar and the date of the public holiday (7th August) formerly kept there, derives its name, as Mgr. Blandamura has kindly informed me, from St. Donatus of Arezzo and not from any alleged St. Donatus of Lecce. The first mention of Donatus of Lecce would seem to be due to Giacomo Antonio Ferrari, the Leccese historian and author of a life of St. Cathal,[25] who, coming across the feast of a St. Donatus, an Irish bishop, in the martyrology on 22nd October (really St. Donatus of Fiesole), turned him into a brother of St. Cathal and made him out to be "episcopus lupiensis in Salentinis." Lanzoni[26] says of Donatus: "Described by Ughelli (IX, 70) as the brother of St. Cathal, Bishop of Taranto [but without the attribute of Saint] he is assigned by him to the year 163. The continuator of *Italia Sacra* at first retained him (X, 125), although transferring him to 173, but later (loc. cit., 199) expunged him, because St. Cathal, the Bishop of Taranto, is presumed to have lived not in the first but in the sixth century. The earliest records

[24] *La Grande-Grèce*, Paris, Lévy, 1881, I, p. 75.
[25] Cf. Ughelli, IX, 94, and Costanzi, op. cit., p. 73.
[26] *Le Diocesi d'Italia*, p. 131.

of St. Cathal make no mention of this alleged brother of his called Donatus. . . . The populace of Lecce, moreover, by a tendency common among all peoples, made them both lead the hermit life in their territory."

§ 8

St. Cathal is credited with having uttered certain 'prophecies' relating particularly to the ruling family on the throne of Naples which were discovered in 1492 in a volume found buried under a lead cross in the Church of S. Pietro della Porta in Taranto, a church which has ceased to exist. Reference to these prophecies, mentioned also by O'Riordan, occurs in many Italian chronicles and memoirs about the end of the fifteenth century.[27] They are obviously spurious, and the Bollandists[28] had already observed: "Prophetiam ipsam ex libro Petri Galatini Ordinis Minorum de Ecclesia destructa, Romae in bibliotheca Araecoeli adservato edidit Morenus in Vita S. Cataldi; quam omittimus, ut rem obscuram, et forte sub nomine Sancti confictam." Dempster, it may be added, in his usual way, took it into his head to ascribe to him also a Book of Homilies.

§ 9

And now, after so much negation and doubt, it may be as well to pass to something positive, the widespread cult which St. Cathal has received and still receives all over Italy, making partial use of the data collected by Blandamura, Cassinelli and De Cristano. This last published with Migliaccio at Naples in 1780, as Part II of, or a Corollary to, Costanzi's book, much information relating to the cult of the saint, "labours performed amid the worries and anxieties of the forum."

[27] Cf. e.g. O. Tommasini, *Diario della città di Roma di Stefano Infessura*, Rome, 1890, p. 272, and A. G. Tononi, 'Note storiche e Rime politiche e morali tra gli atti di un notaio piacentino del sec. XV [Marco Antonio Gatti],' in *Strenna Piacentina* for 1892.
[28] Cf. *AA. SS.*, May, II, p. 576.

It were best to take the provinces separately, beginning as usual with the north of Italy.

At Genoa[29] the feast of St. Cathal was already celebrated towards the end of the thirteenth century on 10th May, although no such feast is to be found in the Roman calendars of the twelfth and thirteenth centuries. The cult of St. Cathal was brought to Genoa very early, most probably—according to Cambiaso—by the traders from southern Italy who frequented that port. The metropolitan Collectionary includes it in all three catalogues with a proper prayer and lessons taken from his Life. The saint also received a cult in the Church surnamed delle Vigne, where an altar was dedicated to him with a chaplaincy founded by the Grillo family, its patrons and protectors. On his feastday there was a choir distribution of fourpence to the canons and twopence to the chaplains according to the Statutes of 1375.[30] At the present day the cult of the saint has completely disappeared.

§ 10

In Lombardy the parish of Mottabaluffi in the province of Cremona is dedicated to St. Cathal. There would seem to have been a chapel there once upon a time belonging to the De Baluffi, lords of that territory, a dependence from the parish of Scandolara Ravaro: it became a parish church in the fifteenth century, taking its title from a church of St. Cathal which stood in the suburbs of Cremona, and was first unconsecrated and then destroyed by the Venetians, along with a number of others in the early fifteenth century.[31] The parish church of Mottabaluffi has a valuable fifteenth century painting, retouched in the eighteenth century, depicting St. Cathal as a bishop vested in pontificals, Our

[29] Cf. Cambiaso, *L'anno ecclesiastico in Genova*, 1917, pp. 11, 157, 285, 311 and 379.

[30] Cf. in the archiepiscopal archives, *Statuti*, N 3, p. 7: Archives of S.M. delle Vigne, *Fabbriceria, Cappellanie*.

[31] As I am kindly informed by Mgr. Illemo Camelli of the Civic Museum. Lubin, *Abb. It. br. not.*, p. 112, says: "Abbatia tit. S. Cathaldi Cremonensis, Canonicorum Regularium Ord. S. Augustini; de qua mentio fit in Codice Taxarum Camerae Apostolicae."

Lady seated with the Child, and St. Joseph leaning on a
pilgrim's staff. The feast is kept there on 10th May. Sufferers
from hernia are particularly devoted to St. Cathal in accordance with an ancient tradition which survives also in Malta
(cf. § 22).

In the province of Mantua there is a district called S.
Cataldo, part of the commune of Borgoforte. There also his
feast is kept on 10th May. The parish church, which dates
from 1550, is dedicated to SS. Florian and Benedict and has
a reliquary which contains "particulas ex ossibus S. Cataldi,"
as appears from a decree of Mgr. De Rubeis, Archbishop of
Tharsus, published in Rome on 8th October, 1743.

§ 11

In Emilia, the parish church of the suburb of Modena,
called S. Cataldo, is dedicated to St. Cathal, and there also
the feast of the saint is kept with great solemnity on 10th May.
A first church of St. Cathal of great antiquity stood under the
pre-Herculean walls of the city between the porta Cittanova
(later St. Augustine) and the porta Ganaceto: it is mentioned
in a bull of Pope Lucius III, dated 1181, together with the
Hospital of St. Cathal as forming part of the property
belonging to the Chapter of the Cathedral of Modena. It
appears in the list of the Modenese churches of the thirteenth
century as belonging to the Monastery of St. Peter, but in a
fifteenth century list as the property of the parish of S. Maria
di Collegara. In the fifteenth century also it absorbed the
neighbouring ancient parish of St. James the Greater. The
first church was knocked down in 1546 and a second larger
church, erected in a locality quite close to the present church,
was consecrated in 1564. A complete list of the names of the
priests of the parish since 1506 is still preserved: it was served
by secular clergy down to 1701. In 1702 it was sub-divided
between the neighbouring parishes of S. Faustino, S. Matteo
and S. Freto, but was reconstituted in 1703 and entrusted to
the care of the Friars Minor, who have served it uninterruptedly ever since. In 1880-82 the present and third church
of St. Cathal was built. It possesses various relics of the saint,

one of which was discovered in 1546 in the high altar during the demolition of the ancient church. There is a Confraternity of S. Cathal which has been in existence at any rate since the eighteenth century.[32]

Guidicini[33] mentions a church of St. Cathal de' Lambertini in Bologna. He states that in 1506 it formed part of the inheritance of Ulysses, the son of the deceased Guidantonio Lambertini and a friar of the Observance of the Order of Minors, in whose inventory it is described as "a great house with the little church of St. Cathal," bordering on the street called del Pavone.

Rimini, also, in the province of Forli, had an ancient parish church of St. Cathal, which stood in the old quarter down by the seashore outside the porta S. Tommaso. The first mention of it occurs in a conveyance of sale made by one Revelone on 20th November, 1168.[34] In 1254 a convent of Dominicans was erected beside the church and they served it down to 1796, when they changed over to the convent of St. Francis Xavier which had belonged to the suppressed Jesuits: but in the following year they were transferred by decree of the Government to the Servite Convent and there, in 1798, they were themselves suppressed. The Convent and Church of St. Cathal were used as a cavalry barracks until they were finally demolished in 1816; now scarcely a memory of them remains and the site of what was once St. Cathal's is now occupied by a new quarter of the city.

In that old Convent of St. Cathal St. Thomas Aquinas may possibly have dwelt; St. Vincent Ferrer certainly did; and Goldoni attended the school of philosophy there for some time. The church had a remarkable collection of pictures which has now been transferred to the civic gallery.[35]

[32] I am indebted for these particulars to some prints kindly given to me by Fr. Samuele Roveda, O.F.M., the present priest-in-charge.

[33] *Cose notabili della città di Bologna*, 1868, IV, 16.

[34] Cf. Tonini, *Storia di Rimini*, II, 423.

[35] I am indebted for these particulars to the courtesy of Mgr. Rubertini, rector of the local episcopal seminary.

§ 12

As for Venice, Blandamura quotes the following passage from Lo Jodice:[36] "The Blessed Giuliana of Collalto, a Benedictine nun, founded a monastery for religious of her order at Venice under the title of SS. Blaise and Cathal. She was its first abbess and she died there in the odour of sanctity; her body is still preserved there uncorrupted."

At Verona, according to De Cristano, a relic of St. Cathal was preserved in the famous monastery of the Santo Spirito. The monastery has now ceased to exist, having been transformed into the present civic hospital, and the relic has disappeared.

§ 13

In Tuscany St. Cathal is honoured only in the neighbourhood of the city of St. Fridian, in the parish of S. Maria a Colle in the commune of Lucca. There the cult is of immemorial antiquity, and it would appear from documents dated 1337 that a Confraternity of the Nativity of Our Lady and of St. Cathal was in existence there at the time. The Confraternity boasts a relic of the saint and a statue: another relic, part of an arm of St. Cathal, has been lost. The feast is celebrated with a great concourse of people on 10th May.[37]

§ 14

Latium shows many traces of the cult of St. Cathal. There used to be a relic even in Rome, in the college of the Irish Franciscans at St. Isidore's, in 1664, but on an examination being made in 1826, it was found to have disappeared.[38]

Cassinelli[39] declares that the famous convent at Gradi belonging to the Dominican Friars at Viterbo had a property called S. Cataldo and a similar statement is made also by De Cristano. A farmstead called S. Cataldo is marked on the Italian Touring Club map (Sheet 27, B. 5), between Acqua

[36] *Memorie storiche di San Cataldo, vescovo e confessore*, Bologna, 1879, p. 132.
[37] Cf. Blandamura, op. cit., p. 68.
[38] Cf. G. Cleary, O.F.M., *Father Luke Wadding and St. Isidore's College, Rome*, Rome. Tip. del Senato, 1925, pp. 223-4.
[39] *Vita di S. Cataldo*, III, cap. XIII, p. 137.

Rossa and Vitorchiano, but I have been unable to obtain
any particulars of this property. There does not appear
to have ever been any cult of St. Cathal in Viterbo.[40]

In the province of Rieti the parish church of Montenero
in Sabina (in the diocese of Poggio Mirteto) is dedicated to
St. Cathal, and his feast is solemnly kept there on 10th May
and attended by crowds from the neighbouring villages as
well; it boasts two relics, one set in the pectoral cross on the
statue, the other in a reliquary made for the purpose. And
still in the province of Rieti great devotion is paid to St.
Cathal in the commune of Cottanello, although the parish
church is entitled after St. Andrew the Apostle. The feasts
are kept there on 8th March and 10th May, when a relic of
the saint is exposed. De Cristano declares that the thaumaturge performed a resounding miracle there in 1760, when he
restored sight to the son of Dr. De Cesaris, the doctor at
Cottanello. A local legend avers that St. Cathal lived in
a grotto close to the village, where a chapel stands at the
present day with a special niche on which the saint is said
to have rested his head when he lay down to sleep.

In the province of Frosinone at Supino (in the diocese of
Ferentino) is the famous Shrine of St. Cathal, the goal of
numerous pilgrimages on the occasion of the feastday on
8th March, and, more particularly, that on 10th May. In
addition to the shrine, which stands in the archpriest's
church dedicated to St. Peter, the parish church is also
dedicated to St. Cathal. A bone, said to have been taken
from the arm of the saint and presented in 1632 by Mgr.
Caracciolo, Archbishop of Taranto, is venerated there in a
silver reliquary shaped like an arm.

There is much devotion to St. Cathal in the commune
of Patrica adjoining Supino, which venerates him as its
protector in chief. The religious feast is kept on 10th May
and the civil celebration deferred until the Sunday within
the octave.

One of the parish churches in Sant' Elia Fiume Rapido
(in the diocese of Monte Cassino and still in the province of
Frosinone) is also dedicated to St. Cathal, contains a large

[40] From information received from the inter-diocesan seminary in Viterbo.

picture of the saint and also boasts a relic. The feast is kept there on the first Sunday in September.

A chapel of St. Cathal is marked on the Italian Touring Club map (Sheet 35, A. 1) near the electric power station on the Liri, at S. Giovanni Incarico, near Ceprano, also in the province of Frosinone.

In Minturno, near Formia (in the province of Rome and the diocese of Gaeta), there is also trace of devotion to St. Cathal. The picture of the saint would seem to have been painted on one of the arches of the Roman acqueduct which was knocked down some forty years back to admit the passage of a new road. A little niche containing an image of the saint has recently been constructed to perpetuate his memory by H.E. Prof. Pietro Fedele, to whom I am indebted for this information. A stretch of land between Minturno and the coast still retains the name Contrada S. Cataldo.

§ 15

In the Marches St. Cathal is one of the patrons of the commune of Esanatoglia, in the province of Macerata, in the diocese of Camerino. His church, greatly revered, is situate about a mile and a half from the village, 2100 feet above sea-level on Monte Consegno, and preserves two relics (a fragment of the skull and a tooth), presented in 1616 by Cardinal Bonifacio Gaetano, Archbishop of Taranto. The feast is celebrated with a solemn procession on 10th May.

§ 16

Crossing over into the Abruzzi, it may be observed that, according to De Cristano (n. 49), there is a tradition of St. Cathal at Pèntima (now Corfinio), the see of the diocese of Valva, near Sulmona. To the neighbourhood of Sulmona belongs a legend of St. Cathal, gathered by A. De Nino,[41] which has been cited as an illustration by Père Delahaye in

[41] *Usi e costumi abruzzesi*, Florence, Barbera, 1887, IV, 194.

his *Légendes hagiographiques*, and deserves to be mentioned because of its interest as a piece of folklore.[42]

De Nino tells the story as follows: "Cathal was a thief and always 'cracked cribs' in company with other members of his gang. His wife, however, was a good soul and unceasingly upbraided her husband, exhorting him to turn over a new leaf. Cathal would hesitate between a 'yes' and a 'no,' only very gradually inclining to a definitive 'yes.' His wife worked like a galley-slave, toiling day and night not to stint the family and to prove to her husband that it was possible 'to get along very nicely' without resorting to burglary. Cathal at last made a firm resolution that he would go and steal no more. One day, however, the rest of the gang, his old companions in theft, wheedled him out of his house with every circumstance of ceremony and quietly did him to death because they were afraid he might 'blow the gaff.' They then carried the corpse into the dead man's cellar and placed it under a cask of wine. His wife, in the interval, had gone out for some messages. A day passed, two days, three days, finally a week; and still Cathal never came home. His wife said: 'Well! he has gone that wicked way again. May God enlighten him!' Three months passed and still there was no sign of Cathal. His wife then took it into her head to sell a little wine to make provision for the family. She sold and sold and sold, but still there was no end of wine. The neighbours remarked: 'How can such a little cask supply such a quantity of wine?' But still there was no end of wine. And they all exclaimed: 'Miraculous! Miraculous!' The Pope with all his cardinals came in procession to Cathal's house. He went all through the cellar but nothing out of the way was to be seen. Just as he was about to take his departure, he caught sight of a lily under the cask. The cask was raised and the lily was found to be growing out of Cathal's mouth. The Pope then exclaimed: 'Cathal is a saint!' "[43]

[42] Brussels, 1927, p. 51. English tr., p. 53.
[43] Père Delahaye regards this last incident as merely an example of the popular imagination getting to work on the fact of a commission having been appointed to examine and report upon rumours of apparently miraculous occurrences.

The commune of Giuliano Teatino in the province and archdiocese of Chieti has St. Cathal for its patron and possesses a wooden statue of the saint said to date back to the sixteenth century. It was presented by Folco de Bosis, a native of Giuliano, who, about 1700, brought it back with him from Taranto. St. Cathal is commemorated with a religious festival only on 10th May: the civil celebration takes place with great pomp on 18th August and is preceded by a novena.

A Masseria S. Cataldo (a farmstead) is marked on the Italian Touring Club map (Sheet 35, A. 6) in the Molise, on the road from Isernia to Fornelli.

§ 17

In Campania, the nearer one gets to Taranto the more numerous become the manifestations of the cult of St. Cathal.

There is a Taverna S. Cataldo marked on the Italian Touring Club map (Sheet 35, B. 3) on the road from Cassino to Mignano in the province of Naples. One of the parish churches of Roccaromana, a commune in the diocese of Teano, is dedicated to St. Cathal, who is looked upon as its patron. The feast days of 8th March and 10th May are solemnly celebrated, and a special feast is kept also on one of the Sundays in September to return thanks to the patron for the immunity granted to the village, from the fifteenth century to the present day, throughout various epidemics of plagues and cholera which have been a sore trial to neighbouring villages. Cassinelli says that in the Church of S. Agnello at Maddaloni, a commune near Caserta, there is an altar dedicated to St. Cathal with a benefice instituted under his name, and that the feast of the saint is regularly kept in that church. In Naples also St. Cathal is associated with St. Agnello.[44] Giovanni Mario Puderico, a Neapolitan noble who died in 1574 after having been Archbishop of Taranto for fifteen years, raised at his own expense the greater part of the basilica of St. Agnello, belonging to the Canons

[44] Cf. Cassinelli, pp. 138-9.

Regular of S. Salvatore, and consecrated the high altar to St. Cathal, adorning it with marble and bas-reliefs, and setting in the midst a picture of the Blessed Virgin with St. Cathal on the right and S. Agnello on the left. Pious Tarantines living in Naples made a practice of going there every year in solemn procession to keep the feast on 10th May.

Cassinelli adds that the parish church of Porta nova at Naples has a benefice under the title of S. Maria delle Grazie and S. Cataldo. St. Cathal is the patron of the commune of Massalubrense in the peninsula of Sorrento. The church, formerly a cathedral, entitled S. Maria delle Grazie, has a chapel dedicated to him in which two relics, the gift of Mgr. G. Capecelatro, Archbishop of Taranto, are venerated. Both feastdays, 8th March and 10th May, are kept.

The province of Salerno had a monastery of Benedictine nuns in the seventeenth century named after St. Cathal at Scala, part of Ravello, in the archdiocese of Amalfi. This monastery, the *insigne decus* of Scala for over two centuries, recently passed into the possession of a Dane and has since been transformed into a hotel. The sisters of the monastery of the Holy Redeemer are said to possess a relic of the saint.[45] Cava dei Tirreni, apparently, once boasted a very ancient Church of St. Cathal mentioned in three documents in the archives of the Benedictines of the Holy Trinity and dated respectively September 1161, March 1165, and December 1165.[46]

In the commune of Campagna there existed as early as 1156[47] a church and a monastery dedicated to St. Cathal, which had been built by the Normans. Only a few traces now remain. St. Cathal is joint patron to this day of the commune of Castelnuovo Cilento: the feast used to be kept there solemnly on 10th May in a little church *extra moenia* which formed an admirable target for lightning, but the wooden statue of St. Cathal inside has always escaped unscathed. A cappella di S. Cataldo is marked on the Italian Touring Club map (Sheet 41, D. 6) at Rocchetta, between

[45] Cf. Blandamura, p. 55.
[46] Cf. Lo Jodice, p. 127.
[47] Cf. Can. A. Rivelli, *Storia di Campagna*.

Cella di Bulgheria and Torre Orsaja, and the long Galleria di S. Cataldo (ibid.) on the railway line from Salerno to Reggio Calabria.

§ 18

In the Puglie, St. Cathal is patron of the commune of Cagnano Varano in the Gargano (province of Foggia), where the feast of 8th March and, more particularly, that of 10th May are kept in the Church of St. Cathal. An ancient statue of the saint is preserved there and a Confraternity also has been instituted.

The province of Bari has a very ancient little Church of St. Cathal at Barletta, near Porta Marina, of which there is record back in the twelfth century. It is maintained at the present day by a flourishing Confraternity, which includes nearly all the seafaring folk in the district, and which, in 1885, presented the church with an artistic silver statue of the saint. An old silver monstrance contains a bone from his arm. The two feast days of 8th March and 10th May were abolished when the universal calendar of the Church was adopted: but a lively popular festival is still held in honour of St. Cathal on the last Sunday in July, when all the fishing boats have returned to Barletta. At Andria, and throughout the diocese of that name, the ancient office of St. Cathal with double rite was recited down to 1883, but, from 1884 onwards, the prayer was taken "ex. comm. Conf. Pont.," and the lessons of the second nocturn were reformed and shortened with the Mass de comm.

At Trani, as at Acquaviva delle Fonti, the liturgical feast on 8th March was celebrated down to 1913 with double rite, the proper lessons of the second nocturn and the Mass de comm.; but, when the calendar of the universal Church was adopted, the feast was abolished. The introduction of the cult of St. Cathal into Corato, of which he is the chief patron, is recorded in a fourteenth century[48] legend. During the plague of 1483 the city remained almost immune through

---

[48] Reproduced in *Apulia, Riv. di Archeol. Filolog. Stor.*, Bari. August 1914, p. 26.

the intercession of the saint. The grateful citizens therefore erected a sumptuous church which, after being long attached to a convent of Franciscan Friars, has now reverted to the parish priest. It contains two relics of the saint. The feasts of 8th March and 10th May are duly celebrated, the latter with a solemn procession. The fair, which was once held there from 3rd to 10th May, was the most important of its kind in the kingdom of Naples. A chapel dedicated to St. Cathal is marked on the Italian Touring Club map (Sheet 38, D. 3) on the shore between S. Spirito and Bari, a masseria S. Cataldo (a farmstead) on Sheet 37, E. 5-6, near Poggiorsini, between Spinazzola and Gravina di Puglia. Putignano once had an ancient chapel dedicated to St. Cathal, which, though now demolished, has bequeathed its name to the locality. Monopoli has venerated the saint since 1476, when the bishop, A. Manfredi, a member of a noble Tarantine family, built a chapel to St. Cathal in the cathedral and entrusted it to a Confraternity which he also instituted. When the cathedral was destroyed, the Confraternity of St. Cathal obtained permission from the Chapter to celebrate the feast of their saint in the reconstructed church where the statue stands vested in pontificals. The feast is kept on the 14th May instead of on the 10th.

In the province of Taranto the liturgical feast of 8th March was celebrated at Castellaneta down to 1913, when the calendar of the universal Church was adopted. As regards the cult paid to its patron, St. Cathal, in Taranto, it should be observed that, until 1913, three feasts were celebrated in the cathedral parish church dedicated to him, the 8th March with double rite of the first class, the 10th May with the same rite and an octave, and the first Sunday in September (the feast of the Patronage) with a major double rite. When the universal calendar was adopted, the first feast ("in depositione S. Cataldi E. C.") was reduced to a double major; the second ("Inventionis die") remained unchanged, while the third ("Patrocinii festo") has been fixed for 3rd September, but without any alteration of rite. On the desert shore of the Gulf of Taranto, close to the mouth of the little river Bevagna, where once stood Fellinum, but a few yards away from the shrine of St. Peter, is the well of St. Cathal. The holy man is said to have rested there after his shipwreck, and the imagination of the populace still attributes medicinal virtues to its waters.

A Ponte di S. Cataldo is marked on the Italian Touring Club map (Sheet 43, B. 6), on the road from Taranto to San Giorgio below Taranto, and a submarine spring in the Mar Grande is called St. Cathal's Ring.[49] In Grottaglie, a commune in the province of Taranto, the cult of the saint goes back to time immemorial and can be proved from documents dating from about the end of the fifteenth century. The Collegiate Church of Grottaglie has a chapel dedicated to the saint, built in 1615 on the initiative of Mgr. Caracciolo, Archbishop of Taranto, who contributed to the expense. High festival is held there on 10th May.

In the province of Brindisi, more particularly in the episcopal see of Oria, the cult of St. Cathal was introduced in 1898 at the instance of Mgr. Gargiulo, and the feast is kept on 10th May.

Lecce contains a monumental church of SS. Nicholas and Cathal built with an abbey attached in 1180 by Tancredi, the last king of the Normans. It has three naves and the whole is profoundly impressive. It underwent many transformations in the eighteenth century at the hands of the Olivetans who served it from 1494 to 1788, but has retained some ancient portals and a thirteenth century fresco.[50] Some eight miles from the city, on the Adriatic, are St. Cathal's Port, the port of the ancient Roman Lupia (Lecce), a fishing harbour, with a St. Cathal's lighthouse, and a bathing place also called after him. The Italian ex-Service Men's Association has recently carried out a land reclamation scheme in the district (the Bonifica di S. Cataldo) and recovered about four thousand acres of what was once marshy and malarial land. The Italian Touring Club map (Sheet 44, C. 4) indicates a hamlet, Case S. Cataldo, near Trepuzzi. At Nardò, as at Alliste, both communes in the

[49] Italian Touring Club *Guide to Southern Italy*, first edition, 1926, p. 685.
[50] Cf. L. De Simone, *Illustrazione dei principali monumenti di Terra d'Otranto*, Lecce, Campanella, 1889, pp. 29-30, and De Giorgi, *La provincia di Lecce*, Lecce, Spacciante, 1888, II, pp. 384-94.

province of Lecce, the cult of St. Cathal was revived in 1899 by Mgr. Ricciardi, a native of Taranto, and his feast is kept there on 10th May.

§ 19

At Bagni di S. Cataldo, part of the commune of Bella in the province of Potenza, between Muro Lucano and Avigliano, the cult of the saint has been kept up *ab immemorabili* in a chapel belonging to Prince Torello di S. Antimo and dedicated to St. Cathal, who has also given his name to the adjoining property and wood (cf. Italian Touring Club map, Sheet 37, F. 2). The little shrine boasts a fine statue of the saint whose feast is kept on 10th May.

A Chapel of St. Cathal is indicated on the map (Sheet 42, A. 4) below Pietrapertosa in the province of Potenza. The commune of Brienza in the same province, but in the diocese of Marsico Nuovo, has St. Cathal for its patron-in-chief, and his two feasts are celebrated there on 8th March and 10th May, with a great concourse of strangers. The consecrated church, once situate in the middle of the village, was later demolished and the site converted into a piazza. The statue of the saint was then housed in the Franciscan Church, now served by priests from the parish church of St. Mary Major of the Assumption. At Gorgoglione, a commune of the province of Matera in the diocese of Tricarico, a statue, much venerated by the faithful, is preserved in the parish church entitled after St. Mary of the Assumption; there the feast is kept on the 20th May instead of on the 10th. A Regione S. Cataldo is indicated on the Italian Touring Club map (Sheet 42, B. 5) north-west of the village. At Saponara di Grumento, a commune of the province of Potenza in the diocese of Marsico Nuovo, there is a shrine of St. Cathal now in ruins, as a result of the earthquake on 16th December, 1857. When the church was destroyed, devotion to the saint ceased, but a memory still remains of the procession which used to take place there on 10th May and a popular adage, "When it comes to Cathal's day, the sun shines and cold's away," is still repeated. A hamlet,

Case S. Cataldo, is marked on the Italian Touring Club map (Sheet 42, E. 4) north of Viggianello (in the province of Potenza and the diocese of Cassano all' Jonio).

§ 20

A chapel dedicated to St. Cathal stood rather more than a mile from Morano Calabro (in the province of Cosenza and the diocese of Cassano all' Jonio), with a hut adjoining for a hermit's dwelling. The chapel has been destroyed, but the district still retains the name of the saint. Cariati (in the province of Cosenza, an episcopal see) has St. Cathal for its patron: the cult was introduced there in the remote past by sailors from Taranto who found it easy to land on those shores and did so frequently. The feast is kept there on 10th May with a large concourse of strangers in a church rather more than a mile from the hut (cf. Italian Touring Club map, Sheet 48, A. 3). The statue is carried there from the cathedral by the populace in solemn procession, left there for a fortnight, and then carried back again amid universal rejoicing. In Cirò Marina, part of Cirò (in the province of Catanzaro and the diocese of Cariati), the parish church, a modern building, is dedicated to St. Cathal, because it stands on the site of an old Chapel of St. Cathal. A relic of the saint is venerated there and his feast kept on 10th May.

§ 21

Crossing over to Sicily, we find a little church dedicated to St. Cathal and containing a statue of the saint in the commune of Gualtieri Sicaminò (in the province of Messina and the diocese of Santa Lucia del Mela), where the feast is celebrated on 10th May. Also dedicated to St. Cathal is the parish church of Gagliano Castelferrato (in the province of Enna and the diocese of Nicosia), whose patron he is. The church, mentioned in a document dated as early as 1334, stands on the highest point of the country and boasts two statues of the saint, the smaller of which is of silver, and a relic with a certificate dated 1612. The feast is kept on 8th March and 10th May, but with special ceremony on 29th, 30th, 31st August and 1st September. On 31st August a great procession takes place, and the ancient statue of the saint is taken for an outing. All during the month of August the faithful, in accordance with a very old custom, go and fulfil their vows of gathering-in the laurel harvest in the distant woods of Caronia, whence they all return together piously to the church and offer the fruits of the harvest to the saint.

In Nicosia also (in the province of Enna and an episcopal see), the cult of St. Cathal is of very ancient date, as may be seen from a missal dated 1346 belonging to the Church of St. Michael. A little Church of St. Cathal, once served by Dominicans, gives its name to a quarter in the city. Enna, formerly Castrogiovanni (the chief town of the province and in the diocese of Piazza Armerina), has a parish church dedicated to St. Cathal and a picture of the saint painted on a pillar and dating from Norman times, with a marked resemblance to another in the cathedral at Cefalù. The map of the Italian Touring Club (Sheet 55, A. 5) shows south-west of Enna, between Monte Cannarella and M. Pasquasia, a regione S. Cataldo: and another regione S. Cataldo is shown south-east of Caltagirone (Sheet 56, C. 1), along the road towards Grammichele.

There is a city of twenty-two thousand inhabitants in the province of Caltanissetta called San Cataldo, with a parish church (recently raised to the dignity of a Collegiate church) dedicated to the saint. The name of St. Cathal was given to the city by its founder, Nicolò Galletti, by permission of Philip III, King of the Two Sicilies; both the princely family of Galletti and the sovereign were greatly devoted to the thaumaturge of Taranto. The name San Cataldo, first given to the place in 1607, was officially registered in 1610.[51] Two feasts are kept every year: on the Sunday after 8th March and on the last Sunday in May, with a great procession. The Guild of St. Cathal numbers about three hundred members, who have their own chapel in the cemetery. In

[51] Cf. Cataldo Urso, *Due secoli di storia del Commune di S. Cataldo*, p. 36.

Gangi also (in the province of Palermo and the diocese of
Cefalù), there is a lively cult of the saint: in the seventeenth
century one of the two parish churches in the commune
was called after him but later became a dependence from the
other, which is the sole parish church at the present day and
is dedicated to St. Nicholas. A relic of St. Cathal, enclosed
in a bronze hand, is venerated there, and the two feasts of
8th March and 10th May are duly kept. In the cathedral
at Cefalù (in the province of Palermo and the seat of a
bishop), on a huge pillar of granite propped against the
great pilaster on the left of the first arch in the transept, an
austere figure of St. Cathal is painted seated in an arm-
chair, his head covered with a bishop's mitre of antique
pattern, and holding in his hands an urn with the representation upon it of two heads, probably those of the martyrs SS.
Vincent and Paul. It dates to Norman times, more precisely
to the reign of King Roger, who began building the cathedral
shortly after 1145. A figure of St. Cathal, similar to that on
the pillar, is carved on a magnificent twelfth century ivory
staff kept in the treasury of the cathedral.

At Palermo, close by the Quattro Canti, a small rectagonal
piazza in the heart of the city, and a stone's throw from the
Norman Church of la Martorana or S. Maria dell' Ammiraglio (1143),[52] with which it is sometimes confused,
stands, on the left side of the via Macqueda, another Norman
church called after St. Cathal, which was already in existence
in 1161, because in that year Count Silvestro de Marsi
buried his daughter Mathilda therein, as may be seen from a
surviving sepulchral inscription. The Church of St. Cathal,
admirably restored by the architect G. Patricolo, in 1884,
preserves better than la Martorana the oriental appearance
of its original architecture with its exterior arches and three
curious little cupolas painted red. The interior is profoundly
impressive: rectangular in shape, thirty feet, roughly, by
twenty-one, it is divided into three naves by six pillars
removed from ancient buildings; the mosaic pavement is the

[52] So called because it was erected during the first half of the twelfth century
in honour of Our Lady by Georgios Antiochenos, grand-admiral of Roger I
and Roger II.

original one, as is also the altar with the cross and the symbols of the four evangelists.

According to Blandamura a full-length figure of St. Cathal is to be seen on one of the pillars of the sacristy, vested in pontificals and wearing the *pallium*, a wand in his right hand and a book in his left. This little Norman church has now been declared a national monument, and, although no longer used for religious purposes, attracts many visitors because of its artistic importance. In the Piazza Marina, still in Palermo, stands the modern Palazzo S. Cataldo, by the side of which, through the vicolo Palagonia all' Alloro, No. 5, the old Palazzo S. Cataldo may be seen. It has some beautifully ornate Renaissance doorways and was once the property of the noble family of S. Cataldo. The Villa S. Cataldo at Bagheria is now a Jesuit novice-house. The cathedral at Monreale, the most beautiful Norman church in all Sicily, adjoining the most beautiful Benedictine monastery in the world, had until 1519 a chapel dedicated to St. Cathal, of which only a fragment remains. A pilaster to the right of the sacristy has a picture in mosaic of the saint vested as a bishop with the *pallium*, carrying a black pastoral staff, not crooked, in his right, and a book in his left hand.

On the Italian Touring Club map (Sheet 49, D. 4) a chapel of St. Cathal is marked on the shore, near Partinico, on the Gulf of Castellamare, and a Torre di S. Cataldo, halfway between Partinico and the sea. It is referred to also by De Cristano on p. 37. At Monte S. Giuliano (in the province and diocese of Trapani), a very old (probably twelfth century) parish church is dedicated to St. Cathal and would seem to have served as a mother church until 1321, the year in which Frederick II of Aragon appointed the Church of S. Maria to be such. The Church of St. Cathal, however, continued throughout many centuries to be the seat of civic assemblies and to preserve traces in its relations with other parishes of its original primacy. It has a relic and a statue of the saint dating from 1781. The feast day there is kept on 10th May. On the Italian Touring Club map (Sheet 49, F. 1), the name of S. Cataldo is given to a district, south-east of Marsala, stretching along the right bank of the river Mazzara, which flows into the sea at Mazzara del Vallo.

§ 22

Memories of St. Cathal are to be found also outside Italy. As regards Malta, Blandamura says on p. 34: "The traveller to the island of Malta may be interested to hear that there exists to this day, near Medina, the ancient capital of the island and almost in the centre of it, 'prope cryptam S. Pauli, et contigua cryptae S. Mariae de spe . . . alia crypta S. Cataldo dicata cum coemeterio, supra quod est hodie parvula ecclesia in honorem ejusdem Sancti consecrata, multumque frequentata a devoto populo propter continuas gratias, quas ibidem ejus intercessione referunt herniosi; qua ex causa ibidem fere semper celebratur missa.'[53] There are, as a matter of fact, no less than six cemeteries to be found in that locality, all of great antiquity and all laid out underground. They are named respectively after St. Agatha, St. Veneranda, St. Cathal, St. Mary della Virtù, St. Paul and the Abbey, the largest of the six, and each has its chapel on top. It may well be that this crypt of St. Cathal is intended to commemorate a sojourn made by our apostle in the course of the journey he had undertaken at a time when ships were still unable to sail in complete safety and independent of one another on long voyages."

De Cristano says that "in France the diocese of Sens contains a parish called after the saint, according to Tillemont, who calls him St. Cartaud. So Castellini wrote to the Bollandists in the Appendix for the month of May; there he performed many miracles."

§ 23

The inference to be drawn from this accumulation of isolated particulars would seem to be that the cult of St. Cathal developed immediately after the invention in 1071 and became widespread after the translation in 1151. The principal propagators of the cult (leaving aside certain

[53] Giov. Franc. De Avila, Vice-Chancellor of the Sacred and Eminent Order of the Knights of Malta, in his *Descriz. dell' isola*, 1647.

relatively recent cases of personal or family devotion and
such as were promoted by the zeal of Tarantine prelates)
seem to have been, ecclesiastically speaking, the Benedictines, and, politically speaking, the Normans, who occasionally worked hand in hand. Dom Lugano[54] observes that,
after the first natural feelings of hostility against the Norman
invaders had subsided, "it was precisely Montecassino which
finally persuaded the Church to become reconciled to the
Normans." The eleventh-century Bishop Drogo, who discovered the body of St. Cathal, was a Norman prelate
consecrated by the Pope to take possession of the diocese of
Taranto immediately after it had been wrested from the
Byzantines.[55] He was present in Montecassino at the consecration of the imposing new basilica by Desiderius on 1st
October, 1071,[56] that is to say, a few months after the
invention of the sacred body, and it is probable that he was
largely responsible for the devotion to the newly discovered
saint, whom he must have considered in some ways his own
special saint, among the Benedictines, in what was their
principal monastery. It should also be observed that the
prayer *Propitiare* in the office of St. Cathal is the same prayer
as that in the office of St. Eneco (1st June), the Benedictine
Abbot of Onia in Spain, who died about the same time.
The Benedictines would seem to have been responsible for
the following foundations: Borgoforte (Polirone: the parish
church of St. Cathal has St. Benedict among its titulars),
Modena (the Monastery of St. Peter was a Benedictine
monastery belonging to the Cassinese congregation), Venice,
S. Elia Fiume Rapido, Maddaloni, Scala and Brienza:
possibly, also, for Genoa and Cremona. The Normans
founded Enna, Cefalù and Monte S. Giuliano; the Benedictines and the Normans together, Campagna, Cava dei
Tirreni, Lecce and Monreale. Dom Lugano in *Italia Benedettina* refers to Benedictine monasteries at Brienza (pp. 211
and 217), Maddaloni (p. 224), S. Maria di Porta Nuova in
Naples (p. 225): and also to a Monastery of St. Cathal at
Oderano, near Salerno (p. 225), founded in 1168 and

[54] *Italia Benedettina*, Rome, 1929, p. 31.
[55] Cf. Blandamura, *Il duomo di Taranto*, p. 42.
[56] Cf. Leo Ostiensis, *Chronicon mon. Casin.*, III, 30.

suppressed in 1550, and to another Monastery of St. Cathal at Taurasio, near Avellino (p. 226), founded in 1193 and suppressed in 1610.

It is also extremely interesting to find Cathal included among the images of saints painted on the pillars of the St. Helena Basilica of the Nativity at Bethlehem, and dating back to the latter half of the twelfth century, i.e., to the time of Raoul (Radulphus), Bishop of Bethlehem, who was of Anglo-Norman blood and died in 1172. The figure of Cathal, to be precise, is painted on the eighth pillar of the principal nave on the left and bears the inscription of his name in Latin and Greek. The same Byzantine artists who worked for the Norman kings in Sicily (e.g., in the Cathedral of Cefalù, la Martorana and the Capella Palatina in Palermo) worked also at Bethlehem. Among the other saints, some twenty in all, represented along with Cathal on the pillars of the Basilica of St. Helena are St. Leonard of Limoges, a great favourite in the Limousin, and St. Bartholomew, both very popular among the Normans in Sicily, and the Scandinavian saints Canute and Olaf, the latter of whom was exceedingly popular among the Norman mercenaries attached to the Byzantine army. This circumstance would seem to indicate that Norman devotion played a conspicuous part in decorating the Shrine of the Nativity. Ever since Tancred planted his standard on the Basilica, the Normans looked upon it as almost their own feudal property. More than ten years before the canonical erection of the bishopric of Bethlehem, Arnaldo, Bishop of Martorano in Calabria, fraudulently seized possession of the Church (10th August, 1099), and it is possible that the first two lawful Bishops of Bethlehem (Aschetino and Anselmo or Anselino) were of Norman blood.[57]

[57] Cf. Vincent and Abel: *Bethléem: le Sanctuaire de la Nativité*, Paris. Gabalda, 1914, pp. 167-75.—"The faded figures upon the columns of the Church of the Nativity at Bethlehem are of about the same period [*sc.* the period of the Frankish occupation]. They consist of single saints including Cnut with both Greek and Latin inscriptions. The occurrence in association with these figures of kneeling persons and coats of arms suggests that they are votive. The iconography is almost entirely Byzantine, though the donors seem to have belonged to the Frankish nobility." O. M. Dalton: *Byzantine Art and Archaeology*, Oxford, 1911, p. 277. Cf. also W. R. Lethaby and others: *The Church of the Nativity at Bethlehem* (Byzantine Research and Publication Fund), London, 1910.

§ 1

OUR pious pilgrimage throughout the various provinces of
Italy in search of traces of Irish sanctity comes to an end
with a strangely pathetic figure whose humility is equalled
only by his dignity. Our last Irish saint links up in the most
curious fashion with the first one encountered on this side
of the Alps, with that St. Ursus, the apostle of the Valle d'
Aosta, who gave his name to so many churches and hospitals,
in which devotion to the Lord must certainly have flourished
throughout the centuries, according to the prophetic words
of Bishop Albert of Ivrea (cf. Ch. X, § 6), in various forms.

The blessed Tadhg brings us down to the end of the
fifteenth century. He belonged to a truly noble, not to say
royal, family in Munster, the family of Mac Carthaigh,
which had given a disciple to Máel-Maedóc Ua Morgair
(St. Malachy), which had built Drishane Castle, near Mill-
street (as it was called), on the road from Mallow to Killarney, the Abbey and Castle of Kilcrea between Cork and
Macroom, and together with Cormac Mac Carthaigh, the
stately and still much visited Blarney Castle, about nine
miles north-west of Cork. "Regia progenies, alto de sanguine, Machar."

§ 2

Tadhg was born in the county of Cork in 1455. Embracing the ecclesiastical career, he received Holy Orders in
Cork, probably at the hands of the Bishop, William Roche,
who, in 1479, succeeded one Jordan.[1] These dates place us
in the thick of the Wars of the Roses (1455-85), which,

---

[1] *The Calendar of Papal Registers, Papal Letters,* XI (1455-64), London,
H.M.S.O., 1921, p. 423, prints a precept or mandate from the *Vatican Register,*
Vol. CCCCLXXX de Curia, 2 and 3 Pius II, issued on the 27 May, 1461,
to the Bishops of Emly and Ros and the Abbot of Fermoy (alias de Castrodey)

fought between the House of Lancaster (the red rose) and the House of York (the white rose), wrought havoc among the nobility of England. Ireland at the time was left very much to herself and her popular history in the textbooks resolves itself essentially into the history of a struggle for supremacy between the two families of Butler and Fitzgerald. While the Anglo-Norman nobles were occupied and preoccupied by the changes of fortune in England and played an active part therein, the nobles of pure Irish descent made war on, or peace with, their neighbours and took sides, in the course of the conflict, as opportunity presented itself or interest dictated.

On the death of one Domnall, Bishop of Ros, a little diocese in the extreme south-west of Ireland (it still exists with an episcopal residence at Skibbereen and as a dependence from the metropolitan see of Cashel), Sixtus IV (1471-84) conceived the design of appointing Tadhg, whose virtue and learning had won universal esteem. He had not, however, attained the age prescribed by canon law for a bishop, but the Pope dispensed him, and, in 1482, Tadhg, aged only twenty-seven, was consecrated in Rome in the Church of S. Stefano del Cacco by the Archbishop of Antivari.

When he returned to his diocese, it was not long before he found himself at odds with a certain Odo, who disputed the legitimacy of his nomination and alleged his own prior appointment to the see. The Anglo-Normans in Cork were Yorkist at the time and hostile to Henry Tudor (later Henry VII, the founder of that ignoble dynasty, 1485-

in the diocese of Cloyne. After reciting that Jordan, Bishop of Cork, is an octogenarian and so old that he cannot exercise the pastoral office in person with the result that many excesses and crimes go unpunished and many goods of the churches and the episcopal *mensa* are in the hands of laymen, it appoints William Roche, Archdeacon of Cloyne, 'of a race of Earls,' to be coadjutor to the said bishop. . . . He is to give an account of his administration and before beginning to act as coadjutor and administrator to take before the three mandatories an oath not to alienate, etc.—Dr. Coulton (*Scottish Abbeys, etc.*, pp. 216-9) notes the emergence of the common informer about this time as an indication of the collapse of the nominal visitation system of monastic houses and the break-down of discipline. Very bad in Scotland, it was complete in Ireland, and, between the years 1418 and 1462, 340 informations from Ireland were laid in Rome, as against 30 from Scotland, one from Wales, none from England, and none from Belgium. The authority for Belgium is Dom Berlière.

1509), the son of a Lancaster; they were opposed by Edmund de Courcy, Bishop of Clogher, and an intimate friend of Tadhg's, in whose favour the bishop had renounced the Abbey of Maur de Fonte vivo, a Cistercian house said to have been founded by Diarmid Mac Cormac mac Carthaigh, King of Desmond, in 1172, and to have received its first members from Baltinglas. The Anglo-Normans in Cork denounced Tadhg to Pope Innocent VIII (1484-92) as a friend of the Bishop of Clogher and an intruder into the see of Ros, to which they maintained Odo was entitled.

The Pope, by a Bull dated 21st August, 1488, denounced Tadhg as a son of iniquity and declared him excommunicate and interdicted. The sufferings of the saintly man can be better imagined than described. But with great dignity, and in order not to scandalise the faithful, he begged the Holy See to institute an inquiry.

From a Bull of Innocent VIII dated 21st April, 1490, we gather that Odo but a few years earlier had surrendered a parish charge in order to enter a convent of Friars Minor, that he had quitted the convent before the year of his noviceship was over, and that in order to recover his cure he had given money and made other presents to the surrogate.[2] Domnall meanwhile had resigned the diocese of Ros in favour of Odo, and had sent him in person as his procurator to Sixtus IV to acquaint him of the resignation; but, while Odo was on his way to Rome, Domnall died. He had resigned before the Pope, hearing of his death, had appointed Tadhg. Both Odo and Tadhg therefore considered themselves to be Bishop of Ros and each resolutely maintained his own point of view. Two years later Innocent VIII, in order to settle the matter, charged Oliviero, Bishop of Sabina, to summon the claimants before him, to invite them both to produce any documents or letters that told in their favour and after mature deliberation to report his

[2] The influence of the Anglo-Norman friars in the Irish Franciscan communities was, it should be observed, very strong towards the end of the thirteenth century, and they, like the Dominicans, were in receipt of regular subsidies from the King of England. Cf. Gregory Cleary, O.F.M., "St. Francis and Ireland," in Studies, an Irish Quarterly Review, Dublin, December 1926, p. 542, and March 1927, p. 56.

judgment in the matter. So it was done. On receiving the Bishop of Sabina's report, Innocent VIII, by the Bull dated 21st April, 1490, and before referred to, declared that Odo must be considered Bishop of Ros by priority of appointment and imposed silence thenceforth on Tadhg: but on the same day and in order to proclaim to the world the latter's innocence, he appointed him bishop of the two dioceses of Cork and Cloyne, which had been canonically united in 1430.[3]

Tadhg thus succeeded the William Roche who had given him Holy Orders and who now freely and spontaneously resigned his own diocese. The Pope rewarded his resignation by assigning to William one-third of the revenues of the episcopal *mensa*. In the Bull dated 21st April, 1490, appointing Tadhg, Innocent VIII publicly declared that he had been appointed and consecrated by Sixtus IV "ecclesiae Rossen tamquam vacanti licet in vero non vacaret," and that he appointed him to the other two dioceses as being worthy of such appointment by reason of the honesty of his life and manners, his prudence and vigilance in things spiritual and temporal and the many other talents and virtues which adorned his character. In view of the troubled times, however, and anticipating fresh difficulties, the Pope by a third Bull of even date addressed Tadhg: "It is Our will and We hereby of Our Apostolic Authority decree that the position and promotion by Us made of your person shall be fully valid even though the churches of Cork and Cloyne should happen to be vacant once again through the death of the said William or for any other reason whatsoever."

But even so the sorrows of Tadhg were not yet at any end. He had been appointed bishop, but he could not take possession of his church, because the property of the episcopal *mensa* had, with the connivance of the Council of Cork and the citizens of Youghal, been sacrilegiously seized by those same Anglo-Norman nobles who had opposed his election to the bishopric of Ros. For two weary years he was compelled to go from village to village in miserable plight,

---

[3] They are now separate again: the residence of the diocese of Cloyne (Clùain-nama) is in Cobh (formerly Queenstown).

recalling in the tribulations he endured the sufferings of Máel Maedóc. He was driven at last to return to Rome, where he persuaded Innocent VIII by letter *motu proprio*, dated 18th July, 1492, sternly to admonish the usurpers, their confederates and adherents, to desist from intermeddling with the property of the two dioceses and trampling under foot the rights of the new bishop.

Pope Innocent died on 24th July, fourteen days only after signing the brief.

Tadhg, confident in the efficacy of a missive from the Holy Father, set out from Rome on his return journey to Ireland.

This great noble and high dignitary of the Church, towards the end of a century full of pride and laxity, started off for his distant diocese without a word to anyone, on foot, unattended, with a stick and a pilgrim's wallet, visiting churches and shrines by the way, seeking hospitality in convents and hospices, like some poor beggar for Jesus Christ's sake. The via Romana, which led from Italy into the Gauls, passed through Ivrea. One evening, late in October, the pilgrim arrived at the fair city situate at the entrance to the valley of the Dora Baltea. He lingered for a moment to say a prayer in the dark shadows of the cathedral before the image of Our Lady of Ivrea, and then walked out of the northern gate of the city in search of a roof under which to pass the night; down the steep slope he went, and took the road to Aosta. He felt ill and weary; he may have been weakened by protracted penances; he may have been exhausted by the long journey: one thing only is certain—the moral martyrdom he had suffered in silence during the past four or five years had broken his heart. He stopped at the door of a hospice. By a mysterious coincidence it was the Hospice of the XXI, already familiar to us, kept by the Canons of St. Ursus of Aosta.

The rector, the Reverend François Chabaud, the vicar-general and official of Monseigneur François Despré, who filled that post from 1483 to 1498,[4] received him charitably; but that same night, or rather, more precisely, at dawn on

[4] Cf. Marguerettaz, *Mémoire sur les hôpitaux anciens du Val d'Aoste*, Bollettino dell' Acc. di S. Anselmo, Aosta 1879, appendix, p. 285.

24th October, 1492, the unknown pilgrim breathed his last. He was only thirty-seven years of age. A brilliant light surrounded the pallet on which he lay at the moment of his passing: the servants, believing that something had caught fire, ran to extinguish the blaze, but there was nothing in the midst of that supernatural radiance but the smiling corpse of their latest guest. The following morning the rector went to report the matter to the Bishop Niccoló Garigliatti and his lordship came in person to see what had happened. He opened the dead man's wallet to find out who he was and marvelled, as did the bystanders, to discover an episcopal cross and a ring and papers describing him as Tadhg, Bishop of Cork and Cloyne in Ireland.

The news sped from mouth to mouth, and the faithful flocked in from the city and surroundings, while some sick folk were miraculously cured. The bishop ordered the body to be borne ceremoniously to the cathedral, where it lay in state for several days: he then had it placed under the table of the altar dedicated to St. Eusebius (later to St. Andrew) with the inscription: "Cava S. Eusebii et sepulcrum B. Taddei Ep. Hib."

§ 3

Ever since then the body has been an object of devotion, and the name of Tadhg venerated with the title 'blessed.' In a fifteenth century breviary used by the clergy of the day a note to the calendar for the month of October states that the blessed Tadhg had performed many miracles, including the curing of a certain Legerio, who was much afflicted by fevers. The *beatus* is mentioned in the pastoral visitations of 1585 and 1647. In 1742 Mgr. M. de Villa had an examination of the body made by three doctors in the city, and a pilgrim's shell and the episcopal ring were found in the coffin.

He placed the sacred remains in a new coffin and had them deposited first in the chapel of the Blessed Sacrament, together with other coffins containing the remains of saints, and afterwards under the high altar in the cathedral, where they rest to this day.

The event is solemnly commemorated by the cathedral chapter on the second Sunday after Easter.

Mgr. Augustine Richelmy (later Cardinal), appointed Bishop of Ivrea by Leo XIII in 1881, in association with Mgr. O'Callaghan, Bishop of Cork,[5] petitioned for official recognition of the cult paid *ab immemorabili* to the blessed Tadhg. A favourable opinion of the Sacred Congregation of Rites, dated 13th August, 1895, which declared him worthy of the honours of the altars, was confirmed by Leo XIII on 26th August of that same year.

In September 1896 a great festival was held in Ivrea in his honour.[6]

[5] A Dominican, long resident in Italy, first as a student, later as master of novices, and finally as prior of the convent of St. Clemente in Rome.

[6] Cf. with reference to the blessed Tadhg, *Analecta Bollandiana*, XV, p. 458. Savio, *Gli antichi vescovi d'Italia: il Piemonte*, p. 179; the *Lives of the Saints of Piedmont*, by Gallizia and Massa, the manuscript histories of Ivrea by Fr. Benvenuti and Canon Robesti (quoted in Ch. X, § 6), Canon Vaudagnotti's *Vita del Card. Richelmy*, the *Numero unico in onore del b. Taddeo Machar*, published by seminarians and other admirers, Ivrea, Tomatis, 1896, and, above all, the little work by Canon Giovanni Saroglia, *Il b. Taddeo Machar vescovo irlandese*, Ivrea, Tomatis, which contains full and precise information.

PART III

THE IRISH RELIGIOUS MOVEMENT AND THE FRANCISCAN MOVEMENT

CHAPTER XXIV

THE IRISH RELIGIOUS MOVEMENT AND THE FRANCISCAN
MOVEMENT

§ 1

"THERE came upon a day to the Apennine valley where
Columban's holy remains are laid [the visit of St. Francis of
Assisi to Bobbio is mentioned by Cardinal Logue in his
'Appeal' for the restoration of the sanctuary (24th November,
1906)]," writes Mrs. Concannon,[1] "one who was destined
to be known through all the world by the very designation
which Columban had chosen for himself [*Peregrinus . . .
pauperculus* (Epist. V, Migne, Vol. 80, c. 274)]. The
'Poverello' of Assisi has much more in common with the
'Pellegrinus . . . Pauperculus' of Bobbio than a self-chosen
designation. So close are the 'conformities' between
Columban and Francis that one can only wonder why they
have not struck the biographers of the latter saint. [Dr.
Shahan has been the only person, as far as I know, to draw
attention to the striking 'conformities' between Columban
and Francis (cf. his article: 'An Irish Monastery in the
Apennines,' *American Catholic Quarterly Review*, July 1901)].
As far as I can recollect, not one of them has recorded the
visit of Francis to Bobbio, and yet the devotion to St.
Columban which it indicated may have had a remarkable
influence on the spiritual development of St. Francis and the
direction of his Order.

"It is not alone that the two saints have taken the same
Great Master for their teacher, and have interpreted His
teachings alike, because they interpreted them literally. It
is not even that the picture we make to ourselves of Francis
standing beneath the oak tree on Monte Alverno with the

---

[1] *The Life of St. Columban*, Dublin, C.T.S., 1915, pp. XVI-XX.   Mrs.
Concannon's notes have been retained within square brackets in the text.

welcoming birds in great multitudes all around him [Fioretti: *First Reflection on the Most Holy Stigmata*] recalls inevitably what Chagnoald saw as he 'ministered' to Columban in the wild fastnesses of the Jura woodlands [*V. Col.*, I, 17]. Little external details of daily life and rule would almost seem to have been borrowed by St. Francis for his brethren from the life and rule of Columban. The dress they wore, the tunic of undyed wool, with a cowl [Joergensen, *Life of St. Francis*, Book II, Chap. I], was the dress of the Irish monks. The 'places' of the earlier Franciscans, little wattled huts with a hedge around them for a *vallum*, might have been reconstructions of an ancient Celtic monastery [Ibid., ii, 4]. Before the door at Rivo Torto [Ibid., ii, 2] we learn there was a great wooden cross, like that which stood before the door of Abbot Athala at Bobbio [*V. Col.*, ii, 6].[2] And if one followed the windings of that same 'twisted river,' one came to little grottoes on the slopes of Monte Subasio, which Francis called 'Le Carceri' [Joergensen, Book II, Chap. ii] and which he used for the same purposes of prayerful retreat for which Columban used his 'Carcair.' Can we doubt but that he borrowed the name from him?

"And the mission of the two men was the same. For Francis it had been defined in the *Legenda Trium Sociorum*, 'pacis et poenitentiae legationem amplectens' [Chap. X, n. 39 (Bollandist Ed.)]. This phrase sums up for Columban also all that was achieved by his life-work. His mission of Peace was carried out in his schools, and in the fields, which his own toil and that of his brethren rescued from the wild barrenness of the *Deserta*. His mission of penance was accomplished in that ministry of 'Soul-Friendship'[3] which did so much to build the laity into the solid masonry of the Church. The symbolism of the Middle Ages, so admirably interpreted for us in the pages of Huysmans' *La Cathédrale*, saw in the laity the stones of the walls of the church, 'of which some were large and some small,' joined together like 'the strong and weak' in the Communion of the Faithful. In that dreadful sixth century in Gaul (of which Gregory

---

[2] Ryan, *Irish Monasticism*, p. 234.
[3] *Anmchara*, cf. Ch. II, § 5 and III, § 2.

of Tours has chronicled the deeds, and pictured the men and women) the walls of the mystic cathedral had well-nigh crumbled away, under the assaults of frightful passions and appetites. 'Religionis virtus pene habebatur. Fides tantum manebat christiana nam penitentiae medicamenta et mortificationis amor vix vel paucis in ea reperiebatur locis,' says Jonas (*V. Col.*, 1, 5). Columban won back the laity to true Christianity—built them up again into the walls of the Church by his ministry of 'Soul-Friendship'—and buttressed them with the many religious communities of men and women who owed their first impulse to Luxeuil. Not unfitting will it seem to one whose mind is open to the interpretation 'of figure and mystery,' that one of Columban's churches was built on the ruins of an ancient Roman Temple of Diana [Miss Stokes, *Three Months in the Forests of France*, p. 54] as if to signify what his mission of 'peace,' in school and field, was to do for the new Christian civilisation of Europe, by consecrating anew the heritage of culture left by Ancient Rome; and one was got by reconsecrating a Christian church defiled by idol-worshippers [*Vita Galli*, auc., Walafrido, Book I, Chap. VI], and a third was built up anew from a half-ruined basilica of St. Peter [*V. Col.*, 1, 30]. So, too, St. Francis restored many churches [Joergensen, op. cit., Book 1, *passim*] and Pope Innocent had a dream wherein he saw him—a 'poor little man,' and meanly clad— hold aloft the mighty structure of the Lateran [Joergensen, op. cit., Book II, 2].

"In that chivalrous conception of saintship, which made Francis see in his companions the 'Cavalieri' of Christ [Wadding, *Annals*, Vol. I, p. 80], we recognise the old Irish idea of the 'Milites Christi.' The Paladins of Charlemagne, the Round Table Knights of Arthur, came to the mind of Francis, as he thought of the relations of himself and his brethren with Christ, their Captain. When we see how readily the warlike metaphor passes to the pen of Columban —whether he writes to the brethren left behind him in Luxeuil, or to Pope Boniface—we are fain to believe that he, too, thought of the knights of his own land, who taught knightliness to Europe.

"One could write a long chapter concerning the 'conform-ities' of Francis and Columban. But enough has been said to show ground for the assertion that, if the Benedictines were the natural heirs of Columban [. . . . even in his own foundations of Luxeuil and Bobbio the Benedictine Rule supplanted that of Columban. An inscription round the antique baldacchino which covered the shrine of Columban at Bobbio bore the inscription 'S. Columbanus, Hibernensis, D. Benedicti discipulus et sectator'], the Franciscans were the true heirs of his spirit. And perhaps therein is indicated a good reason for the wonderful spread of the Franciscan Order in Ireland. When the sons of St. Francis first set foot on Irish soil, they were bringing back to Ireland what she had given Italy centuries before. And this, perhaps, is one of the reasons why the Brown Friar has—much privileged—been always close at hand in the supreme moments of Ireland's heroism, and of Ireland's agony. . . . [The idea has found beautiful expression in Miss Alice Milligan's fine poem, 'The Blessing of the Brown Friar' (*Hero Lays*, p. 44)]."

This long extract contains much that, in my opinion, is well founded and much that is absolutely inadmissible. It is inadmissible in the first place, because it is definitely contrary to historical truth to present St. Francis as deriving from St. Columban, as an imitator almost and a mere reviver of his ideals, with which in all probability he was most imperfectly acquainted and which he eventually identified—according to the common custom of all thirteenth century Italians—with the ideals of St. Benedict.[4] Nor can the suggestion of imitation be supported by such slender arguments as the fortuitous coincidence between the names 'carceri' and 'carcair,' the similarity between the respective habits (that of St. Francis was of direct evangelical inspiration) or the erection of a wooden cross. The entirely Italian origin and character of St. Francis are as a matter of history beyond discussion.

It is inadmissible in the second place, at all events, if the

---

[4] Dante makes no reference of any kind, not even indirectly, to St. Columban in his *Paradiso*.

reader is not to be deceived, to pass over in silence the
enormous differences between the gentle personality of the
seraphic saint and the vehement and haughty personality
of Columban, terrifying in invective and apostrophe, a true
prophet—as the Abbé Martin has well observed[5]—of the
lineage of Elias, Elisha and St. John the Baptist.

That there are points of contact, however, between the
spirit of the Irish movement in the sixth-eighth centuries
and the spirit of the Franciscan movement in the thirteenth-
fourteenth is, in my opinion, perfectly true, and, for this
very reason, in all those matters in regard to which a veil
may be drawn over certain aspects of Columban's character
and he be suffered to stand forth simply as an illustrious
representative of Irish religious sentiment in general, a true
parallel may be sustained between him and St. Francis.

I propose in this last chapter to dwell a little on a subject
of such peculiar interest to Italians and Franciscans and
also because the contrast will permit a useful summary to
be made of the characteristic features of the Irish movement,
whose traces we have pursued so far on Italian soil.

In the preface written by Father Augustine, O.S.F.C.,
to Dom Gougaud's *Gaelic Pioneers of Christianity*,[6] I find
the following (pp. XVIII and XIX): ". . . We seem
to see those Irish confessors of the Faith go forth, sometimes indeed singly, but generally in small bands or in
groups of twelve, following no fixed plan, but, in the
fullness of their trust, leaving themselves to the guidance of
the spirit of God. They usually wore a tunic of undyed
wool to which was attached a capuce like the habit that
was afterwards adopted by the 'sweet St. Francis of Assisi';
and their luggage was confined to little more than a stout
walking-stick, a leathern water-bottle slung to the shoulder,
and a wallet or satchel containing a few choice books and
some relics of the saints. . . . Like the gentle Poverello whose
life and Rule has much in common with theirs, and whose
devotion led him centuries later to the shrine of Columbanus
at Bobbio, they were indeed 'of Christ wholly enamoured'
and had in full and bounteous measure that personal

[5] *Saint Columban*, pp. 174 et seq.   [6] Gill and Sons, Dublin, 1923.

affection which is such a sad want of the present age, but which lit up their hearts with the white-heat of a great passion that no sacrifice could satiate and no suffering subdue."

A reference to the devotional visit paid by St. Francis as an ascertained fact is to be found in the eloquent address delivered by Cardinal Logue at Bobbio on 25th March, 1906: "How pleasant it is to us to think that the little poor man of Assisi made his way one day, unobserved, into the crypt of this basilica and there prostrated himself with oustretched arms before the tomb of our great patron and protector."[7] And further reference is made to the pilgrimage of the seraphic Father in the appeal launched by the same cardinal to the Irish for the restoration of the shrine on 24th November, 1906.

It is recalled, but with a note of interrogation, in the Lenten Pastoral Letter for 1923 of Mgr. P. Calchi-Novati, Bishop and Count of Bobbio:[8] "There is a pious tradition—and why should we not give it credence?—that St. Francis of Assisi made a pilgrimage to this venerable crypt and there gave a fraternal greeting to the great Irish monk."

It may be advisable, however, before proceeding any further to take a rapid glance through the available documents to see what, if anything, they have to relate about this interesting visit.

§ 2

None of the ancient biographers of St. Francis makes any reference to it: and none, so far as I am aware, of the modern. Such information as there is with regard to it is part and parcel only of our general knowledge of the Convent of St. Francis at Bobbio, undoubtedly one of the oldest in the Order, inasmuch as it was founded very probably as early as the first half of the thirteenth century and belonged to the Bolognese Province.[9]

[7] *Irish Eccles. Record*, Vol. XIX, May 1906, pp. 446-50.
[8] Bobbio, Boldini e Foppiani, 1923, p. 19.
[9] Documents relating to its foundation may still possibly be found among the Bobbio papers in the State archives of Turin, also because the site was generously gifted to the Franciscans according to their custom, by the

Fra Salimbene records in his Chronicle[10] that he visited Bobbio in 1249. "Item millesimo supraposito post festum sancti Antonii Paduani, sive Hyspani, qui est ex ordine fratrum Minorum, de conventu Ianuensi recessi cum socio meo (Iohannino de Ollis), et venimus Bobium, et vidimus unam de ydriis Domini, in qua Dominus ex acqua vinum fecit in nuptiis. Dicitur enim esse una ex illis. Si est, Deus novit, cui nota sunt omnia, aperta et nuda. In ea sunt multe reliquie. In altari monasterii Bobii est. Et sunt ibi multe reliquie beati Columbani, quas vidimus. Post hec. venimus Parmam. . . ." He makes no reference to any stay at Bobbio of St. Francis, or, in terms, to the existence there of any convent of the Friars Minor. It is more than probable, however, that the words 'venimus Bobium' should be taken to mean 'to our convent at Bobbio,' as also the following words 'venimus Parmam.'

Gonzaga[11] refers to the 'conventus S. Francisci Bobij' as follows: "Extra istius igitur civitatis muros conventus hic, Seraphico Patri Francisco sacer, atque a 12 fratribus inhabitatus, exsurgit: qui sane antiquissimus est, atque eidem Seraphico patri coëvus: cum, indubia seniorum traditione, ab eo aliquando inhabitatus fuerit. Innititur vero huiusmodi traditio duabus Pontificiis bullis in huius loci tabellario asservatis: quarum altera a Nicolao III Summo Pontiface 30 anno a morte divi patris Francisci, altera vero ab Alexandro IV Pont, itidem max. iij tantum anno post ejusdem patris mortem, data fuit: et utraque hujus sacrae aedis tamquam omnino perfectae, retroque aedificatae mentionem facit. . . ." Here the tradition of St. Francis's visit to Bobbio is found well established and supported by the authority of two papal Bulls, which ought to prove that the convent had been built before his death. There is no respect, however, paid to chronology, for Alexander IV was Pope from 1254 to 1261, and Nicholas III from 1277 to 1280.

Benedictines. The *Codice Diplomatico*, edited by Cipolla and Buzzi, comes down only to 1208.

[10] Cf. Prof. Holder-Egger's edition in *M.G.H.*, *Scriptores*, Vol. XXXII, p. 332, and Dr. G. G. Coulton's *From St. Francis to Dante: a translation of all that is of primary interest in the chronicle of the Franciscan Salimbene* (1221-88), London, Nutt, 1906, at p. 184.

[11] *De origine Seraph. Religionis Franciscanae*, Rome, 1587, Pt. II, p. 268.

Luke Wadding[12] mentions the convent by name but solely with reference to indulgences granted it in 1290 by Nicholas IV (1288-92).[13]

Mgr. Stefano Rebolini of Bobbio has kindly drawn my attention to the *Ordo processionum Cleri Bobiensis*,[14] which, after describing the itinerary of the procession of the 'feria III in Rogationibus usque ad Ecclesiam S. Francisci,' continues (pp. 63 et seq.): "Etsi superioribus annis renovata fuerit haec D. Francisci Ecclesia, una tamen cum adiuncto Coenobio antiquissimae fundationis procul dubio dignoscuntur. Siquidem constans veterum traditio est, eundem Seraphicum Patrem Franciscum aliquando hanc sedem incoluisse prout comprobari videtur, tum ex angusta quadam Cella, in superiori Conventus Dormitorio adhuc extante, quam inhabitasse creditur, tum etiam ex Pontificiis Bullis Alexandri IV 1256 et Nicolai III 1278 editis, et in Tabulario Fratrum asservatis. Olim in hoc coenobio alebantur duodecim Religiosi ad minus, et magna erat Civium erga Seraphicum Institutum devotio, cum omnes ferme Bobienses incolae Tertio S. Francisci Ordini, qui maxime alias floruit in hac Ecclesia, adscriberentur." Here there is mention of something new, the existence of a cell belonging to St. Francis in the convent in Bobbio.[15]

---

[12] *Annales Minorum*, Vol. 5, p. 244, n. 27.

[13] In Vol. XIII, p. 146, n. 75, under the year 1459, he mentions a convent of Poor Clares in Bobbio, called after St. Clare and founded *ante aliquos annos*: and in the same volume, at p. 380, n. 27, under the year 1465, he speaks of "Sorores Monasterii Sanctae Clarae Bobiensis Tertii Ordinis," to whom "omnia et singula conceduntur privilegia et gratiae quomodolibet concessa sororibus quibusvis ejusdem Instituti, sub regimine Fratrum Minorum de Observantia degentibus."

[14] Mediolani, 1756, ap. Fredericum Agnellum. Two earlier editions of 1459 and 1627 respectively are extant.

[15] This *Ordo processionum* mentions also (p. 71) the monastery and church of St. Clare. "Perantiqua est haec S. Clarae Ecclesia, penes quam degunt Sacrae Deo Virgines sub Regulae Seraphici P. S. Francisci, cujus institutum jam fere per sex saecula ab ipsis amplexum, religiose adhuc servatur. Olim supra triginta sorores in hoc asceterio commorabantur, sanctitatis et observantiae fama celebres, quae licet ex antiqua institutione a claustris egredi libere possent, a Pio Papa II anno 1458 supplices petierunt, ut sibi sub arctissima Clausurae custodia et lege vivere imposterum ex solemni voto liceret, quod, prout ex Pontificis litteris ejusdem datis Mantuae primo sui Pontificatus anno, in earundem Archivio asservatis, evincitur, impetrarunt, et huc usque ab ipsis diligenter observatur." The monastery continued to thrive until it was suppressed by Napoleon in 1802.

Flaminio da Parma,[16] on the other hand, makes St. Francis visit Bobbio before the building of the convent and would have him its founder.　He repeats the chronological errors of Gonzaga and says: "It is proper to relate the establishment of the Friars Minor in Bobbio, inasmuch as, although there be no memorial extant to tell us of the same, yet the constant tradition and many coincidences combine to persuade us that this took place at the time of the journey through those parts of the seraphic Father S. Francis. Wadding in divers places, and other writers of the *gesta* of the saintly Father, describe him to us in Lombardy and Piedmont, at one time retracing his steps almost as soon as he had arrived, at another as a solitary traveller on his way to the Gauls and Spain, and on his return thence, making now for Alexandria and Monferrato, and anon for Cuneo, and journeying through the western Apennines of Liguria, passing then through neighbouring Cairo and venturing towards the eastern parts of Liguria itself, and thereafter advancing into the heart of Tuscany.　Now it being certain that the saintly Father crossed the rocky mountains of Liguria, and that, in the course of his travels, he went out of his way to visit the most venerated shrines and even stopped there occasionally for a little while, as in other places also renowned for the virtues of most austere monks and the saints, their founders, as for instance, in Camaldoli and elsewhere, it would seem improbable that, when travelling through the mountains of Liguria, he should not have made a descent to visit the neighbouring shrine and monastery of Bobbio, most renowned all over Italy, and indeed all over Europe, for the sacred bodies there venerated of the most holy abbots, Columban, Athala, Bertulf and Bobulenus, for the most revered Cummian, who quitted his episcopal see in Scotland [*sic*] to go and live the life of a simple monk in that monastery, and for the sanctity of a multitude of other most austere monks.　As it must have been a great consolation for the saintly Father to visit the sacred remains of those holy men in the crypt of the monastery

---

[16] *Memorie istoriche delle chiese e dei conventi dei frati minori dell' Osservante e Riformata Provincia di Bologna*, Parma, 1760, I, p. 4.

church, to admire the edifying lives led by those then numerous monks, to visit those steep places so far withdrawn from the din and tumult of the world, so also he must have longed to build a convent there for the Friars of his Order, and to obtain a site from those venerable monks suitable for his purpose must not have been difficult for him who had obtained from the very generous Benedictine monks both his own beloved little church of the Porziuncola and many other places for the building of convents and the propagation of his Order.

"The respectable, ancient, and, perhaps, also authentic, records of such things would assuredly not be found wanting if the old writings had been preserved in the convent which had been built, but now, there being none of them to be found, there is nothing to go by except only tradition, some scraps of information as to what the ancient edifice was like, and a document or two attesting, if not the foundation, at any rate the antiquity of the convent, well-nigh contemporaneous with the saintly Father. Wadding supposed it to have been built in the very century in which the saintly Father flourished and founded his supposition upon the grant of some indulgences made by the Supreme Pontiff Nicholas IV (Wad., V, year 1290, n. 17).

"Yet are there two memorials still more ancient which were preserved in the convent in the time of Gonzaga and are quoted by the same, to wit: a Bull of Nicholas III, published thirty years, and another of Alexander IV, given only three years, after the death of the seraphic Father (Gonzaga, p. II, *De prov. Bonon.*, num. 3), in which the church and the convent are presumed to have been already built and securely inhabited by religious, inasmuch as Nicholas III grants some indulgences to whoever shall visit in the prescribed form the church of St. Francis at Bobbio in the days dedicated to the same St. Francis, to St. Antony of Padua and St. Clare. And the Bull of Alexander IV shows that in those critical days, in which the dissensions already described were rife between the clergy and the people and the monks, even the poor friars were not exempt from molestation, for an attempt was made to prevent them giving burial in their own church to those devout persons who desired and had taken steps to be buried there; the Supreme Pontiff therefore gave orders that none should offer let or hindrance to them in that regard. The Bull of Nicholas III referred to has gone amissing, but the Bull of Alexander IV is still preserved, and is the sole ancient record left in those archives."

The Bull referred to is reproduced in the *Bullarium Franciscanum*[17] under date 23rd July, 1257 (the third year of the Pontificate of Alexander IV), with the following note: "Ut ex cit. Gonzaga colligi posse videtur: hujus porro loci, Cenobiique meminit Waddingus ad annum 1290, n. 27, sed tantum occasione Indulgentiae illi a Nicolao IV elargitae; caeterum origo ejus adhuc ignoratur, fuitque 5 locus Custodiae Parmensis in Provincia Bononiensi ex veteri Provinciali Ordinis apud Auctorem Polychronici, et Pisanum Conform. XI, Saeculo XV a nostris ad FF. Minores Observantes translatus."

The convent of St. Francis of Bobbio was transferred in 1782 to the province of Turin,[18] where it remained until it was suppressed by Napoleon in 1802. Fr. Corrado refers to it as follows:[19] "Extra huiusce urbis (Bobii) moenia iam ab antiquis temporibus extabat Minorum conventus, quem Ordinis scriptores ex non dubiis monumentis eidem Seraphico S. Francisco coaevum asserunt. Hic conventus Divo P. Francisco dicatus a duodenis Fratribus ut plurimum incolebatur, atque ad Bononiensem Ordinis Provinciam spectabat. Ast anno 1783 huic Divi Thomae Apostoli accessit, in eoque fratres habitavere, spiritualia pro temporalibus subsidia Civibus sedulo praestantes, usque ad annum 1802."

The parchments from the archives of the monasteries of St. Francis and St. Clare suffered the same fate during the Napoleonic régime as those from the archives of St. Columban. They remained in the custody of the sub-prefecture

---

[17] Fr. J. H. Sbaraleae, Romae, 1761, Vol. II, p. 230. Cf. also *Bullarii Franciscani Epitome redegit Conradus Eubel*, Quaracchi, 1908, p. 93, n. 958 in the note.

[18] Cf. P. G. Picconi, *Centone di memorie storiche concernenti la Minoritica Provincia di Bologna*, Parma, Tip. della SS. Nunziata, 1906, tomo I, p. 4.

[19] *Historia et chronologica Synopsis almae prov. Taurinensis de Observantia*, Taurini typ. Castellazzo e Caretti, 1856, p. 104.

of Bobbio until 1815, when they were catalogued and transferred (by way of Voghera and perhaps, also, of Alexandria) to the State archives of Turin, which they had reached as early as 1821.[20] The fabric of the convent of St. Francis and the attached church is still standing: but the church has been turned into a hayloft, while the convent arouses pity owing to the sorry state of squalor to which it has been reduced. Part of it is tenanted by two families of labourers, the rest is uninhabited. The erstwhile sacristy has now been turned into a carpenter's workshop. The whole is the property of Senator the Marchese Obizzo Malaspina, whose ancestors bought it from the State after its suppression in 1802. Two magnificent, age-old yew trees, believed to have been planted by St. Francis, were cut down during the late war.

It is abundantly clear from the foregoing that the tomb of St. Columban was a flourishing centre of Franciscanism early in the thirteenth century, and that the poetic tradition of St. Francis's visit to Bobbio and of his devotion to St. Columban is of very ancient date. But we must be content, in my opinion, to leave it a symbolical, rather than an historical, value. Indeed, the absence of any reference to it by the first biographers of St. Francis, more particularly Tommaso da Celano, who yet records his visit to Alessandria where a miracle took place,[21] the silence of Fra Salimbene, who yet visited Bobbio in 1249, that is to say, only twenty-three years after the death of the Seraphic Father, the silence of Luke Wadding, himself an Irishman, who was yet well aware of the tradition already gathered by Gonzaga, the discrepancy in local memories as to the date of the visit, which, at one time, is placed before, and at another, after the foundation of the convent, all conspire to raise doubts as to its reality. Some sources for the history of Bobbio, which attribute the foundation of the convent to St. Francis, suggest that he probably came up the Val Trebbia on his way from Genoa, where he is said to have held a chapter, to

[20] Achille Ratti, *Le ultime vicende della Bibl. e dell' Archivio di S. Colombano di Bobbio*, Hoepli, Milan, p. 26.

[21] *Vita secunda S. Francisci Assisiensis*, cap. XLVIII.

Piacenza; but the first General Chapter in Genoa was not held until 1244,[22] and Campi denies[23] that St. Francis, in the course of his journeys in Lombardy and France, ever passed through Piacenza.[24]

The visit to Bobbio cannot, on the other hand, be categorically denied, because we are much in the dark as to the itineraries followed by St. Francis in upper Italy, both during the period 1213-15 (the journey to France and Spain) and in 1220 (after his return from the East). Even with regard to the various cities of Lombardy which boast of having been visited by the Saint—Milan, Monza, Treviglio, Oreno, Iseo, Bergamo and Brescia—there is no documentary evidence of any sort and nothing but traditions of varying antiquity.[25]

§ 3

Although a comparison, then, between St. Columban and St. Francis, considered in their characteristic personalities, can scarcely be sustained, and the personal devotion of St. Francis to St. Columban cannot be historically proved, it is nevertheless undeniable—as has been said—that there are similarities between the Irish monastic movement and the Franciscan movement sufficiently striking to impress any dispassionate observer of the two phenomena.

Before considering the substance underlying the similarities, it may be convenient to delay for a moment to examine the real importance of a not unrelated question, which, although it seems to me to be merely formal, yet, owing to the confusions to which it has given rise, might prevent us from attaining to the core of the historical phenomenon and imprison us, so to speak, in a restricted and erroneous conception thereof.

I refer to the question of the Rules.

[22] Cf. Holzapfel, *Manuale historiae Ordinis Fratrum Minorum*, 1909, p. 162.
[23] *Storia Eccl. di Piacenza*, II, Bk. XVI for the year 1221.
[24] Cf. Fr. Andrea Corna, *Storia ed Arte in S. Maria di Campagna (Piacenza)*, Bergamo, Instituto Italiano di Arti Grafiche, 1908, p. 116.
[25] Cf. Fr. P. M. Sevesi, *Gli albori del Francescanesimo in Lombardia*, Saronno, 1930.

The fact is that the Irish monks down to St. Columban never had any real rules and frequently adopted foreign customs such as those of Lérins, which St. Patrick had long ago introduced.[26] Down to the end of the sixth century, that is, until the establishment of the Benedictine Rule, the case was the same in Italy, in the islands of the Tyrrhene Sea, and in the Gauls: the many monasteries established there (including that of Cassiodorus at Vivario and those of Lérins itself and Tours) followed each its own customs and its own special traditions, based in many cases on the rules of Cassian or other Oriental rules, but were without any true and proper written rules.[27] It is not, therefore, surprising, to find that the word 'regula' among the Irish also should not at that time connote in their Vitae of the saints a collection of systematic precepts concerning the religious life, but merely the ascetic teaching of a given saint, imparted orally or by way of example, or else the traditional uncodified observance of some particular monastery. These 'Rules' consist for the most part of pious apophthegms and exhortations in prose or verse.[28] A very brief rule for hermits has been handed down under the name of Columcille.[29] The curious rule of the Culdees attributed to Máel Rúain (792) of Tamlachta (Tallaght, in the County of Dublin) shows some slight development, but as regards monastic rules in the proper sense of the word, drawn by an Irish pen, there is none to be found other than that written in Latin by St. Columban. Although composed for continental monks, it contains many provisions which undoubtedly reflect the habits of the monasteries of Ireland, more particularly those of Bend-chor.

Here it may be observed that the monastic writings of Columban are four in number: the *Regula monachorum*, which deals with the fundamental principles and reasons underlying the monastic life; the *Regula coenobialis*, which deals

[26] Cf. Gougaud, *Christianity in Celtic Lands*, pp. 85 et seq.; Albers, *Aforismi di vita monastica*, pp. 135-44; Martin, *St. Columban*, pp. 4-5 and 192.

[27] Albers, op. cit., pp. 61, 89 and 191, and Martin, op. cit., p. 28.

[28] Ryan, *Irish Monasticism*, p. 411.

[29] Cf. Haddon and Stubbs' *Councils*, II, i, 119-21; Skene, *Celtic Scotland*, II, 508-9 (translation only).

with transgressions by the monks, and the punishments relative thereto; the *Poenitentiale*, which specifies with greater particularity certain of such points; and the *Ordo de vita et actione monachorum*, which contains most admirable instructions or meditations for the spiritual profit of the monks.[30] "Justice requires," writes Dom Lugano,[31] with reference to the *Regula monachorum*, "that attention be drawn to the extraordinary fact that an Irishman, bred to the monastic life in the monastery at Bend-chor, and settling, a wandering missionary, in the heart of the Vosges with Irish and Frankish followers and disciples, should have proposed to them a method of life modelled on the austerities of the ancient Fathers and at the same time tempered by a spirit of wise discretion quite peculiar to the Latins and the Roman Church."

It is the *Regula coenobialis*, however, which is usually considered to be most representative of the Irish monastic spirit and it is upon this especially that criticism has fastened.

The legislation of Columban has been contrasted, as a whole, on the one hand, with the legislation of St. Benedict, and, on the other, with that of St. Francis, and in both cases to its detriment. Compared with the Rule of St. Benedict, it has usually suffered two chief accusations: indeterminateness and excessive rigidity. And these two features are generally alleged to have been the main cause of its rapid decline and later supersession by the Benedictine Rule, which, as it was less rigorous and more exact, so left less scope to the discretion of the individual abbot.[32] Compared with the Rule of St. Francis, it has been charged with excessive rigidity.[33]

[30] Lugano, *San Colombano*, pp. 18-27; the first and the fourth of St. Columban's writings are reproduced according to the critical edition of Otto Seebass in the *Riv. Stor. Benedettina* for the 31 December, 1920, pp. 185 et seq. Migne *P.L,*. LXXX, 216-24 reproduces the edition of Holstenius-Brockie.

[31] Op. cit., p. 18.

[32] Cf. Lugano, op. cit., p. 41; Martin, op. cit., p. 192; Mrs. Concannon, op. cit., p. 277; Cabrol, *L'Angleterre Chrétienne*, p. 189; Gasquet, *Saggio storico della costituzione monastica*, pp. 22-4; Paschini, *Lezioni di storia ecclesiastica*, II, pp. 80-1; Pagnini, *Manuale di storia ecclesiastica*, III, pp. 188-9; and also the observations of Dom Gougaud, op. cit., pp. 225-6 and 405-6.

[33] Cf. Hilarin Felder, O.M., Cap., *Die Ideale des hl. Franziskus*, Freiburg, 1923. There is an American translation of this work, *The Ideals of St. Francis of Assisi*, by Berchmans Bittle, O.M., Cap., London, Burns, Oates and Wash-

"None of the ancient Rules," writes Felder, loc. cit., "omits corporal punishments, i.e., the chastisement of deliberate transgressions with strokes of a rod, whippings, etc. at the hands of a Superior. St. Columban (545-615) was the most inexorable. According to his Rule [Felder cites only the *Regula coenobialis*] the greatest crime and the least peccadillo were alike punished with a thrashing. Anyone forgetting to make the sign of the cross over his spoon at table, anyone omitting 'amen' at the end of a prayer, anyone speaking of himself, anyone excusing himself after a reproof, anyone spitting without just cause, anyone committing any such or any one of a hundred such offences, had to suffer the prescribed penalty. Lashes threatened from all quarters and were duly administered and punctiliously counted out: six, twelve, fifty or a hundred, as the case might be, and to such an extent that a poor monk, with all the goodwill in the world, could scarcely pass a single day with his bones whole.³⁴ The almost barbarous severity of the Rule of St. Columban was such that, apart from any other reasons, the Rule of St. Benedict (480-543) was, from the seventh century onwards, gradually introduced into most monasteries throughout the West. Benedict, being a Roman of gentle breeding and polite education, banished the inexorable system of punishment, without, however, abandoning entirely corporal punishment itself. He ordered

bourne, 1925, but the translator has retained the irritating and confusing German form 'Columba' for 'Columban,' which even Gibbon avoided. I do not understand his reference on page 432 to the English 'translation' of the *Celanese Legends* by Dr. Rosedale, London, Dent, 1904, as 'of very little scientific value.' Dr. Rosedale's work is not a translation, but a careful and laborious collation of the Latin texts in the extant MSS. of Tommaso da Celano, and of the greatest interest. The references to the Italian translation of Fr. Felder's work have been adapted to the pages of the English edition. Cf. pp. 223-4.

³⁴ Cf. Gibbon, *Decline and Fall*, Ch. XXXVII, note 51 (Bury's edition, Vol. IV, p. 68): "Such expressions as my book, my cloak, my shoes (Cassian, *Institut*, L. IV, *c.* 13) were not less severely prohibited among the Western monks (*Cod. Regal.*, Part II, pp. 174, 235, 288), and the Rule of Columbanus punished them with six lashes." Gibbon attributes the austerity of the Rule of Columban to the fact that "he had been educated amidst the poverty of Ireland [i.e. in the sixth century] as rigid perhaps, and inflexible, as the abstemious virtue of Egypt." It was not, however, always lashes: "Si quis non claudit ecclesiam, duodecim psalmos; si quis emittit sputa et contingit altare, viginti quattuor psalmos" . . . and so forth. C.f. s.4 Regula Coenobialis," Migne, *P.L.*, LXXX, col. 222.

in the first place that boys or youths, such as were not intelligent enough to appreciate other forms of punishment, should, if they committed any grave offence 'be punished with extraordinary fasts or severe thrashings to bring them to their senses' (Migne, *P.L.*, LXVI, 533, c. 30). The senior monks were ordered to be thrashed only in cases when, after having been several times reproved, they had not seen fit to mend their ways. Even the statutes of the Cluniac Benedictines (drawn up in 1123) provided for severe corporal chastisement. The back of the delinquent was stripped and he was 'thrashed with a cane in accordance with ancient custom.' The Dominicans likewise faithfully adhered to this custom of having their members stripped and flogged *quantum placuerit praelato*, and, if the superior pleased, flogged again at the feet, first of the superior, and, afterwards, of each of the brethren assembled in session."[35]

The suppression of corporal punishment which St. Francis insisted on so far as his sons were concerned (and yet he mortified his own flesh with an austerity no whit inferior to that of all the other saints, including, therefore, the great Irish saints),[36] shows what a lofty conception he had of penance and his indefectible and unrivalled fidelity to the teaching of Jesus Christ, Who reproved with such efficacious gentleness the woman taken in adultery (John VIII). But the very examples quoted by Felder of rules prescribing corporal punishments show that Columban in this respect was merely following traditions which had received the approval, as conducive to the well-being of souls, of founders of religious communities in all ages, beginning with those early founders of monasteries in the Thebaid:[37] nor should it be forgotten that, if he was more rigorous than others, he was legislating at a time and in the midst of a people notorious for their brutality and immorality: Merovingian

[35] References are (a) for the Benedictine Rule, Migne, *P.L.*, Vol. LXVI, col. 533; (b) for the Statutes of the Cluniac Congregation, ibid., Vol. CIXC, col. 1043; (c) for the Dominican constitutions, I, dist. 23, in Denifle's edition.

[36] "Hoc solo documento," says Tommaso da Celano, II, n. 129, "dissona fuit manus a lingua in patre sanctissimo. Corpus enim suum utique innocens flagellis et penuriis subigebat, multiplicans ei vulnera sine causa."

[37] Albers, op. cit., p. 15 and Ryan, *Irish Monasticism*, pp. 282-5.

Gaul.[38] The judgment of Felder, who would depict Columban as an ignorant barbarian[39] (whereas we know what a great contribution the Irish made at that time to Western civilisation), being based solely on the *Regula coenobialis* and not also on the *Regula monachorum*, the discretion of which is acknowledged by Dom Lugano, ought not, therefore, to lead us into error in any comprehensive estimate of his monastic ideals, much less of the characteristics of the Irish movement as a whole which, although he was undoubtedly one of its most illustrious representatives, had already set in before him and developed in many places, such as Scotland and Northumbria, independently of him, and more particularly, under the influence of Iona. Nor would it do to forget what an important part was left in all the Irish monasteries in the application of the Rules governing the community to the paternal benevolence, the sense of responsibility, and the initiative of the abbot. Columban himself explicitly states that correction should always be more remedial than penal, and that it should therefore vary in its interpretation by an experienced superior with the temperament, the habits, and the needs of the individual.[40]

No religious movement can be judged solely upon the text of a written rule: the facts also must be taken into consideration. "The text of a rule, more particularly one fourteen centuries old, is in part, at any rate, a dead letter; it is only by tradition that it becomes vivified, illuminated, and interpreted," writes Dom Berlière with reference to the Benedictine Rule.[41] And the Benedictine Rule itself, so

---

[38] Martin, op. cit., pp. 70-6.

[39] The tender letter addressed "dulcissimis suis filiis" (Ep. IV, Gundlach, *M.G.H.*, *Epistolae*, III (1892), p. 165), written when the ship, ordered by King Thierry of Burgundy to take Columban and his Irish companions back to Ireland, was about to sail from Nantes in 610, and exhorting them, *viscera sua*, while standing fast by their rule, to conduct themselves with prudence, would be sufficient in itself to dispel any suggestion of the great saint's 'savagery,' if anyone took the trouble to read it.

[40] Martin, op. cit., pp. 57 and 58. And in deference to this same sense of responsibility in the superior, St. Francis, on the other hand, had no hesitation, in certain exceptional cases, in inflicting even on his own brethren appropriate corporal punishment. (Cf. e.g. *Tomm. da Cel.*, II, Nos. 182 and 206).

[41] *L'ordre monastique des origines au XIIème siècle* par D. Ursmer Berlière, third edition, Paris, 1924.

measured and exact, so precise in ordering down to the most trifling detail everything concerning the employment of the day, the allocation of duties, the admission of novices, the taking of vows, and the general government of the community,[42] has not prevented, in the course of centuries, the most extraordinary variation of religious customs, both among solitaries and in communities, and has received the most widely different, not to say opposite, interpretations, as, for example, among Cluniacs and Cistercians.[43] As much may be said of the Franciscan Rule, under which, in the course of centuries, not a few different families have grown up. The text of a rule acquires illumination and value only from the spirit of those who seek to apply it.

I would go further. The texts of rules in the majority of cases never manifest those features which, in the historical development of the respective Orders, are later destined to constitute the peculiar character and the greatest glory of those Orders. St. Columban, for instance, has not a word to say in his rule about the apostolate: yet he was an apostle on his own account and he enabled his disciples (owing to the latitude of the powers reserved to the abbot) to carry out a missionary task marvellous in its range all over the continent of Europe. The Rule of St. Benedict contains no reference to the cultivation of letters: yet the most enduring glory of the Benedictines throughout the ages has been their constant and intense love of learning, the jealous and providential preservation of the means of learning, and the special devotion with which they have employed their profound erudition in doctrine and their liturgical skill to do honour to the Holy Church of Jesus Christ. So also the Rule of St. Francis, the first to take into consideration missionary activity amongst the infidels, mentions such activity only in a few brief words in its last chapter, which is mainly concerned with another matter (the Cardinal Protector of the Order): "Whosoever among the brethren, following divine inspiration, may wish to go among the Saracens and other infidels should ask permission from their

[42] Martin, op. cit., pp. 6 and 192.
[43] Berlière, op. cit., pp. 272-5.

Provincial Ministers. To none, however, should the Ministers give leave to go, except only to those whom they may deem fit to be sent (Rule II, Chapter XII)." The whole marvellous blossoming of Franciscan missionaries, who, within a few decades of their founder's death, had already penetrated—*sicut agni inter lupos*—to the furthest limits of the known world (Giovanni da Pian del Carpine as early as 1245 was abroad in the highways of Central Asia and Giovanni da Montecorvino had reached Peking by 1290) grew out of these few words.[44]

It is obvious, therefore, that anyone presuming to judge a religious movement on the strength of the text of its birth certificate, and not on the strength of the spirit animating it and manifesting itself in the course of that same movement's historical development, may easily fall into grievous error. The Irish movement and, more particularly, that associated

[44] Cf. *The texts and versions of John de Plano Carpini* ["qui missus est Legatus ad Tartaros anno Domini 1246 ab Innocentio quarto Pontifice maximo"]. And *William de Rubruquis* ["de Ordine fratrum Minorum Galli Anno gratie 1253"—William went off at the behest of the King of France] *as printed for the first time by Haklut in* 1598, edited for the Hakluyt Society by C. Raymond Beazley, London, 1903. In April 1278, Pope Nicholas III dispatched a religious mission to the Tartars. Its members were Gerard of Prato, Antony of Parma, John of St. Agatha and Matthew of Arezzo—all Franciscans. Cf. Beazley's *The Dawn of Modern Geography*, Vol. II, London, 1901, pp. 161-2.

Sir C. R. Beazley cites Wadding: *Annales Minorum*, 1733, III, pp. 35-42—On John of Montecorvino, cf. ibid., Vol. III, Oxford, 1901, pp. 161-78. But "among the Latin pioneers of the fourteenth century, there is no one," in Sir Raymond Beazley's opinion, "who has left a travel record of equal range, interest or value," to that of the Franciscan Odoric of Pordenone, whose travels began in 1316. He traversed eastern Asia, sailed from Ormuz to Madras, thence to Java and Cochin China, lived for five years in Peking (1323-8), and returned to Udine by Tibet and Persia. He died in 1331. "During many, if not all of his wanderings, Odoric was not alone: six weeks after his death, the archives of Udine record a payment of two marks 'for the love of God and of Odoric' to his companion, brother James of Ireland; in later years an introduction to the miracle-working remains of the friar is requested from this same James by a Venetian theologian (Asquini, *Vita e Viaggi del B. Odorico*, 1737, p. 206)." Op. cit., p. 255. Sir Raymond Beazley thinks that Brother James was the probable source of Odoric's story of the barnacle goose and its location in Ireland by which Scotland is probably meant. John Lesley, as has already been noticed, claimed it for his own country. There is no evidence that the creature ever grew in Ireland. On Friar James cf. *Materials for the history of the Franciscan province of Ireland* (1230-1450) by Fr. E. B. Fitzmaurice, O.F.M., and A. G. Little, Manchester, The University Press, 1920, pp. 132-3. Simeon Simeonis, another Irish Franciscan, went to the Levant in 1322 and left a remarkable account of the trade of the Massiliots, the Genoese, Catalans and Venetians in Egypt in the early fourteenth century, and the Italian *fondachi* in the Levant. Ibid., pp. 484-91.

with Columban, is not to be judged solely on the basis of some casual written penitential. The Rule of Columban, despite the undeniable severity in disciplinary matters which, undoubtedly, sorely tried the vocation of the monks, had shown considerable power of expansion in the sixth and seventh centuries; and I am of the opinion that its unexpected decline is mainly due to causes of an entirely different nature and cannot be properly explained unless the circumstances in which the Church found itself at the time are borne in mind.

Montalembert[45] has observed that the modest beginnings and the obscure progress of the Benedictine Rule in Gaul have almost escaped the notice of the historian: no outstanding man, no famous saint, contributed by his personal influence to secure that astonishing victory. At Luxeuil and Bobbio the superimposition of the two rules took place under the direct successors of Columban and the complete supersession of the founder's by the Benedictine Rule only fifty years after his death. The Council of Autun, held in 670 and attended by fifty-four bishops under the presidency of St. Léger, who had himself lived at Luxeuil, ordered religious to adopt the Rule of St. Benedict. I would add that it was about the same time that the Rule of St. Benedict superseded in Scotland and Northumbria the Rule of Iona.[46]

Montalembert thinks that the reason for this is to be found "in the much closer and more intimate union of the Benedictine Rule with the authority of the Holy See."

I believe that he has hit the mark.

"We have proved," he continues, "that neither in Columbanus nor among his disciples and offspring was there any hostility to the Holy See and we have quoted proof of the respect of the popes for his memory. Nor had Benedict any more than Columbanus either sought or obtained during his lifetime the sovereign sanction of the Papacy for his institution. But long after his death and at the very time when Columbanus was busied in planting his work in Gaul,

[45] Op. cit., II, pp. 541 et seq. "Why was the Rule of St. Columban rejected and replaced by that of St. Benedict?"

[46] Cf. Albers, op. cit., p. 139.

the man and the saint of genius who occupied the chair of St. Peter, Gregory the Great, had spontaneously impressed the seal of his supreme approbation upon the Benedictine Rule. This adoption of the work Gregory had preluded by the celebration of its author in those famous Dialogues the popularity of which was to be so great in all Catholic communities. The third successor of Gregory, Boniface IV, in a Council held at Rome in 618 and by a famous decree which we reproach ourselves for not having mentioned before, had condemned those, who, moved more by jealousy than charity, held that the monks, being dead to the world and living only for God, were by that reason rendered unworthy and incapable of exercising the priesthood and administering the sacraments.

"The decree of this Council recognises the power of binding and loosing in monks lawfully ordained, and, to confound the foolish assumptions of their adversaries, quotes the example of St. Gregory the Great, who had not been kept back from the Supreme See by his monastic profession, and of many others, who, under the monastic frock, had already worn the pontifical ring. But it especially appeals to the authority of Benedict whom it describes as 'the venerable legislator of the monks' and who had interdicted them only from interference in secular affairs. It proclaims anew, and on the most solemn occasion, that the Rule of Benedict was the supreme monastic law. It impresses a new sanction upon all the prescriptions of him whom another pope, John IV, the same who exempted Luxeuil from episcopal authority, called thirty years later 'the abbot of the city of Rome.'

"Thus adopted and honoured by the Papacy, and identified in some sort with the authority of Rome itself, the influence of the Rule of St. Benedict progressed with the progress of the Roman Church. I own anon that up to the seventh century the intervention of the popes in the affairs of the Church in France was much less sought and less efficacious than in after ages; but it was already undoubtedly sovereign, and more than sufficient to win the assent of all to a specially Roman institution.

"Without weakening the foregoing argument, another explanation might be admitted for the strange course of things which, in the space of a single century, eclipsed the Rule and name of Columbanus, and changed into Benedictine monasteries all the foundations due to the powerful missionary impulse of the Irish apostle. The cause which produced in Western Christendom the supremacy of St. Benedict's institute over that of his illustrious rival, was most likely the same which made the Rule of St. Basil to flourish over all the other monastic rules of the East— namely, its moderation, its prudence, and the more liberal spirit of its government. When the two legislatures of Monte Cassino and Luxeuil met together, it must have been manifest that the latter exceeded the natural strength of man in its regulations relating to prayer, to food, and to penal discipline, and, above all, in its mode of government. St. Benedict had conquered by the strength of practical sense, which in the end always wins the day."

Montalembert declares that he is indebted for this observation to Père Lacordaire. I admire the objectivity of the learned and noble writer and agree with him in willingly acknowledging a secondary value in this factor, but I would also observe that he relates the observation with the express reservation that he does not want "to weaken thereby the value" of his foregoing argument.

Fr. Ferdinando Antonelli, O.F.M., after recalling, in an excellent essay "De re monastica in Dialogis S. Gregorii Magni"[47] that various non-Benedictine monasteries, even in Italy, adopted the Rule of St. Benedict about the end of the sixth and in the course of the seventh centuries, remarks: "Quod factum non solum ex ipsius Regulae excellentia, sed etiam ex favore quo summi Pontifices institutum S. Benedicti prosecuti sunt explicandum videtur."[48]

But the state of the Church in the time of Gregory the Great is the best indication of the probable, not to say imperious, reasons for the assistance required from, and the preference bestowed on, the sons of St. Benedict by the pontiffs.

[47] In *Antonianum*, 1927, p. 435.   [48] Cf. also Ryan, *Irish Monasticism*, p. 412.

On Gregory's accession to the chair of St. Peter (590), the Western Empire was submerged by the barbarian inundation and the Eastern Empire was visibly crumbling. Byzantium had attempted to enslave the Church, had aided and abetted schismatical tendencies, and was utterly incapable for the future of defending the integrity of its territory against the assaults which threatened it on every side. North Africa was still agitated by the Donatist heresy: its faith was flickering out and the country had shown itself ripe for its impending enslavement by Islam. Spain had fallen a prey to the Visigoths and the Suevi, recent converts from Arianism and still sorely in need of religious and civil education. Great Britain had relapsed for more than a century past into paganism owing to the Anglo-Saxon conquest, and only the Britons in Wales and Cornwall and the Irish settlements there kept the faith of Christ alive and the customs of the 'Celtic' Church. The Gauls were Catholic, but ecclesiastical discipline there was lax, while simony and incontinence were rife amongst the clergy. Italy was overrun by the Lombards and with them the forces of Byzantium were desperately engaged: the victors spread their native Arianism and disorder was rampant in ecclesiastical life, paralysed as it was by the violence and distresses of a most disastrous situation. Rome itself, reduced to a state of exhaustion by the Gothic wars and the plague of 566, was falling into ruin, while the new invaders clamoured at the gate.

Gregory had a clear perception of the contribution which the barbarian races were capable of making to the history of the world and the urgent necessity therefore of taking steps for their evangelisation: he also realised and no less clearly, the necessity of supporting the youthful kingdom of the Franks, the personification, as it were, of Christianity in Europe. Were that kingdom to succumb before the simultaneous onslaught of the various hostile forces threatening it, the Church and civilisation were doomed.[49]

The Roman Church, which in its wisdom looks always

---

[49] Cf. Grisar's admirable book, *San Gregorio Magno*, and Berlière, op. cit., pp. 44 et seq., and pp. 60, 62-3.

beyond contingent events, and keeps its gaze ever fixed on the goal assigned to it by Jesus Christ of winning to Him *all* nations, which makes no distinction between conqueror and conquered, because it knows that all authority derives from God and that the material conquerors of to-day will in many cases be the spiritually conquered of to-morrow, which is accustomed to consider all human souls as equally precious, was naturally bound to concern itself both with the conversion of the Anglo-Saxons and with raising the moral level of the Franks and their Church, while keeping them attached to itself. The time was critical in the extreme, and it was necessary resolutely, but still tactfully, to attempt to suppress dangerous national particularisms and to impress the whole body of the Spouse of Christ with the universal spirit of the Roman genius.

Grisar has acutely pointed out[50] that the immediate occasion for the evangelisation of the Anglo-Saxons was offered to Gregory the Great by the fact that Brunhilda, who was on excellent terms with the Pontiff, had succeeded, in 596, in uniting in her own hands the government of all the Frankish States, and that the way to Great Britain, thitherto closed to him under her predecessor Childebert, the ally of the Byzantines in their wars with the Lombards, was thenceforth open once more.

Gregory the Great did not fail to write affectionate letters to Brunhilda and to lavish praise upon her both for the assistance she had given the apostle Augustine and his companions and for the support she had accorded the papal project of convoking a synod to repair the great evils afflicting the Frankish Church. This was his object in dispatching to Gaul yet another of his trusted emissaries, Syriacus, the abbot of his own monastery of St. Andrew on the Coelian Hill. The character of Brunhilda is one of the problems of history and best known to us only through her bitterest enemies:[51] but to the Pontiff who wrote so tactfully to the

[50] Op. cit., p. 235. To say nothing of the fact that Ethelbert, King of Kent, had married Bertha, daughter of Charibert, King of Paris, and by express agreement practised her religion with her own Church and chaplain in Canterbury.

[51] e.g. Jonas of Susa, the inept author of the *Vita S. Columbani*, the chronicle of the pseudo-Fredegarius, the author of the life of St. Didier of Vienne, who

Abbot Mellitus, the first Bishop of London, with reference to certain religious practices bound up with old English pagan traditions, that some "gratification should be outwardly permitted his converts" to the end . . . "that they may the more easily consent to the inward consolations of the grace of God. For there is no doubt that it is impossible to efface everything at once from their obdurate minds . . ."[52] may well be applied, as Grisar observes (p. 269), the words of Cardinal Caraffa: "Principes laudibus demulcebat ut audientes, quales esse debeant, fierent mansuetiores."

Columban's obstinacy in adhering to the Celtic computation of Easter[53] in a letter to that great Pope (c. 600), which seems to have remained unanswered, the refusal of the British monks to lend a hand in the evangelisation of the Anglo-Saxons, the known sympathy of the Irish monks in general for the classics of pagan antiquity whose influence Gregory dreaded,[54] were all so many motives which combined to make him doubt, not the solid and explicit loyalty to Rome of Columban and his sons, but the practical value of the assistance to be derived from them in regard to the more pressing necessities for the time being of the Church which wanted unification and no particularisms, the utmost prudence and no vehemence. Gregory, therefore, had recourse to the Benedictines of his own monastery of St. Andrew on the Coelian Hill for his missions, both to the

was sharply reprimanded by the Pope (*Ep.*, IX, 48) for wasting his time teaching grammar to his pupils instead of attending to the duties of his charge (Cf. Gratian, *Decret.* i, *Dist.* 37, c. 8) and Ratpert of St. Gall, who stigmatises her as "plena daemonis, tenebrarum socia, lucis inimica, omnibus bonis contraria." Gregory of Tours, however, admired her greatly when she first came to Burgundy as a radiant young bride from Spain (*Hist. Franc.*, IV, c. 27), and she had been nobly vindicated by M. Godefroi Kurth, *Études Franques*, Paris and Brussels, 1919, pp. 322-3, and I, p. 438, and Mr. M. V. Hay in *A Chain of Error in Scottish History*, London, 1927, Appendix III. Cf. also an interesting note in Hallam's *Middle Ages*, Vol. I, pp. 5-6, eleventh edition, London, 1856.

[52] Cf. the text of the letter in Bede, *H.E.*, I, 30 (Everyman translation), Grisar, op. cit., p. 294, and *Vita e Pensiero*, 1931, p. 150.

[53] Another letter, twelve years later, addressed this time to Pope Boniface IV (*Ep.*, VI), if in fact by Columban, would seem to suggest that old age had mollified his middle-aged intransigence and that he had abandoned his Irish practice.

[54] Cf. Grisar, op. cit., p. 273 and Lugano, *S. Gregorio Magno e S. Colombano nella storia della cultura latina*, republished from the *Riv. St. Benedettina*, 31st August, 1915.

Anglo-Saxons and the Franks, however foreign such tasks might have been to their rule, because there were no other organised religious orders in existence and because they were, so to speak, of his own household, agents whose fidelity was beyond reproach, interpreters of the directions given by Rome whose prudence was beyond question, because they had been born and bred under the very eyes, almost, of the Holy See.[55] Columban's intransigent attitude towards Brunhilda, his letter to Pope Boniface IV on the question of the Three Chapters,[56] and the accusations made against him by Agrestinus[57] at the Synod of Macon,[58] must have had a certain influence in inducing succeeding pontiffs to contemplate favourably the supersession of the Rule of Columban by the Benedictine Rule; and the occasions on which the Holy See could bring its influence to bear in that direction were those when it was petitioned to grant or confirm the exemption of monasteries from episcopal jurisdiction.[59]

It has been thought proper to dwell a little on the Rule of Columban and the causes of its decline in the course of the seventh century in order to clear the way of prejudices which might easily arise with regard to the spirit animating the Irish movement from the perusal of works by writers so authoritative as Felder without regard to the surrounding historical conditions. The decline of the rule did not, however, modify that spirit or arrest historically the expansion of the Scots religious movement which, as was seen in Chapter II, reached its zenith in the eighth century. Under the Rule of Columban, as under that of Benedict, it was always the same Irish soul which still pulsated.

And now that this obstacle has been cleared out of the way, we can proceed to consider the points of contact between the Irish and the Franciscan movements.

[55] Cf. Lugano, op. cit., pp. 3-7.

[56] Cf. Montalembert, op. cit., Vol. II, pp. 439 et seq.

[57] He had been notary to King Thiery of Burgundy and was afterwards for a time an inmate of Luxeuil. The account of this Synod given by Jonas in his *Vita Col.* cc. IX and X, is particularly interesting.

[58] Cf. Montalembert, op. cit., pp. 468 et seq.

[59] Cf. for the case of Luxeuil, ibid., pp. 274 et seq.

§ 4

No writer has surpassed Felder[60] in demonstrating the perfect limpidity and harmony achieved by St. Francis both in his own life and in the impulse he gave his first followers, through his return, pure and simple but still absolute and whole-hearted, to the spirit of the Gospel.

There is the example of Christ to teach us in every incident and vicissitude of life what we ought to think and do: we must conform to what Jesus Christ said and did. It is an ideal extremely difficult to attain, but a certain guide and an unfailing source of strength. The *alter Christus*, who had the skill to adhere faithfully to that ideal, turned his sojourn on this earth into a spiritual masterpiece, inscribed a poem of such crystalline and linear purity that its match is not to be found in the history of mankind.

The great Irish saints, like all preceding founders of orders, were far from having any conscious vision, so clear, so simple, and so comprehensive, of the goal to be assigned to their sons. But they came near to it, nearer perhaps than any others, in their ardent love for Jesus Christ: a life of prayer and works of charity, example and exhortation, renunciation of the world and apostolic activity in the world. There are only two religious movements in history which, drawing inspiration from the example of Our Lord and His earliest disciples, contemporaneously assumed the three forms, the monastic, the solitary or eremitic, and the apostolic, both for individuals and communities.[61] The lives of St. Francis and the blessed Giles,[62] viewed from this aspect, closely resemble those of St. Colum-cille and St. Columban. They were all four aware that life in community was a wholesome safeguard against the dangers of the solitary life (spiritual egotism and pride of asceticism), and against the danger of "having the dust gather on one's spiritual feet" (St. Bonaventura's "spiritualium pulverizatio pedum," XII, 2) in the course of a wandering life of preaching.

[60] Op. cit., cap. I.
[61] Cf. Martin, op. cit., p. 19.
[62] Felder, op. cit., pp. 303-4.

They are the only two movements which assumed a world-wide mission, not only in extent but also in profundity, not only geographically but also socially. In this respect, also, St. Francis acted with the secure deliberation of genius when he founded the Third Order, while the Irish acted by an obscure instinct and less effectively; but it is impossible not to admit that the crowds which flocked into monasteries and convents in Ireland immediately after the conversion, with the result that the whole island could almost be described as one vast religious community,[63] and the later practice of resort to an *anmchara* or spiritual director, many times before referred to, indicated a desire that all mankind, all classes in society, should participate in the ideal of life "according to the form of the Holy Gospel."[64]

The impulse to peregrinate, so characteristic of the two movements and of them alone, has its source in the same common Biblical origin.

The need to peregrinate far away from everything and everybody beloved is a direct corollary of the feeling that this earthly life is itself a pilgrimage, an exile, in comparison with our heavenly home.[65]

One of the most fundamental distinctions among men is, perhaps, that between the farmer and the shepherd, between those who remain and those who go, between those who

[63] Cf. Dom Gougaud, *Christianity in Celtic Lands*, p. 74.

[64] Apropos the preaching of St. Patrick, Fr. Ryan writes (*Irish Monasticism*, p. 93): "Amid the women folk the proportion desirous of consecrating their lives to God was so great that it surprised himself. They were placed in small groups to assist the clergy in the service of churches, rather than in monasteries proper." St. Patrick's surprise recalls the surprise—if the word be not inapt—of Francis, which induced him to establish the Third Order.

[65] "Advena ego sum apud te, et peregrinus, sicut omnes patres mei," sings the Psalmist, XXXVIII, v. 12: "extraneus factus sum fratribus meis, et peregrinus filiis matris meae," Ps. LXVIII, v. 9: "cantabiles mihi erant justificationes tuae in loco peregrinationis meae," Ps. CXVIII, v. 54. This is the feeling to which Our Lord appeals in Matth. XIX, 29, and the Apostles in 2 Cor. V, 6 et seq., Phil. III, 20, 1 Pet. II, 11 ("tamquam advenas et peregrinos), and especially in Hebr. XI, 12 et seq.: "Propter quod et ab uno orti sunt (et hoc emortuo), tamquam sidera coeli in multitudinem, et sicut arena, quae est ad oram maris, innumerabilis. Juxta fidem defuncti sunt omnes isti, non acceptis repromissionibus, sed a longe eas aspicientes et salutantes, et confitentes quia peregrini et hospites sunt super terram. Qui enim haec dicunt significant se patriam inquirere. Et si quidem ipsius meminissent, de qua exierunt, habebant utique tempus revertendi; nunc autem meliorem appetunt, id est, coelestem," and to it also St. Cyprian (*De mortalitate*) and St. Augustine (*De Cantico novo*) make appeal.

cling to a patch of soil and want to think of it as their very own, and those who wander everlastingly through the boundless gardens of the earth with the feeling that they all belong to God, between the descendants of Cain and the descendants of Abel. And we know that the offerings that found favour in the eyes of the Lord were the offerings of Abel, and that it was to the shepherds that the Angel of God came to proclaim the birth of the Saviour.

I have already dealt at some length, in Chapter II, § 1, with the "peregrinationes pro Christo, pro amore Christi, pro adipiscenda in coelis patria, pro aeterna patria," of the Irish saints,[66] of their continual "sitire ad patriam."

Similar or analogous expressions are of frequent recurrence on the lips of St. Francis and in the earliest Franciscan literature. "The brethren should strive to imitate the humility and poverty of Our Lord Jesus Christ . . . and let them not be ashamed to ask for alms, because Our Lord Jesus Christ, the Son of Almighty God, was not ashamed and was 'poor and a stranger,' and lived on alms, He and the blessed Virgin and His disciples."[67] "Let the brethren appropriate nothing for themselves, neither house, nor land nor anything and as 'pilgrims and strangers' in this world, serving the Lord in poverty and humility, let them go confidently for alms."[68] "Let the brethren be on their guard against receiving churches, dwelling places, and aught else that may be built for them, unless they duly conform to the holy poverty which we have promised in the Rule, sojourning here always as 'strangers and pilgrims'."[69] "Leges enim peregrinorum in filiis suis semper quaesivit, sub alieno videlicet colligi tecto, pacifice transire, sitire ad patriam."[70] "The Minor Friars," says Felder,[71] "devoted themselves to God, not in order to be housed, but because they wished to extend their activities everywhere without ever having in the world a place, however small, which might be called their own. They peregrinated for the 'love of Christ,'

[66] Cf. Dom Gougaud, op. cit., p. 130, and Martin, op. cit., pp. 10 and 30.
[67] *Rule I*, c. 9.
[68] *Rule II*, c. 6.
[69] *The Testament of St. Francis.*
[70] *Tommaso da Celano*, II, n. 59 (Cf. Rosedale (*Legenda Antiqua*), p. 37).
[71] Op. cit., p. 113.

and all they knew were pilgrims' hostels according to the words of the Psalm: 'Thy justifications were the subject of my song in the place of my pilgrimage'."[72]

And the first period of the Franciscan Order, being in conformity with this evangelical principle, was, so to speak, nomadic, like the Irish movement, so that the friars might be able to preach penance to all nations. The triumphs of Aymon of Faversham in 1224 at Paris are as renowned as those of St. Antony in 1231 at Padua.[73] The preaching of these wandering apostles of penance was apt to rouse all classes of the population to the observance of the commandments and the laws of the Gospel, to encourage them to conversion and a change of life, to bring them back to practical Christianity, and, in many cases also, to teach the truths of the Faith to such as were ignorant of them, to convert heretics who denied them, and it therefore reaped that wonderful harvest which earned for Antony the name of 'malleus hereticorum.' These flying troops of Franciscans, flanked, indeed, by fraternal platoons of Dominicans, recall the flying troops of St. Colum-cille among the Picts, of the monks of Lindisfarne among the Angles, of St. Columban and St. Gall in France, Switzerland and Italy.[74]

Here we touch upon the most important point of similarity between the two movements: the apostolate.

It is acknowledged also, but partially, by Felder.[75] "The ancient monks," he declares, "undoubtedly devoted themselves to the apostolic life. But, so doing, they meant no more than that the monk, following the example set by the apostles, bound himself to observe not only the commandments of God, but also the precepts of the Gospel. That they should be obliged, like the apostles, to exterior activity, such as practical evangelization in the proper sense of the term, never entered their heads. Only St. Columban took upon

---

[72] So Douai CXVIII, 54; but cp. the *A.V.* CXIX, 54: "Thy statutes have been my songs in the house of my pilgrimage."

[73] Cf. Felder, op. cit., p. 322.

[74] An early missionary society established in 1312 and in which the Franciscans took part, was called the 'Societas peregrinantium propter Christum.' Cf. Golubovich, *Biblioteca bio-bibliografica della Terra Santa e dell' Oriente francescano* I, p. 228, note 5.

[75] Op. cit., pp. 297-8.

himself the apostolic ministry. There is indeed no reference to any form of missionary activity in his rule; and if he and his disciples acquired undying merit in the preaching of the Gospel, this is due above all to the Irish tradition in accordance with which monasteries were primarily centres for the care of souls. The same is true as regards the later Benedictine Anglo-Saxon abbeys which produced St. Boniface and his disciples. The Benedictine Rule, as such, separated the monk entirely from the world and so prevented his missionary activity in the world."

Stabilitas loci did, in fact, bind the monk forever to the cloister in which he had taken his vows. Gregory the Great made an exception when he employed the sons of St. Benedict on an evangelical mission in a moment of crisis for the Church, at a time when he had no other forces of equal fidelity at his disposal. "But," Berlière admits,[76] "the participation of the [Benedictine] monastic order was neither general nor lasting: with the exception of the Roman mission to England, such participation would seem to have been mainly the monopoly of the Anglo-Saxon and Celtic communities and their settlements on the Continent."

It may be observed in passing that the Anglo-Saxon communities in this particular followed, both chronologically and spiritually, the Irish communities. Wilfred had no sooner become abbot than he turned Lindisfarne into a centre of the Romano-Saxon reaction against the Irish, although the spirit which nourished him was precisely the Irish spirit of evangelization. The Irish influence upon the Anglo-Saxon monks, particularly as regards apostolic activity, is acknowledged by all historians.[77] Dom Berlière himself admits that "one of the great advantages of the contact between Anglo-Saxon and Celtic monachism was the force of expansion the former derived, the impulse given it towards the apostolate. So that the missionary activity of Boniface and his disciples also derives, though at second hand, from the Irish movement." It may be that the real object which Augustine's monks also attained was not so

[76] Op. cit., p. 94.
[77] Cf. Cabrol, op. cit., pp. 187-91.

much the conversion of the Anglo-Saxons (a task performed to a great extent by the Celts, cf. Ch. II, § 3), as the introduction of the Roman genius across the Channel and the elimination of that bane of the Celtic movement, its particularism.

It may confidently be said, in conclusion, that in the Middle Ages the apostolate, in its double aspect of "improving the moral condition of the faithful" (by preaching and confession) and "converting the infidel" (even in the most distant lands) was a fundamental feature only of the Irish monastic programme and the Franciscan.[78] Giovanni da Pian del Carpine and William Rubruck, clothed only in their humble Franciscan cloth, penetrated in the early years of the existence of the Order into the heart of Mongolia[79] much as Cormac and Brendan had penetrated in their *imrama* in the early years of the Irish movement as far as the Orkneys and Iceland.[80]

Although naturally common to all intense religious movements, the fundamental value of liturgical and private prayer is yet specially noteworthy in the two under consideration. The long night orisons and the daily recitation of the entire psalter, the three fifties (*na trí cóecait*), prescribed by many Irish rules and customs,[81] recall the long prayers of Francis, "totus non tam orans quam oratio factus,"[82] and the importance he attached to the daily recitation of the divine office.

Noteworthy also is the predilection of St. Francis for the ancient posture in prayer—the arms raised upright or stretched out crosswise[83]—which is also the *crosfigil* posture so common among the Irish.[84] The *Caeremoniale romanoseraphicum* O.F.M., down to the 1908 edition,[85] enjoined 'ex Ordinis consuetudine,' that the Friar serving Mass

[78] Cf. Gougaud, op. cit., p. 72; Cabrol, op. cit., p. 188; and Felder, op. cit., p. 311.
[79] Cf. Felder, op. cit., p. 316.
[80] Cf. Gougaud, op. cit., pp. 131-3; and Cabrol, op. cit., p. 187.
[81] Cf. Gougaud, op. cit., pp. 90, 332 et seq.
[82] *Tommaso da Celano*, II, No. 95 (Rosedale, p. 53).
[83] Cf. Felder, op. cit., p. 104; St. Bonaventura, X, No. 4.
[84] Cf. Ch. I, § 4; and Gougaud, op. cit., p. 93.
[85] Quaracchi, p. 266.

should recite, between the Elevation and the Pater Noster, six Paters, Aves and Glorias, "genuflexus, brachiis per modum crucis extensis."

The accord between the solitary, the coenobitic, and the apostolic forms of life is another characteristic common to the two movements. St. Francis was not only fond of retiring from time to time into solitude, underneath a cliff or in the heart of a wood, in places later famous such as Greccio, the Celle of Cortona, the Carceri of the Subasio, the Island in the Trasimene Lake, Sartiano and la Verna, but also dictated special instructions 'De religiosa habitatione in eremo,' for his numerous brethren who desired to live either for a time or continuously in hermitages and to devote themselves entirely to a life of uninterrupted reflection and perpetual prayer.[86]

The same feeling manifested itself among the Irish. Reference has already been made (Ch. I, § 4) to their *disert* and their *carcair*. "Even without finally renouncing the advantages of the life in community," writes Dom Gougaud,[87] "it occasionally happened that monks felt the need of giving themselves up for a season to more intense contemplation and severer mortification in solitude; and an island was sometimes chosen for the purpose. But some islands were difficult of access and moreover exposed to the dangers of visits from pirates; those who cared not to face the risk of crossing the waves to find solitude could retire to lonely spots on the mainland, often not far distant from their monastery."

On the deserted rocks of the ocean, where no human soul ventured to approach them, Colum-cille and his disciples sought a retreat still further withdrawn, an asylum still further remote than that of Iona;[88] in solitary places on Iona itself such as Croc an Aingil (the Angel's Hill), the apostle of Caledonia spent his last days in fearful self-discipline.[89] Columban was fond of retreating into the

[86] Cf. Felder, op. cit., pp. 385-7.
[87] Op. cit., p. 100.
[88] Montalembert, Vol. III, pp. 135 et seq.
[89] Ibid, pp. 251 et seq.: ". . . . to such a degree that he grew so emaciated through pious austerity that when he lay in the sand in his cell, as the wind

forests or caves of Gaul to fast for five or six weeks on end
with but a single companion at call or utterly alone. When
we see him reverently surrounded by birds and hares, we
cannot but think of St. Francis, alone, or with Brother Leo
at call, in the island in the Trasimene Lake or amid the cliffs
of la Verna. And St. Columban also spent the last days of
his laborious life in caves and lonely chapels close to Bobbio
(La Spanna, Coli, and elsewhere), imploring between his
fasts the gracious protection of Our Lady.[90] Irish hagiography is full of such legends. It shows us St. Gall, the future
patron of the abbey to which he gave his name, amid the
woods and caves of north-east Switzerland,[91] and St. Sigebert, the patron of Dissentis, in a leafy cell on the St. Gothard
near where the Rhine takes its rise.[92]

And in this life of hermitage the Irish saints found themselves in communion with nature with the same joy, and
exercised over animals the same familiar ascendancy, as give
such a fragrance of poetry to the legends of St. Francis.
Here we find ourselves naturally confronted with a universal
characteristic of sanctity already manifested, in such a
manner as has never been surpassed, in the Lives of the
Fathers of the Desert; but in the legends of the relations
between the Irish saints and animals [93] there are nuances of
Franciscanism which it would be impossible to overlook.

rushed in through the roof, his ribs were distinguishable through his habit,
as the Amra says. . . ." Cf. Keating, Foras feasa ar Éirinn, Dineen's translation,
III, p. 103.

[90] Stokes, Six Months in the Apennines, pp. 187-200.

[91] Montalembert, p. 201.

[92] Ibid., p. 199. Cf. also Ryan, Irish Monasticism, p. 407.

[93] Cf. in Montalembert the beautiful Chapter V, Vol. II, entitled 'The
monks and nature'; Martin, op. cit., p. 10; and also Renan, Poetry of the Celtic
Races, pp. 22 et seq. Colman mac Duach kept a cock, a mouse and a fly, the
cock to crow when it was time for matins, the mouse to rub his ear and wake
him at the appointed time, the fly to settle on the line of his Psalter, where
he had left off reading, and keep his place for him. But the most delightful
tale in hagiology is, perhaps, that of Ciaran of Saigir and his woodland monks,
brother Fox and the rest. The Fox stole his abbot's shoes and the Badger,
being skilled in woodcraft, was set to bring them back. Brother Fox repentant
begged forgiveness and did penance by fasting. Cf. V.S.H., Vita sancti Ciarani
episcopi de Saigir, §§ 5-7, pp. 219-20. "We may well believe many of these
things to be true," Dr. Plummer comments, ibid., p. cxlvii, "without supposing
them to be miraculous, though we may agree with the spirit of Bede's remark
that the more faithfully man obeys the Creator, the more he will regain his
lost empire over the creature." ("Nos idcirco . . . creaturae dominium
perdimus quia . . . Creatori . . . servire negligimus." Vita Cudb., c. 21).

One instance is the story of St. Gall's encounter with the bear, so singularly reminiscent of the meeting between St. Francis and the wolf of Gubbio. St. Gall with a few companions had chosen a place of retreat in the forest, and there "he arranged two hazel boughs in the form of a cross, attached to it the relics he carried round his neck and passed the night in prayer. Before his devotions were concluded, a bear descended from the mountain to collect the remains of the travellers' meal. Gall threw him a loaf and said to him: 'In the name of Christ, withdraw from this valley: the neighbouring mountains shall be common to us but on condition that thou shall do no more harm either to man or beast.' And so the agreement was concluded."[94]

The most ardent love of poverty is another point of contact between the two movements. St. Cadoc admitted nobody into his monastery until he had stripped himself of everything, "even to the last article of dress." Nobody could be received according to the express provision of the rule, unless he were "naked as a shipwrecked man." The phrase is as much of course as any of the most peremptory expressions of St. Francis with regard to poverty.[95] "One day, when, bent by age [St. Colum-cille][96] sought perhaps in a neighbouring island a retirement still more profound than usual in which to pray, he saw a poor woman gathering wild herbs, and even nettles, who told him that her poverty was such as to forbid her all other food. 'See,' he said, 'this poor woman, who finds her miserable life worth the trouble of being thus prolonged and we who profess to deserve Heaven by our austerities, we live in luxury!' When he went back to his monastery he gave orders that he should be served with no other food than the wild and bitter herbs with which the beggar supported her existence."

Even so St. Francis: "If ever he saw anyone poorer than he, forthwith he envied him and feared that in rivalry of poverty he might be beaten by him."[97]

[94] Cf. Montalembert, II, pp. 456-7.
[95] Cf. St. Bonaventura, VII, No. 2. Tommaso da Celano, II, No. 194 (Rosedale, II, p. 32). [96] Cf. Montalembert, III, pp. 258-9.
[97] Tommaso da Celano, II, n. 83. Cf. also the incident narrated in n. 84. So, as Dante says of Bernardo di Quintavalle, his first follower, "Corse e

The earliest Irish monasteries were, as has been observed
in Chapter I, § 4, composed of tiny cells constructed of
wattle and stone without mortar, and surrounded with a
hedge like the laura of Pacomius,[98] and the earliest Franciscan loca at Rivotorto[99] and the Porziuncola. The
churches in either case were just as poor and unpretentious.
The Irish, as St. Bernard testifies, kept as a rule, at any
rate down to the twelfth century, to their custom of building
churches of wood and not of stone.[100] An admirable example
of the spirit of poverty and humility is offered us in the
beginnings of the monasteries at Luxeuil[101] and Bobbio.
This spirit of poverty, it should also be observed, was in
striking contrast to the love of luxury and appearances so
very characteristic of the Anglo-Saxon race, examples of
which may be found, as early as the seventh century, in the
'Oriental pomp' surrounding the consecration of Bishop
Wilfrid[102] by twelve Frankish bishops at Compiègne, in the
almost 'regal luxury' and the imposing edifices in which he
delighted to live, in the grandiose abbeys of St. Peter at
Wearmouth and St. Paul at Jarrow, raised, with the help of
of French and Italian craftsmen, by Benedict Biscop, or
again, in the eighth century, in the luxurious habits of the
English abbesses and nuns which drew such angry protests
from Bede, Boniface and Aldhelm. The Anglo-Saxons of
the higher classes were passionately fond of finery in dress.
Aldhelm—it is pleasant to think of the Abbot of Malmesbury
and Bishop of Sherborne taking his stand at the junction of
two crossroads or on a bridge and there charming a rustic
audience with glees and catches of his own composition, to
his own accompaniment on the harp, until he had gathered
a sufficient crowd and was assured of its attention to the
more serious doctrines he proposed to impart—"wrote a

correndo gli parv' esser tardo." It would be impossible not to refer to the
lovely untranslatable lines in *Paradiso*, XI, 79-117.

[98] Cf. Albers, op. cit., pp. 8-9.
[99] Cf. Felder, op. cit., p. 329.
[100] Cf. *Vita Mal.*, XXVIII, 61 (Migne, *P.L.*, CLXXXII, 1109), the anecdote
of the fanatic who protested against the building by St. Malachy of a stone
oratory at Bend-chor: "We are Scots, not Gauls. Why this frivolity?" and so
forth; and Lugano, op. cit., p. 12.
[101] Cf. Martin, op. cit., pp. 33 et seq.
[102] Cf. Cabrol, op. cit., p. 120.

notable book on Virginity," says the Venerable Bede (*H.E.*, V, 18), "which, in imitation of Sedulius, he composed double, that is, in hexameter verse and prose." The prose tract, 'De laudibus virginitatis,' written in the fantastic, pompous style which he affected—"pomposity," said William of Malmesbury in his life of St. Aldhelm, "is a characteristic of Anglo-Saxon writers, and you can see from their old charters what pleasure they took in abstruse terms and recondite words derived from the Greek"—was dedicated by Aldhelm to Hildelide, Abbess of Barking,[103] and her nuns. If he wished them to understand it, it may be observed in passing, she and her community must have been cultivated to a most uncommon degree. The bishop displays a very particular acquaintance with what he condemns and his description is not without interest. The English women wore undervests of fine linen of a violet colour and over it a scarlet tunic with full skirts and wide sleeves and a hood, both striped and either faced with silk or trimmed with fur. The hair was tastefully (*delicate*) curled with tongs over the forehead and temples. Ornaments of gold in the form of crescents encircled the neck. Bracelets were worn on the arms and rings with precious stones on the fingers, the nails of which were pared to a point to resemble the talons of a falcon.

They wore shoes of red leather and delighted to paint "their cheeks and jaws" 'rubro coloris stibio'. The men dressed in similar fashion, but their tunics were shorter, and they bound their legs with fillets of various colours. On ceremonial occasions both sexes wore blue mantles with facings of crimson silk, ornamented with stripes or vermicular figures. Such was their attire in the world, and such was it, in certain cases, Aldhelm was ashamed to say, in the cloister and the nunnery, although there was an affectation of modesty in the addition to this costume of a veil fastened with ribbons to the head, crossing over the chest and falling

---

[103] Barking, like Faremoutiers, Chelles and Les Andelys (Bede, *H.E.*, III, 8), was a 'double' monastery (ibid., IV, 7). Other such in England were Whitby, Coldingham, Ely and Wimborne. Cf. Leland's *Collectanea*, III, p. 117. At Beverley, a monastery of monks, a college of canons, and a convent of nuns, all obeyed the same abbot. Ibid., p. 100.

to the feet behind, "contra canonum decreta et regularis vitae normam."

The bishop begged to be excused his remonstrance on the ground that "meliora sunt vulnera diligentis quam oscula inimici," and expressed his confidence that in drawing attention to such extravagances he would meet with the general indulgence: "quia neminem specialiter summum severitas castigando exacerbavit: multa quippe genus et species . . . ab invicem differunt."[104] Such abuses were not allowed to pass without censure or condemnation, and it was enacted in councils that canons should be distinguished from monks and nuns, and these from the laity, by their dress, and that such dress should be similar to that worn by persons of the same orders in other Christian countries; but the authority of bishops and the decrees of councils were of no avail against national taste and national vanity. A century later Alcuin is found admonishing the monks of Lindisfarne, Wearmouth, and Jarrow not to glory in the vanity of dress, to prefer the virtues of their profession to the ostentatious display of silk hoods, of bands round the waist, of rings on the fingers, and of fillets round the feet. But the abuse seems to have been ineradicable.[105]

[104] Migne, *P.L.*, LXXXIX, Col. 115, §§ XVII and LVIII. The *De Laudibus Virginum* deals with the same theme in hexameters. Cf. also Lingard: *History of the Anglo-Saxon Church*, third edition, London, 1858, Vol. I, pp. 210-13; and Cabrol, op. cit., p. 205.

[105] Cf. Migne, *P.L.*, 100, *Ep. IX ad Lindisfarnenses*. A final exhortation to the abbot: "Et tu, pater sancte, dux populi Dei, pastor gregis sancti, medicus animorum, lucerna super candelabrum posita . . . sint vestimenta tua gradui condigna. Noli te conformare saeculi hominibus in vanitate aliqua. Inanis ornatus vestimentorum et cultus inutilis tibi est opprobrium ante homines et peccatum ante Deum," col. 151.

Ep XIV: Ad fratres Wirenses (Wearmouth) *et Gyrvenses* (Jarrow): "Nolite conformare vos saeculi homines in vestimentorum vanitate, in ebrietatis luxuria, in joci lascivia, in otiositatis petulantia: sed . . . conversatio vestra Deo sit amabilis et hominibus venerabilis, sicut decet filiis sanctae matris [sc. Ecclesiae] et monachicae vitae alumnos," col. 162.

Ep XV: Ad fratres Gyrvensis (Jarrow) *ecclesiae:* "Quid servis Dei qui monachicae vitae voto se obstrinxerunt inanis vestimentorum pompa quae nec secularibus prodest et multum Deo servientibus obest? (col. 166 and in *Ep. XVI*, col. 168 (to Wearmouth)). Quid vobis vestimentorum? Major exinde erit reprehensio quam laus. Vanitas est enim et superbia et nihil aliud et perditio vitae regularis."

It would be a mistake however, to imagine that the "inanis vestimentorum pompa" was peculiar to English convents. The History of Richer, monk of Saint Remi without the walls of Rheims, contains an account of a synod held at Mont Notre Dame en Tardenais, *c.* A.D. 970, under the presidency of

Far different was it with the Irish monks. The spirit of poverty, which animated many of the Irish saints, e.g., St. Columban, found its most appropriate expression in the same ineradicable predilection as St. Francis had for small communities. "It was the custom of the Irish monks to establish little communities round the principal monastery and to keep them dependent on it; it was thus easier for superiors to govern and there was less risk of any supervening laxity, the bane of overcrowded cloisters."[106]

The same spirit impelled the Irish monks and the Franciscan Friars to use no other means of transport in travelling than their own legs.[107]

Felder[108] deals admirably with the 'knightly sentiment' of St. Francis. 'Christ's Knight' had ceased to be the simple 'miles Christi' of St. Paul (II Tim. ii, 3), of the Fathers and the founders of religious orders down to Benedict; he had become 'God's fool.'[109] The knightly cycles of Arthur and Roland, the Troubadours and the Crusaders, had intervened. It is not difficult therefore to understand why it would be useless to seek for the knightly sentiment as such in the Irish monks of the sixth-seventh centuries. Yet the Celtic spirit, which passed through those centuries and found its ultimate embodiment in the heroic legends which exercised such a fascination upon the Saint of Assisi that he dubbed his friars "Knights of the Round Table,"[110] was sustained by the same indescribable joy as his in serving Christ the King, in serving Him loyally in vassalage, in risking any adventure for His sake, and in proclaiming Him to the whole world like a true knightly troubadour. "They rejected as too profane[111] the ancient tales which had charmed their

Rudolf, Abbot of Saint Remi (III, 40). One complaint against the monks was that they wore furry caps with pointed ears ('pillea aurita'), gorgeous clothes ('vestes lautissimas')—saffron seems to have been regarded with particular disfavour at the synod as an appropriate colour—and shoes with beaks and ears. It was not the only complaint. Cf. Migne, *P.L.*, 100, cols. 98-100, and a curious passage in the *Speculum Charitatis* of Aelred, Abbot of Rievaulx, *P.L.*, 195, III, c. XXVI, 600-5.

[106] Cf. Martin, op. cit., p. 41.
[107] Cf. Gougaud, op. cit., pp. 173-7 and Felder, op. cit., p. 116.
[108] Cf. op. cit., pp. 19, 24-8 and 311-13.
[109] *Joculator Domini, Spec. perf.*, c. 100.
[110] *Spec. perf.*, c. 72.
[111] Cf. Martin, p. 9.

childhood; the adventures of Ossian who dallied so long in the land of youth, to which he had been borne by a woman mounted on a white charger; of Bran, the son of Febal, who went on a visit to the other world, of Arthur whom the fairies carried away with them to the mysterious island of Avalon, so that he returned no more; but they delighted to follow, and not without a pang of envy, the knight Owen and many another hero, who had gone down into St. Patrick's Well, and who, after expiating their sins in a fantastic purgatory, had contemplated with their own eyes what things the Lord reserves for the elect; like the great St. Brendan, too, who had sailed from wonder to wonder until he came at last to the place where the sun sinks into the sea and reached the Fortunate Isles where God will gather the blessed together on the last evening of mankind." And the Celtic legend of the Holy Grail[112] contains the first germ of that religious chivalry, which later developed, with the Crusades, into the Order of Templars and the other semi-military, semi-religious orders. And precisely because of the knightly spirit of their race, the Irish had also the Franciscan 'gaiety' and felt the same need to express it in poetry and music as St. Francis. The Irish made poetry and music almost an integral part of religion, and almost all the great Irish saints have left us hymns or poems. Reference was made in Chapter III, § 1 to the poems of Columban.... "The love and practice of music was a national passion with the Irish," writes Montalembert.[113] "The missionaries and the monks their successors, were also inspired by this passion and knew how to use it for the government and consolation of souls," as, for instance, in the lovely legend of Mo-chuta (St. Carthach), who founded the monastic state of Liss-mor.[114] Colum-cille, the friend and patron of bards and poets, poured forth in song his affection for the foundations which the Lord had allowed him to make, or for the glories of other shrines, or the radiant Brigit, or his trust in Providence when he was forced to flee from King Diarmait. "Among the relics

[112] Cf. Ch. V, § 3.
[113] Cf. op. cit., Vol. III, p. 88. On the passion of Irish saints for music, cf. also Giraldus Cambrensis, *Opp.*, V, 155.
[114] Ibid., pp. 90-1.

of the saints the harp on which they had played found a place. At the first English conquest, the bishops and abbots excited the surprise of the invaders by their love of music and by accompanying themselves on the harp."[115] And it may not be known to everybody that poetry was so deeply rooted in the conquered people that it was proscribed and persecuted by the conquerers as a weapon of insurrection, before and after the Reformation. The minstrel who had succeeded the bard was imprisoned and decapitated as the most dangerous at first of patriots, then later, of papists. He was always at the side of the priest at the celebration of the holy mysteries of the proscribed religion.

"In the annals of the atrocious legislation directed by the English against the Irish people, as well before as after the Reformation, special penalties against the minstrels, bards, rhymers and genealogists who sustained the lords and gentlemen in their love of rebellion and of other crimes are to be met with at every step under Elizabeth, the Stuarts and the Cromwellians."[116]

Everybody knows the predilection of St. Francis for music and singing and the touching incident of the angelic concert which one night at Rieti consoled him, when his eyes were ailing, because, the day before he had been obliged, in order not to offend popular opinion, to refrain from listening to the strains of the friar musician his companion.[117] The author of the Canticle to Brother Sun often sang the praises of the Lord in the French tongue, and at moments of most ecstatic spiritual joy, would make himself a fiddle and a bow from two slender branches of a tree. "Music and song," writes Felder,[118] "played a very important part in the primitive Order of Minors. Spiritual singing was cultivated by Francis and his sons everywhere and in every form: chorales, hymns and proses, the *cantilena* both for the solo voice and in parts, alike in Latin and in the vulgar tongue. And this is one of the main reasons why the Order became so popular in an age so exceptionally and so

[115] Ibid., p. 199.
[116] Ibid., pp. 200-4.
[117] Tommaso da Celano, II, n. 126.
[118] Op. cit., p. 235.

passionately devoted to singing and music. And this makes it the easier also for us to understand why many a troubadour of artistic sensibility came to join the choir of God's poor minstrels, and why their muse, which thitherto had sung of knightly adventures and the praise of women, devoted itself thenceforth to hymns in honour of the eternal love and the Madonna who is the saints' ideal." Brother Juniper and Brother Giles were "excellent fools of God."[119]

The love of poetry and music, common to both Irish and Franciscans alike, is at bottom merely an aspect of their common attitude towards art and life in general, of their common recognition that beauty is a gift from God, of their common need to keep in contact with the soul of the people and to attain to its unsullied sources. The Irish monks were, as mentioned in Chapter III, § 1, the great promoters of the vernacular Gaelic literature, and so, among the literary memorials of the Italian vernacular in the twelfth century the foremost place is occupied by Franciscan compositions ranging from the poetry of the Seraphic Father himself to the verses of Jacopone da Todi, the most intense of the Italian poets who preceded Dante. A similar common effort may be perceived in the utilization and ennoblement of popular decorative motifs, and an analogous attitude may also be descried, in my opinion, towards the rather more complicated problem of literary studies.

The same conflict as had divided the Church in the early centuries was re-enacted on a smaller scale within the Franciscan Order in its early days. Just as in the Church the austere, uncompromising attitude of Tertullian, Arnobius and Lactantius had gradually yielded before the more generous and liberal conceptions of St. Gregory Nazianzen, St. Jerome and St. Augustine, so, within the Franciscan Order, the intransigent puritanism of the Spirituals had gradually yielded before the conception of St. Bonaventura that the world of learning was not necessarily the world of the devil and that, instead of being ignored, it needed to be won for Jesus Christ by being permeated with the spirit of

---

[119] Cf. Tommaso da Celano, *Vita S. Clarae*, c. 6, n. 51; "Vita Fr. Aegidii," in *Anal. Franc.*, III, pp. 105 et seq.

St. Francis.[120] And the Franciscans, in the persons of their great philosophers of the latter half of the thirteenth and the beginning of the fourteenth century (Alexander of Hales, St. Bonaventura, John Duns Scotus, John Peckham, Roger Bacon and Raymond Lully), assumed a position of commanding influence in the field of learning and throughout the fifteenth century played a leading part. Giovanni da Serravalle, Alberto da Sartiano, St. Bernardino of Siena, St. John Capistran, all representative Franciscans, welcomed humanism with undisguised sympathy, while rejecting its pagan excesses. St. Bernardino, who, after his sermons, made bonfires of "the trinkets of vanity" in the market-place, exhorted his listeners to study Cicero together with St. Jerome, and in poverty found it possible still to love beauty. The convents of the Observance bear witness to this day of that love in their delightful situations, the simplicity but supreme elegance of their architectural lines, and the decorations with which they were adorned by artists so renowned as Benozzo Gozzoli, Ghirlandaio and the della Robbias.

This almost native Franciscan sense of harmony with regard to profane learning and art derives from the spirit of the Seraphic Father himself, "who had revalued nature and life in terms of Christianity, who, for all his austerity, was more enamoured, than afraid, of God, who, though closed to pleasure remained open wide to beauty, who in penitence could still be merry,"[121] and finds its perfect counterpart, in my opinion, in the harmony of Irish monasticism in the same respect, as exemplified in Chapters II and III.

Reverting to chivalry, I would observe that the Irish also, like the Franciscans later, were the Knights of the Eucharistic Christ and the Mystic Christ which is the Church. The sacraments of Penance and the Holy Eucharist were little frequented in the Gauls of the sixth century and Christian life languished most miserably. "Such was not the case in Ireland," according to the Abbé Martin.[122] "There the

[120] Cf. Fr. A. Gemelli, *Il Francescanesimo*, Milan, 1932, p. 51 and pp. 120, 134, 426 et seq.   [121] Ibid., p. 138.   [122] Op. cit., p. 71.

abbots treated their subjects in their semi-dioceses rather after the fashion of monks. They had accustomed them to confess their faults, even trifling ones, and to receive from the priest a private penance," appropriate to the needs of their souls. Such was the origin of the penitentials of Finnian, Gildas, Columban and the rest. And this ardent zeal for bringing souls to the tribunal of penance with the object of re-admitting them to the incomparable privilege of the Holy Eucharist was brought over to Europe by the Irish and bore magnificent fruit.[123] The Eucharist, it is common knowledge, was the centre of the whole religious life of St. Francis, and his respect and love for the Body of Christ embraced everything in relation, direct or indirect, with such a mystery, the priests who consecrate and administer It, the sacred vessels which honour and touch It, the churches which house It.[124]

The lover's devotion which St. Francis bore the Roman Catholic Church and the ecclesiastical hierarchy also shone with a dazzling light in that thirteenth century which was so rife with heresy. His Rule unceasingly expresses his veneration for the Pontiff, for bishops, for all the secular clergy, unceasingly inculcates the principle[125] that the Order shall always ask "from the Lord Pope for one of the cardinals of the Holy Roman Church to be governor, protector, and corrector," to the end that all the brethren may be "always subject and submissive at the feet of the same Holy Church and steadfast in the Catholic faith."[126] The heroes of the spiritual life have all felt that outside the Church there is no salvation but only pride, that among mankind, as Lars Eskeland has recently observed, Christ shines resplendent or grows wan, as faith in the Church is radiant or eclipsed.

And fidelity to Rome has been one of the fundamental characteristics of the Irish religious movement from the early days of St. Patrick. The saint in that third dictum attributed to him, part of which, at any rate, rings true, exhorted his

[123] Cf. Mrs. Concannon, op. cit., pp. 147-52 and Mgr. Duchesne, *L'Église au VIème siècle*, p. 549.
[124] Cf. Felder, op. cit., pp. 40-4.
[125] Rule II, cap. XII.
[126] Cf. Felder, op. cit., pp. 56-73.

people to be staunch: "Church of the Scots, nay, of the Romans, as ye are Christians, so be ye also Romans ('Ecclesia Scotorum immo Romanorum, ut Christiani ita et Romani sitis')."[127] St. Columban in his Fifth Letter (c. 612, to Pope Boniface IV) exclaims: "We Irish, who inhabit the extremities of the world, are the disciples of St. Peter and St. Paul and of the other apostles who, under the dictation of the Holy Spirit, compiled the sacred canon. We admit nothing beyond the apostolic and evangelical doctrine. There has never been a heretic, a Jew or a schismatic among us, and the Catholic Faith as it was first delivered to us from you, the successors of the holy apostles, is maintained by us inviolate. . . . We are, as I have already explained, bound to the chair of St. Peter: for however great and far-famed Rome may be, it is that chair alone which makes her great and glorious among us. Although the name of the ancient city, the glory of Ausonia, has been spread throughout the world as something supremely august and far removed from the changing seasons of the common world by the excessive esteem of nearly all the nations, for us you are only august and great since God deigned to become also the son of God, and the Spirit of God, riding on those two high-mettled coursers, the apostles Peter and Paul, the possession of whose dear relics has constituted your felicity, disturbed many waters in the seas of the world and increased by thousands the chariot-teams of countless peoples: so the charioteer in chief, in that race, Christ Himself, a true Father, the Driver of Israel, crossed the broad stream and over the back of dolphins, over the surging main, came at last to us. From that time only are you great and famed, and Rome itself still nobler and more famed, and because

[127] The full text is an exhortation to the Church in Ireland to adopt the liturgical formula "Kyrie eleison, Christe eleison." Mr. Edmund Bishop having pointed out in two articles in *The Downside Review*, December 1899 and March 1900, that such a formula did not reach the Gauls before the sixth century, "its introduction into Italy falling in the fifth century at the earliest, probably in the second half rather than in the first" (cf. his *Liturgica Historica*, Oxford, 1918, pp. 116-36), Prof. Bury was "strongly disposed to think that the third dictum is spurious and was added," perhaps, after A.D. 700, "by a member of the Romanising party to the two genuine dicta" (*Life of St. Patrick*, p. 232). In its present form, however, it may well be merely a useful expansion of an earlier authentic dictum. Cf. § 2 of the *Epistola*.

of the twin apostles of Christ, if I may say so . . . you are almost heavenly, and Rome is the head of the Churches of the world ('vos prope coelestes estis et Roma orbis terrarum caput est ecclesiarum'), excepting only the exceptional prerogative reserved to the place of Our Lord's resurrection."[128]

Such words are proof enough, if any proof be needed, of Grisar's statement that "it is entirely false to insinuate . . . that the Bishops of Rome derived their spiritual authority merely from the external circumstances of their See."[129] St. Kilian,[130] too, hailed Rome as 'the head of the world, the summit of the Catholic faith'.[131]

Many other minor points reminiscent of St. Francis, corollary for the most part to those already made, recur at every step in reading the Lives of the Irish Saints. Allusion may be made in passing to a few facts and incidents gathered, for instance, from the Abbé Martin's *Vie de St. Columban*. St. Columban also was a restorer of churches; he also had the same absolute trust in Providence and prayer for his sustenance and material needs in general, and the same lack of solicitude for the needs of the morrow; he also made no distinction between priests and lay brothers in the life of his community; he also filled his Rule, as Francis his

[128] Cf. Montalembert, II, pp. 441-2; Mrs. Concannon, pp. 233-5; Martin, pp. 160-5; but above all Mr. M. V. Hay's *A Chain of Error in Scottish History*, London, 1927, which contains with much amusing comment on the treatment accorded to this letter by Stokes and others, the text and a translation. The "cara pignora" referred to by St. Columban cannot, however, mean 'beloved descendants,' but, as Mr. Hay suggests in his note, precious, i.e., beloved, relics. Contemporary texts place the construction beyond doubt. The passage cannot be described as simple and the commentators have been shy of translating it.
[129] Cf. *Rome and the Popes in the Middle Ages*, Vol. I, London, 1912, p. 316, also Vol. III, pp. 184 and 348.
[130] Cf. Martin, op. cit., p. 10.
[131] Père Grosjean, S.J., in a review (cf. *Analecta Bollandiana*, 1932, p. 449) of Fr. L. MacKenna's book on the Franciscan bard, Philip Bocht O Huiginn, makes the interesting observation that many traces are to be found in the Irish tradition of a true and proper devotion to the soil of Rome in itself. Cf. the use of the words *rom*, *rúam* in the sense of cemetery from the practice of bringing earth from the sacred City to hallow burial places. Glendalough, reputed to be one of the four best 'Romes' in Ireland, had been hallowed by the earth which Coemgen brought back with him when he returned from Rome (*Vita Coemgeni*, iii, 21), and seven pilgrimages there were the equivalent of one pilgrimage to Rome. Cf. Ch. Plummer, *Bethada Náem nErenn*, Oxford, 1922, II, 156.

first Rule with lessons drawn from the Gospel; he also had
for his first greeting words of peace.

§ 5

At this point we may well ask ourselves: Is there any
explanation to account for similarities so numerous, so
intimate, and so substantial, between the Irish and the
Franciscan movements?

The explanation may be found, in my opinion, in the
ardour and force of expansion which follow every genuine
and profound 'conversion.' In insisting so strongly on
describing his own abandonment of the world as a 'conversion,'[132] St. Francis has given us a hint of the nature of
that most powerful, mysterious impulse, which, in the
thirteenth century, drove humanity after him in multitudes.
The Legend of the Three Companions[133] tells us that, like
Saul on the road to Damascus, he exclaimed one day: "Lord,
what will You have me do?" St. Bonaventura[134] has
repeated to us that cry of his: "Lord, what will You have
me do?" But his conversion was not the conversion of an
individual soul, it was the conversion of an epoch. To
understand the providential value of the appeal made by the
Saint of Assisi, the condition of the Church and society at
large in the thirteenth century should be borne in mind.
Heresies were rampant everywhere, more particularly the
Waldensian and the Albigensian, the persecutions and
impositions of Frederick Barbarossa, Henry VI, Otto IV
and Frederick II were persistent against, and upon, the
Church, the condition of the East after the Fourth Crusade
was disastrous, the States in the north were pitted against
one another in deadly rivalry, the common people in Italy
were struggling to escape from the fetters of feudalism and
to establish the communes, corruption and illiteracy were
rife among the clergy, the usury practised by the Jews was
pitiless in its exactions, misery, vice, ruin and rapine were
everywhere, and Christ was disregarded. The Lord truly

---

[132] Cf. Felder, op. cit., pp. 1-6, 32, 75-80. [133] Cap. II.
[134] Vita di S. F., I, 3.

made use of St. Francis, with St. Dominic by his side, to save the Church and to direct into the main stream of Catholicism the spiritual and social ferment effervescing in a myriad different places and seeking an outlet through a myriad different channels.   Crowds without number, in which beggar jostled king, went after the Little Poor Man. Mankind through the intervention of St. Francis found Jesus Christ again, and having found Him, proceeded, with the convert's enthusiastic love, to follow the Great King and the herald of His Name even to the furthest bounds of the earth.   The same phenomenon occurred in Ireland when she awoke again to the faith of St. Patrick at the highly critical moment of the barbarian invasions.

The Irish monastic movement is dead and buried, the reader may think, while the Franciscan, on the contrary, endures triumphantly.   And he may be tempted to ask: Why should this be?

The question leads the inquirer to seek, beyond the similarities, the differences between the two movements.

But let the limits of the question itself be first determined. If it is true that the Irish foundations have sunk into oblivion, we are, nevertheless, bound to observe that the apostolic spirit, the flame which fired that movement, was never utterly extinguished in Ireland. It remained forever burning in the secular clergy of high and low degree, and in the regular clergy, old and new. Magnificent examples of that spirit are to be found in the heroic resistance offered to the Reformation by both orders, in the manner in which they have followed the national *diaspora* to the Americas, Australia, and South Africa, and in the recent institution of the "Missionaries of St. Columban," gone at a moment's notice to hold the first-line trenches of the Church in China.

Premising thus much, I would suggest that the chief causes of the decline of medieval Irish monasticism (which are also the substantial differences between it and Franciscanism) may be reduced to two: the national character of such monasticism and the lack of organisation.

Whereas the Franciscan movement from the very beginning, during the lifetime of St. Francis himself and by his express will, was decidedly international or, better, universal, Irish monasticism, on the contrary, was national in character and therefore suffered repercussions from the political vicissitudes of the mother country. The decadence of Ireland which set in after the Danish invasion, its gradual conquest later by the Anglo-Normans, and, finally, the material and spiritual usurpations of the Scotch from the thirteenth century onwards, were bound almost inevitably to overwhelm and merge in oblivion the glorious achievements and foundations of the Irish monks.

But besides being national, the Irish monastic movement differed from the Franciscan in its lack of organisation. Some writers have attributed this to the character of the Irish themselves, whom they allege to be devoid of political sense and the spirit of cohesion.[135] My own opinion is that a contributory cause at least was the fact that the Irish foundations were so soon compelled to embrace the rule of the Benedictine Order, whose origin, spirit and objects were so different from their own, and which lacked a central government.

It must, however, be borne in mind that, until the rise of the Mendicant Orders, no religious Order had any central organisation. The efforts made by St. Benedict of Anian in the ninth century to unify the Benedictines at least partially failed in their object; it was achieved early in the twelfth century by the Cistercians, after a fashion. But the Mendicant Orders alone created a true and proper central government with a minister or master-general, the commander-in-chief of all the sons of the Order, with power to issue instructions and to pursue them to the four corners of the globe. There is nothing surprising in this. The province took the place of the abbey, for the simple reason that the Mendicant Orders were really mendicant, whereas the medieval abbeys were also rich and powerful feudatories.

I would take leave to conclude this chapter and my book with some sublime and terrible words of St. Francis:

"Let no man flatter himself with undeserved applause on account of anything that a sinner can do. A sinner can fast

[135] Cf. Gougaud, op. cit., p. 425.

and pray and weep and mortify his flesh, but this one thing he cannot do: 'remain faithful to his Lord.' Therefore of this only should we make our boast, if we return to God that which is His, if, serving Him faithfully, we ascribe to Him whatever He gives us. The greatest enemy of man is his own flesh: for his flesh cannot remember anything to grieve over, cannot foresee anything to be afraid of; its one desire is to abuse the passing moment; and, what is worse, it arrogates to itself and transfers to its own glory that which is given not to it, but to the soul. It preens itself upon its virtues: it goes abroad seeking praise for its vigils and its prayers: it leaves nothing to the soul and would make profit even out of tears."[136]

Ireland has remained faithful to her Lord.

[136] Tommaso da Celano, II, n. 34.

APPENDIX

I WOULD here draw the general attention of students to the great assistance to be derived both in hagiographical and in many other kinds of investigation from the publication of the *Rationes Decimarum Italiae* for the thirteenth and fourteenth centuries inaugurated recently by members of the staff of the Vatican Library in the well-known series "Studi e Testi." The *Rationes* cannot provide a complete list of all the monasteries and churches in Italy at the time, for the reason that they omit foundations belonging to such religious orders as were exempt from tithe, but even so they are a mine extraordinarily rich in statistical information. Each volume contains an appropriate map enabling the reader easily to identify the old with the modern nomenclature. So far only *Tuscia, I, La decima degli anni 1274-80* edited by Mons. Pietro Guidi, and *Aemilia*, edited by Angelo Mercati, Emilio Nasalli-Rocca and Dr. Pietro Sella, have been published and noticed in the *English Historical Review*, Vols. XLVIII, 653, and L, 357 respectively. The reader will be able to judge from the considerable new elements provided by these first two volumes regarding the cult of the Irish Saints what a rich harvest of interesting information awaits other labourers in this field when the publication of the *Rationes* for all the provinces of Italy is completed.

St. Patrick (Ch. VII, § 6).

The church of St. Patrick at Tirli is recorded in *Rat. Dec. Tuscia*, s. No. 720 (tithe for the years 1276-7) as *ecclesia S. Patritii de Curia Tierli*.

St. Brigit of Cell Dara (Ch. VIII, §§ 5 and 7).

The *Rat. Dec. Aem.* mention the church and hospital of St. Brigit in Piacenza s. nn. 5719 and 6015 (fourteenth century) and the *ecclesia S. Brigidae* in Parma s. nn. 4085 (A.D. 1230) and 4743 (A.D. 1299). An *ecclesia S. Brigidae* in the diocese of Bologna, and, more particularly, in the *pieve* of S. Giovanni in Triario, is also mentioned s. n. 2545 (A.D. 1300). This is the church which gave its name to the village of S. Brigida (Italian Touring Club map, sh. 19, A. 1) between Minerbio and Granarolo dell' Emilia.

The *Rat. Dec. Tuscia* record an *ecclesia S. Brigidae de Bagnolo* in the diocese of Arezzo and the parish of Socana (Casentino), in the tithe for the years 1274-5 (no. 1581) and 1278-9 (no. 2293), at a time, therefore, when there is no possible doubt that the titular was the virgin of Ireland. This is not without its importance, because no trace had hitherto been found of any cult of St. Brigit on this side of the Apennines. Cf. also below with reference to St. Brigit at Opaco (Ch. XXI).

St. Columban (Ch. XII, §§ 6, & 8).

The *Rat. Dec. Aem.* record the undermentioned foundations already noted:

(a) In the diocese of Bobbio:

(i) Fourteenth century, no. 6028, *Monasterium S. Col. di Bobbio*;

(ii) Do. no. 6031, *Ecclesia S. Col. de Spelunca* (Cf. Cipolla-Buzzi, III, 265);

(iii) Do. no. 6049 *Ecclesia S. Col. de Caxarco* (Cf. Cipolla-Buzzi, III, 207);

(iv) Do. no. 6050 *Ecclesia S. Col. de Monteforti* (Cf. Cipolla-Buzzi, III, 265).

(b) In the diocese of Bologna:

(i) A.D. 1300 no. 2337, *Ecclesia S. Col. in Bologna*;

(ii) Do., no. 2394 *Monasterium S. Col. in Bologna*.

There is mention also of another church, which had hitherto escaped notice, in the diocese of Bologna: A.D. 1300 no. 2680 *Eccl. S. Columb. de Plumacio*, the present-day Piumazzo (part of the commune of Castelfranco dell' Emilia) in the plain of Bologna between the Panaro and the Samoggia (Italian Touring Club map, sh. 18, A. 4).

The *Rat. Dec. Tuscia* cite in the diocese of Lucca, besides the church in the *pieve* of Segromigno (nn. 4010, 4335, 4965), the present parish church of the village of S. Colombano, part of Capannori, two other churches dedicated to St. Columban (tithe-roll of 1260): one (no. 4829) in the *pieve* of Compito to the south-east of the city of Lucca on Mte. Pisano, and the other (no. 5365) in the *pieve* of S. Gervasio on the hills west of the Arno and south-east of Pontedera. The latter must have been a church of some importance, being taxed at *lit* 260 (Segromigno at 132 and Compito at 31). The same *Rationes Dec. Tuscia* also cite in the diocese of Florence s. n. 566 (A.D. 1276-7) the *eccl. S. Columbani* in the *pieve* of S. Stefano *de Campoli*, which corresponds to the present church of St. Columban at Bibbione.

St. Emilian (Ch. XV, § 2).

The *Rat. Dec. Aem.* record in the diocese of Faenza: n. 2026 *Ecclesia S. Miliani de Faventia;* n. 2085 *Ecclesia S. Miliani de Quarada, plebatus Apri* (now Pidenza, Italian Touring Club map, sh. 19, C. 3), in the county of Faenza which is that referred to by Lanzoni as on the hills above Pergola.

S. Pellegrino (Ch. XVI, §§ 3, 5, 11).

The hospice of S. Pellegrino delle Alpi is mentioned in the *Rat. Dec. Tuscia*, s. no. 5198 as *Hospitale S. Peregrini cum cellis, quas habet in dicto plebatu (de Fosciana)* and is taxed Lit. 200 (tithe-roll of 1260).

The famous *Mansio hospitalis de Altopassu* (Altopascio), which was the wealthiest institution in the diocese of Lucca and flourished as early as the eleventh century, had St. James for titular and SS. Giles and Peregrinus for co-titulars (*Rat. Dec. Tuscia*, p. 250, note 1). The hospital at Lunata (*ibid.*, note 4) had St. Matthew for titular and St. Peregrinus for co-titular.

The church of S. Pellegrino in Lucca is mentioned in the *Rat. Dec. Tuscia*, s. n. 4770 (tithe-roll of 1260). An *ecclesia S. Peregrini de Colline* (n. 4830) is mentioned in the same tithe-roll in the *pieve* of Compito on Mte. Pisano.

A *Hospitale S. Peregrini de Obricolis* (nn. 2708, 2802) is mentioned in the diocese of Chiusi, in the *pieve* of S. Giovanni di Radicofani. This might well be a connecting-link between the churches in the Lucchesia and the church in Viterbo dedicated to the saint.

St. Fridian (Ch. XVII, §§ 9, & 10).

The *Rat. Dec. Aem.* cite in the diocese of Bologna the following three interesting foundations, the first two of which had hitherto escaped notice:

(i) n. 2406, A.D. 1300, *Monasterium S. Fridiani prope Bononiam* (?);

(ii) n. 2848, A.D. 1300, *Monasterium S. Fridiani* in the *pieve* of Casio, near Bagni della Porretta (Italian Touring Club map, Sh. 18, C. 4), the prior of which was, apparently, a certain *Brittellus;*

(iii) n. 2860, A.D. 1300, *Ecclesia S. Fridiani de pàvana:* Pàvana, also near Bagni della Porretta (Italian Touring Club map, sh. 18, D. 4), is now in the diocese of Pistoja.

As to the church of St. Fridian in Bologna it may be recalled that it was appointed for a time (thirteenth century) the national church with peculiar chaplain attached for the German 'nation' frequenting that illustrious university. The Germans were later transferred to St. Dominic's. Cf. Friedländer and Malagola, *Acta nationis Germanicae universitatis Bononiensis,* Berlin, 1887.

The *Rat. Dec. Tuscia* cite in Pisa, besides the monastery of St. Fridian a *Hospitale S. Fridiani* (nn. 3493, 3599) rated at Lit. 28 both in 1275-6 and in 1276-7.

Then follow these churches in the diocese of Pisa:

(i) *ecclesia S. Fridiani de Canneto* (n. 3745) in the *pieve* S. Maria de Cascina on the south bank of the Arno (anno 1276-7);

(ii) *ecclesia S. Fridiani de Gunfo* (nn. 3545, 3707) in the *pieve* of S. Cassiano (S. Casciano) close to present-day Navacchio (annis 1275-7);

(iii) *ecclesia S. Fridiani de Lama* (n. 3720), also in the *pieve* of S. Cassiano (anno 1276-7);

(iv) *ecclesia S. Fridiani de Septimo* (n. 3541) also in the *pieve* of S. Cassiano: the present S. Frediano a Settimo, part of the commune of Càscina (anno 1275-6);

(v) *ecclesia S. Fridiani de Trechese* or *Treccese* or *Tretese* (n. 3766, anno 1276-7) in the *pieve* of S. Giovanni di Calcinaria (a Calcinaja still exists on the north bank of the Arno near Vicopisano), identical, perhaps, with the following:

(vi) *ecclesia S. Fridiani de Trisxi* (n. 3564, anno 1275-6) also in the *pieve* of S. Giovanni di Calcinaria.

Two churches are cited in the diocese of Pistoja:

(i) *ecclesia S. Fridiani de Brugianico* (or *Buggianico*) (note 1198, anno 1276-7) north of Pistoja, near the present station of Vajoni on the railway line Florence-Porretta;

(ii) *ecclesia S. Fridiani de Fabrica* (n. 1349, anno 1276-7) in the *pieve S. Pancratii de Celle,* north-west of Pistoja between Arcigliano and the summit of Mte. Cavalluccio.

In the diocese of Arezzo the *ecclesia S. Fridiani de Calosena* or *Calosina* (n. 1943, anno 1278-9) is cited in the *pieve* of *S. Viti in Versuris* in the valley of the Camerone which flows into the Ombrone from the north, a little above Asciano.

In the diocese of Florence, besides the *canonica S. Fridiani de Florentia* (nn. 34, 204, annis 1274-7) reference is also made to a church *S. Fridiani de Nebbiano* (n. 497, anno 1276-7) in the *pieve* of S. Pietro in Mercato. The village of Nebbiano is still in existence between Castelfiorentino (Val d' Elsa) and Montespertoli.

In the diocese of Lucca the *Rat. Dec.* cite, besides the *canonica* ((n. 4771, anno 1260—n. 4197, 1276-7), the *hospital* (n. 4772, anno 1260) and the *Porta S. Fridiani* (p. 249) in Lucca, the following:

(i) in the *pieve S. Thome Vallis Ariane,* the *ecclesia S.*

Fridiani de Aramo (nn. 4038, 4447, 5034, annis 1260-77). Aramo, part of the commune of Pescia, is up the valley of the torrent Pescia: the church is now a parish church;

(ii) in the *pieve S. Nicholay de Turri* the *ecclesia S. Fridiani de Arsina* (nn. 4035, 4390, 4916, annis 1260-77), north-north-west of Lucca, in the commune of Pescaglia on the Apuan Alps: now a parish church;

(iii) in the *pieve S. Quirici de Casabasciana* the *ecclesia S. Fridiani de Carsciana* or *Crasciana* (nn. 4023, 4568, 5064, annis 1260-77) on the mountains west of the torrent Lima between S. Marcello Pistojese and Bagni di Lucca: still a parish church;

(iv) in the *pieve* of *Arliano* the *ecclesia S. Fridiani de Cassano* (n. 4874, anno 1260), now Compignano, on the hill between Ponte S. Pietro and Massarosa, above the lake of Massaciùccoli; now a parish church;

(v) in the *pieve* of *Controne* the *ecclesia S. Fridiani de Chifenti* (n. 5054, anno 1260) at the confluence of the Lima and the Serchio: now a parish church;

(vi) in the *pieve* of *Triano* the church *S. Fridiani de Crespina* (n. 5317, anno 1260) near Valtirano, north-east of Colle Salvetti;

(vii) in the *pieve* of S. Giorgio *de Brancoli* the church S. *Fridiani de Deccio* (nn. 3945, 4416, 4940, annis 1260-77) near Piazza, on the hills west of the Serchio between Diecimo and Ponte a Moriano: now a parish church;

(viii) in the *pieve* of *S. Gervasio*, the church *S. Fridiani de Forcole* (nn. 4104, 4683, 5385, annis 1260-77). Forcoli is still there and the church a parish church;

(ix) the *plebes S. Fridiani de Lunata* (nn. 4162, 4299, annis 1275-7): Lunata still stands east-north-east of Lucca on the road to Pescia: the church is a parish church;

(x) in the *pieve* of *Massa Buggianese*, the church S. *Fridiani de Malochio* (n. 5232, anno 1260). The village of Malocchio still stands on the mountain north-east of Pescia;

(xi) in the *pieve* of *S. Giovanni de Mosciano* the church *S. Fridiani de Marti* (nn. 4676, 5403, annis 1260-77). The village of Marti still exists near Montopoli in Valdarno, between Pontedera and S. Miniato;

(xii) in the *pieve* of *S. Giovanni de Villa Teransana*, the church *S. Fridiani de Montefegatese* (n. 4561, annis 1276-7). The village of Montefegatesi is part of Bagni di Lucca and the church is now a parish church;

(xiii) in the *pieve* of *S. Macario*, the church *S. Fridiani de Piethano* or *Plossano* or *Piothano* (nn. 3999, 4340, 4887, annis 1260-77). There is a village Piazzano near S. Macario in Monte, north-west of the Ponte S. Pietro; the church is now a parish church;

(xiv) in the *pieve* of *S. Giovanni de Fosciana*, the church *S. Fridiani de Sassi* (nn. 4156, 4542, 5196, annis 1260-77). The village of Sassi, south-south-west of Castelnuovo di Garfagnana, still stands;

(xv) in the *pieve* of *S. Maria di Loppia* the church S. *Fridiani de Sommocologno* (nn. 4523, 5121, annis 1260-77). Sommocolonia, part of the commune of Barga, is now in the diocese of Pisa;

(xvi) in the *pieve* of *S. Maria de Aquis* (=Bagni di Casciana) the church *S. Fridiani de Oscilliano* (nn. 4669, 5341, annis 1260-77). There is still a locality called S. Fridiano on the road S. Ermo-Fauglia, south-west of Osigliano. Cf. also that mentioned in § 9;

(xvii) in the *pieve* of *S. Lorenzo di Segromigno*, the church S. *Fridiani de Valgiano* (nn. 4007, 4331, 4962, annis 1260-77). The village of Valgiano still stands north of Segromigno: the church is a parish church.

In addition the *Rat. Dec.* mention the *monasterium S. Fridiani de Tolli* (p. 251, note 1). It was a nunnery down to 1181 dedicated to St. Fridian, thereafter a monastery called after St. James and the Valle Benedetta. Its exact site has not yet been securely identified.

St. Andrew of Fiesole (Ch. XX, § 2).

S. Martino a Mensola occurs twice (nn. 3 and 251) in the *Rat. Dec. Tuscia* as *Monasterium dominarum S. Martini de Melsola* or *Melsole* and is rated for the year 1274-5 at Lit. 11. 11. 3 and for the year 1276-7 at Lit. 8. 6. 0.

St. Brigit at Opaco (Ch. XXI).

The *Rat. Dec. Tuscia* record the *ecclesia S. Brigidae* in the *pieve S. Martini in Baco* in the diocese of Fiesole s. no. 893 (anno 1274-5) and s. no. 936 (anno 1276-7).

Considering (i) that this saint is venerated in only one church in the world and that dating back to the time of St. Donatus of Fiesole and situate in the diocese of which he was bishop; (ii) that the latest investigations all tend to show that St. Donatus was the most fervent propagandist of devotion to St. Brigit; (iii) that the feast-day of St. Brigit at Opaco coincides with that of the saint of Cell-dara; (iv) that no trace has ever been discovered of any remains of a woman saint at Opaco; (v) that her mysterious appearance at the sick-bed of her brother Andrew at Mensola is for all the world identical with the alleged apparition of St. Brigit to Donatus on his sick-bed at Fiesole (cf. Ch. XIX § 3), I cannot refrain from a suspicion that the saint venerated in the Val di Sieci was originally none other than the illustrious patron of Ireland.

St. Cathal (Ch. XXII, §§ 11 and 13).

The *Rat. Dec. Aem.* record s. n. 3381 (thirteenth century) the *ecclesia S. Cathaldi* in Modena; the *Rat. Dec. Tuscia* a church *S. Cataldi de Petriolo* in the roll of the diocese of Lucca in 1260 (n. 5292). It was in the *pieve* of S. Maria in Monte or S. Maria a Colle on the north bank of the Arno, near Castelfranco and below, a fact which accounts for the cult still rendered to St. Cathal in that parish.

Another ecclesia *S. Cataldi de Pupilliano* (n. 5233) according to the same roll for 1260 stood in the *pieve* of Massa Buggianese (Massa and Cozzile) on the mountain north of Buggiano between Pescia and Montecatini.

INDEX OF PROPER NAMES

Words such as Irish, Ireland, England, English, Celtic, etc., which recur continually are not indexed.

Aaron, St., 283.
Abbey cemetery, 430.
Abbondio, St., 248.
Abbots Langley, 147.
Abel, 81.
Abel, 471.
Abraham, 65, 129.
Abruzzi, 418.
Accia, 300, 312.
Achadh-bo, 80, 162.
Achaius, King, 325, 332.
Acheron, 170.
Achilles, 158.
Acqua Fredda, 254.
Acqua Rossa, 415.
Acquaviva delle Fonti, 422.
Acqui, 301.
Adalbero I, 86.
Adalbero II, 86.
Adam, 59.
Adami, Fr., 241.   [128, 162.
Adamnan, 19, 47, 67, 68, 104, 108,
Adda, 71, 248, 302.
Adelfius, Bishop, 34.
Adelfrid, 70.
Adelgilda, Domna, 295.
Adelgrada, 347.
Adhémar, 20.
Adonic, 103.
Adrian IV, 148, 149.
Adriatic, 402, 424.
Adventurers, 214, 218.
Advocates' Library, 18.
Aedhan mac Gabhrain, 68.
Aedh Mac an Bhard, 23.
Africa, 35, 77, 157, 158.
Africa, South, 490.
Agapit, Pope, 99.
Agata, Sta dei Goti, 230.
Agatha, St., 430.
Aghaboe, 80.
Aghado, 45.
Aghadoe, 406.
Agilbert, 107.
Agilulf, 75, 115.
Aglié, 336.
Agnelli, 302.
Agnello, St., 420, 421.
Agobard, 119.

Agrestius, 468.
Agricola, 31, 32, 33, 35.
Agro Vercellese, 276.
Aidan, St., 56, 70, 71, 84, 108.
Ailpin, 19.
Aisling, 157, 159.
Alaric, 34.
Alba, 19, 253, 293, 314.
Alban, St., 265, 283.
Albano, 148.
Alban's, St., 139, 147, 148.
Albenga, 247, 300, 337.
Albers, Dom B., 290.
Albert, Bishop, 276.
Albert II, Count, 326, 329.
Alberto da Sartiano, 485.
Albert Scotti, 330.
Albigensian, 489.
Albion, 67.
Albona, 261.
Albornoz, Card. E., 308.
Alcazar, 201.
Alclaith, 181, 182.
Alcuin, 24, 110, 120, 121, 126, 480.
Aldfrid, 107.
Aldhelm, 72, 79, 104, 107, 478, 479.
Alessandria, 293.
Alessio, F., 325, 331, 332.
Alexander, 388.
Alexander, Bishop, 383.
Alexander III, 149, 274, 349.
Alexander IV, 350, 448, 449, 451, 452.
Alexander VI, 178.
Alexander of Hales, 485.
Alexandria, 450, 453.
Alfred the Great, 130.
Allen, Card., 96.
Alliste, 424.
Allo, Duke, 380.
Almeria, 337.
Alben, Mt., 359.
Alpes Ubaldinorum, 239.
Alps, 6, 75, 251, 279, 280, 353.
Alsace, 91, 253.
Alseno, 306.
Altenmunster, 80.
Altinum, 265, 266.
Altus prosator, 103.
Alverno, Mt., 442.

Amalefrid, 115.
Amalfi, 421.
Amalric, 248, 304.
Amandus, 115, 295.
Amasianus, 408.
Amator, 42, 235.
Amayden, 95, 338.
Ambrose, St., 124, 234, 235.
Ambrosian Library, 25, 110, 115, 117, 248, 287, 368.
America, 66, 91, 92, 300, 490.
Amiterno, 353.
Ammian Marcellin, 18.
Amondaschi, 312.
Anagni, 350.
Anastasio, S., 250.
Anastasio, Church of, 266.
Anastasius, 35, 105.
Anastasius IV, 148.
Anaunia, 250.
Ancona, 346, 353.
Andrea, S., 293, 296.
Andrea, S. di Borzane, 297.
Andrea, S. di Sestri, 297.
Andreas, Stus, 386.
Andreas, Stus de Carraria, 372.
Andrew, St., 14, 246, 364, 417.
Andrew, St. on the Coelian, 69, 466, 467.
Andrew, disciple of S. Donatus, 386, 388, 395 to 399, 438.
Andria, 422.
Angelo, Ponte Sant, 95.
Angel's Hill, 475.
Angers, 108.
Angles, 19, 37, 70, 472.
Anglesey, 129.
Angleterre, 14.
Anglo-Celtic, 38.
Anglo-Norman(s), 20, 133, 147, 432, 434, 436, 491.
Anglo-Saxon(s), 19, 27, 70, 83, 100, 150, 465 to 468, 473, 474, 478, 479.
Anglo-Saxon Chronicle, 182.
Anglo-Saxon Church, 134, 137.
Angoulême, 20, 82.
Angus, Earl of, 328.
Anian, 491.
Anmehad, 87.
Anna, 182.
Annales Minorum, 154.
Anne, Queen, 179.
Annecy, 279.
Annegray, 72.
Anonimo Ticinese, 285.
Anrìcus Scotus, 336.
Ansan, St., 364.
Anselm, St., 125, 135, 136, 137, 139, 147, 270, 272.

Anselmo, Bishop, 432.
Anselm I, 270, 271.
Anselmo de Scoto, 334.
Ansoald, 81, 85.
Anthony, St., 272, 276.
Antichrist, 48, 205.
Antioch, 408.
Antivari, 435.
Antonelli, F., 28, 464.
Antonine Wall, 32.
Antonino, 397.
Antonio, S., 276.
Antonius, Stus, 448.
Antony of Padua, St., 15, 90, 451, 472.
Antrim, 200, 209.
Antwerp, 17.
Aosta, 244, 246, 253, 265 to 279, 294, 433, 437.
Apennines, 14, 68, 297, 346 to 349, 442, 450.
Apostles, Tombs of the, 346.
Aquila, 288.
Aquileia, 257, 258, 259.
Aquinas, St. Thomas, 282, 308.
Aracoeli, Church of, 412.
Aragon, 429.
Aramo, 375.
Aran, 52, 195.
Aran-mor, 52.
Arce, 27.
Archibald, 328.
Arda, 306.
Ardagh, 406.
Ardennes, 86.
Ardfert, 406.
Ardmacha, 21, 45, 146.
Ards, 200.
Arenula Regis, 308.
Aretino, Leonardo, 262.
Arezzo, 387, 411.
Argonne, 80.
Argyll, 19, 20, 191.
Arian(s), 38, 64, 75, 115, 116, 267, 269, 282, 362, 383.
Arianism, 465.
Aribert, 301.
Ariosto, 180.
Aristotle, 223.
Arles, Council of, 34.
Arley, 189.
Arliano, 363.
Armagh, 45, 47, 107, 128, 131, 132, 134, 136, 138, 140, 141, 142, 174, 194, 197, 198, 205, 208, 217, 219, 234, 315.
Armandus, 295.
Armellini, 94, 95, 96.
Armorica, 37, 63.
Arnaldo, 336, 432.

Arnanus, 78, 81.
Arno, 243, 311, 365, 374, 384, 400.
Arnobius, 484.
Arnolfo, 261.
Arnulf, St., 315.
Arras, 73.
Arrian, 158.
Arsina, 375.
Arthur, King, 33, 37, 182 to 185, 189, 444, 481, 482.
Arthurian, 187.
Artusius, 187
Asaph, St., 182.
Aschatino, Bishop, 432.
Ascoli Piceno, 240.
Ashfield, 70.
Assisi, 442, 447, 481, 489.
Asson, Fr. T., 28, 250.
Asti, 253, 314, 336.
Astigiano, 293.
Astulf, 294, 307.
Athala, Abbot, 443, 450.
Athala, St., 315.
Athanasius, St., 50.
Ath-Cliath, 131, 132, 136, 140.
Athesia, 256.
Ath-Fadat, 45.
Aube, 143.
Aubigny, 73.
Audomar, 78.
Augusta della Vindelicia, 265, 266.
Augusta Praetoria, 266.
Augustine, Fr. O. S. F. C., 442.
Augustine, St., 38, 69, 71, 109, 122, 138, 140, 188, 272, 350, 362, 414, 466, 473, 484.
Augustinian(s), 143, 245, 261, 263.
Augustinus, 109.
Auser, river, 365.
Ausonia, 487.
Austey, Elizabeth, 214.
Australia, 490.
Austria, 75, 89.
Austrians, 359.
Autun, Council of, 462.
Auxerre, 35, 36, 42, 50, 235, 236.
Auxilius, 45.
Avallon, 183.
Avalon, 482.
Avellino, 432.
Avigliano, 425.
Avignon, 148.
Ayeul, St., 73.
Aymon of Faversham, 472.
Azzurrini, B., 344.

Bacco in Toscana, 301.
Bacon, Roger, 485.
Baden, 75.

Badia a Settimo, 311.
Badia Fiesolana, 384, 393, 394.
Badia Polesine, 309.
Badon, Mt., 182.
Baggi, G. B., 26, 237.
Bagheria, 429.
Bagnal, Marshal, 205.
Bagni di Casciana, 375.
Bagni di Lucca, 375.
Bagni di S. Cataldo, 425.
Baithin, 106.
Balagna, 312.
Balbulus, 76.
Baldini, 324.
Baldo, 121.
Balduino, 337.
Balduzzi, Canon, 324, 325, 329, 331.
Bâle, 228.
Ballymore, 209.
Balquhidder, 20.
Baltimore, 198.
Baltinglas, 98, 434.
Baluardo S. Colombano, 311.
Bamborough, 70.
Banaven Taberniae, 39.
Banaventa Berniae, 39.
Bane, Donald, 325.
Bangor, 6.
Bangor-is-Coed, 50.
Banorri, 355, 356.
Baratieri, Count D., 323.
Barbarossa, 301, 489.
Barbiano, 301.
Barcellonnette, 279.
Bardolino, 308, 309.
Barga, 351, 364, 376.
Bari, 184, 346, 422, 423.
Barinthus, 165.
Barking, 479.
Barkley, 202.
Barletta, 422.
Barnabite, 249.
Baronius, Cesare, 16.
Barotti, Bl. Oddino, 244.
Bartholomaeus, Stus., 373.
Bartholomew, 432.
Bartholomew, St., 255, 384
Bartolini, Don Luca, 397.
Barusio, 283.
Basil, St., 464.
Basque, 32.
Bathilda, 78.
Battelli, 167, 180.
Battilano, N., 335.
Battistella, Prof., 180.
Bavaria, 81, 88, 89, 91, 284.
Bavon, St., 292.
Bayeux, 189.
Beadoricesworth, 130.

Bealach, 145.
Beatenberg, 14, 75.
Beatus, St., 14.
Beaulieu, 80.
Bebulf, 258.
Becchignoni, 337.
Becket, St. Thomas, 149.
Bective, 145.
Bede, St., 19, 47, 57, 71, 126, 169, 180, 182, 478, 479.
Bedell, Bishop, 213.
Bedier, 21, 186.
Beer, Rudolf, 115.
Bel, 109.
Belfast, 231.
Belfast Lough, 52.
Belgian, 31.
Belgiojoso, 301.
Belgium, 80, 91, 340.
Belgrano, 330.
Bella, 425.
Belligna, 258.
Belmonte S. Columbano, 292.
Belz, 104.
Bembelia, 299.
Benburb, 215.
Bend-chor, 52, 72, 101, 103, 111, 117, 131, 137, 141, 142, 144, 162, 455, 456.
Benedict, St., 73, 78, 297, 354, 414, 431, 445, 456, 457, 460, 462, 463, 464, 468, 473, 481, 491.
Benedict XII, 308.
Benedict XV, 219.
Benedict Biscop, 478.
Benedict Giovius, 334.
Benedict, St. Rule of, 146.
Benedictine(s), 139, 237, 238, 240, 241, 248, 251, 253, 255, 257, 294, 296, 304, 305, 307, 309, 311, 313, 429, 431, 445, 451, 455, 464, 467, 473, 491.
Benedictine Rule, 456, 459, 462, 463, 468, 473.
Benedictus, S. de Arenula, 95.
Benedictus, S. Sconch, 95.
Benedictus, S. Scottorum, 94, 99, 338.
Benevento, 338.
Benozzo, 311.
Benozzo Gozzoli, 485.
Benti, Don E., 307.
Benvenuti, 275.
Bergamasco, 248.
Bergamo, 237, 255, 305, 454.
Berlière, Dom., 459, 473.
Berlingiero, 404.
Bernadesca, 262.
Bernard, 138.

Bernard, St., 6, 134, 141, 143, 145, 146, 154, 245, 478.
Bernard, St., of Menthon, 268.
Bernard, St., of Rocca d'Arce, 27.
Bernard Scotti, 330.
Bernardino, St., 288, 358, 485.
Berne, 104, 113.
Bernex, 279.
Bernicia, 37.
Bernini, 238.
Berry, 78.
Bertacchi, D., 289.
Bertha, 69.
Berthold, 27.
Bertin, St., 78.
Bertini, 95.
Bertinoro, 292.
Bertrand, 307.
Bertulf, 77, 450.
Bertulf, St., 315.
Berwickshire, 22.
Besançon, 111.
Besson, 268.
Bestagni, 337.
Bethlehem, 432.
Betti, 71.
Bevagna, 423.
Bewdley, 189.
Biagio, St., 294, 309.
Bianco, S. Giovanni, 255, 351.
Biandrate, 295, 296, 313.
Biarii, 324.
Bibbione, 311.
Bicocca, 354.
Bidente, 292.
Biella, 246, 278.
Binbegia, 299.
Bindoli, 353.
Bingen, 80.
Binia, 375.
Birr, 131.
Black Sea, 157.
Black Tom Tyrant, 211.
Blackwater, 110.
Blaise, St., 294, 416.
Blanche, Queen, 330.
Blandamura, Mgr. G., 25, 28, 401, 404, 405, 406, 407, 410, 411, 412, 416, 429, 430.
Blandin, Mt., 80.
Blarney Castle, 433.
Blathmac, St., 61.
Blenheim, 233.
Blessed Virgin, 300.
Blount, Sir Charles, 153, 205.
Bobbiensis, Codex, 114.
Bobbio, 6, 13, 14, 75, 77, 78, 83, 91, 93, 103, 108, 110, 112, 114 to 118, 121, 124, 248, 249, 250, 252, 286,

289, 292, 293, 296, 297, 299, 300 to
304, 306, 308, 312 to 319, 321, 322,
324, 331, 338, 357, 368, 383, 388,
393, 442 to 454, 462, 478.
Bobulenus, St., 315, 450.
Boccaccio, 21, 262.
Bocchetta della Colombana, 305.
Bocchi family, 394.
Boece, 22.
Boehmer, 326.
Boethius, 105.
Boggio, Canon, 277.
Boleyn, Anne, 199.
Bolland, John, 399.
Bollandists, 17, 92, 235, 268, 270, 281,
282, 321, 341, 344, 345, 353, 367,
379, 385, 389, 397, 408, 412, 430.
Bollandus, 15.
Bologna, 24, 240, 250, 307, 308, 314,
321, 326, 329, 350, 356, 358, 359,
372, 384, 385, 415.
Bolognese, 239, 240.
Bolzano, 358.
Bombelio, 300.
Bonaventura, St., 469, 484, 412, 430.
Boncompagni, 243.
Bondoni Guala, 278.
Bonelli, 263.
Bonfiglio, 246.
Boniface IV, 463, 468, 487.
Boniface VIII, 98.
Boniface, Pope, 444.
Boniface, St., 81, 83, 473, 478.
Bonifazi, B., 242.
Bonifica di S. Cataldo, 424.
Bonifort, 286, 287.
Boniprand, 115.
Borbera, 297.
Borgarello, 288.
Borghetto d'Arroscia, 300.
Borghi, Mgr., 397.
Borgo, Church of the, 332.
Borgo a Massano, 375.
Borgoforte, 414, 431.
Borgomanero, Mgr., 296.
Borgo S. Frediano, 374.
Borgo S. Sepolcro, 397.
Borlase, Justice, 213.
Bormida, 297.
Bormida di Spigno, 301.
Bormio, 254, 305.
Borromeo, Card. Charles, 259, 287.
Borromeo, Card. Frederick, 117, 287,
288.
Borzonasca, 357.
Borzone, 299.
Bosco, Don, 276.
Bosham, 71.
Botticino, 255.

Bourcher, 202.
Boyle, 145.
Boyne, battle of the, 221.
Brabant, 198.
Bradamante, 323.
Brakespeare, 147.
Bran, 159, 160, 482.
Brancoli, 363.
Brandano, S., 167.
Brandano, St., 98.
Brandon Hill, 162.
Braughall, Fr., 26.
Brazil, 155.
Breda di Piave, 309.
Bregenz, 74.
Bregia, 132.
Brembana, Val., 245, 255.
Brembo, 302.
Brénaind moccu Altai, 162.
Brendan, St., 52, 65, 160 to 168, 174,
237, 378, 474, 482.
Brescia, 255, 298, 305, 313, 454.
Bresone, 299.
Brest, 221.
Breton, 32.
Breuil, 73.
Brian boroimhe, 132, 133.
Briarius, 158.
Brice, 295, 328.
Bridget, St., 244, 245, 251.
Brie, 73, 79.
Brienza, 425, 431.
Brigid, St., 16, 25, 47, 56, 58, 93, 116.
Brigida, Sta., 248, 250, 251, 322, 399,
400.
Brigit, St., 237, 244 to 250, 256, 260,
266, 271, 275, 277, 278, 294, 321,
324, 325, 331, 332, 383, 385, 388,
389, 392, 395, 396, 399, 400, 482.
Brindisi, 424.
Brioni, 301.
Britain, 18, 33, 35, 37, 72, 78, 101.
Britons, 19, 31, 465.
Brittany, 37, 50.
Brittus, 47.
Broccan, 58.
Brocchi, 397.
Broilum, 73.
Bronda, 245.
Brons, 160.
Brother Sun, 483.
Browne, George, 194, 198.
Brude, 65.
Brugnato, 300, 312.
Brunhilda, 73, 187, 466, 468.
Brunhilde, 187.
Bruno, St., 367.
Brussels, 17.
Brut, 189.

Brythonic, 40.
Brythons, 35, 47, 70.
Buckingham, Duke of, 210.
Bucolics, 104.
Buggiano Alto, 382.
Bughstti, Fr. B., 28.
Bullarini, Don C., 307.
Buonies, 192.
Buonsignore, Don G., 287.
Burano, 265.
Burgh Castle, 79.
Burgianico, 376.
Burgundofara, 73.
Burgundy, 69, 72, 73, 91, 269, 271, 279.
Buriseide, 323.
Burke, 226.
Bury, 40, 235.
Bury St. Edmunds, 130.
Busseya, 267.
Bute, Marquis of, 17.
Buthier, 267.
Butler, 203, 434.
Buzzi, 250, 290, 293, 304, 306, 314, 338.
Byzantines, 431, 466.
Byzantium, 465.

Cabrol, Abbot, 71.
Cacellino, 257.
Cadoc, St., 102, 104, 126, 402, 477.
Cadroe, 83, 86.
Caedwalla, 70.
Caen, 189.
Caerlson-on-Usk, 183, 283.
Caesarius, Bishop, 407.
Caesarius von Heisterbach, 178.
Caginosa, 334.
Cagnano Varano, 422.
Cagno, 256.
Cahors, 78, 81, 85.
Cain, 471.
Cainneih, St., 92, 93, 162.
Cairo, 450.
Calabria, 432.
Calchi-Novati, Mgr. P., 290, 447.
Calderon, 180.
Caledonia, 19, 32, 68, 475.
Calendar of the S.S. of Ireland, 15.
Califani, Padre Giovanni, 308.
Callabà, 255.
Callalta, 309.
Calliano, Don V., 253.
Calo, 344, 345.
Calolzio, 248.
Calporinus, 39.
Caltabellotta, 353.
Caltagirone, 427.
Caltanisetta, 427.

Calvert, Cecil, 198.
Calvi, 96, 312.
Calvin, 20, 272.
Camaggiore, 240.
Camajore, 363.
Camaldolese, 373.
Camaldoli, 450.
Camariano, 293.
Cambiagi, G., 312.
Cambiaso, Mgr. D., 253, 290, 296, 298, 299, 300, 337, 413.
Cambrai, 85, 121, 124.
Camel, 183.
Camerano Casasco, 293.
Camerarius, 23.
Camerino, 418.
Camerlata, 248.
Camillines, 308.
Camillus of Lellis, St., 308.
Campagna, 421, 431.
Campania, 236, 420.
Campi, B., 301, 321, 323, 329, 454.
Campiglia, 275, 375.
Campion, Edmund, 153.
Campione Vecchio, 240.
Campo, 305.
Campofilone, 241.
Camporgiano, 354.
Camugliano, 375.
Canal d'Agordo, 358.
Canal de Ferro, 259, 260.
Candida Casa, 36.
Cannechus, 92.
Canneto, via, 337.
Cannets, 310.
Cannicus, 92.
Canons Regular, 251, 255, 276.
Cantelli, 337.
Canterbury, 17, 96, 134, 136, 137, 138, 140, 147, 151.
Canty, 401.
Canute, King, 130.
Canute, St., 432.
Capannori, 310, 375.
Capecelatro, Mgr. G., 421.
Capella Palatina, 431.
Cape Sta Maria de Leuca, 402.
Capezzano, 364.
Capodimonte, 297, 299.
Caporcorso, 312.
Cappelletti, 93, 409.
Capraja, 234, 235.
Caprino, 256.
Capsoni, Padre S., 282.
Capua, 288.
Capuchin, 244.
Caracciolo, Mgr., 404, 417, 424.
Caradoc, 184.
Caraffa, Card., 467.

Carandini, 28, 276.
Carasco, 357.
Carceri of Subasio, 475.
Cardiganshire, 181.
Caregli di Borzonasca, 299.
Caresana, 295.
Carriarti, 426.
Carinthia, 257, 258.
Carlisle, 37, 144.
Carlow, 26, 45.
Carlsruhe, 113.
Carmignano, 263.
Carmine, Church of, 280, 286.
Carolingian, 24, 82, 85, 118, 237, 297, 327, 383.
Carolus, rex, 331.
Caronia, 427.
Carpi, 355.
Carpignano, 304.
Carpoforo, S. Church of, 282, 283.
Carrickfergus, 221.
Carrick-on-Suir, 203.
Carro, 357.
Carsewell, Bishop, 20.
Cartaud, St., 430.
Carthack, 402, 482.
Carusi, 28.
Cary, Sir Henry, 210.
Casacalistri, 356.
Casal Monferrato, 336.
Casalpusterlengo, 301.
Casatisma, 287, 288.
Casciano, S., 311.
Cascianella, 354.
Cascina, 375, 376.
Casconius, 163.
Casellina, 311.
Casentino, 314.
Caserta, 420.
Cashel, 128, 140, 142, 143, 146, 149, 169, 203, 406, 434.
Cassano al Jonio, 426.
Cassero, 354.
Cassian, 242, 455.
Cassinelli, 412, 416, 420, 421.
Cassino, 420.
Cassino, Monte, 289, 306.
Cassiodorus, 115, 455.
Cassius, St., 374.
Castelbarco, G. di, 309.
Castellamare, 429.
Castellaneta, 423.
Castellarquato, 306, 320.
Castellini, 430.
Castelnuovo Cilento, 421.
Castiglioncello, 240.
Castiglione di Garfagnana, 352.
Castiglioni d'Intelvi, 254.
Castro, 311, 313.

Castrogiovanni, 427.
Catacombs, 293.
Cataldo, S., 401 to 432.
Catania, 184.
Catanzaro, 424.
Cathal, St., 8, 64, 189, 369, 401 to 432.
Cathaldus, Stus, 8.
Cathal's, St. Ring, 424.
Catherine, St., 374.
Catholic Association, 230.
Catholicism, 205.
Cava dei Tirreni, 421, 431.
Cavan, 208, 213.
Cavareno, 250 to 256.
Caxasco, 304.
Ceadda, 84.
Ceananans, 146, 147.
Cecil, Robert, 207.
Cedd, 71.
Cefalù, 427, 428, 431, 432.
Celestine, Pope, 36, 38, 39.
Celestines, 305.
Celestinus, 80.
Celi, G., 291.
Cellac, 141.
Cellach, 71, 174.
Cell-Achid, 72.
Cella di Bulgheria, 422.
Cellan, 79, 104.
Cellanova, 203.
Cell-Cainnich, 92.
Cell-Dara, 57, 58, 244, 251, 450.
Cell-Enda, 51.
Celle of Cortona, 475.
Cell-Lainne, 271.
Cell-Usailli, 45.
Cembrano, 357.
Cencio Camerario, 94, 96.
Cennanensis (Codex), 112.
Centurioni, 337.
Ceprano, 27, 418.
Ceredigion, 181.
Ceredolo, 355.
Cernunnos, 159.
Cerreto, 310.
Certenoli, 296, 299.
Cervignano del Friuli, 260.
Cervo Ligure, 247.
Chabaud, Rev. F., 437.
Chad, 107.
Chagnoald, 443.
Challant, 276.
Chambers, 21, 22, 23.
Chancery, 212.
Channel, The, 283.
Charisius, 104, 318, 319.
Charlemagne, 82, 83, 85, 119, 121, 122, 269, 296, 324, 325, 329, 332, 383, 444.

Charles I, 209, 210, 214, 215, 225.
Charles II, 215, 218, 222.
Charles IX, 209.
Charles, Prince, 210.
Charles Emmanuel I, 117.
Charles the Bald, 85, 105, 124, 385.
Charles the Fat, 85.
Charles the Simple, 129.
Chartularium Imolense, 238.
Chelles, 78.
Cheradi, The, 409.
Chestien de Troyes, 189.
Chiappini, Fr. A., 28.
Chiatri, 378.
Chiavari, 299, 300, 313, 314, 356, 357, 376.
Chiavenna, 305, 334.
Chichester, 136.
Chiemsee, 81.
Chieregato, Fr., 178.
Chieti, 420.
Chifenti, 375.
Childebert, 416.
Childeric, 184.
China, 490.
Christ, 34.
Christopher, St., 254, 363.
Chronos, 158, 159.
Chrysogonios, St., 96.
Chunibald, 284.
Chunradus, 335.
Chur, 254, 304.
Church Island, 386.
Ciampini, 95.
Ciano d'Enza, 355.
Ciaran, 52.
Ciarraige, 162.
Cicero, 104, 116, 117, 118, 485.
Cicognola, 304.
Cima di Piazze, 305.
Cinaedh, 19.
Cipolla, 250, 290, 304, 306, 316, 317, 318, 338.
Cirneo, Pietro, 312.
Cirò, 426.
Cirò Marina, 426.
Cisa, 310.
Cistercians, 134, 145, 146, 254, 294, 311, 460, 491.
Cittanova, porta, 414.
Civardi, Canon, 319.
Cividale del Friuli, 122.
Civitali, Matteo, 351, 352, 381.
Civita Vecchia, 200.
Clairvaux, 143, 144, 145, 147.
Claneboy, 200.
Clanrickarde, 194.
Clare, 207, 222, 240.
Clare, St., 451, 452.

Clarence, Duke of, 192.
Clarendon, Lord, 216, 221.
Claricia, 337.
Claudius, 31, 120, 121, 123.
Cleary, Gregory, O.F.M., 8.
Clement, 84, 86, 120, 127.
Clement VI, 308.
Clement VIII, 308.
Clemente, S., 297, 307.
Clement, St., Church of, 340.
Clepho, 269.
Cleveland, 144.
Clogheen, 406.
Clogher, 174, 434.
Clonfert, 162.
Clonmacnoise, 52, 196, 406.
Clontarf, 132.
Clothaire II, 78.
Clovis II, 78.
Cloyne, 174, 436, 438.
Clúain-ferta, 52, 65, 162.
Clúain-ferta-Brénaind, 101, 162, 318.
Clúain-ferta-Molua, 109.
Clúain-Iraird, 66, 101, 102, 103, 271.
Clúain-mocca-Nois, 101, 109, 271.
Clúain-tarbh, 132.
Clúain-uama, 174.
Cluniac(s), 304, 307, 458, 460.
Cluny, 134, 138.
Clyde, Firth of, 19.
Cnobheresburg, 79.
Coelian Hill, 69.
Coemgen, 52, 54.
Cogitosus, 47, 57.
Cogne, 274, 275.
Cogorno, 299, 357.
Coindire, 141.
Cola di Rienzo, 338.
Colchester, 34.
Colcu, 110.
Coleraine, 208.
Colgan, 15, 16, 17, 90, 91, 92, 318, 367, 406.
Coli, 305, 476.
Collamarini, Signore, 352.
Collegium Nuxii, 332.
Collins, Giovanni, 336.
Collio, 305.
Collis Sti Patritii, 241.
Colman, 71, 80, 88, 249.
Cologne, 83, 87.
Colombani, Marchesi, 292.
Colombarone, 304.
Colonne Scotti, 337.
Columba, St., 19.
Columban(us), St., 8, 13, 14, 16, 47, 52, 64, 69, 72 to 75, 77, 78, 79, 91, 93, 100, 103, 108, 109, 111, 114,

117, 149, 162, 237, 245, 248, 249,
250, 252, 253, 254, 271, 285, 286,
289 to 316, 357, 368, 369, 373, 376,
377, 383, 388, 410, 442 to 446, 450,
453 to 460, 462, 464, 467, 468, 469,
472, 475, 476, 481, 482, 486, 487,
488.
Columbia Univ. Press, 18.
Columbus, 66.
Columcille, 36, 52, 65 to 69, 72, 102,
103, 106, 129, 142, 162, 271, 455,
469, 472, 475, 477, 482.
Comacchio, 314.
Comasco, 314, 334.
Comgall, St., 52, 72, 103, 111, 162.
Commeanus, 317.
Como, 248, 253, 254, 280, 281, 282,
283, 304, 305, 333.
Comparetti, 390·
Compiègne, 478.
Compignano, 375.
Concannon, Mrs. 442.
Conchobar, 172.
Confederates, 214, 215, 225.
Congan, 145.
Conlaed, 57.
Conn, George, 328.
Connacht, 44, 52, 132, 162, 207, 209,
212, 213, 217.
Connor, 141, 142.
Conor O'Brien, 88.
Conrad, Blessed, 374.
Conry, Florence, 15.
Conselice, 238, 239, 240.
Constance, 249.
Constance, Council of, 359.
Constance, Lake of, 74, 187.
Constantine, 86, 283.
Constantinople, 188.
Constantius, Emperor, 283.
Constantius Chlorus, 283.
Continent of Europe, 22.
Contrada S. Cataldo, 418.
Controne, 363.
Corato, 422.
Corazzini, 175.
Corbesassi, 304.
Corbie, 78.
Cordovani, M., 290.
Corfinio, 418.
Coritic, 181.
Cork, 170, 193, 202, 406, 433, 434,
436, 438, 439.
Cormac, 65, 162, 173, 474.
Cormac Mac Carthaigh, 170, 172.
Corman, 70.
Corneliano, 253.
Cornice, 300.
Cornwall, 37, 183, 189, 465.

Corpus Christi College, 17.
Corrado, Fr., 452.
Corsica, 300, 312, 377.
Corte, 309.
Cosenza, 426.
Cosio, 305.
Costa, 296, 309.
Costanzi, 405, 412.
Costa S. Salvatore, 299.
Cottanello, 417.
Count of Faenza, 341, 345.
Courtenay, 202.
Cracavist, 249.
Cranmer, 197, 198.
Crasciana, 375.
Cremona, 122, 223, 326, 413, 431.
Cremona, Girolamo, 352, 370, 381.
Cremonese, 214.
Crescenzi, 326, 328, 333.
Cret, 274.
Cristoforo, S., 274.
Crocan Aingil, 475.
Croce, Sta in Gerusalemme, 98.
Crocette, 284.
Crognolo, 243.
Crollalanza, 322, 325.
Cromer, George, 194,797.
Cromwell, Oliver, 214, 216.
Cromwell, Thomas, 33, 216.
Cromwellians, 483.
Crusade, 482, 489.
Crusaders, 481.
Crux, Sta in Hierusalem, 372.
Cuatto, Mgr., 245.
Cu-Chuimne, 110.
Cuffe, 202.
Cuimine, 318.
Culdees, 455.
Cumberland, 38.
Cumbria, 37.
Cumianus, 317.
Cumin, 317.
Cuminus, 317.
Cumman, 317.
Cummian, St., 76, 108, 315, 450.
Cunedd Wledig, 181.
Cuneo, 245, 253, 293, 294, 301, 450.
Cunibald, 284.
Cunibert, Bishop, 277.
Cunibert, King, 371, 373.
Cuorgnè, 294.
Cuperus, G., 281.
Curti Pasini, G. B., 290, 294, 300, 302
304.
Cusack, Sir Thomas, 196.
Cusio, 248.
Cuthbert, St., 129.
Cybar, St., 20.
Cymri, 181.

Cyran, St., 78.

Da-Bheoc, St., 175.
Da Camino, 256.
Da Celano, Tommaso, 453.
Da Chioggia, Fra. Pietro, 344.
Da Collalto, 256.
D'Adda, 288.
Dagobert I, 78.
Daire-Calgach, 52, 66.
Dair-Inis, 110.
Dair-Mag, 52, 66.
Dal Araide, 52, 72.
Dal Buain, 39.
Dal Cuinn, 44, 45.
Dalg Cais, 132.
Dal-Riada, 19, 67, 68, 70.
Damascus, 146, 489.
Damasus, Pope St., 35.
Da Morzano, 286.
Dane(s), 128, 133, 421.
Danish invasion(s), 64, 333, 340, 491.
Dante, 21, 166, 177, 184, 390, 484.
Danube, 88, 91, 157.
Da Parma, Flaminio, 450.
Da Sangallo, 261, 262.
Da Spettine, 332.
Davagna, 298.
David, junior, 328, 329.
David, il vecchio, 323, 326.
David, King, 143, 144, 146.
David, St., 50, 129, 139, 452.
Davidsohn, 388.
Davis, 207.
Davoragine, Jacopo, 179.
De Albertis, 263.
De Backer, Fr. S. J., 17.
De Baluffi, 413.
De Barry, 156.
De Bosis, Folco, 420.
De Buck, Victor, 16.
De Burgh, 192.
De Canistris, 168, 237, 247.
De Cantellis, 319.
De Cesaris, Dr., 417.
De Challant, 271, 272, 273.
Deccio, 375.
De Claire, Richard, 171.
De Conca, 334.
De Courcy, Edmund, 434.
De Cristano, 412, 416, 417, 418, 430.
Dee, 50.
Defoe, 227.
Deirdre, 187.
Deiria, 37.
Deiva, 300.
De Lance, 277.
Del Aquila, Don Juan, 205, 206.
Delehaye, Père, 283, 284, 418.

Delemont, 75.
Delfino, 259.
Della Chiesa, 268.
Della Robbia, 485.
Del Migliore, 262.
Dell' Orco, 262.
Del Sangue, Paolo, 241.
Deluisa, Signore, 260.
De Lydes, 276.
Demetrius, 158, 159.
Democritus, 385.
Dempster, Thomas, 21, 23, 24, 25,
    282, 328, 329, 389, 399, 405, 412.
De Murofracto, 334.
De Mussi, 331.
De Nino, A., 418, 419.
Denis, St., 121, 122, 186, 385.
Denis the Cathusian, 178.
De Nobili, Ippolito, 352.
De Nobili, Lionello, 348, 351.
De Paul, St. Vincent, 293.
De Pino, 334.
Derby, 274.
Derg, Lough, 175, 178.
Derry, 52, 66, 142.
De Rubeis, Mgr., 414.
Desi, 402.
Desiderius, 78, 325, 332, 431.
De Smedt, Fr., S.J., 17.
Desmond, 172, 194, 196, 200, 201,
    203.
Desmond, King of, 434.
Despré, Mgr. F., 437.
D'Este, Rinaldo, 329.
De Terrinca, 154, 155.
Devereux, Robert, 205.
De Villa, Mgr. M., 438.
Dewi, St., 50.
De Wulf, 125.
Dialogues, St. Gregory's, 360, 361,
    367, 463.
Diana, 248.
Diarmait, King, 482.
Diarmait Mac Murchadha, 96, 129.
Diarmiad Mac Murchadha, 145.
Diaz, 292.
Dicuil, 65, 72, 126.
Didier, 71, 78, 85.
Diecimo, 363.
Digne, 279.
Dinant, 86.
Diocletian, 282, 283.
Diodor the Sicilian, 18.
Dionysiana, 110.
Dionysius, 105.
Di Porcia, 259.
Di Prampero, 258.
Disibod, 80.
Disibodenberg, 80.

Dissentis, 75, 476.
Diuma, 71.
Dobdagrecus, 81.
Dogmael, St., 129.
Dol, 50.
Domenico, S., 384, 394.
Dominic, St., 265, 490.
Dominicans, 277, 278, 427, 458, 472.
Domnach Sechnaill, 45.
Domnall, 141.
Domnall, Bishop, 434, 435.
Don, 250, 256.
Donatists, 435.
Donatus, 104, 126.
Donatus, St., 14, 26, 64, 95, 105, 111,
    123, 248, 249, 321 to 325, 331, 372,
    383 to 396, 410, 411, 412.
Donatus Scotti, 325.
Dondeynaz, Canon, 246, 253, 266,
    267, 277, 278, 294.
Donegal, 15, 175, 208, 209.
Donnaz, 274, 275, 276.
Donnchad, 172.
Donough, 139.
Dora, 275.
Dora Baltea, 276, 437.
Dora Riparia, 294.
Dorigos, 257.
Douai, 229.
Doubs, 75.
Douglas, 326 to 329.
Douglas Scotti, 322.
Dowdall, George, 197, 198.
Down, 44, 129, 142, 200.
Doyle, Dr., 231.
Dresden, 113.
Drihthelm, 169.
Drishane Castle, 433.
Drogheda, 145, 216, 225.
Drogo, 403, 431.
Dromore, 145.
Dronero, 245.
Druids, 43, 44, 47, 59, 102.
Druim Cetta, 102.
Dub-da-chrich, 81.
Dubhgail, 128.
Dubhlochlonnaig, 128.
Dubhthaih, 45, 57.
Dublin, 5, 43, 131, 132, 135, 136,
    137, 140, 146, 179, 192 to 198,
    203, 205, 210, 213, 215, 216, 221,
    226, 228.
Dublin Castle, 226.
Dublin, County, 455.
Duchesne, Mgr., 270.
Dummler, 122.
Dunan, 136.
Duncan, King, 20.
Dun da Leathglais, 128.

Dundalk, 192.
Dungal, 76, 84, 105, 115, 120 to 124,
    126, 127, 385, 392, 393.
Dungal of Pavia, 64.
Dunlop, R., 150.
Dunluse, 204.
Dunshaughlin, 45.
Duns Scotus, 21, 485.
Durrow, 52, 66.
Dyan, Alpicio, 330.
Dymphna, 61.

Eadmer, 138.
Eahfrid, 107.
East Angles, 130.
East Anglia, 37, 130.
Eberger, 87.
Eboria, 42.
Ebroicum, 42.
Eburius, Bishop, 34.
Edgehill, 214.
Edinburgh, 17, 227.
Edmund, St., 96, 130.
Edward, St., the Confessor, 130, 131.
Edward III, 178, 192.
Edward VI, 197, 199.
Edwin, 69, 70.
Eebe, 37.
Egbert, 102, 140.
Egna, 256.
Egypt, 51.
Ehrle, Cardinal, 13, 250, 289.
Einhard, 82, 131, 332.
Eire, 20.
Eireland, 20.
Eleanor, 189.
Elena, 67.
Eleutherius, St., 27.
Elias, 446.
Elias, Abbot, 87.
Elia, Sant, Fiume Rapido, 417, 431.
Eligius, 77.
Elisha, 446.
Elizabeth, 199, 202, 203, 206, 217,
    483.
Ellwangen, 127.
Elphin, 145.
Elsi, St., 77, 78.
Elysian fields, 158.
Elysium, 158, 159.
Emain-Macha, 45.
Emilia, 414.
Emilian, St., 26, 280, 341 to 345, 349.
Emly, 405.
Emma, 130.
Encyclopædia Britannica, 327.
Emmian, 341.
Enda, St., 51, 92, 93.
Endeus, St., 92.

Eneco, St., 431.
English College, 96.
Enna, 426, 431.
Enon, 39.
Entella, 299.
Eoganacht, 318.
Eparchius, St., 20.
Epernay, 85.
Epiphanius, 287.
Epternach, 108.
Erchinoald, 78, 79.
Eri, 20.
Erigena, 105, 124, 125.
Erin, 20, 52, 126, 128.
Eriu, 20, 31.
Ermengarius, 115.
Ermenrich, 127.
Ermo, St., 375.
Erne, 217.
Erode, 330.
Esanatoglia, 418.
Escurial, 117.
Espi, Bernard, 330.
Esposito, Mario, 116, 121, 122, 124, 249, 392, 393.
Essex, 37, 69, 71.
Essex, Earl of, 205.
Eternal City, 235.
Ethelbert, 69.
Ethelhun, 107.
Ethelred, 130.
Ethelwin, 107.
Ethica, 67.
Ethne, 55.
Etna, Mt., 184.
Eucharistic Congress, 5.
Eugenio, Don, 214.
Eugenius III, 144, 145, 148, 374, 406.
Euphemia, Canons Regular of, 320.
Eure, 42.
Europe, Christian, 6, 64, 72.
Eusebius, 76, 85.
Eusebius, St., 246, 295, 296, 488.
Eutyches, 125.
Evreux, 42.
Exilles, 294.

Fabian, St., 308.
Fabbriceria del Carmine, 281-2.
Faenza, 280, 341 to 345, 353.
Faerie Queene, 202.
Failbe, 78.
Falkland, Lord, 210, 211.
Famagusta, 330.
Fanano, 307.
Fanchsa, St., 92.
Fanfani, 263.
Fantuzzi, 94.
Fanucchi, 366, 376, 377.

Fara, St., 73.
Faremoutiers, 73, 111.
Farnborough, 13.
Faro, 73, 77, 85.
Faroe Islands, 65.
Farulph, 342.
Fauglia, 375.
Faulo, 371.
Fausta, St., 374.
Faustin and Giovita, S.S., 255.
Faustino, St., 414.
Faustus, 42.
Favilla, 280, 281.
Fazio degli Uberti, 21.
Febal, 159, 160, 482.
Fedele, Prof. P., 418.
Fedelm, 55.
Fedelm Mac Crimthan, 131.
Federigo, 257.
Felder, 457, 459, 468, 469, 471, 472, 481, 483.
Felice, St., 303, 355.
Felicetti, Don L., 358.
Felicity, St., 364.
Felix, 236.
Felix, Bishop, 371.
Felix, St., 86.
Fella, 258.
Fellinum, 423.
Fenian, 231.
Fer-domnach, 234.
Ferentino, 417.
Ferghil, 80.
Fermanagh, 208.
Fermo, 122, 215, 240, 241, 242.
Ferrante di Ferrara, 330.
Ferrara, 373.
Ferrari, 321.
Ferrari, F., 282.
Ferrari, Giovanni, 411.
Ferrato de Ferrari, 330.
Ferreri, Cesare, 277.
Ferrières, 120.
Fiace, 45.
Fiachna, 318.
Fiacra, St., 73.
Fidolio, 103.
Fiesole, 26, 64, 93, 105, 123, 248, 249, 321, 322, 324, 331, 384, 386, 393, 395, 397, 411.
Filicaja family, 396, 397.
Finan, 71.
Findan, St., 87.
Findbar, St., 367.
Findian, St., 367.
Fingall, 128.
Fingar, 61.
Fingen, 86.
Finnian, 52, 99, 102, 103, 496.

Finnian, St., 367, 368.
Fiorentini, 376, 377, 382.
Fiorentino, Jos., 263.
Firenzuola, 239, 306, 356.
Fis, 168.
Fisher, King, 159.
Fitzgerald, 152 to 156, 193, 228.
Fitzgerald family, 434.
Fitz-Henry, 158.
Fitzmaurice, James, 200, 201, 203.
Fitzsimon, Henry, 17.
Fitz-Stephen, 155, 156.
Fivizzano, 310.
Flaminio, G. A., 344.
Flanders, 206.
Fleming, C. or P., 16, 23, 110, 318.
Flood, Henry, 226, 227.
Florence, 117, 122, 123, 154, 155, 239, 240, 261, 263, 293, 311, 313, 356, 365, 374, 376, 383, 384, 385, 387, 394, 396, 397, 398.
Florentine(s), 155, 263.
Florian, St., 414.
Floridus, Stus Castellana, 273.
Foce delle Radici, 236.
Foggia, 422.
Fogliano, 307.
Fogorty, Dr., 406.
Foillan, 79.
Folco, St., 27.
Follonica, 375.
Folvius, 78.
Fombio, 301.
Fontaines, 72.
Fontana-Buona, 299.
Fontenoy, 223.
Forannan, St., 21, 86, 131.
Forcella, 96.
Forcoli, 375.
Fordun, 39.
Forli, 292, 354, 358, 415.
Formia, 418.
Fornelli, 420.
Fornovo, 354.
Forth, Firth of, 32.
Fortunatae insulae, 157.
Fortunatus, 123.
Fosciana, 364.
Fossano, 244, 245, 294.
Fosses, 79.
Four Masters, 15.
Fox, Charles James, 219, 226.
Framura, 296, 300.   [463, 472.
France, 13, 79, 144, 340, 353, 454,
Francesconi, Don, 292.
Francis, St., of Assisi, 5, 263, 442 to 454, 456, 458, 460, 469, 470, 471, 474 to 477, 481, 482, 483, 485, 486, 488, 489, 490, 491.

Franciscan(s), 191, 382, 423, 445, 446, 471, 472, 474, 482, 485, 489, 490.
Franciscans, Irish, 15.
Franciscan missions, 6.
Franciscan movement, 441, 442.
Franciscan Rule, 460.
Franciscanism, 263.
Francis Xavier, St., 415.
Franco, 85.
Franconia, 80, 91.
Frank Charibert, 69.
Franks, 81, 85, 465, 466, 468.
Frassinoro, 351, 352.
Fredegisus, 120, 122.
Frederick II, 360, 429, 489.
Frediano, 362, 364.
Freising, 80.
French, 343.
Freskin, 328.
Freto, S., 414.
Friars Minor, 155, 435, 450.
Fridian, St., 14, 64, 91, 93, 98, 247, 270, 271, 314, 352, 354, 360 to 377, 382, 383, 386.
Fridolin, St., 75.
Friesland, 107.
Frigdianus, 360.
Frigianus, 361.
Frignano, 346, 347, 355.
Frisians, 107.
Frisons, King of the, 317.
Friuli, 257 to 260.
Frontinus, 104.
Fronto, 116, 117.
Frosinone, 417.
Fruttuoso, S., 297, 299.
Fulco, S., 320, 321, 323, 329, 340.
Fulco Scotti, S., 26, 322, 383.
Fulda, 61, 87, 88.
Fulk, St., 37.
Fursa, St., 79, 83, 169.

Gaddoni, 238, 338.
Gael, 19, 31, 32.
Gaelic, 102, 103.
Gaeta, 418.
Gaetano, Card. B., 418.
Gagliano Castelferrato, 426.
Gail, St., 25.
Gal, Canon, 268.
Galahad, Sir, 160.
Galateo, 411.
Galatinus, P., 412.
Gall, St., 74, 75, 76, 83, 108, 110, 113, 115, 116, 127, 238, 252 to 257, 260, 261, 263, 264, 294, 295, 305, 307 314, 318, 472, 476, 477.
Galletti, N., 427.

Gallicano, 354, 363,
Gallinaria, 234.
Gallinaro, 27.
Gallipoli, 407.
Gallo, S., 255, 260, 263.
Galloglaigh, 191.
Galloway, 36.
Gallowglasses, 191.
Galway, 52, 162, 213, 216, 222, 406.
Gamaliel, 42.
Gams, 408.
Ganaceto, porta, 414.
Gangi, 428.
Garda, 308, 309.
Garfagnana, 310, 314, 346, 352.
Garfagnana, 280.
Gargano, 346.
Gargiulo, Mgr., 424.
Garighetti, Bishop N., 438.
Gasquet, Card., 33.
Gaston de Foix, 343.
Gattinara, 294.
Gaudentius, St., 278.
Gaul(s), 18, 31, 36, 46, 50, 53, 63,
    72, 76, 77, 79, 91, 162, 183, 234,
    235, 247, 333, 437, 443, 450, 455,
    459, 462, 465, 466, 476.
Gavenola, 300.
Gawain, 182, 183, 184, 189.
Gelasius, 142.
Gennaro, S., 363.
Genoa, 179, 236, 247, 286, 296 to 300,
    312, 313, 314, 336, 337, 339, 356,
    413, 431, 453, 454.
Genoese, 286, 298, 312.
Genovesi, via dei, 96.
Geoffrey of Monmouth, 182, 187.
Geoffrey Plantagenet, 182.
George, 115.
George, St., 363.
George III, 226, 227.
Georgius, 104.
Gerald, Archbishop, 403.
Geraldines, 155, 156, 193, 198, 200.
Gerald de Barri, 151, 152, 153.
Geraldy, 155.
Gerard, 27, 336.
Gerard de Gerardi, 154.
Gerardi, 154.
Gerebern, 61.
Germanies, 12, 253, 280, 283, 340, 358.
Germanus, Bishop, 407.
Germanus, St., 35, 36, 39, 42, 50,
    235, 236.
Germany, Southern, 75.
Gerola, 305.
Gertrude, St., 79.
Gervase, 184, 185.

Gervase, St., 280, 283, 285.
Gesuate of St. Joseph, 381.
Ghent, 80, 292.
Gherardi family, 397.
Gherardo Scotto, 337.
Ghirlandaio, 485.
Ghisoni, Fr. R., 237.
Giacomo, 351.
Giacomo, S. de Ponte, 351.
Giamberti, G., 261, 262.
Gianani, 25, 28.
Gianelli, 289.
Gibbon, 17, 33.
Gibellini, 337.
Gilbert, 176.
Gilbert, Sir J. T., 91.
Gildas, 34, 50, 101, 104, 108, 182, 282,
    486.
Giles, Blessed, 469, 484.
Giles, Friar, 256.
Gilla-Chrisst Ua Morgair, 174.
Gilla-easpuic, 137.
Gilla-meic-Liag, 142.
Gilla-na-Naemh, 89.
Gillebert, 137 to 140, 144.
Ginese, S., 364.
Giolla Criost O'Conaire, 147.
Giorgio, S., 307.
Giornale, Araldico, 324.
Giovanni, 323.
Giovanni Battista, S., 363.
Giovanni da Pian del Carpino, 461,
    474.
Giovanni da Serravalle, 484.
Giovanni de Montecorvino, 461.
Giovanni e Paolo, S.S., 99.
Giovanni Gualberto, S., 311.
Giovanni, S., 240.
Giovanni, S. Incarico, 418.
Giovanni, S. in Galilea, 403.
Giovanni the scrivener, 336.
Giovanninello, 312.
Giovio, 334, 335.
Giraldi, 155.
Giraldus Cambrensis, 20, 57, 151.
Girgenti, 353.
Gisbourne, 144.
Giscardi, G., 337.
Gisus, 270.
Giudice, 312.
Giulia, Sta, 300.
Giuliana of Collalto, Bl., 416.
Giuliano, 175.
Giuliano Teatino, 420.
Giulietta, Sta, 304.
Giuseppe, S., 94.
Giussani, 312.
Giustina, Sta, 297, 379, 380, 381, 382.
Giusvalla, S., 297.

Gladstone, 231.
Glan, 80.
Glarus, 75.
Glasnevin Cemetery, 230.
Glastonbury, 33, 176.
Glendalough, 52, 54.
Gloucester, 38.
Godano, 300.
Godsacre, 328.
Godscroft, 325.
Goffredo Scotti, 338.
Goidels, 31.
Goldoni, 415.
Gomorga, 299.
Gonzaga, 448, 450 to 453.
Goodacre, Hugh, 198.
Gordena, 297.
Gordon, Lord George, 227.
Gorgoglione, 425.
Gorgona, 234, 235.
Gorizia, 259.
Gorlois, 182.
Gorno, 238.
Gothard, 295.
Gothard, the Saint, 476.
Gottifridus de Scottis, 95.
Gottschalk, 124.
Gottweich, 88.
Gougaud, Dom, 13, 15, 20, 22, 24,
    25, 54, 60, 73, 93, 100, 101, 135,
    149, 150, 168, 234, 235, 247, 317,
    322, 348, 368, 407, 406, 475.
Gozzoli, 311.
Gradi, 416.
Graf, A., 167, 175, 180, 263.
Grail, 33, 159, 161.
Grammatica, Mgr., 118, 291.
Grammichele, 427.
Grampians, 32.
Granaglione, 356.
Granarolo dell' Emilia, 250.
Grandison, Viscount, 210.
Grange, 26.
Grattan, Henry, 226 to 229.
Gratus, St., 294.
Graveglia, 299.
Gravina di Puglia, 423.
Great Britain, 465, 466.
Great St. Bernard, the, 268.
Greccio, 475.
Greek Fathers, 393.
Green, Mrs. A. S., 14.
Green Isle, 231.
Greenland, 188.
Gregorio, S., 97, 99.
Gregorovius, 337.
Gregory Nazianzen, St., 484.
Gregory of Tours, 443.

Gregory the Great, 69, 109, 138, 140,
    159, 354, 360, 361, 365, 367, 368,
    463 to 467, 473.
Gregory III, 140.
Gregory VI, 312.
Gregory VII, 307, 378.
Gregory IX, 330.
Gregory X, 330.
Gregory XIII, 96, 200, 203.
Grey, Lord, 201.
Grillo family, 413.
Grimald, 127.
Grimaldi, 95, 291, 337.
Grimerio, 320.
Grimhild, 187.
Grimoald, 27.
Grion, 180.
Grisar, Fr., 361, 466, 467, 488.
Grisons, 75, 283.
Grondona, 293.
Grosjean, Fr. P., 17.
Grottaglie, 434.
Guadagni, 293.
Gualdo di Populonia, 370.
Gualdo Tadino, 353.
Gualterio, 243.
Gualtieri Sicaminò, 426.
Gualtiero, Friar, 359.
Guardian Angel, Congr. of, 308.
Guarino, S., 240.
Guascone, Maestro N., 394.
Guasto degli Scotti, 332.
Gubbio, 477.
Guccerelli, 261.
Gueldres, 91.
Guelph, 330.
Guernsey, 189.
Guerra, 368, 370, 371.
Guidalard, Archdeacon, 295.
Guidi, 25, 98.
Guidi, Mgr., 366, 367, 368, 370, 371.
Guidicini, 339, 356, 375, 415.
Guido, Bishop, 277.
Guido Scotti, 323, 329.
Guigone, 336.
Guillaume, St. du désert, 186.
Guillestres, 279.
Guinevere, 182.
Gundulph, 136.
Gunibald, 280 to 283.
Gunifort, St., 280 to 288.
Guntrum, 269.

Hadrian's Wall, 32, 34.
Haemgils, 107, 169.
Hagan, 149.
Hague, 215.
Hainault, 81.
Hampden, John, 214.

Hardicanute, 130.
Harduin, St., 27.
Harold, 130.
Harris, Walter, 90.
Hartgar, 85, 125.
Hartlepool, 56.
Hastières, 86.
Hastings, 130.
Hatton, Sir Christopher, 202.
Hay, M. V., 23.
Hayden, M., 150.
Hebrides, 204.
Heiu, 56.
Helena, St., 432.
Helias Scotigena, 82.
Henry, 176, 177.
Henry II, 88, 147, 151, 155, 189.
Henry VI, 350, 489.
Henry VII 434.
Henry VIII, 33, 191, 193, 194, 196,
    197, 199, 200, 204, 231.
Heraldry, Italian Coll. of, 322, 327.
Hereteu, 56.
Hermengarda, 378, 379.
Hermes, 157.
Herodias, 161.
Hertfordshire, 147, 148.
Hesiod, 157, 385.
Hewald the Black, 107.
Hewald the White, 107.
Hibernensis, 110.
Hiberni, 18.
Hibernia, 18, 20.
Hibernini, 238.
Higden, R., 174.
Highlanders, 20.
Hii, 67.
Hilda, 56.
Hildelide, 479.
Hildoard, 121.
Hilduin, 121.
Hinba, 67, 162.
Hinemar, 124.
Hippolytus, 242.
Hoar, Matthew, 16.
Hoche, 228.
Hogan, Fr. E., 17.
Hogan, Mgr., 62.
Holinshed, 153.
Holland, 220.
Holy Father, 437.
Holy Grail, 482.
Holy Isle, 71.
Holy Land, 402, 408.
Holy Redeemer, 421.
Holy See, 77, 82, 140, 200, 350, 382,
    435, 462, 468.
Holy Sepulchre, 188.
Holy Trinity, 136, 239, 421.

Holy Trinity of the Scots, 91, 93.
Homer, 158.
Honan, 80, 82, 85.
Honoratus, St., 42, 234.
Honorius, 34, 77.
Honorius II, 372.
Honorius of Autun, 125.
Horace, 103.
Horatian, 103.
Hospice of the XXI, 437.
Hospital of the XXI, 276.
Hoxne, 130.
Huelsen, 14, 94, 95.
Hugh, 323.
Hugh, Earl of Tyrone, 205.
Hugh of St. Victor, 125.
Hugo, 324, 325, 326.
Hugo, King, 302, 303.
Hume, David, 325 to 328.
Humility of Our Lady, 308.
Hunaldo, 103.
Hungarians, 258.
Hunneric, 266.
Huntingdon, 176.
Huysman, 443.

I, 67.
Ibar-cind-trachta, 145.
Iceland, 65, 474.
Ider, 184.
Ido, 336.
Igerna, 182.
Ilice, 363.
Illtud, 50.
Imar Ua h Aldhagain, 141.
Immram, 157, 159.
Imola, 238, 240, 344, 356.
Imperia, 247, 300.
Infantino, 410.
Ingono Scotto, 337.
Ingria, 275.
Inguanez, Dom M., 26.
Inis-Celtra, 87, 386.
Inis-lounaght, 145.
Inis Patraic, 128, 144.
Innes, Fr. Thomas, 17, 18, 20.
Innocent II, 143, 144, 258, 300, 312.
Innocent III, 96, 320, 337, 338, 444.
Innocent IV, 97, 98, 350.
Innocent VIII, 434 to 437.
Innocent X, 214.
Innocent XI, 220.
Innocenti, Hospital of, 263.
Insula Sanctorum, 61.
Inventius, St., 283.
Iona, 36, 52, 56, 65, 66, 67, 70, 103,
    106, 110, 128, 135, 162, 271, 318,
    459, 462, 475.
Iora, 67.

Ire, 20.
Ireton, 216.
Irish Augustinians, 243.
Irish Brigade, 223, 340.
Irish College, 230.
Irishery, 20.
Irish Franciscans, 416.
Irish Free State, 231.
Irish Religious Movement, 441, 442.
Isabella d'Este, 179.
Isacchi, 355.
Isaias, 110, 156.
Iseo, 305, 454.
Isernia, 420.
Isidore, St., 19, 91, 416.
Islam, 465.
Isle of Man, 128.
Isola Comacina, 333, 339.
Isolde, 187.
Istria, 251, 261.
Italy, 13, 63, 64, 74, 75, 90, 91.
Ivar, 132.
Iveragh, 141.
Ivrea, 122, 236, 246, 275, 276, 277, 336, 433, 437, 439.
Jacobs Kirche, 88.
Jacopone da Todi, 484.
Jacopo Soprarno, S., 293.
Jacques de Vitry, 178.
James, 328.
James, St., 88, 89, 287, 307, 308, 363, 375, 414.
James I, 195, 207, 208, 215.
James II, 209, 220, 221.
Jarlath, 162.
Jarrow, 128, 478, 480.
Jean, St. de Maurienne, 312.
Jerome, St., 35, 108, 110, 367, 484, 485.
Jerusalem, 88, 186.
Jesuit(s), 153, 415, 429.
Jesus Christ, 458, 460, 466, 469, 471, 484.
Jews, 119, 216.
Joannes, S. in Capite, 372.
Job, 109.
Joergensen, 443, 444.
John, 88.
John and Reparata, S.S., 372.
John, Archb. of Ravenna, 387.
John Capistran, St., 485.
John, Cardinal, 146.
John of Salisbury, 119.
John of Susa, 109, 111.
John of Tynemouth, 368.
John, Prince, 151.
John, son of William, 324.
John, St., 306, 310.

John, St. the Baptist, 336, 363, 364, 446.
John the Deacon, 96, 99, 360.
John the Scot (Erigena), 105, 124, 125, 126, 149.
John I, Bishop, 370, 374.
John II, Bishop, 370, 372.
John IV, 463.
John XVII, 86.
John XXII, 258.
Jonas, 292, 294, 444.
Jones, General, 215.
Jones, Thomas, 17.
Jordan, Bishop, 433.
Josaphat, 47.
Joseph, 47.
Josephe, 160.
Joseph of Arimathea, 33, 160.
Joseph, St., 414.
Joseph the Scot, 105, 110.
Jouarre, 73.
Jovençan, 274.
Jucundus, 75, 267.
Judas, 160, 164.
Julian, St., 265.
Julius Caesar, 18, 31, 216.
Julius, St., 269, 283.
Jumièges, 77, 78.
Juniper, Brother, 484.
Jura, 443.
Juvenal, 104, 116.

Kay, 184.
Keating, 136, 140, 153.
Keenan, 209.
Kehr, 93, 311, 372, 374.
Kells, 146.
Kells, Book of, 112, 113.
Kenney, Dr. J. F., 18, 21, 368.
Kent, 37, 69.
Kentigern, 84.
Kerry, 141, 162, 201, 203, 217, 222, 406.
Kevin, 52.
Kieff, 88.
Kilcolman, 202.
Kilcrea, 433.
Kildare, 26, 57, 155, 192, 193, 231.
Kilian, St., 61, 73, 80, 83, 120, 488.
Kilkenny, 26, 92, 192, 196, 214.
Killaloe, 406.
Killarney, 318, 433.
Killeigh, 72.
Killiany, 51.
Killossy, 45.
Kilmacduagh, 406.
Kilmallock, 200, 203.
King's County, 198, 207.
Kinsale, 206, 209, 221.

Kirke, Rev. J., 20.
Kirkham, 143.
Klagenfurt, 259.
Knox, 20.
Kundry, 161.

Lacordaire, Père, 464.
Lactantius, 484.
Lagamon, 189.
Lagan, 39, 57.
Lagenorum terra, 72.
Lagny, 79.
Lahierius, 399.
Laidaend, 109.
Lambert, 336.
Lambert, Bishop, 307.
Lambert, St., 125.
Lambertini, G., 415.
Lambro, 293, 301, 305, 313.
Lami, 167.
Lammari, 363.
Lancashire, 17, 37.
Lancaster, House of, 434.
Lancelot, 183, 189.
Lanfranc, 135 to 139, 147, 326.
Lanfranc, St., 284.
Lanfrancus de Scota, 335.
Langres, 279.
Lanigan, 41, 247, 389, 406.
Lantosques, 312.
Lanzoni, 24, 25, 28, 94, 235, 236, 265, 266, 270, 284, 341, 344, 345, 349, 353, 407, 409, 411.
Laodiceans, 174.
Laoghaire, 45.
Laon, 124.
Lars Eskeland, 486.
La Spanna, 306, 476.
Lateran, 98, 99, 306, 372, 444.
Lateran, Canons Regular of, 240, 247.
Lateran Council, 320.
La Thuile, 279.
Latium, 92, 416.
Laudabiliter (Bull), 149.
Laurence, St., 19.
Laurentius, 236.
Lavagna, 299.
La Verna, 475, 476.
La Vesubie, 311.
Lawrence, St., 300, 363.
La Zecca, 381.
Laziosi, S. Pellegrino, 354, 358.
Leath Cuinn, 140.
Leath Mogha, 140.
Lecce, 402, 410, 411, 412, 424, 425, 431.
Leger, St., 462.
Legerio, 434.
Leighlin, 145, 231.

Leinster, 45, 52, 57, 58, 72, 98, 132, 198, 207.
Leitrim, 210, 217.
Leix, 198.
Lejay, Paul, 115.
Le Mans, 108.
Leno, 309.
Lenormant, 411.
Lent, 129.
Leo, Brother, 476.
Leo III, 97, 353.
Leo X, 304.
Leo XIII, 439.
Leodegair, 295.
Leoghaire, 55.
Léon, 50.
Leonard, St. of Limoges, 432.
Leonardesque, 114.
Leonardo, 323.
Leone IV, 243.
Leoni, 259, 260.
Lerins, 42, 102, 234, 235, 455.
Lescot, 340.
L'Escot, 340.
Leslaeus, 22.
Lesley, John, 328, 332.
Lesley, John, Bishop of Ross, 23.
Leta, 92.
Letavia, 92.
Leucorroe, 78.
Leuke, 157, 158.
Libya, 157.
Lichfield, 107.
Liége, 79, 85, 124, 125.
Liévin, 80.
Lightfoot, 70.
Ligugé, 50.
Liguria, 168, 246, 253, 297, 309, 313, 357, 450.
Ligurian, 296, 298, 299.
Lilybaeum, 353.
Limerick, 131, 132, 133, 138, 145, 203, 210, 216, 221, 222.
Limoges, 78.
Limousin, 432.
Lincolnshire, 176.
Lindisfarne, 36, 56, 70, 71, 126, 128, 472, 473, 480.
Lindsey, 107.
Lionel, 192.
Lionello, 351.
Liri, 418.
Lisbon, 26.
Lismore, 406.
Liss-mor, 104, 126, 128, 131, 147, 402, 482.
Liuguri, 127.
Livin, 80.
Llan-Badarn, 129.

Llan-Carvan, 50, 102, 104, 129, 167, 402.
Llan-Illtud, 50, 129.
Llan-y-doch, 129.
Llywarch, Henry, 181.
Loannese, 168.
Lobbes, 81.
Locati, U., 326.
Lochlainn, 128.
Lochlannaigh, 128.
Loch-Lem, 318.
Lodi, 301, 302, 303.
Lodigiano, 314.
Lodisio, 300.
Loftus, Chancellor, 17.
Logue, Cardinal, 315, 442, 447.
Loiguire, 127.
Loire, 78, 81.
Lo Jodice, 416.
Lombard(s), 119, 237, 255, 269, 270,
    297, 303, 306, 330, 347, 360, 363,
    371, 387, 465, 466.
Lombard League, 249.
Lombardy, 253, 255, 256, 301, 302,
    324, 337, 347, 401, 413, 450, 454.
London, 34, 208, 218, 219, 467.
Londonderry, 209.
Lonergan, Rev. P., 406.
Longford, 210.
Longinus, 160.
Longrey, 78.
Loppia, 351, 354, 364.
Lorentino, 248.
Lorenzo il Magnifico, 261, 263.
Lorenzo, S. in Servi, 381.
Lorraine, 91.
Losa, 294.
Lot, 182.
Lothair, 241, 380, 383, 385, 387.
Lothair, Emperor, 120, 122.
Lothair II, 126.
Lotharius, 387.
Lothians, 19.
Loto, 300.
Lough Derg, 386.
Louis, King, 330, 387.
Louis II, 126.
Louis XIV, 220.
Louis of Teck, 258.
Louis the Pious, 120, 122.
Louth, 174, 176, 192.
Louvain, 15, 90, 203.
Louvre, Treasury of, 330.
Lowe, E. A., 112, 113, 116.
Lower Austria, 88.
Lubin, 93, 304.
Lucan, 116, 117, 157.
Lucca, 91, 93, 98, 247, 308, 310, 314,
    348 to 352, 354, 360, 362 to 379,
    381, 382, 416.

Lucchesia, 314.
Lucifer, 166.
Lucius III, 272, 274, 381, 414.
Lucius, St., 254.
Ludovicus, 387.
Lugagnano, 255, 306.
Lugano, 25, 28, 69.
Lugano, Dom P., 290, 431, 456, 459.
Luimneach, 132, 137.
Luitprand, 300, 302, 317, 341.
Lully, Raymund, 485.
Lunata, 363, 365, 375.
Lungarno, 374.
Luni, 350, 360, 372.
Luni-Sarzana, 300, 309.
Lupercus, 236.
Lupia, 424.
Lupus, St., 36, 42.
Lusurasco, 306.
Luxeuil, 72, 77, 78, 111, 115, 315,
    444, 445, 462, 463, 464, 478.
Lyons, 97, 119.

Mabinogion, 185.
Macaille, 57.
Mac Alpin, Kenneth, 19.
Macbeth, 20.
Maccabees, 109.
Mac-Carthaigh, 433.
Macchiavellian, 211.
Mac Cormac Diarmid, 434.
Mac Donnell, Charles, 91.
Mac Donnello, 204.
Macerata, 418.
Machar, 433.
Machutus, St., 167.
Mac Mahon, 340.
Mac Mahon Brian Oge, 206.
Mac Neill, Prof., 18, 41.
Macon, Synod of, 468.
Macqueda, via, 428.
Macroom, 433.
Maddaloni, 420, 431.
Madeleine, Col de la, 279.
Madrid, 200.
Maedoc, St., 83.
Mael-dubh, 72.
Mael-Isu-Uah-Ainmire, 136.
Mael-Maedoc Ua Morgair, 134, 140
    to 144, 146, 174, 433, 437.
Mael-Ruain, 455.
Mael-Sechlainn, 122, 145.
Maestri, A., 28, 291, 302, 313.
Mag-bile, 52, 66, 101, 131, 271, 367.
Mai, Card., 117.
Mainz, 80, 87, 88, 265.
Maissana, 357.
Majocchi, 25, 282, 286, 287, 288.
Makaron nesos, 157.

Malachia, 98, 145.
Malachy, St., 140, 145, 433.
Malaspina, Marquis, 319, 453.
Malatesta di Cesena, 241.
Malchus, 136, 137.
Malines, 80.
Mallio, Pietro, 96, 99.
Mallow, 433.
Malmesbury, 72, 478.
Malo, St., 167.
Malplaquet, 223.
Malta, 414, 430.
Ma-lua, St., 83.
Mancini, A., 180.
Mancini, R., 393.
Manfred, King, 241.
Manfred, Scotti, 329.
Manfredi, A., 423.
Manfredo dei Scotti, 323, 326.
Mangilli, 259, 260.
Mantello s. Dubino, 304.
Mantovano, 314.
Mantua, 179, 286, 305, 313, 326, 350, 414.
Manzoli, G., 287.
Marcellus, 76.
Marches, The, 241, 242, 418.
Marcian, 353.
Marciano, 411.
Marcus, 76, 169, 170.
Mare Grande, 409, 424.
Mare Piccolo, 409.
Margherita, Sta, Ligure, 357.
Marguerettaz, 273.
Maria, Sta, a Colle, 416.
Maria, Sta, ad praesepe, 363.
Maria, Sta, a Monte, 372.
Maria, Sta, Capella, 168.
Maria, Sta, Corte-Orlandini, 381.
Maria, Sta, degli Scotti, 94.
Maria, Sta, dell' Ammiraglio, 428.
Maria, Sta, del Conte, 342.
Maria, Sta, delle Grazie, 421.
Maria, Sta, del Popolo, 262.
Maria, Sta, del Porale, 297.
Maria, Sta, del Tiglietto, 297.
Maria, Sta, de Montebello, 372.
Maria, Sta, di Cavour, 277.
Maria, Sta, di Collegara, 414.
Maria, Sta, di Giosafat, 285.
Maria, Sta, di Loreto, 243.
Maria, Sta, di Porta Nuova, 431.
Maria, Sta, di Sturla, 357.
Maria, Sta, Forisportam, 372.
Maria, Sta, Gualtieri, 285.
Maria, Sta, in Duno, 321.
Maria, Sta, in Monte, 364.
Maria, Sta, in Palladio, 97.
Maria, Sta, in Regula, 238.

Maria, Sta, in Sassia, 96.
Maria, Sta, Maggiore, 98.
Maria, Sta, nova, 372.
Maria, Sta, Vallis Salutis, 95.
Mariana, 300, 312.
Mariano, Padre, 262.
Marianus, 148, 263.
Marianus Scottus, 61, 83, 87.
Marie de France, 198.
Marie Madeleine, St., 186.
Mari Gincomo, 312.
Marinus, 277.
Mariscotti, 326, 338, 339.
Mark, St., 33, 408.
Marlia, 310.
Marne, 79.
Marradi, 314.
Marrou, 99.
Marsala, 429.
Marseilles, 159, 296.
Marsico Nuovo, 425.
Martin, Abbé, 446, 485, 488.
Martin V, 286.
Martin, St., 47, 50, 87, 92, 93, 129, 234, 310, 367, 374, 388, 395 to 400.
Martino, S., 240, 363.
Martino, S. di Castrozza, 359.
Martinus, Stus Senarum, 373.
Martorana, 428, 432.
Maryland, 198.
Mary Major, St., 425.
Mary of the Gael, 58.
Mary, Queen, 198, 199.
Mary, St. della Virtú, 430.
Mary Stuart, 207.
Marziano, S., 297.
Maserada, 309.
Maserno, 355.
Massa, 354.
Massa Buggianese, 364.
Massa-Carrara, 310, 352, 376.
Massa di Maremma, 312.
Massalubrense, 421.
Massarosa, 375.
Massani, M., 291.
Masserano, 278, 294.
Masseria, 420.
Matera, 425.
Mattarello, 250.
Matteo, S., 298, 414.
Matthaeus, 110.
Matthew Paris, 176.
Matthew, St., 295.
Maur de Fonte vivo, 435.
Maurice, St., 277.
Maurice de Gerardis, 154, 155.
Mauricius, 88.
Maximian, 282.
Max Muller, 22.

Maynooth, 193.
Mayo, 203, 222.
Mazerolles, 81.
Marzochius, 353.
Mazzara, 430.
Mazzara del Vallo, 430.
Mearns, 39.
Meath, 17, 52, 145, 192, 196.
Meaux, 73, 85.
Medici, 393.
Medina, 430.
Mediterranean, 188.
Meduno, 353.
Meehan, C. P., 16.
Mela, 18.
Melchisedech, 239.
Meldola, 292.
Melk, 88.
Mella, 305.
Mellifont, 145, 206.
Mellitus, 159, 467.
Melo, 81.
Melrose, 143.
Mels, 258.
Meltrid, King, 402.
Menconico, 304.
Mendicant Orders, 155, 491.
Menevia, 50.
Mensola, 92, 93, 388, 396, 397, 399.
Méoties, 288.
Mercati, Mgr., 188, 346, 348, 349, 351, 355.
Mercato Vecchio, 396.
Merchants' Quay, 91.
Merchia, 22.
Mercia, 37, 70, 71, 130.
Mercy, Our Lady of, 388.
Meriadoc, 184.
Merlinus, 187.
Merovingian(s), 85, 458.
Messina, 426.
Metz, 86, 315.
Meyer, W., 168.
Meyronnes, 266, 279.
Mézerolles, 79.
Mezzabarba, S., 282, 286, 288.
Mezzanego, 357.
Mezzola, 305.
Michael,St.,251,303,308,311,346,427.
Michael's, St., 147, 183.
Michael's Abbey, St., 13, 85.
Michele, S. di Pagana, 357.
Micheletto, Mgr., 28.
Micheli, G., 290.
Migliaccio, 412.
Mignano, 420.
Milan, 34, 75, 110, 113, 117, 235, 248, 259, 281, 286, 287, 288, 301, 302, 335, 336, 339, 454.

Milanese, 270, 281, 286, 334, 335.
Milanesi, 262.
Miliucc moccu Buain, 39.
Millianus, 343.
Milligan, Alice, 445.
Minerbio, 250.
Mingarda, 278.
Miniato, S., 364, 375, 376.
Miniato, S. al Tedesco, 364.
Minturno, 418.
Mionghar, 378.
Miquitin, Francesco, 330.
Miquitin, Giovanni, 330.
Mirabello, 288.
Miradolo, 301.
Mirandola, 355.
Missionaries of St. Columban, 490.
Mo-Chuta, 402, 482.
Modena, 184, 346, 350, 352, 355, 356, 414, 431.
Modenese, 307.
Moel-Brigte, 83, 87.
Moel-Isu, 141.
Moena, 350.
Moena di Fiemme, 358, 359.
Moengal, 76.
Moggio, 257 to 260.
Moinan mac Cormaic, 79.
Molazzana, 376.
Molin, Biagio, 259.
Molise, 420.
Mombrione, 301.
Mombrizio, 281, 282.
Mombrone, 301.
Momeliano, 306.
Mommelin, 78.
Monaghan, 206.
Monasterolo-Casotto, 294.
Monastier, 309.
Mondovi, 244, 245, 293.
Monferrato, 450.
Monfestino, 355.
Mongibel, 184.
Mongolia, 474.
Monna Orietta Scotti, 337.
Monopoli, 423.
Monreale, 429, 431.
Monroe, 214.
Monsagrato, 363.
Monserrato, via, 96.
Montagnana, 256.
Montajone, 376.
Montalembert, 20, 462, 464, 482.
Montbar, 279.
Monte Cannarella, 427.
Monte Carlo, 364.
Montecassino, 26, 75, 407, 417, 431, 464.
Montecatini, 364.

Montechiaro d' Asti, 293.
Monte Cimone, 307.
Monteclaro, 293.
Monte Consegno, 418.
Montecorona, 355.
Monte di S. Colombano, 312.
Montedonico, 300.
Montefegatesi, 375.
Monteforte, 304.
Montegiorgio, 240.
Montegranaro, 240.
Monteloro, 383.
Montenero, 417.
Monte Pasquasia, 427.
Montepiccolo, 355.
Monte Pisano, 362.
Monte San Giuliano, 429, 431.
Montespertoli, 376.
Monteventano, 306.
Monti, 240.
Monticelli, 288, 357.
Montignoso, 376.
Montronio, 254.
Monza, 335, 336, 337, 454.
Monzese, 335.
Moonan, G. A., 150.
Moors, 200.
Mor, C. G., 291.
Moralia, in Job, 109.
Moran, Card., 149, 231, 236.
Moranego, 296, 298, 299.
Morano Calabro, 426.
Mordred, 182, 183, 184.
Morenus, 412.
Morgeneu, 126.
Morimondo, 335.
Morison, Fynes, 153.
Morla, via, 305.
Morough, 132.
Mortiera, 294.
Mosburg, 257.
Mosciano, 293.
Moses, 47.
Mostizzolo, ponte di, 256.
Mottabaluffi, 413.
Mountjoy, Lord, 153, 205, 206.
Moville, 52.
Mugrom Ua Morgair, 141.
Muirchertach, 88, 145.
Muir-chu, 57, 236.
Muir-chu-moccu-Mactheni, 42.
Muiredach mace Robartaig, 88.
Muir-n-Iocht, 195.
Mull, 67.
Mumenic, 83.
Munster, 52, 88, 131, 132, 133, 141,
    162, 170, 172, 196, 200, 201, 204,
    206, 214, 401, 402, 433.
Muradello, 306.

Muratori, 40, 358.
Muro Lucano, 425.
Murphy, Denis, 16.
Mynywd, 50, 129.
Myrrdin, 181.

Naas, 45.
Nabe, 80.
Naldi, 326, 329.
Nancy, 117.
Nantes, 129.
Naples, 117, 353, 412, 420, 421, 423,
    431.
Napoleon, 249, 381, 452.
Narbonnese, 119.
Nardo, 424.
Narni, 374.
Nasalli-Rocca, Count, 28, 306.
Natali, Fra. P., 344, 345.
Nativity, Shrine of, 432.
Navarons, 353.
Navigatio Sti. Brendani, 167.
Naviglio, 276, 287.
Nazarius, St., 295.
Nazaro, S., 296.
Narzerius, 115.
Ne, 299.
Neagh, Lough, 39.
Nebbiano, 376.
Nebbio, 300, 312.
Nehemiah Ua Moriertach, 174.
Nenay, 145.
Nendrum, 318.
Nennius, 182.
Neri, St. Philip, 16.
Nesta, 156.
Nestorian, 38.
Neustria, 79.
Newbridge, 21.
Newry, 145.
New York, 18.
Niall, 45.
Niall-noi-giallach, 39.
Nice, 311.
Nicholas, 147, 148.
Nicholas, St., 184, 253, 346, 424,
Nicholas I, 387.   [428.
Nicholas III, 448, 449, 451, 452.
Nicholas IV, 351, 449, 451.
Nicholas V, 351, 397.
Nicholas I de Bersatoribus, 273.
Nicodemus, Gospel of, 33, 160.
Nicolli, 339.
Nicosia, 426, 427.
Niebelungelied, 187.
Ninian, 36.
Nivelles, 79.
Noano, 296, 300.
Nocera Umbra, 353.

Noirmoutier, 78.
Nola, 236.
Nonantola, 253, 307, 355, 356, 374.
Norcia, 353.
Normandy, 129, 288.
Normanni, 20.
Norman(s), 188, 189, 421, 424, 431,
Norris, 202. [432.
Norse, 128.
Norsemen, 79.
North, Lord, 226.
North Africa, 465.
Northern Ireland, 231.
Northmen, 32, 86, 384.
Northumbria, 37, 56, 70, 71, 129, 130,
  135, 459, 462.
Norway, 128, 183.
Nosate, 287.
Notker, 76, 127.
Nottingham, 214.
Novara, 278, 294.
Novate Mezzola, 305.
Novati, 168.
Novati, F., 289.
Noyon, 77, 78.
Nynias, 36.

Oates, Titus, 219.
Obertus Scoto, 334.
O'Brien, 196.
Obsequentius, 362.
O'Byrnes, 210.
O'Callaghan, Mgr., 439.
O'Cleirigh, M., 15.
O'Clery, M., 15, 17.
O'Connell, Daniel, 229, 230.
O'Connor, 198.
O'Connor, B., 15.
O'Connor, Calbach, 192.
O'Connor, Margaret, 192.
O'Conor, Dr. Charles, 113.
Oddino, Blessed, 244.
O'Dempsey, 198.
Oderano, 431.
Odilo, 81.
Odo, 434, 435, 436.
O'Donnell, 194, 206.
Odo Scotto, 337.
Oedipus, 265.
Oengus, 111.
Ofalley, 72, 192, 198.
Oga, 254, 305.
Oge, Garrett, 193.
Ogerio, 336, 337.
Ogham script, 102.
Ognissanti, 154.
O'Hanley, 139.
O'Hanlon, Canon, 284, 319, 368,
O'Hely, 203. [406.

O'Hurley, 203.
Oilean na Naomh, 175.
Olaf, St., 432.
Olaf Cuaran, 135.
Olba, 297.
Olivetans, 424.
Oliviero, Bishop, 435.
Olmo al Brembo, 245.
Oltremarini, 337.
O'Mahoney, 223.
O'Mahony, 340.
O'Mail Chonaire, 15.
Omer, St., 78.
O'More, 198.
O'Neill, 194, 199, 200, 205, 214, 216.
Onia, 431.
Onorato, S. di Patrania, 297.
Opaco, 399, 400.
Opicino de Canistris, 93.
Opizzone di Farignano, 330.
Orange, Prince of, 220.
Oratory della Riva, 355.
O'Reilly, 197.
Oreno, 454.
Oria, 424.
O'Riordan, 406, 412.
Orkneys, 65, 87, 474.
Orleans, 119.
Ormonde, Earl of, 196, 203, 215.
Orso, S., 273.
Orvieto, 242, 338.
O'Sherin, Thomas, 16.
Ospedaletto, 292.
Ossian, 482.
Ossory, 80, 210.
Ostriconi, 312.
Ostro-Gothic, 360.
Ostrogoths, 269.
Oswald, 70, 107.
Oswy, 107.
Othmar, St., 74.
Otranto, 184, 402.
Otto III, 86.
Otto IV, 184, 489.
Otto, Landgrave, 88.
Ottone, Soprano, 304.
Oudenarde, 223.
Oulx, 336.
Our Lady of the Assumption, 363,
Ours, St., 279. [364.
Ovid, 104.
Owen, 160, 175 to 179, 482.
Oxford, 17, 18, 182.
Ozanam, Frederick, 55, 385, 390,
Pacomius, 478. [393.
Paderborn, 88.
Padua, 256, 472.
Padua, St. Antony of, 15.
Padus, 331.

Pagno, 245, 294.
Palagonia all' Alloro, 429.
Palaja, 375.
Palatine, 98, 99.
Pale, 192, 194, 195, 196, 203, 204.
Palermo, 428, 432.
Palestine, 35, 346.
Palladius, 36, 38, 39, 42.
Pallavicino, 312.
Pallium, 140.
Palmaria, 234.
Palmerio, St. Raymund, 250.
Pammachius, 99.
Panaro, 355.
Pancotti, Mgr., 248, 249, 321, 325,
Pannonia, 266.   [326.
Pantaleon, St., 87, 363, 372.
Paolo, S., 409.
Papal Legate, 250.
Papal States, 242.
Paparo, Card. John, 146.
Paparoni, 326.
Papebrochius, 268.
Parenti, John, 263.
Pariana, 354.
Parigi, via, 307.
Paris, 17, 23, 69, 78, 107, 113, 117,
    121, 148, 151, 320, 472.
Parisetti, Ludovico, 351.
Parma, 27, 250, 306, 310, 316, 350,
Parnellites, 231.   [354, 359.
Parsons, Justice, 213.
Partinico, 429.
Parzival, 161.
Parzanica, 305.
Paschal II, 372.
Pasini, Mgr., 292.
Passau, 127.
Passignano, 311.
Passo del Bracco, 300.
Passo del Penice, 304.
Passo di S. Colombano, 312.
Pasté, Mgr., 295.
Pastecca, 286.
Paternus, 88.
Patriarchi, Giovanni dei, 315.
Patrica, 417.
Patricia, 238.
Patricius, 236, 318.
Patrick, 136, 137.
Patrick, St., 5, 6, 25, 39, 40, 41, 42,
    44, 45, 50, 51, 55, 56, 57, 59, 60,
    61, 108, 110, 134, 141, 152, 159,
    160, 165, 173, 174, 176, 190, 191,
    195, 234 to 237, 239, 242, 243, 247,
    295, 356, 362, 379, 455, 486, 490.
Patrick's Purgatory, 175, 177, 179.
Patrick's, St., Well, 482.
Patricolo, G., 428, 429.

Patrizio, S., 238, 239, 240.
Patruccxo, 270.
Paul Giovius, 334, 335.
Paulinus, 236.
Paulinus of Aquileia, 120.
Paulinus of Nola, 123, 188.
Paul V, 47.
Paul, St., 42, 110, 146, 430, 478, 481,
Paul, St., Church of, 278.   [487.
Paul the deacon, 119.
Paul's, St., 136.
Pavana, 376.
Pavareto di Carro, 357.
Pavese, 304.
Pavesi, 321.
Pavia, 93, 121 to 124, 168, 237, 247,
    280 to 284, 286, 287, 288, 301, 302,
    303, 314, 320, 321, 383, 385, 388.
Pavone, 277.
Pavone, via del, 415.
Peada, 71.
Peckham, John, 485.
Pecori Giraldi, 185.
Pedescastellana, 250.
Peebles, 19.
Peking, 461.
Pelagius, 35.
Pélerin, St., 238.
Pélerin, St., d'Auxerre, 353.
Pelleas, 183.
Pellegrinetto, S., 354, 355.
Pellegrino, S., 14, 93, 238, 280, 346,
    348 to 359, 376.
Pellinore, 183.
Pellizzari, A., 291.
Pembroke, Earl of, 191.
Penda, 70, 71.
Pennachi, Fr., 243.
Pentima, 418.
Pera, 386.
Perali, Prof., 243.
Perceval, 183, 189.
Peredeus, Bishop, 310.
Peredur, 160.
Peregrinus pauperculus, 442.
Peregrinus, St., 350, 353, 354, 369.
Pergola, 344.
Pero, 309, 313.
Perona Scottorum, 79.
Péronne, 79, 83, 85, 104.
Perratt, Sir John, 204.
Perrone, Count, 275, 276.
Perugia, 259.
Pesa, val di, 311.
Pescia, 364, 375, 376, 382.
Pesina, 256.
Peter, 115, 146, 347.
Peter, Count, 326.
Peter Damian, St., 188, 343.

Peter of Pisa, 119.
Peter-pence, 83.
Peter, St., 71, 75, 80, 81, 300, 302, 304, 306, 407, 408, 417, 424, 463, 465, 475, 487.
Peter, St., Church of, 267, 268, 274,
Peter, St., in Chains, 274. [275.
Peter, St., Monastery of, 414.
Peter's, St., 353.
Peter the Deacon, 361.
Petroald, 115.
Petrus de Scoto, 335, 336.
Petrus, S., juxta Pistorium, 372.
Pettinari, via dei, 95.
Petty, Sir William, 216.
Peyron, Abbé, 118.
Pezzolo, 293, 301.
Philibert, 77.
Philip III, 14, 330.
Phlegethon, 177.
Piacentine, 331, 332.
Piacentino (i), 306, 321.
Piacenza, 26, 93, 94, 122, 247, 248, 250, 255, 305, 306, 313, 314, 320, 321, 322, 324 to 333, 338, 353, 383,
Piandelagotti, 352, 356.   [388, 454.
Pian delle Fugazze, 309.
Pianello Val Tidone, 306.
Pianta, 292.
Piasco, 245, 277.
Piave, 237, 257.
Piazza, 296, 300.
Piazza Armerina, 427.
Piazza dei Cavalieri, 374.
Piazza Marina, 429.
Piazzano, 375.
Piazzo Basso, 353.
Picardy, 78.
Piccolomini, Aeneas, Syl., 22.
Picts, 19, 32, 34, 65, 67, 87, 472.
Piedicastello, 251.
Piedmont, 244, 253, 279, 293, 334, 336, 450.
Piedmontese Alps, 313.
Piers, Capt. William, 199.
Pietrapertosa, 425.
Pietrasanta, 364.
Pietro, 323.
Pietro, S., 409.
Pietro, S., degli Scotti, 94.
Pietro, S., della Porta, 412.
Pietro, S., di Precipiano, 297.
Pietro, S., di Savignone, 297.
Pietro, S., in Banchi, 297.
Pietro, S., in Campo, 364.
Pietro, S., in Montorio, 208.
Pietro, S., porta di, 310.
Pieve a Fosciana, 349, 354.
Pievepelago, 346.

Pilgrim, 346, 347, 348.
Pinaschi, 312.
Pinerolo, 245.
Pintor, commendatore, 28.
Pippin the Short, 81.
Pisa, 24, 235, 243, 312, 324, 350, 374, 375, 376, 407, 408.
Pistoia, 350, 376.
Pius II, 262, 351.
Pius V, St., 203, 258.
Pius VI, 373.
Pius VII, 381.
Pius XI, 13, 25, 289.
Pizzo dei Tre Signori, 305.
Placentia, 249, 331.
Plautus, 116, 157.
Pliny, 18, 104.
Plocean, 267, 268, 270.
Plummer, Dr. Charles, 17, 18, 349.
Plunket, 229.
Plunket, Bl. Oliver, 219.
Plutarch, 157, 158.
Po, 304, 305, 306.
Poggio Mirteto, 417.
Poggiorsini, 423.
Poitiers, 50, 81, 85, 123.
Pol Aurelien, St., 50.
Pole, Reginald, 193, 198.
Polirone, 431.
Polybius, 157.
Pomponius Laetus, 117.
Pomponius Mela, 157.
Ponna inferiore, 253.
Ponsacco, 375.
Pontecorvo, 27.
Ponte di San Cataldo, 424.
Ponte di San Colombano, 309.
Pontegiacomo, 357.
Ponte Leccia, 312.
Pontenure, 306.
Pontremoli, 357.
Pontremoli di val di Magra, 310.
Ponzate, 248.
Ponziano, S., 381.
Porcile, 357.
Porta Comitis, 341.
Porta della Pescheria, 184.
Porta Marina, 422.
Porta San Frediano, 374.
Porta San Mamolo, 375.
Port Lairge, 132, 136.
Portofino, 299.
Portovenere, 297.
Portugal, 155, 200.
Porziuncula, 451, 478.
Posara, 310.
Postumia, via, 261.
Potenza, 425, 426.
Potitus, 29.

Poyning's Law, 225.
Poverello of Assisi, 442, 446.
Pozzo d'Orvieto, 243.
Pozzuoli, 407.
Prague, 16.
Predazzo, 388.
Premadio, 254, 305.
Presentation of B.V.M., 298.
Prignano, 355.
Prince of Wales, 215.
Priosa di Scorbo, 357.
Priscian, 104, 126.
Probus, 238.
Prosper of Aquitaine, 39.
Protase, St., 280.
Provence, 42, 234, 302.
Prudentius, 104, 123.
Psalms, 109.
Psalter, 109.
Ptolomaic, 122.
Puderico, Giovanni, M., 420.
Puglia, 53.
Puglie, 422.
Pusillana, 280, 282.
Putignano, 423.
Pythagoras, 157.

Quadraginta, SS., de Tarvisio, 373.
Quart, 277.
Quattro Canti, 428.
Queen's County, 198, 207.

Rachau, 402, 405 to 408.
Rada di S. Cataldo, 402.
Radulfus, 432.
Raghan, 406, 407.
Raghlin, 128.
Raheen, 26.
Rainald, Bishop, 403.
Rajna, Pio, 183.
Raleigh, Sir W., 202.
Ramillies, 223.
Rangerius, Bishop, 367.
Ranuccio II, 250.
Raoul, Bishop, 432.
Rapallo, 357.
Rathan (Rathen), 406.
Rath-Breasail, 140.
Rath-Cua, 406.
Rathmullan, 207.
Ratisbon, 88, 89, 148, 169.
Ratpert, 85.
Ratti, Mgr. A., 118, 289, 290.
Ravaldino, Porta, 292.
Ravello, 421.
Ravenna, 94, 115, 238, 265, 266, 269,
Rebais, 73, 78.   [292, 343, 387.
Rebolini, Don Stephen, 28, 291, 306.
Rebolini, Mgr. S., 449.   [317,
Redi, 301.

Reformation, the, 483.
Reggio Calabria, 422.
Reggio Emilia, 307, 310, 350, 351,
Reginaldo, 323.   [354, 355.
Regnans in excelsis (Bull), 203.
Regola, 95, 359.
Regulus, St., 370.
Reichenau, 108.
Reimann, 21.
Remondini, 317.
Renan, 59.
Reno, 384.
Reposi, I., 291.
Restitutus, Bishop, 34.
Revelone, 415.
Revo, 256.
Rezia, 168.
Rhastia, 91, 238, 266.
Rheims, 81, 124, 203.
Rheinau, 87.
Rhine, 76, 81, 87, 91, 167, 476.
Rhineland, 89.
Rhys, Sir J., 32.
Rhys ap Theodor, 151.
Ricciardi, Mgr., 425.
Riccovolto, 356.
Richa, 262.
Richard, 151.
Richard, Abbot, 87.
Richard, St., King, 373.
Richard II, 178.
Richelieu, 214.
Richelmy, Card., 276, 439.
Rieti, 417, 483.
Riez, 42.
Rigg, J. M., 21.
Rigollot, 353.
Rimini, 34, 415.
Rinuccini, G. B., 215, 216.
Rio di S. Colombano, 312.
Rione Rosso, 342.
Riso, Valle del, 238.
Riva di Suzzara, 305.
Rivoli, 334, 336.
Rivo Torto, 443, 478.
Robert, 129, 145, 147.
Robert de Boron, 160.
Robert of Bruce, King, 20.
Robert of Waulsort, 21.
Robolini, 282.
Rocca, E. N., 291.
Rocca Ciglie, 245.
Rocca d'Arce, 27.
Roccaromana, 420.
Rocchetines, 285, 393.
Rocchetta, 421.
Roch, St., 284.
Roche, William, Bishop, 433, 436.
Rochester, 136.

Roding, St., 80.
Rodobald II, 284.
Roger, King, 425.
Rogliano, 312.
Roland, 481.
Rolando di Ripalta, 330.
Rollo, 129.
Romagnano, 250.
Romana, via, 437.
Roman Catholic, 75.
Romanesca, 347.
Romano, San, 281, 283, 285.
Romano-Saxon, 473.
Roman provinces, 18.
Romanus, King, 346.
Romanus de Scotto, 337.
Rombaut, 80.
Rome, 14, 35, 38, 42, 49, 58, 68, 71,
  73, 76, 82, 83, 88, 91, 93, 94, 96,
  98, 99, 115, 130, 137, 139, 140,
  142, 143, 145 to 148, 186, 190, 194,
  200, 203, 205, 208, 214, 235, 243,
  249, 255, 268, 272, 282, 306, 325,
  326, 333, 337, 338, 341, 345, 346,
  368, 372, 378, 379, 387, 414, 416,
  418, 434, 437, 463, 465, 467, 468,
Romescot, 83.   [486, 487, 488.
Romold, 80.
Ronan, 82.
Ronco, 275.
Rongio, 278, 294.
Roncegno, 251.
Ros, 434, 435, 436.
Rosaro, 310.
Rosazzo, 258.
Roscommon, 131.
Roses, Wars of the, 192, 434.
Ross, 23, 194.
Rossano, 334.
Rossetti, B., 289.
Rothe, David, 23.
Rotis, 85.
Roto, prior, 374.
Rouen, 137.
Rouen, St., 80.
Round Table, 189.
Rovereto, 309.
Rovigo, 309.
Roxburgh, 20.
Rubin, 110.
Rubruck, William, 474.
Ruca Sti Ursi, 275.
Rudolf, Blessed, 375.
Rufus, St., 148, 236.
Rupert, St., 284.
Russia, 88.
Ryan, Fr. John, 18.

Sabina, 417, 435, 436.

Säckingen, 75.
Salamanca, 26.
Salerno, 421, 422, 431.
Saletto, 321.
Salimbene, Fra., 21, 448, 453.
Salò, 255.
Saltry, 176.
Saluzzo, 244, 245, 277, 294, 313, 336.
Salvaghi, 337.
Salvaro, S., 256.
Salvator, Stus de Ficarolo, 372.
Salvator, Stus in Mustiolo, 372.
Salvatore, San., 311, 380, 421.
Salvatore, S., in Campo, 95.
Salvatoris Sti Scottorum, 94, 99.
Salvetti, 380, 382.
Salzburg, 81, 122.
Sambuca Pistoiese, 354, 376.
Samson, St., 50.
San Giorgio, 424.
Sansovino, 243, 322, 325.
Santa Lucia del Mela, 426.
Santerno, 239.
Santiago, 185.
Santopadre, 27.
Santorso, 265, 274.
Santo Spirito, 423.
Santo Spirito, Monastery of, 416.
Saorstat Eireann, 231.
Saponara di Grumento, 425.
Saracen(s), 297, 384, 387, 403, 408,
Sardini, Marquis G., 381.   [461.
Saroglia, 266.
Sarsfield, Patrick, 221, 340.
Sartene, 377.
Sartiano, 475.
Sarzana, 310.
Sassi, 376.
Satyrus, 124.
Saul, 489.
Savignone, 297.
Savile, Sir G., 227.
Savinus, 343.
Savio, 23, 267, 269, 270.
Saviour, St., 255.
Savona, 326, 380.
Savorgnan, 259.
Savoy, 272, 279, 312.
Saxons, 35, 37.
Saxonum, Burgus, Schola, Vicus, 96.
Saxony, Elector of, 16.
Scala, 421, 431.
Scandiano, 307.
Scandinavia, 128, 136.
Scandinavian(s), 65, 135, 138, 148.
Scandolara Ravaro, 413.
Scaurus, 97.
Schaffhausen, 87.
Schiaparelli, Luigi, 369.

Schiavi, 306.
Schizzi, 326.
Schmidt, 60.
Schotanus, 340.
Schott, 340.
Schotte, 340.
Schottenhof, 89.
Schottenring, 88.
Scia, 67.
Scoffera, 298.
Scolastica, Sta, 292.
Scoti, 335, 339.
Scoto, G. M., 334.
Scots, 34, 38, 57, 77, 96.
Scots College, Paris, 23.
Scott, 340.
Scott, Michael, 21.
Scotti (Scotus), 18, 22, 78, 79, 85, 95, 150, 338.
Scotti family, 320, 322 to 338.
Scotti, Frederick, 324.
Scotti, Professor, 28, 333, 336.
Scottia (Scotia), 19, 21, 22, 24, 31.
Scottish Benedictine Congr., 88.
Scotto Paparone, 338.
Scotus (see Scotti).
Scozia, 326.
Scriptura Saxonica, 113.
Scriptura Scottica, 113.
Scrivia, 297.
Sebastian, King, 200.
Sebastian, St., 308.
Sebastiano, S., 97.
Secundinus, 55.
Secundus, 45.
Sedgemoor, 222.
Sedulius, 84, 105, 108, 110, 121, 123,
Segetius, 42.   [125, 126, 479.
Segone, 318.
Segromigno, 363.
Selkirk, 19.
Semelano, 355.
Semifonte, 338, 339.
Semorile, 357.
Senator, 235, 237.
Senigallia, 94.
Senio, 239.
Senior, 235.
Sen Raghan, 406.
Sens, 430.
Septimius Severus, 32.
Seraphic Father, 484, 485.
Serbiniano, 94.
Serchio, 310.
Serenus, 159.
Serenus, St., 296.
Sergius II, 387.
Seriana Valle, 237, 238.
Serninus, 45.

Serra Mazzoni, 355.
Sertorius, 158.
Sesia, 278, 295.
Sesto, 258.
Sesto a Meriano, 363.
Sestola, 356.
Sestri Levante, 299, 300.
Set, 64.
Sethus, 103.
Settignano, 395.
Settimo, 311, 374, 376.
Severian, 35.
Severus, Bishop, 36.
Severus and Julius, SS., 269.
Seymour, Jane, 197.
Sezzé, 297.
Sforza, Francesco, 241, 242.
Shahan, Dr., 442.
Shakespeare, 20.
Shannon, 52, 132, 217, 218.
Shanrahan, 406.
Sherborne, 478.
Sholto, 325, 328.
Sholto Douglas, 323, 324.
Sholto du Glasse, 328.
Sicidella, 278.
Sicily, 6, 35, 241, 353, 401, 426, 429, 432.
Siena, 311, 326, 353, 376, 387.
Sigbert, 71.
Sigebald, 309.
Sigebert, St., 476.
Sigestro, 300.
Sigismund, Archpriest, 310.
Sigismund, Emperor, 326.
Sigismund, St., 308.
Signorili, 97.
Sigulf, 120.
Sigurd, 187.
Silaus, St., 14, 26, 352, 369, 378 to 382.
"Silken" Thomas, 193, 195, 200.
Sillan, St., 378.
Sillao, St., 378.
Silvestro de Marsi, 428.
Simancas, 206.
Simnel Lambert, 192.
Simon, St., 321.
Simone, 312.
Sinchell, 72.
Sion, 279.
Siriacus, 466.
Sirinus, 16.
Siro, S., 297.
Sironi, Don, 287.
Sithiu, 78.
Sitric, 132.
Sixtus IV, 434, 435, 436.
Skerries, 144.

Skibbereen, 434.
Skye, 67.
Slebte, 45.
Sletty, 45.
Sliabh Daidche, 162.
Smerwick, 201.
Smith, Sir Thomas, 200.
Societas Scottorum, 330.
Soissons, 124.
Solerio, 276.
Solignac, 78.
Soligo, 256, 257.
Solvatius, King, 323, 324.
Solway, Firth of, 19.
Somerset, 38.
Somhairle Buidhe, 204.
Somme, 79.
Sommocolonia, 376.
Sondrio, 254, 305.
Sorrento, 421.
South Wales, 38.
Spain, 15, 120, 431, 450, 454, 465.
Spanish succession, 223.
Spenser, Edmund, 154, 202, 204.
Spettino, 325, 331.
Spezia, 300.
Spilamberto, 355.
Spinazzola, 423.
Spirito Santo, Borgo, 96.
Spisanelli, 240.
Spottiswood, J., 179.
Stadler and Gindl's Dictionary, 353.
Staffora, val, 304.
Stafford, Viscount, 219.
Stammerer, the, 76.
Stanyhurst, R., 153.
Stefano, S., 297, 298.
Stefano, S., del Cacco, 434.
Stephen, King, 144, 146, 175.
Stephen, St., 246, 276, 363.
Steward, 209.
Stigmata of St. Francis, 356.
St. John, Oliver, 206, 209, 210.
Stockerau, 88.
Stokes, Miss, 14, 163, 166, 306, 317,
    318, 374, 386, 397, 408, 410, 444.
Stornaiolo, Mgr. C., 404, 405.
Strabo, 157.
Stradella, 304.
Strafford, Earl of, 211, 212, 213.
Strangford Lough, 52.
Strasburg, 88.
Strassoldo, 260.
Strathclyde, 36, 37, 130.
Strecker, Karl, 392.
Struppa, 297.
Stuarts, 243, 483.
Stuckley, Sir Thomas, 200.
Stura di Viu, 294.

Stura valdi, 279.
Sturla, 299.
Suabia, 91.
Subasio, Monte, 443.
Suevi, 465.
Suffolk, 79.
Suffred, 378, 379, 380.
Suir, 146.
Sulmona, 418.
Sultan, the, 346.
Summaga, 258.
Supino, 417.
Susa, 294.
Sussex, 37, 71.
Svyskens, 368.
Sweden, 209, 244, 245, 257.
Swedish, 251.
Swift, Jonathan, 226.
Swilly, Lough, 207.
Swiss, 75, 252.
Switzerland, 14, 75, 91, 252, 253, 256,
    257, 258, 261, 279, 283, 333, 472,
Switzers, 257.   [476.
Symphorien, St., 86.
Syrus, St., 321.

Tacitus, 18, 32.
Tadhg, 433 to 439.
Tadhg Machar, Bl., 26, 433.
Tadone I, 323.
Tadone II, 323.
Talbot Press, 18.
Taliesin, 181, 182.
Talhaiarn, 181.
Tallaght, 455.
Tamlachta, 455.
Tancred, 432.
Tancredi, 424.
Taormina, 353.
Tara, 45, 131.
Taro, val di, 306.
Tarantasca, 245.
Taranto, 189, 401 to 405, 407, 408,
    409, 411, 412, 417, 418, 420, 421,
    423, 424, 426, 427, 431.
Tasso, 259.
Tassoni, 180.
Tatti, 281, 282.
Taurasio, 432.
Taverna S. Cataldo, 420.
Teano, 420.
Templars, 330, 482.
Terence, St., 343.
Terni, 353.
Ternoc, 165.
Terragnolo, 309.
Tertullian, 59, 484.
Thalesperian, 310.
Tharsus, 414.

Thebaid, 458.
Theodolinda, 75.
Theodore, 71, 115.
Theodore, St., 382.
Theodoric, 115.
Theodosius, 266.
Theodulf, 119.
Theonestus, St., 265, 266, 268.
Thermae salonis, 347.
Therouanne, 78.
Thetford, 130.
Theutmir, 123.
Thierache, 86.
Thierry, 86.
Thirle, 65.
Thomas, St., 125, 188.
Thomas Aquinas, St., 415.
Thomas de Gerardis, 154.
Thomas of Canterbury, St., 96, 97.
Thomas the Apostle, St., 364.
Thomond, 194.
Thor, 134, 136.
Thorgest, 131, 134.
Three Companions, 489.
Three Levites, Ch. of the, 312.
Thun, 75.
Thuringia, 91.
Ticinese, Porta, 287.
Ticino, 287.
Tidone, val, 306.
Tilbury, 184.
Tillemont, 430.
Tipperary, 196, 202, 207, 406.
Tiraboschi, 355.
Tirechan, 55, 234.
Tir Eoghain, 199, 205.
Tirli, 239, 240, 356.
Tir na n-Og, 183.
Tir Tairngiri, 165.
Titus, 216.
Tnudgal, 169.
Tnuthgal, 169.
Tolla, Val di, 255.
Tomianus, 82.
Tommaso, S., porta, 455.
Tommasini, Fra. A., 555.
Tononi, 245, 330, 386.
Topographia Hibernica, 152.
Torbay, 220.
Torello di S. Antimo, Prince, 425.
Torre d' Arese, 288.
Torre di S. Colombano, 312.
Torre Menapace, 304.
Torre Orsaja, 422.
Torre S. Patrizio, 240, 241, 242.
Torri, 311.
Torriano, 288.
Tortona, 287, 293, 304, 313, 314.
Tortonese, 313.

Totman, 80.
Touring Club, Italian, 294, 304, 305, 306, 319, 375, 415, 416, 420, 421, 424, 429.
Tours, 108, 120, 167, 234, 399, 455.
Tovazzi, Fr. G., 250, 256, 358.
Trajan, Forum of, 243.
Trani, 422.
Trapani, 429.
Trasimene, Lake, 475, 476.
Trassilico, 354.
Trastevere, 96.
Traube, 120.
Trebbia, 75.
Trebbia, val di, 304, 306.
Trent, 250, 251, 358.
Trentino, 256, 309, 350, 358.
Trepuzzi, 424.
Treves, 36, 80.
Treviglio, 454.
Treviso, 256, 265, 309, 313.
Tricarico, 425.
Tricola, 353.
Trim, 195.
Trinitá degli Scoti, 97, 99.
Trinitá, S., dei Pellegrini, 95.
Trinitas, Sta, Peregrinorum, 338.
Trinitatis, Stae, Scottorum, 94, 97, 99.
Tristan, 189.
Troubadours, 481.
Troy, Dr., 228.
Troyes, 36, 42.
Trystanus, 187.
Tuaim, 146.
Tuam, 15.
Tudor, Henry, 434.
Tundale, 160, 169, 170 to 174, 177, 178.
Turanian, 31. [178.
Turgesius, 131.
Turin, 97, 113, 114, 117, 118, 121, 122, 123, 236, 244, 277, 279, 294, 452, 453.
Turlaugh, 132. [452, 453.
Turraza, Canon G., 248, 254.
Turris Patritia, 241.
Tuscan(s), 347, 348, 357, 359, 377.
Tuscany, 167, 309, 347, 369, 375, 384, 385, 399, 416, 450.
Tuscia Marittima, 299.
Tyburn, 219.
Tyrconnell, 207, 221.
Tyrone, 205 to 209, 214.
Tyrrhene Sea, 234, 455.

Ua-Briain, 132.
Ua-h-Anglé, 139.
Ua Heilighe Padraig, 203.
Ua Hurthuile, 203.
Uberti, Fazio degli, 180.
Udine, 257, 259, 260, 353.

Ughelli, 28, 268, 315, 316, 318, 411.
Ugo, 342.
Ui-Neill, 66.
Ulaid, 40, 44, 362.
Ulfilas, 116.
Ulidia, 72.
Ulster, 44, 45, 52, 162, 204, 206 to 209, 212, 213, 215, 217, 218, 231, Ultan, 58, 79. [362.
Ulysses, 415.
United Irishmen, 228.
Urban II, 272.
Urban VIII, 272.
Urbana, 256.
Ursanne, St., 75.
Ursiana basilica, 266.
Ursiano, St., 266.
Ursicino, S., 266.
Ursicinus, St., 77.
Ursius, St., 265.
Ursitz, St., 75.
Ursus, St., 64, 93, 244, 245, 246, 265 to 279, 294, 368, 377, 383, 433, 437.
Ussher, Archbishop, 153, 210, 312.
Uther Pendragon, 182.
Uzzone, 301.

Vaccoli, 364.
Vacheresse, 279.
Valais, 279.
Val Brembana, 353.
Valdarno, 364.
Val d'Elsa, 338.
Val di Castello, 364.
Val di Fraina, 305.
Val di Lamola, 307.
Val di Nievole, 364.
Val di Sieci, 383, 399, 400.
Val di Taro, 297.
Valdostani, 267.
Valerius Maximus, 104.
Valery, St., 78.
Val Fella, 260.
Valgiano, 275.
Valladolid, 206.
Vallanzengo, 278.
Vallanzengo Biellese, 246.
Vallarsa, 309.
Vallata, 304.
Valle Ariana, 364.
Valle d'Aveto, 296.
Valle del Bitto, 305.
Valle Uzzone, 293.
Vallis Soquanae, 275.
Vallombrosa, 311.
Valprato Corsonera, 275.
Valprato Pianetto, 275.
Valsoana, 275.

Valtellina, 254, 304, 305, 314.
Valtesse, 305.
Val Trebbia, 453.
Valva, 418.
Vandrille, St., 77.
Van Ginkel, G., 222.
Vannes, St., 86.
Vaprio d' Adda, 302.
Vara, val di, 300.
Varaita, 245.
Varenna, 334, 335, 336.
Variana, 293.
Varzi, 304.
Vasari, 262.
Vatican, 110, 113, 117, 118, 345.
Vatican City, 243.
Vecchia, Guglielmo della, 330.
Vecchiano, 376.
Vegetius, 104.
Vejano, 265.
Velici, 300.
Venantius, 360.
Veneranda, St., 430.
Veneto, 256.
Venice, 167, 256, 258, 259, 265, 416,
Venzone, 258. [421.
Vercellese, 270.
Vercelli, 93, 94, 125, 246, 247, 265, 268, 273, 278, 294, 295, 336, 339.
Verdun, 86.
Vernasca, 306.
Verona, 122, 256, 298, 313, 326, 409,
Veronese, 308, 313, 314. [416.
Versilia, 364.
Vertova, 237, 238.
Verulamium, 283.
Vespucci, 397.
Vestal Virgins, 56.
Vesulana, 249.
Vézelay, 186.
Vicenza, 265, 266.
Vicobarone, 306.
Vico-Vallari, 364.
Victor, St., 304.
Vienna, 113, 117.
Vienne, 81, 89.
Viezzero, 257.
Viggianello, 426.
Vignale, 299, 375.
Vignati, Mgr., 404.
Vigoleno, 323, 326.
Vikings, 87, 128, 129, 131.
Viktor, St., 85.
Viktorsberg, 76.
Villa, 274.
Villa Basilica, 363, 375.
Villach, 259.
Villafranca di Lunigiana, 257.
Villalbese, 288.

Villani, Giovanni, 367.
Villanterio, 288.
Villari, 167, 175, 180.
Villar S. Costanzo, 245.
Villiers, George, 209.
Vincent, St., 373.
Vincent Ferrer, St., 415.
Vincent and Paul, SS., 428.
Vincenzo, S., 362, 364.
Vindersi, S., 297.
Viola Bormina, 305.
Virgil, 81, 104, 120, 385, 390, 402.
Virginensis, 98.
Virginia, 210.
Visconti, 285, 287, 301, 330.
Visigoths, 405.
Vitale, R. M., 28.
Vitaletti, 168.
Viterbo, 267, 357, 358, 416, 417.
Vitorchiano, 417.
Viu, 294.
Vivario, 115, 455.
Voghera, 304, 314, 453.
Voldarico, I., 257, 258.
Volterra, 350, 376.
Volto Santo, Il, 370.
Vosges, 456.
Vulgate, the, 367.

Wace, Maistre, 189.
Wadding, Luke, 23, 91, 154, 449 to
Wagner, A., 175.   [453.
Wagner, R., 161, 187.
Wahlund, C., 168.
Walaricus, 78.
Walburga, St., 373.
Waldensian, 489.
Waldeve, 143.
Waldo, 122.
Wales, 37, 50, 51, 54, 63, 402, 465.
Walla, 114, 124.
Wallenus, 143.
Walprand, Bishop, 310, 371, 373.
Walsingham, 204.
Walvanus, 187.
Wandregisilus, 77.
Warbeck, Perkin, 193.
Ward, Hugh, 15, 23.
Ware, 154.
Ware, Sir James, 90.
Waterford, 132, 136, 137, 138, 202,
221, 401, 406.
Waters, E. G. R., 167.
Waulsort, 21, 86.
Wearmouth, 478, 480.
Weber, 309.
Weih-Sanct-Peter, 88.
Wentworth, Thomas, 211.

Weser, 37.
Wessex, 37, 130.
West Indies, 216.
Westminster Abbey, 52, 131, 138.
West Munster, King of, 318.
Westphalia, 88.
West Saxons, 373.
Whigs, 226.
Whitby, 56, 70.
White, Stephen, 15, 23.
Whitgift, Archb. of Canterbury, 17.
Whithorn, 36.
Whiting, Richard, 33.
Wicklow, 52, 210.
Wigbert, 107.
Wigtownshire, 144.
Wilhelmo, 336.
Wilfred, 71, 473, 478.
Wiligelmo, 184.
William, 115, 325, 326, 328, 333.
William I, 322, 324.
William de Barri, 151.
William of Malmesbury, 479.
William of Orange, 220, 221, 222.
William Rufus, 137.
William the Conqueror, 130, 184.
Willibald, St., 373.
Willibrord, 107.
Wilmart, Dom, 96 to 99.
Wiltshire, 72.
Winchester, 136, 183.
Witto, 120.
Wolfenbüttel, 117.
Wolfram von Eschenbach, 161.
Wunibald, St., 373.
Würzburg, 80, 83, 120.

Yarrock, 144.
Yellow Ford, 205.
York, 34, 138, 140, 143.
York, House of, 434.
Yorkshire, 37, 70, 144.
Youghal, 110, 155, 436.
Yvanus, 187.

Zaccherini, 238, 338.
Zachary, Pope, 81.

Zanoni, Canon, 261.
Zenobius, 388.
Zerbo, 288.
Ziano Piacentino, 306.
Zita, St., 374.
Zoagli, 357.
Zorigo, 257
Zurich, 113, 257.
Zwinglianism, 179.